Frommer's®

South Africa

4th Edition

by Pippa de Bruyn

W9-CHE-015

Here's what the critics say about Frommer's:

"Amazingly easy to use. Very portable, very complete."

—*Booklist*

"Detailed, accurate, and easy-to-read information for all price ranges."

—*Glamour Magazine*

"Hotel information is close to encyclopedic."

—*Des Moines Sunday Register*

"Frommer's Guides have a way of giving you a real feel for a place."

—*Knight Ridder Newspapers*

WILEY

Wiley Publishing, Inc.

About the Author

Pippa de Bruyn was born in Durban, raised in Johannesburg, and has now settled in Cape Town. She is an award-winning journalist and is also a coauthor of *Frommer's India*.

Published by:

Wiley Publishing, Inc.

111 River St.
Hoboken, NJ 07030-5774

ISBN-13: 978-0-7645-9888-3
ISBN-10: 0-7645-9888-0

Editor: Alexis Lipsitz Flippin
Production Editors: Suzanna R. Thompson, M. Faunette Johnston
Cartographer: Anton Crane
Photo Editor: Richard Fox
Production by Wiley Indianapolis Composition Services

For information on our other products and services or to obtain technical support, please contact our Customer Care Department within the U.S. at 800/762-2974, outside the U.S. at 317/572-3993 or fax 317/572-4002.

Wiley also publishes its books in a variety of electronic formats. Some content that appears in print may not be available in electronic formats.

Manufactured in the United States of America

5 4 3 2

Contents

5 Whale Coast & Garden Route: The Western Cape   158

6 Undiscovered Wilderness: The Eastern Cape   218

7 Africa's Big Apple: Jo'burg Plus Safari Excursions   238

8 Big-Game Country: Kruger National Park & Environs   287

9 Kingdom of the Zulu: KwaZulu-Natal   338

10 Thundering World Wonder: Victoria Falls & Vicinity   375

11 Original Eden: Botswana   390

by Keith Bain

Appendix: South Africa in Depth   413

Index   428

List of Maps

An Invitation to the Reader

In researching this book, we discovered many wonderful places—hotels, restaurants, shops, and more. We're sure you'll find others. Please tell us about them, so we can share the information with your fellow travelers in upcoming editions. If you were disappointed with a recommendation, we'd love to know that, too. Please write to:

Frommer's South Africa, 4th Edition
Wiley Publishing, Inc. • 111 River St. • Hoboken, NJ 07030-5774

An Additional Note

Please be advised that travel information is subject to change at any time—and this is especially true of prices. We therefore suggest that you write or call ahead for confirmation when making your travel plans. The authors, editors, and publisher cannot be held responsible for the experiences of readers while traveling. Your safety is important to us, however, so we encourage you to stay alert and be aware of your surroundings. Keep a close eye on cameras, purses, and wallets, all favorite targets of thieves and pickpockets.

Frommer's Star Ratings, Icons & Abbreviations

Every hotel, restaurant, and attraction listing in this guide has been ranked for quality, value, service, amenities, and special features using a **star-rating system.** In country, state, and regional guides, we also rate towns and regions to help you narrow down your choices and budget your time accordingly. Hotels and restaurants are rated on a scale of zero (recommended) to three stars (exceptional). Attractions, shopping, nightlife, towns, and regions are rated according to the following scale: zero stars (recommended), one star (highly recommended), two stars (very highly recommended), and three stars (must-see).

In addition to the star-rating system, we also use **seven feature icons** that point you to the great deals, in-the-know advice, and unique experiences that separate travelers from tourists. Throughout the book, look for:

Finds	Special finds—those places only insiders know about
Fun Fact	Fun facts—details that make travelers more informed and their trips more fun
Kids	Best bets for kids and advice for the whole family
Moments	Special moments—those experiences that memories are made of
Overrated	Places or experiences not worth your time or money
Tips	Insider tips—great ways to save time and money
Value	Great values—where to get the best deals

The following **abbreviations** are used for credit cards:

AE	American Express	DISC	Discover	V	Visa
DC	Diners Club	MC	MasterCard		

Frommers.com

Now that you have the guidebook to a great trip, visit our website at **www.frommers.com** for travel information on more than 3,000 destinations. With features updated regularly, we give you instant access to the most current trip-planning information available. At Frommers.com, you'll also find the best prices on airfares, accommodations, and car rentals—and you can even book travel online through our travel booking partners. At Frommers.com, you'll also find the following:

- Online updates to our most popular guidebooks
- Vacation sweepstakes and contest giveaways
- Newsletter highlighting the hottest travel trends
- Online travel message boards with featured travel discussions

What's New in South Africa

"**A** decade after its first free election slammed the door on apartheid," wrote *Time* magazine, "the rainbow nation is shining brighter than ever—and starting to take on its thorniest problems."

With consumer confidence and productivity at an all-time high, the former is for the most part true, while the latter was dramatically proved on June 14, 2005, when President Thabo Mbeki fired his popular deputy Jacob Zuma, the result of a recent court case in which Zuma's relationship with the accused was described as "generally corrupt." The democracy may be young, but it is thriving, as is the economy, and the energy and enthusiasm of its "buppies," as South Africa's newly moneyed black professionals are called, are palpable proof. Sadly, at least for foreign visitors, this confidence is reflected in a strong rand, which at press time was hovering around R6.70 to the dollar (this is also the figure used to translate rand figures in this book—but keep in mind that rates fluctuate, so before budgeting for your holiday, check the exchange rate and adjust accordingly). Despite the impact that a stronger currency has had on tourism, it remains one of the South Africa's growth industries (surpassing even gold in its total contribution to gross domestic product), with numbers up by 13% in 2004 in Cape Town alone—this, together with touring the Garden Route and going on safari, remains the focus of most visitors, and to this end the fourth edition focuses on these areas in depth, with side

trips and major gateways covered, as well as a new chapter on itineraries to help plan a great vacation. Enjoy!

CAPE TOWN & THE WINELANDS

With yet another slew of awards under her belt, the Mother City remains an essential stop on any visit to southern Africa, though the distance works to preclude cheap package junkets. As a result, the city keeps producing one boutique guesthouse after another, the best of which is the new **Cape Cadogan,** though the recently enlarged **African Villa** still offers superb value, and **Les Cascades** in Bantry Bay has the best sea views for your money.

Given that one of the accolades Cape Town was given in 2004 was "Best City in the World to Eat Out," reviewing this burgeoning sector has become increasingly challenging. Sadly, the best of these, The Restaurant, closed (lauded chef Graham Shapiro was poached by a large law firm, for whom he now exclusively caters, provoking much resentment from his loyal followers), but foodies are now advised to book at least one meal at **Aubergine** in Cape Town central, and then overnight in Franschhoek, the picturesque Winelands town that is justifiably known as its gourmet capital.

With South Africa hosting the 2010 World Cup Soccer, big plans are afoot to upgrade the city's infrastructure, including the creation of a rapid-transport link between the airport and the city center. These kinds of innovations are to be welcomed, but if you're like me, you may prefer Cape Town as she currently is—laid-back and a bit old-fashioned, with a somewhat exclusive air. So get here soon! For details on Cape Town and environs, see chapter 4.

WESTERN & EASTERN CAPES
With the enduring popularity of Cape Town within easy striking distance of the vast plains of the Klein Karoo and the Eastern Cape, it was only a matter of time before these previously degraded cattle and sheep farms were rehabilitated and filled with the wildlife that roamed here for centuries before the arrival of the colonists and their guns. Their growing popularity is not only about ease of access—being malaria-free, these reserves appeal to those traveling with children or those who prefer to avoid the potential side effects of malaria medication.

Of the growing vacation options in the Western Cape, the 54,000-hectare (133,380-acre) **Sanbona Wildlife Reserve** is still the best, both for the beauty of its landscape (particularly if you have a preference for arid, blue-horizoned landscapes) and the luxury of the accommodations and facilities. Spend a few days unwinding here, and you will certainly see elephant, rhino, and lion (and a myriad other species), but Big 5 fans be warned: Leopards here are very elusive. The reserve is also off **Route 62,** a rural road that leads through the Little Karoo. "The Route Less Traveled" has become increasingly popular, with a wonderful array of places to stay and dine, and it's highly recommended as a way to the Garden Route. Along the Garden Route you can still find superb value for money (like the gorgeous Treetops suite at **Moontide Guest Lodge** in Wilderness) and tip-top accommodations: Both **Pezulu** in Knysna and the **Grand** in Plettenberg Bay made it into *Condé Nast Traveler*'s 2005 Hot List—not bad going for one province in competition with 60 countries!

While the Western Cape has increased its wildlife conservancies, by far the biggest growth in reserves has taken place in the Eastern Cape, with **Addo Elephant National Park** leading the way: After securing a $5.50-million grant from the World Bank in 2004, a further 45,000 hectares (111,150 acres) was secured, and lion, buffalo, rhino, and spotted hyena have been introduced. The plan—to be completed in 5 to 10 years—is to feature the "Big 7" (lion, leopard, rhino, buffalo, elephant, southern right whale, and great white shark), with 240,000 hectares (592,800 acres) of land and 120,000 hectares (296,400 acres) of marine area under park control. Travelers on a budget can opt to stay in the main camp, but if your dollar can stretch that far, luxurious **Gorah** is the top choice, located in a concession inside the park. For the hardcore design-conscious, the 20,000-hectare (49,400-acre) **Kwandwe Private Game Reserve** is still the top choice in the Eastern Cape, particularly if you stay in the intimate **Ecca Lodge** (opened late 2003), which embraces a modern Africa look; parents in need of on-tap nannies should look no further than the reserve's **Lalibela Game Lodge.** For details on the Western and Eastern Capes, see chapters 5 and 6.

GAUTENG & SAFARI EXCURSIONS
While Johannesburg has always had numerous large-scale hotels, intended primarily for business travelers, the city has seen a boom of late in the number of small luxury B&Bs and guesthouses catering to the tourist market. These represent excellent value and bring contemporary style to an otherwise rather fusty market (this is particularly true of the new **Peech Hotel,** conveniently located near Melrose Arch, and the **Parkwood,** northwest of Melville). More important, Johannesburg is becoming an increasingly safe and sophisticated metropolis,

with ongoing signs of urban renewal, cosmopolitanism in its arts and entertainment industries, and a visibly affluent black middle class. The city's skyline has changed considerably with the addition of the **Nelson Mandela Bridge,** and the new **Constitution Hill** development is an additional tribute to the process of democratization and the ongoing concern with social freedom. But perhaps the most exciting developments have taken place in the malaria-free reserves, **Welgevonden** and **Madikwe,** that lie within easy striking distance of the bright lights of the city. Both have seen numerous lodges opening to cater to the increased interest in tracking the Big 5 in a malaria-free environment. The award for best newcomer goes to CC Africa's stylish new **Madikwe Safari Lodge,** which combines top-end accommodations (each guest room comes with its own private plunge pool), quality game-viewing, easy access (it's a 3-hr. drive or a 45-min. flight from Jo'burg), and exceptionally good value relative to the Kruger lodges. Nearby, the new **Madikwe Hills** adds spectacular views to the mix. Built on an elevated rise, guest rooms are spread out on a rocky outcrop; there's a spa and a colonial-themed lounge and bar area. For details on Gauteng and environs, see chapter 7.

KRUGER & ENVIRONS   The growth in lodges has occurred mostly inside Kruger itself, in the new concession earmarked for private development; sadly, all still are competing for top dollar. Of these, **Singita**'s concession in the far eastern sector of Kruger National Park, augmented with **Singita Sweni,** the most private, exclusive, and intimate of all the private game lodges in the region, and situated just 5 minutes (on foot) from Singita Lebombo, is the one to book. If the price strikes you as just too steep, opt instead for a few nights at **Rhino Walking Safaris,** another private concession within Kruger, where game drives are complemented by on-foot safaris; you can also book an authentic bush sleeping experience at their **Rhino Post Camp.** Almost all the other luxury lodges recently opened in and around Kruger are overpriced, given that they bring nothing new to the experience. In Sabi Sand, adjacent to Kruger, the new **Lion Sands Ivory Lodge** offers every modern convenience at the highest possible price, while **MalaMala** has created the new, exclusive **Rattray's Lodge,** with rates starting at $1,700 double. **Sabi Sabi** also plans to launch a new lodge, having recently acquired Londolozi's Safari Lodge. Also in Sabi Sand, **Exeter** has expanded and upgraded quite extensively, and offers a range of options—from the midrange ex-MalaMala **Kirkman's Kamp** to upscale **Leadwood Lodge,** which has become a very classy act. A recent addition to the Manyeleti Reserve is **Tintswalo,** which is pricier than neighboring **Honeyguide,** an old Frommer's favorite for value-hunters. In the far north of Kruger, Wilderness Safaris has recently opened **Pafuri Camp** in the 24,000-hectare (59,280-acre) Makulele concession. Remote and far from the maddening safari crowds of southern Kruger, the new camp is designed to appeal to those looking to get away from it all. For details on Kruger and environs, see chapter 8.

KWAZULU-NATAL   News here is also concentrated on new safari options, though the city of Durban, with its fascinating mix of Indian, African, and colonial influences, is also undergoing an urban rejuvenation, and the massive cash injection from beachfront developments like **Suncoast Casino, uShaka Marine World,** and **Wilson's Wharf** has sparked a property boom. Best of all, you can now overnight in total luxury (its interiors were created by Durban-designer Boyd Ferguson, who put Singita on the map) at good-value **Leadwood Lodge** in Tala Private Game Reserve, a 3,000-hectare (7,410-acre) wildlife conservancy a mere 45 minutes west of Durban. If ticking off the Big 5 is more important to you (and you'd like to combine it with turtle tracking, close-up encounters with dolphins, whale-watching, and snorkeling off species-rich reefs—second only to Australia's Great Barrier Reef), you need to head farther north to new **Thanda Game Reserve,** a 5,000-hectare (12,350-acre) reserve just beyond Hluhluwe, and then east to **Thonga Beach Lodge,** another newcomer, this time overlooking the coral sands of Mabibi, a castaway's fantasy come true. For details on KwaZulu-Natal, see chapter 9.

VICTORIA FALLS, ZIMBABWE In 2005 Robert Mugabe, Zimbabwe's dictatorial president, unleashed his henchmen on his long-suffering population with Operation Murambatsvina (literally translated as "Drive Out Trash/Rubbish"). The result: a smoky pall over every city and town (including Vic Falls Village), as homes (mostly shacks but also permanent homes, the owners of whom were accused of "illegally" gaining title deeds) were set afire and the hapless residents "relocated" to more "desirable" rural locations. Although foreign visitors are not in any way directly threatened by Mugabe's policies, the staff who serve you on the Zimbabwean side are, and you may prefer not to have to face the desperation of people on the street. Still, they need the tourist dollar as never before, and accommodations on the Zimbabwean side of Victoria Falls are often available at excellent prices. **Matetsi River Lodge,** in particular, represents very

affordable luxury in the bush, with great game-viewing opportunities, while the century-old **Victoria Falls Hotel** has dropped its rates considerably and still offers old-world charm. On the Zambian side, **Tongabezi** has begun a much-needed upgrade of its accommodations; its newly refurbished Tree House—carved from the rock and hanging right over the Zambezi River—is one of the most romantic rooms in Africa. The **River Club** remains a perennial favorite. For details on Vic Falls and Zimbabwe, see chapter 10.

BOTSWANA With concessions hard to come by, there hasn't been much movement in the game-rich Okavango Delta, but in May 2005 Wilderness Safaris opened a new luxury camp to the north of Mombo: **Vumbura Plains,** a private concession sharing a border with the Moremi Game Reserve in the delta's extreme north. With access to varied habitats, the new camp offers *mokoro* (canoe) trips, boating, bush walks, and excellent game-viewing in 4WD Land Rovers; vehicles enjoy traversing rights over almost 52,000 hectares (128,440 acres). The camp consists of two totally separate lodges, each with seven luxury guest rooms linked by raised walkways, outdoor showers, and private *salas* (gazebos). Vumbura charges top dollar; if you prefer something more affordable, Abercrombie & Kent's new **Baines' Camp** is quite lovely. The open public viewing deck, lounge, and dining area overlook a lagoon where hippos wallow and play, providing endless entertainment. The camp has only five guest units, ensuring exclusivity, and the atmosphere is one of laid-back elegance. For details on Botswana, see chapter 11.

1

The Best of Southern Africa,

People come to southern Africa for its natural beauty, wildlife, and sunshine, and few leave disappointed. With an immensely varied terrain supporting a rich diversity of fauna and flora, the region offers a correspondingly diverse range of experiences. Whether you're here on safari, on a self-drive tour through the vast hinterland, or simply on vacation in one of the world's most beautiful regions, this chapter will help you experience the very best southern Africa has to offer.

1 Unique Southern African Moments

- **Spotting Zebra Grazing on the Mountain from the Highway** (Cape Town): Zebra, wildebeest, and various antelope graze on Table Mountain's slopes, literally minutes from the city center. Look out for them from the highway as you drive in from the airport. See chapter 4.

- **Enjoying the Sunset from Table Mountain** (Cape Town): From this great vantage point, you can watch the sun sink into the Atlantic Ocean, turning the Twelve Apostles a deep pink; then walk across the tabletop to the lip and watch the city lights start to twinkle and the dusky outline of the hinterland mountains under a moonlit sky. See chapter 4.

- **Feeling Humbled at Mandela's Prison Cell** (Cape Town): Tours of Robben Island are pretty restrictive, but looking into the tiny cell where Nelson Mandela spent the majority of his time in prison leaves few unmoved. Further insights are provided by guides, some of whom were incarcerated at the same time as Mandela, in what came to be known as the "University of Robben Island." See chapter 4.

- **Getting Caught Up in the Cape Minstrels Carnival** (Cape Town): Every New Year, brightly dressed troupes of "coloured" (mixed-race) men and children dance through the streets of Cape Town, singing to the quick-paced strum of banjos and the thump of drums. This tradition was inspired by American minstrels who came to the Cape in the late 1800s, but the celebration actually dates back to 1834 when slaves took to the streets to celebrate their liberation. See chapter 4.

- **Watching Whales from White Sand Dunes** (Western Cape): At De Hoop Nature Reserve's Koppie Alleen, the massive white dunes stretch deep beneath the sea, turning its blue hue into a hypnotic turquoise. This is the perfect place to watch the Southern Right whales that come to breed off the Overberg Coast—said to offer the best land-based whale-watching in the world. See chapter 5.

- **Walking Through Carpets of Flowers** (Northern Cape): In this annual miracle of almost spiritual proportions, the semi-arid and seemingly barren West Coast bursts into life after the first spring rains. More than 2,600 species of flowers literally carpet the Namaqualand plains for a few weeks before subsiding back into the soil for another year-long wait. See chapter 5.

- **Visiting the World's Largest Open-Air Gallery** (Western Cape, Eastern Cape, and KwaZulu-Natal): Created by the San hunter-gatherers, an ancient civilization all but destroyed by the migrating Nguni and white settlers, these rock-art paintings date back between 100 and 20,000 years, and document the history and spiritual beliefs of these gentle people. More than 15,000 sites are scattered throughout the country. See chapters 5, 6, and 9.

- **Jiving with Jo'burg Jollers to the Sounds of Kwaito** (Gauteng): The best place to experience the melting pot of Rainbow Nation culture, and to celebrate the emergence of a cohesive national identity, is on the dance floors grooving to *kwaito,* South Africa's own homegrown version of house. Look out for performances (or recordings) by Brothers of Peace (BO), Mandoza, Mafikizolo, Zola, M'Du, Mzekezeke, Kabelo, Mapaputsi, Bongo Maffin, or Mzambiya. See chapter 7.

- **Freezing Your Butt Off on an Early-Morning Game Drive** (Limpopo Province, the North-West, Mpumalanga, and Botswana): Winter (May–Aug) is considered to be the best time of the year to go on safari, as animals are the most visible, but be prepared: Rangers set off in their open-topped vehicles before dawn, when temperatures are barely above zero. See chapters 7, 8, and 11.

- **Seeing Virgin Maidens Dance the Zulu King's Reed Dance** (KwaZulu-Natal): Experience a scene that has been enacted for hundreds of years as you join some 15,000 Zulus, many dressed in tribal gear, to watch the virgin maidens dance for the Zulu Prince Gideon, who would traditionally pick a wife here. See chapter 9.

- **Soaking Up Victoria Falls** (Zimbabwe): The sight of more than 500 million liters of water a minute thundering into the Batoka Gorge, creating soaring rainbows and a mist of drenching spray, will never leave you. Enjoy the view with a champagne breakfast on Livingstone Island. See chapter 10.

- **Rafting the Churning Waters of the Zambezi** (Victoria Falls, Zimbabwe): There is absolutely nothing like hearing this mighty river pound past, drowning the guides' last-minute instructions as you plunge into swirling white waters, with fitting names like "the Muncher" and "Boiling Pot." See chapter 10.

- **Drinking the Waters of the Delta** (Okavango Delta, Botswana): As you're poled along in your *mokoro* (dugout canoe), past palm-fringed islands and aquatic game, sample the life-giving waters of the delta. Simply scoop up a handful (keeping an eye out for crocs!) and take a sip. See chapter 11.

2 The Wildest Animal Encounters

- **Staring Down a Roaring Lion** (private game reserves in Mpumalanga, Limpopo Province, the North-West, and Botswana): Tourists are notoriously hungry for shots of big cats, and if you spend 2 nights at one of the top private game reserves, you will certainly get close to lions and leopards, often on the first drive. If you're lucky enough to get close enough to have your vehicle shuddering from the powerful noise that erupts from the king of the jungle's gut, you are talking a truly wild-animal encounter. See chapters 7, 8, and 11.

- **Waiting for a Leopard to Finish Its Dinner** (private game reserves, the North-West, Mpumalanga, KwaZulu-Natal): Holing up in your room while a leopard gnaws its dinner outside your door might happen at any of the private game-reserve lodges that are set in the bush. Animals roam freely in this environment, and if dinner happens to be on your patio, celebrate the fact that you're not it and plunder the minibar. See chapters 7, 8, and 9.

- **Stalking a Rhino on Foot** (Kruger National Park, Hluhluwe-Umfolozi Reserve): Tracking rhino is no mean feat: They can smell humans up to 800m (2,624 ft.) away. Being on foot, with only the sounds of the bush and your beating heart as you crouch just meters from an animal as large as a tank, is unbeatable. For the best rhino-tracking experience, stay at Royal Malewane lodge, in the Thornybush game reserve. You will almost definitely track white rhino on the Bushman, Wolhuter, and Napi trails run by Kruger National Park, as well as on the Umfolozi trails run in Hluhluwe-Umfolozi. See chapters 8 and 9.

- **Swimming with Penguins** (Boulders Beach, Cape Town): This is a beautiful place to swim; large boulders create natural swimming pools shared by the only land-breeding colony of jackass penguins. Watch them waddle and dive through the crystal-clear waters, which are slightly warmer than the Atlantic seaboard side—cold comfort, considering how icy that is. See chapter 4.

- **Baiting Great White Sharks** (Hermanus and Mossel Bay, Western Cape): Descend in a steel cage to meet Jaws up close and personal. Specialist tour operators offer controversial cage diving off Dyer Island in "Shark Alley," where Great Whites hunt the resident seal population. Sharks swim within spitting distance of cages—not that there's much to spit when your mouth is dry with fear. See chapter 5.

- **Watching Rare Turtles Nest** (Zululand, KwaZulu-Natal): In November and December, the female leatherback and loggerhead turtles leave the safety of the sea at night to lay their eggs above the high-tide mark on the northern beaches of KwaZulu-Natal. Two months later, hatchlings scramble out of their nests and make a run for the ocean. Only one or two out of every thousand make it to maturity; those that do, return to the same beach to produce the next generation. See chapter 9.

- **Avoiding a Territorial Hippo** (Victoria Falls, Okavango Delta): The upper reaches of the Zambezi and the Okavango Delta's watery channels are best explored by gliding along in a canoe, or *mokoro,* but you're also more than likely to meet a hippo this way. Always treat them with respect—despite a relatively docile appearance, they are Africa's most dangerous mammal, and responsible for more deaths than crocodiles or lions. See chapters 10 and 11.

3 The Best Private Game Lodges & Camps

- **Singita** (Sabi Sands Reserve and Kruger National Park): Singita offers the best game lodge experience in Africa, with a choice of styles, from plush colonial to the last word in contemporary Afro-chic. Elevated private viewing decks let you immerse yourself in the tranquillity of the bush without leaving your suite. Add top-notch rangers, a roving masseuse, exquisite food, and a connoisseur's selection of wines, and you're assured an unforgettable stay—the only difficulty is deciding which lodge you prefer. See chapter 8.

- **Londolozi Bateleur and Tree Camps** (Sabi Sands Reserve, Mpumalanga): Londolozi is the flagship lodge of safari operator CC Africa, who set the standard in luxury bush accommodations (CC Africa also manages the recently opened Madikwe Safari Lodge, incidentally the best malaria-free option in southern Africa). While Londolozi is not as grand or exclusive as Singita, it is justifiably famed for its leopard sightings. See chapter 8.

- **Honeyguide Tented Safari Camp** (Manyeleti Reserve, Mpumalanga): If the thought of a luxury hotel in the bush leaves you cold, Honeyguide's tented camp delivers a more authentically *Out of Africa* experience—right down to the sunken baths and cheeky local elephants. The lack of commercial activity in the Manyeleti Reserve and the relatively low rates are also extra pluses. See chapter 8.

- **Royal Malewane** (Thornybush Reserve, Limpopo Province): With privately situated suites that offer every luxury, this is all about deep relaxation, enhanced by the recently expanded spa. If you can bear to leave your private pool and large viewing deck (or in-room lounge and fireplace, lit for you in winter), the on-foot tracking is the best in the country. See chapter 8.

- **Leadwood Lodge** (Tala Private Game Reserve, KwaZulu-Natal): This reserve is not Big 5 country (it does have buffalo, rhino, giraffe, and antelope), but it is the new showcase for the team that created Singita's award-winning interiors—hardly surprising, then, that it made it onto *Condé Nast Traveler*'s 2005 Hot List. It's also the most affordable option listed here, and a mere 40 minutes from Durban International Airport. See chapter 9.

- **Jao Camp** (Okavango Delta, Botswana): Not only is this camp located in one of the finest concessions in the delta, but it is also one of the most gorgeous camps on the continent, bringing elegant Balinese design elements to bear on an otherwise classic African lodge. See chapter 11.

- **Mombo Camp** (Moremi, Okavango, Botswana): At the confluence of two river systems, Mombo has long been regarded as one of the best game-viewing spots in Africa, attracting large numbers of plains game and their attendant predators—leopard, wild dog, and lion are frequently sighted here. See chapter 11.

- **Jack's and San Camps** (Makgadikgadi Pans, Botswana): Desert reserves have a very special effect on the spirit, and these classic 1940s safari camps, situated under palm trees on the fringe of the pans, offer one of the most unusual experiences in Africa. (For a more luxurious desert lodge—we're talking swimming pools and top-end service—head for Tswalu, in the Kalahari.) See chapter 11.

4 The Best National Parks & Provincial Nature Reserves

De Hoop Nature Reserve (Whale Coast, Western Cape): A magnificent coastal reserve featuring deserted beaches, interesting rock pools, beautiful *fynbos* (uniquely diverse shrublands), a wetland with more than 200 bird species, and a number of small game. Very limited accommodations in simple huts ensure that the reserve is never crowded. See chapter 5.

Tsitsikamma National Park (Garden Route, Western Cape): Stretching from Storms River Mouth to Nature's Valley, this coastline is best explored on foot via the 5-day Otter Trail. If you're pressed for time, or if the trail is full, take the 1km (just over ½-mile) walk to the mouth, or complete the first day of the Otter Trail, which terminates at a beautiful waterfall. See chapter 5.

• **Goegap Nature Reserve** (Namaqualand, Northern Cape): This is one of the best places in Namaqualand to witness the floral transformation after the first spring rains. A recommended way to explore the reserve is to hire a bike and complete the two trails that traverse the reserve. Grazing among the flowers are zebra, springbok, and the stately gemsbok, or oryx. See chapter 5.

• **Kgalagadi (Kalahari) Transfrontier Park** (Northern Cape): This is one of the largest conservation areas in Africa—twice the size of Kruger—yet because of the long distances you need to travel to reach it, this desert reserve is seldom included in the first visitor's itinerary. Pity, for it is starkly beautiful, with red dunes, blonde grasses, and sculptural camelthorn trees contrasting with cobalt-blue skies. Despite its aridity, the reserve supports a number of predators, including the famed black-maned "Kalahari" lion, hyena, wild dog, and cheetah. See chapter 7.

• **Pilanesberg National Park** (the North-West): This reserve is one of southern Africa's most accessible (just 2 hr. from Johannesburg), which is both a blessing and a drawback, depending on whether you have serious time constraints or a need for solitude. Lying on the eroded remains of a 1.4-billion-year-old extinct volcanic crater—one of only three in the world—the 58,000-hectare (143,260-acre) reserve supports more than 35 large mammal species. See chapter 7.

• **Madikwe Game Reserve** (the North-West): Rapidly gathering momentum as one of the country's most sought-after getaways, this 75,000-hectare (185,250-acre) reserve offers highly diverse ecozones (including Kalahari sandveld), allowing it to support an unusual range of species—which is why it's been dubbed the "Magnificent 7" reserve (cheetah and wild dog being added to the lineup of usual suspects). Best of all, it's malaria-free. See chapter 7.

• **Kruger National Park** (Mpumalanga and Limpopo Province): One of Africa's greatest game parks, with probably the best-developed infrastructure, Kruger is the most cost-effective, do-it-yourself way to go on safari. Most accommodations are pretty basic but clean, functional, and affordable; and the park teems with wildlife. Good news for connoisseurs is that there are an increasing number of classy private concessions, where the finest lodgings are available—at a price. See chapter 8.

• **Greater St Lucia Wetland Park** (Zululand, KwaZulu-Natal): This World Heritage Site encompasses five distinct ecosystems, including the croc-rich estuary, the Mkhuze savanna, and offshore coral reefs. It is also close to Hluhluwe-Umfolozi, the province's largest Big 5 reserve, which supports the densest rhino population in Africa. See chapter 9.

- **The Kosi Bay Nature Reserve** (Maputaland, KwaZulu-Natal): This chain of four lakes, fringed by lush and varied vegetation (marsh forests, mangroves, giant swamp figs, dune forests, raffia palm forest) and home to rare birds (Pels fishing owl and the palm nut vulture) and tropical fish, is a delight for hikers and birders, though it takes some commitment to get to this northeastern corner of South Africa. See chapter 9.

- **The uKhahlamba-Drakensberg Park** (KwaZulu-Natal): The Drakensberg in its entirety is spectacular, but if you have time to visit only one region, head north for the Amphitheatre. One of the most magnificent rock formations in Africa, it is also the source of South Africa's major rivers, the Vaal, the Orange, and the Tugela. Rolling grasslands, breathtaking views, and crystal-clear streams can be explored only on foot or horseback. See chapter 9.

- **The Victoria Falls National Park** (Victoria Falls, Zimbabwe): This World Heritage Site offers the most stupendous views of the 1,000m-wide (3,280-ft.) falls, and the constant spray, crowned by a permanent rainbow, sustains a lush and verdant rain forest. See chapter 10.

- **Moremi Game Reserve** (Botswana): No visit to Botswana would be complete without a trip to Moremi, which makes up much of the eastern shores of the delta and offers arguably the best game-viewing in southern Africa. Covering an area of 487,200 hectares (1,203,384 acres), including woodlands, wetlands, waterways, islands, and pans, this reserve is home to lion, elephant, cheetah, wild dog, leopard, buffalo, and more than 500 species of birds. See chapter 11.

- **Chobe National Park** (Botswana): This park includes the fabulous game areas of Savuti and Linyanti—river systems that provide life for abundant game including lion, leopard, wild dog, and elephant; the Chobe River is in fact the best place to see elephant in Africa, and from the boats that operate along its shores it's possible to see dozens of them swimming across the rivers between Botswana and Namibia. See chapter 11.

5 The Best Beaches

- **Long Beach** (Cape Town): This 4km-long (2½-mile) stretch of sand—almost as wide as it is long—is the city's best place to go horseback riding. Even if you don't have time to ride it, stop to admire it from the overlooking cliffs of the Chapman's Peak Drive. See chapter 4.

- **Clifton** (Cape Town): The city's most beautiful beach is just minutes from the city center, and where Cape Town's most gorgeous creatures like to parade. It's also the most wind-free area in Cape Town—handy when the southeaster, known locally as the Cape Doctor, is driving you mad. Divided by large boulders into First, Second, Third, and Fourth beaches, it is accessible only via steep steps. Other great city beaches include Camps Bay and Llandudno. See chapter 4.

- **De Hoop Beach** (Whale Coast, Western Cape): Tall white dunes sliding into the sea, coves, evocative limestone outcrops, an aquamarine sea, and picture-perfect rock pools make this reserve's beaches the most glorious in the Overberg, if not the entire Cape. See chapter 5.

- **Noetzie** (Garden Route, Western Cape): One of the closest beaches to Knysna is also the most charming, not least because of the crenellated castles overlooking it. If the sea is too wild, take a dip in the lagoon that meanders into it. See chapter 5.

- **Plettenberg Bay** (Garden Route, Western Cape): It's a toss-up between Lookout and Robberg beaches, but safe to say that "Plett," as the locals call it, has the best beaches on the Garden Route. Pity about the monstrous houses that overlook them. Head for Lookout for a view of the distant Outeniqua Mountains, and Robberg for whale-watching. See chapter 5.

- **Wild Coast** (Eastern Cape): The entire Wild Coast is renowned for its magnificent, deserted coastline; but since **Port St Johns** is one of the more accessible points, you may wish to head straight here and laze away the sultry days on Second Beach, a perfect uninhabited crescent, fringed with tropical vegetation. For total seclusion, head for Umngazi, a few miles south, or north to the new Gwe Gwe Lodge in Mkambati. See chapter 6.

- **Mabibi and Rocktail Bay** (Maputaland, KwaZulu-Natal): With the "Holiday Coast" surrounding Durban largely ruined by an uninterrupted ribbon of development, you'll need to head north, past the Greater St Lucia Wetland to the beaches of Maputaland. For Robinson Crusoes who like their luxury, Thonga Beach Lodge at Mabibi and Rocktail Bay lodge offer total seclusion on the coast for a limited number of guests. See chapter 9.

6 The Best Outdoor Adventures

- **Throwing Yourself Off Lion's Head and Landing on Camps Bay Beach** (Cape Town): It's a breathtaking ride hovering over the slopes of Table Mountain. As you slowly glide toward the white sands of Camps Bay, lapped by an endless expanse of ocean, you'll have time to admire the craggy cliffs of the Twelve Apostles. See chapter 4.

- **Kayaking to Cape Point** (Cape Town): Kayaking is the most impressive way to view this towering outcrop, the southwesternmost point of Africa. It's also the ideal opportunity to explore the rugged cliffs that line the coastline, with numerous crevices and private coves to beach yourself on. See chapter 4.

- **Mountain Biking Through the Knysna Forests** (Garden Route, Western Cape): Starting at the Garden of Eden, the 22km (14-mile) Harkerville Red Route is considered the most challenging in the country. Its steep, single-track slip paths take you past indigenous forests, silent plantations, and magnificent coastal fynbos. See chapter 5.

- **Bungee Jumping Off Bloukrans River Bridge** (Garden Route, Western Cape): The real daredevils do the highest bungee jump in the world in just their birthday suits, leaping 216m (708 ft.) and free-falling (not to mention screaming) for close to 7 seconds. See chapter 5.

- **Surfing "Bruce's Beauties"** (Cape St Francis, Eastern Cape): Bruce's Beauties, the waves featured in the 1960s cult classic *Endless Summer,* form an awesome right-point break. They need a massive swell, however, and don't work very often; the same goes for Supertubes, hailed the "perfect wave," in nearby Jeffrey's Bay. See chapter 6.

- **Surfing the Mighty Zambezi River** (Victoria Falls, Zimbabwe): Not content with merely rafting down the Zambezi, adrenaline-seekers can plunge into the churning waters attached to nothing more than a boogie board and ride the 2m- to 3m-high (6½–9¾-ft.) waves. See chapter 10.
- **Riding an Elephant Through the African Wilderness** (Mpumalanga, Victoria Falls, and Botswana): This is a great way to explore the bush, not only because of the elevated view and

the proximity with which you can approach animals, but because you won't feel safer—no one in the jungle messes with an elephant. See chapters 8, 10, and 11.

- **Tracking Big Game on Horseback** (Mashatu and Okavango Delta, Botswana): You haven't lived until you've outraced a charging elephant on the back of you trusty steed—experience Africa as the pioneers did by taking a 3- to 10-day horse safari in the Mashatu Game Reserve, or explore the western delta bordering the Moremi Game Reserve. See chapter 11.

7 The Best Places to Discover South African Culture & History

- **Diagonal Street** (Johannesburg, Gauteng): On one side of the street, *sangomas* (healers) enter a pungent *muti* (folk medicine) shop to purchase jars of crushed baboon skull, lizards' feet, and crocodile fat, while on the other, accountants flashing cellphones exit the glass walls of "Diamond House," the gleaming high-rise designed by Chicago architect Helmut Jahn. It is this kind of contrast that makes Johannesburg such an electrifying experience. See chapter 7.
- **The Hector Pieterson Memorial** (Soweto, Gauteng): When schoolchildren took to the streets on June 16, 1976, in a peaceful protest against the decision to use Afrikaans as the sole means of instruction in schools, police opened fire, killing, among others, young Hector Pieterson. This was a turning point in the battle against apartheid. Widespread riots and international condemnation followed, and nothing would ever be the same. The best way to see it is with a township tour. See chapter 7.
- **Apartheid Museum** (Gauteng): Few other museums are able to achieve

the emotional impact generated by this rich reminder of South Africa's ugly past. The collection of images, audiovisual presentations, and intimate tales of human suffering and triumph in the face of adversity is staggering; raw and vivid, the journey from oppression to democracy is powerfully evoked here. See chapter 7.

- **Cradle of Humankind** (Gauteng): Having shot to fame in 1947 with the discovery of a 2½-million-year-old hominid skull, the region continues to produce fascinating finds about the origins of mankind. Tours with paleontologists introduce you to many intriguing aspects of human evolution, in an area that has remained unchanged for millions of years. See chapter 7.
- **Voortrekker Monument** (Pretoria, Gauteng): This massive granite structure commemorates the Great Trek—in particular, the Battle of Blood River (fought between Trekkers and Zulus on Dec 16, 1838)—and remains hallowed ground for Afrikaner nationalists. See chapter 7.
- **Robben Island** (Cape Town): A prison for political activists since the

17th century, including its most famous prisoner, Nelson Mandela, the island was commonly known as the "Alcatraz of Africa." Today the island is a museum and a nature reserve, and a tangible symbol of South Africa's transformation. See chapter 4.

• **Bo-Kaap** (Cape Town): This Cape Malay area, replete with cobbled streets and quaint historical homes, was one of the few "nonwhite" areas to escape destruction during the apartheid era, despite its proximity to the city. A walk through the streets should be combined with a visit to the **District Six Museum,** which commemorates a less fortunate community. Visible today only as large tracts of cleared land on the southern outskirts of town (opposite the Bo-Kaap), this once vibrant suburb was razed to the ground in the '60s. See chapter 4.

• **Wuppertal Moravian Mission Station** (Cederberg, Western Cape): Located at the end of a long, dusty road in the Cederberg Mountains, Wuppertal remains unchanged to this day and is both architecturally and culturally a living legacy of the early missionaries. Other mission stations worth visiting are Elim and Genadendal, both in the Overberg. See chapter 5.

• **The Nelson Mandela Museum** (Umtata, Eastern Cape): A homegrown tribute to Africa's greatest statesman, with posters, photographs, and videos documenting his life and work. Among the interesting memorabilia are the many gifts from adoring admirers. See chapter 6.

• **Rorke's Drift and Isandlwana** (Battlefields, KwaZulu-Natal): These two Anglo-Zulu War battlefield sites, within walking distance of each other, encompass both the British Empire's most humiliating defeat and its most heroic victory in the colonies. At the Battle of Isandlwana, more than 1,300 armed men were wiped out by a "bunch of savages armed with sticks," as the mighty Zulu nation was then referred to. Hours later, 139 British soldiers (of which 35 were ill) warded off a force of 4,000 Zulus for 12 hours, for which an unprecedented 11 Victorian Crosses were awarded. See chapter 9.

• **Kwa Muhle Museum** (Durban, KwaZulu-Natal): Excellent user-friendly displays explain how the "Durban System" not only exploited the indigenous peoples, but also made them pay for its administration. It's a good introduction to the discriminatory laws that preceded apartheid. See chapter 9.

• **The Vukani Collection** (Eshowe, KwaZulu-Natal): While most Westerners head for the cultural villages to gain some insight into Zulu tribal customs and culture, Vukani is where Zulu parents take their children. With the largest collection of Zulu artifacts in the world, this is a highly recommended excursion, particularly for those interested in crafts. Note that if you aren't venturing this far afield, the **Campbell Collection** in Durban is an alternative. See chapter 9.

8 The Most Authentic Culinary Experiences

• **Ordering a Cape Malay Dish** (Cape Town): Typified by mild, sweet curries and stews, this cuisine is easy on the uninitiated palate. The most authentic restaurant is Biesmiellah, located in the Bo-Kaap in Cape Town, but many of the top restaurants in the Cape incorporate Cape Malay spicing in creative ways. See chapter 4.

- **Lunching in the Vineyards** (Winelands): Set aside at least one afternoon to lunch in the Winelands overlooking vine-carpeted valleys. Recommended options include the lovely terrace at **Constantia Uitsig** (© **021/794-4480**), on the Constantia Wine Route, and a window table at **La Petite Ferme** (© **021/876-3016**), overlooking the lush Franschhoek Valley. See chapter 4.

- **High Tea at the Nellie** (Cape Town): Regularly voted the top hotel in Africa, the Mount Nelson has been serving up the best high tea south of the equator for over a century. Luxuriate on sofas under chandeliers as plates piled high with cucumber sandwiches and cream puffs are served to the strains of the tinkling pianist. A graciously colonial experience, and a relative bargain at R100 ($15) a head. See chapter 4.

- **Braaing Crayfish on the Beach** (West Coast, Western Cape): The West Coast all-you-can-eat beach *braais* (barbecues) are legendary, giving you an opportunity to try a variety of local fish. Your best bet is Muisbosskerm, near Lamberts Bay, an ideal spot if you want to combine a trip to the Cederberg. See chapter 5.

- **Eating with Your Fingers:** You'll find that the African staple *pap* (maize-meal prepared as a stiff porridge that resembles polenta) is best sampled by balling a bit in one hand and dipping the edge into a sauce or stew—try *umngqusho,* a stew made from maize kernels, sugar beans, chiles, and potatoes, and said to be one of Nelson Mandela's favorites. You're most likely to sample pap on a township tour (see chapters 4, 6, and 7).

- **Dining Under the Stars to the Sounds of the Bush** (private game reserves throughout southern Africa): There's nothing like fresh air to work up an appetite, unless it's the smell of sizzling food cooked over an open fire. Happily, dinners at private game reserves combine both more often than not. Weather permitting, meals are served in a *boma* (a reeded enclosure), or in the bush in riverbeds or under large trees. Armed rangers and massive fires keep predators at bay.

- **Chewing Biltong on a Road Trip:** *Biltong,* strips of game, beef, or ostrich cured with spices and dried, are sold at farm stalls and butcher shops throughout the country. This popular local tradition that dates back to the Voortrekkers is something of an acquired taste, but it's almost addictive once you've started.

Planning Your Trip to Southern Africa

Most first-time visitors to South Africa are amazed at how sophisticated the infrastructure is here, but it's still a developing country—the high levels of poverty can be disturbing, and service standards can be patchy. Although generally smaller than those in Europe and the United States, South Africa's major cities offer all the same facilities, and it's a good idea to start your southern African trip here. Unless you're heading into really remote areas (which some Botswana camps constitute), don't worry about finding what you need: Anything you've forgotten can be bought here, credit cards are an accepted form of payment, and you're as likely to be affected by water- or food-borne illnesses as you would be back home. You'll also find a reasonably efficient tourism infrastructure, with plenty of services and facilities designed to help you make the most of your trip. Start by browsing the Web and contacting your local travel agent. Or simply read this chapter.

1 The Regions in Brief

SOUTH AFRICA

South Africa once consisted of four large provinces with borders created during the country's colonial past. These were where, by law, the white population resided. The black "tribes" were crammed into a number of shamefully small, quasi-independent homelands peppered throughout the country. After the 1994 elections, which finally saw Nelson Mandela the rightful leader of the "New" South Africa, the country was redivided into nine new provinces, but with the exception of Gauteng, spatial integration of the races has been slow.

For the first-time visitor, there are usually three crucial stops: a trip to **Big-Game Country,** most of which is located in **Mpumalanga** and the **Limpopo Province,** a visit to **Cape Town** and its **Winelands,** and, time allowing, a

self-drive tour of the **Garden Route** in the Western Cape.

THE WESTERN & EASTERN CAPE

The least African of all the provinces, the Western Cape is also the most popular, primarily due to the legendary beauty of its capital city, **Cape Town,** the neighboring **Winelands,** and the scenic coastal belt called the **Garden Route,** which winds through South Africa's well-traveled Lakes District. It also offers some of the best beach-based whale-watching in the world on the **Overberg Coast;** the world's most spectacular spring flowers display on the West Coast, north of Cape Town; and in the **Karoo,** the quaint *dorps* (small towns) that typified rural Afrikaans culture. The mountains and hills that trail the coastline are a botanist's and hiker's dream, with the Cape Floral Kingdom—an awesome array of more

Southern Africa

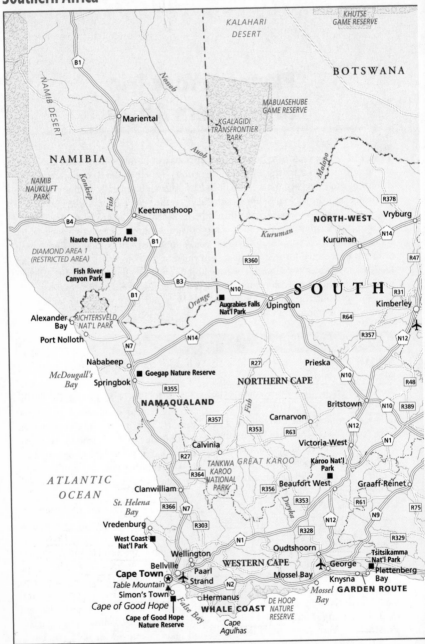

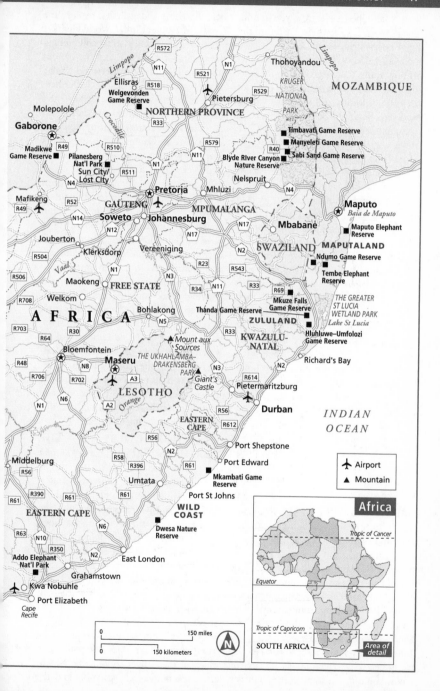

R572
R518
R521
N11
N1
Thohoyandou
Limpopo
Ellisras
Welgevonden
Game Reserve
R529
MOZAMBIQUE
KRUGER
NATIONAL
PARK
Pietersburg
Molepolole
NORTHERN PROVINCE
R33
Gaborone
Crocodile
R579
Timbavati Game Reserve
Manyeleti Game Reserve
R40
Sabi Sand Game Reserve
R49
R510
Madikwe
Game Reserve
Pilanesberg
Nat'l Park
Sun City/
Lost City
R511
N1
N11
Blyde River Canyon
Nature Reserve
Nelspruit
N4
Mafikeng
Pretoria
Mhluzi
N4
Maputo
Baia de Maputo
R52
GAUTENG
MPUMALANGA
R49
N14
Soweto
Johannesburg
N17
Mbabane
Maputo Elephant
Reserve
N12
N17
MAPUTALAND
Jouberton
Vereeniging
N2
SWAZILAND
Ndumo Game Reserve
Klerksdorp
R504
R23
R543
Tembe Elephant
Reserve
R506
N1
N3
R69
Maokeng
FREE STATE
R34
N11
R33
Mkuze Falls
Game Reserve
THE GREATER
ST LUCIA
WETLAND PARK
Lake St Lucia
R708
Welkom
Bohlakong
Thanda Game Reserve
A F R I C A
N5
ZULULAND
R703
R30
R33
KWAZULU-
NATAL
Hluhluwe–Umfolozi
Game Reserve
R64
Mount aux
Sources
Bloemfontein
THE UKHAHLAMBA-
DRAKENSBERG
PARK
Richard's Bay
R48
N8
Maseru
R706
R702
Giant's
Castle
N3
R614
LESOTHO
A3
Pietermaritzburg
N2
A2
Orange
Durban
N1
N6
R56
EASTERN
CAPE
INDIAN
OCEAN
R612
Middelburg
R56
R58
Port Shepstone
N2
R396
R61
Port Edward
R61
R390
R61
R61
Umtata
Mkambati Game
Reserve
Port St Johns
EASTERN CAPE
WILD
COAST
R63
N10
N6
R350
Dwesa Nature
Reserve
Addo Elephant
Nat'l Park
N2
East London
Kwa Nobuhle
Grahamstown
Port Elizabeth
Cape
Recife

✈ Airport
▲ Mountain

Africa

Tropic of Cancer

Equator

Tropic of Capricorn

SOUTH AFRICA

Area of
detail

0   150 miles
0   150 kilometers

than 8,000 species—a treat year-round. The Eastern Cape is where you'll find the Big 5 reserves closest to Cape Town (also malaria-free), as well as two of the country's top trails: the **Otter Trail** in the Tsitsikamma National Park, the exit point of the Garden Route; and the **Wild Coast,** bordering KwaZulu-Natal.

Established as a port in 1652, Cape Town was the first gateway to southern Africa from Europe, and still retains more of a colonial feel than any other major city. It is cut off from the rest of the country by mountain ranges and has its own distinctive climate—cool, wet winters and hot, windy summers—ideal for the wine and deciduous fruits that further cocoon the Cape's inhabitants from the harsh realties of the hinterland. This geographic insularity, and the wounds inflicted by apartheid, have bred their own set of unique problems, however. Gang warfare and drug trafficking in the Cape Flats—a region created by the notoriously draconian Group Areas Act, which relocated people of color to housing projects on the outskirts of town—as well as the increased rancor of the swelling homeless (further exacerbated by the stream of economic refugees from the Eastern Cape and beyond) are serious problems. In a city this size, such problems are hardly unusual, but what is surprising is how cut off from them you'll feel as a visitor.

GAUTENG & FREE STATE Situated on the inner plateau, or highveld, the Free State and Gauteng were originally covered with grasslands. In the Free State this made way for farming, while the discovery of gold in the late 19th century was to change the Gauteng landscape irreparably. Today Johannesburg International Airport is the biggest and busiest in sub-Saharan Africa, and Jo'burg (or Jozi, as **Johannesburg** is also referred to by locals) its busiest city. Here in the "Place of Gold" you can visit some of the country's best museums and galleries; explore the **Cradle of Humankind,** a World Heritage Site where paleontologists are still probing the origins of mankind; and the famous gold mines of the **Witwatersrand** ("ridge of white waters"). Miners dig deeper here than anywhere else in the world, and although gold resources are starting to dwindle, all the country's major industries are based in Gauteng. Johannesburg's northern suburbs blend almost seamlessly into **Pretoria,** or **Tshwane,** as the country's administrative capital is in the process of being renamed, and the resulting urban sprawl covers most of the province and houses an estimated population of five to seven million. Downtown Johannesburg's northern suburbs blend almost seamlessly into **Pretoria,** the country's administrative capital. Jo'burg is where you'll see the growing black middle class flexing its financial muscle and where Africans from all over the continent congregate to shop, party, and get down to business—all of which makes it one of the most exhilarating cities on the continent, not least because it is so predatory: Despite huge improvements in crime prevention and control, it is still advisable to act with due caution while visiting this area.

THE NORTH-WEST & THE NORTHERN CAPE This is *Thelma and Louise* territory, perfect for people who like taking road trips past endless horizons with little sign of human habitation. The North-West is not as arid as the neighboring Northern Cape and is much more accessible; its most famous attraction—**Sun City** and its centerpiece, the **Palace of the Lost City**—can be visited as a day trip from Johannesburg or Pretoria. The region also offers easy access to malaria-free Big 5 game reserves, the best of which is **Madikwe,** which has seen a number of new lodge openings in the past 2 years but is still less congested than much of the Kruger region. The Northern Cape is the least accessible and the least populated province in South Africa, and—perhaps as a consequence—has some of the most beautiful scenery in the world, though the starkness of the desert reserves won't strike a chord in everyone. But no one can remain unmoved in the spring when the first rains transform the vast arid plains of Namaqualand into horizon-filled fields of flowers, making this an ideal side trip from Cape Town.

MPUMALANGA & THE LIMPOPO PROVINCE To the east of Gauteng and the Free State lies the **Escarpment**—the end of the Drakensberg mountain range that rises in the Eastern Cape, running up the western border of KwaZulu-Natal before dividing Mpumalanga and the Limpopo Province into the high- and lowveld. Traveling through the Escarpment to reach the lowveld's **Big-Game Country,** you will find some of the country's most gorgeous views, the world's third-largest canyon, the largest man-made forests in the world, and the country's first gold-rush towns, one of which has been declared a living monument. Traveling east on scenic mountain passes, you will drop thousands of feet to the lowveld plains before reaching Big-Game Country. If you want to see Africa's wild animals on a budget, **Kruger National Park** offers the best deal on the continent—a high density of game combined with spotlessly clean, albeit spartan, accommodations. But for the well-heeled (or visitors wanting that once-in-a-lifetime treat), Kruger is now also home to several high-end **private concessions,** combining ultra-luxury lodgings with fantastic game-viewing. Along Kruger's western flank, with no fences between, lie the **private game lodges** in the **Sabi Sand, Manyeleti,** and **Timbavati reserves,** which offer a variety of experiences—from over-the-top-decadent luxury chalets with private plunge pools to rough huts with no electricity. Closer to Johannesburg, the malaria-free **Welgevonden** reserve offers a Big 5 alternative for those with limited time.

KWAZULU-NATAL Hot and humid in summer, warm and balmy in winter, the KwaZulu-Natal coast offers excellent beach holidays, with temperatures never dropping below 61°F (16°C), and the Indian Ocean kept warm by the Mozambique Current, which washes past its subtropical shores. Unfortunately, this is no well-kept secret, and development along much of its south and north coasts (Durban being the center) has resulted in another paradise lost and an endless string of ugly, indifferent vacation and timeshare beach resorts. There are exceptions, the best of which lie north, like the **St Lucia Wetland Park,** Africa's biggest estuary and home to large populations of Nile crocodile and hippo, and within easy striking distance of **Hluhluwe-Umfolozi,** the province's largest Big 5 resort.

After Cape Town, **Durban** is the most enjoyable city in the country to visit, with great museums, arts and crafts, restaurants, the busiest port in Africa, and an interesting blend of cultures—besides the Zulu, the largest indigenous group in South Africa, the biggest population of Indians outside of India resides here. It is also well situated, should you be interested in combining a visit to a Big 5 game reserve with diving or snorkeling, taking one of the historic battlefields tours, or hiking through the majestic Drakensberg range. With a proposed new international airport in Durban scheduled for completion in 2009, this relatively undiscovered region is set to offer the Cape some stiff competition.

ZIMBABWE

A country of great natural beauty, Zimbabwe has a wide variety of habitats: In the West lie the expanses of the Kalahari sand; traveling east, you pass through woodland savanna and open grassland, until, in the East, you come up against the lush montane forests of the Eastern Highlands. However, with President Robert Mugabe's relentless pursuit of a land "redistribution" policy, as well as serious food shortages, press oppression, and victimization of opposition party members, the Zimbabwean dollar remains in free fall. Although this means there are bargains to be had, traveling can be difficult, not least due to fuel and food shortages. Thankfully, the country's primary attraction, **Victoria Falls,** is within striking distance of Botswana and bordering Zambia, making it easy to reach and safe to visit. Chapter 10 deals with the best way to experience what has justifiably been described as one of the wonders of the world, from both the Zimbabwean and Zambian sides.

BOTSWANA

Straddling the Tropic of Capricorn in southern Africa, Botswana is truly one of the last pristine wilderness areas on the continent. Roughly the size of France, it is bordered by Namibia to the west and north, Zimbabwe to the east, and South Africa to the south.

A sparsely populated country of just over one million inhabitants, Botswana offers a varied wilderness experience, from forest to salt pan, bushveld to rolling savanna, ancient lake beds to palm-fringed islands. The waterless Kalahari covers two-thirds of its surface, so it is nothing short of incredible that it is also home to one of the world's largest inland delta systems—the **Okavango Delta,** highlight of Botswana. This 15,000-sq.-km (5,850-sq.-mile) inland flood plain fans out in the northwestern corner of the country, creating a paradise of palms, papyrus, and crystal-clear channels and backwaters. The life-giving waters provide a much-needed oasis for birds and animals, and consequently unparalleled opportunities for humans to view them.

In addition to the delta, Botswana has **Chobe National Park** to the northeast, a 12,000-sq.-km (4,680-sq.-mile) park that is famed for its huge elephant herds, while to the southeast are the spectacular wide-open spaces of **Makgadikgadi** and **Nxai Pans.** Time (and money) allowing, a visit to these areas are essential to your southern Africa itinerary.

2　Visitor Information

SOUTH AFRICA South African Tourism (**www.southafrica.net**).

In the U.S. 500 5th Ave. 20th Floor, Suite 2040, New York, NY 10110 (© 212/730-2929; newyork@southafrica.net). For brochures, call © 800/782-9772. Los Angeles office: © 310/643-6481.

In Canada 4117 Lawrence Ave. E., Suite 2, Ontario M1E 2S2 (© 0416/966-4059).

In the U.K. Ms Nolwazi Mdluli, 6 Alt Grove, London SW19 4DZ (© 0870/1550044 for brochure line; info.uk@southafrica.net).

In Australia Bangu Masisi, Level 1, 117 York St., Sydney, NSW 2000 (© 61-2-9261-5000; info@southafrica.net).

ZIMBABWE Zimbabwean Tourism Authority (**www.zimbabwetourism.co.zw**).

In the U.S. 128 E. 56 St., New York, NY 10022 (© 212/486-3444).

In Canada Zimbabwe High Commission, 332 Somerset St., West Ottawa, Ontario K2P OJ9 (© 613/237-4388).

In the U.K. Zimbabwe High Commission, 429 Strand, London WC2R OQE (© 44-207-240 61 69; zta.london@btclick.com).

Tips Websites to Surf for the Latest Happenings

The official South African tourism website, **www.southafrica.net**, offers a comprehensive listing of events taking place throughout the country and links you to **www.africaexperts.com**, a division of Goway Travel that specializes in safaris and vacations to suit various budgets (like the 11-day itinerary for $1,999, including airfares; click on "SA Stories"). For the latest news, reviews, and tips and overviews on countries throughout Africa, go to **www.getawaytoafrica. co.za**, the site of Africa's best-selling travel magazine; for more general views, you may also want to take a look at **www.africanexplorer.co.za**, a virtual magazine that features some of the country's top local journalists, like Heather Dugmore. To find out what's happening in South Africa, from politics to art exhibitions, visit **www.mg.co.za**, the home page for the *Mail & Guardian*, South Africa's best national newspaper. To get a live, close-up view of the action in Big-Game country, click on **www.africam.co.za**.

In Australia The High Commission, 11 Culogoa Circuit, O'Malley, Canberra ACT 2606 (✆ **02/6286-2700**). There is no representation in New Zealand.

BOTSWANA Botswana Tourism (**www. gov.bw**).

In the U.S. The Embassy of the Republic of Botswana, 1531–3 New Hampshire Ave. NW, Washington, DC 20036 (✆ **202/244-4990**).

In the U.K. 6 Stratford Place, London W1N 9AE (✆ **0207/499-0031**).

3 Entry Requirements & Customs

Citizens of the United States, the E.U., the U.K., Canada, Australia, and New Zealand need only a valid passport and return ticket for a 90-day stay in South Africa and Botswana. Upon entering S.A., you will automatically be given a free entry permit sticker. However, please note that under South Africa's Immigration Act of 2002, in force since April 7, 2003, the passport must contain at least one unused page for endorsements. Visitors wanting to stay for a longer period will have to apply formally for a visa, as opposed to relying on the automatic entry permit. For more information, visit the South African Home Affairs Department website at http://home-affairs.pwv. gov.za.

To enter Zimbabwe, U.S., Canadian, Australian, and New Zealand citizens are issued visas on arrival for US$30/US$45 (single/multiple entry); U.K. citizens are charged up to £100 for a multiple-entry visa. Note that visa fees are subject to frequent change due to diplomatic unease between the Zimbabwe government and many other states. You can also obtain your visa in advance for US$60/US$75 (single/double entry), which will reduce the amount of time you need to spend at any border post; consult your travel agent in this regard or, to simplify the process (at a price), use Travel Document Systems, 925 15th St. NW, Suite 300, Washington, DC 20005 (✆ **202/638/3800; www.traveldocs.com**). A Zambian visa costs US$40 if purchased in advance from the consulate (£40 if you are U.K. citizen). Day visitors to the Zambian side of Victoria Falls can purchase a US$10 day visa at the bridge. If you plan to stay on the Zambian side but are transferring from Victoria Falls airport in Zimbabwe, your lodge—given warning—can arrange

Tips　Phone Home: Calling to & from South Africa

To call southern Africa from another country: Dial the international access code (United States or Canada 011, United Kingdom or New Zealand 00, Australia 0011) plus the country code (the country code for South Africa is 27; for Zimbabwe, it is 263; for Botswana, it is 267), plus the local number minus the 0.

To make an international call from South Africa: Dial 09, then the country code (United States or Canada 1, UK 44, Australia 61, New Zealand 64), the area code, and the local number.

To charge international calls from South Africa: Dial AT&T Direct (✆ 0-800-99-0123), Sprint (✆ 0800-99-0001), or MCI (✆ 0800-99-0011).

At press time, AT&T Direct, Sprint, and MCI did not have international toll-free access numbers from Zimbabwe or Botswana.

To make a local call: Drop the country code and add a zero (0) to the city code (except in Botswana, which has no city codes). At press time, you did not have to dial the city code when calling from within the city limits, but Telkom has been threatening to change this since 2003; it's best to ask your host or dial directory assistance on ✆ 1023. Note also that if you are using a mobile phone, you always need to enter the city code before the telephone number.

Mobile/cell numbers: Be aware that numbers that start with the codes 082, 083, 084, 072, and 073 are mobile or cell numbers, and these codes must not be dropped.

Looking for a number: In South Africa: Call directory assistance at ✆ 1023 for numbers in South Africa, and ✆ 0903 for international numbers. To track down a service, call ✆ 10118.

a visa waiver for Zambia; you will then need only a multiple-entry visa for Zimbabwe.

To enter Botswana, you require a passport valid for 6 months, sufficient funds to finance your stay, and outgoing travel documents. Holders of U.S., Commonwealth, and most European passports do not require visas.

For additional information on entry requirements, travelers may contact the embassies listed under "Visitor Information," above.

PASSPORT INFORMATION

Allow plenty of time before your trip to apply for a passport; processing normally takes 3 weeks but can take longer during busy periods (especially spring). And keep in mind that if you need a passport in a hurry, you'll pay a higher processing fee. When traveling, safeguard your passport in an inconspicuous, inaccessible place like a money belt and keep a copy of the critical pages with your passport number in a separate place. If you lose your passport, visit the nearest consulate or embassy of your native country as soon as possible for a replacement. Passport applications are downloadable from the Internet sites listed below.

Note: The websites listed provide downloadable passport applications as well as the current fees for processing passport applications.

FOR RESIDENTS OF THE UNITED STATES

If you're applying for a first-time passport, you need to do it in person at 1 of 13 passport offices throughout the United States; a federal, state, or probate court; or a major post office (though not all post offices accept applications; call the number below to find the ones that do). You need to present a certified birth certificate as proof of citizenship, and it is wise to bring along your driver's license, state or military ID, and social security card. You also need two identical passport-size photos (2×2 in.), taken at any corner photo shop (not one of the strip photos, however, from a photo-vending machine).

For people 16 and older, a passport is valid for 10 years and costs $55; for those under 16, it's valid for 5 years and costs $40. If you're over 16 and have a valid passport that was issued within the past 12 years, you can renew it by mail and bypass the $15 handling fee. Allow plenty of time before your trip to apply; processing normally takes 3 weeks but can take longer during busy periods (especially spring). For general information, call the **National Passport Information Center** (*(C)* **877/487-2778;** http://travel.state. gov).

FOR RESIDENTS OF CANADA

You can pick up a passport application at one of 28 regional passport offices or most travel agencies. The passport is valid for 5 years and costs C$85, C$35 for children 3 to 15, and C$20 for children under 3. Applications, which must be accompanied by two identical passport-size photographs and proof of Canadian citizenship, are available at travel agencies throughout Canada or from the central **Passport Office, Department of Foreign Affairs and International Trade,** Ottawa K1A 0G3 (*(C)* **800/567-6868;** www.dfait-maeci.gc.ca/passport). Processing takes 5 to 10 days if you apply in person, or about 3 weeks by mail.

FOR RESIDENTS OF THE UNITED KINGDOM

To pick up an application for a standard 10-year passport (5-year passport for children under 16), visit the nearest Passport Office, major post office, or travel agency. You can also contact the **United Kingdom Passport Service** at *(C)* **0870/571-0410** or visit its website at www.passport. gov.uk. Passports are £33 for adults and £19 for children under 16, with an additional £30 fee if you apply in person at a Passport Office. Processing takes about 2 weeks (1 week if you apply at the Passport Office).

FOR RESIDENTS OF IRELAND

You can apply for a 10-year passport, costing €57, at the **Passport Office,** Setanta Centre, Molesworth Street, Dublin 2 (*(C)* **01/671-1633;** www.irlgov.ie/iveagh). Those under 18 and over 65 must apply for a €12 3-year passport. You can also apply at 1A South Mall, Cork (*(C)* **021/272-525**) or over the counter at most main post offices.

FOR RESIDENTS OF AUSTRALIA

Apply at your local post office or passport office, or search the government website at www.dfat.gov.au/passports. Passports for adults are A$144 and, for those under 18, A$72.

FOR RESIDENTS OF NEW ZEALAND

You can pick up a passport application at any travel agency or Link Centre. For more information, contact the **Passport Office,** P.O. Box 805, Wellington (*(C)* **0800/225-050;** www.passports.govt. nz). Passports for adults are NZ$80 and, for those under 16, NZ$40.

CUSTOMS

When entering South Africa, items for personal use are duty-free. Goods intended as gifts or trade are duty-free up to the value of R3,000 ($448) and thereafter taxed at 20%. You're allowed to bring in up to 2 liters of wine, 1 liter of spirits, 50 milliliters of perfume, 250 milliliters of eau de toilette, and 200 cigarettes or 20 cigars or 250 grams of tobacco.

The above restrictions on alcohol, perfume, and tobacco also apply to Zimbabwe and Botswana.

Before leaving your home country, register your foreign-made electronic equipment with Customs.

WHAT YOU CAN TAKE HOME & IMPORT RESTRICTIONS

Returning **U.S. citizens** who have been away for at least 48 hours are allowed to bring back, once every 30 days, $800 worth of merchandise duty-free. You'll be charged a flat rate of duty on the next $1,000 worth of purchases. Any dollar amount beyond that is dutiable at whatever rates apply. On mailed gifts, the duty-free limit is $200. Be sure to have your receipts or purchases handy to expedite the declaration process. *Note:* If you owe duty, you are required to pay on your arrival in the United States, by cash, personal check, government or traveler's check, or money order, and in some locations, a Visa or MasterCard.

To avoid having to pay duty on foreign-made personal items you owned before you left on your trip, bring along a bill of sale, insurance policy, jeweler's appraisal, or receipts of purchase. Or you can register items that can be readily identified by a permanently affixed serial number or marking—think laptop computers, cameras, and CD players—with Customs before you leave. Take the items to the nearest Customs office or register them with Customs at the airport from which you're departing. You'll receive, at no cost, a Certificate of Registration, which allows duty-free entry for the life of the item.

With some exceptions, you cannot bring fresh fruits and vegetables into the United States. For specifics on what you can bring back, download the invaluable free pamphlet *Know Before You Go* online at **www.cbp.gov**. (Click on "Travel," and then click on "Know Before You Go! Online Brochure") Or contact the **U.S. Customs & Border Protection (CBP)**, 1300 Pennsylvania Ave., NW, Washington, DC 20229 (© **877/287-8667**), and request the pamphlet.

For a clear summary of **Canadian** rules, write for the booklet *I Declare*, issued by the **Canada Border Services Agency** (© **800/461-9999** in Canada, or 204/983-3500; www.cbsa-asfc.gc.ca). Canada allows its citizens a C$750 exemption, and you're allowed to bring back duty-free one carton of cigarettes, one can of tobacco, 40 imperial ounces of liquor, and 50 cigars. In addition, you're allowed to mail gifts to Canada valued at less than C$60 a day, provided they're unsolicited and don't contain alcohol or tobacco (write on the package "Unsolicited gift, under $60 value"). All valuables should be declared on the Y-38 form before departure from Canada, including serial numbers of valuables you already own, such as expensive foreign cameras. *Note:* The C$750 exemption can be used only once a year and only after an absence of 7 days.

U.K. citizens returning from **a non-E.U. country** have a Customs allowance of: 200 cigarettes; 50 cigars; 250 grams of smoking tobacco; 2 liters of still table wine; 1 liter of spirits or strong liqueurs (over 22% volume); 2 liters of fortified wine, sparkling wine, or other liqueurs; 60cc (mL) perfume; 250cc (mL) of toilet water; and £145 worth of all other goods, including gifts and souvenirs. People under 17 cannot have the tobacco or alcohol allowance. For more information, contact HM Customs & Excise at © **0845/010-9000** (from outside the U.K.,

020/8929-0152), or consult their website at www.hmce.gov.uk.

The duty-free allowance in **Australia** is A\$400 or, for those under 18, A\$200. Citizens can bring in 250 cigarettes or 250 grams of loose tobacco, and 1,125 milliliters of alcohol. If you're returning with valuables you already own, such as foreign-made cameras, you should file form B263. A helpful brochure available from Australian consulates or Customs offices is *Know Before You Go*. For more information, call the **Australian Customs Service** at © **1300/363-263,** or log on to www.customs.gov.au.

The duty-free allowance for **New Zealand** is NZ\$700. Citizens over 17 can bring in 200 cigarettes, 50 cigars, or 250 grams of tobacco (or a mixture of all three if their combined weight doesn't exceed 250g), plus 4.5 liters of wine and beer, or 1.125 liters of liquor. New Zealand currency does not carry import or export restrictions. Fill out a certificate of export, listing the valuables you are taking out of the country; that way, you can bring them back without paying duty. Most questions are answered in a free pamphlet available at New Zealand consulates and Customs offices: *New Zealand Customs Guide for Travellers, Notice no. 4.* For more information, contact **New Zealand Customs,** The Customhouse, 17–21 Whitmore St., Box 2218, Wellington (© **04/473-6099** or 0800/428-786; www.customs.govt.nz).

U.K. citizens returning from a non-E.U. country have a Customs allowance of 200 cigarettes, 50 cigars, or 250 grams of smoking tobacco; 2 liters of still table wine; 1 liter of spirits or strong liqueurs (over 22% volume); 2 liters of fortified wine, sparkling wine, or other liqueurs; 60 milliliters perfume; 250 milliliters of toilet water; and £145 worth of all other goods, including gifts and souvenirs. People under 17 cannot have the tobacco or alcohol allowance. For more information, contact **HM Customs & Excise,** Passenger Enquiry Point, 2nd Floor, Wayfarer House, Great South West Road, Feltham, Middlesex TW14 8NP (© **0181/910-3744,** or 44/181-910-3744 from outside the U.K.), or consult their website at www.open.gov.uk.

Canadian citizens returning are allowed a C\$500 exemption (note that this can be used only once a year and only after an absence of 7 days), as well as 200 cigarettes, 1 kilogram (2.2 lb.) of tobacco, 40 imperial ounces of wine or liquor, and 50 cigars. In addition, you're allowed to mail gifts to Canada from abroad at the rate of C\$60 a day, provided they're unsolicited and don't contain alcohol or tobacco (write on the package "Unsolicited gift, under \$60 value"). All valuables should be declared on the Y-38 form before departure from Canada, including serial numbers of valuables you already own, such as expensive foreign cameras. For a clear summary of Canadian rules, write for the booklet *I Declare,* issued by **Revenue Canada,** 2265 St. Laurent Blvd., Ottawa K1G 4KE (© **613/993-0534**).

The duty-free allowance in Australia is A\$400 or, for those under 18, A\$200. Personal property mailed back should be marked "Australian goods returned" to avoid payment of duty. Upon returning to Australia, citizens can bring in 250 cigarettes or 250 grams of loose tobacco, and 1,125 milliliters of alcohol. If you're returning with valuable goods you already own, such as foreign-made cameras, you should file form B263. A helpful brochure, available from Australian consulates or Customs offices, is *Know Before You Go.* For more information, contact **Australian Customs Services,** GPO Box 8, Sydney, NSW 2001 (© **02/9213-2000**).

The duty-free allowance for **New Zealand** is NZ\$700. Citizens over 17 can bring in 200 cigarettes, 50 cigars, or 250 grams of tobacco (or a mixture of all three if their combined weight doesn't exceed 250g), plus 4.5 liters of wine and beer, or 1.125 liters of liquor. New Zealand currency does not carry import or export restrictions. Fill out a certificate of export, listing the valuables you are taking out of the country; that way, you can bring them back without paying duty. Most questions are answered in a free pamphlet available at New Zealand consulates and Customs offices: *New Zealand Customs Guide for Travellers, Notice no. 4.* For more information, contact **New Zealand Customs,** The Customhouse, 17–21 Whitmore St., Box 2218, Wellington (© **04/473-6099** or 0800/428-786; www.customs.govt.nz).

4 Money

CASH

For the most favorable rates, change money at banks (the exception to this is Zimbabwe, where the bank exchange rate is far from favorable; because of the huge differences in exchange rates, the best currency in Vic Falls is foreign, including traveler's checks).

The **South African currency unit** is the **rand** (R), with 100 cents making up R1. Notes come in R10, R20, R50, R100, and R200. Minted coins come in 1-, 2-, and 5-rand denominations, and 1, 2, 5, 10, 20, and 50 cents—small change doesn't buy much; use it for tips. Sadly, for foreign visitors, at any rate, the rand has continued to gain in strength and in May 2005 was hovering at R6.70 to US$1 and R11 to £1. While a few doomsayers continue to predict a fall in the rand's fortunes, there are certainly no indicators at this time to support this, so you shouldn't delay your vacation in hopes of a drop in the rand's value.

In the unlikely event that you will need local currency while visiting Vic Falls (see "Money Matters" in chapter 10), note that the monetary unit in **Zimbabwe** is the **Zimbabwe dollar,** abbreviated as Z$ and comprising 100 cents. Notes come in denominations of Z$2, Z$5, Z$10, Z$20, Z$50, and Z$100. The conversion rate at the time of going to press was US$1 = Z$810, or £1 = Z$1,304. Note that travelers to Zimbabwe are usually required to pay for all lodging with credit cards or internationally convertible currency such as U.S. dollars or British pounds.

The **pula** (which, incidentally, means "rain") is the official currency of **Botswana.** One pula (P) is divided into 100 thebe. Bills come in P1, P2, P5, P10, P20, and P50, and coins in 1t, 2t, 5t, 10t, 25t, 50t, and P1. This is the most expensive region in southern Africa; at press time, the exchange rates were P5.44 to US$1 and P9.70 to £1.

For up-to-the-minute currency conversions, go to www.xe.com/ucc.

TRAVELER'S CHECKS

Note that credit cards are generally accepted throughout southern Africa, particularly MasterCard and Visa (less so American Express), and you can use them to draw cash at ATMs, which you'll find throughout South Africa, making traveler's checks somewhat redundant.

You can get traveler's checks at almost any bank. American Express offers denominations of $10, $20, $50, $100, $500, and (for cardholders only) $1,000; you can also purchase them in South African rands. You'll pay a service charge ranging from 1% to 4%. You can also get American Express traveler's checks over the phone by calling © **800/221-7282;** by using this number, Amex gold and platinum cardholders are exempt from the 1% fee. AAA members can obtain checks without a fee at most AAA offices or by calling © **866/339-3378.**

Visa offers traveler's checks at Citibank locations nationwide, as well as several other banks. The service charge ranges between 1.5% and 2%; checks come in denominations of $20, $50, $100, $500, and $1,000. Call ✆ **800/732-1322** for information. MasterCard also offers traveler's checks. Call ✆ **800/223-9920** for a location near you.

ATMs

ATMs offering 24-hour service are located throughout South Africa. ATMs are linked to a national network that most likely includes your bank at home. **Cirrus** (✆ **800/424-7787;** www.master card.com) and **PLUS** (✆ **800/843-7587;** www.visa.com) are the two most popular networks; check the back of your ATM card to see which network your bank belongs to. Be sure to check the daily withdrawal limit before you depart, and make sure your PIN is valid.

CREDIT CARDS

American Express, Diners Club, Master-Card, and Visa are accepted at most hotels, restaurants, and stores in South Africa, though the latter two are the most popular here. Many lodges in Botswana do not accept credit cards (though in all

likelihood you will be booking and paying for these ahead of time as part of a safari). For the most part, however, you'll find credit cards to be invaluable when you travel. They are a safe way to carry money and provide a convenient record of all your expenses, and they generally offer relatively good exchange rates. You can also withdraw cash advances from any bank (though there's often a relatively hefty withdrawal fee, so make sure the amount you draw is big enough to make it worth your while). At most banks, you don't even need to go to a teller; you can get a cash advance at the ATM if you know your PIN. If you've forgotten your PIN or didn't even know you had one, call the phone number on the back of your credit card and ask. It usually takes 5 to 7 business days, though some banks will provide the number over the phone if you pass security clearance. Keep in mind that when you use your credit card abroad, most banks assess a 2% fee above the 1% fee charged by Visa or Master-Card or American Express for currency conversion on credit charges. But credit cards still may be the smart way to go when you factor in things like exorbitant ATM fees and high traveler's check exchange rates (and service fees).

5 When to Go

Because southern Africa is such a large area, with each region offering different seasonal benefits, the time you go should help determine where you go.

SOUTH AFRICA

The summer months (Nov–Feb) tend to attract the majority of visitors (particularly from Europe). Fortunately, the country is big enough to absorb these increased numbers without causing the discomfort most people associate with busy seasons. Be aware, however, that accommodations prices do increase in summer, some by as much as 80%; and if you dislike crowds,

you should try to avoid South Africa's busiest school holidays, which take place over December and the Easter long weekend. Spring (Sept–Oct) and autumn (Mar–Apr) are considered by many to be the best times to visit, when temperatures are not quite so high (the balmy to baking days of Feb–Mar are particularly popular in Cape Town). Winter (June–Aug) brings substantial benefits, too: From July to November are the months when the Southern Right whales migrate to the Cape's southern coast, providing guaranteed sightings. From May to August are considered the best months for sighting big game: The foliage is less dense, malaria areas offer a lower risk, and many of the private game reserves drop their prices substantially. This is also a good time to visit Botswana and Zimbabwe, though Victoria Falls will not be in full flood (Zimbabwe is a summer rainfall area), and malaria remains a high risk year-round in both these areas. Cape Town gets winter rainfall during what it calls its Green Season (May–Aug), though there are always sunny breaks. Thanks to the year-round sunshine that the Garden Route and Karoo enjoy, any time is a good time to tour this region.

Weather Chart for Southern Africa

Cape Town, South Africa

	Jan	Feb	Mar	Apr	May	June	July	Aug	Sept	Oct	Nov	Dec
Temp. (°F)	61/79	59/79	57/77	54/73	50/68	46/64	45/63	45/64	46/66	50/70	55/75	59/77
Temp. (°C)	16/26	15/26	14/25	12/23	10/20	8/18	7/17	7/18	8/19	10/21	13/24	15/25
Rainfall (in.)	0.6	0.7	0.7	2.0	3.5	3.3	3.5	3.1	2.0	1.4	.5	.6

Johannesburg, South Africa

	Jan	Feb	Mar	Apr	May	June	July	Aug	Sept	Oct	Nov	Dec
Temp. (°F)	59/79	57/77	55/75	52/72	46/66	41/61	41/61	45/66	48/72	54/75	55/77	57/77
Temp. (°C)	15/26	14/25	13/24	11/22	8/19	5/16	5/16	7/19	9/22	12/24	13/25	14/25
Rainfall (in.)	4.5	3.8	2.9	2.5	0.9	0.3	0.3	0.2	0.1	2.7	4.6	4.3

Victoria Falls, Zimbabwe

	Jan	Feb	Mar	Apr	May	June	July	Aug	Sept	Oct	Nov	Dec
Temp. (°F)	65/85	64/85	62/85	57/84	49/81	43/76	42/77	47/82	55/89	62/91	64/90	64/86
Temp. (°C)	18/30	18/30	17/30	14/29	9/27	6/24	6/24	8/28	13/32	17/33	18/32	18/30
Rainfall (in.)	6.6	5	2.8	1.0	0.1	0	0	0	0.7	1.1	2.5	6.8

Maun, Botswana

	Jan	Feb	Mar	Apr	May	June	July	Aug	Sept	Oct	Nov	Dec
Temp. (°F)	66/90	66/88	64/88	57/88	48/82	43/77	43/77	48/82	55/91	64/95	66/93	66/90
Temp. (°C)	19/32	19/31	18/31	14/31	9/28	6/25	6/25	9/29	13/33	18/35	19/34	19/23
Rainfall (in.)	4.3	3.2	2.8	1.0	0.3	0.1	0	0	0	1.2	2.0	3.8

THE CLIMATE

Depending on where you are, average maximum temperatures can vary from 80°F/27°C (Cape Town) to 90°F/32°C (Kruger National Park) in the summer, and from an average 69°F/21°C (Cape Town) to 77°F/25°C (Durban) in winter. While summer is the most popular time, high humidity in KwaZulu-Natal can make for muggy days, and gale-force winds often occur in Cape Town and Port Elizabeth. Winter visitors would be well advised to pack warm clothes—despite higher average temperatures than in the United States or Europe, South Africa is simply not geared for the cold, and insulation and central heating are low on the priority list. Temperatures in the interior fluctuate wildly in winter; you're best off layering.

RAINFALL

South Africa is generally considered an arid region, with two-thirds of the country receiving less than 500 millimeters (20 in.) of rain a year. In the interior, rain usually falls in the summer, and spectacular thunderstorms and the smell of damp earth bring great relief from the searing heat. The Garden Route enjoys rain year-round, and in Cape Town and surrounds, the rain falls mostly in the winter, when the gray skies are a perfect foil for the burnt-orange strelitzias, pink proteas, and fields of white arum lilies—not to mention the perfect accompaniment to crackling fires and fine South African red wines.

HOLIDAYS

If you are traveling during the South African school holidays (check exact dates with South African Tourism), make sure you book your accommodations well in advance. Flights can also be impossible, particularly over the Christmas holidays (usually early Dec to mid-Jan). Easter holidays (usually the end of Mar to mid-Apr) can also be busy, while the Kruger is almost always packed during the winter vacation (mid-June to mid-July). There's another short school break in spring, from late September to October 7.

Public holidays in South Africa include New Year's Day; March 21 (Human Rights Day); Good Friday, Easter Sunday and Monday; April 27 (Founders/Freedom Day); May 1 (Workers Day); June 16 (Soweto/Youth Day); August 9 (Women's Day); September 24 (Heritage Day); December 16 (Day of Reconciliation); Christmas Day; and December 26 (Boxing Day).

ZIMBABWE

Zimbabwe's climate is similar to that in South Africa's northern provinces, with a summer rainy season and most of the rainfall occurring between December and mid-March. Summers are warm to hot (late Oct and Nov–Dec can be uncomfortable), and winters are mild. Malaria is still a danger in many areas, there are tsetse flies in parts of the Zambezi Valley and in the southeast, and be aware that certain rivers, lakes, and dams are infected with bilharzia. Victoria Falls are often at their fullest from January to mid-April, at the end of the rainy season,

though this is also when the mist created by the falling water may obscure the view, and malaria-carrying mosquitoes are at their most prolific. Temperatures are pleasantly reduced from May to October (81°F/27°C). Many think the best time to see the falls is from August to December, when the view is clearer (though the flow of the water is at its lowest). From June to December is high season for many of the upmarket lodges, which raise their prices during these months.

Holidays in Zimbabwe are New Year's Day, Good Friday through Easter Monday, April 18 (Independence Day), May 1 (Workers Day), April 25 (Africa Day), August 11 (Heroes Day), August 12 (Defense Forces Day), Christmas Day, and December 26 (Boxing Day).

BOTSWANA

Botswana has a pleasant subtropical climate with low humidity. Rain falls during the summer months, from November to March—this is a great time to visit the delta if you're interested in birds and plants, but it can get very hot. From April to September, the days are mild to warm, but temperatures drop sharply at night and early in the morning, particularly around June and July. Most consider these 2 months the best time to visit the delta, when the rain that falls on the Angolan bushveld plains seeps down to create what is referred to as the "flood." At this time, waterlilies bloom, countless aquatic creatures frolic in the water, and a huge diversity of game from the surrounding dry areas moves into the delta.

Holidays in Botswana are New Year's Day, January 2 (public holiday), July 1 (Sir Seretse Khama Day), Good Friday, Easter Monday, May 1 (Labour Day), and Ascension Day (40 days after Easter), third Monday and Tuesday in July (President's Day), September 30 (Independence Day), Christmas, December 26 (Boxing Day).

CALENDAR OF EVENTS

A comprehensive list of events with dates for the current year can be found on www.south africa.net; alternatively, check with the regional tourism branch—see relevant chapters for contact details.

January

Cape Minstrels Carnival, Cape Town. Festive Cape Malay or "coloured" groups compete and parade, dressed in colorful outfits, through the city's streets, singing and jiving to banjo beats. Several days in January.

Spier Arts Festival, Spier Estate, Stellenbosch, Winelands. The Western Cape's premier arts festival features local and international opera, classical music, comedy, jazz, and drama at the Spier Amphitheatre. January to March.

Shakespeare Open Air Festival, Maynardville, Wynberg, Cape Town. Pack a picnic to enjoy this annual Shakespeare play performed in the Maynardville Gardens. Mid-January.

Duzi Canoe Race, Pietermaritzburg, KwaZulu-Natal. The country's most prestigious canoeing event covers the 115km (71 miles) between Pietermaritzburg and Durban. Late January.

J&B Metropolitan Horse Race, Kenilworth Race Course, Cape Town. The Western Cape's premier horse-racing event is Cape Town's excuse to party, and attracts many of the city's socialites. Last Saturday in January or first in February.

South Africa Open, new venue every year. South Africa's golfing greats battle it out on one of the country's premier courses. Mid- or late January.

February

Sangoma Khekheke's Annual Snake Dance, Zululand, KwaZulu-Natal. Some 6,000 to 8,000 Zulus gather to slaughter cattle and dance under the auspices of Sangoma Khekheke. Late February.

Dance Umbrella, various venues, Johannesburg. A platform for the best contemporary choreography and dance in South Africa. Mid-February to mid-March.

March

Cape Argus Cycle Tour, Cape Town. The largest of its kind in the world, this race attracts some 30,000 cyclists and covers 105km (65 miles) of Cape Town's most scenic routes. Second Sunday of every March.

Cape Town International Jazz Festival, Cape Town. The best local jazz talent joined by international greats (often including a great lineup from all over Africa) perform for enthusiastic audiences for 2 days; go to www.cape townjazzfest.com. Late March.

Klein Karoo National Arts Festival, Oudtshoorn, Western Cape. Showcases the country's best, with many productions (often in Afrikaans) premiering here. Predominantly drama, as well as excellent dance and music acts. End of March or early April.

April

Two Oceans Marathon, Cape Town. This 56km (35-mile) scenic route attracts some 12,000 athletes. Easter Saturday.

May

Cape Times Waterfront Wine Festival, V&A Waterfront, Cape Town. With some 400 wines from 95 estates and wineries represented, and a great selection of South Africa's finest cheeses, this has got to be the easiest way to sample some of the culinary wonders of the Cape. Unlimited tastings in 2005 cost R65 ($9.70). Early May.

June

Comrades Marathon, Pietermaritzburg, KwaZulu-Natal. More than 13,000 runners participate in this 89km (55-mile) race, which started in 1921. Mid-June.

Standard Bank National Arts Festival, Grahamstown, Eastern Cape. The largest arts festival in the Southern Hemisphere features performances from cutting-edge to classical. Pack warm woolies. Late June to early July.

July

Knysna Oyster Festival, Knysna, Garden Route, Western Cape. The festival encompasses the Forest Marathon, a mountain-bike cycling tour, a regatta, a golf championship, and flea markets. First Friday to second Saturday of every July.

S.A. Fashion Week, Sandton Convention Centre, Johannesburg. A great showcase of the abundance of new Afro-centric design talent. Late July.

Rothmans July Handicap, Greyville Racecourse, Durban. This horse-racing event has a stakes of 1 million rand ($149,254). First Saturday of every July.

Mr Price Ocean Action, Durban beachfront. This world-class watersports- and beach-related tournament includes what is still referred to as the Gunston 500, one of the world's premier surfing events. Mid- or late July.

August

Namaqualand Wild Flower Season, Western and Northern Cape. From mid-August on (sometimes later, depending on rain), the semi-arid West Coast is transformed into a floral paradise with more than 2,600 species in bloom. August to October.

Jomba Dance Festival, Elizabeth Sneddon Theatre, Durban. A 10-day contemporary dance festival featuring the best of KwaZulu-Natal's considerable dance and choreography talent. Late August to early September.

September

Haenertsburg and Magoebaskloof Spring Festival, Limpopo Province.

Flowering azaleas, cherry blossoms, and crabapples are celebrated with a crafts market, carnival, exhibitions, and evening events. Call for dates.

Arts Alive International Festival, Johannesburg. This urban arts festival features local talent and international stars. Includes the Jazz on the Lake Concert held at Zoo Lake. Call for dates.

Whale Festival, Hermanus, Western Cape. The Whale Festival includes drama performances, an arts ramble, a crafts market, and whale-route lectures and tours. Late September to early October.

Darling Wildflower and Orchid Show and Hello Darling Arts Festival, Arcadia Street, Darling, West Coast. Combine a trip to see the flowers with a show at Evita se Perron hosted by Pieter Dirk Uys, South Africa's most famous female impersonator. End of September.

International Eisteddfod of South Africa, Roodepoort, Gauteng. This competitive international music and dance festival features entrants from some 30 countries—gospel choirs are the S.A. highlight. Late September to early October

King Shaka Day Celebrations and the **Zulu Kings Reed Dance,** Zululand, KwaZulu-Natal. King Shaka Day sees all the Zulu heads, from Chief Buthelezi (leader of the IFP party) to Prince Gideon, dressed in full traditional gear, addressing their minions in a moving day celebrating Zulu traditions. Later in the month some 15,000 Zulu maidens participate in the colorful Reed Dance, in which the king would traditionally choose a new wife. Prince Gideon, mindful of the AIDS crisis, uses the opportunity to address some of the issues affecting the nation today by abstaining. Both events are highly recommended.

October

Shembe Celebrations, Zululand, KwaZulu-Natal. The prophet Shembe, the fourth successor of the first prophet, presides over a congregation of some 30,000 who gather to hear his words; Sundays, when Shembe leads the crowds into prayer-dancing, are the highlight. Last 3 weeks of October.

December

Mother City Queer Project, Cape Town. This masked costume ball features some 10 dance zones and costumed teams celebrating Cape Town's vibrant and creative queer culture. The best party of the year. Early December.

Million Dollar Golf Challenge, Sun City, North-West Province. This high-stakes tournament attracts the world's best golfers. Call for exact dates.

Appletiser Summer Sunset Concerts (Kirstenbosch Gardens, Cape Town). Start of the new season; pack a picnic and get there by 4:30pm to grab a choice spot on the lawn before the concert starts at 5:30pm. Program runs to March.

Vortex New Year's Eve Rave Party (Grabouw, Cape Town surrounds). An almost weeklong nonstop camp-out party where Cape Town's hippest hippies pay homage to the beat from dusk to dawn.

6 Planning Your Safari

What are the safari options available?

Wildlife viewing is the reason most set their sights on southern Africa. As a result, a number of ways to experience the bush have been developed. You can opt for a **self-drive safari** in a national park, fly straight to a luxurious lodge in a **private game reserve,** or—best of all—combine the two. The more adventurous take their chances on a specialist safari and go on **foot, horseback, bike, canoe,** or even on the back of an **elephant.** If you're keen to walk the wilderness accompanied by an experienced, armed game ranger, the trails in **Umfolozi,** 30,000 hectares (74,100 acres) of pristine bush and savanna (with no roads or paths other than those created by animals), are rated by experienced hikers as South Africa's best, particularly the 4-day **Traditional Trail** (see chapter 9). Alternatively, the walking safaris in **Kruger National Park,** which offers a choice of seven separate wilderness trails, are also highly recommended (see chapter 8). For game spotting on horseback, book a safari with

Equus Safaris in the Waterberg Mountains (see chapter 7), take a day ride in a reserve in the **Victoria Falls** vicinity (see chapter 10), or saddle up in Botswana (see chapter 11). Other Botswana highlights include cycling safaris offered in **Tuli,** quad-bike safaris at **Jack's Camp** in the Makgadikgadi Pans, and *mokoro* (dugout canoe) safaris in the **Okavango Delta**—one of the best ways to get around the waterways, unhindered by buzzing motors or gas fumes. If you've always had a soft spot for the pachyderm, you can now mount your very own elephant and go tracking in almost all the game-viewing regions, but the best experience is in **Abu Camp** in the delta (chapter 11).

Which country should I focus on?

South Africa has the best-managed national parks in Africa, as well as some of the most luxurious private reserves; but if you're looking for the original untamed Eden, nothing beats Botswana, particularly the Okavango Delta. This is largely due to a government policy aimed at low-density, high-cost tourism. So be warned:

Little here comes cheap. Until the land-grab and economic crisis is resolved in Zimbabwe, visiting here should be restricted to Victoria Falls, which is close to the Botswana and Zambian border.

How do I get around between reserves?

In South Africa, the **major reserves** are concentrated in **Mpumalanga and the Limpopo Province** (chapter 8), and you can reach them by flying directly to Johannesburg or Cape Town, then catching a connecting flight to an airport in or near the reserves, and hiring a car or arranging a transfer with your lodge. Or you can opt for the 4- to 5-hour (or more if you include the Blyde River Canyon) drive from Johannesburg; the scenery is pleasant, and there are fabulous lodging options located in the forests and farms along the way.

To reach **KwaZulu-Natal**'s reserves, most of which are in Zululand, fly from Johannesburg or Cape Town to Durban or Richard's Bay airport. The closest reserves is 30 minutes away, while the biggest, Hluhluwe-Umfolozi, is a 3-hour drive from Durban airport (2 hr. from Richard's Bay).

Port Elizabeth is the airport closest to the **Eastern Cape reserves**—most a mere 20 to 90 minutes' drive away. Best of all, these reserves are malaria-free. Visiting one of these is ideally the start or exit point of a 7-hour driving trip along the Garden Route to or from Cape Town, a wonderfully scenic drive with great choices in lodgings.

From South Africa you'll have to fly via Johannesburg or Cape Town to get to **Botswana's reserves and camps,** most of which are reached by charter flight from Maun or Kasane.

For recommended safari operators that include the cost of flights to and around southern Africa, see "Package & Escorted Tours" in "Getting There," later in this chapter.

What should I do if I'm on a budget?

By far the best budget option is to rent a car and drive yourself around the reserves, concentrating on the national parks (like Kruger) and/or the provincial reserves (like Hluhluwe-Umfolozi). The roads in these reserves are in good condition, so you won't need a four-wheel-drive. There are a number of advantages besides cost: You can set your own pace, take in more than one environment (many visitors, for instance, combine a trip to Kruger with a KwaZulu-Natal reserve trip), and bring the kids (many private game reserves don't accept children). Kruger accommodations are usually in semiserviced ron-dawels (pronounced "ron-*da*-villes," these are round, thatch-roof cottages with kitchens and en-suite bathrooms) that offer excellent value for money (around R480/$72 a night). Cheaper units won't have their own kitchen, but all feature a fridge, tea-making facilities, and a barbecue area. Linens and towels are also provided. Most rest camps have a shop selling supplies, including basics like dishwashing liquid, wood, firelighters, tinned foods, frozen meat, toiletries, and aspirin; you can also purchase field guides here. Most also have a restaurant serving breakfast, lunch, and dinner. Try and combine this with at least 2 nights in a private reserve (for reasons below)—the best Big 5 budget options close to Kruger are **Honeyguide** and **Umlani.** These range from R2,700 to R4,600 ($403–$687) a night for two, including game drives and all meals. The best Big 5 budget option close to Hluhluwe are the **tented** camps at **Mkuze Falls** (R2,640–R4,200/$394–$627) and **Thanda Private Reserve** (R3,240–R3,600/$484–$537)—all rates are for two people and include game drives and meals. If seeing the Big 5 isn't on your agenda, the most luxurious safari experience (with interiors by the team responsible for award-winning

Singita) for the least amount of money is to be had a 30-minute drive from Durban at **Tala Leadwood Lodge** (R3,000–R4,500/$448–$672 double, including game drive and all meals).

Do I need to visit a private reserve?

The best reason to visit a private reserve is that you are guaranteed to see more animals, and you will learn more about the intricacies of the bush. Visitors are taken for game drives in an open-topped vehicle by an armed and knowledgeable ranger, usually helped by a tracker, and in radio communication with other vehicles. Sightings are excellent on game drives (at least two of the Big 5 in one drive), and it's great to have your questions answered without having to flip through a book. In certain reserves, like **Sabi Sand, Timbavati, Thornybush,** and **Phinda,** rangers are allowed to drive off-road, taking you almost within touching distance of animals. A typical day starts with a 3-hour, early-morning game drive, where eight (or fewer, at the more expensive lodges) guests are accompanied by a game ranger and tracker—followed by a large cooked breakfast, possibly in the bush. A guided walk is generally offered before lunch, and afternoons are spent relaxing at the pool or on a viewing deck. Night drives take place during the sunset/early evening hours, with drinks (sundowners) served in the bush, and the last hour or so is spent driving with a spotlight. Night drives can be incredibly dull (it's pitch black) or totally exhilarating, with nocturnal predators stalking—and killing—prey, a rare but privileged sighting. Dinners are large, often buffet, and often served under the stars by firelight.

What's the difference between private reserves? Should I visit more than one?

It's definitely worth combining reserves, moving to new landscapes that support different species. If this is your first time, it's worth choosing a Big 5 reserve—the presence of lion, leopard, rhino, elephant, and buffalo usually means a great concentration of other species as well. The Big 5 reserves flanking Kruger (**Sabi Sands, Manyeleti, Timbavati**) and the new **concessions inside the Kruger** are your best bet in South Africa—there are no fences between them and Kruger, creating a massive wilderness area where game moves freely. Sabi Sands is the private reserve that has the highest concentration of both game and luxury lodges. Another Big 5 reserve well worth looking at is **Madikwe** in the North-West, where a number of excellent new lodges have opened in the past couple of years. With a more varied terrain, it sustains a wider variety of species, including cheetah, than any of the other Big 5 reserves.

Although the reserves surrounding Kruger are typical of the African bush and savanna, the **Okavango Delta** offers a lush landscape that attracts an incredible variety of bird life (not to mention a dense concentration of game)—and is a must on any safari itinerary. Then there are the desert reserves like **Tswalu, Kgaligadi Transfrontier Park,** and **Makgadigadi Pans**—with huge horizons and stark landscapes, these support species that have adapted to the harsh conditions, like cheetah and gemsbok (oryx). By contrast, **KwaZulu-Natal**'s semitropical climate creates a more junglelike environment—beautiful, but spotting animals is a little more difficult in dense foliation—and a safari can be combined with diving and snorkeling excursions.

I've heard that malaria medication can have side effects, and I want to take my children. Are there malaria-free reserves worth visiting?

In many ways, the most attractive malaria-free reserve is **Makweti**, but it's

> ### ⟨Tips⟩ Wilderness Etiquette
>
> Because southern Africa is constantly afflicted by drought and tap water is not recycled, try to use as little water as possible, even in cities. Don't stray from paths—this leads to erosion. If you're in a four-wheel-drive vehicle, do not thunder along unspoiled dunes or bush. If you smoke, be sure to extinguish matches and cigarettes, and carry the butts with you—they take more than 20 years to biodegrade. Never touch, scratch, or wet rock art. Never approach wildlife if they appear in any way disturbed by your presence—rules regarding marine animals are particularly strict.

also worth looking at the options in **Welgevonden,** a pretty reserve very close to Johannesburg with numerous lodges, as well as the reserves in the **Western** and **Eastern Cape.** Used as a tack-on to the Garden Route, the relatively uncluttered landscape of Sanbona in the Eastern Cape and the Big 5 reserves in the Eastern Cape are great for game-viewing. Staff and programs are often geared specifically for children (particularly at Lalibela), but the landscape is not typical bushveld.

I've decided on the private reserve. How should I choose my lodge?

It's worth mentioning that some of the larger lodges simply feel like plush hotels. Select a private lodge that takes no more than 8 to 12 guests per camp—this means you are given very personal service and the peace to absorb your surroundings, and privacy is paramount—units are usually set far apart, often with luxuries like private plunge pools. If, however, you want to get a real feel for the bush, consider tented bush camps, where essentials like hot water and en-suite bathrooms are standard features, but canvas walls allow the sounds of the bush to connect you with the outdoors. If you don't mind living out of a suitcase, moving from camp to camp is the ideal way to see different environments as well as plentiful game; and nowhere does it get as good as Botswana—see chapter 11 for a listing of

safari operators who specialize in this area, as well as for a detailed description of the type of accommodations available.

If I'm visiting a private reserve, do I still need to include a national park or provincial reserve in my itinerary?

Not necessarily. In a national park or provincial reserve, you are, after all, in a closed vehicle, you can't leave the road, and you're not trained to spot animals in the bush. On the other hand, you may appreciate the relative privacy: There's nothing like spotting a cheetah on the side of the road, with no other soul in sight—a privilege you'll never have in a private reserve, where other guests are onboard, and another vehicle is on the way as soon as an animal is spotted.

When's the best time to go on safari?

The dry winter months (June–Oct, particularly Oct) are considered best. That's when the vegetation has died back and animals are easier to see and concentrated around the diminishing sources of water. Unless it was a particularly wet summer, the malaria risk is also considerably lower. But spring and summer bring their own benefits: Many animals have young (there's nothing quite as delightful as a baby giraffe), the vegetation is lush and often flowering, and colorful migrant birds adorn the trees. It is more difficult to spot animals in spring and summer,

Where & When to See Game

	Jan	Feb	Mar	Apr	May	June	July	Aug	Sept	Oct	Nov	Dec
Kruger National Park	P	P	P	F	F	G	E	E	E	E	G	F
Private Game Reserves	G	G	G	G	G	E	E	E	E	E	E	G
Moremi & Okavango Delta	G	G	G	G	E	E	E	E	E	E	E	G
Chobe	F	F	F	G	G	E	E	E	E	E	E	G
Makgadikgadi & Nxai Pan	E	E	E	E	G	F	F	P	P	P	F	G

E = Excellent, G = Good, F = Fair, P = Poor

however, and you'll almost definitely need to spend time in a private reserve if you want to be assured of seeing big game.

How long do I need to spend on safari?

To honestly say you've experienced the bush, you'll need a minimum of 3 nights and 2 full days, preferably 4.

How safe am I on safari?

You are undertaking a journey through a landscape where wild animals abound, and irresponsible behavior could result in death. Malaria is also a serious threat—potentially fatal. See "Staying Healthy," below, for tips on how to ensure you survive your safari.

I've heard that walking safaris are the best way to experience the bush. Is this true?

In a sense, yes. Guided by an armed ranger, you will see many things that people in cars blindly cruise by, and the experience of spotting rhino just yards away on foot is unforgettable. The emphasis, however, is not on tracking game (no ranger would take you within striking distance of a big cat) as much as it is on understanding the intricacies of the relationships in the bush and communing with nature. The ranger is armed, so there is no real danger (though a ranger was recently trampled to death by an elephant in Hluhluwe-Umfolozi, so be aware that these seemingly gentle giants need to be treated with the utmost respect), and the wilderness trails in Kruger and Hluhluwe reserves enjoy an unblemished safety record for visitors.

What should I pack?

Pack light, particularly if you are taking a charter plane to Botswana, which currently allows only one soft-sided bag weighing 10 kilograms (22 lb.). Choose colors that blend in with the bush: Gray, brown/beige, and khaki are best. Loose cotton clothing tends to be the most comfortable and protects your limbs from mosquitoes. If you intend to walk, you'll need long pants to protect you from prickly vegetation and ticks, as well as comfortable hiking boots. A warm sweater, a coat, long pants, a scarf, and gloves are recommended during evening game drives in winter (May–Aug); you'll also need warm sleepwear. A fitted broad-brimmed hat, swimwear, good sunglasses, and sunscreen are essential in summer. Though many lodges supply insect repellent, pack your own, as well as every other malaria precaution (see "Health, Safety &

Insurance," below). And, of course, don't forget binoculars and a camera (a telephoto lens is ideal) and, if you're not using digital, plenty of film, though you can usually purchase more at the camp. If you bring a video camera, pack a 12-volt adapter for charging the batteries (keep in mind, however, that electricity isn't always supplied on safaris).

7 Other Active Vacations

Surrounded by oceans and with a diverse landscape that includes forests, rivers, mountains, and large tracts of pristine wilderness, southern Africa is the ideal destination for outdoor adventure. For more details on any of the activities mentioned below, see the "Staying Active" sections in specific chapters. For a complete list of operators specializing in adventure pursuits, purchase the *Getaway Adventure Guide* or go to **www.getawaytoafrica.com** for details.

The Western Cape (which includes Cape Town) and Victoria Falls are the two adventure centers of southern Africa. Both are well serviced by one-stop shops where staff will advise and make bookings for every adventure activity available. In Cape Town, visit Long Street, which is littered with one-stop adventure shops offering similar services; for personal attention, stop at **Detour**, 234 Long St. (© **021/424-1115;** www.detourafrica.co.za), owned and run by the helpful Shawn Petre. The most helpful outfit in the vicinity of Vic Falls is **Safari Par Excellence** (© **260/3/32-0606;** www.saf-par.co.za).

ABSEILING With numerous mountainsides to drop off and a number of rivers to drop into, the Western Cape offers the most scenic abseiling (rappelling) options in South Africa; see chapters 4 and 5 for details.

BALLOONING For the best hot-air balloon views, head for the Pilanesberg game reserves in the North-West and drift over the savanna looking for big game. A close second is to sample a glass of wine while soaring over its source in the Winelands of the Western Cape. For information on ballooning operators, see chapters 4 and 5.

BIRD-WATCHING Situated on one of the world's biggest continents, with a range of totally different environments, the southern African region offers hours of rewarding bird-watching, and many species occur nowhere else but here. The best areas are Ndumo and Mkhuze in KwaZulu-Natal, the bush savanna of Mpumalanga and the Limpopo Province, and the Okavango Delta in Botswana. For the best bird-watching safaris in southern Africa, contact **Peter Lawson** (© **27/13/741-2458;** www.lawsons.co.za).

BOARDSAILING (WINDSURFING) The most exhilarating windsurfing spots are in the Scarborough and Kommetjie area on Cape Town's western seaboard, off the Cape Point coast, and at Langebaan on the West Coast, where the wind comes up almost every afternoon (see chapters 4 and 5).

BUNGEE/BRIDGE-JUMPING You can take the highest bungee jump in the world at **Bloukrans River Bridge**— 216m (708 ft.), which rather makes the 65m (213 ft.) from the Gouritz River Bridge seem like child's play. Both these jumps are on the Garden Route, Western Cape (see chapter 5). At 104m (341 ft.), the world's second-highest bungee jump is off the Victoria Falls Bridge (see chapter 10).

CANOEING & KAYAKING Canoes can usually be rented wherever there's water—check the regional chapters or with the local tourism bureaus. This is certainly a great way to explore the upper reaches of the Zambezi River (see chapter 10) and South Africa's "Lakes District" in the Garden Route (see chapter 5). Kayaking is offered along the coast as well as on certain rivers, but takes considerably more practice. Gliding through the waters in a dugout canoe (called a *mokoro*) in the delta is one of the highlights of a trip to Botswana (see chapter 11).

DIVING   You'll need to take a recognized dive course before plunging down in the deep to meet some of the 2,000 species that live off the African shores. If you're doing it here (and this is one of the cheapest places in the world to do so), make sure the organization is part of the **South African Underwater Union (SAUU),** which is affiliated with agencies worldwide. Sodwana Bay in northern KwaZulu-Natal is the most popular dive destination (see chapter 9). The Cape coast is good for wreck-diving. For more information, contact **SAUU** (© **27/21/930-6549**).

FISHING   With more than 2,500km (1,550 miles) of coastline, rock, and surf, anglers are spoiled for choice here. The confluence of the warm Indian Ocean and the cold Atlantic is responsible for one of the highest concentrations of game fish in the world, including marlin. June through November are particularly popular months on the KwaZulu-Natal coast, for which you need no license (see chapter 9). Spear fishermen won't leave disappointed, either; for more information, contact SAUU (see "Diving," above). Trout fishing is also extremely popular, particularly in the Dullstroom area (Mpumalanga), the Drakensberg (KwaZulu-Natal), and the mountains of the Western Cape. For more information, call the **Federation of S.A. Flyfishers** (© **27/11/462-6687**). For organized fly-fishing holidays, contact **Ultimate Angling** (© **27/21/686-6877**).

GOLFING   Courses in KwaZulu-Natal and the Western Cape are usually very

beautiful and incorporate the natural environment. Unique to Africa are the courses where you may bump into wild animals (in Mpumalanga and the Limpopo Province, in particular). Many of the best courses have been designed by world champion and Johannesburg native Gary Player.

HANG- & PARAGLIDING   To combine flights with beautiful scenery, head for Wilderness in the Western Cape, considered the best area for coastal flying, or dive off Lion's Head for a bird's-eye view of Cape Town. To fly alone, you'll need to complete a course here or ensure that your license is recognized. If you've never flown before, simply do a tandem flight with an instructor. See relevant chapters for schools or clubs in the various regions.

HIKING   South Africa has the most comprehensive trails network in Africa, from short rambles to tough 2-week hikes covering everything from fragrant botanical gardens, indigenous forests, savanna, and *fynbos*-clad mountains to uninhabited coastlines. Unique to Africa are trails in game reserves where you may encounter big game on foot, the best of which are the Umfolozi trails in KwaZulu-Natal. Also keep an eye out for **"kloofing"** trails, on which you follow a river through a mountain gorge (kloof), swimming and clambering your way out. Most of the best hiking trails are in the Western Cape and KwaZulu-Natal, as well as in Mpumalanga and the Limpopo Province. Hikers may wish to contact the **National Hiking Board of South Africa** (© **012/336-7500**) or consider purchasing *The Complete Guide to Walks and Trails in Southern Africa,* by Jaynee Levy (Struik).

MOUNTAIN BIKING   For pure scenic splendor, the best trails are in the Western Cape. Explore the Cape's Winelands, Table Mountain, Cape Point, or the indigenous forests and superb coastline of the Garden Route. Bikes can be rented wherever there are trails. For more information, read *Guide to Mountain Bike Trails in the Western Cape,* by Paul Leger (Red Mill Publications).

MOUNTAINEERING The most challenging and popular mountains are in KwaZulu-Natal (Drakensberg) and the Western Cape (Table Mountain, Cederberg). Table Mountain alone offers more than 500 routes. Some of the best mountains are privately owned, but local climbing clubs can provide permits. For more information, contact the **Mountain Club of South Africa** (ℂ 27/21/465-3412).

PARACHUTING (SKYDIVING) You need no previous experience to do a same-day jump—simply complete an accelerated free-fall course or try a tandem jump. For the best views, leap into the skies above Stellenbosch in the Cape's Winelands (see chapter 4), then reward yourself with some serious wine tasting after the event.

RIDING There are horse trails throughout southern Africa, ranging from 2-hour excursions around town surrounds (Noordhoek Beach in Cape Town is particularly recommended) to weeklong expeditions. One of the best wilderness experiences is found in the Limpopo Province (see chapter 8). If horses aren't your bag, you can mount an ostrich in Oudtshoorn (chapter 5), a camel in Cape Town (chapter 4), or an elephant in Victoria Falls or Botswana (chapters 10 and 11).

SAILING You'll find the yacht facilities in South Africa excellent, with winds averaging 15 to 25 knots. Offshore sailing requires that you belong to a recognized

yacht club; to find out more about local harbor regulations, contact **South African Sailing** (ℂ 27/21/511-0929; www.sailing.org.za).

SHARK-CAGE DIVING Unlike scuba diving, this requires no experience. Great White sharks are baited by operators who lower cages (usually containing two persons) into the water to view this protected species feeding close up. This activity is offered in the Western Cape—off Dyer Island, near Hermanus; and in Mossel Bay, Garden Route. See chapter 5.

SURFING For many, Jeffrey's Bay in the Eastern Cape (chapter 6) represents the surf mecca of Africa; but KwaZulu-Natal's Durban, with its year-round warm weather and water and consistently good waves, is South Africa's real surfing center.

WHITE-WATER RAFTING Commercial river running is a well-developed industry, and no experience is necessary if you're escorted by a reputable outfit (that is, registered with **South African Rafting Association [SARA]**). The Zambezi below Victoria Falls offers one of the greatest adrenaline trips on water and is not to be missed, even if you've never rafted before. The biggest wildwater after this is the Tugela River in KwaZulu-Natal (runnable only in summer). Other rivers worth rafting are the Blyde in Mpumalanga, an 8km (5-mile) descent with grade 3 to 5 rapids; the Doring (late Aug to Sept) and the Palmiet in the Western Cape; and the Orange in the Northern Cape—the latter offers the most relaxing rafting trip. Ask what you should wear or bring when making a booking. For details, see the "Staying Active" sections in chapters 5, 8, and 10.

8 Health, Safety & Insurance

STAYING HEALTHY

Visiting southern Africa should pose no serious threat to your health: Hospitals are efficient (though in an emergency you'd be better off going to a private hospital—facilities are better and you'll avoid a lengthy wait), hygiene is rarely a problem, tap water is safe, stomach upsets from food are rare, there are no weird tropical viruses, and medical aid is generally always within a 2-hour drive. Procedures, particularly dental and plastic surgery, are, in fact, so highly rated (and relatively inexpensive) that there is now a roaring trade in safari-surgery holidays. That said, there are a few things to watch out for. Malaria in certain areas is problematic, AIDS is rampant, bilharzia and tick-bite fever can be unpleasant, and precautions against the summer sun are essential. Plus, if you're used to civilized, law-abiding drivers, you'll find South African road manners leave a lot to be desired, and drunk driving can be a problem.

Unless you're already covered by a health plan while you're abroad, it's a good idea to take out medical travel insurance, particularly if you're going to participate in adventure activities (see the section on travel insurance below). Be sure to carry your identification card in your wallet.

Pack prescription medications in your carry-on luggage. Carry written prescriptions in generic, not brand-name form, and dispense all prescription medications from their original labeled vials. Also bring along copies of your prescriptions in case you lose your pills or run out. If you wear glasses or contact lenses, pack an extra pair.

Contact the **International Association for Medical Assistance to Travelers** (IAMAT; © 716/754-4883 or 416/652-0137; www.iamat.org) for tips on travel and health concerns in the countries you'll be visiting. The United States **Centers for Disease Control and Prevention** (© 800/311-3435; www.cdc.gov) provides up-to-date information on necessary vaccines and health hazards by region or country.

For up-to-date travel advisories, log on to the **State Department website** (http://travel.state.gov) or www.fco.gov.uk/travel (in the U.K.), www.voyage.gc.ca (in Canada), or www.smartraveller.gov.au or www.dfat.gov.au/consular/advice (in Australia).

OF SPECIAL CONCERN

AIDS   South Africa has more people living with AIDS than any other country in the world—if you're entering into sexual relations, use a condom. There's no real risk that you'll contract the virus from medical treatment.

BILHARZIA   Do not swim in dams, ponds, or rivers unless they are recommended as bilharzia-free. Symptoms are at first difficult to detect—tiredness followed by abdominal pain and blood in the urine or stools—but are effectively treated with praziquantel.

CREEPY CRAWLIES   You are unlikely to encounter snakes—they are shy, and, with the exception of puff adders, they tend to move off when they sense humans approaching. If you get bitten, stay calm—very few are fatal—and get to a hospital. Scorpions and spiders are similarly timid, and most are totally harmless. To avoid them, shake out clothing that's been lying on the ground, and be careful when gathering firewood. If you're hiking through the bush, beware of ticks; tick-bite fever is very unpleasant, though you should recover in 4 days—to remove ticks, smear Vaseline over them until they let go.

INOCULATIONS   No shots are necessary, unless you're from a country where yellow fever is endemic, in which case you'll need a vaccination certificate. As a general precaution, you might want to make sure your polio and tetanus shots are up-to-date, and ask your doctor or a travel-health specialist about vaccinations for hepatitis.

MALARIA   Parts of northern KwaZulu-Natal, the Kruger National Park and surrounding reserves, Zimbabwe, and Botswana are all high-risk malaria zones, though some become low-risk areas in the dry winter months (see **www.travel clinic.co.za** for a map). Both Hluhluwe-Umfolozi (KwaZulu-Natal) and the Kruger are usually low-risk areas from May to September (generally, this means no medication is necessary, though other protective measures are advisable; see below), but please note that this depends on the rainfall during the previous summer. Always check with a travel clinic or contact malaria@mweb.co.za. Another useful website is www.meditravel.co.za.

Do I need to take drugs?

If you are entering a high-risk zone for the first time, a course of anti-malarial tablets (prophylactic), for which you will need a prescription, is essential. What is prescribed is dependent on your health profile, but the latest antimalarial drug, Malarone (or Malanil, as it also known as), is the most effective (98%) and has the fewest side effects, and you have to take it only 1 day before entering a malarial area and continue the course for only 7 days after you leave the area. The downside is, at R35 to R40 ($5.20–$6) a tablet, taken daily, it's quite expensive, and available in South Africa only at travel clinics (see websites above). Larium is 91% effective but has strong potential side effects so should be started 2 weeks prior to entering the area, to allow you to switch if necessary (this should happen within 3 days). Side effects may include depression, anxiety, disorientation, dizziness, insomnia, strange dreams, nausea, or headaches; the principal contraindications are a history of anxiety, psychiatric problems, or epilepsy. If you've taken Larium before and suffered no side effects, you can start the course 1 week before. If you do suffer side effects, the medication is usually changed to an antibiotic containing Doxycycline—a daily tablet taken 1 day before. Both Larium and Doxycycline need to be taken 28 days after leaving the area—and make sure to take your full course of tablets.

Are tablets enough?

Keep in mind that as no prophylactic is totally effective, your best protection is to avoid being bitten. Sleep under a mosquito net, if possible; burn mosquito coils or plug in mosquito destroyers if you have electricity; wear loose, full-length clothing; and cover exposed skin with insect repellent.

How do I know if I've got it?

The flulike symptoms—fever, diarrhea, headaches, and joint pains—can take up to 6 months to develop. Consult a doctor immediately—a delay in treatment can be fatal.

What if I'm traveling with kids or I'm pregnant?

Taking medication is not advisable for children under the age of 5 and pregnant women. Your best bet is to choose a malaria-free Big 5 reserve: Pilanesberg and Madikwe in the North-West, Welgevonden in the Limpopo Province, and those located in the Eastern Cape (see "Planning Your Safari," earlier in this chapter). In the dry winter months, the Kruger and the Hluhluwe-Umfolozi reserve in Zululand (3 hr. from Durban) have a very low risk.

SUN Remember that the sun doesn't have to be shining for you to burn—wear a broad-brimmed hat at all times, and apply a high-factor sunscreen or total block—at least initially. Wear sunglasses that reduce both UVA and UVB rays substantially, and stay out of the sun between 11am and 3pm. Children should be kept well covered at the beach; it can take as little as 15 minutes for an infant's skin to develop third-degree burns.

STAYING SAFE

IN THE CITIES The rules are the same as all over the world, though the high incidence of crime warrants extra caution in southern African cities. Always be aware of the people around you, whether you're walking down a busy city street or driving through a deserted suburb—if you sense danger, act on your instincts. Don't flash expensive jewelry or fancy cameras; wear handbag straps across the neck, and keep a good grip on items. Don't walk any of the major city-center streets after dark, especially if you're alone. Keep your car doors locked at all times, particularly in Johannesburg (it's a good idea to also lock your room, even in hotels, and don't open the door unless you're expecting someone). Avoid no-go areas like Hillbrow and Berea, the inner-city suburbs of Johannesburg, and find out from your hotel or host how best to get where you're going and what's been happening on the streets recently. Finally, if confronted by an assailant, keep calm, and don't resist in any way.

With such widespread poverty, you will inevitably have to deal with beggars, some of them children. Money is often spent on alcohol or drugs; should you feel the need to make a difference, donating to a relevant charity, such as a street shelter, or to the excellent "One Love" campaign (see chapter 4) is the best way to assist. Some beggars offer services, such as watching or cleaning your car. There is no need to feel intimidated, and how much you decide to tip them is entirely personal, though with unemployment running as high as 40%, this is the best way to help the many who need the dignity of some semblance of employment as much as your small change.

TOURING THE COUNTRYSIDE
Do not pick up hitchhikers, and if you're on a self-drive holiday, hire or keep a cellphone with you to call the **Automobile Association of South Africa (AA; ℰ 0800/03-3007)**, should you break down, or the police, should you feel under threat. If you are at a remote site or beach, be aware of who is there when you approach the spot, and don't leave your

car if you don't feel safe. Also be aware of suspicious persons approaching you at a remote site; again, a cellphone, with the correct emergency numbers on speed dial, is recommended for peace of mind.

IN THE GAME RESERVES Visitors to the national parks and reserves should bear in mind at all times that they are in a wilderness area: Even those animals that look cute are wild and should not be approached. If you're on a self-drive safari, make sure you get out of your vehicle only at designated sites. While most rest camps in the national parks are fenced for your protection, this is not the case with lodges and camps situated in private reserves: Animals, including dangerous ones like hippos, lions, and elephants, roam right through them. After dark it's essential that you are accompanied to and from your room by a guide. Even when you're in a safari vehicle on a game drive, your ranger will caution you not to stand up, make sudden or loud noises, or otherwise draw attention to yourself. Occasionally, the ranger may leave the vehicle to track game on foot; always remain seated in the vehicle. It is probably not necessary to point out that lions and crocodiles are dangerous; however, hippos kill more humans in Africa than any other animal, and you should take this seriously. Hippos may look harmlessly ponderous, but they can move amazingly fast and are absolutely lethal when provoked. Even some of the smaller animals should be treated with a great deal of respect: The honey badger is the most tenacious of adversaries, and even lions keep their distance.

INSURANCE
Check your existing insurance policies and credit card coverage before you buy travel insurance. You may already be covered for lost luggage, canceled tickets, or medical expenses. The cost of travel

insurance varies widely, depending on the cost and length of your trip, your age and health, and the type of trip you're taking, but expect to pay between 5% and 8% of the vacation itself. For information on **car-rental insurance,** go to the "By Car" section of "Getting Around," later in this chapter.

TRIP-CANCELLATION INSURANCE

Trip-cancellation insurance helps you get your money back if you have to back out of a trip, if you have to go home early, or if your travel supplier goes bankrupt. Allowed reasons for cancellation can range from sickness to natural disasters to the State Department declaring your destination unsafe for travel. (Insurers usually won't cover vague fears, though, as many travelers discovered who tried to cancel their trips in Oct 2001 because they were wary of flying.) In this unstable world, trip-cancellation insurance is a good buy if you're getting tickets well in advance—who knows what the state of the world, or of your airline, will be in 9 months? Insurance policy details vary, so read the fine print—and make sure that your airline or cruise line is on the list of carriers covered in case of bankruptcy. A good resource is **"Travel Guard Alerts,"** a list of companies considered high-risk by Travel Guard International (see website below). Protect yourself further by paying for the insurance with a credit card—by law, consumers can get their money back on goods and services not received if they report the loss within 60 days after the charge is listed on their credit card statement.

Note: Many tour operators, particularly those offering trips to remote or high-risk areas, include insurance in the cost of the trip or can arrange insurance policies through a partnering provider, a convenient and often cost-effective way for the traveler to obtain insurance. Make sure the tour company is a reputable one, however: Some experts suggest you avoid buying insurance from the tour or cruise company you're traveling with, saying it's better to buy from a "third party" insurer than to put all your money in one place.

For information, contact one of the following recommended insurers: **Access America** (© 866/807-3982; www.access america.com), **Travel Guard International** (© 800/826-4919; www.travelguard. com), **Travel Insured International** (© 800/243-3174; www.travelinsured. com), or **Travelex Insurance Services** (© 888/457-4602; www.travelex-insurance. com).

MEDICAL INSURANCE For travel overseas, most health plans (including Medicare and Medicaid) do not provide coverage, and the ones that do often require you to pay for services upfront and reimburse you only after you return home. Even if your plan does cover overseas treatment, most out-of-country hospitals make you pay your bills upfront, and send you a refund only after you've returned home and filed the necessary paperwork with your insurance company. As a safety net, you may want to buy travel medical insurance, particularly if you're traveling to a remote or high-risk area where emergency evacuation is a possible scenario. If you require additional medical insurance, try **MEDEX Assistance** (© 410/453-6300; www.medex assist.com) or **Travel Assistance International** (© 800/821-2828; www.travel assistance.com; for general information on services, call the company's Worldwide Assistance Services, Inc., at © **800/777-8710**).

LOST-LUGGAGE INSURANCE On international flights (including U.S. portions of international trips), baggage coverage is limited to approximately $9.07 per pound, up to approximately $635 per checked bag. If you plan to check items more valuable than the standard liability, see if your valuables are covered by your homeowner's policy, get baggage insurance as part of your comprehensive travel-insurance package, or buy Travel Guard's BagTrak product. Don't buy insurance at the airport, as it's usually overpriced. Be sure to take any valuables or irreplaceable items with you in your carry-on luggage, as many valuables (including books, money, and electronics) aren't covered by airline policies.

If your luggage is lost, immediately file a lost-luggage claim at the airport, detailing the luggage contents. For most airlines, you must report delayed, damaged, or lost baggage within 4 hours of arrival. The airlines are required to deliver luggage, once found, directly to your house or destination free of charge. If you plan to check items more valuable than the standard liability, you may purchase "excess valuation" coverage from the airline, up to $5,000.

9 Specialized Travel Resources

TRAVELERS WITH DISABILITIES

Most disabilities shouldn't stop anyone from traveling. There are more options and resources out there than ever before.

While not as sophisticated as those in first-world countries, facilities are generally satisfactory, with a growing number of tourist attractions designed to be disability-friendly. All major airlines can provide assistance, and Avis and Budget offer cars with automatic transmissions and hand controls. Note that many of the national parks, including the Kruger, as well as the KwaZulu-Natal Nature Conservation Service (KN NCS) camps, have specially adapted huts. **Titch Tours** (© 27/21/686-5501; titcheve@iafrica. com) plots tailor-made trips, from car hire to arranging guides, for the physically and visually challenged throughout southern Africa. Other companies specializing in tours throughout the country for travelers with disabilities are **Flamingo Adventure Tours** (© 021/557-4496; www.flamingotours.co.za) and **Wheelchair Travel Club** (© 011/725-5648/ 50; wheeltra@mweb.co.za). The **National Council for the Physically Disabled** (© 27/11/726-8040; www.ncppdsa.co. za) will advise on equipment rental in all the major cities.

U.S. organizations that offer assistance to disabled travelers include **MossRehab** (www.mossresourcenet.org), which provides a library of accessible-travel resources online; **SATH** (Society for Accessible Travel & Hospitality; © 212/447-7284; www.sath.org; annual membership fees: $45 adults, $30 seniors and students), which offers a wealth of travel resources for all types of disabilities and informed recommendations on destinations, access guides, travel agents, tour operators, vehicle rentals, and companion services; and the **American Foundation for the Blind** (**AFB**; © 800/232-5463; www.afb.org), a referral resource for the blind or visually impaired that includes information on traveling with Seeing Eye dogs.

For more information specifically targeted to travelers with disabilities, the community website **iCan** (www.ican online.net/channels/travel/index.cfm) has destination guides and several regular columns on accessible travel. Also check out the quarterly magazine **Emerging Horizons** ($14.95 per year, $19.95 outside the U.S.; www.emerginghorizons. com) and *Open World* magazine, published by SATH (see above; subscription: $13 per year, $21 outside the U.S.).

GAY & LESBIAN TRAVELERS

South Africa's constitution outlaws any discrimination on the basis of sexual orientation, making it the most progressive gay policy in the world. Cities are gay-friendly, with Cape Town often called "the gay capital of Africa." (See "The Great Gay EsCape" in chapter 4 for details on gay-friendly accommodations and nightlife, written by Cape Town's most celebrated queen.) More information about gay-friendly or gay-only places and events can be found in the *Pink Map,* a free pocket-size guide available at Cape Town tourism desks or the more comprehensive *Cape Gay Guide.* Or simply contact the official gay info center **Atlantic Tourist Information** (© 27/21/434-2382; www.arokan.co.za).

Wanderwomen is a personalized women's-only travel agent; visit www.wanderwomen.co.za or call © 021/788 9988.

Remote rural areas may be less accepting, with both blacks and whites tending to be very conservative, so take care when venturing off the beaten tourist track. Zimbabwean President Robert Mugabe is a virulent homophobic, but establishments at Victoria Falls are safe to visit as a couple.

The International Gay and Lesbian Travel Association (IGLTA; © 800/448-8550 or 954/776-2626; www.iglta.org) is the trade association for the gay and lesbian travel industry, and offers an online directory of gay- and lesbian-friendly travel businesses; go to their website and click on "Members."

SENIOR TRAVELERS

South Africa is not a difficult destination for seniors to navigate, with driving on the "wrong" side of the road probably the most intimidating aspect you'll have to face. Admission prices to attractions are often reduced for seniors (known as "pensioners" in South Africa), so don't be shy about asking for discounts, and always carry some kind of identification, such as a driver's license, that shows your date of birth. Accommodations discounts are unusual; national parks, for instance, offer special rates, but these tend to be for South African nationals only.

In the United States, **AARP** (formerly known as the American Association of Retired Persons), 601 E St. NW, Washington, DC 20049 (© **888/687-2277;** www.aarp.org), offers members a wide range of benefits, including *AARP: The Magazine* and a monthly newsletter, and can offers tours through international affiliates like Collette Vacations and Globus. Anyone over 50 can join.

FAMILY TRAVEL

South Africa is regarded as the most child-friendly country in Africa, with plenty of family accommodations options, well-stocked shops, sunshine, safe beaches, high hygiene standards, animals, and babysitters and burgers on tap. Hotels usually provide discounts for children under 12, and children under 2 sharing with parents are usually allowed to stay for free. Ages and discounts vary considerably, however, so it's best to check beforehand. South Africa also has a large number of excellent self-catering cottages, hotels, and guest lodges. Bear in mind that most private game reserves will not accept children under 12, and since prophylactics are not recommended for those under 5, choose a malaria-free area, or visit during a dry winter (see "Malaria," above).

STUDENT TRAVEL

The **International Student Identity Card (ISIC)** offers substantial savings on rail passes, plane tickets, and entrance fees. It also provides you with basic health and life insurance, and a 24-hour help line. The card is available for $22 from **STA Travel** (© **800/781-4040** in North America; www.sta.com), the biggest student travel agency in the world. If you're no longer a student but are still under 26, you can get an **International Youth Travel Card (IYTC)** for the same price from the same people, which entitles you to some discounts (but not on museum admissions). (*Note:* In 2002, STA Travel bought competitors **Council Travel** and **USIT Campus** after they went bankrupt.

It's still operating some offices under the Council name, but it's owned by STA.) **Travel CUTS** (© **800/667-2887** or 416/ 614-2887; www.travelcuts.com) offers similar services for both Canadians and U.S. residents. Irish students may prefer to turn to **USIT** (© **01/602-1600;** www.usitnow.ie), an Ireland-based specialist in student, youth, and independent travel.

South Africa has a large number of lodges and activities catering to the growing backpacker market—in Cape Town,

contact **Africa Travel Centre** at © **27/ 21/423-5555** (www.backpackers.co.za); this is a recommended backpackers resource near the center of town, with comfortable accommodations and an excellent travel desk aimed at the budget traveler.

Alternatively, become a member of **Hostelling International** before you leave; contact the South African branch for local bookings (© **27/21/421 7721;** www.hisa.org.za).

10 Getting There

BY PLANE
TO SOUTH AFRICA

You can fly directly to Johannesburg and Cape Town, the major airport hubs in South Africa. From both of these airports you can fly into airports adjoining the Kruger National Park or the surrounding private game reserves in Mpumalanga and the Limpopo Province (many have their own airstrips), and to Durban in KwaZulu-Natal (a 3-hr. drive from the Zululand reserves). Port Elizabeth, the exit or start of a Garden Route trip, is a short flight from Cape Town or Johannesburg. To add Botswana to a trip to South Africa, you will have to fly via Maun, gateway to the Okavango, or Kasane, gateway to Chobe. Vic Falls can also be reached from Kasane, or you can fly to Livingstone (the Zambian town nearest the Falls) or Victoria Falls airport in Zimbabwe. For details on getting to each province, go to the "Arriving" sections in each chapter.

From the U.S., the only direct flight to South Africa is with **South African Airways (SAA;** © **800/722-9675;** www.fly saa.com) or **Delta Air Lines** (© **800/ 221-1212;** www.delta.com). Both fly directly from New York (JFK) to Johannesburg (at 17 hr., this is the longest nonstop commercial flight in the world), and nonstop from Atlanta to Johannesburg

and Cape Town; alternatively you can fly from Washington, D.C.; Los Angeles; Miami; or San Francisco via a European capital with a European carrier like Air France or Virgin. This is also how you will fly from Montreal or Toronto.

From the United Kingdom, **SAA** (© **0171/312-5005;** www.flysaa.com) and **British Airways** (© **0181/897- 4000;** www.british-airways.com) offer the most direct flights. **British Airways** (© **800/AIRWAYS;** www.british-airways. com) also operates a number of flights from New York to South Africa via London. Connection time is usually no longer than an hour, and flights continue on to Johannesburg, Cape Town, and Durban. **Virgin Atlantic Airways** (© **800/862-8621** in the United States, or 0293/747-747 in Britain; www.virgin-atlantic.com) also flies daily from New York to Johannesburg via London, and offers a few direct flights from London to Cape Town. Alternatively, check out any of the European carriers, such as **KLM** (© **800/447-4747** in the U.S., 08705/ 074074 in the U.K., or 800/505-747 in Australia; www.klm.com), which flies via Amsterdam, and **Air France** (www.air france.fr), which flies via Paris.

From Australia and New Zealand, contact **SAA** (© **02/9223-4448**) or **Qantas** (© **13-13-13;** www.qantas.com.au).

TO ZIMBABWE

The easiest way to get to **Victoria Falls International Airport** (© 263/13/ 4250) is to fly via Johannesburg; contact either **SAA** (© 27/11/978-1763; www. flysaa.com) or **British Airways Comair** (© 27/11/921-0222)—both fly daily. **Nationwide Air** © 011/327-3000; www.flynationwide.co.za) flies daily directly from Johannesburg to **Livingstone,** the closest town on the Zambian side of the falls.

Victoria Falls is not far from Kasane, in Botswana; this is accessible with **Air Botswana** (see below).

TO BOTSWANA

No matter where you're coming from, you'll probably have to make a connection in Johannesburg. If the delta is your destination, you'll need to fly to Maun, the airport just south of the Okavango Delta: **Air Botswana** is the only international carrier that flies here directly from both Johannesburg and Cape Town (© 267/686-0391; fax 267/686-0598 in Botswana; © 27/11/975-3614 in Johannesburg). The toll-free number in the U.S. and Canada is © **800/518-7781,** where it's marketed through Air World Incorporated. In the U.K., call **BA Travel Shops** (© 0207/707-4575). Air Botswana also flies from Johannesburg to Kasane (ideal to reach the Chobe reserve), and from Kasane to Victoria Falls.

In the unlikely event that you will want to visit Gaborone, the capital, **Air Botswana** also flies from Johannesburg to **Sir Seretse Khama International** (© **267/395-1921**), as do SAA and **British Airways.**

To charter a light aircraft, contact an air-charter company that operates small planes from Maun to all the delta camps. Note that strict luggage restrictions currently apply: 10 to 12 kilograms (22–25 lb.), preferably packed in soft bags. Charter prices vary, so be sure to compare the following companies' prices for the best deal: **Sefofane** (© **267/686-0778**) is recommended; alternatively, **Mack Air** (© **267/686-0635**) or **Delta Air** (© 267/ 686-0044).

FINDING THE BEST AIRFARE

Keep in mind that high season for the Okavango is in winter (June/July–Sept/ Oct), and for South Africa in summer (Sept/Oct–Apr)—during peak season (Dec–Feb), it can be difficult to get a flight at the last minute. A great way to see the country is to travel overland from, say, Johannesburg or Hoedspruit/Nelspruit (in Big-Game Country) to Cape Town via Durban; or to drive the Garden Route, then fly back from Port Elizabeth to Cape Town. Purchasing an "open-jaw" ticket will allow you to arrive in one city and depart from another.

The benefits of researching and booking your trip online can be well worth the effort in terms of savings and choice. These days, Internet users can tap into the same travel-planning databases that were once accessible only to travel agents. Sites such as **Travelocity, Expedia,** and **Orbitz** allow consumers to comparison-shop for airfares, access special bargains, book flights, and reserve hotel rooms and rental cars.

PACKAGE & ESCORTED TOURS

Before you start your search for the lowest airfare, you may want to consider booking your flight as part of a travel package such as an escorted tour or a package tour.

Escorted tours are structured group tours, with a leader. The price usually includes everything from airfare to hotels, meals, tours, admission costs, and local transportation. *Note:* Since escorted tour prices are based on double occupancy, the single traveler is usually penalized.

Package tours are simply a way to buy airfare and lodging, or book a safari, at the same time. For far-off destinations like South Africa or Botswana, they can be a smart way to go; by using a reputable operator, you put your trip in the hands of someone who knows the area well enough to help you plan the best vacation for your interests. Note that you will pay for the operator's expertise, however, and this book is designed to help you create your own great itinerary.

Packages vary widely. Keep in mind that though we recommend companies based in Africa, it is usually easiest to book their services through a representative in your home country. Most of the U.S.- and U.K.-based operators listed below and elsewhere in the book represent several reputable African-based companies. For more safari and tour operators, also see individual chapters, particularly the Botswana chapter, which covers the best in the business.

Companies specializing in top-end safaris and sightseeing trips throughout southern Africa are **Abercrombie & Kent** (www.abercrombiekent.com), **Ker & Downey** (www.kerdowney.com), and **Orient-Express Safaris** (www.orient-express.com).

If you're looking for a smaller agency that specializes in Africa as a destination, contact Judy Udwin at **Mushinda**, P.O. Box 421665, Atlanta GA 30342 (© **404/843-0046**; mushinda@mindspring.com). Judy visits all her lodges personally and will tailor an itinerary around your needs and tastes. South African–born Julian Harrison (© **800/545-1910**; www.premiertours.com; info@premiertours.com) is another U.S.-based operator worth contacting—he is consistently named one of *Condé Nast Traveler*'s Top Travel Agents in the U.S. and offers safaris that range from the do-it-yourself, eco-conscious, participation type to high-end luxury, and combines these with general sightseeing trips to suit the individual. Premier also acts as an air consolidator and offers some of the lowest airfares to Africa. Be sure to double-check

your accommodations bookings before you depart, and insist that there are no ad hoc changes once you have arrived.

For safari-specific trips, particularly to Botswana and Namibia, the highly recommended **Wilderness Safaris** (© **27/11/883-0747**; www.wilderness-safaris.com) specializes in putting together excellent itineraries that cover visits to a variety of their camps, located in the best wilderness areas throughout southern Africa. They are recommended for the quality of their guides (and staff in general) and—with a maximum of eight guests on any safari—the quality of the experience.

Another good local company is **Pulse Africa** (© **27/11/327-0468**; www.africansafari.co.za), specialist tour planners to eastern and southern Africa as well as the Indian Ocean Islands—the staff has an excellent eye for quality accommodations and will put together anything from gastronomic and horticultural tours to fishing and horseback safaris.

For escorted tours of the bush, particularly in the South African reserves, with the focus primarily but not exclusively on bird-watching, contact **Peter Lawson** (© **27/13/741-2458**; www.lawsons.co.za). Not only is he excellent company, but he also loves what he does and puts together itineraries to suit any budget.

Born Free Safaris, 12504 Riverside Dr., North Hollywood, CA 91607 (© **800/372-3274**; fax 818/753-1460; www.bornfreesafaris.com), is another solid operator with trips from the Cape to northern safari locales, though their moderate/budget options are not as good as those suggested in this book.

Alternatively, take a look at **"South African Stories"** (www.africaexperts.com), which offers itineraries like the affordably priced "Cape & Kruger" (in mid-2005 this 11-day itinerary cost only $1,999, including airfare from New York), as well as a large cross section of the most interesting ways to travel in South Africa.

For those travelers who prefer the freedom of independently customizing and booking their trip online, **e-gnu** offers soup-to-nuts trip implementation to exotic locales. Among their offerings are luxury bush lodges and wilderness camps in South Africa, Botswana, and Zimbabwe (www.e-gnu.com).

GETTING THROUGH THE AIRPORT

With the federalization of airport security, security procedures at U.S. airports are more stable and consistent than ever. Generally, you'll be fine if you arrive at the airport **2 hours** before your flight; if you show up late, tell an airline employee and they'll probably whisk you to the front of the line.

Bring a **current, government-issued photo ID** such as a driver's license or passport. Keep your ID at the ready to show at check-in, the security checkpoint, and sometimes even the gate. (Children under 18 do not need government-issued photo IDs for domestic flights, but they do for international flights to most countries.)

In 2003, the TSA phased out **gate check-in** at all U.S. airports. And **e-tickets** have made paper tickets nearly obsolete. Passengers with e-tickets can beat the ticket-counter lines by using airport **electronic kiosks** or even **online check-in** from your home computer. Online check-in involves logging on to your airline's website, accessing your reservation, and printing out your boarding pass—and the airline may even offer you bonus miles to do so! If you're using a kiosk at the airport, bring the credit card you used to book the ticket or your frequent-flier card. Print out your boarding pass from the kiosk and simply proceed to the security checkpoint with your pass and a photo ID. If you're checking bags or

looking to snag an exit-row seat, you will be able to do so using most airline kiosks. Even the smaller airlines are employing the kiosk system, but always call your airline to make sure these alternatives are available. **Curbside check-in** is also a good way to avoid lines, although a few airlines still ban curbside check-in; call before you go.

Security checkpoint lines are getting shorter than they were during 2001 and 2002, but some doozies remain. If you have trouble standing for long periods of time, tell an airline employee; the airline will provide a wheelchair. Speed up security by **not wearing metal objects** such as big belt buckles. If you've got metallic body parts, a note from your doctor can prevent a long chat with the security screeners. Keep in mind that only **ticketed passengers** are allowed past security, except for folks escorting disabled passengers or children.

Federalization has stabilized **what you can carry on** and **what you can't.** The general rule is that sharp things are out, nail clippers are okay, and food and beverages must be passed through the X-ray machine—but that security screeners can't make you drink from your coffee cup. Bring food in your carry-on rather than checking it, as explosive-detection machines used on checked luggage have been known to mistake food (especially chocolate, for some reason) for bombs. Travelers in the U.S. are allowed one carry-on bag, plus a "personal item" such as a purse, briefcase, or laptop bag. Carry-on hoarders can stuff all sorts of things into a laptop bag; as long as it has a laptop in it, it's still considered a personal item. The Transportation Security Administration (TSA) has issued a list of restricted items; check its website (www.tsa.gov/public/index.jsp) for details.

Airport screeners may decide that your checked luggage needs to be searched by hand. You can now purchase luggage locks that allow screeners to open and relock a checked bag if hand searching is necessary. Look for Travel Sentry certified locks at luggage or travel shops and Brookstone stores (you can buy them online at www.brookstone.com). These locks, approved by the TSA, can be opened by luggage inspectors with a special code or key. For more information on the locks, visit www.travelsentry.org. If you use something other than TSA-approved locks, your lock will be cut off your suitcase if a TSA agent needs to hand-search your luggage.

FLYING FOR LESS: TIPS FOR GETTING THE BEST AIRFARE

Keep in mind that high season for the Okavango is in winter (June/July–Sept/Oct), and for South Africa is in summer (Sept/Oct–Apr)—during peak season (Dec–Feb), it can be difficult to get a flight at the last minute. A great way to see the country is to travel overland from, say, Johannesburg or Hoedspruit/Nelspruit (in Big-Game Country) to Cape Town via Durban; or to drive the Garden Route, then fly back from Port Elizabeth to Cape Town. Purchasing an "open-jaw" ticket will allow you to arrive in one city and depart from another.

Here are some ways to keep your airfare costs down.

- Passengers who can book their ticket **long in advance,** who can **stay over Saturday night,** or who **fly midweek** or **at less-trafficked hours** may pay a fraction of the full fare. If your schedule is flexible, say so, and ask if you can secure a cheaper fare by changing your flight plans.

- You can also save on airfares by keeping an eye out in local newspapers for **promotional specials** or **fare wars,** when airlines lower prices on their most popular routes. You rarely see fare wars offered for peak travel times, but if you can travel in the off-months, you may snag a bargain.

- Search **the Internet** for cheap fares.
- Try to book a ticket **in its country of origin.** For instance, if you're planning a one-way flight from Johannesburg to Bombay, a South Africa–based travel agent will probably have the lowest fares. For multileg trips, book in the country of the first leg; for example, book New York–London–Amsterdam–Rome–New York in the U.S.
- **Consolidators,** also known as bucket shops, are great sources for international tickets, although they usually can't beat the Internet on fares within North America. Start by looking in Sunday newspaper travel sections; U.S. travelers should focus on the *New York Times, Los Angeles Times,* and *Miami Herald.* For less-developed destinations, small travel agents who cater to immigrant communities in large cities often have the best deals. *Beware:* Bucket shop tickets are usually nonrefundable or rigged with stiff cancellation penalties, often as high as 50% to 75% of the ticket price, and some put you on charter airlines, which may leave at inconvenient times and experience delays. Several reliable consolidators are worldwide and available on the Net. **STA Travel** is now the world's leader in student travel, thanks to their purchase of Council Travel. It also offers good fares for travelers of all ages. **ELTExpress (Flights.com; © 800/TRAV-800;** www.eltexpress.com) started in Europe and has excellent fares worldwide, but particularly to that continent. It also has "local" websites in 12 countries. **FlyCheap** (© **800/FLY-CHEAP;** www.1800fly cheap.com) is owned by package-holiday megalith MyTravel and so has especially good access to fares for sunny destinations. **Air Tickets Direct** (© **800/778-3447;** www.air ticketsdirect.com) is based in Montreal and leverages the currently weak

Canadian dollar for low fares; it'll also book trips to places that U.S. travel agents won't touch, such as Cuba.

• Join **frequent-flier clubs.** Accrue enough miles, and you'll be rewarded with free flights and elite status. It's free, and you'll get the best choice of seats, faster response to phone inquiries, and prompter service if your luggage is stolen, if your flight is canceled or delayed, or if you want to change your seat. You don't need to fly to build frequent-flier miles—**frequent-flier credit cards** can provide thousands of miles for doing your everyday shopping.

11 Getting Around

With a well-maintained and well-organized road system, a good range of car-rental companies, and the best internal flight network on the continent, a combination of flight and road travel is recommended in South Africa—that is, you overland to a certain point and then fly out. If you have time on your hands, nothing beats the romance of rail—if you can afford it, steam into Johannesburg or Cape Town on the Blue Train (see below). At the other end of the scale, those with a tight budget can opt to travel by bus: The major intercity bus companies are reliable for long-distance hauls, and some are fairly flexible; for this, the Baz Bus, which offers a hop-on, hop-off service on interesting routes throughout the country, is unbeatable.

Traveling in Zimbabwe and Botswana is not as straightforward—public transport is unreliable, roads can be bad, fuel in Zimbabwe can be scarce, and help can take a long time coming in the event of a road emergency. Safest, particularly with limited time, is to fly directly to your intended destination with transfers prearranged.

BY PLANE

If you have limited time to cover Africa's large distances, flying is your best bet, though internal flights can be very expensive. The good news for anyone planning to fly around the country is that, as a result of pressure created by the budget airlines **Kulula.com** and newcomer **1Time** (see below), South African Airways (SAA) is now slashing many of its fares. Although the latter two specialize in heavily discounted fares and are well worth looking into, SAA often offers cheaper flights for passengers booking through the Web. Despite the relative increase in discounted fares on established routes, these seats fill fast, so book early.

Details for the domestic airlines servicing all of the major cities in South Africa are as follows: **SA Express** and **SA Airlink** (both domestic subsidiaries of SAA; ✆ 27/11/978-1111; www.flysaa.com), **Nationwide** (✆ 27/11/390-1660; www.flynationwide.co.za), **BAComair** (✆ 27/11/921-0222; www.ba.co.za), **Kulula.com** (✆ 086/158-5852; www.kulula.com), and **1Time** (✆ 086-1752846; www.1time.co.za). All the lodges recommended in this book will arrange to charter a flight into the reserve (at a competitive rate) if time is of the essence.

BY CAR

Given enough time, this is by far the best way to enjoy South Africa—you wind along relatively empty and well-maintained roads through some of the most spectacular scenery in the world. Certainly in urban centers, you'll need a car (or taxi) to get around because public transport in the cities is generally not geared toward tourists and can be unsafe (though Cape Town is slowly getting its act together). All the major car-rental companies have agencies here, and there are a host of local companies as well. All offer much the same deals, but cars are in big demand and short supply during the busiest period (Nov–Jan), so book well in advance.

Prefer a home on wheels? **Britz Africa** (© **27/11/396-1860**; fax 27/11/3961937; www.britz.co.za) offers fully equipped camper vans and four-wheel-drive vehicles, and will pick you up in your vehicle from the airport. Britz currently charges R1,195 ($178) a day for a double-cab four-wheel-drive pickup for between 5 and 20 days.

CAR RENTALS   You'll need a driver's license to rent a car—your home driving license is good for 6 months—and most companies in South Africa stipulate that drivers should be a minimum of 21 years (in Botswana you must be 25 or older). Armed with a letter of authority from the rental agency, vehicles rented in South Africa may be taken into Botswana and Zimbabwe, though this requires 72 hours' notice, and additional insurance charges are applicable. You can leave the vehicle in these countries for a fee; in South Africa, you can hire a one-way rental car to any of the major cities. All the major companies have branches in South Africa, including Avis (www.avis.com), Hertz (www.hertz.com), and Budget (www.budget.com); the latter usually offers a slightly more competitive rate. Note that it's best to prebook your vehicle, particularly if you're traveling during the peak season (Dec–Feb).

Car-Rental Insurance   Before you drive off in a rental car, be sure you're insured. Hasty assumptions about your personal auto insurance or a rental agency's additional coverage could end up costing you tens of thousands of dollars—even if you are involved in an accident that was clearly the fault of another driver.

Even if you already hold a private auto insurance policy, coverage probably doesn't extend outside the United States. Before you leave, find out whether you are covered in the area you are visiting, whether your policy extends to all persons who will be driving the rental car, how much liability is covered in case an outside party is injured in an accident, and whether the type of vehicle you are renting is included under your contract.

Most major credit cards provide some degree of coverage as well—provided they were used to pay for the rental. Terms vary widely, however, so be sure to call your credit card company directly before you rent.

ON THE ROAD IN SOUTHERN AFRICA

GASOLINE   Fuel is referred to as "petrol" and is available 24 hours a day in major centers. At press time, 1 liter cost approximately R4.90 (73¢; 4 liters is approximately 1 gal.). Gas stations are full serve, and you are expected to tip the attendant R2 to R5 (30¢–75¢). *Note:* Credit cards are not accepted as payment.

ROAD CONDITIONS & RULES   In South Africa, you'll find an excellent network of tarred roads, with emergency services available along the major highways; you cannot rely on this sort of backup on road conditions in Zimbabwe or Botswana. Driving in all three countries is on the left side of the road—repeat the mantra "drive left, look right," and wear your seatbelt at all times; it's mandatory, and, in any case, driving skills on the road vary considerably. A broken line means that you may pass/overtake; a solid line means you may not. Generally the speed limit on national highways is 120kmph (74 mph), 100kmph (62 mph) on secondary rural roads, and 60kmph (37 mph) in urban areas.

BREAKDOWNS   The **Automobile Association of South Africa (AA)**

extends privileges to members of AAA in the United States and the Automobile Association in Britain. The local emergency toll-free number is ℂ **0800/03-3007.**

BY TRAIN

Shozoloza Mail (ℂ **086/000-8888**) runs most of the intercity rail services; ticket prices for first class are comparable to a bus ticket to the same destination. Second class costs considerably less but is inadvisable from a comfort and safety point of view. Coupes in first class take only two people, making them ideal for couples. Note that the journey from Johannesburg to Cape Town takes 27 hours—longer than the bus.

If the journey is as important as the destination, splurge on a trip with the world-famous **Blue Train** (ℂ **27/12/334-8459;** www.bluetrain.co.za). This luxury hotel on wheels currently runs between Pretoria/Johannesburg and Cape Town, and makes a few trips along the Garden Route. Travel amid beautiful scenery, dining on fine food in plush surroundings (marble en-suite bathrooms, fabric-lined wardrobes, a personal butler to take care of your every need). Another luxury option (less famous, but making in-roads—it was voted the World's Leading Luxury Train in the 2004 World Travel Awards)—is **Rovos Rail** (ℂ **27/12/421-4020;** www.rovos.co.za). Rovos covers the same routes as the Blue Train and offers a number of exciting options, like the 13-day journey to Tanzania or the 9-day journey to the Kruger, Durban, Garden Route, and Cape Town.

If you like the romance of rail but can't face the steep fares, book a **Premier Class** coupe from Cape Town by calling ℂ **012/334 8459** (make sure when booking that this is the special Premier Class coupe on the once-weekly train, not First Class on the daily train). The Premier Class train arrives in Pretoria/Johannesburg from Cape Town every Wednesday and departs for Cape Town from Pretoria/Johannesburg every Thursday. It costs R2,050 ($306) per person one-way (all-inclusive).

BY BUS

The three established intercity bus companies are **Greyhound, Intercape,** and **Translux.** There's not much to choose among them, though Greyhound offers a pass to frequent users. Johannesburg to Cape Town takes approximately 19 hours. An alternative to these is the 22-seater **Baz Bus,** which offers a flexible hop-on, hop-off scheme aimed at backpackers and covers relatively inaccessible areas—definitely the best way to explore the Garden Route, the Eastern Cape (including the Wild Coast), Drakensberg, and the area around the Mpumalanga reserves if you can't afford a rental car or guided tour. The two most popular routes are Cape Town to Port Elizabeth (traveling the Garden Route with stops at various backpackers' lodgings), at a cost of R810 ($121) one-way (from Port Elizabeth, you can then travel via the Wild Coast to Durban); and Cape Town to Johannesburg via Drakensberg, at a cost of R1,900 ($284) one-way, with recommended stops along the way.

- **Baz Bus National** (www.bazbus.com) In Cape Town, ℂ **27/21/439-2323.**
- **Greyhound** (www.greyhound.co.za) In Johannesburg, ℂ **27/11/276-8500;** in Cape Town, ℂ **27/83-915 9000** or 27/21/505-6363; in Port Elizabeth, ℂ **27/41/363-4555;** in Durban, ℂ **27/31/334-9170.**
- **Intercape** (www.intercape.co.za) In Pretoria/Tshwane, ℂ **27/12/3284556;** in Cape Town, ℂ **27/21/380-4400.**
- **Translux** (www.translux.co.za) In Johannesburg, ℂ **27/11/774-3333;** in Pretoria/Tshwane, ℂ **27/12/315-4300;** in Cape Town, ℂ **27/21/449-3333;** in Port Elizabeth, ℂ **27/861589282;** in Durban, ℂ **27/861589282.**

12 Tips on Accommodations

The choice of accommodations can make or break a holiday, and with South Africa's enduring popularity, this is one area worth tying up before you leave. The selection in this book covers a wide variety of budgets, but all share the common ability to delight, be it because of a fabulous location, special decor, or beautiful views. If, however, you have trouble deciding without a photograph, the following is highly recommended: **Portfolio** (www.portfoliocollection.com) brings out an attractive range of free booklets profiling the full spectrum of options across the country. The "B&B Collection" offers fair to excellent budget options, some in quite luxurious surroundings—if anything, you now have almost too many choices, but if you stick to the "Luxury" and "Great Comfort" options, you're likely to be delighted at the good value. In the "Retreats Collection" the focus is upmarket guesthouses; top of the range is the "Country Places Collection," which includes some of the best game lodges in the country. Each review comes with at least one photograph—with more on their website.

Other collections that show some discernment before charging the (usually hefty) fee to establishments featured are **Superior Choices** (www.superiorchoices.com) and **Exclusive Getaways** (www.getaways.co.za).

Portfolio, Superior Choices, and Exclusive Getaways all have game lodges in their collections, but if a safari is the primary reason you're heading south, you'd be well advised to take a look at the excellent selection in **Classic Safari Camps of Africa** (www.classicsafaricamps.com).

Note: South Africa has a great selection of self-catering options—good for families or for those wishing to prolong their stay—and thanks to restaurant delivery services in most urban centers, you won't even have to cook. See individual chapters for suggestions, try to track down the excellent "Budget Getaways," or go to **www.farmstay.co.za** for more off-the-beaten-track options.

FAST FACTS: South Africa

For "Fast Facts" for Victoria Falls and Livingstone and for Botswana, see chapters 10 and 11, respectively.

American Express **In South Africa** Report card loss to the National Call Center Johannesburg branch at © 27/11/359-0200. Other branches are located in Cape Town, Johannesburg, Durban, Port Elizabeth, Pretoria, and Richard's Bay; see regional chapters.

Banks & ATM Networks See "Money," earlier in this chapter.

Business Hours Shops are generally open Monday to Friday from 8:30 or 9am to 4:30 or 5pm, and Saturday from 8:30am to 1pm. In smaller towns, they often close between 1 and 2pm. Many of the larger shopping malls (like the V&A Waterfront) are open from 9am to 9pm daily. South African "cafes" (local minimarts) are usually open from 7am to 8pm daily; some stay open until 10pm. Public offices open at 8am and close at 3:30pm Monday to Friday. Bank hours are usually Monday to Friday from 9am to 3:30pm, and Saturday from 8:30am to 11am. Banks often close from 12:45 to 2pm in rural areas.

Currency See "Money," earlier in this chapter.

Drugstores Drugstores are called "chemists" or "pharmacies"; ask the local tourism bureau for directions, see city listings, or look under "Pharmacies" in the Yellow Pages.

Electricity Electricity in southern Africa runs on 220/230V, 50Hz AC, and sockets take round- or flat-pinned plugs. Most hotel rooms have sockets for 110V electric razors. Bring an adapter/converter combination, but also be aware that many bush camps do not have electricity at all.

Embassies & Consulates The U.S. Embassy in Pretoria is located at 877 Pretorius St., Arcadia, Pretoria, ℂ 27/12/431-4000. Other offices are in Johannesburg, ℂ 27/11/644-8000; Cape Town, ℂ 27/21/421-4280; and Durban, ℂ 27/31/305-7600.

Emergencies Ambulance: ℂ 10177 or 999. Police: ℂ 10111. Fire: Consult the front pages of the local telephone directory for brigade numbers.

Holidays See "When to Go," earlier in this chapter.

Information See "Visitor Information," earlier in this chapter.

Language There are 11 official languages in South Africa, but English dominates as the lingua franca here, as well as in Botswana and Zimbabwe. It's often a second language, though, so be patient, speak slowly, and keep a sense of humor.

Liquor Laws Most liquor stores (called "bottle stores" in South Africa) are closed on Saturday afternoons and Sundays.

Lost & Found Be sure to tell all of your credit card companies the minute you discover your wallet has been lost or stolen, and file a report at the nearest police precinct. Your credit card company or insurer may require a police report number or record of the loss. Most credit card companies have an emergency toll-free number to call if your card is lost or stolen; they may be able to wire you a cash advance immediately or deliver an emergency credit card in a day or two. Visa's U.S. emergency number is ℂ **800/847-2911** or 410/581-9994. American Express cardholders and traveler's check holders should call ℂ **800/221-7282**. MasterCard holders should call ℂ **800/307-7309** or 636/722-7111. For other credit cards, call the toll-free number directory at ℂ **800/555-1212**.

Identity theft and fraud are potential complications of losing your wallet, especially if you've lost your driver's license along with your cash and credit cards. Notify the major credit-reporting bureaus immediately; placing a fraud alert on your records may protect you against liability for criminal activity. The three major U.S. credit-reporting agencies are **Equifax** (ℂ 800/766-0008; www.equifax.com), **Experian** (ℂ 888/397-3742; www.experian.com), and **Trans Union** (ℂ 800/680-7289; www.transunion.com). Finally, if you've lost all forms of photo ID, call your airline and explain the situation; they might allow you to board the plane if you have a copy of your passport or birth certificate and a copy of the police report you've filed.

Magazines **Getaway** (www.getawaytoafrica.com) is an excellent monthly travel magazine that covers destinations throughout Africa and is well worth purchasing for cheap accommodations listings and up-to-date information. *SA City Life* carries entertainment listings for all three major cities, as well as features of local interest. *Eat Out* (www.eat-out.co.za), *Wine Magazine Top 100 Restaurants Guide* (www.winemag.co.za), and *Style Restaurant Guide* (www.stylemagazine.co.za) cover most of the top restaurants in South Africa; *Eat Out* is the most discriminating. The CNA and Exclusive chains sell these as well as international press and magazines.

Maps See "Getting Around," earlier in this chapter.

Newspapers The weekly *Mail & Guardian* (www.mg.co.za) is one of the most intelligent papers and comes out every Friday with a comprehensive entertainment section. Local papers include the *Star* or the *Sowetan* in Johannesburg, the *Cape Times* and *Argus* in Cape Town, the *Natal Mercury* in Durban, and the *Eastern Province Herald* in Port Elizabeth. *Business Day* is South Africa's version of the *Wall Street Journal* or *Financial Times*.

Police Call ✆ **10111**.

Taxes A value-added tax (VAT) of 14% is levied on most goods and services; check that it's included in any quoted price. Foreign visitors can claim VAT back on goods with a cumulative value of over R250 ($37) by presenting the tax invoice (make sure it has a VAT registration number on it) together with their passport at a VAT refund office (airports, selected shopping centers, and visitor bureaus) before departing. Call ✆ **021/934-8675** to find out where and hours.

Telephone & Fax For telephone tips, see "Phone Home: Calling to & from South Africa," earlier in this chapter. If you have problems getting through to anyone, or if you need a new number, use the directory assistance service by dialing ✆ **1023** for numbers in South Africa, and ✆ **0903** for international numbers. Be patient, speak slowly, and check spellings with your operator.

Pay phones require a minimum of 80¢ for a local call; because hotels often charge a massive markup, it's worth purchasing a telephone card (used in specific pay phones) for international calls—these card pay phones are also often the only ones working. Cards are available from post offices and most news agents, and come in units of R20 ($3), R50 ($7.45), R100 ($15), and R200 ($30).

Vodacom has 24-hour desks at all major international airports offering mobile phones for rent—a recommended option if you haven't prebooked your entire holiday. Alternatively, bring your own phone with you; check that the handset is GSM and will be compatible with the S.A. frequency (900/1800). You can use your U.S. SIM card in South Africa to receive calls from home, but making local calls will cost a lot; it's best to purchase a local SIM card and a pay-as-you-go airtime card.

Time Zone South Africa is 2 hours ahead of GMT (that is, 7 hr. ahead of Eastern Standard Time).

Tipping Add 10% to 20% to your restaurant bill, 10% to your taxi. Porters get around R4 (60¢) per bag. There are no self-serve garages; when filling up with fuel, tip the person around R2 to R5 (30¢–75¢). It's not unusual to leave some money for the person cleaning your hotel room. Be generous if you feel the service warrants it—this is one of the best ways to alleviate the poverty you may find distressing.

Useful Telephone Numbers **Computicket** (② **27/11/340-8000** in Johannesburg; ② **27/83/915-8000** in Cape Town and Durban) is a free national booking service that covers cinema and concert seats, as well as intercity bus tickets; payment can be made over the phone by credit card. In South Africa, call directory assistance at ② **1023** for numbers in South Africa, and ② **0903** for international numbers.

Water Tap water is safe to drink in all city and most rural areas. Always ask in game reserves.

Weather You can see what tomorrow's weather will be in every region at www.weathersa.co.za. Alternatively, call ② **082 162.**

3

Suggested Southern Africa Itineraries

Given that most people fly to southern Africa to witness firsthand Mother Nature at her most powerful—from the wonder of seeing a leopard haughtily surveying you from a branch, her bloodied paw carelessly slung over her kill, to the haunting majesty of the white-cloud "tablecloth" billowing down Cape Town's Table Mountain, the focus here is on various ways of doing just that.

1 The Real Relaxer: Cape Town & the Winelands in 1 Week

You've chosen to stay put in one region and relax. Sensible, really: You're in one of the most beautiful cities in the world, surrounded by vineyard-carpeted valleys and a whale nursery off the coast—why rush off?

Day ❶: Cape Town

Having arranged for an airport transfer with your lodgings (where you have booked for 4 nights), spend the first day sleeping late and book a spa treatment for the afternoon at one of the recommendations in chapter 4. Then take a stroll around the **Victoria & Alfred Waterfront** in the late afternoon before dining at **Den Anker** (for delicious Belgian-inspired cuisine) or the more brassy, flashy **Baia** (for seafood)—make sure to book ahead for either (in the summer, even before you leave home), and request a table with a view of iconic **Table Mountain.** Alternatively, if you want to watch Capetonians at play, head for the tiny piazza at **Cape Quarter** and grab an outside table at one of the surrounding eateries there.

Day ❷: Kirstenbosch Botanical Gardens & Southern Suburbs

Hopefully you're now feeling fully recovered on day 2, as your car should be delivered to you this morning. Spend the morning on the eastern slopes of Table Mountain exploring **Kirstenbosch Botanical Gardens** (or, if you're a beach lover, take a book to **Camps Bay,** where you can simply cross the road when it's time to lunch). From Kirstenbosch, make your way farther south to lunch at the manor house at **Constantia Uitsig,** for pastoral vineyard views and old-style elegance. Or skip lunch altogether and take high tea at the **Mount Nelson,** Africa's grandest and most colonial hotel. If you have the energy, ascend **Table Mountain** in the late afternoon to watch as the sun sinks into the western horizon and the city lights come twinkling on.

Day ❸: Cape Peninsula

The third day should see you complete the Peninsula drive described in chapter 4, where the highlights are getting off the beaten track in the **Cape Point Nature Reserve** and cruising the awesome **Chapman's Peak Drive** when the sun starts to

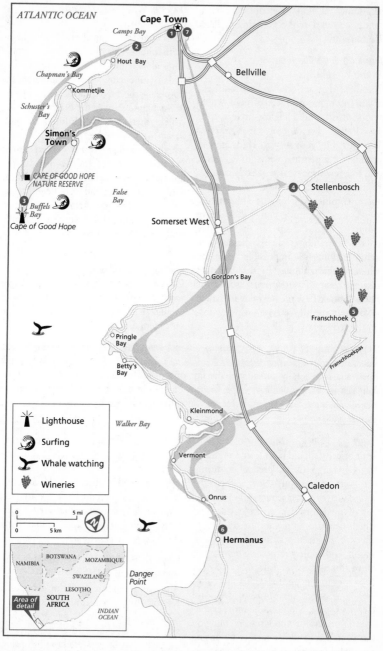

ATLANTIC OCEAN

Cape Town

Camps Bay

Hout Bay

Bellville

Chapman's Bay

Kommetjie

Schuster's Bay

Simon's Town

CAPE OF GOOD HOPE NATURE RESERVE

False Bay

Stellenbosch

Buffels Bay

Cape of Good Hope

Somerset West

Gordon's Bay

Franschhoek

Pringle Bay

Franschhoekpas

Betty's Bay

Kleinmond

Walker Bay

Vermont

Caledon

Lighthouse

Surfing

Onrus

Whale watching

Wineries

Hermanus

0   5 mi

0   5 km

NAMIBIA   BOTSWANA   MOZAMBIQUE

SWAZILAND

LESOTHO

Area of detail   SOUTH AFRICA

Danger Point

INDIAN OCEAN

set. Lunch at Kalk Bay; dine on fresh, tender calamari at the **Chapman's Peak Restaurant.**

Days ❹ & ❺ Franschhoek & the Winelands

The next day, set off for **Franschhoek,** 79km (49 miles) from Cape Town, where you should spend 2 nights, preferably at **La Petite Ferme** or **Le Quartier Français.** On your way to Franschhoek, arrange for a personal wine guide to take you to a few wine estates in **Stellenbosch** to sample the Cape's best. While you're there, consider lunching at **Tokara** (the views are beautiful), and try to leave enough time to sleep off the possible effects of imbibing such delicious fare before tackling the impossible: choosing where to have dinner in this gourmet heaven. After a leisurely start, ascend the **Franschhoek Pass** the next day for lunch at Le Petite Ferme; reserve a window seat on the terrace well in advance.

Day ❻: Whale-Watching in Hermanus

You could easily spend another night in Franschhoek (for the choice of restaurants alone!) but, if it's whale-watching season (June–Nov), keep heading south, traversing the Franschhoek and Viljoens passes before joining the N2 at Grabouw (where there is a delightful farm stall, Peregrine, if you're feeling peckish), which will take you to **Hermanus,** "whale-watching capital of the world," approximately 112km (69 miles) from Cape Town. Spend the night here (preferably at the **Marine**) before returning to Cape Town, this time taking the magnificent **Coastal Road** to rejoin the N2 at Gordon's Bay.

Day ❼: Cape Town

Celebrate your last night in Cape Town with a meal at **Aubergine** if you're a foodie, or back at **Den Anker** if you're sentimental.

2 The Quick Fix: Botswana, Vic Falls & Cape Town in 1 Week

Botswana is generally considered the last untouched wilderness in Africa, Victoria Falls is a world wonder, and Cape Town is one of the most beautiful cities on earth. A week covering these sights will leave you with unparalleled memories.

Days ❶, ❷ & ❸: Okavango Delta

Your priority should be at least 3 nights in the Okavango Delta, preferably during the wet season (July–Nov), when the abundance of game attracts a huge number of predators. It's worth noting that you'll need to book up to a year in advance at the top camps during peak season, and while you may be tempted to move around between camps, it really is a good idea to stay put for such a short stay. The top lodges are **Mombo, Jao,** and **Chief's Camp.** Mombo, the most expensive, is pricey for good reason, but you can stretch your dollar further by opting for slightly more affordable alternatives, such as **Kwetsani, Duba Plains, Sandibe, Chitabe,** or **Baines' Camp,** all

of which offer superb wildlife experiences—although not quite on the same level as the first three options. Another recommended alternative is **Abu Camp,** where the elephant-back safaris are unparalleled and you are ensured a completely different experience to that of the standard game experience.

Days ❹ & ❺ Chobe National Park/Victoria Falls

After your time in the delta, transfer to Kasane for a couple nights' sojourn at Chobe National Park, where elephant sightings are believed to be the very best on earth. You have a plethora of options here, but one of the most luxurious and accessible is **Chobe Chilwero:** Near the

The Quick Fix: Botswana, Vic Falls & Cape Town in 1 Week

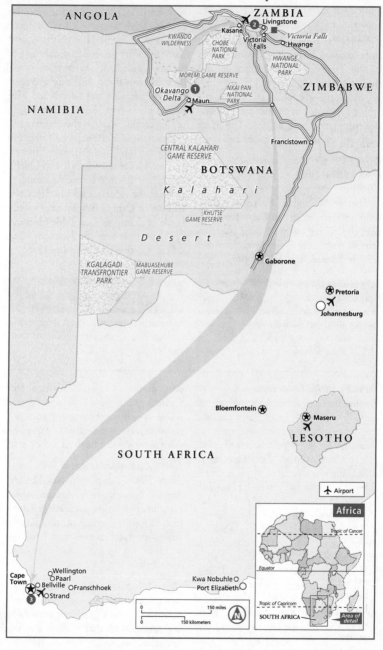

northern town of Kasane, and overlooking the Chobe River, Chilwero also organizes day trips to **Victoria Falls,** just an hour away. Alternatively, you can skip Chobe National Park altogether and charter a direct flight from Maun to Livingstone and overnight at one of the options discussed in chapter 10; for colonial pampering, nothing beats **The River Club,** on the banks of the Zambezi.

Days ⑥ & ⑦ Cape Town & the Winelands

Whether you go to the Zambezi or Chobe, you'll need to fly via Johannesburg or Maun to get to **Cape Town** the next day. There are wonderful places to stay all over town, but given that your time is limited, opt for lodging in the City Bowl (a natural amphitheater created by Table Mountain and the encircling arm of Signal Hill) or the Atlantic Seaboard, if it's summer; see chapter 4 for the top choices. If the weather is bad, book a personalized wine tour and spend the day sampling the superb red wines produced in the Stellenbosch region's tasting rooms, many of them heated with crackling fires. If the sun's out, spend the day doing the Cape Peninsula drive (see chapter 4). Or sleep in late and lunch at the Cape Quarter before browsing the shops in the vicinity. End your last day on **Clifton** or **Camps Bay beach,** or with a bottle of champagne on **Table Mountain** as the sun sets over the Southern Hemisphere, toasting your next trip here.

3 Going on Safari: The Best of the Best, No Expense Spared, in 10 Days

For the southern African safari experience of a lifetime, you really need to experience Botswana's Okavango Delta, a desert reserve, and the abundant wildlife of South Africa's Kruger Park region.

Days ① to ⑥: Botswana

Fly directly from either Johannesburg (or Cape Town) to Maun in Botswana, and spend 4 nights at one or more of the top Okavango Delta camps: whether **Mombo, Jao,** or **Chief's Camp** (the latter being an equally luxurious but slightly more affordable option; note that you need to book up to a year in advance if you plan to go during high season, when the delta is flooded and the attendant wildlife abundant). Alternatively, if you want to complement the standard game-drive experience you'll have in Kruger, book into **Abu Camp,** where all game-viewing takes place on elephant back, and accommodations are of an exceptionally high standard. Spend your first day relaxing and recovering from your long journey, watching the wildlife from the privacy of your deck. You'll wake the next day refreshed and ready for a day's intensive game-viewing. From the pristine delta, move on to spend 2 nights at **Jack's Camp** in Botswana's Kalahari wilderness, where the desolate desert landscape is nature at its most surreal; take a quad-bike safari to view some **Bushman rock art.**

Day ⑦: Zambia/Victoria Falls

From Jack's Camp, you can charter a flight to Livingstone, in Zambia, where a night at the colonial style **River Club**—located on the edge of the Zambezi River—provides a romantic base from which to visit the spectacular sight of **Victoria Falls.**

Day ⑧: Johannesburg

Return to Johannesburg (directly from Livingstone) for a heady night in Africa's Big Apple: If all that wildlife and those serene nights under African skies have you itching for some club action, **Kilimanjaro,** in Melrose Arch, is the place to

Two Safaris: One Splurge, One Budget

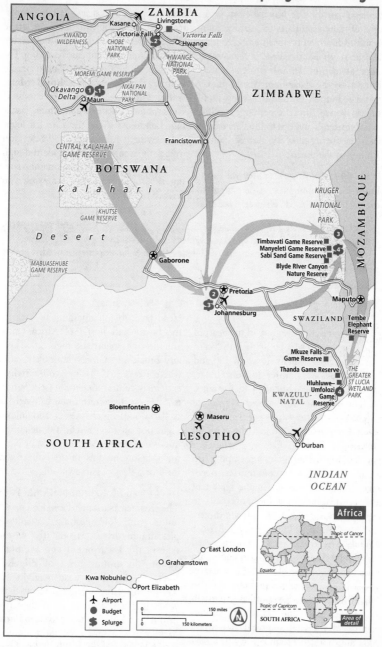

ANGOLA

ZAMBIA

Kasane ✈
Livingstone ✈

KWANDO
WILDERNESS

Victoria Falls
CHOBE
NATIONAL
PARK

Victoria Falls ▣

Hwange

MOREMI GAME RESERVE

HWANGE
NATIONAL
PARK

NXAI PAN
NATIONAL
PARK

Okavango ✈ ❶ 💲
Delta ✈ Maun

ZIMBABWE

CENTRAL KALAHARI
GAME RESERVE

Francistown ✈

BOTSWANA

K a l a h a r i

KRUGER

NATIONAL

PARK

MOZAMBIQUE

KHUTSE
GAME RESERVE

D e s e r t

Timbavati Game Reserve ▣ ❸
Manyeleti Game Reserve ▣ 💲
Sabi Sand Game Reserve ▣

MABUASEHUBE
GAME RESERVE

Gaborone ✪

Blyde River Canyon
Nature Reserve

Maputo ✪

❷ ✪ Pretoria
❸

Johannesburg

SWAZILAND

Tembe
Elephant
Reserve

Mkuze Falls
Game Reserve ▣

THE
GREATER
ST LUCIA
WETLAND
PARK

Bloemfontein ✪

✪ Maseru

LESOTHO

SOUTH AFRICA

Thanda Game Reserve ▣

Hluhluwe- ▣
Umfolozi ❹
Game
Reserve

KWAZULU-
NATAL

✈
Durban

INDIAN
OCEAN

○ East London

○ Grahamstown

Kwa Nobuhle ○
○ Port Elizabeth

✈ Airport
● Budget
💲 Splurge

0   150 miles

0   150 kilometers

🇳

Africa

Tropic of Cancer

Equator

Tropic of Capricorn

SOUTH AFRICA

Area of
detail

be (you can dine at **Moyo** before, or in one of the restaurants in nearby Norwood). Or, if you prefer listening to local live acts, go to **Bassline** in Newtown. Top attraction for daytime viewing should be the **Apartheid Museum.** Or do as Jo'burgers do and just shop—and unless you're after something specific, avoid the malls and opt to lunch at one of the pavement cafes in trendy Fourth Avenue in Parkhurst.

Days ❾ & ❿: Kruger National Park
From Johannesburg it's an easy flight to the world-renowned **Kruger National Park,** along South Africa's eastern border. Here, a choice of ultraluxurious game lodges offer smart design, impeccable comfort, and excellent game-viewing. For the absolute best options, choose among **Singita, Londolozi,** and **Royal Malewane.** The latter is the best choice if you're interested in on-foot rhino tracking, Londolozi is the ultimate for leopard-viewing, while Singita will bowl you over with its sophisticated modern design and opulence—oh, and the game-viewing is also superb. Leave knowing you really have done it all.

4 The Affordable Southern African Safari in 14 Days

Though it ain't gonna come cheap, the Great African Safari experience needn't empty your wallet.

Days ❶ to ❹: Botswana: Okavango Delta
Begin your bush adventure in the heart of the Okavango Delta by flying into Maun and chartering a flight (between $85 and $170 one-way) transfer to your lodge, where you should spend 3 to 4 nights. Either book at **Oddballs,** a 20-minute flight from Maun, where per-person rates start from below $200 a night, with an overnight mokoro camping safari; or arrange a 3-day all-inclusive camping trip with Detour (www.detourafrica.co.za), which should run you in the region of $350. If you have a bit more cash to splash, opt for one of the private camps: An excellent choice is CC Africa's **Sandibe Safari Lodge** with rates between $860 and $1,080 for two, depending on the season, or one of Wilderness Safaris' "Classic" camps, ranging from $860 to $1,190 (double). **Kwetsani** is a particularly fine option and in the same conservancy as the heftily priced Jao, so at $1,200 to $1,740 (double), it offers relatively good value—some visitors even prefer it for its intimacy.

Day ❺: Johannesburg
Head back to Johannesburg to soak up the hustle and bustle of Africa's most vibrant city; spend the night at a **bed-and-breakfast** in Melville or Parkwood, where R800 ($119) buys you a stylish, extremely comfortable room (see "Where to Stay: Northwestern Suburbs [Melville & Parkwood]" in chapter 7), and enjoy a night out on the town in the neighborhoods of Melville, Melrose Arch, or Newtown, before heading to the Kruger area for 4 or 5 days of game-viewing.

Days ❻ to ❿: Kruger National Park
The Kruger National Park lies just 5 hours from Johannesburg, and it's a pleasurable drive, particularly if you take in the **Escarpment** and overnight at the old mining town of **Pilgrim's Rest.** Alternatively, head straight for **Rissington Inn,** a good place to base yourself if you want to make day trips into the park. If you want to sleep in the park, you can save even more money: Rates here start at R480 ($72) for a comfortable, clean en-suite unit in one of the rest camps. If you can book well

enough in advance, the **Lower Sabie** and **Olifants rest camps** are the ones to choose; spend 2 nights at each. Again, if your budget can stretch this far, take a look at augmenting your national park experience with a sojourn at **Rhino Walking Safaris** (R3,900–R5,800/ $582–$866 double), a fabulous private concession within Kruger itself, or **Honeyguide**'s two smart-casual tented camps (R3,600–R4,600/$537–$687) in the adjacent **Manyeleti Reserve**—effectively the same game-viewing land, as it shares an unfenced border with Kruger.

Days ⑪ to ⑭: KwaZulu-Natal

Head south to the subtropical **Hluhluwe-Umfolozi Game Reserve** in KwaZulu-Natal, and join one of the Wilderness Trails in the pristine 25,000-hectare (61,750-acre) **Umfolozi wilderness area,** where armed rangers will take you within spitting distance of a large variety of wildlife. Considered the best on-foot safari experience in southern Africa, the all-inclusive price for 4 nights ranges between R1,400 and R2,480 ($209–$370) per person. The fastest way to get here is to fly from Kruger to Richards Bay and arrange a transfer to Hluhluwe; see chapter 9.

4

The Mother City:
Cape Town & the Winelands

Cape Town, the oldest city in southern Africa, is regularly heralded as one of the most beautiful on earth. The massive sandstone bulk of Table Mountain, often draped in a flowing "tablecloth" of clouds, forms an imposing backdrop, while minutes away, pristine sandy beaches line the cliff-hugging coast. Mountainous slopes sustaining the world's most varied botanic kingdom (some 9,000 species strong) overlook fertile valleys carpeted with vines, and driving from the highway you can spot zebra and wildebeest grazing unperturbed by the hubbub below. Every year brings a slew of new awards ("best value for money," "best city in the world to eat out in," "best destination in Africa and Middle East"), leaving no doubt that Cape Town is now a permanent fixture on the map of global hot spots. Yet the city feels—and is—very different from the rest of Africa.

Situated in the country's far southwestern corner, Cape Town is physically separated from the rest of the continent by a barrier of mountains. The hot, dry summers and cool, wet winters are Mediterranean, while the Atlantic Ocean is as frigid here as it is off the coast of Maine. Unique, too, is the Cape's architectural heritage—Cape Dutch homesteads, neo-Gothic churches, Muslim minarets, and English-inspired Georgian and Victorian buildings speak of the influences of a multifaceted colonial past.

Inevitably, colonialism has left its mark on the residents of Cape Town as well; the majority of the population is made up of the mixed-blood descendants of European settlers, Asian slaves, and indigenous people. This Afrikaans-speaking group is referred to as the "coloureds," a divisive designation conferred during the apartheid era, when they were relocated behind Table Mountain into the grim eastern interior plain known as the Cape Flats. Since the scrapping of influx control in 1986, this area has seen phenomenal growth, and today squatter towns form a seamless ribbon of cardboard-and-corrugated-iron housing that most visitors only glimpse on their way from or to the airport. Cape Town's newest residents come from the poverty-stricken Eastern Cape, others from as far afield as Somalia, Angola, and Mozambique, making it one of South Africa's fastest-growing cities—and unfortunately, the gangster-ridden Cape Flats have made it the most violent.

Although violent crime is mostly contained in these areas, visitors to Cape Town should take the same precautions they would in any large city—don't wear expensive jewelry or flash fancy cameras, and be aware of where the latest crime spots are—ask your hosts before you begin exploring, particularly the mountain or deserted beaches; sadly, you're usually best off where there are plenty of other people or where access is controlled.

Many who come to Cape Town choose to just whip straight out from the airport to the Winelands, where you can stay amid some of the best-preserved examples of Cape Dutch architecture and sample award-winning wines. This is a great area in which to base yourself if you're looking for a relaxing, rural escape, with the bright lights of the city a mere 60-minute drive away; the coastal town of Hermanus, "capital" of the Whale Coast, a 70-minute drive away; and the lakes, lagoons, and forests of the Garden Route an easy 4- to 5-hour drive along the N2. Alternatively, visit the Winelands or Whale Coast as a day trip, and base yourself here, overlooking the Atlantic Ocean, where the sun sets on an unbelievably azure sea. Regardless of where you choose to stay, you will leave Cape Town wishing you had more time to explore, so do try to keep your itinerary flexible.

1 Orientation

ARRIVING

BY PLANE   Following a R250-million ($37-million) upgrade, **Cape Town International Airport** (℡ 021/937-1200) is both comfortable and efficient, and is now served by 21 national and international airlines. The unprecedented popularity of the destination (an increase of a million passengers in under 2 years) has, however, led to some delays; call ℡ 086/727-7888 to check arrival times. (*Note:* If you've arrived early or are waiting for a connection, you can now relax in a Rennies Travel "Premier Club" lounge, which offers the same facilities as a first-class lounge; entry costs R120/$18 in the international terminal and R60/$8.95 in the domestic terminal.) The airport is a 22km (14-mile) drive from the center of town, so it should take no longer than 20 to 30 minutes to get into the city and surrounds (set aside twice that amount of time during the evening rush hours of 4–6pm). The **Magic Bus Shuttle** (℡ 021/505-6300; capemagic@magicbus.co.za) offers a door-to-door service; from the airport to the city center costs around R140 ($21)—ideally, you should book this a day or two in advance. Alternatively, contact **Sean Casey** (℡ 082/954-4867; seancasey12@hotmail.com), who offers the same service for similar rate. You'll find taxis directly outside the terminals; the same trip costs in the region of R180 ($27), but you can usually bargain this down. Just make sure you agree on a price up front. Car-rental desks are located inside the arrival terminals, and a Bureau de Change stays open for international flights; the rates aren't always the best, so use an ATM instead.

BY CAR   If you're traveling directly from Johannesburg, you will drive in on the N1, traveling past the Winelands area of Paarl. From Port Elizabeth, via the Garden Route, you'll approach the city center on the N2, passing Stellenbosch in the Winelands. The N2 splits into the M3 (the highway that connects the southern suburbs to the City Bowl suburbs) and Eastern Boulevard, which joins the N1 as it enters the perimeter of town. The entrance to the Waterfront is clearly signposted off here.

BY BUS   The main intercity buses, **Greyhound, Intercape,** and **Translux,** all terminate at the junction of Strand and Adderley streets. Note that the **Baz Bus**—a minibus service aimed at backpackers—offers a more flexible hop-on, hop-off option throughout the country. (See chapter 2 for regional numbers.)

BY TRAIN   The luxurious **Blue Train** (℡ 021/449-2672) and **Rovos Rail** (℡ 012/315-8242) roll in to Cape Town station from Johannesburg/Pretoria and at certain times of the year from the Garden Route; see chapter 2 for details. If you love rail travel, a charming alternative (and certainly more affordable) is to book a Premier

Class coupe from Johannesburg/Pretoria on **Shozoloza Mail** (© **086/000-8888**), South Africa's main line passenger services. The train departs for Cape Town from Pretoria/Johannesburg every Thursday (and departs for Johannesburg/Pretoria every Tues) and costs R2,050 ($306) per person one-way (all-inclusive). It's worth noting that the bus is quicker, albeit not as comfortable (the Trans-Karoo to Jo'burg is 25 hr., and the bus takes 18 hr.).

VISITOR INFORMATION

You'll find a Cape Town tourism desk at the airport (© **021/937-1234;** international terminus daily 7am–5pm, domestic daily 8am–midnight), but the best place to gather information is at **Cape Town Tourism** (© **021/426-4260;** www.cape-town.org; Mon–Fri 8am–6pm, Sat 8:30am–2pm, Sun 9am–1pm). Located in the **Pinnacle Building,** at the corner of Burg and Castle streets, this is the best bureau in South Africa, with a number of knowledgeable staff on hand to assist with anything from specialized tour bookings to transport queries and general information. Also present is a wine bar where you can do wine tastings and arrange for exports, a foreign exchange desk, a VAT desk (to claim back the VAT on your purchases; see chapter 2 for details), and an Internet cafe. There are literally hundreds of brochures, but look for the **Footsteps to Freedom Cape Town City Guide** (www.footstepstofreedom.co.za) and the series of special-interest maps—from the *Arts & Crafts Map* to the *Pink Map,* there's something to suit everyone. Shuttles to the city's top attractions, the hop-on hop-off Cape Town Explorer bus (see "Getting Around," below), and city walking tours depart regularly from here.

If it's more convenient, you could visit the Cape Town Tourism office located at the **Waterfront Clock Tower** (© **021/405 4500**). It offers similar services but has longer hours (9am–9pm). Two **Public Assistance** kiosks (© **021/426-5792**) are located in St George's Mall and the Company Gardens; besides offering general information, they sell parking cashcards here as well as "One Love" booklets containing coupons that entitle the bearer to a hot meal at a charity aimed at reuniting the homeless with their families; these can be a handy salve to your conscience when faced with the city's street children.

Note: The **SAA-Netcare Travel Clinic** (© **021/419-3172;** www.travelclinic.co.za), which offers expert advice and medical services (inoculations, malaria tablets) should you be traveling farther afield, has moved to 1107 Pickbell Parkade, 58 Strand St. **MTI Medi-Travel International** offers a similar service but, again, may be more conveniently located in the Waterfront Clock Tower (© **021/419-1888;** www.medi travel.co.za).

CITY LAYOUT

Cape Town lies on a narrow peninsula that curls southward into the Atlantic Ocean. Its western and eastern shores are divided by a spinal ridge of mountains, of which Table Mountain is the most dramatic landmark. The city center, located on the western shore, is known as the **City Bowl,** the "bowl" created by the table-topped massif as backdrop, flanked by jagged Devil's Peak to the east and the embracing arm of Signal Hill to the west. Upmarket residential suburbs range along these slopes (Tamboerskloof, Higgovale, Oranjezicht, and Gardens are where you'll find a plethora of lovely guesthouses), with views north overlooking the city center and harbor, where the **Victoria & Alfred Waterfront** is situated at the icy waters of Table Bay.

Within easy striking distance from the City Bowl and the Waterfront are the dense, built-up suburbs of tiny **De Waterkant** (arguably Cape Town's most fashionable suburb, and a must-see destination for shoppers who hate malls), Victorian **Green Point,** and high-rise **Sea Point.** Moving farther south, the western slopes of the Cape Peninsula mountain range slide almost directly into the sea, and it is here, along the dramatic coastline referred to as the **Atlantic seaboard,** that you can watch the sun sinking from Africa's most expensive real estate. Of these, the beaches of **Camp's Bay** ⊛ and **Clifton** ⊛⊛⊛ are the most conveniently located—easily reached from the City Bowl via Kloofnek, they are a mere 10- to 15-minute drive from the city center.

Traveling along the Atlantic seaboard is the most scenic route to Cape Point, but the quickest route is to travel south along the eastern flank of the mountain, via the M3, past the **southern suburbs** of Woodstock, Observatory, Rondebosch, Claremont, Wynberg, Kenilworth, Bishopscourt, and Constantia (the closest wine-producing area to the city, some 30 min. away, this vies with the Atlantic seaboard as pure real-estate wealth), and then snake along the False Bay seaboard to the Point. These eastern slopes, which overlook False Bay (so called by early sailors who mistook it for Table Bay), are the first to see the sun rise, and have price tags still affordable for locals (though with the recent boom in property, even this is set to change).

East of the peninsula are the **Cape Flats,** where the majority of so-called "Cape coloureds" live (see "The Coloured Class: Rise & Demise of a New 'Race'" in the appendix), and the **"black townships"** of Gugulethu, Langa, Nyanga, and Khayalitsha, reached via the N2. The N2 also provides access to the airport and the Winelands, which lie north of it. **Stellenbosch,** unofficial capital of the Winelands, is just over an hour's drive from the center of town, and from here the pretty valley of **Franschhoek,** some 85km (53 miles) northeast of Cape Town, is reached via the scenic Helshoogte Pass. A quicker route to Franschhoek is via the northern-bound N1, the highway that connects Cape Town to **Paarl,** a 40-minute drive from the center of town.

Pick up a free city map at the tourism office or consider investing in a detailed street atlas like *Mapstudios A–Z Streetmap,* sold at most newsagents.

Finally, if you get lost, don't despair—with Table Mountain as a visual guide, it's difficult to stay lost for long.

THE NEIGHBORHOODS IN BRIEF

CITY BOWL Within striking distance of the Waterfront, beaches, and Winelands, and in easy reach of most of the city's best restaurants, the residential suburbs that flank the bowl are the most convenient place to stay. Opt to stay in the one of the elegant guesthouses on the mountain slopes of the upmarket suburbs of Oranjezicht, Higgovale, and Tamboerskloof, with excellent views of the city and harbor.

VICTORIA & ALFRED WATERFRONT The Waterfront is considered one of the most successful in the world, and one of Cape Town's top attractions. Hotels have glorious sea and mountain views, and many shopping, dining, and entertainment options are right at your doorstep; but you'll pay for the privilege of staying here (the cheap options aren't worth it), and it's a little out of touch with the rest of the city.

DE WATERKANT, MOUILLE POINT, GREEN POINT & SEA POINT These border the Waterfront, and as such are also conveniently close to the city, with a number of value-for-money options. De Waterkant, in particular, is so close its accommodations are listed under "City Bowl," below; the neighborhood has evolved into the city's most chi-chi shopping area, with cobbled streets and a gorgeous square (Cape Quarter) surrounded by restaurants. The Mouille Point and Sea Point beachfront has been largely ruined by the construction of dense high-rise apartments, and pockets along Sea Point's Main Road are hangouts for hookers and drug dealers. This area used to be the heart of Cape Town's nightlife, and is experiencing a slow but sure comeback. You'll find a number of excellent restaurants on Main Road, but exercise caution after dark.

ATLANTIC SEABOARD 🏵🏵🏵 If you're looking for a beach holiday, there is only one place to be: the Atlantic seaboard, where Table Mountain drops steeply into the ocean, creating a magnificent backdrop to the seaside "villages" of Bantry Bay, Clifton, Camps Bay, Bakoven, and Llandudno. Besides offering the most beautiful beaches (of which Camps Bay is the most accessible, with a string of restaurants and cocktail bars), you'll find gorgeous people strutting their stuff on these pristine, fine white sands, and truly awesome sunsets.

HOUT BAY Surrounded by mountains, this charming town has its own harbor, and marks the start of the breathtaking **Chapman's Peak Drive** 🏵🏵🏵 (finally reopened in 2004), which snakes past Noordhoek, Kommetjie, and Scarborough before reaching the Cape Point Nature Reserve. These seaside towns have retained a quaint villagelike feel, but are a little far from the city's attractions and restaurants to base yourself.

FALSE BAY Distance from city attractions and the Winelands is also the drawback of these suburbs, which are (driving south to north) **Simon's Town** 🏵, Fish Hoek, **Kalk Bay** 🏵, St

James, and Muizenberg. The sea is a few degrees warmer on this side of the mountain, however, and because this part of the coast faces east, dawn can be breathtaking, though at the expense of any sunsets.

SOUTHERN SUBURBS The two worth highlighting are Observatory and Constantia. **Observatory** (less than 10 min. from town), with its quaint Victorian buildings and narrow streets, offers a number of good restaurants and an interesting bohemian feel—its proximity to both the University of Cape Town and Groote Schuur hospital makes for a particularly eclectic mix of people. Considered less brash than the Atlantic seaboard, the oak-lined streets and old, established mansions of **Constantia** 🏵🏵 are arguably the city's most exclusive addresses, with the lush surrounds of the Cape's oldest wine-producing area attracting the rich and famous who prefer their privacy to the glare of the sun-soaked hoi polloi.

CAPE FLATS This is where the majority of "coloureds" (the apartheid name for people of mixed descent) live, many forcibly relocated from District Six (a now-razed suburb adjacent to the city) by apartheid policies. The residents of the Cape Flats suffer from high unemployment and a lack of cohesive identity and hope, and the area has become a fertile breeding ground for drug-fueled gangster wars. Even farther east are the "black suburbs" (historically referred to as "townships") of Gugulethu, Langa, and Nyanga, and the vast shantytowns and new residences of Khayalitsha (visible from the N2 as you drive into town from the airport). To get a balanced view of Cape Town and a real insight into South Africa's history, a visit to these areas is highly recommended; see "Getting Around," below, for township tours.

WINELANDS No trip to Cape Town would be complete without at least a day spent here; indeed, many prefer to stay here for the duration of their visit— Cape Town lies no more than an hour or so away, the airport 45 minutes. The university town of **Stellenbosch** ★★ is the cultural center of the Winelands, and its oak-lined streetscape offers the greatest sense of history. However, **Fran-schhoek** ★★★—reached via either Stellenbosch or Paarl—is located in the prettiest of the wineland valleys, and is considered the Winelands' cuisine capital; if you visit only one wine-producing region, make sure it's Franschhoek. Deciding where to stay is ultimately a matter of availability; places situated on wine estates with views of the vineyards

and mountains are most desirable. The town of **Paarl** is not as attractive, but the surroundings, on gracious wine farms and old estates, offer great accommodations options.

NORTHERN SUBURBS With their kitsch postmodern palaces and endless "first-home" developments, these suburbs don't really warrant much attention (though Lagoon Bay, a new hotel development in Milnerton, may change this). However, if you're heading north to see the West Coast, you should consider stopping at Blouberg Beach for the postcard view of Table Mountain across the bay. To reach Blouberg Beach, take the R27 Marine Drive, off the N1.

2 Getting Around

Contained by the mountain, the city center is small enough to explore on foot. Public transport in Cape Town is marginally better than that in other South African cities—shuttle buses connect the tourism bureaus located in the center and the waterfront with top attractions such as the Table Mountain cableway, Camps Bay, and Kirstenbosch, while trains will take you to the southern suburbs and False Bay beaches (though the latter hardly hold an unblemished safety record). However, to move at will, or to explore the Atlantic seaboard, Cape Point, or the Winelands, you're better off renting a car. The roads are relatively empty of traffic, parking is (with the exception of the city center) easy to find, and signs are easy to understand.

BY PUBLIC & PRIVATE TRANSPORTATION

BY TRAIN If you're heading to the southern suburbs, Paarl, or Stellenbosch, contact **Cape Metropolitan transport information** (✆ 0800/656-463) for routes and fares. Trains, however, are not always reliable, clean, or safe; choose first-class cars with other occupants, and watch your bags. A better option is to take the spectacular cliff-hugging route along the False Bay seaboard to Simon's Town aboard **Biggsy's Restaurant Carriage & Wine Bar** (✆ 021/788-7760), with breakfast, lunch, or snacks en route; the return from the city station takes 2½ hours; tickets are R24 ($3.60) per person, excluding drinks and meals. Breakfast is an extra R32 ($4.75; "champagne" breakfast R47/$7), lunch is R72 ($11), and snacks run at about R15 ($2.25).

BY BUS The most useful way to get around the city is with **Cape Town Explorer,** a hop-on, hop-off bus that visits the city's top attractions, departing from the tourism offices from 10am to 3pm (see "Organized Cruises & Tours," below). Municipal buses depart from the center of town (principal terminals are around the Golden Acre shopping center on Adderley St.) to various points of interest, including Sea Point and Hout Bay. Contact **Golden Arrow** (✆ 080/121-2111) for routes, times, and fares. A **V&A Waterfront bus** (✆ 021/408-1000) leaves from Adderley Street (in front of the

"One Love": The R2 Coupon That Can Make a Difference

The most distressing aspect of exploring the city is the number of homeless children you'll find begging at traffic intersections and cruising in groups along the street. Although these children, having run from deeply dysfunctional "home" environments, deserve sympathy, visitors are urged not to give them money, as this effectively condemns them to a life on the streets. If you want to act, One Love is a new charity that provides locals and visitors with an interesting option: booklets with coupons entitling the bearer to a hot meal and drink at the charity's premises, where the children are then assessed by social workers who work to reunite and rehabilitate these broken families. You can purchase these booklets from **Public Assistance kiosks** (℗ 021/426-5792), located in St George's Mall and the Company Gardens.

station) every 15 minutes from 6am to 11pm daily; the trip costs R2.60 (40¢); alternatively, head for the tourist bureau, where shuttles are regularly departing (maximum 10-min. wait) for the Waterfront (R25/$3.75), Kirstenbosch (R60/$8.95), Table Mountain cable car (R40/$5.95), and airport (R120/$18 for one; R150/$22 for two; can arrange pickup from hotel).

BY CAR Cape Town is a relatively car-friendly city with a minimum of traffic jams and enough parking lots to warrant driving into town—try the **Picbel Arcade** (entrance off Strand St.), the **Golden Acre Parking Garage** (entrance off Parliament St.), the **Pay & Display** on the Grand Parade (entrance off Buitenkant St.), or the **lot** opposite **Heritage Square** (entrance off Shortmarket St.). It can be difficult to find parking on the street, but if you do, you'll need to purchase an **Addo parking card** (℗ 021/712-0307); look for the city police (dressed in black-and-white uniforms) or traffic officers (in blue uniforms), who will assist. Self-appointed "parking attendants" will offer to watch your car; although you are under no obligation to reward these irritants, it is customary to tip those who are clearly hired by local businesses (they will usually wear some kind of bib or hand over a card) on your return; R2 to R5 (30¢–75¢) is adequate, depending on how long you've been.

You'll find numerous car-rental companies in Cape Town. For a cheaper deal, try **Easy Rent-A-Car** (℗ 021/424-3951), **Value** (℗ 021/696-2298), or **Imperial Economy** (℗ 021/465-4729). For a one-way rental to another province, you'll have to use a company with nationwide offices, such as **Avis** (℗ 021/424-1177), **Budget** (℗ 021/418-5232), **Hertz** (℗ 021/400-9630), or **Imperial** (℗ 021/421-5190). **Felix Unite** (℗ 021/425-5371) acts as a rental broker and gives good-value fixed-rate deals. To feel the wind in your hair, rent a **classic convertible** ℗ 021/423-1800; www.moto stars.com) and tool stylishly along the coast in chauffeur-driven comfort.

BY TAXI Much cheaper than a metered taxi are **Rikkis,** which keep prices down to R10 to R16 ($1.50–$2.40) by continuously picking up and dropping off passengers en route. These open-sided, three-wheeled vehicles will drop you off anywhere in the City Bowl, the Waterfront, or Camps Bay; call ℗ 021/423-4888 for a pickup anywhere in these areas (or hail one) from 7am to 7pm weekdays, Saturday 8am to 4pm. Metered taxis don't cruise the streets looking for fares; you'll have to phone. It's expensive, but it's also the best and safest form of transportation after dark. Contact

Sea Point Taxis (© 021/434-4444; R8/$1.20 per km) or Marine Taxis (© 021/434-0434; R10/$1.50 per km).

BY BIKE   Hire a Harley (© 021/434-2603; www.harley-davidson-capetown.com; R1,000/$155 per day) or a flashy **BMW** (© 021/794-7887; www.sa-motorcycle-tours.com; prices dependent on length of tour and whether you choose to be accompanied by a guide). If all you want is to get from the beach to the city, zip around on a Vespa from **Vespa Café** (© 021/426-5042; R200/$30 per day) Alternatively, get off the road and rent a mountain bike from **Downhill Adventures** (© 021/422-0388). **Rent 'n Ride** (© 082/881-1588) supplies bicycles as well as jet skis, though the latter may well be banned by the time this comes to print.

ORGANIZED CRUISES & TOURS

Note that these tours concentrate on the city and immediate surroundings; for tours farther afield, like four-wheel-drive journeys up the West Coast, or whale and dolphin safaris on the Whale Coast and Garden Route, see chapter 5.

ON FOOT   The 3-hour **"Footsteps to Freedom"** (© 083/452-1112) guided walk departs Monday to Saturday at 10:30pm from Cape Town Tourism and covers all the top attractions in the city center. It's a good way to get oriented and come to grips with Cape Town's multifaceted history. The tour costs R100 ($15).

BY BOAT   One of the best vantages of Cape Town is undoubtedly from the sea. Tours cost from R30 ($4.45) per person, depending on the duration and destination, with a sunset cruise from the harbor to Clifton highly recommended (R150/$22). The **Boat Owner and Charter Association** (call Ms. Pollet at © 021/418-0134) offers a large range of vessels to cater to all interests, but it's worth highlighting the following enterprises: The **Waterfront Boat Company** (© 021/418-5806; www.waterfrontboats.co.za) has a 18m (58-ft.) gaff-rigged schooner called *Spirit of Victoria* that cruises the Table Bay and Blouberg area, and a luxury motorboat, *Condor,* that cruises to Clifton Bay. The company also has a whale-watching permit (May–Dec) that allows controlled approach to within 50m (164 ft.). *Tigresse* (© 021/419-1510), a luxury catamaran, provides another great way to get to Clifton. Alternatively, get your pulse racing and strap up with **Atlantic Adventures** (© 021/425-3785), who set off at 120kmph (74mph) across Table Bay in a rubber duck. In Hout Bay harbor, **Drum Beat Charters** (© 021/791-4441) and **Circe** (© 021/790-1040) both offer 40-minute trips to see the Cape fur seals on Duiker Island (R35/$5.20 adults; trips leave at 8:45 and 9:30am daily).

BY BUS   A large number of operators offer driving tours of the city and its surrounds—recommended companies that offer tours in minibuses include the well-established **African Eagle** (© 021/464-4266) and **Legend Tours** (© 021/697-4056).

   Cape Town Explorer (© 021/511-1784; R90/$13) offers a 2-hour, 15-minute tour aboard an open double-decker bus—given that your ticket is valid for the day and that you can hop on or off at any stage, this is a great way to get around the top attractions; catch it from 9:30am outside Ferryman's Pub at the Waterfront (from 9:40am at Cape Town Tourism, or call at any time to find the location of the bus closest to you) and hop off at any of the designated points along the tour, which includes various city museums, the cable car, and Camps Bay. Last round is at usually around 5pm but could be later or earlier, depending on the season; best to call ahead. **Hylton**

Ross (℡ 021/511-1784) and **Atlas** (℡ 021/460-4700) are long-standing operators offering a variety of half-day, full-day, and 4-day tours. To choose, check the selection at www.hyltonross.co.za.

BY AIR   For an aerial tour of the city or peninsula, contact **Civair Helicopters** (℡ 021/419-5182). **Federal Air** (℡ 021/934-1383) offers scenic flights as far afield as Bushmanskloof game reserve in Cederberg (see chapter 5), **Aquilla** (℡ 021/712-1913) takes to the sky in microlights, and **ThunderCity** (℡ 021/934-8007) caters to adrenaline junkies with expensive tastes—an hour ride in one of their fighter planes costs from R28,000 to R73,000 ($4,179–$10,896).

TOWNSHIP TOURS   For a more holistic view of the still essentially segregated Cape Town community, a township tour is essential. The tourism bureau will put you in contact with a "Trail of Two Cities" operator: A tour initiated for the 2002 World Summit on Sustainable Development, this introduces the visitor to some of the interesting entrepreneurs working in the poorer areas of the city, from the likes of Golden Nongawuza, who, after a vivid dream, started making flowers from discarded cans in his Khayalitsha shack, to Victoria Mxenge, who has a group of previously homeless women cultivating arum lilies. **Tana-Baru Tours** (℡ 021/424-0719) and **Grassroute Tours** (℡ 021/706-1006) provide insight into the Cape Muslim culture of the Bo-Kaap and the forced removals from District Six, and also takes you through the predominantly black communities of Langa, Gugulethu, and/or Khayalitsha. **One City Tours** (℡ 021/387-5351) and **Thuthuka Tours** (℡ 021/433-2429) concentrate on interesting aspects of the black Cape Town community; the latter offers recommended Gospel Tours, Evening Jazz Tours, and Xhosa Folklore Tours, where you can witness ancestor rituals and *umcimbi* rites. For more on these, see "Cultural Sights: Cape Muslim to Khayalitsha," later in this chapter.

SPECIALIST TOURS   **Daytrippers** (℡ 021/511-4766) specializes in combining hiking, biking, and sea kayaking with sightseeing tours of the peninsula. For specialist **wine tours,** see "The Winelands," later in this chapter.

FAST FACTS: Cape Town

American Express Main local offices are in the city center at Thibault Square (℡ 021/425-7991) and at the Waterfront, Shop 11A in Alfred Mall (℡ 021/419-3917). City center hours are from 8:30am to 4:30pm Monday through Friday. Waterfront hours are from 9am to 7pm Monday through Friday, and from 10am to 5pm Saturday and Sunday.

Airport See "Arriving," earlier in the chapter.

Area Code The area code for Cape Town and surrounding Winelands is **021**.

Babysitters Contact **Supersitters** (℡ 021/439-4985; www.supersitters.net; R30/$4.45 per hour before midnight, thereafter R40/$5.95 per hour). Contact Mary Poppins (℡ 021/674-6689 or 083/454-1282; vicky@icon.co.za; R450/$67 per day) for au pair placements.

Bookstores For books on Cape Town and South Africa, head for **Traveller's Bookshop** (℡ 021/425-6880) or **Exclusive Books** (℡ 021/419-0905), both in Victoria Wharf, Victoria & Alfred Waterfront.

Car Rentals See "Getting Around," above.

Climate See "When to Go," in chapter 2.

Doctors & Dentists Call © 021/671-3634 or 021/671-2924 for a 24-hour referral service. **SAA Netcare Travel Clinic** is located in the Fountain Medical Centre, Adderley Street (© 021/419-3172). **MTI Medi-Travel International** is in the Clocktower, Waterfront (© 021/419-1888).

Driving Rules See "Getting Around," above.

Drugstores See "Pharmacy," below.

Embassies & Consulates **U.S.:** 4th floor, Broadway Centre, Heerengracht Street (© 021/421-4280); **Canada:** 19th floor, Reserve Bank Building, corner St Georges Mall and Hout Street (© 021/423-5240); **U.K.:** 15th floor, Southern Life Centre, 8 Riebeeck St. (© 021/405-2400).

Emergencies For an ambulance, call © 10177; for police, call © 10111; in case of fire, call © 021/535-1100; for a sea rescue, call © 021/449-3500.

Hospitals **Groote Schuur** (© 021/404-9111) in Observatory is the Cape's largest hospital; **Somerset Hospital** (© 021/402-6911) at the Waterfront may be more conveniently located. However, for immediate attention in more salubrious surrounds, you're best off heading for a private clinic (this is why medical insurance is so advisable). **The Chris Barnard Memorial Hospital** (© 021/480-6111) in the center of town, at 181 Longmarket St. **Claremont Hospital** (© 021/670-3400) is closest to Constantia. Contact **Mediclinic** (© 021/883-8571) if you're in Stellenbosch in the Winelands.

Hot Lines **Automobile Association** (for vehicle breakdown, © 082/161-11); **Rape Crisis** (© 021/447-9762 for 24-hr. advice and counseling).

Internet Access There are numerous Internet cafes all over the city, but the Cape Town Tourism offices (see "Visitor Information," earlier in this chapter) are probably the most convenient place to surf, given the volume of hard-copy information at your disposal. Alternatively, ask your host for the nearest Internet access.

Maps See "City Layout," earlier in this chapter.

Mobile-Phone Rental You can rent a phone in the International Arrivals terminal at the airport from **MTN Rentals** (© 021/934-3261) or from **Cellucity,** Kiosk 5, Victoria Wharf Centre, Waterfront (© 021/418-1306), for about R18 to R40 ($2.70–$5.95) a day.

Newspapers & Magazines The morning paper, *Cape Times,* and the more sensationalist afternoon and evening paper, *Argus,* are sold at most street corners. You'll find international titles at the Waterfront (see "Bookstores," above).

Pharmacy **Lite-Kem** (© 021/461-8040), at 24 Darling St., opposite the city post office, is open Monday through Saturday from 7:30am to 11pm and Sunday from 9am to 11pm. **Sunset Pharmacy** (© 021/434-3333), in Sea Point Medical Centre, Kloof Road, is open daily from 8:30am to 9pm.

Post Office The central branch is located on the corner of Parliament and Darling streets (© 021/464-1700), on the second floor. Hours are Monday through Friday from 8am to 4:30pm (Wed from 8:30am), and Saturday from 8am to noon.

Restrooms The city's large population of homeless people means that the hygiene of public restrooms can be of varying quality. You're best off going to a coffee shop or restaurant, or visiting a gas station.

Safety The formation of the Central City Improvement District (CCID), the installation of closed-circuit cameras, a dedicated city police force, and 24-hour care centers for Cape Town's street children has resulted in a drastic reduction in crime in the city center. This is no reason to let down your guard, however. Muggings can be avoided by taking the same precautions you would in any large city. Be aware of street children, many of whom beg at large intersections. Visitors are requested to give them food coupons (inquire at the CCID Kiosks in St George's Mall and Company Gardens) or make a donation to one of the childcare centers rather than provide them with cash, which keeps them on the streets. Note that it is inadvisable to pull over and stop on the N2 (the airport highway), and it's worth traveling with a cellphone in case your car breaks down. For detailed advice, pick up a brochure on safety from any tourism office.

Spa & Salon Treatments There are numerous wellness centers and hotel spas (p. 92), but if you're in the city and just want a 1- or 2-hour pampering session, the most convenient option, with a wide range of therapies, is **S.K.I.N.**, on the Waterfront (© **021/425-3551**).

Taxis See "Getting Around," earlier in this chapter.

Weather Call © **082/231-1640**.

3 Where to Stay

Cape Town's popularity has produced an ever-expanding list of accommodations options, and many seasoned globetrotters contend it offers the best selection of guesthouses in the world, though the increased competition has yet to produce a concomitant drop in rates in the top-end sector. That said, recent heated debates on the potential impact of a handful of greedy operators on the city's reputation as a great-value destination, not to mention the rand's bullish performance, have led to a stabilization in prices for the first time in a decade.

The City Bowl (which includes the residential suburbs on the slopes of Table Mountain), Waterfront, and Camps Bay remain the most popular areas to stay, with most options listed here providing great views and/or good access to restaurants, attractions, and beaches. If you're traveling between May and September, it's worth checking on low-season (or "green-season") rates, but with the city's popularity spreading throughout the year, discounted rates may be harder and harder to come by.

Note: The airport is no more than a 20- to 30-minute drive from most hotels, so it's not necessary to move to an airport hotel for early-morning or late-night flights; instead, try to arrange for an early or late check-in to coincide with your flight. All the places listed below will arrange airport transfers.

CITY BOWL

For easy access to sights, top restaurants, and beaches, you can't beat the **City Bowl.** The **city center** itself has a few options worth considering, the best of which are the following: If you like your hotels old style, the **Holiday Inn Cape Town** (© 021/ 488-5100; www.southernsun.com), a block from the tourist office, is a brash '70s (tons of brass and glass) high-rise with great views; a mountain-facing standard room on the 30th floor will run you R995 ($149) double. Alternatively, the new **Arabella Sheraton Grand Hotel** (© 021/412-8200; www.arabellasheraton.com/capetown), part of Cape Town's super-slick Convention Centre, offers rooms from R1,400 ($209). If you prefer boutique-style hotels, the elegant and intimate **Cape Heritage Hotel** (© 021/424-4646; R1,040–R1,800/$155–$269 double) on Heritage Square provides immediate access to some of the city's best restaurants; take a look at its tasteful colonial-themed interiors at www.capeheritage.co.za. The more mod **Metropole** (© 021/424-7247; R1,200–R1,375/$179–$205) is styled along the lines of a downtown New York boutique hotel, with a hip restaurant and a chic bar frequented by a primarily gay clientele. Check it out at www.metropolehotel.co.za. Slightly on the outskirts (a 10-min. walk to the center), but better situated for restaurants (it's right on the vibrant cafe-and-dining strip of Kloof St.), **Hippo Hotel** (© 021/423-2500; www.hippotique.co.za) is not as self-conscious as the Metropole, and offers better business facilities, including multimedia personal computers in every room, 24-hour complimentary ADSL broadband, electronic safes that accommodate laptops, and DSTV and DVD players. It's also good value, at R900 ($134) double (R675/$101 single). Moving east, the **Cape Town Hollow** (www.capetownhollow.co.za), located directly opposite the Company Gardens (Cape Town's "Central Park"), offers double

---

Tips **Great Self-Catering Options**

Renting an apartment or home can be a good value-for-money option for longer stays, particularly for families, and thanks to Mr Delivery (see "Where to Dine," later in this chapter), you won't even have to cook. A good option is **Cote-Sud Apartments** (© 021/422-5124; www.cotesud.co.za; R500–R900/ $75–$134 for two, depending on season)—four tasteful two-bedroom apartments with separate entrances and a communal pool conveniently located on busy Kloof Street (plenty of dining options within walking distance and literally a stone's throw from an excellent pizzeria and useful minimart). Proprietor Robyn is very flexible, so it's worth dealing with her direct; book an upstairs apartment for views. Located in the city's hippest urban suburbs, **Village & Life** (© 021/422-2721; www.villageandlife.com) runs a variety of self-catering accommodations options (almost all featured on their website), in three "villages": **De Waterkant** (City Bowl with harbor views), **Camps Bay,** and the **Waterfront.** All three are within walking distance of coffee shops and restaurants. **Icon Villas and Vistas** (© 021/424-0905; www.icape.co.za) deals with a broad spectrum of upmarket suburbs (and as far afield as Franschhoek and Knysna) and price ranges (apartments and homes R350–R15,000/$52–$2,239 per day). Another website worth checking out is **www.cliftononsea.com,** which offers an excellent range of accommodations options sleeping from 2 to 10 people, most with pools and all with superb sea and sunset views of Africa's "Cote d'Azure." Prices range from R350 to R1,000 ($52–$149) per person per night. At the top end of the scale (we're talking butlers, chauffeurs, and chefs, should you so require), take a look at **www.capeportfolios.com.**

Where to Stay in Cape Town

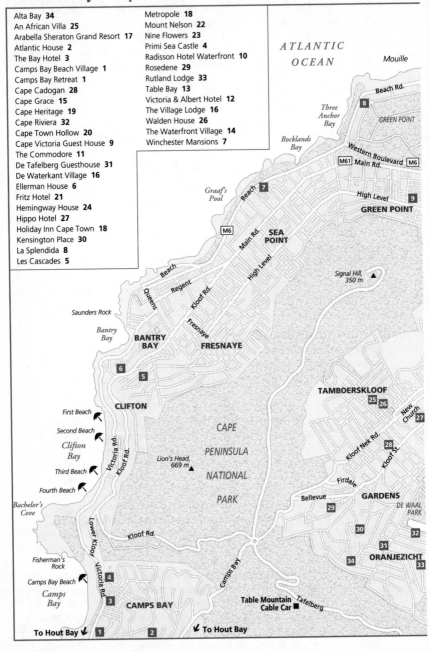

Alta Bay **34**
An African Villa **25**
Arabella Sheraton Grand Resort **17**
Atlantic House **2**
The Bay Hotel **3**
Camps Bay Beach Village **1**
Camps Bay Retreat **1**
Cape Cadogan **28**
Cape Grace **15**
Cape Heritage **19**
Cape Riviera **32**
Cape Town Hollow **20**
Cape Victoria Guest House **9**
The Commodore **11**
De Tafelberg Guesthouse **31**
De Waterkant Village **16**
Ellerman House **6**
Fritz Hotel **21**
Hemingway House **24**
Hippo Hotel **27**
Holiday Inn Cape Town **18**
Kensington Place **30**
La Splendida **8**
Les Cascades **5**

Metropole **18**
Mount Nelson **22**
Nine Flowers **23**
Primi Sea Castle **4**
Radisson Hotel Waterfront **10**
Rosedene **29**
Rutland Lodge **33**
Table Bay **13**
Victoria & Albert Hotel **12**
The Village Lodge **16**
Walden House **26**
The Waterfront Village **14**
Winchester Mansions **7**

*ATLANTIC
OCEAN*

Mouille

Beach Rd.

*Three
Anchor
Bay*

8

GREEN POINT

*Rocklands
Bay*

M61 Main Rd. **M6**

Western Boulevard

High Level **9**

GREEN POINT

*Graaf's
Pool*

Beach **7**

M6

Main Rd.

**SEA
POINT**

High Level

Signal Hill,
350 m ▲

Beach

Queens

Regent

Kloof Rd.

Fresnaye

Saunders Rock

*Bantry
Bay*

**BANTRY
BAY**

FRESNAYE

6

5

First Beach

CLIFTON

Second Beach

*Clifton
Bay*

Victoria Rd.

Kloof Rd.

CAPE

*Lion's Head,
669 m* ▲

PENINSULA

Third Beach

Fourth Beach

*Bachelor's
Cove*

Lower Kloof

NATIONAL

PARK

*Fisherman's
Rock*

Kloof Rd.

Victoria Rd.

Camps Bay Beach

4

*Camps
Bay*

3

CAMPS BAY

To Hout Bay ↙ **1**

2

↙ **To Hout Bay**

TAMBOERSKLOOF

25 **26**

New Church

27

Kloof Nek Rd.

28

Kloof St.

Firdale

Bellevue

GARDENS

29

DE WAAL
PARK

30

31

32

34

ORANJEZICHT

33

Camps Bay

Table Mountain
Cable Car ■

Tafelberg

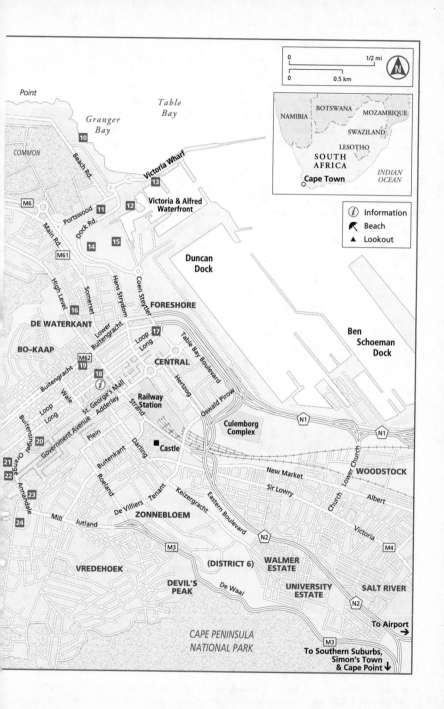

rooms for a very reasonable R595 to R990 ($89–$148), depending on the season. It has a pretty exterior, is popular with package tourists, and enjoys a great location (make sure you book a room overlooking the gardens), but the decor is dull. Decor is also not the primary reason to book into **Nine Flowers,** but with doubles at R600 ($90), the rather stark rooms are very comfortable indeed, and again you are a few minutes' walk from the city center (details below). But a few blocks away is the eclectically furnished **Dunkley House** (© 021/462-7650; www.dunkleyhouse.com); rooms are a tad pricier, at R700 to R1,150 ($104–$172) double, but it has real character and a pool.

These are the best city center options, but given Cape Town's geography, my money remains on one of the options located in the residential suburbs that tumble down the mountain slopes, most with fabulous views of the "Bowl"—of the accommodations listed below, the **Mount Nelson** is still the classiest option, **The Village Lodge** and **An African Villa** share the honors for "best value," and **Alta** and **Cape Cadogan** can both claim "best newcomer."

VERY EXPENSIVE

Mount Nelson ✸✸✸   The worst thing about staying here is how difficult it is to leave—the "Nellie," as she's affectionately known, is a 10-minute stroll through the Company Gardens to the center of the city, yet the great pink ship is adrift in 3.6 hectares (9 acres) of mature gardens that offer all the tranquillity of the country. Service standards are unparalleled, and rooms (particularly those in the Hof Villa, the main hotel building, and the sublime garden cottages around the adults' pool) elegant and soothing. Having opened her doors in 1899 to accommodate the passengers of the Union and Castle lines, the undisputed grand dame of colonial hotels became a little fusty over the years, but with some clever refurbishing (by world-renowned Cape-based designer Graham Viney, who has a real flair for sophisticated old-world charm) and the opening of the slinky Planet bar, the likes of Colin Farrell and Nicholas Cage now mingle with nouveau riche ladies in large hats and doddering aristocrats in cardigans. A massive breakfast buffet and light meals are served in the **Oasis** restaurant, overlooking the large pool and gardens. The elegant **Cape Colony restaurant** (see "Where to Dine," later in this chapter) offers more formal dining in a wonderful old-fashioned atmosphere. Even if you don't opt to stay here, make sure you set aside an afternoon to imbibe in the Nellie's legendary high tea. *Tip:* While this is a deservedly firm favorite, do take a look at Ellerman House (later in the chapter), which is the seaside alternative.

76 Orange St., Gardens 8001. © 021/483-1000. Fax 021/483-1782. www.mountnelsonhotel.orient-express.com. 201 units. R3,460–R5,130 ($516–$766) double, depending on season; R5,120–R11,970 ($764–$1,787) suite. Dec 18–Jan 5, 7-night minimum stay. AE, DC, MC, V. **Amenities:** 2 restaurants; bar; 2 pools; 2 tennis courts; gym; salon; room service; laundry; squash. *In room:* A/C, TV, minibar, hair dryer, DVD.

EXPENSIVE

Alta Bay ✸✸   It opened its doors only at the end of 2004, but already this discreet, well-bred guesthouse has seen plenty of repeat business. Located on the steep slopes of wind-free Higgovale (the City Bowl's most prestigious suburb), Alta comprises only six suites, but with most of them on separate levels with private courtyards or decks, and a great sense of space and light throughout, you'll never feel claustrophobic or invaded. Furnished with all the modcons you'd expect from a guesthouse in this price category, and with what has become signature South African Modern (clean angular lines softened with suede, leather, and timber; neutral warm colors; a few ethnic touches; and high-quality fabrics—not a faux zebra skin in sight), the house also offers plenty of access to the outdoors, either through large doors that lead to the shaded and lush garden, or gorgeous vistas of the sparkling city below. A personal favorite, the Bay Room, has simply marvelous views, fringed with pines, and the biggest bathroom by far; book it if you can. This is a smart, comfortable choice that, like the Cadogan (see below), will appeal to the design conscious, but do also look at Les Cascades, later in this chapter.

12 Invermark Crescent, Higgovale 8001. ⓒ **021/487-8800.** Fax 021/487-8822. www.altabay.com. 6 units. High season R2,100 ($313) suite; low season R1,200 ($179). Rates include breakfast. AE, DC, MC, V. **Amenities:** Honesty bar; pool; laundry; airport transfers. *In room:* A/C, TV, hair dryer, wireless PC connection, DVD/CD.

Hemingway House 🎭🎭   This is a fabulous, romantic guesthouse, the kind that regularly makes it into interior design magazines. If you're traveling with a group or planning a small wedding, I can't think of a better place to host a house party. Featuring four plush rooms built around a serene courtyard with pool, the house can accommodate a maximum of eight guests, all of whom have access to the entire house (including a classy English/Provençal country-style kitchen that would delight anyone who actually wants to cook, and an outdoor, undercover lounge adjacent to the pool, furnished with comfortable couches that invite hours of reading, and warmed in the evenings by a wood-burning fire). The many personal touches mean the house has a wonderful lived-in ambience; it feels more like staying in the home of a friend who just happens to have impeccable taste—potentially a negative if you like anonymity. Other drawbacks are the fact that it has no view and it's not exactly cheap; opt for the better-value Garden Suite or Courtyard Bedroom (R1,800/$269)—they're a tad smaller but just as gorgeously furnished, with four-poster beds and antiques.

1–2 Lodge St., Cape Town 8001. ⓒ/fax **021/461-1857.** www.hemingwayhouse.co.za. 4 units. R1,800–R2,500 ($269–$373) double. Rates include breakfast. AE, DC, MC, V. **Amenities:** Dining room (chef on request); honor bar; pool; limited room service; laundry. *In room:* A/C, TV/VCR, hair dryer, heated towel rails.

Kensington Place 🎭🎭🎭   This award-winning boutique hotel is, like Alta Bay, situated in the prestigious residential area of Higgovale, with beautiful views of the city, harbor, and mountain. A sense of real opulence pervades; each bedroom is the size of a minisuite, with expensive finishes and luxurious fabrics throughout. Beds are dressed in pale cotton linen, and bathrooms have underfloor heated marble and custom-made bathtubs. The best rooms have balconies overlooking the city—ask for one (no. 1, 2, or 3) on the top floor for the best city views. The plunge pool is surrounded with timber decking and has a comfortable outdoor lounge area replete with billowing curtains—a calm oasis from bustling Kloof Street, with its excellent restaurant choices, a short stroll away. Despite its small size, service is excellent, but some may find the atmosphere a little stuffy, and the seaside alternative, Les Cascades, offers better value.

38 Kensington Crescent, Higgovale 8001. ⓒ **021/424-4744.** Fax 021/424-1810. www.kensingtonplace.co.za. 8 units. High season R2,000–R2,400 ($299–$358) double; low season R1,300–R1,500 ($194–$2240) double. Rates include breakfast. AE, DC, MC, V. Children 16 and over only. **Amenities:** Pool; 24-hr. room service; massage; laundry; wireless Internet connection; Virgin Active membership. *In room:* TV, minibar (1 room only), hair dryer, DVD.

MODERATE

Cape Town has a few more guesthouses worth looking at in this price category, all of them in gorgeous homes located high up on the slopes of Oranjezicht, with great views of the city and harbor lights.

Cape Riviera (✆ 021/461-8535; www.caperiviera.co.za; R710–R1,200/$106–$179 double) is efficiently manager-run and has the added advantage of overlooking the Molteno reservoir. Rooms, furnished in dark wood and white, are somewhat stark (no art on the walls or any personal touches) but equipped with all the comforts (air-conditioning, minibar, Internet connection, TV). It has a large pool (currently a little exposed to the street, which, incidentally, is lined with some of the best-looking homes in Cape Town). Book room no. 1.

Rutland Lodge (✆ 021/461-7062; www.capeboutiquehotel.com; R1,300/$194 double) is owner-run, which is potentially a little claustrophobic, but the three rooms on the top floor (each with semiprivate decks) have phenomenal views and are tastefully decorated with all the modcons—perfect to lounge around with sundowners as the city lights come on. (Given that you pay the same for the two rooms downstairs, I would insist on one of these.) A large, lovely pool completes the picture.

De Tafelberg Guesthouse (✆ 021/424-9195; www.detafelberg.com; R880–R1,450/$131–$216 double) accommodates 16 and has equally wonderful views from most of the rooms, as well as a great breakfast "room"—a deep covered balcony overlooking the pool and city.

The Cape Cadogan ★★★ (Value)
One of the original farmhouses built on the slopes of Table Mountain, this elegant double-storied Georgian is in the heart of Gardens (the residential suburb adjacent to the city center) and has been carefully transformed into a luxurious guesthouse, with 12 well-groomed en-suite bedrooms decorated with a mix of contemporary and antique furnishings that never lapse into the mundane or pedestrian. Lovely touches such as a plush Victorian chair or gilt-framed mirror offset the cool white-and-gold minimalism, while the travertine bathrooms with twin basins, double-volume showers with twin heads, glass partitions, and separate baths or showers will suit the most ardent hydro-addict. The best rooms have private courtyards or balconies. The ones to book are nos. 2 and 8, both huge, beautifully furnished, and airy (although no. 8 is preferable, not only because it is even bigger, but also because it is above room no. 2, where ceilings are high but not entirely soundproof). Good "standard" room choices are nos. 4 (with a small balcony), 3 (best bathroom), and 6 and 7 (overlooking the street). Situated just off vibey Kloof Street, with its many restaurants, brasseries, and interior design shops, this is not the most peaceful option (for that, book at Alta or Hemingway), but staff are wonderfully laid-back and efficient (for instance, they will arrange for cutlery and crockery, should you choose to have a restaurant meal delivered from nearby Café Gainsborough or Mr Delivery). Given the convenience and level of comfort, the Cadogan offers good value in its category.

5 Upper Union St., Gardens, Cape Town 8001. ✆ 021/480-8080. Fax 021/480-8090. www.capecadogan.com. 12 units. High season R1,200–1,500 ($179–$224) double; low season R900 ($134). Rates include breakfast. AE, DC, MC, V. **Amenities:** Bar; pool; laundry; ADSL Internet access; airport transfers. *In room:* A/C, TV, minibar, hair dryer, tea- and coffee-making facilities.

De Waterkant Village ★★ (Value)
Situated in the oldest residential area of Cape Town, amid partly cobbled streets and quaint Cape Malay architecture, De Waterkant has an almost European feel, and places you in the heart of what has become Cape Town's most fashionable shopping district, with loads of restaurants and nightlife options within strolling distance. Village & Life offers some 60 fully serviced self-catering apartments and cottages (and a new backpackers)—either surf the website or specify when booking whether you want a plunge pool and/or a really good view

(luxury or superior category), and whether you prefer modern furnishings or a Cape cottage style. Note that while some of the high-season prices quoted may appear a tad steep, these are usually for two- or three-bedroom cottages, hence the good-value tag. Staff will stock your cottage with food and other items, given prior warning (but be warned that service standards are a little lax—laundry, for instance, can be a problem). If you don't care to self-cater, a good-value option is the elegantly furnished **De Waterkant House,** a B&B that has a small plunge pool and lounge overlooking the harbor; book the large **Harbour View suite** (R820–R900/$122–$134 double, depending on season), which comprises the entire top floor and has stunning views. See "Where to Dine," later in this chapter, for the numerous dining options here.

Note: If the Village is full, or you want to check out the full spectrum on offer in this area, take a look at **Cedric's Lodges** (© 021/425-7635; www.newsinafrica.co.za; R900–R1,100/$134–$164 double) or contact **De Waterkant Lodge and Cottages** (© 419-1097; www.dewaterkant.co.za).

1 Loader St., De Waterkant 8001. © 021/409-2500. Fax 021/418-6082. www.dewaterkant.com. 74 units. Cottages high season R1,000 ($149) standard, R1,300 ($194) luxury, R1,900 ($284) superior; low season R800 ($119) standard, R1,000 ($149) luxury, R1,350 ($201) superior. De Waterkant House high season R680–R900 ($101–$134) double; low season from R500 ($75). AE, DC, MC, V. **Amenities:** Pools (some cottages feature private plunge pools, also the De Waterkant House); tourist information center; babysitting; laundry. *In room:* A/C (some cottages), TV, hair dryer.

Rosedene ★★ Perched high above Table Bay, where Table Mountain meets the slopes of Lion's Head, this charming Balinese-themed guesthouse offers good views of the city and mountain. There's also quick access to Camps Bay and Clifton beaches, and to the cableway; and the restaurants at the top end of Kloof Street are just a stroll away. (If you want to order in, the staff will set up a table for you.) Ask for room nos. 8 through 11—situated on the top floor of this two-story building, they have the best views. The small, sundrenched top-floor patio is where you can lounge around while watching the cloud "tablecloth" tumbling down Table Mountain. Rosedene also trades in Bali furniture and artifacts—you may choose to ship home half your room! It's a small lodge, but 24-hour reception ensures that guests' needs are well tended.

28 Upper Kloof St., Higgovale 8001. © 021/424-3290. Fax 021/424-3481. www.rosedene.co.za. 12 units. High season R1,200 ($179) double; low season up to 40% discount. Rates include breakfast. AE, DC, MC, V. Children by arrangement. **Amenities:** Bar; plunge pool; limited business services; laundry. *In room:* A/C (room nos. 8–11), TV, minibar, hair dryer.

The Village Lodge ★★ *Value* This newcomer (opened Dec 2004) is compact, stylish, and modern, and ideally situated on Napier Street—like Loader Street, right in the heart of historic De Waterkant, and a short stroll from its world-class restaurants and shops, and some of the city's best nightlife options. Room nos. 5 and 6, each with a small terrace overlooking the city, are currently the most spacious (there are plans to extend the lodge), but if you're watching your budget, opt for one of the smaller rooms, which are equally tasteful (all grays and whites, with satin-ribboned pillows adding a splash of color). Relax on the rooftop terrace, which has a pool and bar and a fabulous mountain and city backdrop. If you're spending only a few nights in the city and want to be in the heart of the action, there is no better option, but space is tight and it doesn't have the tranquillity of, say, Alta or Cadogan.

49 Napier St., De Waterkant 8001. © 021/421-1106. Fax 021/421-8488. www.thevillagelodge.com. 7 units. High season R900–R1,200 ($134–$179) double; low season R500–R750 ($75–$112). Rates include breakfast. AE, DC, MC, V. **Amenities:** Restaurant; bar; pool; laundry. *In room:* A/C, TV, minibar, wireless Internet access.

Walden House 🏠 This quiet, turn-of-the-20th-century guesthouse offers stylish rooms in one of the city's oldest residential areas. White features are predominant—from the floorboards to the linen—with many wicker touches. The R950 ($142) rooms are slightly on the small side but comfortable (although men may find them a tad feminine), and with a choice of twin rooms or queen-size beds. The spacious garden suite (R1,080/$161) offers the best value and is a personal favorite, but the most popular room remains the upstairs **luxury suite,** with a door opening onto the first-floor veranda that provides a great view of Table Mountain. Kloof Street, with its large selection of restaurants, is just a short drive away. While this is a very pretty option and well managed, if you're looking for a little more action, De Waterkant House offers comparable accommodations, for less money, in a much more trendy, vibrant area, and the more modern An African Villa, located nearby, is a much better value.

5 Burnside Rd., Tamboerskloof 8001. © 021/424-4256. Fax 021/424-0547. www.walden-house.com. 8 units. R950 ($142) double; R1,280 ($191) suite. Rates include breakfast. AE, DC, MC, V. Children 12 and over only. **Amenities:** Limited room service; laundry. *In room:* TV, minibar, hair dryer, heated towel rails, complimentary bottle of wine.

INEXPENSIVE

Unless your taste runs to minimalist, **Parker Cottage** (© **021/424-6445;** www.parker cottage.co.za; from R750/$112 double) is another good option—the decor is a little more fussy than the guesthouses listed below, but it's very pretty and extremely professionally run. On the other end of the scale (a dearth of art or decorative touches), **Nine Flowers** (© **021/462 1430**) is easy walking distance from the city center (just as well, as there are no parking facilities) and costs R600 ($90) a night. If you're on a serious budget, consider booking a double room in one of the city's first-rate backpacker lodgings: The **Backpack** (© **021/23-4530;** www.backpackers.co.za; R285/$43 double, R360/$54 en-suite double) is one of the oldest and most successful; it's clean, with a busy courtyard, cafe, bar, travel center, shuttle bus, and pool, and an easy stroll from the nightlife and restaurant options along Kloof and Long streets.

An African Villa 🏠🏠 *Value* It takes a special talent to transform a tiny 19th-century double-story Victorian semidetached house into a chic "African-Zen" boutique-style guesthouse, but this is exactly what owners Louis and Jimmy have achieved, through skillfully reworking spaces, using a clever mix of ethnic and modern furniture, and offsetting muted modern tones and earthy textures with playful touches of vivid color. The combination of style, good value, and a very warm and welcoming environment has proved a winning formula, so much so that the two adjoining terrace homes are now part of the Villa, offering a wonderful warren of public spaces—beautifully dressed, of course—all leading to a lovely outdoor area with plunge pool and timber loungers. The rooms on the second floor are marginally preferable to those on the ground, but it is the three suites, each with doors that lead to the Victorian balcony overlooking the street, that are the ones to go for. The greatest drawback is its sheer popularity, but the good news is that Jimmy's own home, the 1894 **Liberty Lodge,** has four charming B&B units; ask for one of the en-suite rooms on the first floor—they share a balcony with more lovely views of the city. All options are walking distance to restaurants.

Reception for all 3 options at 33 De Lorentz St., Tamboerskloof 8001. © **021/423-2162.** Fax 021/423-2274. www.capetowncity.co.za. 17 units. R650–R1,040 ($97–$155) double. Ask about discounts. Rates include breakfast. AE, DC, MC, V. **Amenities:** Pool; laundry; free Internet access. *In room:* A/C (some), TV, hair dryer.

Fritz Hotel *(★ (Value*   Situated off Kloof Street (the "restaurant strip") on the outskirts of the city (a 5-min. walk to the center), and furnished with an eclectic selection of Art Deco and '50s pieces (clearly a passion for owner Arthur Bisig), the Fritz Hotel is a bargain. Ask for room no. 6, 7, 12, or 14; these open onto the first-floor veranda, with room nos. 6 and 14 by far the biggest. Each of the patio suites on the ground floor has a small garden area. Room no. 11 is small but has a great view of Table Mountain from the bed. Breakfasts and drinks are served in the courtyard, which— like the whole hotel—has a lovely relaxed atmosphere.

1 Faure St., Gardens 8001. ✆ 021/480-9000. Fax 021/480-9090. www.fritzhotel.co.za. 13 units. High season R600–R750 ($90–$112) double; low season R425–R500 ($63–$75) double. Rates include breakfast. AE, DC, MC, V. **Amenities:** Bar; business services; laundry. *In room:* TV, fax, minibar, hair dryer on request.

WATERFRONT
VERY EXPENSIVE

Cape Grace *(★★★ (Kids*   The Cape Grace is the classiest option in the Waterfront and was the hotel of choice when the Clintons were in town (although this may have more to do with security considerations). Certainly the difference between this hotel and the Mount Nelson is primarily one of location; the Cape Grace is in a marina, situated on its own promontory and surrounded by water on all three sides, while the Nellie is surrounded by lush gardens. But it also doesn't have the graciousness of the century-old Mount Nelson and, from an exclusivity point of view, cannot compete with the Ellerman. That said, the luxury (standard) rooms truly are luxurious, in both size and furnishings, with French doors opening onto mountain or harbor views; superior rooms are slightly larger, with walkout balconies. For an extra R215 ($32) in either category, you can bag one of the "loft" rooms, which are both larger and have the best views. The two- and three-bedroom suites, with fully equipped kitchens, are ideal for families. In fact, the Cape Grace prides itself on its reputation as the most family-oriented luxury hotel in the country: Kids are welcomed with their own cards and gift hampers, and are read stories and provided milk before bed; plus, the hotel rents anything from a car seat to a pram.

The lively **Bascule** regularly hosts some great New World DJs (it's packed with singles on the prowl on Fri), and the newly refurbished restaurant, **one.waterfront,** is regularly voted one of the top restaurants on the Waterfront.

West Quay, V&A Waterfront 8002. ✆ 021/410-7100. Fax 021/419-7622. www.grace.co.za. 102 units. High season R4,180–R4,998 ($624–$746) double, R7,750 ($1,157) 1 bedroom, R10,220 ($1,525) 2 bedrooms, R12,425 ($1,854) 3 bedrooms and penthouse; low season R3,380–R4,300 ($504–$642) double, R6,650 ($993) 1 bedroom, R8,765 ($1,308) 2 bedrooms, R10,850 ($1,619) 3 bedrooms. All rates include breakfast. Children under 12 stay free in parent's room. AE, DC, MC, V. **Amenities:** Restaurant; bar; spa; pool; concierge; room service; babysitting; laundry; well-stocked library. *In room:* A/C, TV, minibar.

Table Bay *(★★*   Competing with the Mount Nelson, Ellerman, and Cape Grace as the preferred location for the rich and famous, this glitzy hotel is located in a prime position on the Prince Alfred Breakwater—views are standard features here. It doesn't have the sense of exclusivity or privacy of the aforementioned competitors (Michael Jackson is reputed to have stayed here because he *wanted* to hear his fans chanting in the parking lot), but the service standards are equally high; best of all, it's ideal for shopaholics: The hotel is directly connected to the Waterfront's Victoria Mall. The public spaces (designed by the Lost City team) are superb, but standard rooms are small and dull; opt for a luxury room or suite (or a room at the Cape Grace) instead.

Quay 6, V&A Waterfront 8002. ⓒ 021/406-5000. Fax 021/496-5656. www.suninternational.com. 329 units. High season R3,865–R4,825 ($577–$720) double, R6,500–R18,400 ($970–$2,746) suite; low season R2,190–R3,625 ($327–$541) double, R4,900–R13,800 ($731–$2,060) suite. AE, DC, MC, V. **Amenities:** 2 restaurants; bar; pool; gym; spa; business services; salon; room service; laundry. *In room:* A/C, TV, minibar, hair dryer.

EXPENSIVE

An alternative to the Victoria & Alfred (but not as well situated) is the **Commodore** (ⓒ **021/415-1000;** www.legacyhotels.co.za; high season from R2,080/$310 double). Located 300m (984 ft.) from the Portswood entrance to the V&A Waterfront, the Commodore offers comfortable rooms at relatively low rates, making it very popular with tour groups. Business-class rooms cost a negligible R50 ($7.70) more than standard rooms in season but feature extras like minibars, are more spacious, and offer the best views.

Radisson Hotel Waterfront ✸✸ *Value*   The Radisson (formerly the Villa Via) is located on the outskirts of the Waterfront (500m/1,640 ft. from the entrance), but enjoys an exceptional setting—right on the sea. It offers the best value for money on the Waterfront, particularly in winter, but be warned: Although service is well meaning, standards can lag. That said, almost every room—furnished in dark blues and gold, with a nautical theme—has an excellent sea view. The infinity pool (irritatingly small) is right on the ocean's edge, and two catamarans, moored in the Waterfront, are available for guests' use. **Tobago's,** the hotel restaurant, has an excellent reputation, and the outside terrace overlooking the ocean is a popular meeting place for locals after work.

Beach Road, Granger Bay 8002. ⓒ 021/441-3000. Fax 021/441-3560. www.radissonsas.com. 182 units. High season R2,240–R2,460 ($334–$367) double, R3,320 ($496) suite, R4,200 ($627) 2-bedroom; ask about low-season rates. Children sharing stay free. AE, DC, MC, V. **Amenities:** Restaurant; bar; pool; day membership to the adjacent golf club; complimentary access to a nearby health club; spa; business and secretarial services; salon; room service; laundry. *In room:* A/C, TV, minibar, hair dryer, tea- and coffee-making facilities.

Victoria & Alfred Hotel ✸   Situated alongside the Alfred Basin's working dock, in the historic 1904 North Quay warehouse now called Alfred Mall, this hotel is the most centrally located Waterfront choice. (*Note:* Although the Radisson is not as conveniently located, it offers better views, a pool, and similar rates.) Bedrooms, dressed in wrought iron and veneer, are disappointingly bland, but they are spacious, each featuring a king-size bed. Rooms on the second floor, particularly nos. 225 through 234, have the best views. The in-house restaurant has a reasonably good reputation and is particularly popular for breakfast; you can dine alfresco while enjoying the excellent view of Table Mountain. The **Green Dolphin,** one of Cape Town's premier (but pricey) jazz venues, is in the same building, and **Den Anker,** one of the best Waterfront restaurants, is a short stroll away.

Pierhead, Waterfront 8002. ⓒ 021/419-6677. Fax 021/419-8955. www.vahotel.co.za. 68 units. R1,995–R2,725 ($298–$407) double. Children 2–12 stay in parent's room for R90 ($13), or R425 ($63) for extra bed. AE, DC, MC, V. **Amenities:** Restaurant; bar; access to nearby health club; regular shuttle bus to city center; room service; massage; babysitting; laundry. *In room:* A/C, TV, minibar, hair dryer, trouser press, DVD player, wireless Internet connection, tea- and coffee-making facilities.

GREEN POINT & SEA POINT

These suburbs are close to town and the Waterfront, but ironically (considering their location at the beginning of the Atlantic seaboard), the lay of the mountain makes access to beaches a little more time-consuming than from the City Bowl. That said, the area offers views of the sea and good value, particularly when compared with accommodations in the adjacent Waterfront. If none of the below appeals, check out the delightful **Cape Victoria Guest House** (© 021/439-7721; www.capevictoria.co.za; R660–R1,350/$99–$201), run by excellent hostess Lily (whose architect son converted the building); it has been featured in numerous design magazines.

EXPENSIVE

Winchester Mansions ★★   Built in the 1920s in the Cape Dutch style, this gracious low-slung hotel faces the sea, though a busy road and broad swath of park lie between it and the ocean. The hotel has recently converted its loft space into standard rooms and suites; these feature classy modern interiors, with earthy tones and dark wood. The original standard rooms are furnished in rich colors offset by cream walls, and exude an old-fashioned charm (a few antiques, floral artworks); the best options are the Winchester rooms, though you must specify a sea-facing room (no additional charge). The pool has also been enlarged and a wellness spa added. Incidentally, the Winchester bar and restaurant is very popular with locals, particularly on Sunday, when a jazz brunch is served to the strains of live music in the beautiful colonnaded central courtyard, built around a fountain and encircled with trees. Family accommodations are available.

221 Beach Rd., Sea Point 8001. © 021/434-2351. Fax 021/434-0215. www.winchester.co.za. 76 units. High season R1,650–R1,950 ($246–$291) double, R2,150–R3,450 ($321–$515) suite; low season R1,100–R1,350 ($164–$201) double, R1,450–R2,200 ($216–$328) suite. Rates include breakfast. AE, DC, MC, V. **Amenities:** Restaurant; bar; pool; room service; laundry. *In room:* A/C (now in all rooms), TV, minibar, hair dryer, tea- and coffee-making facilities, under-carpet heating.

INEXPENSIVE

La Splendida ★ *Value*   If you can't afford the Waterfront or Atlantic seaboard, but want to be close to the ocean, this is a great option. Just minutes from the Waterfront and the city center, this small hotel is separated from the sea only by a road and offers the best value-for-money views in town. The Art Deco exterior wouldn't look out of place in Miami, and the interiors are very comfortable. You have your choice of mountain- and sea-view rooms—a sea-view room is worth the extra R70 ($10); note that the penthouse can sleep four. Pack your in-line skates, as the seafront promenade stretches all the way past Sea Point. Meals are served at the ground-floor restaurant, which opens onto a terrace; sadly, the pool has been removed. A potential drawback in winter (June–Aug) is the noise from the foghorn—this is, after all, the closest that boats leaving the harbor come to shore before turning out to sea, and the foghorn makes sure it stays that way.

121 Beach Rd., Mouille Point 8001. © 021/439-5119. Fax 021/439-5112. www.lasplendida.co.za. 24 units. High season R795–R865 ($119–$129) double, R1,025 ($153) suite, R1,250 ($187) penthouse; low season R575–R635 ($86–$95) double, R785 ($117) suite, R890 ($133) penthouse. AE, DC, MC, V. Children by arrangement. **Amenities:** Restaurant/bar; room service; massage; babysitting; laundry. *In room:* A/C, TV, minibar, hair dryer on request.

ATLANTIC SEABOARD

For most visitors to the Cape, waking up to a seascape and strolling down to the beach take first prize, but you'll need to shell out for the privilege (and book early!). **Camps Bay** has by far the most options and offers the city's most easily accessible beach, lined with dozens of sea-facing bars, coffee shops, and restaurants. It's also a mere 10-minute drive from the center of town. The area has numerous B&Bs (check out www.portfoliocollection.com), but be warned: Good taste and great location seem to enjoy an inverse relationship here, and you're really paying for the sea view. There are a few exceptions, of course, the most notable of which is gorgeous Atlantic House, reviewed below. If you're on a budget, take a look at **Camps Bay Beach Village** (www. villageandlife.com)—its studio apartments, built around a heated pool, offer great value at R500 to R850 ($75–$127) double. In fact, with the addition of Camps Bay Retreat and The Bay Hotel to their portfolio, Village & Life now has a virtual monopoly on accommodations options in Camps Bay. For accommodations in **Clifton,** you're looking at climbing a lot of steps (the beach lies below relatively steep cliff paths that meander among homes and boulders) and, in summer, dealing with a lot of traffic. It's not the most convenient place to stay, and no doubt as a consequence has a dearth of guesthouses; here you're best off renting your own bungalow and living like a local (see "Great Self-Catering Options," earlier in this chapter). Neighboring **Bantry Bay** has two excellent options (reviewed below).

VERY EXPENSIVE

Atlantic House ✿✿✿   This is the best-dressed joint in Camps Bay, on a par with Kensington in the City Bowl, but with the added benefit of an endless ocean horizon. Public spaces are gorgeous—dark timber boxes framing the blue sky and sea—and belie its size: The house accommodates only 10 guests, but no expense has been spared, with wonderful touches like a large fish tank where tropical fish oversee the breakfast diners and a great photographic mural that covers the entire double-volume stairwell. But it is the rooms that are the real winners, the kind you'd be happy to cut short a day of sightseeing so you can luxuriate in womblike luxury. The three seaview rooms on the top floor are the most popular, but the garden room, which has a private outdoor area and alfresco shower, is the biggest and charming. The room downstairs (no. C6) on the pool level is less private. A manager is always on duty (the two I met were absolutely charming), but, given the perfection of the decor, oversights like a skewed lampshade and untended bits of garden could potentially grate. *Note:* Atlantic House is not to be confused with Atlantic View.

20 St. Fillians Rd., Camps Bay 8005. ✆ 021/437-8120. Fax 021/437-8130. www.atlantichouse.co.za. 5 units. R1,300–R2,200 ($194–$328) double. Rates include breakfast. AE, DC, MC, V. **Amenities:** Bar; heated pool w/music; laundry. *In room:* A/C, TV, minibar, hair dryer, DVD, Internet connection.

The Bay Hotel ✿✿   The Bay Hotel's shopping mall architecture is a bad reminder of the 1980s, but if you're a beach lover, the location, directly opposite Camps Bay's palm-lined beachfront, more than makes up for it. Rooms facing the sea are pricey, but because this is the hotel's raison d'être, you should probably shell out or consider one of the cheaper alternatives (like the more elegant Atlantic House or Les Cascades). Service is good (it is, after all, a member of the Small Luxury Hotels of the World) though not in the same class as, say, Ellerman House (see below). This is basically the choice for those who want to be in the hub of Camps Bay's restaurants and bars, within walking distance of the beach, and prefer the anonymity and facilities that come with large hotels.

Victoria Rd., Camps Bay 8005. ✆ 021/438-4444. Fax 021/438-4455. www.thebay.co.za. 78 units. High season R2,450 ($366) non-sea-facing double, R5,030 ($751) sea-facing double, R6,690 ($999) suite, R10,890 ($1,625) penthouse; low season R1,400 ($209) non-sea-facing double, R3,020 ($451) sea-facing double, R3,190 ($476) suite, R5,190 ($775) penthouse. AE, DC, MC, V. Children 12 and older only. **Amenities:** 2 restaurants; 2 bars; heated pool; fitness room; concierge; salon; room service; massage; laundry. *In room:* A/C, TV, minibar, hair dryer.

Camps Bay Retreat ✿   Earl's Dyke Manor was built "on a site to be envied, on the spur of the mountain as it juts out between two ravines," as a gushing society reporter described it after the manor was completed in 1920. Surrounded by streams, with paths tumbling down the lush gardens to a mountain pool, this gracious old-world home offers a wonderful glimpse into a bygone lifestyle, with much of the public space still furnished with the belongings of the grande dame of the house, Trudi Knacke, who sold the property to Village & Life in 2002. While it was a provisio to retain the architecture, the new owners have sadly not worked with the era, and rooms, while perfectly functional, are cheaply furnished and ignore the period and grandeur of the home. (Note that Deck House, the adjoining property, is marketed under the same name but is not the same experience.)

7 Chilworth Rd., The Glen, Camps Bay 8005. ✆ **021/437-8300.** Fax 021/426-5088. www.campsbayretreat.com. 6 rooms (Deck House also has 6 rooms). High season R1,100 ($164) double, R2,200 ($328) suite; low season R1,000 ($149) double, R1,800 ($269) suite. Rates include breakfast. AE, DC, MC, V. **Amenities:** Lunch and snack menu; honesty bar; 2 pools; spa/salon; business center; laundry. *In room:* TV, minibar, hair dryer, DVD, tea- and coffee-making facilities.

Ellerman House ★★★ Situated on a spectacularly elevated site overlooking the Atlantic Ocean and premier suburb of Bantry Bay, this gorgeous Relais & Châteaux member is in a class of its own, and—with only 11 rooms—the most exclusive address in Cape Town. Once the stately residence of Sir John and Lady Ellerman, the house has been meticulously restored to its original early-20th-century splendor, with renovations and additions blending seamlessly. The views, which evoke comparisons with the Riviera, are a feature of almost every window (of which there are many) and balcony, and the sheer grace and style of the place makes you feel like royalty. If you're staying in room no. 6 (no view) or room no. 3 (view, but no balcony), spend your days on the broad patio (where drinks and meals are served) or in the terraced garden with a large pool, from where you can see forever. For a view from your bathtub, book room no. 1. The chefs create each day's menus around fresh produce and will honor any special requests. Personally, I think it's the best choice to be had in Cape Town.

180 Kloof Rd., Bantry Bay 8001. ✆ **021/430-3200.** Fax 021/430-3215. www.ellerman.co.za. 11 units. R3,500–R5,700 ($522–$850) double; R8,100 ($1,209) suite. Rates include airport transfer, breakfast, laundry, tea/coffee, drinks (except wine and champagne), and ad hoc secretarial services. AE, DC, MC, V. Children 14 and over only. **Amenities:** Dining room; bar; pool; gym; sauna; concierge; business services; room service; massage; laundry; library; wine cellar. *In room:* A/C, TV, minibar, hair dryer.

EXPENSIVE

Les Cascades ★★★ *Value* Situated high on the Bantry Bay cliffs, this beautifully appointed boutique villa exudes class and comfort, and with high levels of service offers the best value on the Atlantic seaboard. Rooms are spacious and finished in warm, modern earth tones that contrast with the blue sky and sea, with fantastic views from your private deck area of what appears to be the edge of the world. The "villa" rooms, located in a beautiful sandstone house at the base of the guesthouse, are smaller, and finishes are not quite so expensive, but the rooms are still gorgeous and offer superb value for money at R1,200 ($179). Featuring a classy mix of African, Indian, and Balinese influences, public spaces seamlessly flow onto decks with pools; snag your couch on the main pool deck early and order a bottle of bubbly at sunset. Hosts Luc and Els are always on hand to assist with anything from tour bookings to arranging lunch and dinner (during summer you can dine here), and their eye for the finer things in life means that everything from the choice of wine in your minibar to the selection of cold meats at breakfasts is spot on.

48 De Wet Rd., Bantry Bay 8005. ℂ 021/434-5209. Fax 021/439-4206. www.lescascades.co.za. 10 units. High season R1,200–R2,100 ($179–$313) double; low season up to 40% discount. AE, DC, MC, V. **Amenities:** Dining room/bar; 3 pools; business services; room service; laundry. *In room:* A/C, TV, minibar, hair dryer.

Primi Sea Castle 🐾 (Kids)   Situated directly across the beach, these apartments (all with sea views) are the self-catering, child-friendly alternative to The Bay Hotel. The open-plan living areas, recently redecorated in shades of brown and beige, are pretty tasteless but feature sleeper couches and modern, fully equipped kitchens. The sidewalk cafes, restaurants, bars, and Camps Bay supermarket are all within strolling distance. *Note:* If you need to be surrounded with good taste in order to relax, the decor here could be a real drawback. For better (but pricier) self-catering options, I suggest you take a look at www.lionsview.co.za or www.balibay.co.za; alternatively, take a look at what's on offer at www.villageandlife.com.

15 Victoria Rd., Camps Bay 8005. ℂ 021/438-4010. Fax 021/438-4015. 8 units. High season R1,600 ($239) standard, R2,100 ($313) luxury, R3,150 ($470) superior; low season R950 ($142) standard, R1,260 ($188) luxury, R1,890 ($282) superior. Rates include a continental breakfast. Children under 12 stay free in parent's room. Superior rooms are self-catering and can accommodate up to 4 people. AE, DC, MC, V. **Amenities:** Pool (some apts have plunge pools/Jacuzzis); concierge; laundry. *In room:* TV, underfloor heating.

SOUTHERN SUBURBS

If the beach isn't your scene, and you prefer your landscape filled with mountains and trees, you'll find blissful peace in **Constantia,** the wine-producing area closest to the city, some 20 to 30 minutes away (halfway between the city and Cape Point). Closer to town is **Bishops Court** and **Newlands,** home to landmark rugby stadiums and the world's largest rugby museum; it's ideal for sports fans, though much of it is bland middle-class suburbia. It does have some large, gracious lodging properties that may suit the older traveler who wants to be pampered; besides those reviewed below, take a look at the Vineyard Hotel's gorgeous new **Riverside Deluxe Suites** (ℂ 021/657-4500; www.vineyard.co.za; from R1,840/$275 double) or the guesthouses listed at www.thelastword.co.za: smart, spacious rooms in high-security homes concentrated in the southern suburbs, and offering comforting touches like chauffeurs on tap and discreet managers to administer advice and arrange tours.

At the other end of the spectrum is bohemian **Observatory,** a mere 7 minutes from the center of town, and a multiethnic area popular with artists, hippies, students, and backpackers.

To get a sense of the location of the following places, see the "Peninsula Driving Tour" map, later in the chapter.

Cellars-Hohenort Hotel 🌟🌟   Recently selected for the Gold List by *Condé Nast Traveller UK,* this hotel has expansive views of the densely forested eastern slopes of Table Mountain behind, and the valley and mountains towering above False Bay in front. A genteel hotel that would suit the older traveler looking for an out-of-town, cheaper alternative to the Mount Nelson, it is also an oasis of sorts, but traveling to town or the seaboard can be a hassle. Antique furnishings and original artworks adorn the original Hohenort manor house; this is also where the best rooms are located. All rooms are comfortably furnished with floral fabrics adorning the king-size or twin beds. Considerable pluses are the beautiful 3.6-hectare (9-acre) garden, and the dining: chefs David Godin and Martha Williams work wonders—this is, after all, a Relais & Châteaux member, and well deserving of this distinction: **The Greenhouse** (where Prince Philip, incidentally, hosted his World Fellowship dinner) is one of the best

Finds **B&B** *Ubuntu*

To experience real *ubuntu,* and the warm spirit of African hospitality, you can arrange to spend a night in one of the city's "townships," or black suburbs. Portfolio has approved four B&Bs (**Kopanong, Majoro's, Luyolo's,** and **Malebo's**), and recommends that you combine your transfer and overnight stay with a **Township Music Tour** (for bookings, call (✆ **021/790-8826** or 021/426-4260). Khayalitsha now even has its very own backpackers lodge (R100/$15 per night), called **eKasie,** located near Kopanong; for a totally different cultural experience, a night at one of these establishments cannot be recommended highly enough.

restaurants in Cape Town, and the **Cape Malay Kitchen** provides an excellent introduction to regional cuisine.

P.O. Box 270, Constantia 7848. (✆ 021/794-2137. Fax 021/794-2149. www.cellars-hohenort.com. 53 units. High season R2,650–R3,500 ($396–$522) double, R4,600–R6,800 ($687–$1,015) suite, R10,000–R12,000 ($1,493–$1,791) Madiba Villas; low season R2,150–R2,900 ($321–$433) double, R3,800–R5,900 ($567–$881) suite, R9,000–R11,000 ($1,343–$1,642) Madiba Villas. Rates include breakfast. AE, DC, MC, V. Children 12 and over only. **Amenities:** 2 restaurants; 2 bars; 2 swimming pools; full-scale golf green (designed by Gary Player); tennis; salon; room service; laundry; croquet lawn. *In room:* TV.

Constantia Uitsig 🐾🐾   Part of the Constantia Wine Route, the aptly named Constantia Uitsig (*uitsig* means "view") has commanding vistas of the surrounding vineyards and mountains, and there's a calm sense of rural peace on this working wine farm. Even so, it's the food that draws people here: The farm boasts three tip-top restaurants (see "Where to Dine," below), of which **Uitsig** and **La Colombe** are regularly ranked by food critics in their top 10 Cape restaurants. It's wonderful to simply roll back to one of the 16 well-appointed suites dotted in the butterfly- and bird-filled gardens, the Cape Dutch architecture echoing that of the 17th-century manor house. Uitsig's lawns extend onto a cricket oval—with its unhindered view of the mountains and distant sea, and attractive Victorian pavilion, it's a popular destination for players and enthusiasts from around the world. *Note:* If Uitsig is full, or if you're a keen golfer, check out the 18-hole championship golf course at **Steenberg Country Hotel** ((✆ **021/713-2222;** www.steenberghotel.com; from R2,350/$351 double), another beautifully restored 17th-century wine farm.

Spaansgemacht Rd., P.O. Box 32, Constantia 7848. (✆ 021/794-6500. Fax 021/794-7605. www.constantiauitsig.co.za. 16 units. High season R2,300–R2,800 ($343–$418) double, R3,300–R4,800 ($493–$716) suite; low season R1,500–R1,700 ($224–$2540) double, R2,000–R2,800 ($299–$418) suite. AE, DC, MC, V. **Amenities:** 3 restaurants; lounge; pool; room service; babysitting; laundry. *In room:* TV, minibar, hair dryer, tea- and coffee-making facilities.

FALSE BAY

This is a very laid-back choice, probably more suited to the older traveler or someone who's been to Cape Town before and loved the naval atmosphere and Victorian architecture of Simon's Town. Staying here, you are well positioned for major attractions like the penguins at Boulders (within walking distance) and Cape Point (some 10 min. away), but it's 40 minutes from the city center. Families should definitely consider the **British Hotel Apartments** (www.british-hotel.co.za; R300–R380/$45–$57 per person)—lovely, large old-fashioned apartments in a Victorian-era hotel with sea

Tips Destination Spas

Less than a decade ago, a South African "spa" was little more than a Jacuzzi, and beauty treatments were limited to facials and "pedis." But with the advent of tourism (not to mention high-flying new émigré arrivals), pampering has become a multimillion-rand industry, with numerous options. Here's a roundup of the best.

BEST URBAN RETREATS Situated on Mouille Point's trendy Beach Road, with views of Table Mountain and the sea, **Sérénité Lifestyle Rituals** (*©* 021/ 434-2950; www.serenite.co.za) is a minimal, light-filled space that combines stone, wood, steel, glass, and slate with a palette of sorbet shades. After a Self Renewal Ritual (R590/$88 for 2 hr., including a body polish, hot sheet wrap, and "chakra" massage), grab a light bite at the adjoining bistro. Located on the first floor of the Waterfront's Commodore Hotel (see "Where to Stay," above), **S.K.I.N Care Clinic** (*©* 021/419-3090; www.skinon line.co.za) offers slick, fuss-free interiors and personal attention. The Ayurvedic Head Massage (R300/$45 for 45 min.) is recommended, as are the full body scrub and Dead Sea Mud wrap and steam (R365/$54 for 1 hr.). Alternatively, head for the **Camelot Spa** (*©* 021/406-5904; www.suninternational. com/resorts/tablebay) at the Table Bay Hotel for a diverse range of treatments—a "holistic stir-fry" to give you that get-up-and-go after a long-haul flight; the Ayurvedic treatment (R400/$60 for 2 hr.) is recommended. **The Spa at the Cape Grace** (for hotel guests only; see "Where to Stay," above) is African-inspired, offering exotic options like the Thaba treatment: an application of *intelezi* (a heavenly aloe vera and eucalyptus gel) to the ankles, wrists, biceps, and head by two therapists who then use a *knobkerrie* (a traditional African stick) to relieve tension and stimulate muscle tone. For 360-degree city views, you can't beat the 19th floor of the Arabella Sheraton Grand Hotel, where you'll find **Altiraspa** (*©* 021/412-8200; www.arabella sheraton.com/capetown); try an hour in the state-of-the-art Hyrdothermal Capsule, followed by a Balinese Synchronised Massage and a steam bath, and then cool off in the pool before kicking back on a giant waterbed overlooking the city—whew! The newly opened **Angsana Spa** at the Vineyard Hotel (*©* 021/657-4500; www.vineyard.co.za) is where you'll see Capetonians in the know leaving fresh-faced and in the pink. Managed and created by the award-winning Banyan Tree Spa team, it's stocked with Thai therapists

views. **Simon's Town Quayside Lodge,** off Jubilee Square, St Georges Street (*©* 021/ 786-3838; www.quayside.co.za; R775–R975/$116–$146 double), is part of the Simon's Town Harbour development, with a number of shops and Bertha's Restaurant below, right on the water. Most of the rooms, decorated in a pleasant nautical theme, have French doors opening onto beautiful views of the False Bay coast and Simon's Town yacht basin. And last but not least, if you're looking for accommodations right on the beach, take a look at some of the options in Kommetjie (near Cape Point), of which the **Beach House** (www.littleruo.co.za), a self-catering thatched cottage, and who offer divine treatments like Ibu's Secret (R480/$72 for 90 min.), a full-body massage followed by a jasmine and frangipani body polish.

BEST WINELANDS SPA   Located on the Simonsvlei Road between Franschhoek and Paarl, **Santé Winelands Hotel and Wellness Centre** (© 021/875-8100; www.santewellness.co.za) is a super-size spa with all the frills (even the showers have settings that range from tropical rain to mountain mist, infused with aromatic essential oils). But the main attraction is the a la carte menu of signature Vinotherapy treatments that utilize the antioxidant property of grapes.

BEST SEASIDE SPA   What more could you want than to succumb to the ultimate relaxation while looking out to sea? The best place to do so is at the exclusive **Birkenhead House Spa** (see "Where to Stay: Hermanus" in chapter 5), where you can choose from a variety of holistic massages (on the deck overlooking the bay or down on the beach below), body polishes, and specialized skin-care treatments. In Cape Town, **The Sanctuary Spa** (© 021/437-0677; www.12apostleshotel.com) at The Twelve Apostles, which lies between mountain and sea on the stretch between Camps Bay and Llandudno, offers seven Eastern-inspired treatment rooms built inside a grotto using natural materials like stone and wood. If you want to check out the seaview, ask for an outdoor massage around the pool.

BEST MEDICAL SPA   Cape Town Medi-Spa (© 021/422-5140; www.float.co.za) is functional and understated, not big on decor but focused on offering you the best of both worlds: modern medical techniques (there's a resident plastic surgeon, homeopath, dermatologist, and GP) and ancient Eastern healing (an assortment of body treatments, plus yoga or Pilates).

BEST HEALTH & WEIGHT-LOSS SPA   If your main aim is to lose weight as well as improve your sense of well-being, head for **St Francis Health Centre** (© 046/625-0927; naturecure@imaginet.co.za) in the Eastern Cape. A 6-day course (R4,686/$699; includes a personal consultation, cleansing diet, swimming and aquaerobics, daily steam baths and massages), and you're guaranteed to return home looking better than you left.

—*Sally Munro, Travel Editor,* Condé Nast House & Garden

the **Long Beach** (www.thelongbeach.com), a luxury B&B villa, are tops. Kommetjie is far from the action, but with these accommodations you won't really feel much like leaving.

4 Where to Dine

For centuries Cape Town has set the table for a varied and increasingly discerning audience, who have raved about its world-class fare (in 2004 British Airways' *High-Life* rated it the best city in the world in which to eat out), augmented by historical

Where to Dine in Cape Town

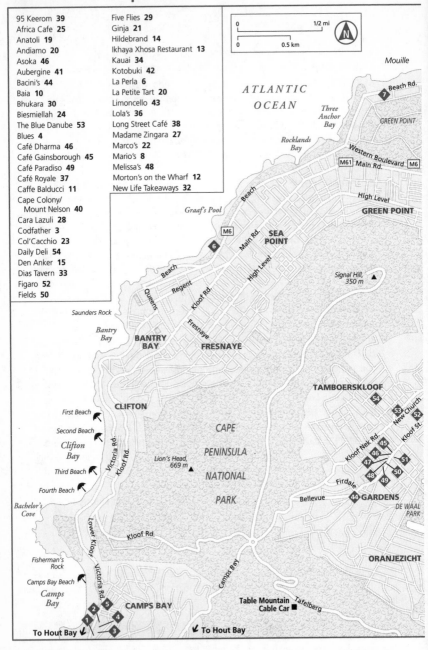

95 Keerom **39**
Africa Cafe **25**
Anatoli **19**
Andiamo **20**
Asoka **46**
Aubergine **41**
Bacini's **44**
Baia **10**
Bhukara **30**
Biesmiellah **24**
The Blue Danube **53**
Blues **4**
Café Dharma **46**
Café Gainsborough **45**
Café Paradiso **49**
Café Royale **37**
Caffe Balducci **11**
Cape Colony/
  Mount Nelson **40**
Cara Lazuli **28**
Codfather **3**
Col'Cacchio **23**
Daily Deli **54**
Den Anker **15**
Dias Tavern **33**
Figaro **52**
Fields **50**

Five Flies **29**
Ginja **21**
Hildebrand **14**
Ikhaya Xhosa Restaurant **13**
Kauai **34**
Kotobuki **42**
La Perla **6**
La Petite Tart **20**
Limoncello **43**
Lola's **36**
Long Street Café **38**
Madame Zingara **27**
Marco's **22**
Mario's **8**
Melissa's **48**
Morton's on the Wharf **12**
New Life Takeaways **32**

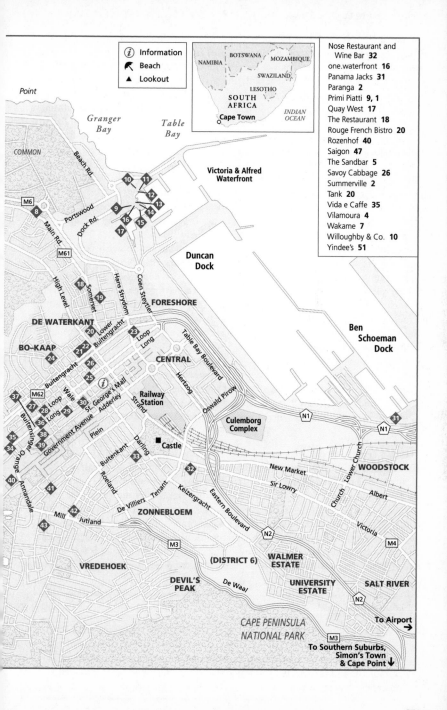

Nose Restaurant and
  Wine Bar **32**
one.waterfront **16**
Panama Jacks **31**
Paranga **2**
Primi Piatti **9, 1**
Quay West **17**
The Restaurant **18**
Rouge French Bistro **20**
Rozenhof **40**
Saigon **47**
The Sandbar **5**
Savoy Cabbage **26**
Summerville **2**
Tank **20**
Vida e Caffe **35**
Vilamoura **4**
Wakame **7**
Willoughby & Co. **10**
Yindee's **51**

venues and great views. For harbor settings and Table Mountain views, head for the Waterfront; for uninterrupted ocean views and great sunsets, the Atlantic seaboard is tops. But whatever you do, enjoy at least one lunch or dinner in the Winelands, where you can drink in views of the vineyards and mountains along with a selection of fine Cape wines. For people-watching, head for the cobbled square in the new Cape Quarter in De Waterkant, or the cafes and coffee shops of Kloof Street (particularly around Vida e Caffé), or just sink into a sofa for high tea at the Mount Nelson. If you like to window-shop for your dinner, take a stroll along Victoria Road in Camps Bay, the restaurant strip that lines the beachfront—a great place to dine in summer, when the sun sets around 8 or 9pm, but a little brash and overheated for my taste; I'd head back over the Nek to Kloof Street, the road that runs down the slope of Table Mountain into Long Street, or settle on one of the recommendations below.

If you're setting off for Cape Point, a journey that will take you the better part of the day, try to time lunch at one of the recommended restaurants in the Constantia area, among the vineyards, or one overlooking the False Bay coast.

Finally, make sure to sample at least one dish inspired by the unique hybrid of Cape cultures. For traditional fare, you can't get more authentic than Biesmiellah in the Bo-Kaap, but there's more to Cape cuisine than *bobotie* and *denningvleis*. Cape Town's scenic setting and regular influx of cosmopolitan visitors has attracted some of the world's top chefs, many of whom are creating a new and exciting "modern Cape" cuisine, combining local ingredients with elements of the Portuguese, Dutch, French, German, English, Indian, and Malaysian influences that have made up the city's multicultural past. Bon appetit.

Tip: Serious foodies might want to pick up a copy of *Rossouw's Restaurants,* a new annual guide to Cape Town and Winelands restaurants, featuring the opinions of patrons rather than critics, and useful index listings (from "alfresco" and "intimate" to "seaside" and "veg-friendly"). If you don't agree with a write-up, you can join the team and send in your own comments at **www.rossouwsrestaurants.com**.

CITY BOWL

There is simply not enough space to cover the many superb restaurants concentrated in this area, so in some cases a mention will have to suffice. Located at 102 New Church St. is the **Blue Danube** (✆ **021/423-3624**), where owner-chef Thomas Sinn is considered one of the top chefs in Cape Town (he has featured in almost every foodie's top 10 selection since the early '90s), but personally I find his food a little too fussy. **Madame Zingara,** located on 192 Loop St. (✆ **021/426-2458**), is another name you'll encounter when looking for recommendations; owner-chef Richard Griffin has a reputation for originality (his filet with chocolate-chile sauce is legendary), but I prefer his new sister restaurant (literally next door), **Cara Lazuli,** reviewed

---

Tips Eating In

If you're staying in a B&B or self-catering, contact **Mr Delivery** (✆ 021/423-4177 in City Bowl; ✆ 021/439-9916 in Sea Point; ✆ 021/761-0040 in Constantia) and ask them to drop off a menu. Mr Delivery delivers meals from more than 20 restaurants and takeout joints (some of which are described below), as well as groceries, directly to your door.

The Dining Mile

If you like looking at venues before deciding where to eat, take a stroll down Kloof Street. This is the road that runs parallel to Kloof Nek, which takes you up the saddle of the mountain and over into Camps Bay. Aside from the spots reviewed in full, the street has some lively and eclectic dining choices.

Start at the top, where **Bacini's** (© 021/423-6668; ask for a table outside, next to the faux waterfall) serves up great pizzas in a family-oriented atmosphere, then stroll down the hill to **Cafe Paradiso** 🎭🎭, 110 Kloof St. (© 021/423-8653), a sprawling terra-cotta villa with Italian-style decor and Mediterranean-style food that will delight those bored with modern haute cuisine. This is an ideal all-day or balmy evening venue: Book a table under a tree or umbrella on the terrace outside—the interior is dull and you'll miss the view of the city—and peruse the no-nonsense menu, which features plenty of vegetarian options. A personal favorite is the tender Greek lamb, served warm on a cold shredded spinach salad and topped with homemade mayo.

Next up, a block down from Melissa's (see review below) and the vegetarian-only Fields, is **Saigon** 🎭🎭, corner Kloof and Camp (© 021/424-7669), an elevated venue with great views that specializes in Vietnamese cuisine (don't miss the crystal prawn spring rolls: steamed prawns, carrots, cucumber, noodles, basil, mint, and a peanut sauce). **Asoka "Son of Dharma,"** 68 Kloof St. (© 021/422-0909), next door, doesn't look like much from the outside, but it's a great spot—an open-plan house artfully renovated around a central courtyard and tree, with soothing lighting and groovy music—highly recommended for a pre- or postdinner drink. The vibe, created by Cape Town's happening, young (mid-20s and up) crowd, is great, but you'll find better food across the road at **Yindee's** 🎭🎭🎭 (© 021/422-1012), Cape Town's best Thai restaurant (at least, according to its loyal following).

A little farther down is **Cafe Gainsborough** 🎭🎭, 64 Kloof St. (© 021/422-1780), a casual bistro-type restaurant built around an open-plan kitchen. Get there early (no bookings) to grab a table on the sidewalk and enjoy the view of Table Mountain. The small menu has Flemish overtones.

Numerous takeout joints and casual eateries follow, but the next good cluster occurs at the junction of Kloof with Park Road. Head up Park Road and look for **Figaro** (adjacent to Greens, which, incidentally, offers good-value salads, burgers, and light meals), where lawyers tuck into bottles of Fauchon and the best sandwiches in town under chandeliers. Back on Kloof, and a little farther down, is **Vida e Caffé**, 34 Kloof St. (© 021/426-0627), where the city's trendiest come to quell their addiction to the best coffee in town. **Lola's**, 228 Long St. (© 021/423-0885), within walking distance from here (Kloof merges with Long), is where, in their own words, "faggy Afro-trash meet to slip-sexy music." This is in the heart of the Long Street stretch that fills with backpackers and offers the city's most vibrant nightlife, particularly in summer (see "Cape Town After Dark," later in this chapter).

below. **Ginja** is another that keeps getting rave reviews, not least because of its location in a wonderful dilapidated double-volume space on 121 Castle St. (© 021/426-2368), but the "fine fusion" strikes me as rather fussy. But an unreserved thumbs up to **Aubergine,** 39 Barnet St. (© 021/465-4909), where the unassuming Harold Bresselschmidt conjures up magical combinations: Fabulous vegetarian options include the aubergine and Gorgonzola parcels wrapped in potato and served with a sublime pine-nut sauce, and his reasonably priced bistro menu comes with suggested wines by the glass to accompany each inspired creation—a great way to sample some of South Africa's best wines.

EXPENSIVE

Africa Café ★★ AFRICAN   Portia and Jason de Smidt have expanded to ever bigger premises, beautifully decorated by Portia, where you can sample a great selection of traditional dishes from all over Africa. Meals are brought to your table in bowls—a "communal feast" shared in the African tradition—and you can eat as much as you want. Dishes include the Malawi *mbatata* balls (sweet potato and cheese rolled in sesame seeds), West Coast mussels served in a Cape Malay coconut sauce, Tunisian *briouats* (potatoes and garlic in phyllo pastry), Ethiopian *sik sik wat* (lean, succulent lamb in a mild berbere and paprika sauce), Moroccan *zeilook* (aubergine, dhania, and garlic dip), Tanzanian mango chicken (strips of chicken filet, a little tough, in a tangy sauce), and South African *ithanga* (pumpkin and cinnamon fritters)—all served with warm Xhosa potbread. Leave space for the Egyptian *basboussa* (semolina cake with almonds and yogurt) and Moroccan almond fritters. There's a great moment when the wooden floorboards start to shake as the ululating staff dance through the restaurant with real unrestrained joy. All in all, it's a very touristy experience, but still well worth it.

Heritage Sq., 108 Shortmarket St., Cape Town. © 021/422-0221. Reservations essential. Set-price menu R135 ($20) per person. AE, DC, MC, V. Mon–Sat 6:30–11pm.

The Cape Colony ★★★ INTERNATIONAL/MODERN CAPE   It's been rated as one of the top 10 hotel restaurants in the world; The Cape Colony remains the grandest venue in Cape Town: the perfect place to celebrate a wedding anniversary or special

---

⌒Finds Where Are the Africans?

Although recommended, Africa Café and Moyo (at Spier) essentially cater to the well-heeled Western traveler, and many visitors come away nonplussed at how European all the Cape Town dining options (and diners) are. If you'd like to sample South African cuisine along with other Africans (for considerably less money), head for the balcony of the **Pan African Market,** Long Street (© 021/426-4478), for lunch with the traders, or **Marco's Place,** 15 Rose St. (© 021/423-5412). More touristy, but a very authentic "nonrestaurant" experience, is a meal arranged at **Lelapa (The Home;** © 021/694-2681) in Langa—best to arrange this along with a township tour. Another venue worth considering is **Ikhaya Xhosa Restaurant** in the Waterfront Clocktower (© 021/418-3728), not least because almost every element, from staff recruitment to the wine choices on offer, is linked to an empowerment initiative, though you're still likely to find the majority of black faces on the side that's doing the serving. When it comes to social transformation, Cape Town is taking its time.

Tips **High Tea at the Nellie**

High tea at the **Mount Nelson** (© **021/483-1198**; R85/$13; daily 2:30–5:30pm) is a Cape Town institution: crustless cucumber and salmon sandwiches in a vast sea of tarts and cakes, served buffet style in an elegant chandeliered room littered with comfortable armchairs to sink into while you hum to the sounds of a tinkling piano (or escape to the verdant gardens). It's a wonderful way to experience the grande dame's gracious ambience and watch the creatures who frequent her.

---

birthday. Its wonderfully plush ambience is created by the discreet yet attentive service, live classical or jazz music (which never overwhelms), and old-fashioned decor—right down to the individual table lamps that create soft pools of light on the impeccable table appointments. Food is excellent, from both a flavor and presentation point of view, though, again, it may be the atmosphere that makes it all look and taste so good! The menu changes regularly, but new executive chef Stephen Templeton has kept old Cape Colony classics like the smoked crocodile served with spinach, red onion, and a samosa wafer, and the delicately spiced Cape Malay chicken and prawn curry, while adding a few of his own signature dishes; he serves a mean Caesar salad, but the more adventurous would be well advised to try the popular springbok pie, served with root vegetables and a Pinotage jus.

Mount Nelson Hotel, Gardens (entrance off Kloof St.). © **021/483-1850.** Main courses R75–R120 ($11–$18); prawns R265 ($40). AE, DC, MC, V. Daily 7:30–10pm.

Five Flies ⭐⭐ FRENCH/INTERNATIONAL Located in the old Netherlands Club and the adjacent Rembrandt House (which dates back to 1754), this is one of the classiest venues in the Cape. Even better is the news that the man who put Five Flies on the map, French-classic-trained Gerard Reidy, is back as head chef. The menu—which offers any combination of two, three, or four courses for a set price—is about to be changed, but generally Reidy leans toward the unfussy side of haute cuisine. At press time, the slow-roasted duck with wok-fried vegetables and Oriental plum sauce was a winner, as was the roast kingklip with a basil-and-pine-nut crust and cumin sauce (served on grilled red pepper and sweet-potato mash), and the medallions of beef filet, served with mushroom duxelles, spinach, and hollandaise sauce.

   Tip: It's worth asking if a tour group is booked and, if so, asking to be seated in a room far from them, in case they turn raucous. And if you are looking for a discreet and elite corner for two, book the "wine cellar," a quiet candlelit room that is only occasionally disturbed by your waiter collecting one of the fine vintage wines. You'll have plenty of space to get down on one knee!

16 Keerom St., Cape Town. © **021/424-4442.** Reservations essential. 2 courses R110 ($16); 3 courses R140 ($21); 4 courses R160 ($24). AE, DC, MC, V. Mon–Sun noon–3pm; daily 7–10:30pm.

Savoy Cabbage ⭐⭐ INTERNATIONAL This stylish restaurant celebrates the European trend for "sophisticated peasant food," and if you like the more interesting cuts of meat, you'll find this one of the country's best. Starters are particularly exciting, like the absolutely delicious (though unassuming sounding) tomato tart; the pear, plum, pepper cheese, and walnut salad; the sugar-cured springbok with soba noodles and mango relish; and the salad of grilled lamb filet with capers, anchovies, and buffalo mozzarella. Recommended mains include the sweetbreads with lemon, chives, and mushrooms; the lamb- and rice-filled cabbage rolls poached in broth; and the spatchcocked quail with oats and green peas and a white-wine sauce—chef Peter Pankhurst's latest offering. The venue—a narrow double-volume L-shape with old brick walls exposed and juxtaposed with glass-and-steel fittings—is as interesting as the food, though the opening of 95 Keerom has put this somewhat in the shade. The back entrance connects you to Heritage Square's central courtyard—consider an after-dinner drink upstairs at the Po-Na-Na Bar to mingle with Cape Town trendies.

101 Hout St., Heritage Sq. ℭ 021/424-2626. Reservations recommended. Main courses R70–R150 ($10–$22). AE, DC, MC, V. Mon–Fri noon–2:30pm; Mon–Sat 7–10:30pm.

MODERATE

Bhukara 🎭🎭 NORTH INDIAN   Sabi Sabharwal met his Afrikaans wife in Italy and followed her home, an act of love for which Capetonians are truly grateful. A decade later, Bhukara is still considered the best Indian restaurant in the country; certainly, it's the city's most stylish (though acoustics are a problem when the place is full). That said, the menu is limited to northern India dishes, specializing in rich Mughal food and tandoori barbecues—a pity, given the freshness of southern Indian spicing. Meats are tender and the flavors full and vibrant, however: Make sure you try the legendary butter chicken. Chefs leave no fat on meat and use only the freshest ingredients, including the spices. Their motto, "Only the best will do, whatever the cost," must be what kept Shakira and Michael Caine coming back for more.

33 Church St., Cape Town. ℭ 021/424-0000. Reservations recommended. Main courses R49–R84 ($7.30–$13); prawns R139 ($21). AE, DC, MC, V. Mon–Sat noon–3pm; daily 6:30–11pm.

Biesmiellah 🎭 (Value CAPE MALAY   A number of places offer Cape Malay fare, but none is as authentic as Biesmiellah. Run by two generations of the Osman family in the historic Malay quarter of Bo-Kaap, Biesmiellah has been serving the local Cape Muslim community and, increasingly, tourists for 2 decades. The *denningvleis,* a sweet-sour lamb cutlet stew flavored with tamarind and served with saffron rice, almonds, raisins, and mashed potatoes, is recommended, as is the *pienang* curry, a beef cutlet stew prepared with bay leaves. In keeping with Muslim tradition, no alcohol is allowed on the premises. Biesmiellah also offers takeout—try the *roti* (flatbread) stuffed with cubed mutton.

2 Upper Wale St., Cape Town. ℭ 021/423-0850. Reservations recommended. Main courses R57–R70 ($8.50–$10). AE, DC, MC, V. Mon–Sat noon–10pm.

Cara Lazuli 🎭🎭 MOROCCAN   Unless you've booked the courtyard (comprising a single table under the stars) or one of the terrace tables, this is not the place to come for a quiet romantic evening. It is a warren of semiprivate spaces done up in rich colors and textures, some of which are often booked out for small parties of raucous revelers. And what with a seminaked Hindu god wandering around to paint faces, or a python-draped belly dancer, or tarot readings in the hall, it's as much showtime as restaurant. But don't let that put you off—the food is fantastic and the atmosphere embracing—you're as likely to be handed a glass of sparkling as the birthday girl, and there's always a convivial group sharing a cigarette break on the small veranda. Quite possibly the most delicious starter I've ever had is "skewers arabesque": marinated fish of the day, wrapped in vine-leaves and chargrilled, served with a sweet-chile and coriander dip. Follow this with a simple, hearty tagine (slow-cooked in a clay pot), served with fragrant couscous and roasted vegetables.

11 Buited St., City Center. ℭ 021/426-2351. Reservations essential. Main courses R56–R84 ($8.35–$13). AE, DC, MC, V. Mon–Sat 7pm–closing.

95 Keerom ★★★ ITALIAN This urbane restaurant—modern in the very best sense (unpretentious and comfortable)—is proof that the Cape Town dining scene has come of age. Not only because it feels good to walk through (intimate spaces downstairs showcase the building's age with raw brickwork, offset with slate and glass, and plenty of wood; upstairs an ancient olive tree serves as organic centerpiece), but because the food is simple and straightforward, service is excellent, and owner Giorgio hasn't felt the same compunction to charge high prices just because he can. It's affordable glam, and Capetonians love it. The waitstaff is excellent, and Giorgio visits every table to ensure that the evening is going as expected. The menu is extensive, but start with one of the carpaccio choices and follow with the tuna, cooked "New York" style with anchovies, capers, olives, and tomatoes (incidentally, Giorgio has purchased his own boat to ensure fish is truly fresh). For the more carnivorous, the pork loin, rolled with spinach and ricotta and served with mushroom sauce, is a definite hit.

95 Keerom St., City Center. ℭ 021/422-0765. Reservations essential. Main courses R65–R100 ($9.70–$15). AE, DC, MC, V. Mon–Fri noon–3pm; Mon–Sat 7–11pm.

Rozenhof ★★ CONTINENTAL Located in a house that dates back to 1852, Rozenhof has been delivering the same understated menu since 1984, unfazed by passing fads and the mushrooming of competition. The food is delicious, the service

---

Finds Going Local

If ever there was a queue worth watching, the early-morning caffeine addicts at **Vida e Caffé**, 34 Kloof St. (ℭ 021/426-0627) will do. From those carefully created don't-care student coiffures to queens sporting impeccable labels and girls in inappropriate micro-minis, a table armed with a cappuccino and a Quattro (four-cheese) muffin is the place to watch the city's producers, photographers, students, designers, and edgy housewives hard at (net)work. To view the more laid-back Capetonian in his natural lair, grab a pavement table at super-friendly **Daily Deli**, 13 Brownlow Rd., Tamboerskloof (ℭ 021/426-0250), and order the aubergine bake, followed by a piece of cheesecake. Both are open daily, but not at night. If you like the idea of pizza but could do without the cheese (obviously a victim of colonic irrigation), the best ever is to be found at **Limoncello**, 8 Breda St. (ℭ 021/461-5100), a tiny restaurant in Gardens frequented by locals who love the ultra-thin, "white-based" crispy pizza base (tomato-free), topped with smoked salmon (or aubergine), lemon juice, and fresh rocket (arugula). Or opt for the tender baby squid, flash-fried with chile and garlic. But when it comes to Italian (and Capetonians will curse me for sharing this), you'd be hardpressed to beat **Magica Roma,** located in the unassuming suburb of Pinelands, not far from the city center (15 min.), but way off the tourist track. It's jammed full night after night with a (mostly suburban) clientele who know and appreciate that excellent service and superb northern Italian fare (everything on the menu is recommended) don't come at this price anywhere else. Reservations are very much advised.

intelligent (waiters have usually served at Rozenhof for some time), and the ambience warm. Diners are seated in one of three rooms, ensuring an intimate experience even when the restaurant is full. Many of the dishes have remained unchanged since the restaurant opened; the cheese soufflé starter with herb-and-mustard cream is a must, as is one of the linefish preparations—try it almond-crusted on leeks and braised in citrus butter. The crispy roast duck is also an old favorite, glazed with mandarin and ginger and served with a warm orange vinaigrette. The restaurant also offers an extensive, well-chosen wine list.

18 Kloof St., Gardens. ✆ 021/424-1968. Reservations recommended. Main courses R56–R90 ($8.35–$13). AE, DC, MC, V. Mon–Fri 12:30–3:30pm; Mon–Sat 7–10:15pm.

INEXPENSIVE

Café Royale 🏆🏆 GOURMET BURGERS   A better burger you won't find anywhere—be it the lamb with mint (amusingly referred to as the "baaa baaa" burger); the fish of the day with mango, peppadew, and coriander salsa; the "big bird" (ostrich with beetroot relish); or the "fat bastard" (double everything). All patties are made on the premises and come with garlic aioli sauce, lettuce, tomato, caramelized onion, and cucumber, and your choice of chips, salad, or sweet-potato wedges. It's hip and trendy, and if you're lucky you'll be served by a Gwyneth Paltrow look-alike. Eat your heart out, McDonald's.

273 Long St., Cape Town ✆ 021/422-4536. Average burger R35–R40 ($5.20–$5.95). AE, DC, MC, V. Mon–Sat noon–11:30pm.

Col'Cacchio 🏆🏆 *Kids* PIZZA   If you like your pizza base thin and crispy, Col'Cacchio is the best in town (though little Limoncello is a David-like contender; see "Going Local," above). Recommended choices include the Tre Colori (smoked salmon, sour cream, and caviar) and the Prostituto (avocado, bacon, feta, and spinach). Salads are large and fresh (try the smoked chicken and pepperdew), and service is fast. It's a large and laid-back venue (with a child-friendly staff; ask for a bit of dough to "shape and bake").

Seeff House, 42 Hans Stridom Ave. ✆ 021/419-4848. Main courses R30–R54 ($4.45–$8.05). AE, DC, MC, V. Mon–Fri noon–11pm; Sat 6–11pm.

Dias Tavern *Value* PORTUGUESE   A bit of a dive, with red plastic chairs alternating with plastic-covered booth seats, but Dias is famous for its delicious steak dishes, and you won't find a fellow tourist in sight. Try their *espetada* (chunks of marinated sirloin, skewered and carried, flaming hot, to the table) or *trinchada* (cubes of sirloin in a garlic and wine sauce). Not the venue for vegetarians, Dias does not bother with vegetables; meals are served with a choice of marge-spread bread or potatoes. Unless you enjoy eating to the live accompaniment of a wannabe Julio Iglesias, don't dine here on Friday or Saturday evenings. *Note:* If you're craving a meat fix in more salubrious surroundings, **The Famous Butcher's Grill** in the Day's Inn on Buitengracht Street (✆ **021/422-0880**) is regularly rated one of the top in the country.

15 Caledon St., Cape Town. ✆ 021/465-7547. Main courses R25–R62 ($3.75–$9.25). AE, DC, MC, V. Mon–Sat noon–late.

Melissa's 🏆🏆 ITALIAN/DELI   A delicious buffet of eight great salads (roasted beetroot and feta, for example, or baby tomatoes soaked in balsamico with fresh basil and coriander), a selection of two to three quiches (try the roasted vegetables and cream cheese) and two pasta dishes (spinach and ricotta, beef chorizo and chile), as

---

> ## Tips Vegetarian?
>
> This is a carnivorous country (you'll still hear the joke that chicken is served as a side order to red meat in some rural areas), but thankfully, veggie Capetonians are blessed with a number of options: **Fields,** 84 Kloof St. (© **021/423-9587**), a health-shop-cum-deli, serves strictly vegetarian- and vegan-only meals and freshly squeezed juices in a casual environment; unfortunately, it closes in the evenings between 7 and 8pm. A few blocks down the road, in the Kloof Lifestyle Centre, there's **Kauai,** which serves a good selection of vegetarian dishes (and every meal has a nutritional breakdown) as well as every conceivable health drink (this is, incidentally, a health-food chain). Closer to the city center, **Lola's,** 228 Long St. (© **021/423-0885**), is a buzzing pavement cafe.

---

well as a selection of the best cakes and tarts in town make this one of Kloof Street's most popular eateries (and one of the best delis in town). With limited table seating and a window bar stacked full of magazines (ideal for solitary diners), you'd be well advised to get here early. Self-service only. Everything in the well-stocked continental deli is delicious, and it's ideal for picnics or healthful hotel-room snacks.

94 Kloof St., Cape Town. © **021/424-5540**. Meals weighed by the plate; average R30–R45 ($4.45–$6.70). AE, MC, V. Mon–Fri 7:30am–8pm; Sat–Sun 8am–8pm. Also in Constantia (© **021/794-4696**) and Newlands (© **021/683-6949**).

WATERFRONT

Because of space constraints and the strength of the competition in the City Bowl, I have included no full reviews of restaurants on the Waterfront. This is not to say that there aren't a few restaurants you should consider visiting, regardless of the fact that they are located in one of the city's biggest and busiest tourist attractions. First among the recommended choices is **Den Anker** ✹✹✹, Pierhead (© **021/419-0249**; ask for a map at one of the information desks in Victoria Wharf), which warrants a trip just to wolf the freshest West Coast mussels, washed down with Belgian beer, in a casual atmosphere with great harbor and mountain views. Rabbit, simmered in Belgian beer and served with applesauce and potato croquettes, is another specialty, and the steaks are out of this world.

In the Victoria Wharf shopping center proper is **Willoughby & Co** ✹✹✹, lower level (© **021/418-6116**), arguably the best place in town for fresh, unpretentious seafood dishes and the top sushi option in town; certainly, it doesn't get any fresher. *Note:* If Willoughby's is too busy, an alternative venue very much on a par and also located in the mall is **Cape Town's Fish Market** (© **021/418-5977**).

If eating in a mall in the most beautiful city in the world depresses you, head upstairs to the terrace at **Baia Seafood Restaurant** (© **021/421-0935**) for linen table clothes and great harbor and mountain views; the food's good, too, but most locals think it's overpriced.

If you're simply looking for a break from shopping, grab a deep leather sofa at **Caffe Balducci,** Quay 6, Victoria Wharf (© **021/421-6002**). With the exception of the carpaccio, the Italian/Californian–inspired food isn't that great, but the cappuccinos, cakes, and atmosphere make up for it—this is the most elegant cafe in the Waterfront, and great for people- (and fashion TV–) watching.

Another Victoria Wharf option that cooks all day is **Primi Piatti** (© 021/419-8750), offering unbelievably good-value pasta dishes, equally good thin-based pizzas, and faster-than-lightning service.

For a more refined atmosphere, **one.waterfront** ✦✦✦ (© 021/410-7100) in the Cape Grace is considered the best hotel restaurant in the Waterfront. Almost totally surrounded by water, with tranquil views across the marina, this is an elegant choice, but not the place to come for plain cooking. Chef Bruce Robertson delights in complex flavors, hence such favorites as marinated beef in truffle oil, topped with duck liver pâté, and served with pommes William and Madeira sauce.

Finally, no review of Waterfront restaurants would be complete without a mention of **Panama Jacks** ✦✦✦, Quay 500 (© 021/448-1080), the celebrated seafood restaurant that predates the Waterfront development (and is still in the old working harbor section—that is, a long walk from the mall and tower precinct). Head for the Royal Cape Yacht Club and take the second road left—it has no view or elegance, but serves superb, simple seafood dishes steamed, grilled, or flambéed (fresh crayfish [lobster] is the specialty). Globetrotters who are bored with over-attentive service and fusion-fussy meals love it.

DE WATERKANT

It has always enjoyed a reputation as a Cape Town nightlife hotspot and center of the gay scene, but De Waterkant has in the past 2 years also developed into the city's most exciting shopping precinct (see "Shopping," later in this chapter). But one needs sustenance to plunder, and the restaurants and eateries in and around the new Cape Quarter don't disappoint. Around the central cobbled courtyard are four options, all with tables spilling out around the central fountain: **Tank** (© 021/419-0007), with its oversize fish tank and ego, is great for sushi (they're very proud of the fact that their sushi master, Arata Koga, is rated seventh in the world) and for people-watching—*if* you can get a table outside. Indoors, the acoustics can be a problem, but head right to the back banquette seats for views of the city skyline. Equally popular but more casual is **Andiamo** (© 021/421-3687), which has a small but good Italian menu and testosterone-strong staff pumping up the action. Food is good, but when it's packed, tables are a little too close together and the vibe is frenetic. Inside the actual deli-shop, you'll find the greatest selection of edible items this side of the Equator—this is a good place to stock up for a picnic, or gifts for foodie friends. Across the tiny piazza is the **Nose Restaurant and Wine Bar** (© 021/425-2200), which serves superb wines by the glass, with personal write-ups by the owner to ease the selection process. Food is perfectly serviceable, too, and the atmosphere is a great deal more laid-back than Andiamo, which you can watch buzzing from your table. In the other corner, **Rouge French Bistro** (© 021/418-3671) does an excellent range of crepes, but only at lunchtime. These are all good, but if it's a cup of coffee or tea you're after, with a delicious light meal, don't miss the gorgeous **La Petite Tart,** on the "outside" of the Quarter, on Dixon Street (© 021/425-9077). Owned and run by Jessica, a French model who has successfully re-created her own little bit of the Left Bank here, it has the longest "tea-list" in town and the most wonderful tart selection (apricot and almond is a big favorite); if you're more savory-minded, opt for a traditional croque-monsieur or quiche (try the bleu cheese and artichoke).

MOULLE, SEA & GREEN POINT

One more establishment in the Sea Point area deserves a mention: Not much has changed at **La Perla** ✦✦, Beach Road (© 021/434-2471), the Italian restaurant that opened on the Sea Point promenade in the '60s, with waiters who have made this a career choice dishing up excellent pasta dishes (albeit old-fashioned toppings—no sign of Jamie Oliver here) and truly superb seafood.

Anatoli ✦ *Finds* TURKISH Housed in an old, gutted warehouse with exposed bricks and draped Persian carpets creating a spacious yet warm environment, Anatoli has been serving up Cape Town's best Turkish *mezze* (appetizer) platter since 1986. Served with loaves of bread so freshly baked they're too hot to touch, mezze choices are carried to the table on huge wooden trays, each bowl more delectable than the next. Waiters will run you through the dishes. Don't miss the hot potato rolls made with cheese, egg, chile, and parsley, and baked in phyllo; the cold tabouleh made with cracked wheat, mint, tomato, and cucumber; or the seriously good *dolmades* (stuffed grape leaves). Choose a selection to share, and don't bother with mains. A great choice if you're looking for an informal, relaxed evening.

25 Napier St., Green Point. ✆ 021/419-2501. Mezze (appetizers) R18 ($2.70) each; main courses R55 ($8.20). AE, DC, MC, V. Tues–Sun 6:30–11pm.

Mario's ✦✦ *Finds* ITALIAN Don't let the unprepossessing decor fool you; the kitchen serves authentic Italian cuisine, and a long list of Capetonian regulars will attest to it. Mario passed away back in the early 1980s, but his widow, Pina, single-handedly kept the family business growing, now ably assisted by her daughter Marlena and son Marco. The menu features everything you'd expect from an Italian restaurant (pasta is homemade and delicious), but the specials—almost as numerous as the menu items—are what's really likely to get your mouth watering. Pheasant, guinea fowl, quail, wild duck, rabbit—you name it, Pina cooks it.

89 Main Rd., Green Point. ✆ 021/439-6644. Main courses R42–R75 ($6.25–$11). AE, DC, MC, V. Tues–Fri and Sun 10:30am–2:30pm; Tues–Sun 6:30–10:30pm.

Wakame ✦✦ SEAFOOD/SUSHI Although some locals rue the day the old Harbour Tavern (a kitsch '70s relic) closed down, anyone who loves an ocean view while imbibing its fresh bounty, skillfully sliced, diced, wrapped, and/or cooked, will raise a glass of sake to the team who transformed it into the elegant Wakame. This is the best place to eat with a sea view. An airy interior where Japanese chefs display their skill steps down (to maximize the number of seats with a view), and ceiling-length glass doors fold back entirely to reveal a postcard-perfect view of the tankers and containerships sailing in and out of the nearby harbor. Sushi and sashimi are made to order, but here service can be tardy; besides, Wakame has a great menu to choose from. Seared tea-smoked tuna served on wasabi mash is flavorful, and the shrimp and butter sauce is simply delicious, but the top rating goes to the sesame-crusted tuna, served on bok choy and topped with slivers of deep-fried sweet potato. Unlike any of the Atlantic Seaboard options (see below)—all of which (with the exception of Blues) suffer from a certain brashness, their glorious views tainted by a low-level aggression on the part of the waitstaff—the atmosphere here is laid-back, and the food a great deal more innovative.

Corner of Beach Rd. and Surrey Place, Moulle Point. ✆ 021/433-2377. Reservations recommended for dinner in season. Main courses R68–R92 ($10–$14). AE, DC, MC, V. Daily noon–2:30pm and 7–9:30pm.

ATLANTIC SEABOARD: THE SUNSET STRIP

When the summer sun starts its slow descent into the ocean, you simply have to be on the Atlantic seaboard soaking up the last of its pink rays. Victoria Road, the street that hugs Camps Bay's palm-fringed beachfront, is where you'll find the most options, all with good-to-glorious views of the ocean and white-sand beach.

A general note of caution: In season the atmosphere can be a bit frenzied, and any genuine desire to service needs or produce noteworthy food takes a backseat to trying to turn over as many tables as possible (Blues being the notable exception); if you're looking for a more laid-back seaside alternative, head for Wakame in Moulle Point (see above).

La Med, the Glen Country Club, clearly signposted off Victoria (✆ 021/438-5600), is a rather tacky indoor/outdoor bar in a sublime location, with lawns that run into the ocean. The standard pub grub, beer garden, and sheer size (it seats over 500) can attract a rowdy crowd; for better-looking drinking partners, keep south down Victoria Road into Camps Bay proper. First up is the **Sandbar** (✆ 021/438-8336), one of Camps Bay's oldest sidewalk bistros, and known to serve a mean strawberry and mango daiquiri and great salads.

Even better views are to be had from the options housed in the Promenade Centre, which enjoys the choicest position on the Atlantic seaboard. Best dressed is **Paranga** (✆ 021/438-0404), on the first floor but elevated, with great cushy banquette seating along the walls (book seats 35–38 for best views); food is nothing to write home about and quite pricey, but during the late summer evenings, the venue is pretty unbeatable. Above is **Summerville** (✆ 021/438-4016), for more great views and excellent fresh fish. But if it's the coolest cocktail bar in Cape Town you're looking for, you'll have to climb one more flight of steps to reach **Eclipse** (✆ 021/438-0883). Furnished only with couches (on which you'll find Pamela Anderson look-alikes lounging about) and with a strict waitstaff policy (only the gorgeous need apply), it offers a surreally beautiful view to contend with all that flesh. Alongside these newer options is the stalwart **Blues** (✆ 021/438-2040), also with great views and the most old-fashioned (read: grownup) establishment on the Promenade. You often need to book a dinner table days before, proof that with a sublime location (and waiters with good teeth), you can get away with inconsistent cuisine standards. The **Blues Cafe,** above, which has DJs playing world music on Thursday, is a great deal more trendy (as offspring usually are). Adjacent to Blues is **Baraza** (✆ 021/438-1758), finished in muted earth tones and furnished with comfortable sofas, with a counter that runs the length of the window to offer more elevated views of the sunset strip. Adjoining Baraza is **Vilamoura** (✆ 021/438-1850), which serves mainly Portuguese fare, even though the baroque interior with Miro-style murals is anything but. Below is **Café del Mar** (✆ 021/438-0156), which serves light meals all day and well into the night. Farther along you'll find another **Primi Piatti** (✆ 021/438-2923); like its sister establishment in the Waterfront, this offers excellent thin-based pizzas and delicious pastas (veal's not bad, either), and lightning-fast service.

SOUTHERN SUBURBS

The Constantia wine estate, Uitsig, is fortunate enough to house three fabulous dining options: The first, Constantia Uitsig, is reviewed in full below because the venue—an old Cape Dutch farm that dinner guests have the run of—is simply the best, but most rate the food at **La Colombe** (✆ 021/794-2390) higher. Chef Frank Dangereux specializes in classic Provençal cuisine (even the French say you won't taste better anywhere in France), so if you have a soft spot for rich reduction sauces, book here, but bear in mind you'll have to forfeit the sublime view Constantia Uitsig offers. Best-case scenario: Sample both! If you're in the mood for more casual fare, at friendlier prices, Constantia's

Spaanschemat River Café (© 021/794-3010) is where local legend Judy Badenhorst is again dishing up superb deli-style food (as well as more substantial items such as succulent linefish or Karoo-lamb burger with cucumber/mint relish) in a garden setting. Her smoked salmon and scrambled eggs crepe, topped with chives and hollandaise sauce, is one of the best breakfasts in town.

Another Constantia option worth considering, not least for its lovely garden setting, is the **Greenhouse** (© 021/794-2137) at the Cellars-Hohenort hotel, where chef David Godin works wonders; in fact, the hotel was included in *Condé Nast Traveler*'s 2005 Gold List (featuring the top 108 hotels in the world), specifically in the food category. Martha Williams shares this honor for her fantastic work, ensuring that sister restaurant, the **Cape Malay Kitchen,** sets a similarly high standard.

VERY EXPENSIVE

Buitenverwachting ★★★ INTERNATIONAL/MODERN CAPE   Like Uitsig, Buitenverwachting (meaning "Above Expectation") is situated on one of the historic Constantia wine farms, with lovely views and an exceptional reputation. But Buitenverwachting is more formal and more expensive, and from a consistency point of view, the food is also better—it wows almost everyone who eats there and tends to make it into the top three of every food critic's Cape listing. Austrian chef Edgar Osojnik combines local ingredients with international techniques and flavors, like preparing kingklip in the tandoor and serving it with gingered bisque and basmati-pea samosas, or creating a creamy polenta-spinach soup and topping it with *osso buco* tartlets. Crayfish

---

Kids Family-Friendly Restaurants

Most city restaurants have limited space, but **Deer Park Café** (© 021/462-6311) opens onto a children's park in Vredehoek, Cape Town, and is open for breakfast, lunch, and early dinners. Besides the park, the menu is a big drawing card: lots of healthful organic vegetables and free-range meat dishes; great cappuccinos, too. The outdoor seating and coloring books at **Cafe Paradiso** ★, 110 Kloof St. (© 021/423-8653) make this a popular, good-value venue (with delicious food) for parents in the know. If the kids are clamoring for pizzas, check out nearby **Bacini's** (p. 97) or head into town to **Col'Cacchio** (© 021/419-4848)—ask for a bit of dough to make 'n' bake in the pizza oven. The old stalwart **McDonald's** (© 021/419-3715), in Green Point, has a kids' playground; for a better-quality burger, the best city option is **Colorado Spur Steakranch** (© 021/426-5321), on Kloof Street; it has an indoor playground, and child-friendly staff hand out balloons, coloring paper, and crayons. The most child-friendly venue on the beach is **Dunes Bar & Restaurant** (© 021/790-1876), in Hout Bay: Relax at a table with your feet in the sand and watch junior check out the swings and climbing frame—don't forget the sunblock. **Wharfside Grill** (© 021/790-2130), also in Hout Bay, has a great harborside location and offers kiddie portions. If you're on your way to or back from Cape Point, pop in at **Barnyard Farmstall** (© 021/712-6934) in Tokai for great country fare amid bales of straw and strutting roosters.

Tips **Picnic Fare**

Table Mountain is one big garden, and its "tabletop" makes a great picnic venue, as does Kirstenbosch, particularly during the summer when sunset concerts are held every Sunday from December to March. You can order a picnic hamper from the **Picnic Company** to be delivered to your door (© **021/706-8470;** R90/$13 per person plus R50/$7.45 delivery). But for a real feast, take your pick at **Melissa's,** 94 Kloof St. (© **021/424-5540**), or order a picnic basket, replete with cutlery. **Giovanni's,** 103 Main Rd., Green Point (© **021/434-6893**), is a real Italian deli with mouthwatering prepared meals and sandwiches. To picnic on one of Cape Point's deserted beaches, check out the fare at Kalk Bay's **Olympia Café** (© **021/788-6396**).

A great Winelands option is **Le Pique Nique** (© **021/870-4274**), at the gorgeous Boschendal Estate, where you can buy a hamper filled with local delicacies and spread out on their oak-shaded lawns.

---

is pan-fried and served with a Buiten-Brut bisque and spaghettini-artichoke bake. End with the "chocolate variation"—it's a masterpiece. A less pricey option is **Café Petit** in the courtyard, which is open for lunch. You can also arrange for takeout picnic fare.

Klein Constantia Rd., Constantia. © 021/794-3522. www.buitenverwachting.co.za. Reservations essential. Main courses R95–R138 ($14–$21); crayfish R290 ($43). AE, DC, MC, V. Tues–Fri noon–1:30pm; Tues–Sat 7–8:30pm; Cafe Petit lunches from R68 ($10) Tues–Sat 11:30–3:30pm.

EXPENSIVE

Constantia Uitsig ✶✶✶ INTERNATIONAL/ITALIAN   Situated on the Constantia wine route, Uitsig (literally, "Views") combines perfect mountain and vineyard views with a predominantly Italian menu. Chef Frank Swainston tries to update his menu, but patron pressure has ensured you will have the following choices, all recommended: paper-thin fish carpaccio, served with avocado; *bouchée de moules* (mussels in puff pastry in a spinach-and-saffron veloute); jointed wild duck with porcini mushrooms; grilled springbok loin served with a caramelized honey and lemon sauce; and the legendary *trippa alla Florentina* (a tomato-based tripe with carrots, celery, and onions). Swainston's Marquise au Chocolat is the most sinful dessert ever made. Sadly, consistency has become a bit of a problem, with some dishes simply not up to par, but the staff is superb at assisting with new choices, and it still rates tops as an overall experience.

Spaanschemat River Rd. © 021/794-4480. www.constantiauitsig.co.za. Reservations essential. Main courses R77–R120 ($11–$18). AE, DC, MC, V. Daily 7:30–9:30pm; Tues–Sun 12:30–2:30pm. June–Sept closed Mon lunch.

FALSE BAY: TRAVELING TO CAPE POINT

If you're traveling through Muizenberg or staying in the vicinity, make sure you book a table at **Railway House,** 177 Main Rd. (© **021/788-3251**). Located above the station, it has great sea views and a good, unfussy menu. You'll find the best False Bay restaurants in the charming and increasingly trendy fishing village of Kalk Bay. The **Harbour House** ✶✶, Main Road (© **021/788-4133**), is a great summer venue, one of the few places on the entire coast where you can sit with the ocean crashing on the rocks just below. Linefish are listed in chalk on the board and scratched off as they disappear down the hungry mouths of patrons.

If you feel like eating equally fresh fare but something other than seafood, **Olympia Cafe & Deli** ☆☆, Main Road, diagonally opposite the turnoff to Harbour House (© **021/788-6396**), is an excellent deli-restaurant serving light meals to the trendy bohemians that now frequent this side of the mountain. **Cape to Cuba,** Main Road (© **021/788-1566**), is a truly fabulous place to pop into for a cocktail—eclectically decorated with mismatched chairs, numerous chandeliers, and Catholic kitsch on rich, saturated-color walls, it's extremely comfortable, and the mojitos are knock-dead delicious; pity the food isn't up to scratch. Moving out of Kalk Bay, it's worth noting that **Bon Appetit** ☆ (© **021/786-2412**), a small, unprepossessing French restaurant on the main road running through Simonstown, is considered one of the best in the city. Leaving Simonstown to approach Cape Point, you'll see the **Black Marlin,** Main Road (© **021/786-1621**), a venue that enjoys one of the best sea views in the Cape, making it a popular tourist spot; seafood is the specialty, so order the linefish—and ask for all three butters (lemon, garlic, and chile) on the side.

Note that if you haven't had a chance to eat on the False Bay side, or have decided to approach Cape Point from the Atlantic seaboard, the **Chapman's Peak Restaurant,** Main Road, just before you ascend the Peak (© **021/790-1036**), is famous for its fresh calamari and fish—served still sizzling in the pan with fat fries—and wide veranda with views of the small fishing harbor. It's a jolly, unpretentious place that long predates Cape Town's burgeoning restaurant scene yet still pulls in the punters from all over the city.

5 Exploring Cape Town

From ascending its famous flat-topped mountain to indulging in the sybaritic pleasures of the Winelands, Cape Town has much to offer sightseers. You could cover the top attractions in 3 days, but to really get a sense of how much the city and surrounds have to offer, you'll need to stay at least a week.

THE CAPE PENINSULA NATIONAL PARK

Nowhere else in the world does a wilderness with such startling biodiversity survive within a dense metropolis; a city housing some three million people effectively surrounds a national park, clinging to a mountainous spine that stretches from the massif of Table Mountain to the jagged edges of Cape Point. Hardly surprising, then, that the city's best attractions are encompassed by the Cape Peninsula National Park: world-famous **Table Mountain,** also known as Hoerikwaggo, "Mountain of the Sea"; the dramatic **Cape Point,** most southwesterly tip of Africa; the unparalleled **Kirstenbosch Botanical Gardens,** showcase for the region's ancient and incredibly varied floral kingdom; and **Boulders,** home to a colony of rare African penguins. Ascending

---

Tips Cape Town Pass for Savings

If you plan to do some intensive sightseeing, look into purchasing a **Cape Town Pass.** Available in 1- (R275/$41), 2- (R425/$63), 3- (R495/$74), and 6-day (R750/$112) options, the credit card pass entitles you to free entry to some 50 top attractions, and comes with a 160-page guide profiling them. (Almost all the attractions reviewed below are included in the pass, with the notable exception of the Table Mountain cableway.)

Cape Town Attractions

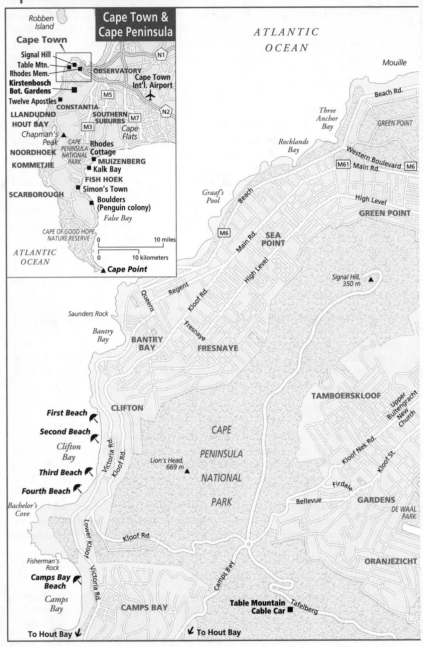

Cape Town & Cape Peninsula

ATLANTIC OCEAN

Robben Island

Cape Town

Signal Hill
Table Mtn.
Rhodes Mem.
Kirstenbosch Bot. Gardens
Twelve Apostles
LLANDUDNO
HOUT BAY
Chapman's Peak
NOORDHOEK
KOMMETJIE
SCARBOROUGH

OBSERVATORY
Cape Town Int'l. Airport
N1
M5
N2
M7
SOUTHERN SUBURBS
Cape Flats
M3
CONSTANTIA
CAPE PENINSULA NATIONAL PARK
Rhodes Cottage
MUIZENBERG
Kalk Bay
FISH HOEK
Simon's Town
Boulders (Penguin colony)
False Bay

CAPE OF GOOD HOPE NATURE RESERVE

ATLANTIC OCEAN

0   10 miles
0   10 kilometers

▲ **Cape Point**

ATLANTIC OCEAN

Mouille

Beach Rd.

Three Anchor Bay

GREEN POINT

Rocklands Bay

Western Boulevard M6
M61 Main Rd.

Graaf's Pool

Beach

High Level

GREEN POINT

M6

Main Rd.

High Level

SEA POINT

Signal Hill, 350 m ▲

Queens

Regent

Kloof Rd.

Fresnaye

Saunders Rock

Bantry Bay

BANTRY BAY

FRESNAYE

TAMBOERSKLOOF

Upper Buitengracht
New Church

CLIFTON

First Beach

Second Beach

Clifton Bay

Third Beach

Fourth Beach

Bachelor's Cove

CAPE

PENINSULA

NATIONAL

PARK

Lion's Head, 669 m ▲

Victoria Rd.

Kloof Rd.

Kloof Nek Rd.

Kloof St.

Firdale

Bellevue

GARDENS

DE WAAL PARK

Fisherman's Rock

Camps Bay Beach

Camps Bay

CAMPS BAY

Lower Kloof

Victoria Rd.

Kloof Rd.

Camps Bay

ORANJEZICHT

Table Mountain Cable Car

Tafelberg

To Hout Bay ↓

↙ To Hout Bay

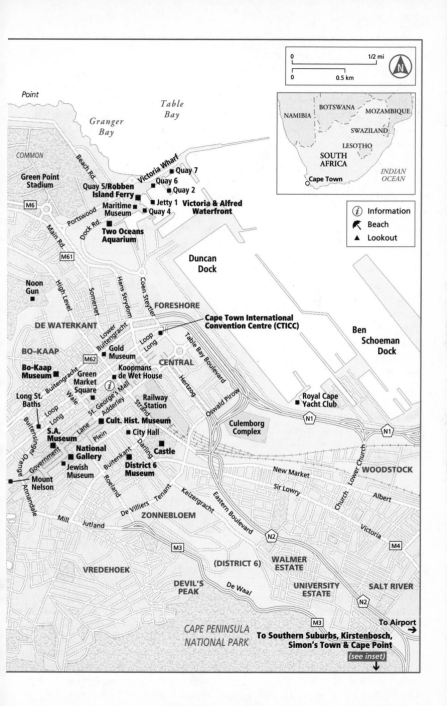

Point

Granger Bay

Table Bay

COMMON

Green Point Stadium

M6

Quay 5/Robben Island Ferry

Victoria Wharf

Quay 7
Quay 6
Quay 2
Jetty 1
Quay 4

Maritime Museum

Two Oceans Aquarium

Victoria & Alfred Waterfront

Duncan Dock

Ben Schoeman Dock

Beach Rd.

Portswood

Dock Rd.

Main Rd.

M61

High Level

Somerset

Hans Strydom

Coen Steytler

Noon Gun

DE WATERKANT

BO-KAAP

Bo-Kaap Museum

Long St. Baths

S.A. Museum

National Gallery

Jewish Museum

Mount Nelson

Lower Buitengracht

M62

Gold Museum

Koopmans de Wet House

Green Market Square

St. George's Mall

Adderley

Strand

Railway Station

Cult. Hist. Museum

City Hall

Castle

District 6 Museum

FORESHORE

Cape Town International Convention Centre (CTICC)

Loop
Long

Table Bay Boulevard

Hertzog

CENTRAL

Oswald Pirow

Culemborg Complex

Royal Cape Yacht Club

N1

N1

Buitengracht

Loop
Long

Wale

Buitensingel

Orange

Government

Plein

Lane

Buitenkant

Darling

Roeland

De Villiers

Tenant

Keizergracht

Eastern Boulevard

New Market

Sir Lowry

Church

Lower Church

WOODSTOCK

Albert

Victoria

Annandale

Mill

Jutland

ZONNEBLOEM

M3

VREDEHOEK

(DISTRICT 6)

WALMER ESTATE

N2

M4

DEVIL'S PEAK

De Waal

UNIVERSITY ESTATE

SALT RIVER

N2

CAPE PENINSULA NATIONAL PARK

M3

To Airport →

To Southern Suburbs, Kirstenbosch, Simon's Town & Cape Point
(see inset)
↓

0   1/2 mi
0   0.5 km
N

NAMIBIA   BOTSWANA   MOZAMBIQUE
SWAZILAND
LESOTHO
SOUTH AFRICA
Cape Town
INDIAN OCEAN

ⓘ Information
↖ Beach
▲ Lookout

111

Fun Fact **A Devil of a Wind**

Legend has it that the "tablecloth," the white cloud that tumbles over Table Mountain, is the work of retired pirate Van Hunks, who liked nothing more than to climb Devil's Peak and smoke his pipe while overlooking Cape Town. One day the devil, not happy that someone was puffing on his patch, challenged him to a smoking contest. Needless to say, the competition continues to rage unabated, particularly in the summer months. The downside of this magnificent spectacle is that hurricane-force winds will simultaneously whip around Devil's Peak and rip into the city at speeds of up to 150kmph (93mph). The "Cape Doctor," as the southeaster is often called, is said to clear the city of pollution, germs, and litter; but most just wish Van Hunks would give it up and stop infuriating the devil. For sanity's sake, head for the Atlantic seaboard, where the most protected beach is Clifton. Alternatively, escape to the Winelands, or visit in March and April, when the wind usually dies away completely.

Table Mountain warrants half a day, as does a visit to Kirstenbosch—though you could include it as part of a (rather rushed) daylong Peninsula Driving Tour, which encompasses Boulders and Cape Point; for details, see "Farther Afield: Discovering the Peninsula," later in this chapter.

Table Mountain 🦆🦆🦆   This huge, time-sculpted slab of shale, sandstone, and granite that rose from the ocean some 250 million years ago is Cape Town's most instantly recognizable feature. Recently incorporated into the Cape Peninsula National Park, thereby affording it the highest level of protection, the flat-topped mountain dominates the landscape, climate, and development of the city at its feet, and provides Cape Town with a 6,000-hectare (14,820-acre) wilderness at its center.

The best view of the mountain is from Table Bay (another good reason to take the Robben Island tour; see below), from where you can get some idea of the relative size of the mountain—while the city shrinks to nothing, the "Mountain of the Sea" can be seen from 150km (93 miles) at sea. Other views of the mountain are no less beautiful, particularly from the wooded eastern flanks of **Constantiaberg,** which greet the sun every morning, and the bare buttresses of a series of peaks named the **Twelve Apostles,** who are kissed by its last rays. The fact that the mountain alone has more plant varieties (some 1,470 species) than the entire British Isles is flaunted with pride, and it is thought to be the most climbed peak in the world, with some 350 paths to the summit.

You can ascend the mountain on foot or via cable car and, once there, spend a few hours or an entire day exploring. The narrow table is 3km (1¾ miles) long and 1,086m (3,562 ft.) high. **Maclear's Beacon** is its highest point. The upper cable station and restaurant are on the western edge, from where you can view the Twelve Apostles towering over Camps Bay. Walk eastward, and you'll have a view of the southern suburbs. The back table, with its forests, *fynbos* (shrublike vegetation), and the reservoirs that supply Cape Town with its water, is a wonderful place to hike, but much of it is off-limits.

By cable car: Cars depart every 15 minutes from the lower station at Tafelberg Road (© **021/424-8181**) daily (weather permitting) between 8 and 8:30am until between 6 and 9pm, depending on the season. A round-trip ticket costs between R80 and R110 ($12–$16) for adults, and R40 and R58 ($5.95–$8.65) for children, depending on the season (free for children under 4). Operating since 1929 but upgraded in 1997, the Swiss-designed cable car has a floor that rotates 360 degrees, giving everyone a chance to gape at the breathtaking views during the 4-minute journey up. The upgrade has meant that queues are now much shorter—even during the busiest months from November to April, the longest you'll wait is 30 minutes. Afternoons are generally less crowded.

On foot: The most commonly used route to the top is via **Platteklip Gorge**—the gap is visible from the front, or north face, of the mountain. The route starts just east of the lower cable station (see below) and will take 2 to 3 strenuous hours. Be sure to bring water. A more scenic route starts at the Kirstenbosch Botanical Gardens and climbs up the back via **Skeleton Gorge.** It's steep, requiring reasonable fitness, but should take approximately 2 hours to the summit. Rather than walk another hour to the upper cable station, most return by walking down via **Nursery Ravine.** Be aware that the mountain's mercurial weather can surprise even seasoned Capetonians—more people have died on Table Mountain than on Mount Everest. Don't climb alone, stick to the paths, and take water and warm clothes. For guided hikes, contact **Table Mountain Walks** (✆ 021/715-6136). The **Mountain Rescue** number is ✆ 10177 or 021/948-9900. Note that four new overnight hiking trails are scheduled to open over the next 3 years. The first is the **Table Mountain Trail,** which kicks off in September 2005 and provides comfortable lodgings and baggage portering for R950 ($142) a night. Hikers will be able to book through the South African National Parks website (www.sanparks.org) from June 2005 on.

Boulders ✶✶   A few minutes from the center of Simon's Town, on the way to Cape Point, is the turnoff to pretty Boulders, named after a cluster of large granite boulders that have created a number of small sheltered bays and provided sanctuary for a breeding colony of African penguins (formerly known as "jackass penguins" because of their braying). You can swim at the main beach, which the penguins visit, but the best place to view them is from the raised boardwalk overlooking Foxy Beach; they are a treat to watch, and almost human in their interactions. A monogamous species, the penguins mate in January and nest from February to August.

The Boulders (off M4), Simon's Town. ✆ 021/786-2329. R15 ($2.25) adults, R5 (75¢) children. Daily 8am–6:30pm.

Cape of Good Hope Nature Reserve ✶✶✶   The Cape of Good Hope Nature Reserve is most famous for **Cape Point,** the farthest tip of the Cape Peninsula. There are a number of drives and picnic sites in the reserve, which is home to baboons, zebra, eland, red hartebeest, ostrich, and the pretty bontebok. (Be aware that the baboons, which have become habituated to humans, can be dangerous; don't approach them, keep your car windows closed, and never feed them.) The usually windswept reserve can be pretty bleak, but the coastal views are arresting, and the beaches—which are seldom visited—are almost always deserted. The walks from Gifkommetjie and Platboom

---

Tips Beware the Giant Hamsters

On a visit to Table Mountain, you will certainly encounter the **dassie,** or rock hyrax, on the summit. These large, furry, rodentlike animals are (despite appearances) related to elephants, and although they are relatively tame, they do bite.

Beach on the west coast (incidentally, a good place for windsurfing) are recommended, or follow the turnoff to Bordjiesdrif or Buffelsbaai Beach on the east coast, where you can swim in protected tidal pools or even *braai* (barbecue). At Buffelsbaai, you can see the remains of one of the more than 20 ships that have wrecked on this coast.

Most head straight for Cape Point, taking the funicular (R31/$4.60 round-trip; 8 or 10am to 5 or 5:30pm, depending on season) to the viewing platforms surrounding the old lighthouse (built too high, it was often obscured by mists) and walking to the "new" lighthouse—built after yet another liner wrecked itself on the coast in 1911 and the most powerful on the South African coast. The spectacular view from these cliffs, towering more than 180m (600 ft.) above the lashing ocean, is truly "bird's-eye"—hundreds of seagulls wheel below. *Note:* Despite the T-shirt slogans and the name of the Cape Point restaurant, this is not the meeting place of two oceans; that would be Cape Agulhus, to the southeast of Cape Point.

Entrance off M4 and M65. ✆ 021/780-9204. R35 ($5.20) adults, R10 ($1.50) children 2–16. Oct–Mar daily 6am–6pm; Apr–Sept daily 7am–5pm.

Kirstenbosch Botanical Gardens ★★★
Situated on the eastern slopes of Table Mountain, Kirstenbosch is the third-most-visited attraction in Cape Town and is without a doubt one of the most beautiful gardens in the world, its shaded lawns and gurgling streams the perfect antidote to the searing summer heat (though winter brings some of the best blooms). With the cultivated sections seamlessly blending into the adjoining nature reserve, some 8,000 of South Africa's 22,000 plant species (including a giant baobab tree) grow here. There are a number of themed walks and areas; as an introduction to the indigenous flora, the fynbos walk is recommended. Of historic interest are the remains of the wild almond hedge that Jan Van Riebeeck planted in 1660 to demarcate the colony from the indigenous Khoi. Easiest is to hire an audioguide or avail yourself of the free guided garden walks that take place on Tuesday, Wednesday, and Saturday, or take a golf cart tour (R20/$3). **Summer sunset concerts ★★★** are held every Sunday at 5:30pm from December to March and feature some of Africa's best acts (as well as a few mediocre options)—call to find out what's on. At the main entrance there are two restaurants (✆ 021/762-9585): the self-service **Fynbos** (9am–5pm) and adjacent **Silver Tree,** serving a la carte lunches and dinners. Lovely venue and views, but the food is nothing to write home about, and increasingly pricey. Locals and visitors in the know avoid these tourist traps and opt to enter through Gate 2 and breakfast or lunch at the charming **Tea House** (✆ 021/797-4883), a small thatched building with tables outside that boasts a great menu, well priced and proudly advertising the use of organic ingredients: no MSG, no preservatives, no margarine.

Rhodes Ave. (off the M5), Newlands. ✆ 021/799-8899, or 021/761-4916 on weekends. www.nbi.ac.za. R22 ($3.30) adults, R5 (75¢) children 6–18. Concerts R35 ($5.20) adults, R10 ($1.50) children. Sept–Mar daily 8am–7pm; Apr–Aug daily 8am–6pm. Tours: Free guided garden walks every Tues at 9am and Sat at 11am; forest walk is Wed at 9am. Audioguides for self-guided tours (R30/$4.45). Specialized themed tours are offered monthly; call to see what's on. Golf-cart tours (R20/$3) depart every hour from 8am.

Rhodes Memorial
Rhodes Memorial was erected in honor of Cecil Rhodes, the man who, incidentally, donated the land for Kirstenbosch Gardens in 1902. Rhodes made his fortune in the Kimberley diamond mines and became prime minister of the Cape in 1890. A true British imperialist, he "owned" Zimbabwe (previously known as Rhodesia), and it was his lifelong dream to see a Cape-to-Cairo railway line built so that the "sun would never set on the British Empire." The memorial is an imposing

---

Fun Fact **Every Breath You Take**

The air at Cape Point is believed to be particularly pure—hence the establishment of one of the World Meteorological Organization's 20 Global Atmosphere Watch stations here, which monitors long-term changes in the chemistry of the earth's atmosphere.

---

granite staircase flanked by lions and overlooking the Cape Flats and Table Bay. In one of the Cape's most bizarre juxtapositions, herds of wildebeest and zebra graze on the slopes around the memorial, oblivious to rubberneckers driving the M3 below. An informal restaurant behind the memorial has outdoor tables with some of the best views in Cape Town—a great breakfast venue.

Off the M3 (De Waal Dr.), Groote Schuur Estate (signposted turnoff just after the University of Cape Town). © 021/689-9151. Free admission. Daily 8am–7pm (8am–6pm off season).

ATTRACTIONS IN THE CITY BOWL

Cape Town is South Africa's oldest and most pleasant city center, featuring a combination of Cape Dutch, Georgian, Victorian, and 20th-century architecture, all framed by the backdrop of Table Mountain. Hardly surprising, then, that Cape Town is also the only South African city that, with the efforts of the Cape Town Partnership, is slowly transforming itself into a residential enclave, with many of the city's period buildings (like the Art Deco Mutual Heights and new Mandela Rhodes Place, incorporating an entire block) being redeveloped into apartments and hotels, with retail and restaurant outlets planned to service these new city dwellers.

The major axis, **Adderley Street,** runs past the railway station, cutting the city in half. East of Adderley is the **Castle of Good Hope, Grand Parade,** and **City Hall.** West are the more charming shopping areas, the best of which, **Long Street** and **St George's Mall** (a pedestrian street), run parallel to Adderley. **Greenmarket Square,** a lively flea market surrounded by coffee shops, lies between these two streets and Longmarket and Shortmarket streets. South of Adderley Street (where it takes a right turn at The Slave Lodge and melds with Wale St.) is the **Company Gardens,** a green lung where most of the museums are situated.

The city is small, so the best way to get to know it is on foot (or by carriage—see Castle review below); you can either take a 3-hour guided walking tour, which departs from the tourism office at 10:30am (offered by knowledgeable guides, these are highly recommended) or enjoy your own pace: Start at the Castle, then head down Darling Street to Adderley Street. Either turn right to look at the brilliant blooms trading at Trafalgar flower market before continuing up Darling to browse the markets and shops at Greenmarket Square, Church Street, and Long Street, or turn left onto Adderley to complete a loop that takes in The Slave Lodge, the Company Gardens, the National Gallery, and/or the South African Museum before returning down Queen Victoria Street or Long Street to Greenmarket Square.

Castle of Good Hope ★★   Built between 1666 and 1679, the castle—really a pentagonal fortress typical of the Dutch defense system adopted in the early 17th century—is the oldest surviving building in South Africa, and marks the original shoreline. Once the hub of civilian and administrative life, the long-serving castle is still the regional headquarters of the South African Defence Force, though the most invasive force it's ever dealt with are the tourists ambling through its ramparts (and more recently, some 5,000 camp brides and other gay revelers at "The Wedding," an annual masked ball that was hosted here in 2002). The fort combined local materials (note the slate paving stones, taken from Robben Island in the 17th c.) with European imports (the bell at the entrance was cast in Amsterdam in 1697) and looks much as it has for centuries.

Get here at 10am sharp or noon if you want to see the Key Ceremony, a kind of "Changing of the Guard" (Mon–Fri only). There are also 30-minute tours departing at 11am, noon, and 2pm (ask about the many ghosts that wander its ramparts), or you can explore on your own. Unless you're fascinated with colonial military might, you can give the **Military Museum** a miss, but don't miss the **William Fehr Collection.** An arch-conservationist, Dr. Fehr (1892–1968) collected paintings and graphics that provide insight into the early colonists and how they were to change the face of the Cape completely, like Thomas Baines's painting *The Greatest Hunt in Africa* which depicts the slaughter of 30,000 animals in honor of the visiting Prince Alfred.

During the day, light meals and refreshments are served in the central courtyard at **Die Goewerneur Restaurant** (Mon–Sat 9am–4pm). For reservations, call © 021/787-4895. (Note that at press time you could catch a horse and carriage from the castle to the Company Gardens at 10:30am and 2pm, with plans to increase to four daily rides.)

Corner of Buitenkant and Strand sts. © 021/787-1249. R20 ($3) adults, R10 ($1.50) children. Mon–Sat 9am–4pm. William Fehr: Mon–Sat 9:30am–4pm.

The Slave Lodge ✦ Built in 1679 to house the Dutch East India Company's slaves, this building now houses the South African Cultural History Museum. The museum has just completed a long-overdue overhaul of its exhibits, and aims to provide a greater focus on the colony's slave history as well as the story behind Cape Town's multicultural makeup. A recent success was the "Hands That Shape Humanity" exhibit: the world's largest humanitarian art exhibition, in which well-known personalities from around the world (the likes of Isabel Allende, Marion Jones, Carlos Santana, Desmond Tutu, and so on) shared their inspirations and wisdom. Permanent exhibits are drawn from the lives of the early Cape colonists, with various artifacts from the 17th, 18th, and 19th centuries on display, and drawings and photographs that give visitors an idea of what Cape Town looked like before the land-reclamation project and development of the mountain's slopes.

49 Adderley St. © 021/460-8200. Daily 10am–4pm. R10 ($1.50) adults, R3 (45¢) children.

Fun Fact All that Glitters . . .

The **Gold of Africa Museum** is the newest addition to Cape Town's attractions, housing an African collection of gold artifacts purchased from the Barbier-Mueller Museum in Geneva for R11 million ($1.6 million). Created in Mali, Senegal, Ghana, and Cote d'Ivoire during the 19th and 20th centuries, the collection is a refreshing change from the mostly Eurocentric designs available commercially, and the intention is to foster an appreciation for and pride in African design. The museum is housed in the historic **Martin Melck House,** Strand Street (© 021/405-1540; R20/$3 per person), constructed in 1781 as the parsonage for the pretty Lutheran Church, located next to the house.

South African Museum and Planetarium ⚐   Founded in 1825, South Africa's old-est museum has excellent ethnographic displays, with displays on traditional medicine, the use of wood (used to tell the time), and African mathematics and alphabetic symbols. The Lydenburg heads, which date back to around A.D. 500, are some of the earliest examples of African art, as is the collection of San rock paintings—a must-see if you are not able to view these in the natural "open-air" gallery of the Cederberg or Drakensberg. The natural-history side includes a few fascinating exhibits, particularly the fossil gallery, with evidence dating life back 300 million years providing valuable insight into the now-barren Karoo; and the four-story whale well, hung with two massive whale skeletons. Others, like the stuffed *kwagga* (an extinct relative of the zebra) foal, are simply macabre.

Between Government Ave. and Queen Victoria St. ℂ 021/481-3800. Museum R10 ($1.50) adults, R5 (75¢) children 3–16. Planetarium show R20 ($3) adults, R6 (90¢) children 3–16. Museum daily 10am–5pm. Planetarium show Mon–Fri 2pm; Sat–Sun noon, 1, and 2:30pm (children's show at noon); Tues 8pm.

South African National Gallery ⚐⚐⚐   This small gallery, started with an initial donation by Victorian randlord Sir Abe Bailey, has room to exhibit only 5% to 8% of its collection of more than 8,000 artworks. Despite this, and despite a lack of fund-ing, it is considered by many to be the country's premier art museum, with many art-works reflecting South Africa's turbulent and painful history. Under the expert guidance of Marilyn Martin, the gallery has collected works neglected by other South African galleries, including rare examples of what used to be considered crafts, such as Ndebele beadwork and *knobkierries* (fighting sticks). The gallery also often hosts excel-lent traveling exhibitions, the most recent being a superb retrospective of one of South Africa's greatest living artists, William Kentridge, put together by MOMA.

Government Ave. ℂ 021/467-4660. R10 ($1.50) adults, R5 (75¢) students and children. Tues–Sun 10am–5pm.

ATTRACTIONS AT THE WATERFRONT

Redevelopment of this historic core started in the early 1990s, and within a few years the Victoria & Alfred Waterfront had been rated as the best of its kind, successfully inte-grating a top tourist attraction with southern Africa's principal passenger and freight har-bor. Views of Table Mountain and the working harbor, as well as numerous restored national monuments and a wide array of entertainment options, attract an estimated 20 million visitors a year. The smells of diesel and fish mingle with the aromas wafting from pavement bistros, tugboats mingle with catamarans, and tourists mingle with, well, tourists. (If you're seeking tattooed sailors and ladies of dubious repute, you'd be better off taking a drive down to Duncan Dock, where the large working ships dock.)

A rather sanitized place, the Waterfront contains some **400 stores** that are open until 9pm daily, and there is a choice of more than **70 restaurants,** as well as **11 main-stream-movie screens** (ℂ 021/419-9700) and 7 **art-movie screens** (ℂ 021/425-8222). (The **IMAX theater,** showing predominantly wildlife movies, was closed at press time, but there were plans to reopen; call ℂ 021/419-7364.) Don't limit your exploration to the Victoria Wharf shopping center, which feels like any other mall in a large city—take a stroll from Quay 5 to Pierhead Jetty. Beer lovers should make the detour to **Mitchell's Brewery** to sample the excellent handmade ales (ℂ 021/419-5074; tours Mon–Fri 3pm). The Waterfront is host to the **S.A. Maritime Museum** (ℂ 021/405-2880), a rather dry exhibition consisting mostly of model ships. Its floating exhibit, the **SAS *Somerset,*** the only surviving boom-defense vessel in the world, is moored on North Quay, but is currently under repair and closed until further notice.

Cultural Sights: Cape Muslim to Khayalitsha

On the slopes of Signal Hill—the arm that stretches out of Table Mountain to overlook the city and harbor—is the suburb of **Bo-Kaap.** Home to a section of the Cape's Muslim community (often referred to as the Cape Malays, despite the fact that only 1% of their forefathers, skilled slaves imported by the Dutch, were born in Malaysia), this is one of the city's oldest and most interesting areas, though its character is somewhat under threat from property speculators and foreign investors keen to own a piece of the city's quaintest suburb. Narrow cobbled streets lead past colorful 19th-century Dutch and Georgian terraces and tiny mosques; try to visit at sunrise and sunset when the air is filled with the song of the muezzins in their minarets, calling the community to prayer.

Start at the **Bo-Kaap Museum** ⍟, 71 Wale St. ((℗ **021/481-3939**; Mon–Sat 9:30am–4:30pm; R5/75¢ adults, R2/30¢ children). The museum gives some idea of the furnishings of a relatively wealthy 19th-century Cape Muslim family. One block south, at Dorp Street, is **Auwal,** South Africa's oldest mosque, dating back to 1795, and said to be where Afrikaans was first taught.

The protected historic core of the Bo-Kaap ranges from Dorp to Strand streets, and between Buitengracht and Pentz streets—the best way to experience them is on foot, with a local guide, like **Tana-Baru Tours** ⍟⍟ ((℗ **021/ 424-0719**). A 2-hour tour ends with tea and traditional Malay cake at a private home (R100/$15 per person) or a five-course informal lunch (R125/$19). (Its 3-hr. "Route of Many Cultures" tours is also recommended as one of the most authentic ways of understanding how segregation tore communities apart, with guides providing personal accounts while visiting District Six and the Cape Flats.)

Alternatively, head up steep Longmarket on your own and stop for tea and traditional *melktert* (milk tart) at the **Noon Gun Tea Room and Restaurant** ⍟, 273 Longmarket St. ((℗ **021/424-0529**). The name "Noon Gun" derives from the Signal Hill cannon fired by the South African Navy daily at noon—a tradition that has informed Capetonians of their imminent lunch break since 1806. The tearoom features magnificent views of the city and mountain, and serves authentic Cape Malay fare.

The charm of the Bo-Kaap provides some measure of what was lost when **District Six** was razed; opposite the Bo-Kaap, and clearly visible from any raised point, this vacant land is located on the city's southern border. When bulldozers moved in to flatten the suburb in 1966, an estimated 60,000 Cape Muslims (referred to as coloureds) were living in what was condemned as a ghetto by the apartheid hardliners. Much like Sophiatown in Johannesburg, District Six housed people from every walk of life—musicians, traders, teachers, craftsmen, *skollies* (petty criminals), hookers, and pimps—and was one of South Africa's most inspired and creative communities, producing potent poets, jazz musicians, and writers. When the bulldozers finally moved out, all that was left were a few churches and mosques—in a weird attempt at morality, religious buildings were exempt from the demolition order. The community was relocated piecemeal to the Cape Flats—a name that accurately describes both the geography and psychology of the area. Many believe that Cape Town's current gangster problems, spawned in the fragmented, angered, and powerless Cape Flats communities, are a direct result of the demise of District Six.

Renamed Zonnebloem (Sunflower), the so-called white area of District Six remained largely vacant, as even hardened capitalists spurned development in protest, and only the state-funded Cape Technicon was ever built on the land (purchased, incidentally, for R1/15¢). Restitution is finally underway, with a "homecoming ceremony" held in November 2000 and construction of homes for some of the more than 1,700 wrongly evicted resumed in April 2003. Life will never be the same here again, but most hope that by returning the stolen land to the original families, the damage done to the national psyche can be reversed. Until then, the scar on the cityscape is a constant reminder.

Most organized tours of District Six include a trip to **Gugulethu** and **Langa,** two of Cape Town's oldest "townships," as black suburbs are still referred to, and the shantytowns of **Khayalitsha.** While you can self-drive to craft centers like Sivuyile Tourism Centre in Gugulethu (see "Shopping," later in this chapter), to get an in-depth understanding of how "the other half" of Cape Town lives, a tour is definitely recommended. Other than Tana-Baru (see above), you could book a tour with **Grassroots** (② 021/706-1006) or **Legend Tours** (② 021/697-4056). Most kick off from either the Bo-Kaap or District Six museums, then head for a short visit to the townships to visit a crafts center, an "informal" home, a *shebeen* (traditional drinking house), and a housing project; both can extend the tour to include Robben Island, though you don't really need a tour guide to visit the latter. The highly recommended **One City Tours** ★ (② 021/387-5351) concentrates on the experiences of the black Cape Town community: "Ekhaya" concentrates on history from a black perspective, "The Gospel Truth" takes you to different church services in the townships, and the "Shebeen Crawl and All That Jazz" is a nocturnal pub crawl through the townships. **Township Crawling** (② 021/689-9705 or cellphone 082/478-8028) is also recommended, and includes a visit to a traditional healer; call Laura or Thandile. **Township Music Tours** ★ (② 021/790-8826) specializes in introducing visitors to the sounds of Mbanqanga, Afro-jazz, and marimba and percussion; after eating at an informal township restaurant, guests are taken to a shebeen for a session of live music.

If you do only two things on the Waterfront, you should book a **boat trip,** preferably to Robben Island, and visit the **Two Oceans Aquarium** (see below). Most cruises (see "Organized Cruises & Tours" earlier in the chapter), including the Robben Island ferry, take off from Quay 5. *Steamboat Vicky* (© **083/651-0186;** R30/\$4.45), which tools around the harbor, takes off from North Quay. From May to December you can also book a whale-watching cruise with the **Waterfront Boat Company** at Quay 5 (© **021/418-5806;** all viewing is strictly controlled to within 50m/164 ft.).

Robben Island ★★★   To limit access to the delicate ecosystem of the island, only tour groups organized by the Department of Arts, which manages the Robben Island Museum (encompassing the entire island), are allowed to land on the island, declared a World Heritage Site in 1999. Visitors are transported via the *Makana* or the *Autshumato,* luxury high-speed catamarans that take approximately 25 minutes. (The views of Table Mountain and Cape Town as you pull out of the harbor are fantastic—don't forget your camera.) The 45-minute bus tours of the island provide passing glimpses of the **lepers' church and graveyard;** PAC leader **Robert Sobukwe's house,** where he was imprisoned; the **"warden's village,"** a charming collection of houses and a school; the **lighthouse; World War II fortifications;** Robben Island's **wildlife** (a variety of antelope, ostrich, and African penguins); and the **lime quarry,** worked by political prisoners (take sunglasses—the brightness ruined many inmates' and wardens' eyes). The tour's highlight is the prison, where you can view the tiny cell in which Mandela spent 18 of his 27 years of imprisonment. To make the experience even more poignant, an ex–political prisoner conducts this part of the tour, giving a firsthand account of what it was like to live here. Tours take 3½ hours (including boat trip) and can feel very restricted—to get a real feel for the village (not to mention the most spectacular sunset view of Table Mountain), it's worth trying to arrange a night in one of the old wardens' cottages: A fascinating counterpoint to the more publicized prison, the village seems stuck in time, its deserted streets and low fences conjuring up the nostalgic 1950s. You can make inquiries through **Rabia** (© **021/409-5182**); preference is given to groups or people doing research or engaged in some artistic endeavor. Don't expect any luxuries, and take your own picnic hamper with bottled water. Rabia can also organize special tours on request.

Tickets and departure from the Clocktower terminal on Quay 5, close to Jetty 1. © **021/419-1300.** R150 (\$22) adults, R75 (\$11) children 4–17. Ferries depart every hour 9am–3pm. Tours may be increased to include sunset tours in summer, and decreased in winter or because of inclement weather—please call ahead.

Two Oceans Aquarium ★★★ *Kids*   This is by far the most exciting attraction at the Waterfront itself. From the brightly hued fish found on coral reefs to exhilarating encounters with the Great White sharks, more than 3,000 live specimens are literally inches from your nose. Besides the Indian and Atlantic underwater tanks displaying the bizarre and beautiful, there are a number of well-simulated environments, including tidal pools, a river ecosystem, and the magnificent Kelp Forest tank. The walk through the aquarium (30–90 min., depending on how long you linger) ends with an awesome display on deep-sea predators. There are child-height window benches throughout and a "touch pool" where kids can touch kelp, shells, and anemones. On weekends kids are entertained in the Alpha Activity center with face painting and puppet shows. Predators are fed at 3:30pm daily (the large sharks on Sun).

Between New Basin and Dock Rd. © **021/418-3823.** R60 (\$8.95) adults, R28 (\$4.15) children 4–17. Daily 9:30am–6pm.

My, what an inefficient way to fish.

Ring toss, good. Horseshoes, bad.

Faster! Faster! Faster!

We take care of the fiddly bits, from providing over 43,000 customer reviews of hotels, to helping you find our best fares, to giving you 24/7 customer service. So you can focus on the only thing that matters. Goofing off.

travelocity
You'll never roam alone.

Island of Tears

The remarkably varied history of Robben Island goes back some 400 years. It has served variously as a post office, a fishing base, a whaling station, a hospital, a mental asylum, a military base, and—most infamously—as a penal colony, for which it was dubbed "South Africa's Alcatraz." The banished have included Angolan and West African slaves, princes from the East, South African chiefs, lepers, the mentally insane, French Vichy POWs, and, most recently, opponents of the apartheid regime. But all that changed on September 24, 1997, when the Robben Island Museum was officially opened by its most famous political prisoner.

The island, once the symbol of political oppression and enforced division, was to be transformed into a symbol of reconciliation. In Mandela's words, "Few occasions could illuminate so sharply the changes of recent years; fewer still could bring to sharp focus the challenges ahead." Rising to this challenge is an eclectic complement of staff—artists, historians, environmentalists, ex–political prisoners, and ex-wardens. It's hard to imagine how a group of people with such diverse backgrounds and ideologies could work together, but it seems anything is possible once you've established common ground—in this case, the 586 hectares (1,447 acres) of Robben Island.

Patrick Matanjana, one of the prison tour guides, spent 20 years behind bars on the island. Now he spends time at Robben Island's bar, fraternizing with the very people who upheld the system he was trying to sabotage. "They know me; they respect me," he says when asked what it's like to sit and drink with former enemies. "We are trying to correct a great wrong. They also buy the drinks," he grins. The island's ironies don't end here. Even the bar, the Alpha 1 Officers' Club, has historic significance: This is where Patrick's latrine bucket would have been emptied in the 1960s and 1970s, before the prisoners had access to toilets (not to mention beds, hot water, or adequate nutrition).

Despite the radical changes, the remaining ex-wardens, now mostly in charge of island security, do not want to leave. "You cry twice on Robben Island," explains skipper Jan Moolman, who first stepped onto the island in 1963 as one of PAC leader Robert Subukwe's personal wardens. "The day you arrive, and the day you have to leave."

For the many day-trippers, all it takes is the sight of Mandela's cell.

6 Farther Afield: Discovering the Peninsula

THE CONSTANTIA WINE ROUTE

Groot Constantia is a good place to start your exploration of the Cape's oldest and closest Winelands, an area that comprises eight wineries, the most famous being **Groot Constantia, Klein Constantia, Buitenverwachting, Uitsig,** and **Steenberg.** All feature Cape Dutch homesteads, oaks, and acres of vineyards, and because they're about 30 minutes from town, spending time here is definitely recommended, particularly if you aren't venturing into the surrounding Winelands. If you're looking for an

Finds **Vin de Constance**

Constantia's famous dessert wine, so treasured by the great names of 18th-century Europe (even Jane Austen was moved to describe its "healing powers on a disappointed heart"), is today made in much the same way by Klein Constantia (part of the Constantia estate until 1712). Visit Klein Constantia to sample this nectar—you can purchase it only from the estate—if you're lucky enough to find some in stock, or look for it on wine lists.

ideal luncheon venue, look no further than Buitenverwachting or Uitsig—both are located on the eastern slopes of the Constantiaberg, with views of vineyards and the distant sea, and both are renowned for their cuisine (see "Where to Dine," earlier in this chapter).

Groot Constantia ★★   Groot Constantia was established in 1685 by Simon van der Stel, then governor of the Cape, who reputedly named it after his daughter Constancia and planted the Cape's first vines. A century later, the Cloete family put Constantia on the international map with a dessert wine that became the favored tipple of the likes of Napoleon, Bismarck, King Louis Philippe of France, and Jane Austen (see "Vin de Constance," above). An outbreak of phylloxera in the 1860s bankrupted the family, however, and the land lay fallow until 1975, when substantial replanting began. Today Groot Constantia is known for its reds, particularly the Gouverneurs Reserve. In addition to tasting the wines in the modern cellars here, you can visit a small museum showing the history of the manor, as well as the beautiful Cape Dutch house itself, furnished in beautiful late-18th-century Cape Dutch furniture. Behind the house are the old cellars, originally designed by French architect Louis Thibault; note the celebrated pediment sculpted by Anton Anreith in 1791. The cellars now contain an interesting museum of wine. A cozy, pleasant restaurant, **Jonkershuis** (*©* **021/794-6255**), serves traditional Cape Malay dishes, and **Simon's** (*©* **021/794-1143**)—surrounded by vineyards and lawns—is where the locals can be found quaffing from the extensive wine list and marveling at the pinkness of the seared tuna or lamb.

M3, take the Constantia turnoff; follow the Groot Constantia signs. *©* **021/795-5140**. R10 ($1.50) museum; R20 ($3) wine tasting; R25 ($3.75) wine tasting and cellar tour. Daily 10am–5pm.

DRIVING TOUR   **A PENINSULA DRIVE**

Start:	Take the M3 out of town; this follows the eastern flank of the mountain, providing access to the southern suburbs.
Finish:	Kloof Nek roundabout in town.
Time:	The full tour will take at least 1 full day.

Not all the sites listed below are must-sees; personal interest should shape your itinerary. That said, get an early start, and make an effort to fit Kirstenbosch and Groot Constantia into the morning, leaving Cape Point for the afternoon and Chapmans Peak drive for the evening. Because this is a circular route, it can also be done in reverse, but the idea is to find yourself on the Atlantic seaboard at sunset.

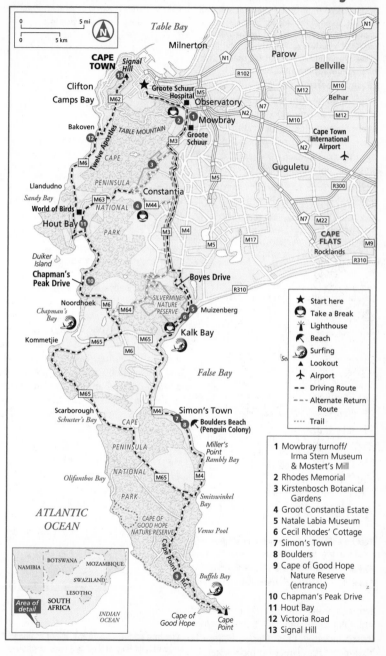

Peninsula Driving Tour

Table Bay

Milnerton

CAPE TOWN
Signal Hill

Clifton
Camps Bay

Bakoven

Llandudno

Sandy Bay

World of Birds

Hout Bay

Duiker Island

Chapman's Peak Drive

Noordhoek

Chapman's Bay

Kommetjie

Scarborough
Schuster's Bay

ATLANTIC OCEAN

Olifantbos Bay

Cape of Good Hope

Cape Point

Groote Schuur Hospital

Observatory

Mowbray

Groote Schuur

Constantia

Boyes Drive

Silvermine Nature Reserve

Muizenberg

Kalk Bay

False Bay

Simon's Town

Boulders Beach (Penguin Colony)

Miller's Point
Rambly Bay

Smitswinkel Bay

Venus Pool

Buffels Bay

CAPE OF GOOD HOPE NATURE RESERVE

Cape Point Rd.

Parow

Bellville

Belhar

Cape Town International Airport

Guguletu

Cape Flats

Rocklands

Table Mountain

Cape Peninsula National Park

5 mi
5 km

N

Legend

★ Start here
☻ Take a Break
🗼 Lighthouse
Beach
Surfing
▲ Lookout
✈ Airport
-- Driving Route
--- Alternate Return Route
··· Trail

1 Mowbray turnoff/ Irma Stern Museum & Mostert's Mill
2 Rhodes Memorial
3 Kirstenbosch Botanical Gardens
4 Groot Constantia Estate
5 Natale Labia Museum
6 Cecil Rhodes' Cottage
7 Simon's Town
8 Boulders
9 Cape of Good Hope Nature Reserve (entrance)
10 Chapman's Peak Drive
11 Hout Bay
12 Victoria Road
13 Signal Hill

Area of detail

NAMIBIA
BOTSWANA
MOZAMBIQUE
ZIMBABWE
SWAZILAND
LESOTHO
SOUTH AFRICA

INDIAN OCEAN

As you approach the Groote Schuur Hospital on your left, scene of the world's first heart transplant in 1967, keep an eye out for the wildebeest and mountain zebra grazing on the slopes of the mountain. Art lovers should consider taking the Mowbray turnoff to the:

❶ Irma Stern Museum

Stern, a follower of the German expressionist movement—and acknowledged as one of South Africa's best 20th-century artists—was also an avid collector of Iberian, African, and Oriental artifacts. The museum, on Cecil Road (℃ **021/685-5686;** Tues–Sat 10am–5pm; R7/$1.05), also exhibits new talents.

Back on the M3, still traveling south, you will pass Mostert's Mill on your left, another reminder of the Cape's Dutch past, and look out for a turning on your left to:

❷ Rhodes Memorial

You can see the imposing memorial high up on the slopes on your right (see "The Cape Peninsula National Park," earlier in this chapter); the restaurant behind the memorial has awesome views, so break here for tea or breakfast if you have the time, or return another day. Back on the M3 you will pass a series of imposing ivy-clad buildings—the **University of Cape Town,** built on land donated by Rhodes. If you're interested in colonial architecture, you can make an appointment to visit **Groote Schuur,** also donated by Rhodes and designed by Herbert Baker, "the architect of the Empire," and up until the end of Mandela's term, the official government residence; call Alta Kriel (℃ **021/686-9100**).

From here the suburbs become increasingly upmarket. Take the turnoff to:

❸ Kirstenbosch Botanical Gardens

Consider visiting Kirstenbosch (you'll need at least an hour, preferably more) before heading through the suburbs of Bishop's Court and Wynberg for Constantia. See "The Cape Peninsula National Park," earlier in this chapter.

If you've decided against Kirstenbosch, you may have time along the way to visit the:

❹ Groot Constantia Estate

You can visit the 17th-century manor house and wine museum, and possibly try a wine tasting (see above). Alternatively, set aside a full afternoon to travel the full Constantia Wine Route, visiting at least three estates.

Keep traveling south on the M3 until it runs into a T-junction, then turn left to the next T-junction, where you join the M4; turn right and look out for Boyes Dr. for the gorgeous elevated views of False Bay. This short detour of the coastal route is often less congested than the narrow road that runs through the coastal suburbs of Muizenberg, St James, and Kalk Bay, though you'll miss much of the interesting turn-of-the-20th-century architecture. If this interests you, try to time your visit for a Monday and make an appointment to view the:

❺ Natale Labia Museum

Built in the Venetian style, the **Natale Labia Museum,** on the main road (℃ **021/788-4106;** Mon by appointment only; R5/$75¢) was the sumptuous home of the Count and Countess Labia, and is a fabulous example of the holiday homes built by Cape Town's glam society in the last century, when the False Bay coast used to be the favored seaboard of the wealthy randlords.

Another attraction on Muizenberg's Main Rd. (also called the Historical Mile) is:

❻ Cecil Rhodes's Cottage

This house, on the main road (℃ **021/788-1816;** Mon–Fri 9:30am–4:30pm, Sat–Sun 10am; donation welcome), is the place where Rhodes purportedly died—a remarkably humble abode for a man who shaped much of southern Africa's history. If you enjoy this area and want more information, visit **Peninsula Tourism,** in the Pavilion Building, Beach Road (℃ **021/788-1898**).

Continue on Main Rd. to the quaint fishing village of Kalk Bay, which has a number of good places to eat and junk shops to browse.

TAKE A BREAK
Whether you've taken Muizenberg's main road or Boyes Drive, stop in at quaint **Kalk Bay** to browse the antiques shops, galleries, junk shops, and retro-modern boutiques. You can lunch here: Try the excellent **Olympia Deli** for light meals, or, for ocean views, try **Cape to Cuba** or **Harbour House;** see "Where to Dine," earlier in this chapter.

The drive then resumes its way south along the M4 to Fish Hoek and the naval village of:

7 Simon's Town

This vies with Kalk Bay as the most charming of the False Bay towns, lined with double-story Victorian buildings, which is why many regular visitors to the Cape choose to stay here. If you feel like lingering, visit the **Simon's Town Museum,** Court Road (© 021/786-3046; Mon–Fri 9am–4pm, Sat 10am–4pm, Sun 10am–1pm), or take a 40-minute cruise around the bay (© 021/786-2136). For more details on what the town has to offer, visit the **Simon's Town Tourism Bureau,** also on Court Road (© 021/786-5798).

If you're hot and bothered, don a bathing suit and join the penguins at nearby:

8 Boulders Beach

View the large breeding colony of jackass (African) penguins that settled here in the early 1980s, much to the horror of the residents, who now have to deal with the attendant coachloads of tourists.

From Simon's Town, it's 15 minutes to the entrance to the:

9 Cape of Good Hope Nature Reserve

Once inside, take the Circular Drive to spot game, or head for one of the usually deserted beaches; if you're pressed for time, head straight for Cape Point (see "The Cape Peninsula National Park," earlier in this chapter). From the nature reserve, it's a relatively straightforward—and spectacular—drive back to town (if Chapman's Peak is open; if not, see tip above). Take the M65 left out of the reserve past the **Cape Point Ostrich Farm** (© 021/780-9294; daily 9:30am–5pm, tours are R25/$3.75 and include coffee), and travel through the pretty coastal town of **Scarborough** (passing the aptly named **Misty Cliffs**) and **Kommetjie** (you can opt to bypass Kommetjie, but note that this has some fabulous beachfront accommodations options) to **Noordhoek.**

Noordhoek has a famously beautiful beach, the aptly named Long Beach (make sure you don't walk it with valuables), but if you're pressed for time, follow the signs and head north to ascend the exhilarating:

10 Chapman's Peak Drive

Built between 1915 and 1922, this winding 10km (6¼-mile) drive must rate as one of the top in the world, with cliffs plunging straight into the ocean, dwarfing the vehicles snaking along its side. Not surprisingly, hundreds of international car commercials have been shot here. Note that this opened as a toll road in 2003; the fee is R22 ($3.30) (credit cards accepted).

From Chapman's Peak, you descend into:

11 Hout Bay

Here you could either stop for the most delicious calamari on the veranda at the Chapman's Peak Hotel, or head for the harbor and book a cruise to view the seal colony and seabird sanctuary on **Duiker Island** (see "Organized Cruises & Tours," earlier in this chapter), or visit the **World of Birds Sanctuary** in Valley Road (© 021/790-2730; 9am–5pm daily; R45/$6.70 adults, R30/$4.45 children 3–16), home to more than 330 species; it's a big hit with kids.

From Hout Bay, you can now take the coast-hugging:

⑫ Victoria Road (or M6)

Take this road to town—with any luck this will coincide with sunset, or you'll have a moon to guide you.

Follow the M6 through Camps Bay and turn right at the sign KLOOF NEK ROUND HOUSE to snake up the mountain to the Kloof Nek roundabout and take the turnoff to:

⑬ Signal Hill

The views from the hill are breathtaking, particularly at night, when the twinkling city lies spread before you.

7 Surf & Sand

You'll find Cape Town's most beautiful beaches along the Atlantic seaboard, with Clifton, Camps Bay, and Llandudno the most popular. A combination of four beaches semiseparated by large granite boulders, gorgeous **Clifton** has Blue-Flag status, is often the only place where the wind isn't blowing, and is good for swimming (albeit freezing), but it's a long walk back through the cliff-hugging village to your car. **Camps Bay** offers easy access and a few rock pools, and has numerous bars and cafes within strolling distance. You can also hire loungers and umbrellas on the beach (in season), even summon a personal masseuse; for the latter, call ℂ **082/940-7465.** Laid-back **Llandudno** is one of the city's prettiest beaches, though parking can be a real problem during high season. **Sandy Bay,** adjacent to Llandudno, is the Cape's only nudist beach. Reached via a narrow footpath, it is secluded and popular with gay men and wankers—this is not a great spot for women, unless you're in a group. The pristine, empty 8km (5-mile) stretch of **Long Beach** 𝕱, featured in a thousand television commercials, is best traversed on horseback. On the False Bay side, where the water is 2° to 3° warmer, the best place to swim is with the penguins at **Boulders** (although on a bad day you may have to contend with gawking tourists as well).

8 Especially for Kids

Many of the Waterfront activities have been designed with children in mind, making it Cape Town's foremost family destination. The top attraction here is the **Two Oceans Aquarium.** Face painting, drawing, and puzzles are on offer in the aquarium's Alpha Activity center, and staff often arrange sleepovers and excursions to interesting and educational locations for ages 8 to 12. Call ℂ **021/418-3823** to find out what special kids' entertainment will be available when you're in town. On the way, stop at the **Scratch Patch,** where kids literally scratch through mounds of semiprecious stones, selecting their own "jewels," after which they can play a round of crazy golf.

Catch the kiddies' **Blue Train** in Mouille Point (ℂ **021/434-8537;** Mon–Fri 3–5pm, Sat–Sun 11–5pm); next door is a maze and an outdoor putt-putt (crazy golf) course. In town, the noon **Planetarium** show is held every Saturday and Sunday, where they attempt to answer simple astronomy questions, like "Why is the sky blue?" and "Is the sun round?" To get there, take a stroll along Government Avenue (enter from Orange St., opposite Mount Nelson) armed with a bag of nuts to feed the almost-tame squirrels. Afterward, take high tea in the **Mount Nelson gardens,** or head for **Deer Park Café,** a child-friendly restaurant that opens onto a public play-park. End the day by ascending **Table Mountain** in the rotating cable car—the ride alone is a thrill for kids, but the views are equally rewarding; pack a picnic, but don't forget the sunblock, hats, and a warm layer, should the weather turn.

A gentler experience is to chill out with a picnic next to a burbling stream at **Kirstenbosch Gardens,** or head for the shady oaks at **Le Pique Nique,** Boschendal, near Franschhoek. Then visit **Butterfly World** (© 021/875-5628), where 22 different species of butterfly flit about a tropical garden, or **Drakenstein Lion Park** (© 021/863-3290), a sanctuary for captive-born lions—both are near Paarl. Other kid-friendly attractions in the Paarl area include **Le Bonheur Crocodile Farm** (© 021/863-1142).

Closer to town is a walk through the **World of Birds Sanctuary,** Valley Road (© 021/790-2730), in Hout Bay; then take one of the cruises to **Seal Island,** departing from Hout Bay Harbour. **Imhoff Farm** (© 021/783-4545) in Kommetjie offers country-style refreshments, camel rides, horseback riding, crafts shops for kids, and a snake and nature park to entertain.

When all else fails, there's always the beach. Try **Boulders,** where the temperature is slightly warmer, tidal pools are safe, and the penguins add unique entertainment value. Visit the **Warrior Toy Museum** (© 021/786-1395) on Georges Street, Simon's Town, on your way.

9 Staying Active

For one-stop adrenaline shopping, head straight for **Detour Travellers Shop,** 234 Long St. (©/fax **021/424-1115** or 082/875-9496; www.detourafrica.co.za), where Shaun Petre will organize bookings for almost every adventure activity under the sun (for numbers not available below, contact them directly). This is also where bookings to Botswana and Victoria Falls can be made, as well as many specialized overland and safari trips throughout southern Africa.

ABSEILING   **Abseil Africa** (© **021/424-4760**) will throw you 100m (328 ft.) off Table Mountain—attached to a rope, of course (R250/$37). But their best trip is **Kamikaze Kanyon** ⚐: a day's kloofing (scrambling down a river gorge) in a nature reserve, ending with a 65m (213-ft.) waterfall abseil (R550/$82).

BALLOONING   Board a balloon in the early morning and glide over the Paarl Winelands—the 1-hour flight (R1,550/$231 per person) takes off every morning from November to April, and includes a champagne breakfast at the Grande Roche. Contact **Wineland Ballooning** (© 021/863-3192).

BIRD-WATCHING   The peninsula attracts nearly 400 species of birds; Kirstenbosch Botanical Gardens, Cape Point, and Rondevlei Nature Reserve are some of the best areas for sightings. For guided tours of the area and farther afield, contact **Birdwatch Cape** (© 021/762-5059; www.birdwatch.co.za).

BOARDSAILING & KITE-SURFING   Big Bay at Blouberg (take R27 Marine Dr. off the N1) provides consistent wind, good waves, and a classic picture-postcard view of Table Mountain. Another popular place is Platboom, off the Cape of Good Hope Nature Reserve, and Milnerton Lagoon. Contact Lucian at the **Kite Shop** (© 021/421-6231). Or head north for Langebaan Lagoon (see chapter 5).

BOATING   The most exhilarating boating experience is called oceanrafting, reaching speeds of up to 130kmph (81 mph) across Table Bay in a 12-seater inflatable (© **021/425-3785**; www.atlanticadventures.co.za; R250/$37). For more options, see "Organized Cruises & Tours," earlier in this chapter.

CANOEING/KAYAKING **Felix Unite** (© 021/670-1300) offers relaxing river trips on the tranquil Breede River—the closest is the Wine Route Adventure, which includes tasting wines of the area and costs R395 ($59) per person. **Real Cape Adventures** (© 021/790-5611; www.johanloots@mweb.co.za) covers almost every sea-kayaking route on the West and Southern coasts and caters to all levels of ability—request a trip to the rugged coastline of Cape Point.

DIVING Wreck diving is popular here, and the coral-covered wrecks at Smitswinkel Bay are particularly worth exploring. Also Maori Bay, Oak Burn, and Bnos 400. Call **Dive Action** (© 021/511-0815; www.diveaction.co.za). (For shark-cage diving at Hermanus, 1 hr. away, see chapter 5.)

FISHING **Big Game Fishing Safaris** (© 021/674-2203) operates out of Simon's Town on a 12m (39-ft.) catamaran and offers bottom/reef fishing (as well as crayfish lunches, sundowner cruises, on-board skeet shooting, and shark-cage diving). Trout fishing is popular in the crystal-clear streams found in the Du Toits Kloof Mountains near Paarl and in Franschhoek, where salmon trout is a specialty on every menu. For guided trips, call Tim at **Ultimate Angling** (© 021/686-6877); for general advice, tuition, and permits in Franschhoek, contact Mark at **Dewdale Fly Fishery** (© 021/876-2755).

GOLFING The **Royal Cape** (© 021/761-6551) has hosted the South African Open many times. **Milnerton Golf Club** ⛳ (© 021/552-1047; www.milnerton golfclub.co.za) is the only true links course in the Cape, with magnificent views of Table Mountain, but is best avoided when the wind is blowing. **Rondebosch** (© 021/689-4176) and **Mowbray** (© 021/685-3018)—both located off the N2—have lovely views of Devil's Peak (the latter course is the more demanding). **Clovelly** (© 021/782-1118), in Fish Hoek, is a tight course requiring some precision. **Steenberg** (© 021/713-2233) is the course to play in Constantia.

In the Winelands, the Gary Player–designed **Erinvale** ⛳, Lourensford Road (© 021/847-1144) in Somerset West is considered the best, but **Stellenbosch** (© 021/880-0103), on Strand Road, is another worthwhile course, with a particularly challenging tree-lined fairway.

HIKING Most hikers start by climbing Table Mountain, for which there are a number of options (see "Table Mountain," earlier in this chapter); call the **Mountain Club** (© 021/465-3412). For hikes farther afield, contact **Cape Eco Trails** (© 021/785-5511) or Ross at **High Adventure** (© 021/447-8036)—as a trained climbing instructor, Ross can spice up your walk with some exhilarating ascents. If you're staying in Stellenbosch, the trails (5.3–18km/3.25–11 miles) in the mountainous **Jonkershoek Nature Reserve** are recommended. Recommended reading for hikers: *Day Walks in and Around Cape Town,* by Tim Anderson (Struik), and Mike Lundy's *Best Walks in the Peninsula* (Struik).

HORSEBACK RIDING Take an early-morning or sunset ride on spectacular Long Beach, Noordhoek, by contacting **Sleepy Hollow** (© 021/789-2341; R150–R250/ $22–$37 for 90 min.). For beach rides closer to town, contact **Horse Riders** (© 082/409-9699), in Hout Bay (R150/$22 per hour). To ride among the vines on horseback or in a carriage, stopping for wine tastings, see "Getting Around" in "Franschhoek" and "Stellenbosch," later in this chapter.

MOUNTAIN BIKING There are a number of trails on Table Mountain, Cape Point, and the Winelands, but the Tokai Forest network and Constantiaberg trails are the best; contact **Day Trippers** (© 021/511-4766; R315/$47) for guided rides on the

Constantiaberg and Cape Point; **Downhill Adventures** (✆ **021/422-0388;** www. downhilladventures.com; R350–R550/$52–$82) for guided rides on Table Mountain, Cape Point, and Winelands. Call Bobby (✆ **082/881-1588;** R400/$60 a day; delivery or collection R85/$13) for bike rentals only.

PARAGLIDING   Soar off Lion's Head for a jaw-dropping view of mountains and sea, and land at Camps Bay Beach or La Med bar for cocktails at sunset; another rated flight is over the Franschhoek valley. This is truly an exhilarating trip that will leave you feeling high; no prior experience is necessary (R750/$112). Contact Barry at **Birdmen** (✆ **082/658-6710;** www.birdmen.co.za) or Ian at **Paraglide Cape Town** (✆ **082/727-6584;** www.tandemparagliding.co.za).

SANDBOARDING   South Africa's answer to snowboarding takes place on the tallest dunes all around the Cape; contact **Downhill Adventures** (see above) for trips and tuition (✆ **021/422-0388**).

SKYDIVING   Freefall for up to 30 seconds, attached to an experienced instructor. Tandem dives are offered off the West Coast, some 3,600m (11,808 ft.) over Melkbosstrand; contact **Skydive Cape Town** (✆ **082/800-6290;** www.skydivecapetown.za. net; R1,200/$179).

SURFING   The beaches off Kalk Bay reef and Noordhoek are considered hot spots, but Muizenberg and Big Bay at Blouberg (take R27 Marine Dr. off the N1) are good for beginners; for the daily surf report, call ✆ **082/234-6340. Downhill Adventures** (✆ **021/422-0388**) has a surf school with all equipment provided; if all you need is equipment or advice, call **Matthew Moir** (✆ **083/444-9442**).

WHALE-WATCHING   Hermanus, just over an hour's drive on the N2, is one of the world's best land-based spots (see chapter 5). Call the **Whale Hot Line** (✆ **083/ 910-1028**). For the best whale-watching in the city, drive along the False Bay coast, or contact Evan at **Atlantic Adventures** (✆ **083/680-2768**), which operates trips out of the V&A Waterfront. Contact the **Waterfront Boat Club** (✆ **021/418-5806/5;** www.waterfrontboats.co.za) for trips in Table Bay, departing from the Waterfront.

10 Shopping

You'll find a large selection of shops and hundreds of street hawkers catering to the African arts-and-crafts market; because very little of it is produced locally, however, you pay a slight premium—and, of course, the better the gallery, the larger the premium. Beadwork, however, is a local tradition; a variety of beaded items is for sale at the tourism bureau, also the place to pick up an *Arts & Crafts Map*. But Cape Town shopping now offers a great deal more than naive wooden carvings and beaded trinkets. Sophisticated "Eurocentric" products with superb local twists are finding their way into design-savvy shops all over the world, and, from minimalist handbags made with richly patterned Nguni hides to gorgeous lamps made with polished horn or porcupine quills, you'll find them here, particularly in the De Waterkant area, for far less. For more listings, page through the annual *Time Out Visitor's Guide*. And remember that you are entitled to a 14%VAT refund before you leave.

GREET SHOPPING AREAS
DE WATERKANT

In just 2 years, this area has developed into the most exciting shopping precinct in town, with lovely cobbled streets and a great selection of coffee shops and restaurants.

You could start anywhere, but the main streets are Jarvis and Waterkant and, of course, the Quarter (a cobbled square) itself. Whatever you do, don't miss the **Africa Nova, Fibre Designs,** or **Louise Hennigs** (all details listed below). Also worth a visit are **VEO Gallery,** 8 Jarvis St. (© 021/421-3278), the best of the art galleries here; **Pierre Cronje,** Jarvis House (© 021/421-1249), with top-quality solid timber furniture; and **India Jane,** Waterkant St., selling flowing fabrics in feminine prints.

CITY CENTER

In the heart of the city center, the cobbled **Greenmarket Square** (Mon–Sat 9am–4pm) is brimful of traders selling clothing, crafts, and souvenir or gift items. Weather permitting, it's worth browsing here just for the atmosphere, as well as Church Street's cobbled walkway. To get to the square, walk straight up Shortmarket Street (stop in at **Streetwires** at 77 Shortmarket St. to view the largest selection of wire and bead crafts in the city, or check it out at www.streetwires.co.za). Take your first left onto Long Street for the **Pan African Market,** probably the best place to pick up African crafts in Cape Town (see "Best Buys," below). Follow the flow of the traffic to the pedestrianized section of **Church Street.** Street traders deal in antiques here, and there are a number of interesting shops. Check out the **Cape Gallery,** 60 Church St. (© 021/423-5309), for fine artworks with an emphasis on plant, animal, and birdlife, and **Imagenius,** on the corner of Long and Church sts. (© 021/423-7870), specializing in contemporary South African art and ceramics. **Gilles de Moyencourt,** 54 Church St. (© 021/424-0344), deals in overpriced but interesting Africana and other quirky antiques; the **Collector,** 52 Church St. (© 021/423-1483), trades in the expensive end of what they term "tribal" artifacts and antiques. Don't miss **African Image,** on the corner of Church and Burg (see below), and their cafe, where you can sample a range of coffees from Africa—incidentally, the home of the coffee bean. Art lovers should stop in at **Cape Gallery,** 60 Church St. (© 021/423-5309), and the **Association of Visual Arts,** 35 Church St. (© 021/424-7436).

Keep walking down Church Street to **St George's Mall**—a pedestrian street that runs the length of town. Buskers and street dancers perform here, and a small selection of street hawkers peddle masks and sculptures. For a larger selection, head 1 block down to Adderley Street, cross via the Golden Acre, and browse the station surroundings, where the streets are paved with wood and soapstone carvings. It's also paved with pickpockets, so don't carry valuables here. If you've had your fill of African crafts, head back up to **Long Street** and walk toward the mountain. This is the city's most interesting shopping street—lined with Victorian buildings, Long Street houses antiques shops, galleries, gun shops, porn outlets, hostels, and cafes/bars, as well as Turkish baths. Be on the lookout for **Baobab Mall** (210 Long St.) for more African arts and crafts.

WATERFRONT

Shopping here is a far less satisfying experience than in the bustling streets of town or the gentrified cobbled streets of De Waterkant; at the end of the day, Victoria Wharf is simply a glam shopping center with a nice location. There are, however, a few gems, like **Out of Africa** (next to Exclusive Bookshop), for a fantastic, albeit pricey, range of items from all over the continent. And if you're looking for a dress or shirt that will really make heads turn—we're talking uniquely African designer wear—head straight upstairs for **Sun Goddess** (© 021/421-7620). Outside the shopping center, in the old offices of the Port Captain (on the way to the Clocktower), is the truly excellent selection of sculptures, jewelry, tableware, textiles, ceramics, and furniture at the **African Trading Post,** Pierhead, Dock Road ((©) 021/419-5364; www.atp.co.za); spread over three stories, this is worth a visit even if you're not buying.

BEST BUYS

SOUVENIRS & GIFTS FROM AFRICA

Africa Nova Arguably the best of its kind, this large selection of contemporary handmade African goods has been chosen by someone with a real eye; it's where craft really starts to meet art. Best of all, it's located on the cobbled Cape Quarter square, right next to Andiamo deli. 72 Waterkant St. (©) 021/425-5123.

African Image This store offers a well-chosen selection of authentic crafts and tribal art ranging from headrests and baskets to beadwork and cloth. Church St. (©) 021/423-8385.

Amulet Goldsmiths Add value to the world's safest investment by commissioning Gerika and Elizabeth, the city's most talented duo, to make a contemporary jewelry item (or simply pick one up at their studio). 14 Kloofnek Rd., Tamboerskloof. (©) 021/426-1149.

A.R.T. Gallery This gallery sells brightly hued African-motif tableware, created by popular ceramist Clementina van der Walt, as well as a selection of textiles, woodwork, baskets, and ceramics created by up-and-coming local artists. Main Rd., Kalk Bay. (©) 021/788-8718.

Heartworks It's more of a crafts showcase, but items here are chosen with a modern design slant; look for beautiful ceramics and bead- and wirework. Gardens Centre, Mill St. (©) 021/465-3289 (satellite store on Kloof St.).

Louise Hennigs Louise has a real passion for quality leather (zebra, Nguni, snake, ostrich), and a classic design approach. Her tiny shop in trendy De Waterkant is filled with handcrafted leather accessories (the most beautiful Nguni bags ever made), as well as a few choice artworks by friends. Sadly, she may move; viewing will then be by appointment only. 13 Jarvis St. (©) 082/423-9394. lhennigs@mweb.co.za.

Pan African Market Three stories of rooms overflow with goods from all over Africa, from tin picture frames to large, intricate carvings and beautiful pieces of beadwork. There's also a small cafe with traditional food on the first-floor balcony. 76 Long St. (©) 021/426-4478.

Philani Flagship Printing Project Vibrant hand-painted textiles created by a group of Xhosa women whose training was funded by the Department of Welfare. Choose among various designs, made into T-shirts, scatter pillows, wall-hangings, placemats, aprons, cards, and oven mitts. 5 Old Klipfontein Rd., Crossroads. (©) 021/374-9160.

Vlisco This shop has the widest range of vibrant traditional African fabrics, as well as clothing, like the shirts made popular by Mandela. 45 Castle St. (diagonally opposite Cape Town Tourism in town). (©) 021/423-2461.

SOPHISTICATED AFRICAN INTERIOR DESIGN

African Light & Trading Mix together a sophisticated design eye, an obsession with luxury materials, and a large dose of playfulness, and you might just come up with one of the wonderful furniture items produced by Trevor Dykman. Using his trademark *shagreen* (the skin of the sand shark, in wonderful colors), mirror, leather, chrome, fur, lacquer, walnut-wenge, and maple-veneer, he consistently produces the kind of object that sets an entire room apart. Upper Canterbury St., City Center. (©) 021/462-1490. www.altrad.co.za.

The Great Gay EsCape

Cape Town has become one of the great international gay destinations—like sister cities San Francisco, Sydney, and Miami, this is a sexy seaside spot, with a variety of queer things to do. Promoted as "The Gay Capital of Africa" (South Africa's constitution is the only one in the world to expressly protect the rights of homosexuals), Cape Town's queer tribes are rich and varied, with different events and venues catering to their needs. The international stereotypical GWM (gay white male) subculture exists here as elsewhere, with a mix of muscle men, fashion victims, fitness freaks, and a handful of drag queens. Local lesbian life is more low-key—more along the lines of ceramics classes and having meetings about making documentaries about women.

Most gay-friendly venues are situated in and around the City Bowl, particularly the "De Waterkant Queer Quarter" in Green Point, Sea Point's Main Road, and the mountain end of Long Street. The "De Waterkant Queer Quarter"—west of the city in Green Point, centered on Somerset Road and running up the slopes of Signal Hill to Loader Street—is where you'll find the best selection of clubs, bars, bathhouses, cafes, and guesthouses. Check the local press, *The Pink Map,* or visit www.cape-town.org for more information. **Wanderwomen** (© **021/788-9988;** www.wanderwomen. co.za) is a personalized women's-only travel agent.

A GAY NIGHT OUT   Traveling from town to Green Point, the first stop worth considering is the buzzy **Manhattans,** 74 Waterkant, corner of Dixon (© **021/421-6666**), a friendly, chatty bar with a good-value restaurant, which gets busy after 9pm nightly. (Sun roast specials are also recommended.) Farther along is **Village Café,** corner of Napier and Waterkant streets (© **021/421-0632**), a charming little coffee shop/restaurant, good for a breakfast or daytime relax; just down the road is the more trendy **Dutch.** You can walk from here to Somerset Road, where you'll find **Bronx,** corner Napier and Somerset Road (© **021/419-9216**), a very popular late-night bar with an entertaining dance floor; open from 9pm to 4am nightly, with different events (like karaoke on Mon). Currently, the sexiest club is **Sliver and Sliver Upstairs,** 27 Somerset (© **021/421-4799**), playing funky house Tuesday to Sunday. **Bar Code,** 18 Cobern St., off Somerset (© **021/421-5305**) is a men's-only leather cruise bar—ask at the bar about the underwear parties and leather nights. Still in the same area, but getting steamier, the **Hot House,** 18 Jarvis St. (© **021/418-3888**) is a European-style men's-only leisure club, with sauna, steam room, and outdoor sun deck with spectacular views over the city and the harbor.

Colonial House Design   Another interior shop producing wonderful furniture and accessories with a unique African twist—a one-stop shop if you're looking to furnish an upmarket game lodge. Shop A17 Cape Quarter, De Waterkant. © 021/421-1467. www.colonial house.co.za.

Back in town you'll find **On Broadway,** 88 Shortmarket St. (✆ 021/418-8338), a great cabaret and theater restaurant, with excellent shows (in summer season, book early for *Mince,* featuring some of South Africa's best female impersonators). Moving to Long Street, **Lola's,** corner of Long and Buiten (✆ 021/423-0885), is the queerest vegetarian joint in town, with an Afro-trash crowd and slip-sexy music. Just around the corner, on Loop Street, are **Madame Zingara** and **Cara Lazuli** (✆ 021/426-2458)—these cozy, exotic restaurants are a delight and most welcoming to new visitors.

BEST BEACHES Clifton's **Third Beach** is where you'll find international male models parading in garments so tight you can tell what religion they are. **Sandy Bay** is Cape Town's nudist beach, with discreet cruising at the far end of the main beach. But beware: The freezing ocean will bring you down to size.

GAY EVENTS Cape Town's biggest queer celebration and Africa's biggest gay circuit party is the annual **MCQP Costume Party,** held during the MCQP Festival. It's a massive fancy-dress costume ball held at great venues (2002 was at the Castle, the oldest building in Cape Town and still the regional HQ of the S.A. Defense Force!) and attended by thousands of queers of all ages and persuasions, with some 10 dance floors playing a rich variety of music. A new theme is explored each year. (For details, go online at www.mcqp.co.za.) Also worth planning around is the **Pink Loerie Festival,** held at the end of May, when some 5,000 camp revelers take to the streets of Knysna, on the Garden Route—a welcome extension to a trip to Cape Town, with plenty of gay-friendly places to stay along the way. Call ✆ 044/386-0011.

RECOMMENDED GUESTHOUSES There are a variety of options to be had in **De Waterkant Village** (see "Where to Stay," earlier in this chapter), which is situated in the heart of the Queer Quarter, within easy walking distance of clubs and bars. **Amsterdam Guest House,** 19 Forest Rd. (✆ 021/461-8236; www.amsterdam.co.za), is an extremely popular men's-only guesthouse situated on the slopes of the city, with a pool, Jacuzzi, sauna, and the like. **Parker Cottage,** Carstens, Tamboerskloof (✆ 021/424-6445; www.parker cottage.co.za), is a neat, graciously decorated Victorian home away from home that will suit the older traveler. Alternatively, you can peruse the options listed earlier in the book, all of which are gay-friendly.

—*Andre Vorster, Cape Town's most celeb queen and "mother"*
of MCQP (Mother City Queer Projects)

Fibre Designs The best carpet shop on the continent, with the most exciting designs, in wonderful color combinations. You'd be hard-pressed to find any of the items anywhere else in the world. This is a perfect global match, with carpets designed in Africa and woven by master weavers in the East. 3 Jarvis St., De Waterkant. ✆ 021/418-1054. www.fibredesigns.co.za.

LIM   This tiny shop produces some of the city's best examples of home-grown simple, modern furniture and accessories, be it an asymmetrical Mozambican vase, a paper-thin Shapiro salad bowl, or a leather cube footrest. 86a Kloof St. ✆ 021/423-1200.

FINE ART
The Bell-Roberts Gallery   Host to regular, interesting exhibitions by up-and-coming artists. 199 Loop St. ✆ 021/422-1100.

Erdmann Contemporary   Heidi Erdmann has a real knack for unearthing new talent; she's also the agent for Conrad Botes, one of South Africa's best exports, and very affordable here. 63 Shortmarket St. ✆ 021/422-2762.

Everard Read Gallery   For one of the best selections of South African art, particularly African landscapes and wildlife paintings, this is your best bet—be warned, though: You won't find a bargain here. 3 Portswood Rd, Waterfront. ✆ 021/418-4527.

Joào Ferreira Gallery   Also a good bet for contemporary works by artists like William Kentridge—whose video work *History of the Main Complaint* has a room all to its own in the Tate Modern in London—which Joào both exhibits and sources. 80 Hout St. ✆ 021/423-5403.

FOOD
Andiamo   The best deli in town, with a huge selection of imported goodies but plenty of local produce, too. Cape Quarter. ✆ 021/421-3687.

Atlas Trading Co.   Re-create the mild, slightly sweet curry flavors of Cape Malay dishes back home by purchasing a bag of mixed spices from the Ahmed family, proprietors of Atlas. 94 Wale St. ✆ 021/423-4361.

Joubert & Monty   This is one of the best places to sample good biltong; try a bit of kudu and beef—ask for the latter to be slightly moist and sliced. Waterfront. ✆ 021/418-0640.

WINE
Caroline's Fine Wine Cellar   Caroline has an exceptional nose for finding those out-of-the way gems most Capetonians, let alone visitors, simply don't have the time or know-how to track down. Arguably the best wine shop in Cape Town. V&A Waterfront. ✆ 021/425-5701. Also at 15 Long St. (✆ 021/419-8984).

Steven Rom   This liquor merchant has a large selection in stock but will also track down and order anything you request (even once you're home) and arrange freighting. Galleria Centre, 76 Regent Rd., Sea Point. ✆ 021/439-6043. www.winecellar.co.za.

11 Cape Town After Dark

Pick up a copy of the monthly *Cape etc.* or the annual *Time Out* magazine. Alternatively, the weekly *Mail & Guardian* covers all major events, as does the local daily *The Argus*—look in the "Tonight" section, or Friday's insert "Top of the Times" in the *Cape Times.* You can book tickets to theaters and movies and most major music/party events by calling **Computicket** (✆ **083/915-8000;** www.computicket.co.za) and supplying your credit card details.

THE PERFORMING ARTS
Critics in the Mother City, as elsewhere, pull no punches, so watch the press. Anything directed or produced by Martinus Basson or Mark Fleischman is not to be

missed. In summer, take in one of the outdoor concerts (see below). Take a look at what's on at the city's **ARTscape Theatre** (© 021/421-7839) or **Baxter Theatre,** Main Road, Rondebosch (© 021/685-7880). If you like your entertainment light, the **Theatre on the Bay,** Camps Bay (© 021/438-3301) hosts a frothy mix of comedies and farces, **On Broadway,** Shortmarket Street (© 021/418-8338), is the city's best cabaret venue, and the **Independent Armchair Theatre,** Lower Main Road, Observatory (© 021/447-1514; www.armchairtheatre.co.za), is a lounge-style theater that hosts an irregular, cult-variety selection of offbeat comedy shows.

OUTDOOR CONCERTS

Summer brings a wealth of fantastic outdoor concerts; tops for venue are the Sunday **Kirstenbosch Summer Concerts** (© 021/799-8783, or 021/761-4916 weekends): Bring a picnic and relax to great music, from jazz bands to Cape Minstrel troupes, popular acoustic groups to the Philharmonic Orchestra, while the sun sets behind the mountain. Concerts start at around 5pm, but get there early in order to secure your patch of lawn. **Maynardville Open Air Theatre,** Church and Wolf streets, Wynberg, hosts an annual Shakespeare play against a lush forested backdrop—performances vary from year to year but invariably put a contemporary spin on the Bard. Free concerts are held at the **V&A Waterfront Amphitheatre** (© 021/408-7600); acts range from winners of school talent contests to good jazz. It's worth taking the 30-minute drive to Stellenbosch, where you can choose between the lineup at **Oude Libertas Amphitheatre,** Adam Tas Road (© 021/809-7473), and the generally superior **Spier Summer Festival,** Spier Wine Estate (© 021/809-1158; www.spier.co.za), which serves up local and international opera, theater, and music acts. Note that you can catch a steam train to Spier from the Waterfront, and make a night of it by dining at Moyo, their Pan-African restaurant.

THE CLUB, BAR & MUSIC SCENE

During the summer season, Cape Town becomes one big party venue. Get into the mood with sundowners at a trendy bar in Camps Bay (see "Where to Dine: Atlantic Seaboard: The Sunset Strip," earlier in this chapter) or with a bottle of bubbly on a well-situated beach (though, strictly speaking, this is illegal, so be discreet) or the top of Table Mountain. You will, however, want to pace yourself—getting to *any* party before 11pm will see you counting barstools. Listings below were hip at press time, but like most cities, sell-by dates are unpredictable. To play it safe, expect good nights out from Wednesday onwards, and head for one of the following two areas: **Long Street,** particularly the mountain end (near the Turkish Baths), is the central city's hot party area. Here the best bar by far is **Jo'burg,** frequented by a self-styled selection of hipster trendies, and owned by local character Bruce Gordon—he's the one with the barcode tattooed on his arm, done in 2003 when he was exhibited as an artwork at the National Gallery. Next door (well almost) is **Lola's** (© 021/423-0885), a casual corner cafe that attracts an eclectic mélange of gay, bohemian, and backpacker types; across the road, single-malt devotees frequent the plush leather settees of **Kennedy's Cigar Bar** (© 021/424-1212). The other big party strip, catering to a (generally speaking) older, more sophisticated audience, is in Green Point, once known as Cape Town's "Gay Quarter," but now simply the Cape Quarter.

Note that **Lower Main Road** in Observatory, Cape Town's "bohemian" suburb, is another good place to hang out if you're into a grungier atmosphere—from **Café Ganesh** (© 021/448-3435) to over-the-top baroque **Touch of Madness** (© 021/448-2266).

LIVE MUSIC

It's off the beaten tourist track, but you can catch regular Cape jazz sessions featuring hot artists like pianist Hotep Galeta and guitarist Alvin Dyers at **West End,** College Road, Athlone (© 021/637-9132). The **Green Dolphin Restaurant** at the V&A Waterfront (© 021/421-7471) caters to the supper-club jazz enthusiast, attracting a good lineup of local and international performers (the food is pretty mediocre and pricey). **Manenberg's Jazz Café** at the Clock Tower Precinct, V&A Waterfront (© 021/421-5639), serves up an array of jazz flavors geared toward the tourist trade. **CD Wherehouse,** V&A Waterfront (© 021/425-6300), South Africa's finest specialist music store, sometimes showcases in-store performances; call for times, or pop in to purchase a good selection. (The **African Music Store,** 134 Long St., is incidentally another good place to purchase African music.) Back in town, **Mercury Live** is hardly the most slick or sophisticated venue, but it's still the only place in the city where you'll find a regular lineup of original South African bands. Downstairs at the broom-cupboard-size **Mercury Lounge,** 43 de Villiers St., Zonnebloem (© 021/465-2106; www.mercuryl.co.za), you can catch a cutting-edge selection of up-and-coming local acts.

CLUBS

Bossa Nova 🎭🎭 Looking to shake that newly suntanned kaboos? Bossa Nova plays the best Latin dance music and jazz. Also good for sundowner cigars on the balcony—ah, another tough day in Africa. 43 Somerset Rd., Greenpoint. © 021/425 0295.

Bronx 🎭🎭🎭 Two levels of dance floor and all the characters you'd expect at Cape Town's most established gay club. Very straight friendly, this is undoubtedly still one of the better parties on a Friday or Saturday night. 35 Somerset Rd., Greenpoint. © 021/419-9216.

Dockside The biggest club in South Africa, Dockside is more like a mall with 5 dance floors and 14 bars with every type of music, from jazz, commercial house, '80s, and even some karaoke. It's big and not always pretty, but the sound and lighting system puts others to shame. Century City Blvd. © 021/552-7303.

The Fez 🎭🎭 The Fez faithful who flock to one of Cape Town's oldest clubs seem to get younger every year. The dance floor is always full, but the Moroccan-themed VIP area upstairs is much cooler. Still one of the best places to dance all night. Themed nights specialize in African house and hip-hop. 38 Hout St., Central City. © 021/423-1456.

Galaxy 🎭🎭🎭 The home of the local radio station's Goodhope FM's big parties and a favorite with the coloured community, this is off the tourist track. Expect to sweat a lot, unless it's a famous Galaxy foam party. A great place to party with a lot of bumping and grinding into the wee hours to the sounds of house, R&B, hip-hop, and live music. College Rd., Rylands Estate, Athlone. © 021/637-9132.

Hemisphere 🎭🎭🎭 Located on the 31st floor in the Cape Town CBD, this club has fantastic views of the Mother City and Table Mountain. Lounges lead into dance floors, which lead into bars, but the excellent soul and funk music will keep you under the glitter ball all night. Get there early; the elevator is slow. Riebeeck St. © 021/421-0581.

Mink 🎭🎭 New Cape club Mink combines simple and elegant decor with fab lighting to create the most sophisticated atmosphere in Cape Town. The cocktail menu is designed by S.A.'s top barman, so save space to sample a few bites. 24 Shortmarket St., CBD. © 021/422-3262.

169 on Long ★★   One big dance floor and a balcony overlooking Long St[ ]is perpetually crowded with people. It's a hot spot on the CBD's club street strip[ ]features a very mixed crowd. Regular weekday parties and special events include de[ ]house and hip-hop nights. 169 Long St. ℂ 021/426-1107.

Opium ★★★   In the heart of the De Waterkant clubbing area, Opium is the hottest place to spot Cape Town's globe-trotting models, sip cocktails, and boogie the night away to some funky house music. Even if you're not into beautiful people, come for the big dance floors and relaxed vibe. 6 Dixon St., De Waterkant. ℂ 021/425-4010.

Purgatory ★★   Also located in De Waterkant, Purgatory is Cape Town's answer to a '40s supper club, and offers a more exclusive vibe; if it's not pumping, simply step into neighboring Opium. 8 Dixon St., De Waterkant. ℂ 021/421-7464.

Rhodes House ★★★   Situated in one of Cape Town's historic mansions, well-dressed Rhodes House has for many years been regarded as *the* place to be seen in Cape Town. Still seriously stylish, this multiroomed venue is great for checking out the rich and famous, and the gorgeous models that attend to them. 60 Queen Victoria St., Gardens. ℂ 021/424-8844.

BARS

Alba.Lounge ★★   The classiest lounge-bar in the Waterfront, this waterside venue is unpretentious and comfortable; even children are welcome here. It's the perfect place to unwind after a full day's shopping or before wandering to a Waterfront restaurant. Pierhead, V&A. ℂ 021/425-3385.

Asoka ★★   A favorite with the inner-city "boho" set, this intimate Balinese-styled venue, complete with comfy seating in a courtyard centered on an old tree, is apparently steeped in feng shui. Whatever the reason, it attracts a cool mix. 68 Kloof St. ℂ 021/422-0909.

Baraza ★★   This funky bar with great elevated views of Camps Bay's palm-fringed beach still pulls a crowd who lounge around sipping cocktails and watching the sun go down. The Promenade, Victoria Rd., Camps Bay. ℂ 021/438-1758.

Bascule ★   A tiny whiskey bar and wine cellar situated on the edge of the yacht marina. Wednesday and Friday are when the city's singles come to prowl—nights to avoid. Cape Grace Hotel, V&A Waterfront. ℂ 021/410-7100.

Buena Vista Social Café ★★   This small Cuban-themed cafe is the ideal spot to enjoy laid-back jazz flavors and the best mojitos in town. Main Rd., Green Point. ℂ 021/433-0611.

Eclipse ★★★   Situated on the beachfront of renowned Camp's Bay, Eclipse has a small dance floor, a busy bar, and a large balcony overlooking the picture-perfect sunset and beach. The cocktails (made with fresh fruit) are superb; weekends can get very crowded. Victoria Rd., Camps Bay. ℂ 021/438-0883.

Po Na Na Souk ★★★   End your day in an inner-city oasis where you can slowly sip a cocktail as you relax on a balcony overlooking the historic Heritage Square courtyard or cozy up with cushions in a fully winterized indoor area. A great place to people-watch. Heritage Sq., 100 Shortmarket St., City Center. ℂ 021/423-4889.

EVENTS

MCQP ★★★   More than just an excuse to party in a funny frock, Cape Town's "Mother City Queer Party" has mushroomed from an annual gala costume party to a party in up to 10 different party zones. Venue changes annually. .co.za.

tival 🏵🏵🏵   Local and international artists combine in S.A.'s elebrating its fifth year in 2005, the Jazz Festival attracts thou- around South Africa and abroad for the huge variety of differ- varieties. Check the schedules closer to the time and be ready for plenty of crowds. www.nsjfcapetown.co.za.

J&B Met   It's a horse race, but no one really watches the ponies. As one of the biggest events of the Cape Town social calendar, the J&B Met attracts the cream of S.A.'s best-dressed celebrities (and a few clots, too). www.jbmet.co.za.

12 The Winelands

South Africa has 13 designated wine routes, of which the area called the Winelands— comprising the routes of Helderberg (Somerset West), Stellenbosch, Paarl, and Fran- schhoek—is by far the most popular. While the towns are all within easy driving distance from each other, there are over 250 estates and farms to choose from, and first-time visitors are advised to concentrate on those that offer a combination of his- toric architecture, excellent wines, and/or views of the vineyard-clad mountains. True oenophiles should refer to the box "Selecting Your Cape Wines," later in this chapter, and spend the day with an expert who can tailor-make your tour to suit your specific interests (see "Exploring the Winelands," below). You can treat the Winelands as an excursion from Cape Town or base yourself here—no more than 30 to 75 minutes from the bright lights of the city, this is a great area to immerse yourself in rural peace and fine wines. Accommodations options are also excellent, with many offering bet- ter value than their Cape Town counterparts. If you have time to concentrate on only one area, make it Franschhoek, the prettiest (though most touristy) of the Winelands valleys, with the best selection of award-winning restaurants; or Stellenbosch, which has a charming historic center and the densest concentration of estates—this is also the area that produces (by general consensus) the best selection of wines. Both are within easy driving distance of one another, via the scenic Helshoogte Pass.

EXPLORING THE WINELANDS

This is a large, mountainous area, and you're best off exploring it by car so that you can choose your own estates and pace. Don't try to cover the entire Winelands in a day; tackle no more than four to six estates a day, and don't forget to book a luncheon table with a vineyard view. If you're serious about your wine, take a personalized guided tour with a specialist (tours offered by large companies or prearranged by the Wine Desk tend to focus on large producers). For tailor-made trips into selected and often lesser- known cellars, accompanied by a true wine lover, you can't beat a tour with **Stephen Flesch.** Former chairman of the Wine Tasters Guild of S.A., Stephen personally knows many of the winemakers and proprietors of the top wine estates, and has a thorough knowledge of South African wines that spans 4 decades. He will take into account your particular interests or preferences, and tailor a personalized itinerary, including a delightful lunch at a restaurant or estate (he is, after all, secretary of Cape Town's Slow Food Convivium). Rates are R1,100 ($164) per day per person double, R450 ($67) extra for each additional person (half-day starts at R750/$112). You can contact him at 📞 **021/705-4317,** but it's advisable to book well in advance by e-mailing him at sflesch@iafrica.com. If Stephen is unavailable, **Keith van der Schyff**

The Winelands

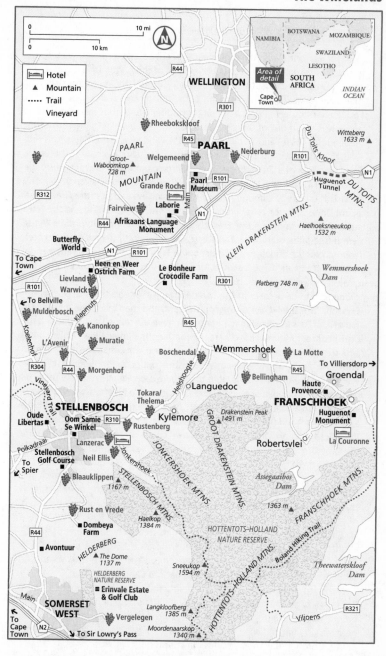

Three Dramatic Wineland Drives

Wines seem to thrive in the most beautiful environments. If you want to see as much of the landscape as possible, try one of these **Wineland drives** for a terrific—and breathtaking—overview of the region. Traversing four mountain ranges and encompassing both Franschhoek and Stellenbosch, the **Four Passes Route** will take a full day, including a few stops for wine tastings and lunch. Head out of the city center on the N2, bypassing the turnoff for Stellenbosch (R310) and Somerset West (R44), and ascend the Hottentots Holland Mountains via **Sir Lowry's Pass,** with breathtaking views of the entire False Bay. Take the Franschhoek and Villiersdorp turnoff, traveling through the town of Grabouw, and traverse the Groenland Mountains via **Viljoen's Pass.** This takes you through fruit-producing valleys and past the Theewaterskloof Dam. Look for a right turn marked Franschhoek, and ascend the Franschhoek Mountains via the **Franschhoek Pass** , stopping at La Petite Ferme (see later in this chapter) for tea or lunch with a view. Drive to Stellenbosch via the equally scenic **Helshoogte Pass** , stopping at Boschendal to tour the historic Cape Dutch Manor House. Take the R310 back to the N2, or overnight in Stellenbosch.

The second drive takes in the Breede River Valley and the historic town of Tulbagh. Take the N1 out of town, past Paarl, and then tackle the majestic **Du Toit's Kloof Pass** (if you've made a late start, take the tunnel). Once through the Du Toit's Kloof Mountains, you are approaching the Breede River Valley, a less publicized wine-producing region, but no less attractive than the more famous Winelands areas, and producing wines with a distinctive berry flavor. Keep an eye out for the turnoff to the right marked Rawsonville, then follow the signs north (left) to Goudini Spa and **Slanghoek** ; stop here to taste the award-winning Noble Late Harvest. This scenic back road meets the R43 in a T-junction—turn left and follow the signs to the small town of Wolseley before taking the R46 to Tulbagh. Once there, stroll down charming Church Street to admire the Cape Dutch and Victorian buildings, perfectly restored after an earthquake damaged them in 1969, and lunch at **Paddagang** (© **023/230-0242**): Their traditional *waterblommetjie bredie* (waterlily stew) is delicious. After lunch you might want to sample one of the Tulbagh Estate's wines before overnighting at **Hunters** (© **023/230-0582**; R500–R540/$75–$81 double, depending on season). Alternatively, head back to Wolseley, this time taking the R303 to Wellington via **Bain's Kloof Pass** , a spectacular pass created by the father of the celebrated master engineer responsible for the Swartberg Pass outside Oudtshoorn. From Wellington, follow the signs to Paarl or Franschhoek, where you could overnight, or head for the N1 and back to Cape Town.

The third drive, another full day, takes you along the dramatic **Coastal Route** to Hermanus, snaking along cliffs that plunge into the ocean, before turning off to sample the wines growing in the Hemel en Aarde (Heaven and Earth) valley. For more details on this drive, see "The Coastal Route: Gordon's Bay to Hermanus" in chapter 5.

((C) 082/443-6480), based in Stellenbosch, is also highly recommended, as much for his discreet company as his wine knowledge.

If you prefer the idea of a self-drive tour, then purchase a copy of *John Platter's South African Wines* (or visit www.platteronline.com before you leave)—updated annually and now in its 25th printing, it's still the best in the business. The definitive guide to wine in South Africa not only lists each of the 974 producers and their wines, but provides star ratings, and though the writers are careful not to say anything nasty, you very quickly learn to read between the lines. Alternatively, read the box "Selecting Your Cape Wines," below, written by the editor of the Platter guide, and work your way through his suggestions!

Note: Even though the majority of wine estates accept credit cards for wine purchases, you should keep some cash on hand—most estates charge a fee (R5–R25/75¢–$3.75 per person) for a wine-tasting session.

STELLENBOSCH

46km (29 miles) E of Cape Town

The charming town of Stellenbosch was founded in 1679 by Gov. Simon van der Stel, who, among other achievements, built Groot Constantia and planted hundreds of oak trees throughout the Cape. Today Stellenbosch is, in fact, known informally as Eikestad, or "City of Oaks." The beautifully restored and oak-lined streetscapes of **Dorp, Church,** and **Drosdty** make Stellenbosch the most historic of the Winelands towns (it has the largest number of Cape Dutch houses in the region), but outside of the historic center much is suburban sprawl. But this is also a university town, site of the country's most prestigious Afrikaans university, with attendant coffee shops and student bars, and it also promotes itself as the cultural center of the Cape, with a number of great theater options. Contact the Tourism Bureau to find out what's on at the open-air amphitheaters at **Oude Libertas** and **Spier.**

ESSENTIALS

VISITOR INFORMATION Stellenbosch Tourism Bureau ((C) 021/883-3584; www.stellenboschtourism.co.za) is by far the most helpful in the Winelands, and you'd be well advised to head to their office as soon as you arrive—besides giving expert advice on where to stay and what to do, they provide the excellent "Discover Stellenbosch on Foot" leaflet (R3/45¢), which indicates more than 60 historical sites with accompanying text. The Tourism Bureau is located at 36 Market St. (summer hours Mon–Fri 8am–6pm, Sat 9am–5pm, Sun 10am–4pm; winter hours Mon–Fri 9am–5pm, Sat 9:30am–4:30pm, Sun 10am–4pm). Adjacent is the **Adventure Centre** ((C) 021/882-8114; www.adventure shop.co.za), which lists a huge variety of activities in the region.

GETTING AROUND   In Town   Guided walking tours (90 min.) leave the Tourist Bureau every day at 10am and 3pm. For historic and twilight walks in town at a time that's convenient for you, contact **Sandra Krige** ((C) 021/883-9633; hkrige@ iafrica.com). The town center is small enough to explore on foot, but you can rent a bicycle from **Piet se Fiets** ((C) 021/887-3042; R15/$2.25 per hour, R65/$9.70 per day).

To Wine Estates   See "Exploring the Winelands," above, for specialist tours and self-drive tips. Note that if you don't want to drive, you can visit five Stellenbosch wine estates by using the hop-on, hop-off **Vinehopper bus** ((C) 021/882-8112; R135/$20 per person) To explore the Spier estate on horseback, contact **Horse Rides at Spier** ((C) 021/881-3683).

EN ROUTE TO STELLENBOSCH FROM CAPE TOWN

Vergenoegd ★★★ opened the doors of its old Cape Dutch homestead to the public at the end of 2003—great news for red-wine lovers; in fact, the combination of superbly smooth red wines and the gorgeous setting make this quite possibly my favorite estate in the Winelands, so don't miss it (© **021/843-3248;** Mon–Fri 8am–5pm, Sat 9:30am–12:30pm).

Vergelegen ★★★ (© **021/847-1334;** daily 9:30am–4pm; call for tour times) is the other must-see estate on the Somerset West or "Helderberg" Wine Route, which lies a few miles from Stellenbosch. Vergelegen (Far Location) was built by reprobate Willem Adriaan van der Stel, who took over from his father as governor of the Cape in 1699, only to abuse his power by building Vergelegen on land that did not actually belong to him and by using the Dutch East India Company slaves and resources to compete with local farmers. He was sacked in 1707 and the farm demolished and divided. Today this beautifully restored wine estate, surrounded by gorgeous gardens, is known to be Mandela's favorite, as well as the only one to host Queen Elizabeth II and the Clintons during their respective state visits. The estate restaurant, the **Lady Phillips** (© **021/847-1348**), serves excellent meals in a wonderful atmosphere; in summer the **Rose Terrace,** an alfresco venue, is the place to sample a glass of estate wine with a sandwich or quiche. There is a R10 ($1.50) entry fee; cellar tours are a further R10 ($1.50); wine tasting (Mon–Sat) from R5 (75¢).

To get to Stellenbosch from here (some 20 min. away), head back to the R44 and turn right (at the Lord Charles Hotel). Red-wine lovers are advised to look out for the sign to **Rust en Vrede (Rest and Peace)** ★★★ along the way—turn right onto Annandale Road to sample these raunchy reds (© **021/881-3881;** Mon–Fri 9am–5pm, Sat 9am–4pm in season). Families should turn left and head for **Spier** (© **021/809-1100;** daily 9am–5pm; you can assemble your own picnic at their deli). Among the many activities on offer at Spier are scenic horseback rides through the estate's vineyards, as well as an outdoor activity center; their Cheetah Conservancy, where you can see these slinky creatures up close, is also very popular. A little farther along the R44 is the turnoff for **Blaauwklippen** (© **021/880-0133;** Mon–Fri 9am–4:45pm, Sat 9am–4pm), where from October 1 to April 30 you can take a coach ride through the vineyards (call ahead to book); also look for the delightful **Waterford**—a wonderful example of the Cape's love affair with Tuscany (© **021/880-0496**).

WHAT TO SEE & DO IN TOWN

If you have time for only one historic stop in town, make it the **Village Museum** ★★★, 18 Ryneveld St. (© **021/887-2902;** Mon–Sat 9am–5pm, Sun 2–5pm; admission R15/$2.25), which comprises the Schreuderhuis Cottage (1709), the Cape Dutch Blettermanhuis (1789), the Georgian Grosvenor House (1803), and the Victorian Murray House (1850). Each house has a guide done up in period dress, and the artful styling of the furniture, combined with the accessible explanations on the architecture and fashion of these eras, make these the best house museums in the country.

From here head south along Drosdty Street, turn right onto Dorp Street, and then stroll down the oak-dappled street to **Oom Samie Se Winkel** ★ (© **021/887-2612;** 9am–5:30pm weekdays, 9am–5pm weekends, till 6pm in summer), a Victorian-style general dealer bursting at the seams with knickknacks, and a great place to pick up souvenirs, such as step-by-step *bobotie* spice packs, dried-fruit rolls, and dirt-cheap enamel plates. It has a charming tearoom, complete with sunning cats and clucking chickens, behind the shop.

THE STELLENBOSCH WINE ROUTE

This is the oldest in the country, with more than 100 estates and farms to choose from, almost all of which are reached via the three major roads radiating from the town center. Note that it's worth double-checking opening times if you're traveling over the weekend. If you head southwest on the R306, you should consider visiting the 300-year-old **Neethlingshof** (℃ **021/883-8988;** Mon–Fri 9am–5pm, Sat–Sun 10am–4pm; in high season [Aug–Jan] hours are extended) just for the pleasure of driving up its gracious pine-lined avenue—once there, however, you may find the experience relatively commercial, though it's worth it to taste their Noble Late Harvest. To reach **Zevenwacht** (℃ **021/903-5123;** Mon–Fri 8am–5pm, Sat–Sun 9:30am–5pm)— one of the prettiest wine estates in the country, with a manor house on the edge of a tranquil lake and views all the way to the ocean—take the M12 to Kuilsriver.

Most of the wine estates are located off the R44, which runs north to Paarl. First stop should be the beautiful **Morgenhof** to sample the merlot and chardonnay (℃ **021/889-5510;** Mon–Fri 9am–4:30pm, Sat–Sun 10am–5pm; Nov–Apr hours extend to 5pm), followed by **L'Avenir** (℃ **021/889-5001;** Mon-Sat 9am–5pm) to try the Pinotage. The turnoff for tiny **Muratie,** still one of the most noncommercial estates, is next. This is a must if you like port (beware—the nonvintage is as easy to drink as grape juice!) and berry-rich red wines (℃ **021/865-2330;** Mon–Fri 9am–5pm, Sat–Sun 10am–4pm). Muratie is followed by **Kanonkop** (℃ **021/884-4656**), famous for its reds; the equally acclaimed **Warwick** (℃ **021/884-4410**); and **Le Bonheur** (℃ **021/875-5478**)—all on the road to Paarl.

Some of the best estates on the Stellenbosch wine route are located on the Helshoogte Pass, which links Stellenbosch with Franschhoek; see "Stellenbosch to Franschhoek: The Helshoogte Pass," below, for recommendations.

Fun Fact Drinking with a Conscience

A decade after the transition to democracy, our wine industry is still grappling with how to redress the economic and social injustices resulting from apartheid-era policies, such as the lack of land ownership by blacks and "coloureds," the shortage of qualified black winemakers and viticulturists, widespread unemployment, and rampant alcohol abuse. Significant change is in progress, however, through macro-initiatives such as the **Wine Industry Transformation Charter,** being finalized at press time under the auspices of a Black Economic Empowerment (BEE) Steering Committee. Integral to the charter will be a scorecard, in which wine industry participants will accumulate points commensurate with their performance in such key areas as equity, asset ownership, land reform, shareholding, skills development, procurement practices, and more. Broader developments such as these should bolster the individual transformative efforts of those like **New Beginnings** (℃ 021/863-8612), the first black-owned wine farm in the country. Subsequent empowerment efforts worth noting are **Thandi Wines** (℃ 021/886-6458), **Reyneke Wines** (℃ 021/881-3517), **Bouwland** (℃ 021/865-2135), **Van Loveren** (℃ 023/615-1505), and **Buthelezi Wines** (℃ 021/461-9590). A powerful behind-the-scenes influence, and a vintner in his own right, is urbane Jabulani Ntshangase of **Thabani Wines** (℃ 021/883-9640).

Finally, if you're tired of tasting wine, take the 10km (6¼-mile) circular drive through the **Jonkershoek Nature Reserve,** stopping for lunch at **Lanzerac**—ask for a map from the Tourism Bureau. This is also where you'll find **Neil Ellis** (✆ **021/ 887-0649;** Mon–Fri 9:30am–4:30pm, Sat 10am–2pm), another estate producing superb wines.

WHERE TO STAY

In Stellenbosch it makes sense to stay within the historic center—attractions and a great selection of restaurants and coffee shops are only a short stroll away along the oak-lined streets. Given this, the best option is River Manor (see below), but you may also want to investigate the following. **Roosenwijn Guest House** ✿ (✆ **021/883-3338;** www.stellenguest.co.za) offers comfortable rooms tastefully decorated in Afrikaans-Afro chic for between R620 and R680 double ($93–$101), depending on the season. Given its location (a 2-min. walk from the center) and the attractive decor, this is the best deal in town, but it doesn't have a great pool or any real garden to speak of. Opposite is **Bonne Esperance** (✆ **021/887-0225;** www.bonneesperance.com; R590/$88 double), which you should consider only if you can get an upstairs room, specifically no. 5, 14, or 15. Even more central, but not as good value, are **Eendracht** (✆ **021/ 883-8843;** www.eendracht-hotel.com; R578–R1,238/$86–$185), which has bright but impersonal rooms and no real public spaces right in the center of historic Dorp Street; and **D'Ouwe Werf:** The oldest inn in South Africa, popular for its old-fashioned hospitality, this has—in the original building—some wonderful rooms, but many are of the bland hotel variety (✆ **021/887-1608;** www.ouwewerf.com; R990–R1,390/$148–$207).

If you don't mind having to drive everywhere, you should also take a look at **Summerwood** (✆ **021/887-4112;** www.summerwood.co.za; R1,300/$194 double), a top-caliber guesthouse situated on the Jonkershoek Road. Your hosts, Ann and Christian Baret, offer an intimate atmosphere (only nine rooms, of which I recommend no. 8 for best views), large rooms, and a great pool and garden. If you find guesthouses too claustrophobic and Lanzerac too pricey, I'd opt for **Devon Valley Hotel** ✿ (✆ **021/865-2012;** www.devonvalleyhotel.com; high season R1,170/$175 double, low season R940/$140): Situated a few kilometers outside of town, amid rolling hills carpeted with vines, it's popular with conference groups, but the location is great; book the cellar rooms for best views.

Lanzerac Manor & Winery ✿✿✿ ⟨Kids⟩ The Lanzerac remains one of the top luxury options in the Winelands, with a historic manor, and outlying rooms and suites sublimely situated amid rolling vineyards in the beautiful Jonkershoek Valley, with spectacular views of the Helderberg mountain range from every angle. The standard "classic" rooms, furnished in reproduction antiques and expensive fabrics, are comfortable, but for real privacy, opt for one of the huge luxury rooms situated in separate suites in the gardens. The Lanzerac's position as the Winelands' most upmarket hotel (this excludes the classy intimate guesthouses you'll find in Franschhoek) is challenged only by stalwart Grande Roche and newcomer The Winelands Hotel and Wellness Centre, and though it's not as slick as its Paarl competitors, some would appreciate the fact that the Lanzerac is very laid-back. It also welcomes children, with huge lawns for them to romp on.

Lanzerac Rd., Stellenbosch 7599. ✆ 021/887-1132. Fax 021/887-2310. www.lanzerac.co.za. 48 units. High season R2,700–R3,900 ($403–$582) double, R5,350–R8,060 ($799–$1,203) suite; low season (June–Sept) R1,520–R2,180 ($227–$325) double, R2,910–R4,350 ($434–$649) suite. Rates include breakfast. Children's rates on request. AE, DC,

MC, V. **Amenities:** 3 restaurants; bar; cigar lounge; 3 pools; room service; babysitting; laundry. *In room:* A/C, TV, mini-bar, hair dryer, tea- and coffee-making facilities, underfloor heating.

River Manor & Spa ★★   A few minutes' stroll from the historic attractions of Stellenbosch, this charming guesthouse, comprising two interlinked properties and a brand-new spa, is situated on an oak-lined road that follows the course of the Eerste River. Colonial-themed rooms are graciously outfitted (historical prints, turn-of-the-20th-c. trunks, and plenty of wicker) and very comfortable, but the real reason this gets my vote are the great public spaces. Two pools are surrounded by table- and lounge-dotted lawns, and for those who want to escape the sun, deep verandas have comfortable chairs and striped awnings. The best-value rooms are no. 6 (R1,320/$197 double), which has a semiprivate, comfortably furnished veranda attached, and, to a lesser extent, no. 14, which is also a little more private than most classic rooms; other than these, you're better off booking a superior room. A number of restaurants are within walking distance. *Note:* If you're watching your budget, Roosenwijn (see above) is an excellent alternative, except in summer, when you'll want a pool.

No 6. The Avenue, Stellenbosch 7600. ✆ 021/887-9944. Fax 021/887-9940. www.rivermanor.co.za. 16 units. R950–R1,904 ($142–$284) double. Rates include breakfast. Children by request only. MC, V. **Amenities:** 2 pools; room service; laundry. *In room:* A/C, TV, hair dryer.

WHERE TO DINE

Stellenbosch does not have the caliber of restaurants Franschhoek is famed for, but there are a few stalwarts that seldom disappoint. Recommended restaurants within walking distance of the historic center are the **Greek Kitchen,** 42 Ryneveld St. (✆ **021/887-7703**), a small, laid-back place with outdoor seating and excellent slow-roasted lamb; the nearby **Fishmonger,** Ryneveld Street (✆ **021/887-7835**), with fresh, simple seafood; and, around the corner, **Decameron,** 50 Plein St. (✆ **021/883-3331**) now vies with **Al Frascati,** 18 Mill St. (✆ **021/883-9623**) as the best Italian restaurant in town. Oenophiles should head for **Wijnhuis** (✆ **021/887-5844**) in the Dorpsmeent Complex on Andringa Street, where you can dine on average Mediterranean-type fare with a tasting of the region's best wines (R25/$3.75 to sample six). If you feel like sampling authentic north Indian, don't miss the new satellite of Bhukara on the corner of Dorp and Bird streets (see full review in "Where to Dine: City Bowl," earlier in this chapter).

Moving out of town, **33 Stellenbosch,** on the Vlottenberg Road (✆ **021/881-3793**), is, like 96 Winery Road (see below), a highly rated country-style restaurant. Set to challenge Franschhoek's culinary dominance is the newly opened **Terroir** (✆ **021/880-8167**), opened by Michael Broughton (the man behind Broughton's, his much-acclaimed restaurant in Johannesburg) and Nic van Wyk (ex–sous chef from La Colombe). The emphasis at Terroir is firmly French—expect bouillabaisse, foie gras, truffles, and plenty of rich reductions. Finally, no overview of Stellenbosch eateries would be complete without a mention of the Pan-African buffet (R150/$22) served at **Moyo,** on the Spier estate (✆ **021/809-1100**); this is a great summer night option when the treetops are lit up, the drummers and dancers are writhing in the candlelight, and the canvas-covered outdoor lounge areas look their most romantic and inviting. Combining the theatrical with interesting dishes from across the continent, Moyo is a recommended, albeit touristy, night out.

96 Winery Road ★★ *Finds* MODERN SOUTH AFRICA   This is one of the most unassuming and unpretentious restaurants in the Cape, yet it has a loyal following of

Selecting Your Cape Wines

South African wineries produce well over 5,000 individual wines—a veritable cornucopia, with obvious appeal for the vinously intrepid, but a somewhat daunting prospect for the visitor trying to decide which bottle to choose from a long restaurant wine list. Fortunately, in South Africa, as in many other wine-producing countries, there are a select number of vintners who consistently turn out good-to-excellent products at prices that are reasonable, even after sometimes steep restaurant markups.

THE STALWARTS   Anything vinified by Charles Back of **Fairview** is likely to satisfy, even impress. Ditto the output of Pieter Ferreira and Charles Hopkins of **Graham Beck,** Gary and Kathy Jordan of **Jordan Winery,** Abrie Beeslaar of **Kanonkop Estate,** Neil Ellis of **Neil Ellis Wines,** Johan Malan of **Simonsig,** the Grier family of **Villiera,** or André van Rensburg of **Vergelegen,** the *homme sauvage* of South African winedom. **Alto Estate,** something of a Cape institution, is also still much admired for its powerful cabernets and red blends.

Other stalwarts who invariably deliver quality and value across a spectrum of styles include Beyers Truter of **Beyerskloof,** David Finlayson of **Glen Carlou,** Mike Dobrovic of **Mulderbosch,** Adi Badenhorst of **Rustenberg,** Abrie Bruwer of **Springfield Estate,** Gyles Webb of **Thelema Mountain Vineyards,** and Marc Kent of **Boekenhoutskloof** (note his alternative label, **Porcupine Ridge,** which offers exceptional value for money). Edgier, but equally reliable, are the inspired fabulations of Bruce Jack and his fellow envelope-pushers at **Flagstone Winery.**

BOUTIQUE WINES   Definitely worth sampling—if you can find them—are the following small wineries producing low-volume "boutique" wines. **De Trafford** and **Rudera,** both owned and run by husband-and-wife teams, can be depended on to impart much pleasure for a fair price. **Hamilton Russell Vineyards,** internationally renowned for elegant pinot noirs and chardonnays, is another must; also the family-run **Jacobsdal,** noted for resonant hand-crafted Pinotages; **De Toren** for confident, expressive Bordeaux-style reds; and **Le Riche Wines,** showcasing the fine-tuned red-wine-making skills of Francophile owner Etienne le Riche.

If the notion of small family wineries specializing in a particular wine style or grape variety appeals to you, make a point of trying the beautiful Rhône-styled reds produced by biodynamicist Eben Sadie and wife, Magriet, of **Sadie Family Wines;** the cool, upland sauvignon blanc of **Iona** proprietors Andrew and Rosie Gunn; the resolutely retro **Luddite** Shiraz, fashioned by man-mountain Niels Verburg and diminutive wife, Penny; and the sleek, scented **Axe Hill** "port" of Cape Wine Master Tony Mossop and partner Lynn.

PICK OF THE PINOTAGE   No self-respecting local wine list would be complete without a Pinotage. South Africans claim Pinotage as their own, the grape having been created in Stellenbosch in the 1920s as a cross between pinot noir and cinsault (then locally known as hermitage). As contemporary critics are quick to confirm, Pinotage comes in a truly bewildering variety of styles, from juicy-fruity and early drinking to ponderous and demanding of long maturation. The **Pinotage Association** (www.pinotage.co.za) annually anoints a Pinotage Top Ten in which names like **Beyerskloof, Kanonkop, Kaapzicht, Tukulu, DeWaal/Uiterwyk,** and **L'Avenir** regularly feature. My own recommendations would also include the liltingly fragrant **Laibach,** the value-for-money **Cape Bay** (part of the Longridge portfolio), and the outstanding new Ashbourne from the aforementioned **Hamilton Russell Vineyards.**

BEST CAPE BLENDS   Relatively new within the local arena is the so-called Cape Blend, a red wine usually containing a significant quantity of Pinotage. South Africans, true to form, disagree on virtually everything about this emerging category, including the optimum proportion of Pinotage. Fortunately, the best of these characterful and unique blends speak for themselves, as a tasting of **Kaapzicht**'s Steytler Vision, **Warwick**'s Three Cape Ladies, **Grangehurst**'s Nikela, and **Welgemeend Estate**'s pioneering Amadé will attest to.

LOCAL ICONS   I admit, rather regretfully, that South Africa cannot yet boast of a wine of the iconic stature of a Latour, or a true cult wine such as Valandraud or Screaming Eagle. Still, the country does have a small but growing number of internationally recognized wines, as well as a clutch of new wines that have the potential to attain lasting international repute. For the visiting connoisseur, the must-taste labels would probably include the **Rust & Vrede** Estate Blend (cabernet, Shiraz, and merlot), **Kanonkop** Paul Sauer and **Meerlust** Rubicon (both Bordeaux-style reds), **Boekenhoutskloof** cabernet sauvignon, **Veenwouden** merlot, **Klein Constantia** sweet elixir, Vin de Constance; and **Boplaas**'s opulent Cape Vintage Reserve Port.

The potential icon/cult wines make for a fascinating and varied tasting experience, and you really shouldn't pass up an opportunity to savour all or some of the following personal selections: **Sadie Family** Columella (Shiraz, Mourvèdre) and Palladius (chenin blanc, Viognier, chardonnay, grenache blanc), **Engelbrecht & Els** Ernie Els, **Capaia Wines** Capaia, **Vilafonté Wines** Series C and Series M (Bordeaux-style reds), and the multiawarded **Rudera** chenin blanc. Also, being readied for launch at the time of writing, the long-gestated flagship red from **Tokara,** and the brilliant Syrah-Viognier from **Ridgeback.**

—Philip van Zyl, wine lover and editor of the annual John Platter Wines, *the most respected guide to wine in South Africa*

locals who appreciate the informal atmosphere; unfussy, delicious food; great wine list; and excellent service (this is one place where waiters really know their wines). The menu changes every 6 months (with fresh and seasonal menu changes daily), but established favorites include Karoo shoulder of lamb; fresh Saldanha Bay mussels; pork belly strips served on sweet potato with homemade tomato chutney; crispy duck, roasted with ginger and sage and served on creamy potato bake; seared Norwegian salmon, served with a miso sauce on a vermicelli-noodle stir-fry; and the legendary dry-aged steaks. In season, bookings need to be made weeks in advance.

Zandberg Farm, Winery Rd., Helderberg region. ✆ 021/842-2020. Reservations recommended. Main courses R60–R82 ($8.95–$12). AE, DC, MC, V. Daily noon–5pm; Mon–Sat 7am–10pm.

Tokara ✿✿ MODERN SOUTH AFRICA   You'll find a few good options on the Helshoogte Pass (which links Stellenbosch to Franschhoek), but if you like your meals augmented with stunning views, Tokara is the place to stop. And if you're not eyeing the vistas, there is the architecture to admire—effortlessly floating over the mountain slope, with plenty of space, a lack of clutter, and great artworks, this is easily the best-looking modern wine-tasting venue in the Western Cape. Of course, the menu produced by the experimental chef Ettienne Bonthuys is worth the stop, too, though his penchant for mixing his meats (calamari and oxtail, oysters and steak) and rich sauces may not appeal to the timid or health-inclined. That said, simpler fare is always on offer, and this remains a personal favorite for lunch (the views are gone by nightfall).

Helshoogte Pass. ✆ 021/808-5959. Main courses R65–R98 ($9.70–$15). AE, DC, MC, V. Tues–Sat noon–3pm and 7–10pm.

FRANSCHHOEK

33km (20 miles) E of Stellenbosch; 79km (49 miles) E of Cape Town via Stellenbosch; 85km (53 miles) SE of Cape Town via Paarl

If you plan to overnight in the Winelands, the prettiest valley by far is Franschhoek (French Corner), the land Simon van der Stel gave the French Huguenots fleeing religious persecution in 1688. This minute valley, surrounded by soaring mountains, is so lush a local once compared it to "living in a lettuce"; aside from its scenic advantages, it boasts the highest concentration of top-quality restaurants in Africa, and a number of excellent accommodations options. It's very faux French, however, and some complain that it's become too touristy, but relative to the other Winelands options, it's easy to navigate and still offers the most rural atmosphere, with dirt tracks a few blocks from the main road, and glorious views wherever you look.

ESSENTIALS

VISITOR INFORMATION   Make sure to pick up one of the helpful maps and a great regional brochure at the **Franschhoek Tourism Bureau,** on the main road going into town, at 85 Huguenot Rd. (✆ 021/876-3603; Mon–Fri 9am–6pm, Sat–Sun 9am–4pm; hours are extended Oct–Apr).

GETTING AROUND   The town is small enough to traverse on foot, but to visit the wine farms you will need to hire a car, taxi, or specialist guide. For the latter, see "Exploring the Winelands," earlier in this chapter; for shuttle services, transfers, and general tours, contact **Franschhoek Experience** (✆ 083/234-4038) or **Winelands Tours** (✆ 082/774-2790). For wine-tasting expeditions on purebred Arab horses, contact **Paradise Stables** (✆ 021/876-2160; www.paradisestables.co.za; R325/$49) or **Steinmetz Arabians** (✆ 021/876-2570). If you'd like to tour the region on a bike, rent one for R90 ($13) per day from **Bike Point** (© **083/235-3260**); for cycling tours, take a look at **Cycling Holidays** (www.cyclingholidaysouthafrica.com).

STELLENBOSCH TO FRANSCHHOEK: THE HELSHOOGTE PASS

From Stellenbosch the R310 heads over the scenic Helshoogte Pass, linking it with Franschhoek and Paarl, both of which lie some 30 minutes from the center of Stellenbosch. If you're heading to Franschhoek from Stellenbosch, follow the R310 for 2km (1¼ miles) before turning left into Ida's Valley and heading for **Rustenberg** (© **021/887-3153;** Mon–Fri 8:30am–4:30pm, Sat 9am–12:30pm). This gorgeous estate is renowned for its red wines, as well as its peaceful and beautiful setting, with a historic manor house contrasting with a tasting center and state-of-the-art milking parlor. Stop for lunch at **Tokara** for the fine views (see review above), or push on to visit the beautifully maintained Cape Dutch estate of **Boschendal** ⍟⍟⍟ (© **021/ 870-4200;** 8:30/9:30am–4:30/5pm; wine tastings on Sun only in season [Nov–Apr]). Together with Vergelegen and Constantia, Boschendal is the Winelands' most photographed estate, combining an excellent manor house museum with beautiful grounds and great wines. Boschendal also offers three different dining experiences: The luncheon buffet (© **021/870-4272;** R195/$29) is served in the original wine cellar, with a huge buffet table covered from end to end with tasty traditional Cape Malay and South African dishes as well as lighter treats like venison carpaccio with Satsuma preserve, watercress with local goat's cheese and walnuts, and Franschhoek specialties like smoked salmon trout (a type of trout with salmon-hued flesh). If you're not that hungry, head for the wrought-iron tables under the oaks at **Le Café** and order one of the delicious quiches (the delicious traditional *bobotie* is recommended). From October to April, you can purchase a **picnic hamper** (R95/$14) to enjoy on the lawns shaded by more ancient oaks. (Ask about the full-moon picnics, held Dec–Mar.)

THE FRANSCHHOEK WINE ROUTE

The following estates, all clearly signposted off Main Road and its extension, Huguenot Road, are recommended. **La Motte** (© **021/876-3119;** Mon–Fri 9am–4:30pm, Sat 10am–3pm), which has been producing wines for 3 centuries, is worth stopping at to sample its red wines; the same is true of **Rupert & Rothschild** (© **021/876-1648;** by appointment only). If you're hungry, head for **Moreson Soleil de Matin** (© **021/876-3055;** Tues–Sun 11am–5pm; May–Nov until 4pm), where the sauvignon blanc is a good choice with lunch at the estate's delightfully relaxed **Bread & Wine Restaurant** ⍟ (Wed–Sun noon–3pm), worth visiting for its oven-fresh foccacia alone, served with Mediterranean-style dips. Pop into **Grande Provence Wines** (© **021/876-3195;** daily 9am–5pm) to sample the semisweet Angels Tears wine, and **Mont Rochelle Mountain Vineyards** (© **021/876-3000;** Sept–Apr daily 10:30am–6pm), still owned by a descendant of the French Huguenots, for its glorious setting. In fact, if it's setting you're after, double back and head onto the dirt track to **Glenwood Vineyards** (© **021/876-2044;** Mon–Fri 9am–1pm); besides enjoying the drive, you can sample one of the estate chardonnays.

A visit to the **Cabriere Estate** (© **021/876-2630;** tastings and cellar tours Mon–Sat 11am and 3pm) is also recommended—and not just for the excellent bubbly. Every Saturday at 11am you can witness a demonstration by winemaker Achim von Arnim, who uncorks his bottles by slicing the neck off with a sabre, followed by an in-depth (2-hr.) tasting and tour (R25/$3.75 per person).

The boutique-style **Boekenhoutskloof** (℃ **021/876-3320**) produces internationally acclaimed wines, particularly the reds—tastings, conducted by the winemaker himself, are by appointment only, one well worth making. If you get there between 9am and 1pm, you don't need an appointment to visit **Stony Brook,** another boutique-style winery where tastings are held by owners Nigel and Joy in their home, a wonderfully informal and personal experience (℃ **021/876-2182**).

Huguenot Road intersects with Lambrecht Road at a T-junction at the base of the Franschhoek Mountains. Opposite is the **French Huguenot Monument,** erected in honor of the French Protestant refugees who settled here between 1688 and 1700. Its three arches symbolize the Holy Trinity. Turn left to drive the Franschhoek Pass for lunch at **La Petite Ferme**—a must, if you can get a table; see below.

WHERE TO STAY

Franschhoek's property boards have prices quoted in rands, euros, and dollars—proof of its popularity with visitors from all over the world who fall in love with the valley and want to own a piece of it. As a result, there has been a mushrooming in accommodations options. But frankly, you'd be hard-pressed to beat the following recommendations. Included is the gorgeously decorated **La Residence,** the sumptuous summer residence of the owner of Domaine des Anges, a vineyard on the outskirts of Franschhoek. Its five suites are by far the best dressed in the valley, but located in the town (www.laresidence.co.za). Also take a look at **Klein Genot (Little Pleasure),** which offers six large suites on a beautiful wine farm off the appropriately named Green Valley Road (www.kleingenot.com). If you're on a budget, or just want to be left alone, a number of self-catering cottages are situated on wine farms, some with swimming pools and/or fireplaces and featuring lovely mountain and vineyard views. **Klein Dassenberg Cottages** (℃ **021/876-2107;** www.kleindassenberg.co.za; from R400/$60 double), **Blueberry Hill** (℃ **021/876-3362;** R500/$75 double), **Vineyard Cottages** (℃ **021/876-3194;** R175/$26 per person), and the idyllic **Bird Cottage** (℃ **021/876-2136;** R140/$21 per person) are all recommended. If you want to be in town, book the picture-postcard-cute **Lavender Cottage** (℃ **021/876-2666;** R200/$30 per person). Fly fishermen should book the cottage at **Three Streams** (℃ **021/876-2692;** R800/$119)—it's renowned for its smoked trout, and visitors have exclusive access to one of the farm's trout dams.

Auberge Clermont 🐾🐾 Located on a working wine and fruit farm, in an old wine cellar, painted cream and offset with pale blue, this auberge is inspired by the tastes and colors of Provence—the gardens, redolent with the scent of lavender and roses, are an integral part of this theme. Rooms are large and comfortably decorated; bathrooms are equally spacious, with double basins, separate showers, and heated towel racks. Opt for one of the two loft rooms for a greater sense of privacy. Breakfast is served in the breakfast room or in the courtyard under the 140-year-old oak trees. For families, a spacious three-bedroom, two-bathroom self-catering farmhouse is set in a formal French garden.

Robertsvlei Rd., Franschhoek 7690. ℃ **021/876-3700.** Fax 021/876-3701. www.clermont.co.za. 6 units. R950 ($142) double; R1,300 ($194) villa. Rates include breakfast, except for villa. Ask about winter (May–Sept) discounts. AE, DC, MC, V. **Amenities:** Dining room/bar; small pool; tennis court; limited room service; laundry. *In room:* TV w/satellite channels, hair dryer, underfloor heating.

L'Auberge du Quartier Français 🐾🐾🐾 This auberge, voted best Small Hotel in the World by *Tatler* in 2005, is the most expensive option in the valley, but the fact

that it is "in" the valley (rather than overlooking it, like La Couronne or La Peti
is a drawback. That said, it means you can roll back to your room after gorging
superb restaurants (see "Where to Dine," below). The hotel also offers compliment.
transport within the valley, so you can take your pick of other wining and dining suggestions. Rooms encircle a central courtyard with verdant gardens and a large oval pool,
and are huge, comfortable, and stylish, featuring luxuries like wood-burning fireplaces.
Book room no. 16, which also has a totally private seating area in the garden. (In room
no. 14, the seating area is screened off by vegetation). Note that the two suites come with
an additional bathroom and bedroom and their own private pool, ideal for families. Le
Quartier has also opened a Screening Room, which serves up mainstream and art-house
movies along with gourmet popcorn to guests and locals.

16 Huguenot Rd. © 021/876-2151. Fax 021/876-3105. www.lequartier.co.za. 17 units. R2,700 ($403) double;
R5,000 ($746) suite. Inquire about the great winter specials. AE, DC, MC, V. **Amenities:** 2 restaurants; bar; pool; room
service; beauty therapy and bath menus; complimentary transport in valley. *In room:* TV, A/C, minibar, hair dryer,
CD/DVD.

La Cabriere Country House ★★ (Value)

A good choice if you want to be within walk-
ing distance of the village, yet surrounded by views and vineyards, La Cabriere Country
House has only five guest rooms, each luxuriously and individually decorated with a
blend of African and Provençal fabrics, furniture, and *objets*. The well-traveled owners
have incorporated all the best elements of guesthouses they've visited in various parts of
the world, ensuring attention to detail not normally expected in this price range. Three
of the rooms have fireplaces, and all have French doors that lead out into the garden with
its Koi pond, inviting swimming pool, and gorgeous mountain and vineyard vistas.
Breakfasts are lavish affairs enjoyed poolside or in the privacy of your room.

Middagkrans Rd., Franschhoek 7690. © 021/876-4780. Fax 021/876-3852. www.lacabriere.co.za. 5 units. R1,350
($201) double. Rates include breakfast. Ask about winter discounts. AE, DC, MC, V. Children over 15 accepted. **Ameni-
ties:** Dining room; pool; laundry. *In room:* A/C, TV, minibar, hair dryer, fireplace (some).

La Couronne ★★

Once the holiday home of the president of the Ivory Coast, La
Couronne (The Crown) is on a hill overlooking the Franschhoek valley and mountains; the views from every window of this luxuriously appointed hotel are thus marvelous (although not as sweeping as the La Petite Ferme suites that perch below the
pass across the valley). Public spaces are comfortable and elegant, but with the addition of two new wings over the years (particularly the most recent "bunkered in" Vineyard Wing), the room decor has become increasingly standardized, losing its exclusive
boutique air and feeling more like a hotel chain. Best rooms are still those in the original "Manor" House (ask for room no. 5) and room nos. 15 to 18 in the Garden Wing.
The restaurant, which has always had an excellent reputation (and wonderful views),
is now under the direction of Roger Clement, the Swiss-trained chef who has presided
over kitchens in several top hotels around the Western Cape.

Robertsvlei Rd. (turn right at the monument), Franschhoek 7690. © 021/876-2770. Fax 021/876-3788.
www.lacouronnehotel.co.za. 17 units. High season R1,800–R2,700 ($269–$403) double, R2,950–R5,500
($440–$821) suite; low season (May–Oct 15) R1,100–R1,600 ($164–$239) double, R2,350–R4,600 ($351–$687)
suite. Rates include breakfast. AE, DC, MC, V. **Amenities:** Restaurant; cigar bar; pool; room service; babysitting; laundry; trout fishing. *In room:* A/C (some rooms), TV, hair dryer.

La Petite Ferme ★★★

Despite the fact that this is not a hotel, these spacious
B&B suites, located in separate cottages below the Franschhoek Pass, are a personal
top Winelands choice, particularly the aptly named Vista suite, which is the most private of the five. The La Petite Ferme vineyards are within touching distance, and

valley and mountain views, enjoyed from your king-size bed or
with plunge pool. Rooms are spacious and tastefully decorated,
comforts needed for a wonderful stay, and the staff is intelligent
ons and dinners can be enjoyed at the adjacent restaurant or at
s the road; alternatively, staff will arrange for transfers into the
y tours of the wineries. Some may find the suites a little cut off
from the action—at around 6pm, the restaurant closes, and staff is now a phone call
away—but I consider this level of privacy, in this kind of location, priceless.

Franschhoek Pass Rd., Franschhoek 7690. ℂ **021/876-3016.** Fax 021/876-3624. lapetite@iafrica.com. 5 units. Standard Luxury R1,200 ($179); Vista R1,600 ($239); Deluxe R2,400 ($358) double. Rates include breakfast. AE, DC, MC, V. No children under 16. **Amenities:** Restaurant; room service (day only); laundry. *In room:* TV, minibar, hair dryer, DVD (in Vista and Deluxe), tea- and coffee-making facilities, fireplace, plunge pool, undercarpet heating.

WHERE TO DINE

Franschhoek calls itself "the gourmet capital of the Cape," and with good reason. Not
only are an increasing number of restaurants now fixtures on the global foodie map,
but Franschhoek is also renowned for its produce, particularly its rainbow trout,
cheese (it hosts the annual S.A. Cheese Festival), and hand-crafted Belgian chocolates.
Chocoholics should book **The Chocolate Experience** (ℂ 021/876-4092); to sample
some of the 40-odd farmhouse cheeses, pop into **La Grange Fromagerie** (ℂ 021/
876-2155)—also, incidentally, where you will find the locals on Friday evenings during the summer months, when La Grange hosts its jazz evenings from 5 to 8pm.
Besides the restaurants reviewed below, **Klein Olifantshoek** (ℂ 021/876-25666) is
worth considering—you can take a look at these and other menus at the tourism
bureau in town. And if all the fine dining is too much for your senses (not to mention your waistline), opt for **French Connection** (ℂ 021/876-4056). The brainchild
of Matthew Gordon of Haute Cabriere, this is an informal pavement-style bistro
located on the main road, and a favorite with the Franschhoek locals. Alternatively,
head for **Bread & Wine** (ℂ 021/876-3692), situated at the La Motte estate.

Haute Cabriere Cellar Restaurant ⋒⋒⋒ INTERNATIONAL/MODERN CAPE
The ideal dinner venue (in contrast with La Petite Ferme, where views make it ideal
for lunch), the rose-covered "Russian bunkhouse" is almost hidden from the road, and
the vaulted ceiling gives it a modern medieval feel. Only the well-respected wines of
this estate—handpicked to complement each of Matthew Gordon's dishes—are
served, and there are no appetizers or main courses, just full or half-portions or shared
platters to mix and match. The menu is seasonal; start with oysters and a celebratory
flute of Pierre Jourdan Brut Savage (summer), or the *tian* (casserole) of four types of
Franschhoek salmon trout served with Belle Rose (winter); then try the roasted loin
of springbok in a Cape Malay spice jus with corn tempura (summer), or grilled Scottish salmon with creamed spinach and potato galette and horseradish (winter). Finish
with Belgian chocolates (handmade in the valley under the Huguenot label) with Fine
de Jourdan potstill brandy (brandy distilled in a traditional copper pot) and coffee.

Pass Rd. ℂ 021/876-3688. Portions R60–R120 ($8.95–$18). AE, DC, MC, V. Daily noon–3pm; Fri–Mon 7–9pm.

La Petite Ferme ⋒⋒⋒ COUNTRY If you are spending only 1 day in Franschhoek,
make sure you lunch here: Book a table on the all-weather veranda, order the signature
deboned smoked rainbow trout served with a creamy horseradish sauce, and allow
plenty of time to drink in both the view and one of the farm's great wines. Even the locals
can't resist dining here—situated on the Franschhoek Pass with a breathtaking view of

the entire valley, this family-owned and -managed restaurant has arguably the best setting in South Africa. Food is refreshingly simple—if the trout doesn't appeal, try the Portuguese-style calamari, marinated in red wine and grilled, or the Mediterranean-style lamb. End with La Petite Ferme's own plums, poached in red wine and served with meringues and ice cream.

Pass Rd. ⓒ 021/876-3016. Reservations essential. Main courses R58–R90 ($8.65–$13). AE, DC, MC, V. Daily noon–4pm.

Le Quartier Français ✶✶✶ INNOVATIVE CONTINENTAL/BISTRO For years this has been considered by many to be the best in Franschhoek—and in this haute cuisine environment, that takes some doing. To focus more exclusively on her innovative flavor combinations, executive chef Margo Janse has now separated the restaurant into two sections: **iCi,** the more laid-back bistro-style restaurant serving delicious but relatively simple meals (grilled sirloin with garlic butter and charred tomato salad; wood-roasted pork chop served with apple relish and a cannelloni bean and chorizo ragout; and pan-roasted kingklip fish served with avocado, lime, and mint, and a yellow pepper broth), and the **Tasting Room,** where she flexes her award-winning capabilities (voted Best Restaurant in the Middle East & Africa by *Restaurant* magazine in 2005). Here the dinner-only menu changes daily, and guests can choose from a four- (R240/$36), six- (R400/$60), or eight-course meal (R600/$90) that showcases her passion for culinary innovation.

Corner of Berg and Wilhelmina sts. ⓒ 021/876-2151. iCi main courses R50–R75 ($7.45–$11); Tasting Room R240–R600 ($36–$90). AE, DC, MC, V. Year-round daily 7–9pm. iCi lunch daily noon–2:30pm.

Reuben's ✶✶✶ ECLECTIC BISTRO A wonderful rags-to-riches story, Reuben, who grew up in Franschhoek, was working as a barman in Chamonix when a staff shortage sent him to the kitchen, where he met Richard Carstens, one of the most respected chefs in S.A. (now working at Lynton Hall in Kwazulu-Natal). Six months later, he followed Carstens to Monneaux, and then left for Cambridge, where he opened Bruno's, before returning to his hometown in 2004 to open his own restaurant. By the end of the year, Reuben's experimental comfort food, sensibly priced, was the talk of the town (and possibly precipitated "haute" stalwarts like Janse and Gordon's break into "bistro"-style cuisine), and in 2005 he was voted Chef and Restaurant of the Year by the *Eat Out* team. The menu changes regularly, but expect innovative use of local ingredients, like salmon trout fish cakes served with a poached organic egg, watercress, and lime butter, or the divine mascarpone and bleu cheese tart with tomato jam. Recommended mains include the smoked paprika Indian prawn risotto, served with avocado ice cream, and the grilled quail with grapes, tarragon, mascarpone, beetroot, and orzo. End with lemon and passion fruit curd tart with moskonfyt ice cream. Success has never been more deserved.

19 Huguenot Rd., Oude Stallen Centre. ⓒ 021/876-3772. Main courses R58–R74 ($8.65–$11). AE, DC, MC, V. Wed–Mon noon–3pm and 6–9:30pm.

Topsi & Company ✶✶✶ INNOVATIVE COUNTRY/VEGETARIAN Featured in Robert Carrier's *Great Dishes of the World* (Smithmark Publishing), Topsi is often described as "the doyenne of Cape chefs"; her honest home-style cooking is refreshing, her ebullient presence in the open-plan kitchen and dining room a delight. Located in an unassuming building off the main road, and furnished with portraits, rugs, mismatched wooden furniture, and a parrot, Topsi serves interesting cuts like calves' liver, baked and served on parsnip purée, or no-nonsense but delicious basics like her filet of trout baked on a bed of leeks and thyme, with baby potatoes and beet-root, or shredded duck and crunchy cabbage served in a crepe with nectarines and satay sauce. Topsi's vegetarian daughter ensures wonderful nonmeat options like the ricotta, spinach, and butternut crepe-cake with tapenade and caramelized apple stack. *Note:* Topsi's is unlicensed.

7 Reservoir St. W. (next to the library). ℂ **021/876-2952.** Main courses R50–R80 ($7.45–$12). AE, DC, MC, V. Wed–Mon noon–2:30pm and 7–9pm.

PAARL

33km (20 miles) NW of Franschhoek; 56km (35 miles) E of Cape Town

Paarl is named after the great granite rocks that loom above the town—the first Euro-pean party to visit the area in 1657 watched the dawn sun reflecting off the glistening boulders after a night of rain, and named it Peerlbergh (Pearl Mountain). These 500-million-year-old domes are one of the world's largest granite outcrops, second only to Ayers Rock in Australia. The town's large size makes it a less attractive destination than the chi-chi village of Franschhoek and the oak-lined avenues of Stellenbosch, but there are a number of excellent wine estates to visit (get a map from the information bureau), and Main Street, with its 2km (1¼-mile) stretch of beautifully preserved buildings, is worth taking a leisurely drive along. Most visitors also find a visit to the **Taal Monument** (the large phallic sculpture clearly visible on the slopes of Paarl Mountain) worthwhile—the views of the valley and False Bay are excellent. To get here, drive down Main Street, passing the KWV headquarters on your left, and look for the signs to your right.

ESSENTIALS

GETTING THERE To get to Paarl from Franschhoek (some 30km/19 miles northwest), retrace your footsteps down Huguenot Road and take the R303 to Paarl (off the main road, after the turnoff to La Motte). Once in town, look for the first traffic circle and turn left onto Market; keep going until Market meets Main Street.

VISITOR INFORMATION The **Paarl Information Bureau** (ℂ **021/872-3829;** www.paarlonline.com; Mon–Fri 8:30am–5pm, Sat 9am–1pm, Sun 10am–1pm) is at 216 Main St.

WHERE TO STAY

Unlike Stellenbosch or Franschhoek, it's not really ideal to stay in town—despite boasting some rather beautiful buildings, Paarl is not the most attractive Winelands town. Just as well, then, that a good selection of Cape Dutch homestead-cum-guest-houses are situated in the Paarl/Wellington area, some on working wine farms, the best of which are described below. If you'd prefer to be alone, in a secure (gated) vine-yard estate, book one of the two delightful cottages at **Diemersfontein;** the "honey-moon cottage" is particularly cute (ℂ **021/873-5050;** www.diemersfontein.co.za; R800/$119 double)—rooms don't offer as good value. Diemersfontein also boasts an excellent restaurant, **Seasons** (beautiful views to match the food), and produces my favorite Pinotage. If you'd like to include some serious pampering in your itinerary, then take a look at the **Winelands Hotel & Wellness Centre,** a new luxury hotel located on a working wine estate near Paarl, and recently voted one of the "16 Best Spas on Earth" by *UK Elle* magazine (ℂ **021/875-8100;** www.santewellness.co.za; from R2,200/$328 double).

Bartholomeus Klip ✿✿✿   Okay, so this luxury country lodge is not, in fact, in Paarl, but located some 30 minutes' drive away on a working wheat and sheep farm. But this is a wonderful base from where you can combine a bit of wildlife viewing (the 4,500-hectare/11,115-acre nature reserve is stocked with buffalo, zebra, wildebeest, gemsbok, eland, springbok, bontebok, and hartebeest) with wine tastings and a day trip to the city (a 75-min. drive away), or just really unwind. Accommodations are in a restored Victorian homestead, elegantly furnished in period style. There are only five bedrooms; the best option by far is the beautiful suite, which has its own entrance and a private veranda with great views. Alternatively, you can stay in a small farmhouse called Wild Olive House. It's a truly peaceful place, with little to do but enjoy the exceptional food (included in the rate), laze around on loungers—the large, deep, farm-style pool is wonderful—and walk, cycle, or drive through the reserve.

Elandskloof Mountains, Hermon. ✆ 022/448-1820. Fax 022/448-1829. www.parksgroup.co.za. 5 units. High season (Sept–Mar) R2,500 ($373) double, R2,750 ($410) suite; low season (May–Aug) R1,800 ($269) double, R2,700 ($403) suite. Rates include brunch, high tea, 3-course dinner, and all game activities. AE, DC, MC, V. No children under 16. **Amenities:** Dining room; pool; laundry; game drives; game walks; canoeing; mountain biking. *In room:* Hair dryer.

Grande Roche ✿✿✿   Located in a beautifully restored 18th-century Cape Dutch estate, surrounded by lush gardens and with the Drakenstein Mountains as dramatic backdrop, this—together with Lanzerac—is the most expensive accommodations option in the Winelands. It has all the amenities you'd expect from a classy hotel (not to mention a top-rated restaurant, **Bosman's,** see below), and even though it's only minutes from Paarl's town center, the mountain and vineyard views that embrace the homestead create a relaxing country atmosphere. The doubles have integrated lounges/bedrooms and are extremely luxurious and roomy, so no need to book a suite. Most rooms also come with private terraces. Service is tip-top—a request for train information was doggedly researched by one of the managers. Many people come for the relaxing spa treatments; it's not unusual to see robe-clad guests blissfully wandering the grounds. *Note:* The hotel is closed from mid-May to July 31.

P.O. Box 6038, Paarl 7622. ✆ 021/863-2727. Fax 021/863-2220. www.granderoche.co.za. 34 units. High season (Oct–Mar) R2,240–R3,680 ($334–$549) double; R5,200 ($776) honeymoon suite. Dec 12–Jan 10 5-night minimum stay. Low season (Apr–May and Sept) R1,680–R2,630 ($251–$393) double; R4,000 ($597) honeymoon suite. Rates include breakfast. AE, DC, MC, V. Children 4 and over only. **Amenities:** Restaurant; bar; 2 pools (1 heated); fitness center; spa; salon; room service; massage; laundry. *In room:* A/C, TV, minibar, DVD (some) underfloor heating (some).

Palmiet Valley ✿✿   Situated on a working wine farm in a historic homestead dating back to 1717, Palmiet Valley is arguably the most beautifully furnished guesthouse in the Winelands, with lovely antiques in every room (book one with a fireplace if you're traveling in winter). Once outdoors, you can enjoy beautiful views of the surrounding vineyards and craggy mountains from every angle, including the terrace and decent-size pool. Four-course dinners are served in the period-styled dining room at one table; you can request a more private option if you like. A chauffeur-driven limo is available for daily charter or airport transfers.

P.O. Box 9085, Klein Drakenstein 7628. ✆ 021/862-7741. Fax 021/862-6891. www.palmiet.co.za. 10 units. R950 ($142) junior suite; R1,490 ($222) double; R1,690 ($252) cottage room double; R1,890 ($282) honeymoon suite. Winter rates 20% less. Rates include breakfast. MC, V. **Amenities:** Dining room; bar; pool; room service; laundry; wine tasting; mountain bikes; horseback riding. *In room:* A/C, hair dryer, CD player, tea- and coffee-making facilities, fireplaces (some).

Roggeland ✿✿   The visitors who book at Roggeland—another gracious Cape Dutch homestead in the Klein Drakenstein Valley—are a who's who of traveling writers and foodies, all of whom rave about this 300-year-old estate. World-famous chef Robert

Carrier called it an inspiration, *Travel + Leisure* described it as one of the world's 20 best hotels, and the *New York Times* named it the preferred choice of hotels in the Winelands. Furnishings are more fusty than at Palmiet (food is the main reason to come here), but rooms are spacious and comfortable, the location is tranquil, and the service discreet and efficient.

P.O. Box 7210, Northern Paarl 7623. ✆ **021/868-2501**. Fax 021/868-2113. www.roggeland.co.za. 11 units. R520–R970 ($78–$145) double. Rates include breakfast and 4-course dinner with predinner wine. AE, DC, MC, V. **Amenities:** Restaurant; pool; mountain bikes. *In room:* Hair dryer, tea- and coffee-making facilities.

WHERE TO DINE

If Bosman's is closed during your stay, head into town to the **Restaurant at Pontac** (✆ **021/872-0445**), where chef Craig McGeean presides over an exciting menu (smoked salmon is paired with baked pear cheesecake, lamb loin with cardamon carrot cake). Alternatively, **Seasons at Diemersfontein** (see "Where to Stay," above), a boutique winery in the Wellington area, serves up contemporary country-style meals, very reasonably priced; gorgeous views (and wines) make it an ideal luncheon stop (✆ **021/873-2671**).

Bosman's Restaurant ★★★ INTERNATIONAL/MODERN CAPE   The first and only hotel restaurant in Africa to achieve Relais Gourmand status, and listed one of the top 10 in the world by *New Straits Times,* Bosman's has been wowing local and international food critics alike for years. Menus change regularly, but there are always a number of set-menu choices (including a "Flavors of the Cape" sampler, a low-fat menu, and a vegetarian-only menu), or you can opt for the a la carte. Popular starters are the Cape Crustacean salad with chile dressing or hot olive oil served with peppercorn beef sashimi with wasabi-centered jus. Cherry crepe–wrapped springbok loin with black peppercorn and Pinotage jus is another winner, and the coffee savarign filled with fynbos honey ice cream is a pretty perfect ending. Unfortunately, the fabulous cuisine can be marred by service that confuses sophistication with cloying formality, and a request for a glass of tap water is likely to be met with an upturned nose. Small price to pay, however, when you're dining on the restaurant veranda on a glorious star-filled night with a warm breeze and vineyards stretching out before you.

Plantasie St. (in the Grande Roche Hotel). ✆ **021/863-2727**. Reservations essential. 3-course lunch menu R175 ($26); dinner set menu R380–R520 ($57–$78); main courses average R140 ($21). AE, DC, MC, V. Sept–May daily 7–10:30am, noon–2pm, and 7am–9pm. Closed mid-May to July 31.

Rhebokskloof ★★ SOUTH AFRICAN/CONTINENTAL   Located in what is called "The Victorian Restaurant and Terrace," this is a great luncheon venue with a superb setting overlooking the estate's manicured lawns and lake—book a seat on the

---

⟨ *Fun Fact* ⟩ The Last Step to Freedom

Paarl made headlines when President Mandela, who spent his last years here under house arrest, took his final steps to freedom from the Victor Verster prison on the outskirts of town on February 11, 1990. This was the first time South Africans could see how 27 years of incarceration had changed Mandela. Many, in fact, had never seen his face—under the Prisons Act, not even old pictures were allowed to be published.

terrace for shady, alfresco dining in summer, or near the fireplace for warmth in winter. Chef Elton Flack changes his menu at least four times a year and alternates between a light, value-for-money luncheon menu and a slightly more robust (and pricey) dinner menu. Recommended starters include the braised duck and brown onion soup, served with julienned vegetables and potato and honey dumplings, and crocodile carpaccio served with rocket leaves, toasted pumpkinseed, and chevin goat's cheese. Heavier but no less delicious is the house specialty: Trio of Game, comprising grilled springbok loin on a grape confit and merlot sauce, roast kudu filet wrapped in red spinach and phylo pastry with a creamy thyme sauce, and lightly smoked impala loin with a tomato and roasted garlic jus, served with homemade tagliatelli and sautéed wild mushrooms.

Rhebokskloof Estate, Agter Paarl. ℂ 021/869-8386. www.rhebokskloof.co.za. Reservations essential in season. Main courses R40–R75 ($5.95–$11) lunch, R60–R105 ($8.95–$16) dinner. AE, DC, MC, V. Thurs–Mon 8:30am–9:30pm; Tues–Wed 8:30am–5:30pm. (In-season hours are extended.)

Whale Coast & Garden Route: The Western Cape

The Western Cape, Africa's southwestern-most tip, is the most popular tourist destination in South Africa, and with good reason. Aside from the sybaritic pleasures of Cape Town and its wine routes (see chapter 4), a vast Southern Right whale nursery stretches along the Cape's southern coast. Some of the best land-based whale-watching sites in the world are in the Overberg, with whales migrating to its shallow coastal basin to mate and calve from mid-July to November. The Whale Coast, of which the coastal town of Hermanus is the unofficial capital, is an easy (and beautiful) 90-minute drive from Cape Town, but there's plenty to do and lovely places to stay, should you choose to spend a few days here.

East of the Overberg are the coastal lakes and forests of the Garden Route, fringed by the majestic mountains that separate it from the ostrich farms and vineyards of the Klein Karoo, and the distinctive architecture of the small settlements dotted in the vast arid plains of the Great Karoo. This is a wonderful part of the world to explore by car, and although you can drive the entire Garden Route from Cape Town in approximately 5 to 6 hours, you should spend at least 2 nights along the route—preferably more—to discover the beauty off the beaten N2 track. It's a great place to do nothing but unwind—but this scenic coastal belt, which encompasses South Africa's "Lakes District," also takes pride of place on the itinerary for adrenaline junkies, with a rush of activities ranging from the highest bungee jump in the world to cage-diving for Great White sharks.

Moving north from Cape Town, along what is simply known as the West Coast, you'll find numerous treasures, among them laid-back open-air beach restaurants, the bewitching Cederberg Mountains, and—after the first rains fall, usually in August—the annual miracle of spring, when the seemingly barren plains bloom with spectacular flower displays. You can explore the West Coast on a day trip, but to find yourself alone, surrounded by a floral carpet as far as the eye can see, you'll need to take a side trip to Namaqualand in the Northern Cape.

1 Staying Active

ABSEILING Take a 45m (148-ft.) abseil (rappel) in the Kaaimans River in Wilderness, then canoe out (R225/$34 per person). Call **Eden Adventures** (© **044/877-0179**). Even more exhilarating is canoeing over to Knysna's Western Head in the Featherbed Nature Reserve—not least because the drop here is 70m (230 ft.) and is followed by a 90-minute quad-bike ride. Contact **S.E.A.L.** (© **083/654-8755** or 044/382-5599; **www.sealadventures.co.za**; R470/$70). If you don't fancy clinging to a cliff, both offer a range of canoeing trips.

> **Fun Fact** **Africa's Floral Kingdom**
>
> The **Cape Floral Kingdom** covers .04% of the world's land surface, yet it contains 24,000 plant species and is considered the most diverse of the world's six floral kingdoms—comparable only to the Boreal Kingdom, which comprises all of Northern America, Europe, and Asia. Popular indigenous species that have found their way into gardens across the world include the gardenia, red-hot poker, arum lily, strelitzia (bird of paradise), agapanthus, gladioli, and freesias.

BLACK-WATER TUBING   Not quite as exhilarating as white-water rafting, but equally spectacular, is a half-day spent floating on a tractor-tire inner tube down the Storms River. Once you enter the narrow gorge, you can look up to see nothing but the dramatic cliff face, dripping ferns, and a sliver of sky above. Trips cost R345 ($51) per person, including kit and lunch. **StormsRiver Adventures** (© **042/281-1836;** www.stormsriver.com) offers this and a host of other activities in the Tsitsikamma area, including a 110m (361-ft.) abseil, marine tours, and scuba-diving.

BOARDSAILING & KITE-SURFING   If you get your rush from the combined power of water and air, Langebaan Lagoon on the West Coast is considered one of the best sites in South Africa, particularly in the early afternoon, when the wind picks up. Book lessons and rent equipment from the **Cape Sports Centre** in Langebaan (© **022/772-1114;** www.capesport.co.za).

BOATING   You can cruise the ocean all along the coast; recommendations can be found under each section.

BUNGEE/BRIDGE-JUMPING   There are two sites: The original **Gourits River bridge-jump** (© **044/697-7001;** R170/$25 per person), between Albertinia and Mossel Bay on the N2, is a 65m (213-ft.) jump. The **Bloukrans River bridge-jump** (© **042/281-1458;** R580/$87 per person), 40km (25 miles) east of Plettenberg Bay, is the highest bridge-jump in the world, a stomach-churning 7-second, 216m (708-ft.) free fall. Both operate daily from 9am to 5pm.

CANOEING   Naturally, one of the best ways to explore South Africa's "Lakes District" is via its many waterways. Canoes can be rented throughout the area—contact the local tourism bureau wherever you are. Recommended canoe trips are the 3-day guided **Wilderness Canoe Trail** (R340/$51 per person) starting at the Ebb & Flow rest camp at Wilderness National Park (© **044/877-1197**), and the 2-hour **Keurbooms River Canoe Trail** ★★★, near Plettenberg Bay (© **044/535-9648**). The latter is unguided and takes you 7km (4¼ miles) upstream through totally untouched vegetation, to an overnight hut where you're assured of total privacy. The luxury of solitude will cost you R400 to R520 ($60–$78) per person per night, depending on the day; all you have to supply is food. For various catered overnight canoe trips, or half-day trips, contact Anna (BSC Zoology) at **Blue Sky Adventures** (© **044/343-1757**). For sea-kayaking tours of the marine-rich ocean in Plettenberg Bay, contact **Dolphin Adventures** (© **044/384-1536** or 083/590-3405; www.dolphinadventures.net).

DIVING   There are two snorkeling and diving routes in Tsitsikamma National Park: **StormsRiver Adventures** (© **042/281-1836;** www.stormsriver.com) provides guides, equipment, and dive courses. Gear and guides can also be rented from **Diving Adventures** (© **044/533-1158**) in Plettenberg Bay; ask about Jacob's Reef, another good spot off the Plett coast. The **Heads Adventure Centre** (© **044/384-0831**) can assist with any diving queries or equipment rentals in the Knysna area, where there are a number of wrecks to explore. The **Mossel Bay Diving Academy** (© **082/896-5649**) specializes in dives west of Knysna.

GOLFING You're really spoiled for choice on the Garden Route, which has all but supplanted KwaZulu-Natal as South Africa's "Golf Coast." The almost unrestricted (and unpoliced) development of new courses in the past 4 years, however, has produced a groundswell opposition from locals who fear that the environmental impact of these thirsty lawns for the well-heeled are still to be felt.

In George The George Golf Club course 🏌🏌 (© **044/873-6116**) will run you R330 ($49), while the **Fancourt** 🏌🏌🏌 links course and Bramble Hill course (© **044/804-0000**) will cost R650 to R850 ($97–$127) and R220 ($33), respectively; if you're not up to par, sign up with the Fancourt Golf Academy. Fancourt has two other Gary Player–designed championship courses, but you have to stay at Fancourt to play these.

In Knysna Pezula 🏌🏌 (originally named Sparrebosch; © **044/384-1222**), a relatively new links course designed by Ronald Fream and David Dale, is perched atop the Knysna East Head cliffs along with a hotel where you can overnight in luxury. It costs R400 ($60) to play Pezula.

In Plettenberg Bay Choose between the challenging 18-hole course in evergreen surrounds at the **Plet Country Club** (© **044/533-2132;** R280/$42) and the Gary Player–designed **Goose Valley** 🏌 (© **044/533-0846;** R300/$45).

In Hermanus Top course here is at **Arabella Country Estate,** 20 minutes from Hermanus, voted one of the country's top 10 courses; like Pezula and Fancourt, it has a luxury hotel with a spa for golf widows. Call © **028/284-0000** (R550/$82).

HIKING Garden Route This is a walker's paradise, and one of the best ways to experience this is with the **Garden Route Trail** 🏌🏌, an easy 5-day coastal walk (all luggage portaged) that takes you from the forests of the Wilderness National Park to the Featherbed Nature Reserve in Knysna and includes a trip on the Outeniqua Choo-Tjoe steam train (www.gardenroutetrail.co.za). For serious hikers, the following four are worth noting: the 108km (67-mile) 7-day **Outeniqua Trail** 🏌 (© **044/382-5606**), which takes you through plantations and indigenous forests (shorter versions available); the 64km (40-mile) 5-day **Tsitsikamma Trail** 🏌🏌 (© **044/874-4363**), an inland version of the more famous Otter Trail, which includes long stretches of *fynbos* (hardy indigenous evergreen vegetation) as well as forests and rivers; and the 27km (17-mile) 2-day **Harkerville Trail** 🏌🏌 (also called the Mini Otter Trail, and a good alternative), which features forest and coastal scenery (© **044/302-5606**). Best of all is the 42km (26-mile) 5-day **Otter Trail** 🏌🏌🏌, South Africa's most popular trail. It's a tough coastal walk, taking you through the **Tsitsikamma National Park,** past rivers and through indigenous forests, with magnificent views of the coast; its popularity means it must be booked at least a year in advance (© **012/426-5111;** www.san parks.org). The 3-night **Dolphin Trail** is a new luxury trail in the Tsitsikamma, with all luggage portaged, comfortable fully catered accommodations, plenty of time for lolling in tidal pools, and trained field guides accompanying walkers (© **042/280-3699;** www.dolphintrail.co.za). If you don't have the time (or energy!) for overnight trails, the 10km (6.25-mile) **Pied Kingfisher Trail** in Wilderness National Park follows the river through lush indigenous forest to a waterfall; the 9.5km (5.6-mile) **Kranshoek Walk** in the Harkerville Forest is another great forest environment, and the 9km (5.5-mile) **Robberg Trail** in Plettenberg Bay is definitely worth exploring for its wild coastline and whale-watching opportunities.

West Coast   Avid hikers are advised to find out more about the **Cederberg Wilderness Area,** which lies some 3 hours north of Cape Town—with its strange twisted rock formations and tea-colored streams, this is a hiker and climber's paradise, plus it's off the beaten track (© **022/931-2088**).

HORSEBACK RIDING   In Hermanus   Contact **Klein Paradys Equestrian Centre** (© **028/284-9422** or 083/240-6448).

In Swellendam   Short or full-day excursions in the Langeberg Mountains are offered by **Two Feathers Horse Trails** (© **082/956-9452**).

In Knysna   Cherie's Riding Centre (© **082/962-3223**) offers scenic trails along the Swartvlei Lake and forests, as well as a beach ride that includes a light lunch. **Forest Horse Rides** (© **044/388-4764**) takes small groups through the Knysna forests. For multiday horse safaris and shorter beach rides, contact **Great** (© **082/835-9110;** www.great.co.za).

In Plettenberg Bay   Contact **Equitrailing** (© **044/533-0599**) to explore fynbos and forests in this area.

MOUNTAIN BIKING   In and Around Wilderness   To tour the foothills of the Outeniqua Mountains (close to George), contact **Eden** (© **044/877-0179**); the half- and full-day tours often combine other activities. Eden also cycles the Swartberg Pass—thankfully, only down!

In Knysna   All three of the Diepwalle State Forest trails are ideal for mountain biking, particularly Harkerville, which has four color-coded routes: The Harkerville red route, which includes forest, fynbos, and the craggy coastline, is considered one of the best in South Africa—book early. For more information on trails in the **Knysna State Forests,** contact Mrs. van Rooyen (© **044/302-5606**) or Jacques at **Knysna Cycle Works** (© **044/382-5153;** www.knysnacycles.co.za). For guided tours and bike rentals, contact **Outeniqua Biking Trails** (© **044/532-7644**). For half- to 5-day mountain-biking tours of the region, including an add-on option to cycle with the Big 5 in Botswana, contact **Mountain Biking Africa** (© **082/783-8392;** www.mountain bikingafrica.co.za).

PARAGLIDING & GLIDING   Wilderness is considered South Africa's best site for coastal flying, particularly from August to May. Paragliding courses last 7, 10, and 14 days, or you can take a flight with a qualified instructor. Experienced pilots can rent equipment. Contact Bruce Watney from **Wings Over Wilderness** on his mobile phone (© **082/412-6858**) or at wow@atlantic.net. If you're based in Knysna and are loathe to travel, contact **Smile High** (© **044/384-0308** or 082/652-1952).

For a bird's-eye view of Plettenberg Bay, call **Stanley Island** (© **044/535-9442**); the two-seater glider flight is 30 minutes and costs R380 ($57) a person.

QUAD BIKING   Traverse a 20km (12-mile) trail in the Featherbed Nature Reserve. Call **S.E.A.L. Adventures** (© **044/382-5599** or 083/654-8755; R280/$42 per person).

SANDBOARDING   It's like snowboarding, only on sand. Contact **Downhill Adventures** (© **021/422-0388**) to surf the dunes on the coastal road to Hermanus.

SHARK-CAGE DIVING   In Hermanus   This has become a hugely popular activity, with a number of operators offering a similar service for more or less the same price; for more, see "Exploring the Overberg & Whale Coast," below.

In Mossel Bay   Shark Africa ★★★ (© **082/455-2438** or 044/691-3796) is the only operator in Mossel Bay, so your close-up encounter with a Great White is likely to be less crowded and frenzied than in Gansbaai. Cost is R1,200 ($179) for the shark-cage dive, R900 ($134) for viewing from boat only (closed Dec school holidays); you get a 50% reduction on the shark cage dive in the unlikely event that you don't see a Great White.

SKYDIVING/PARACHUTING   Try dropping from a height of 900m (2,952 ft.) with **Skydive Citrusdal** (© **021/462-5666**), based in the citrus-growing area 90 minutes north of Cape Town. With 1-day training for the novice costing R625 ($93), including the first jump, and additional jumps costing R150 ($22), this is one of the cheapest drops from a plane in South Africa.

SURFING   Top spots in the Western Cape include **Inner and Outer Pool and Ding Dangs** at Mossel Bay, **Vic Bay** (a good right point break), and **Elands Bay** ★, the best spot on the West Coast. For more information, e-mail Paul at nirvan@ilink.nis.za. Call **Ocean Life Surf Shop** (© **044/533-3253**) for rentals in Plett; see chapter 4 for rentals in Cape Town.

WHALE-WATCHING   Some of the best land-based whale-watching in the world happens on the Overberg coast, particularly Hermanus (see "Exploring the Overberg & Whale Coast," below), and the Garden Route from June to October/November. For boat-based encounters, note that only 13 to 20 boat-based whale-watching permits are issued for the entire South African coast—so make sure your operator has a permit. Boats are allowed to approach no closer than 50m (164 ft.), but the whales, curious, will often swim right up to the boat. See relevant sections below for recommended companies.

WHITE-WATER RAFTING   **Felix Unite** (© **021/670-1300**) runs rafting trips on the Breede River near Swellendam, but it's pretty tame when compared with the Doring River, considered the best in the Western Cape and running from mid-July to mid-September. **River Rafters** (© **021/712-5094**) organizes all-inclusive weekend trips for R895 ($134) per person. Base camp is 4 hours from Cape Town, in the Cederberg area. River Rafters also runs 4-day year-round trips on the Orange River, on the border with Namibia.

2 Exploring the Overberg & Whale Coast

During the 17th century, the Dutch settlers saw the jagged Hottentots Holland mountain range as the Cape Colony's natural border, beyond which lay what they called Overberg: literally, "over the mountain." Today this coastal area—wedged between the Cape Peninsula and the Garden Route, with mountains lining its northern border and the ocean on its south—encompasses a vast patchwork of grain fields, fruit orchards, and fynbos-covered hills.

There are two main routes through it: the **N2,** which traverses its northern half and is the quickest way to reach the Garden Route; and the slightly more circuitous and scenic **Coastal Route,** which is highly recommended, particularly during the whale-watching months.

Known as "the graveyard of ships," this rugged coastline is pounded by both the Atlantic and Indian oceans, which meet at L'Agulhus, Africa's most southerly point. East of this point is Arniston (Waenhuiskrans to locals), a bleak fishing village overlooking a magnificent turquoise bay; and De Hoop Nature Reserve, which vies with the Garden Route's Tsitsikamma as the most beautiful coastal reserve in South Africa. The Overberg gives visitors the opportunity to view a wealth of rare fynbos (see "Africa's Floral Kingdom," earlier in the chapter), as well as sightings of South Africa's national bird, the endangered blue crane.

Another sanctuary-seeker is the Southern Right whale; these return in increasing numbers every spring to mate and nurse their young off the "Whale Coast." The towns of Hermanus and Die Kelders, which overlook Walker Bay, and Koppie Alleen in De Hoop Nature Reserve are considered the best locations for viewing these oddly elegant, 60-ton, callus-encrusted cetaceans.

THE COASTAL ROUTE: GORDON'S BAY TO HERMANUS

You can reach Hermanus in about 80 minutes via the N2, but the coastal route, which adds another 20 to 30 minutes to the journey, and snakes along the sheer cliffs of the Hottentots Holland Mountains as they plunge down to the oceans below, is the recommended route. To take it, head for **Gordon's Bay,** an easy 40-minute drive from Cape Town on the N2, and take the coastal route (R44) out of town. Keep an eye out for **whales** and **dolphins** in False Bay as you descend the cliffs and bypass the Steenbras River mouth and Koeelbaai (pronounced "cool-buy"), a beautiful beach and break favored by surfers. Between rocky outcrops along this stretch of coast, you'll find small sandy coves shaded by ancient milkwood trees and grassy sunbathing areas.

Having crossed the Rooiels River (named after the red alder trees that grow in the riverine bush up the gorge, and twisting through another beautiful and usually deserted beach) you head through fynbos-covered hills passing the Buffels River and the sprawling holiday village of **Pringle Bay.** Just past Pringle Bay, where the R44 cuts inland past the Grootvlei marshlands, is a less traveled detour to **Cape Hangklip** (pronounced "*hung*-clip"—literally, "hanging rock"). This 460m-high (1,509-ft.) wedge of rock was often mistaken for Cape Point, which, incidentally, is how False Bay came by its name. After skirting three lagoon-type lakes—estuaries blocked by coastal dunes—you reach **Betty's Bay,** home to a remarkable number of ugly holiday cottages, one of only two land-based colonies of jackass penguins (the other is in Cape Town), and the beautiful **Harold Porter Botanical Gardens** (© **028/272-9311;** Mon–Fri 8am–4:30pm, Sat–Sun 8am–5pm; R8/$1.20). Take one of the four trails up the mountain to the **Disa Kloof Waterfall** (duration 1–3 hr.) to appreciate the beauty of the Cape's coastal fynbos.

If you need to stop for lunch or want a five-star hotel experience attached to one of the country's best 18-hole golf courses (with the requisite spa for golf widows), stop at the **Sheraton's Western Cape Hotel & Spa,** situated on **Arabella Country Estate.** The estate's lawns run into the Bot River lagoon, which provides lovely views, and the hotel offers every comfort known to man. Call © **028/284-0000** or visit **www.arabella sheraton.co.za;** rates start at R3,190 ($476) a room, but discounts are not unheard of.

The R44 now heads northeastward in the direction of Caledon, while the road to Hermanus branches eastward from the inland side of the Palmiet Lagoon. This is called the R43; take it and keep an eye out for the R320 turnoff, which will take you past the vineyards of the **Hemel-en-Aarde** (literally, "Heaven and Earth") Valley. Here, you can go on wine tastings at the small but excellent selection of farms that

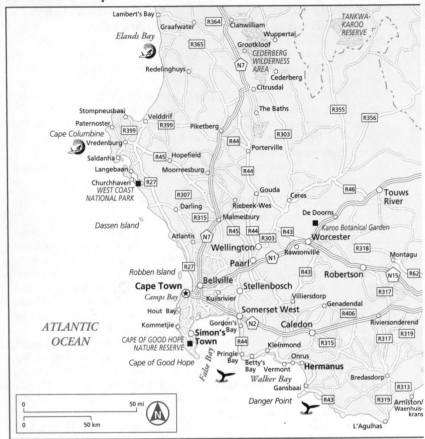

make up the **Hermanus Wine Route** (see "What to See & Do," below), stopping for lunch along the way (see "Where to Dine," below).

HERMANUS

With a backdrop of mountains, a large lagoon and long white beach, deep rock pools, and a wealth of coastal fynbos, **Hermanus** was destined to develop into one of South Africa's premier holiday resorts. The best times to visit Hermanus are autumn and spring, when aficionados come from afar to view the whales in **Walker Bay.** Humpback, Brydes, and Minke whales make occasional appearances, but the bay is essentially frequented by Southern Right whales.

Whales aside, there are seven **wine farms** in the Hemel-en-Aarde Valley to visit, the opportunity to have a **close encounter with a Great White shark** (see "Staying Active," earlier in this chapter), **long beaches** to walk, and a number of **good trails** in the Walker Bay and Fernkloof nature reserves. With Hermanus as your base, the **picturesque villages** of Arniston and Elim are only a day's excursion away.

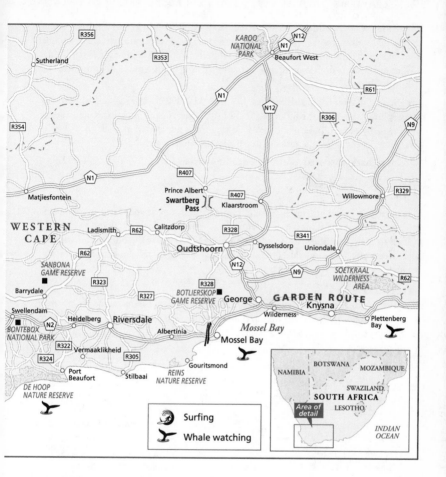

ESSENTIALS

VISITOR INFORMATION The excellent **Hermanus Tourism Bureau,** the Old Station Building, corner of Mitchell and Lord Roberts Street (© **028/312-2629;** www.hermanus.co.za) is open Monday through Saturday from 9am to 5pm, and from August to April on Sunday from 10am to 3pm.

GETTING THERE   By Car To rent a car, see "Cape Town: Getting Around," chapter 4. Hermanus lies 112km (69 miles) east of Cape Town via the N2 (just under an hour). The N2 route is a pretty drive, but the winding coastal route from Gordon's Bay, at times snaking along cliffs that plunge into the sea, is simply breathtaking (see "The Coastal Route: Gordon's Bay to Hermanus," above).

By Bus Contact **Hylton Ross** (© **021/511-1784**) for scenic day trips to Hermanus via the coastal route on Wednesday or Sunday.

GUIDED TOURS   Whale & Dolphin Safari (© **044/382-3815;** www.exploresouthafrica.co.za) offers a 4-day marine tour from Cape Town to Port Elizabeth via

Hermanus. Call **Fernkloof Nature Reserve** (© **028/312-1122**) to find out about specialized fynbos tours. For an insight into the greater community, take a walking tour of the Hermanus township, Zwelihle, the first black township established in the Overberg, with Wilson Salukazana, a registered SATOUR guide and proprietor of **Ubuntu Tours** (© **073/214-6949**).

By Boat   **Walker Bay Adventures** (© **028/314-0925**) runs 2-hour sundowner cruises on the lagoon for R80 to R100 ($12–$15) per person, and also rents a variety of seaworthy vessels. A variety of sea-kayaking tours are offered as well. See "Whale-Watching," below, for operators with permits for whale-watching.

On Horseback   Contact **Klein Paradys Equestrian Centre** (© **028/284-9422**).

WHAT TO SEE & DO
SURF & SAND
The sweeping 30km (19-mile) curve of **Grotto Beach** can be seen from most vantage points of Walker Bay. This is a great family beach, made for long walks and swimming. Closer to town, **Voëlklip** is a popular swimming beach where the hip youth hang out; the closest beach, **Langbaai** (pronounced "*lung*-buy"), offers the best bodysurfing, though currents can render it hazardous.

WILDFLOWERS
The **Fernkloof Nature Reserve** (© **028/313-0300**), which overlooks the town, offers more than 50km (31 miles) of hiking trails to explore the coastal fynbos of the region, as well as providing great views of Walker Bay.

WINE TASTING
The wineries that comprise the **Hermanus/Walker Bay Wine Route** are almost all located on the R320, known as Hemel-en-Aarde Valley; see "The Coastal Route: Gordon's Bay to Hermanus," above. (The exceptions are Mauroma and Erica, both near the picturesque village of Stanford.) The oldest and most respected of the Walker Bay wines are **Bouchard Finlayson** (© **028/312-3515**) and **Hamilton Russell** ✸✸✸ (© **028/312-3595**). The latter has the dubious distinction of producing South Africa's most expensive wines—a chardonnay and a pinot noir—but admittedly they are absolutely delicious, with the chardonnay voted one of the top 20 in the world. You can sample them for free, but you will be hard-pressed to walk away without a purchase. Tastings are held in a beautiful setting, Monday to Saturday from 9am to 12:30pm. Another winery worth seeking out, with glorious valley and lake views, is **Sumaridge** (© **028/312-1097**), the valley's newest. You can settle for just a tasting (daily 10am–3pm) or a picnic, arranged by calling ahead (© **083/636-1180**)—though you'll find a wonderful restaurant, Mogg's Country Cookhouse, nearby (see below).

WHALE-WATCHING
The once-threatened Southern Right whale (a protected species since 1946) is enjoying a major comeback, with the population on the South African coastline nearly doubling over the past decade. In recent years, as many as 2,000 whales have followed the annual migration from Antarctica, to flirt, mate, and calve in the warmer waters off the southern Cape coast.

One can clearly view these playful, gentle giants—sometimes at a distance of only 10m (33 ft.)—from the craggy cliffs that run along the Hermanus shoreline. For the best sightings, take the 12km (7½-mile) cliff path from New Harbour east to Grotto Beach and the lagoon. Beware of the waves—a young visitor was swept off the rocks in 2000 and drowned. Also recommended are the terraces above the Old Harbour, where a telescope and a plaque provide basic information about the bay and its whales.

Hermanus is very proud of the fact that it is the only town in the world to have a "whale crier": During whaling season, Wilson Salukazana walks the town streets blowing a kelp horn in a sort of Morse code to alert the town's inhabitants to the presence and whereabouts of whales. If you don't understand the code, never mind; Salukazana also wears a sandwich board and carries a mobile phone (© **073/214-6949**). Contact him direct for reports of the latest whale sightings, or contact the museum (© **028/ 312-1475**).

For assured "up-close" encounters, consider boarding a boat with a license to approach the whales (up to 50m/164 ft.). Bank on paying about R600 ($90); some of the longest-running operators are **Ivanhoe Sea Safaris** (© **082/926-7977**), **Southern Right Charters** (© **082/353-0550**), and **HFC Boat–based Whale Cruisers** (© **082/ 369-8931**).

Note: The limestone cliffs of De Kelders, southeast along the R43, provide a superb view of Walker Bay and the whales, and are never as crowded as Hermanus in season.

SHARK-CAGE DIVING

Fancy coming face to face with a Great White? Since the likes of Nicolas Cage, Ruby Wax, Richard E. Grant, and Andie MacDowell have (the latter trio for a reality-TV program called *Celebrity Shark Bait*), cage diving has become almost as mainstream as whale-watching. Boats leave from Gansbaai (a coastal town some 30km/19 miles east of Hermanus) and head out to Dyer Island Nature Reserve. This and nearby Geyser Island are favorites of the jackass penguin and seal breeding colonies, whose pups are an all-time favorite Great White shark snack—so much so that they call the channel between the islands "Shark Alley." The sharks are baited (highly contentious, I might add), and you stand an excellent chance of seeing one from the cage (or the boat, if you prefer to keep your distance)—the best time of the year is April to mid-June/July.

A number of operators offer a similar service for more or less the same price, but **White Shark Projects** (© **021/405-4537**; www.whiteshark.co.za) is one of the longest running and most respected (the company was instrumental in getting the white shark protected under S.A. law and was the recipient of the 2004 SKAL International Ecotourism Award). The rate is R1,000 ($149) per person and includes pickup from hotel or guesthouse (in Cape Town or Hermanus), a full buffet breakfast, a day at sea on a customized catamaran, dive equipment, a White Shark Lecture (given on board), lunch, tea, and return transfer. Note that you don't need to be a certified diver to descend in the cage. Another operator worth noting, particularly if you are a woman, is **Sharklady.** Equally committed to conservation and education, it's the only commercial hands-on women-only operator in the industry (© **028/312-3287**; www. sharklady.co.za).

WHERE TO STAY

Hermanus itself is not a particularly attractive town. With the streetscape away from the sea, it's reminiscent of any sprawling suburbia in the world; either opt for one of the following recommendations, all of which have grand sea views, or base yourself near the charming village of Stanford, a 15-minute drive inland, at a little gem called **Blue Gum Country Estate** (© **028/341-0116**; www.bluegum.co.za). A 52-hectare

(130-acre) farm, this tranquil retreat has only 10 rooms, each with private verandas and idyllic views of the mountains and gardens; its comfortable styling is rather like what Martha Stewart would have created if she hadn't been otherwise occupied in recent years. Rates start at R840 ($125) for two (R1,590/$237 in peak summer season)—this includes breakfast and a sumptuous high tea; set-menu dinners at R180 ($27) per person are worth writing home about.

Auberge Burgundy 🦀   Auberge Burgundy is conveniently located opposite the Old Harbour and the **Burgundy** restaurant (see "Where to Dine," below); a number of other dining options are also within easy walking distance. Almost every room has something to recommend it (except for some unfortunate fabric choices), and each comes with a walk-in dressing room. Request a room with a balcony that overlooks the ocean (although those that overlook the garden, which in spring is redolent with the scent of roses and lavender, aren't bad, either). Still, aside from a savings in price, it doesn't compare with Auberge Provence (below).

16 Harbour Rd., Hermanus 7200. ℂ 028/313-1201. Fax 028/313-1204. www.auberge.co.za. 18 units. From R880 ($131) double; R2,500 ($373) 3-bedroom penthouse. Rates include breakfast. AE, DC, MC, V. Children over 12 only. **Amenities:** Restaurant; pool; limited room service; laundry. *In room:* TV, minibar, hair dryer, tea- and coffee-making facilities, under-floor heating, heated towel rails.

Auberge Provence 🦀🦀   Set on the cliffs overlooking Walker Bay, just meters from the whale-watching path that meanders above it, this Provençal-style guesthouse is planned around a central courtyard pool. Interiors are stylish, with large stone fireplaces for the winter months; the exterior features a rustic stone facade, heavy wooden shutters, and wrought-iron balconies. All five rooms are extremely spacious (there are even separate dressing rooms), soothingly tasteful, and very comfortable: You can luxuriate in your queen-size beds while watching the whales, snug under goose-down duvets and cotton percale linen. Go all out and book the Lavender Suite if you want your own private plunge pool, or the huge Overberg Suite—a double-story suite with a private lounge, courtyard, and Jacuzzi. You'll be close to the village with its selection of good restaurants and shops, but you'll have to get in your car if you want to spend a day on the beach.

25 Westcliff Dr., Hermanus 7200. ℂ **028/312-1413**. Fax 028/312-1423. www.aubergeprovence.co.za. 6 units. R1,600 ($239) double; R2,200 ($328) suite. Rates include breakfast (rate depending on size of room); ask about winter specials. **Amenities:** Pool; laundry; library. *In room:* Minibar, hair dryer, tea- and coffee-making facilities.

Birkenhead House 🦀🦀🦀   A glam boutique hotel decorated in the Ian Shrager tradition, this exclusive guesthouse is aimed at a slightly younger market than the Marine, or at least those who like to mingle in a closed environment (no one but the maximum 22 hotel guests is allowed on the premises). Decor is eclectic—French baroque meets 21st-century modern, with a few pieces of kitsch thrown in for good measure—with white and cream the predominant colors throughout. The public spaces (of which there are several) are wonderfully over-the-top (massive gilded mirrors, French antiques, Philippe Starck lights, chandeliers, large Disneyesque white couches), but not all bedrooms are created equal. The top choice by far are nos. 1 and 2, built right at the front of the "house," with the only unobstructed views of the sea. Not even the honeymoon suite comes close. Officially opened in May 2003, at press time it still had a few rough edges, but because it's owned by the same couple who brought us Royal Malewane (one of the most beautiful game lodges flanking the Kruger), these kinks will hopefully be smoothed out in time. Neither of the three pools is big enough for my liking, but Hermanus's best swimming beaches flank the rocky outcrop on which the hotel is built.

7th Ave., Voelklip, Hermanus 7200. © **028/314-8000.** Fax 028/314-1208. www.royalmalewane.com. 11 units. R3,800–R5,950 ($567–$888) double. Rates include all meals, local beverages (excellent wines), tea, coffee, laundry. AE, DC, MC, V. Call for winter and extended stay rates. No children under 12. **Amenities:** Gourmet dining; 2 pools; gym; spa; laundry; all excursions arranged. *In room:* TV, minibar, hair dryer, DVD player.

Grootbos Private Nature Reserve ★★★ *Kids* Surrounded by 1,600 hectares
(3,952 acres) of fynbos fauna, a 1,000-year-old milkwood garden, and indigenous gardens a few minutes east of Hermanus, this is the best place in the Western Cape to learn about the eccentricities of the smallest and most diverse floral kingdom in the world. Guests are accommodated in either the original **Garden Lodge,** in 11 privately situated stone-and-timber cottages—each a fully equipped open-plan house with large fireplace, multilevel sun decks, and views of Walker Bay and the surrounding fynbos vegetation; or the newly opened **Forest Lodge,** which has wowed even arch-urbanites like Brad Pitt. Framed by a glass-and-steel structure, each of the 10 private suites is built from local sandstone rock and grass thatching that blends in with the surroundings, and from your bathtub you can watch the Southern Right whales breaching in Walker Bay. You can take a fynbos drive in the reserve every morning with one of the resident botanists, and evening walks or boat tours in Walker Bay with the resident marine biologist. Guests are also welcome to walk, ride, or bike through the reserve, which features—among other rarities—porcupine, lynx, and bushbuck. Picnic on your own private stretch of beach or dine out on a five-course meal at the Garden Lodge restaurant, with its sweeping views of the bay.

Off the R43, 33km (20 miles) east of Hermanus. Mailing address: P.O. Box 148, Gansbaai 7220, South Africa. © **028/384-8000.** Fax 028/384-8040. www.grootbos.com. 21 units. High season R4,600 ($687); low season R3,680 ($549). Rates include all meals and activities; minimum 2-night stay. Children's rates on request. AE, DC, MC, V. **Amenities:** Dining room; bar; pool; children's programs; babysitting; laundry; horseback riding; guided walks and drives. *In room:* TV, minibar, hair dryer, fireplace.

Marine Hotel ★★★ Situated on the craggy cliffs close to the town center and Old
Harbour, this grand dame of Hermanus (built in 1902) has wonderful views of Walker Bay and its whales. Rooms face either the sea or the courtyard (with pool); others have distant views of the mountain. Rooms are all tastefully furnished and finished in soothing mute colors, but even if you're not here to see the whales, it's worth spending an additional R800 ($119) for a luxury room, as this is the best-value category to feature gorgeous ocean views (note that one luxury has a mountain/pool view, so do specify). Guests can choose to relax in the comfortable wicker-furnished sea-facing bar or the pool terrace, or head for an invigorating swim in the large tidal pool below the cliffs. This Relais & Châteaux establishment also offers a choice of excellent restaurants: No prizes for guessing what the critically acclaimed **Seafood at the Marine** specializes in, but it's the **Pavilion** (serving a larger variety of meals) that has the view. The hotel also has the de rigueur beauty spa.

Marine Dr., Hermanus 7200. © **028/313-1000.** Fax 028/313-0160. www.marine-hermanus.co.za or www.collection mcgrath.com. 42 units. R2,250–R2,800 ($336–$418) double, depending on season; R3,050–R3,700 ($455–$552) luxury double, depending on season; R4,000–R5,600 ($597–$836) suite, depending on type and season. AE, DC, MC, V. No children under 12. **Amenities:** 2 restaurants; bar; pool; spa; concierge; room service; laundry. *In room:* A/C, TV, minibar, hair dryer, DVD player, ISDN, under-floor heating, heated towel rails.

WHERE TO DINE

For a relatively small coastal town, Hermanus offers a plethora of dining options, but foodies in search of super-fresh organic ingredients, innovatively combined and presented with unpretentious home-style flair (and averaging no more than R60/$8.95 for mains), should head out into the glorious countryside—either east to the quaint village of Stanford, where Mariana and husband Peter tend their vegetable garden as carefully as their guests in the cottage known as **Mariana's Home Deli & Bistro** ✦✦ (✆ 028/341-0272; Fri–Sun lunch only; no credit cards). If Mariana's is full (and it has become very popular), another Stanford stalwart is **Paprika** (✆ 028/341-0662; Wed–Sat only), where owner-chef Robin chalks up seasonal specialties on the blackboard outside (anyone for roast beetroot and avocado salad?). Alternatively, head west to the Hemel en Aarde Valley and **Mogg's Country Cookhouse** ✦✦ (✆ 028/312-4321; Wed–Sun). Having passed (and hopefully sampled) the five wineries along the way, you'll find Mogg's at the very end of a dirt track—a thoroughly rustic venue where mother-and-daughter team Josie and Jenny serve up a small a la carte menu that changes weekly; expect delicious combinations like roasted tomato and pepper soup, calamari with caper mayonnaise or chicken medallions, or rocket and cherry tomatoes on homemade tagliatelli. If the very presence of the ocean helps to work up an appetite, try **Milkwood** (✆ 028/316-1516), a casual seafood restaurant located just above the Onrus beach (a short drive west of Hermanus), which scores top ratings for location and views; the food's not bad, either—you can't go wrong with a plate of oysters, followed by linefish and washed down with the region's delicious Birkenhead beer.

Back in town you'll almost certainly want a sea view while imbibing its bounty: other than Bientang's Cave (reviewed below), the **Burgundy** (opposite Old Harbour; ✆ 028/312-2800)—located in the oldest building in Hermanus (the stone-and-clay cottage was built by a Swedish boat builder in 1875)—is a casual eatery serving simple fare like the Moroccan fish (grilled linefish in chile crust, served with *tzatziki*, a Greek cucumber sauce), or springbok *bobotie* (mild Malay curry) with pumpkin fritters. Make sure to book a table on the veranda or lawn—both overlook Walker Bay. A great location can sometimes be a drawback (management may be tempted to rest on their laurels)—if recent news reports are to be believed, the Burgundy's service has been less than deferential. If you want a more fine-dining atmosphere (where the staff is more professional), book a seaview table at the **Pavilion** at the Marine Hotel (see above), or specify the same at **Meditterea** (✆ 028/313-1685). Meditterea has a great seafood selection (the pesto kingklip is a good option), but if you're stuffed to the gills with seafood, the house specialty is slow-roasted—we're talking 15 hours—lamb. Lastly, if you're in the mood for Italian, **Rossi's** (✆ 028/312-2848) is rated as Hermanus's best, and **Marimba Café** is the place to go if you want to sample traditional African fare in a laid-back environment (✆ 028/312-2148).

Bientang's Cave ✦ ⓚⓘⓓⓢ SEAFOOD   Few restaurants in the world can best this location—a cave in the rocks just above the sea, with the most fabulous view of Walker Bay and the whales at play. Predictably, seafood is Bientang's specialty. Try one of two fresh linefish, grilled daily—the snoek with apricot, a traditional South African combination, is recommended. With the fresh sea breeze to build up an appetite, you might want to order one of the buffet options. Option A (R195/$29) gives you a chance to sample almost every item on the menu. Alternatively, opt for B, a choice of six salads, followed by bouillabaisse (tomato-based soup with calamari, prawns, mussels, linefish, and saffron), a choice of two linefish, and dessert—a steal at R170 ($25). A kids' menu is available for smaller appetites.

Off Marine Dr., next to Old Harbour, Hermanus 7200. ℂ **028/312-3454.** Reservations essential. Main courses R50–R130 ($7.45–$19). AE, DC, MC, V. Daily 11:30am–4pm; Fri–Sat 7–9pm.

Seafood at the Marine 🗬🗬🗬 FUSION SEAFOOD   Generally considered the best seafood restaurant in the entire Overberg region, with executive chef Christian injecting Continental creativity into the natural local bounty drawn from the ocean and fertile valleys. Start with chilled cucumber and coconut soup, marinated *concasse* of tomatoes, or tempura prawns and vegetables, served with a lemon-grass vinaigrette. Popular main courses include Rich Man's Fish and Chips, served in the *Financial Mail;* a ravioli of prawns and creamed leek; and pan-fried prawns with basil and lemon butter and shaved Parmesan, served on homemade angel-hair pasta. The muted modern Cape Cod–style decor, like the rest of the hotel, is wonderful, but the restaurant sadly has no sea view.

The Marine Hotel. ℂ **028/313-1000.** Reservations recommended. 3 courses R160 ($24); 2 courses R130 ($19). AE, DC, MC, V. Daily noon–2pm and 7–9:30pm.

MORE WHALE COAST DESTINATIONS

Two coastal destinations east of Hermanus well worth visiting are the village of **Arniston** 🗬🗬 and the **De Hoop Nature Reserve** 🗬🗬🗬. To reach either, head east to Stanford on R43, then turn northeast on R326 before turning right and heading south for Bredasdorp. Once there, you can go either immediately south on R316 toward Arniston, or north on R319 for De Hoop. If, however, you want to take a side trip to Africa's southernmost tip, where the Indian and Atlantic oceans meet, turn south on R319 for **L'Aghulus.** Barring the interesting facts of its location, the place itself has little to recommend a visit, unless you wish to view the wreck of the freighter *Meisho Maru 38* or visit the **Lighthouse Museum** (ℂ **028/435-6078**), built in 1849 and now a satellite of the Shipwreck Museum in Bredasdorp. The adjacent coffee shop and restaurant (open daily) is where Lydia Brown serves good home-style cooking. If you are taking the R319 south, don't miss a turn through the tiny town of **Elim.** Established as a Moravian mission station in 1824, the town remains unchanged and is still inhabited by Moravian church members who make their living from harvesting fynbos.

Arniston, a small fishing village and popular getaway, lapped by a startling turquoise sea, lies only 24km (15 miles) south of Bredasdorp on R316. If you see signs for WAENHUISKRANS, don't panic—Arniston, named after a British ship that wrecked here in 1815, is also officially known by its Afrikaans name, Waenhuiskrans, which

---

⌒Moments Fish Stew by Candlelight

One of the most authentic experiences in the Overberg has to be dining in the heart of the Kassiesbaai community—on a prearranged night, you can delight in pan-fried yellowtail and green bean stew, prepared by the local fisher-women and served by candlelight in one of the century-old fishing cottages. The meal costs R90 ($13) per person; to book, call Lillian Newman (ℂ **028/445-9760** or 076/150-1755). Lillian, a resident of Kassiesbaai, can also arrange for a guided tour.

refers to the limestone cave that is big enough to house a *waen* (wagon). For centuries, the local fishermen have been setting out at first light to cast their lines and returning at night to the quaint lime-washed, thatched cottages clustered on the dunes overlooking the sea—these dwellings, some of which date back 200 years, have collectively been declared a national monument and are picture-postcard pretty, though doubtless less romantic to live in. You can take a wander through the sandy streets of what is called the **Kassiesbaai community** 𝕣 on your own, but it's more considerate to visit with the local community guide. Then take a stroll along the unspoiled coastline.

The **De Hoop Nature Reserve** 𝕣𝕣𝕣 (© 028/425-5020; entry R20/$3 per person) has what many consider to be the best whale-watching spot on the entire coast, a huge dune appropriately called "Koppie Alleen" (Head Alone), but most visitors are here to explore one of the most beautiful coastal reserves in the world—51km (30 miles) of pristine white beach dunes, limestone cliffs, rock pools, wetlands, coastal fynbos, and no one to disturb the peace but zebra, several species of antelope, and more than 260 species of birds. Once in the reserve, there are limited routes (you can drive to the beach or accommodations), so the reserve is best explored on foot (ask about the Vlei Trail). Do note that the reserve hours (7am–6pm) are strictly enforced, and that visitors intending to overnight should report to the reserve office no later than 4pm on the day of arrival.

WHERE TO STAY & DINE

If the thought of self-catering at De Hoop sounds like too much work, **Buchu Bushcamp,** which adjoins the reserve, has six simple 2-bedroomed thatched and timber chalets (R700/$104 per chalet) and a restaurant; best of all Rory, a conservationist who used to head up the team at De Hoop, offers guided walks in the reserve. Contact the camp at © 028/542-1602 or visit www.buchu-bushcamp.com.

The Arniston Hotel 𝕣   This is the best hotel in the region, with a great location directly opposite the exquisitely colored sea. It's a place to come for a real sense of getting away from the rat race, but not from some of its better byproducts, like room service. The luxury sea-facing rooms are a vast improvement over the standard sea-facing rooms, and while the pool-facing rooms are less windy (yes, the wind often blows here), it's a shame to miss out on the surreal view. Dining is good, particularly the linefish, but if you're spending more than 1 night, do try to book a meal in the Kassiesbaai fishing community (see "Fish Stew by Candlelight," above).

P.O. Box 126, Bredasdorp 7280. © 028/445-9000. Fax 021/445-9633. www.arnistonhotel.com. 30 units. R1,100 ($164) double; R1,790 ($267) for recommended luxury sea-facing units. Rates include breakfast. AE, DC, MC, V. **Amenities:** 2 restaurants; bar; pool; room service; babysitting; laundry; boating; cycling. *In room:* A/C (some), TV, hair dryer, tea- and coffee-making facilities.

De Hoop Nature Reserve 𝕣 *Kids*   This is one of the most peaceful places on earth, with only a handful of people to explore the 36,000-hectare (88,920-acre) reserve (see above) once the gates close for nonresidents at 6pm. The small self-catering cottages are very basic—two bedrooms, one bathroom, and an open-plan kitchen and dining room—and there is no shop or restaurant, but they are comfy. Pack an overnight picnic (there is a large Pick 'n Pay in Hermanus or if you're coming from Cape Town, go on a shopping splurge at Melissa's in Kloof St., or pop into Peregrine farm stall along the way) and maybe something to barbecue; each cottage has its own *braai* (barbecue) site (wood is sold at the reserve entrance), and there's nothing quite like a fire crackling under a star-spangled sky. As only three cottages are equipped with bedding and towels, make sure you book these slightly more "luxurious" units—they also enjoy a better location. De Hoop is ideal for young children—it has a game trail, a wetlands trail, and endless sand dunes and coves to romp in, but no TV. Check-in time is currently between 2 and 6pm; it's probably a good idea to call ahead to make sure this is still the case.

Wydgeleë, Private Bag X16, Bredasdorp 7280. Bookings and inquiries ℂ **028/425-5020**. Reserve ℂ 028/542-1253. Fax 028/425-5030. www.capenature.org.za. 10 units, each with 4–6 beds. R320–R600 ($48–$90) basic cottage/4 people; R480–R600 ($72–$90) luxury cottage/4 people; R80–R100 ($12–$15) per extra person. Campsites R130 ($19). AE, MC, V.

3 Swellendam & the Overberg/Breede River Valley Interior

Swellendam: 220km (136 miles) E of Cape Town

Most people who choose to drive through the Overberg interior (as opposed to its Whale Coast) are on their way to the Garden Route and may rush through and completely bypass the excellent pit stops and side trips along the way. Ideally, try to set aside enough time to take the R62 detour (see "The Route Less Traveled," below), which means veering north from Swellendam and traveling through the small towns of Barrydale, Ladismith Calitzdorp, Oudtshoorn, and Prince Albert. This makes for a great road trip, and the empty, arid spaces are a great contrast to the later lushness of the Garden Route.

Leaving Cape Town, you will ascend **Sir Lowry's Pass** ⭐⭐ to reach the fruit-growing areas of Grabouw and Elgin (the area, incidentally, produces 65% of South Africa's apple export crop) and the first of many farm stalls dotted along the way. **Peregrine** ⭐⭐⭐ (opposite the Grabouw turnoff) is one of the oldest and still one of the best—stop here for fresh farm produce and various traditional "road trip" treats (see the appendix) like *biltong* (air-dried meat strips) and *droë wors* (air-dried sausage). The adjacent bakery is also excellent—the pies (try the springbok), *melktert* (custard tart), and *koeksisters* (deep-fried dough soaked in syrup) are sublime.

The first detour you might consider is the R406, which loops past the villages of **Genadendal** and **Greyton.** Genadendal is the oldest Moravian mission village in Africa, with buildings dating back to 1738. The **Genadendal Mission and Museum Complex** documents the activities of the missionaries and their flock. For guided tours, call ℂ **028/251-8582** (Mon–Thurs 8:30am–5pm; Fri 8:30am–3:30pm; Sat 9am–noon).

Greyton, a few minutes farther east on the R406, was developed much later and by a more affluent community—this is still very much the case, as is evidenced by the recent boom in property prices, inflated by affluent Capetonians looking for a safe, secure, and pretty bolthole. Set at the foot of the Riviersonderend Mountains, with many beautifully restored Victorian and Georgian buildings, it's a great place to stop for lunch—grab a table on the stoep (veranda) at the **Oak & Vigne** (ℂ **028/254-9037;** open daily, closed for dinner). If you feel like spending the night, your best bet is **Greyton Lodge** (ℂ **028/254-9876;** R295–R495/$44–$74 per person, depending on season), a cozy country inn that has an excellent reputation for its dining and wine list. Other than strolling the streets, the main attraction here is the 14km (8.5-mile) **Boesmanskloof Trail,** which traverses the mountains to the town of McGregor. A good alternative is the 9km (5.5-mile) walk to **Oak Falls**—the highlight of the route—instead. For information, call ℂ **028/254-9414.**

The Route Less Traveled

To reach the Garden Route from Cape Town, it's worth considering an alternative route, highly recommended for its empty roads, spectacular mountain scenery, vineyard valleys, small-town architecture, and wide-open plains. With no detours or stops, this scenic route will take approximately 90 minutes more than traveling directly to the Garden Route along the N2, but ideally you should plan to overnight 2 to 3 nights along the way. To help plan your journey, look at the comprehensive listings on www.route62za.co.za. Suggested route is as follows:

Travel north from Cape Town on the N1, on the toll road that takes you through the **Du Toitskloof Tunnel**. Time allowing, bypass the tunnel and traverse the **Du Toitskloof Pass**—the soaring mountain and valley views from the 1:9 gradient road are well worth the extra 15 minutes.

At Worcester, capital of the Breede River region, the **Karoo Desert Botanical Gardens** (© 023/347-0785; Mon–Fri 7:30am–1pm and 2–4:30pm; Aug–Oct also Sat–Sun 9am–4pm), off Roux Road, are definitely worth viewing, particularly in spring (admission R12/$1.80). The gardens showcase the weird and wonderful plants from the country's semi-arid regions.

From here, head southeast on the R60 to Robertson, keeping an eye out for **Graham Beck**'s cellar and tasting room (© 023/626-1214; Mon–Fri 9am–5pm, Sat 10am–3pm), worth a stop if you like sparkling wine—the award-winning nonvintage *brut* is used at presidential inaugurations, and many consider the vintage *brut* (made from 100% chardonnay grapes) the best *methode champenoise* in the country.

From Robertson (where you should make time to sample the superb wines of **Springfield** [© 023/626-3661]—where, incidentally, my favorite sauvignon blanc, the aptly named "Life from Stone," is produced), it's another 20km (12 miles) southeast to Ashton, where you should plan to stop at **Fraai Uitzicht 1798**. Located in the midst of vineyards and orchards, this wonderful *auberge* and restaurant is no longer a well-kept secret, so reservations are essential in the summer, particularly on weekends (© 023/626-6156). It's definitely worth overnighting here to indulge (as you should) in the six-course menu, matched with wines from the region. If Axel and Mario are unable to

SWELLENDAM

Swellendam, a pretty town situated at the foot of the Langeberg Mountains and appropriately billed as "the historic heart of the Overberg," is the perfect halfway stop (for lunch or the night) for visitors driving from Cape Town to the Garden Route directly via the N2.

ESSENTIALS

VISITOR INFORMATION   The **Swellendam Tourism Bureau** is in the Oefeningshuis at 36 Voortrek St. (© **028/514-2770;** Mon–Fri 8am–5pm, Sat 9am–noon).

GETTING THERE   By Car   The quickest way to get to Swellendam is via the N2, as described above. Alternatively, you can travel the more attractive mountain and semidesert routes (see "The Route Less Traveled," above).

accommodate you, there are two other choices: Either trundle a bit farther south to Bonnievale and dine on fine country fare at **Jan Harmsgat Country House** ((©) **023/616-3407**) before overnighting at nearby Swellendam, or traverse the 10km (6¼-mile) **Cogmanskloof Pass** 🔆 to the pretty town of **Montagu** 🔆, where there are a number of B&Bs. Either book one of the four garden cottages at Aasvöelkrans ((©) **023/614-1228**; www.aasvoelkrans.co.za), a delightful guesthouse located on a stud farm at the foot of the Langeberg Mountains, or a room at **Mimosa Lodge** in the center of town ((©) **023/614-2351**). Take an evening stroll and admire the town's Victorian architecture and soaring brick-red mountains, or enjoy a therapeutic dip in the nearby hot springs (it's worth noting from an aesthetic point of view, however, that these have been ruined by the resort that's sprung up around them). The **springs** ((©) **023/614-1050**) are a constant 109°F (43°C) and are open daily from 8am to 11pm, for R25 ($3.75) per person.

From Montagu you can retrace your footsteps through the **Cogmanskloof Gorge** to rejoin the R60 south to Swellendam, but the better route by far is to take the road east to Barrydale (if you need to a pit stop, **Clarke of the Karoo** is the best restaurant here; (©) **028/572-1017**). Along the way you'll pass signs for **Sanbona Wildlife Reserve,** a beautiful 54,000-hectare (133,380-acre) reserve that now stocks the Big 5; time (and money) allowing, make this your next stop. Next up is the small village of **Calitzdorp;** leave enough time for a short stop to taste some of the Cape's best fortified wines at **Boplaas** ((©) **044/213-3326**) and **Die Krans** ((©) **044/213-3314**). If you have the time to spend another night on the R62, **The Retreat at Groenfontein** ((©) **044/23-3880;** www.groenfontein.com) is the place to do so—20km (12 miles) northeast of Calitzdorp, this comfortable Victorian farmhouse lives up to its name, with wide-open, unpopulated spaces and breathtaking views of the Swartberg mountains. By overnighting here, you also ensure that you arrive in Oudtshoorn before dark to tackle the Swartberg Pass. Then overnight at Prince Albert—highly recommended; see "Where to Stay," later in this chapter—before traveling on southward to George and the pleasures of the Garden Route.

By Bus   Intercape, Translux, Greyhound, and **Baz Bus** pass through daily on their way to the Garden Route. See chapter 2 for contact details.

GETTING AROUND   On Foot   This is the best way to explore the small village and Drostdy Museum complex. Hiking trails in the nearby Marloth Nature Reserve lead into the Langeberg Mountains; for permits and maps of hikes, including the popular but tough 5-day Swellendam Trail, contact the reserve office ((©) **028/514-1410** or 072/601-4145).

On Wheels   Bontebok National Park ((©) **028/514-2735;** daily 7am–7pm) lies 7km (4¼ miles) out of town and is accessible by car or mountain bike. Rent bikes from **Swellendam Backpackers Lodge** ((©) **028/514-2648;** R60–R114/$8.95–$17 per day).

On Horseback   Short or full-day excursions in the Langeberg Mountains are offered by **Two Feathers Horse Trails** (✆ **082/956-9452** or 082/494-8279).

HISTORIC SWELLENDAM

Back in the early 1700s, the Dutch East India Company was most perturbed by the number of men deserting the Cape Colony to find freedom and fortune in the hinterland. Swellendam was consequently declared a magisterial district in 1743, making it the third-oldest white settlement in South Africa and bringing its reprobate tax evaders once again under the Company fold. In 1795 the burgers finally revolted against this unwanted interference and declared Swellendam a republic, but the Cape's occupation by British troops later that year made their independence rather short lived. Swellendam continued to flourish under British rule, but a devastating fire in 1865 razed much of the town. Almost a century later, transport planners ruined the main road, Voortrek Street, by ripping out the oaks that lined it, ostensibly to widen it. Two important historical sites to have survived on this road are, at no. 36, the **Oefeningshuis** (where the tourism bureau is located), built in 1838, and, at no. 11, the over-the-top baroque **Dutch Reformed Church,** built in 1901.

The **Drostdy Museum complex** 🏛🏛 (✆ **028/514-1138**) comprises the Drostdy, the Old Goal and Ambagswerf (Trade's Yard), Mayville House, and Zanddrift, now an excellent daytime restaurant. The Drostdy was built by the Dutch East India Company in 1747 to serve as residence for the *landdrost* (magistrate), and features many of the building traditions of the time: yellowwood from the once abundant forests, cowdung and peach-pit floors, elegant fireplaces, and, of course, Cape Dutch gables. The Drostdy also houses an excellent collection of late-18th-century and early-19th-century Cape furniture in the baroque, neoclassical, and Regency styles.

WHERE TO STAY & DINE

Swellendam's small-town rural ambience is starting to change, as a number of young entrepreneurs, both local and foreign, have opted to drop out and live the rural life, opening quirky or modern alternatives to the more traditional options reviewed below. One, in particular, deserves a mention: **Bloomestate,** owned by Dutch couple Miranda and Niels, will suit younger travelers with a preference for contemporary design. Miranda and Niels designed most of the furniture and fittings, utilizing the skills of local craftsmen (or, if all else failed, importing Philippe Starck). The new rooms, spacious and pleasing to the eye (albeit slightly bland), have been built on a single raised platform (pity they're not totally separate suites), with doors opening onto landscaped gardens and a heated saltwater pool and Jacuzzi. Rates are R750 to R1,100 ($112–$164) double, including breakfast (✆ **028/514-2984;** www.bloom estate.com). If your taste runs to the more traditional, another good option, with suites and cottages scattered in the gardens of a historic Cape Dutch National Monument, is **Augusta De Mist Country House** (✆ **028/514-2425;** www.augus-tademist.com; R200–R450/$30–$67).

The best place to eat dinner is still **Herberg Roosje;** for a more fine-dining experience, try **Klippe Rivier** (see below for reviews on both), though the **Old Mill** (✆ **028/514-2790**), where Belgian owner Nikki serves up Flemish delicacies (like slow-stewed rabbit) and quirky takes on new ingredients (try the venison quiche), is also proving popular. But if you're just looking for a caffeine fix or want to eavesdrop on the local gossip, stop in at the quirky **Colour & Coffee** (✆ **028/514-3723**).

Herberg Roosje Van De Kaap ✰✰ *Value*   Conveniently located opposite the Drostdy Museum, this quaint country inn is the ideal place to stay over on your way to the Garden Route. Some of the rooms are a bit on the small side, but the tasteful furnishings and general welcoming ambience more than make up for this—if you want more space, book one of the garden suites or the honeymoon suite. The inn has no lounge, but guests tend to gather around the sparkling pool and the equally charming restaurant, **Roosje Van De Kaap,** which serves a la carte meals with an Italian slant in an informal atmosphere—definitely consider eating here even if you don't stay. Pizzas are popular, as is the Cape Duo (*bobotie,* curried lamb) and the filet Roosje, tender beef medallions prepared in garlic butter and herbs—an all-time favorite.

5 Drostdy St., Swellendam 6740. ℭ/fax **028/514-3001.** www.roosjevandekaap.com. 9 units. R490–R660 ($73–$99) double. Rates include breakfast. MC, V (note that using your credit card carries a small surcharge here). **Amenities:** Restaurant; pool; laundry. *In room:* Hair dryer on request.

Klippe Rivier Country House ✰✰✰   This Cape Dutch homestead, dating back to the 1820s, is by far the most luxurious address to overnight in Swellendam, though it's pretty pricey and service can be a tad snooty. Furnished with beautiful antiques and run like a small luxury hotel, Klippe Rivier lies on the outskirts of town, which means you'll have to drive to visit the Drostdy Museum. Choose between the spacious downstairs suites (each with its own fireplace and walled-in garden) and the more contemporary upstairs suites (each with a private balcony overlooking the mountains and gardens). For total privacy and stunning mountain views, request the honeymoon cottage, set well away from the main house. Klippe Rivier has its own vegetable gardens and orchards. The three-course dinners featuring country-style cooking (R160/$24) can last several hours, concluding in the library or lounge with coffee and chocolate truffles.

Box 483, Swellendam 6740. ℭ **028/514-3341.** Fax 028/514-3337. www.klipperivier.com. 7 units. R1,790 ($267) double. Rate includes breakfast. Call for winter specials. AE, DC, MC, V. No children under 8. **Amenities:** Dining room; pool; limited room service; laundry. *In room:* A/C, fans, hair dryer, fireplace (downstairs rooms only), heaters.

4 Exploring the Klein Karoo & the Garden Route

The Garden Route, with recommended detours into the Klein Karoo, has become the country's most popular tourist destination after Cape Town, drawing visitors year-round to its indigenous forests, freshwater lakes, wetlands, hidden coves, and long beaches. You can traverse mountains, explore caves, bike through forests, encounter a white shark, visit an ostrich farm, paraglide onto the beach, or boat down the many rivers and lakes of South Africa's most famous garden. The mountains that range along the Garden Route's northern border beckon with a series of spectacular passes that cut through to the Afrikaans hinterland of the Klein Karoo. Besides providing a stark contrast to the lush coast, the dusty *dorpies* (little towns) dotted throughout this arid area have developed a distinctive architectural style, the best-preserved examples being found in the tiny hamlet of **Prince Albert** ✰✰✰. **Oudtshoorn** ✰✰ is the center of the Klein Karoo, and this is where you'll find the Klein Karoo region's most famous attractions: ostrich-farm tours, the Cango Caves, and the **Swartberg Pass** ✰✰✰, a dramatic road trip connecting Oudtshoorn with Prince Alfred.

The narrow coastal strip that forms the Garden Route stretches from the rural town of Heidelberg in the west to Storms River Mouth in the east; and from the shore of the Indian Ocean to the peaks of the Outeniqua and Tsitsikamma coastal mountain ranges. This is the official boundary description, but for many, Mossel Bay or George marks the entry point in the west, and Port Elizabeth the eastern point of the route. (See chapter 6 for transport details to and from Port Elizabeth and the nearby hamlet of Jeffrey's Bay.)

Highlights of this region include the Wilderness National Parks "Lakes District," with some of the Garden Route's loveliest coastline; Knysna's lagoon- and forest-based activities; and Plettenberg Bay, which combines some of South Africa's best swimming beaches with beautiful fynbos and forest surrounds in areas like the Crags. The real "garden" of the Garden Route, however, is the Tsitsikamma National Park, where dense indigenous forests interrupted only by streams and tumbling waterfalls drop off to a beautiful coastline.

Time allowing, the best way to reach the Garden Route is via the Klein Karoo.

OUDTSHOORN, PRINCE ALBERT & THE KLEIN KAROO

The Klein (Little) Karoo—a sun-drenched area about 250km (155 miles) long and 70km (43 miles) wide—is wedged between the coastal mountains that separate it from the Garden Route and the impressive Swartberg mountain range in the north. To reach it from any angle, you have to traverse precipitous mountain passes, the most spectacular of which is the Swartberg Pass, connecting the Klein Karoo with its big brother, the Great Karoo. Unlike this vast dry land that stretches well into the Northern Cape and Free State, the "little" Karoo is watered by a number of streams that flow down from the mountains to join the Olifants River. Grapes grow here (Calitzdorp produces some of the country's best port), as does lucerne (alfalfa), which is why farmers in the region were able to successfully introduce the ostrich—lucerne is a favorite food of the ostrich.

Today the **ostrich farms,** together with the **Cango Caves**—a series of subterranean chambers some 30km (19 miles) from Oudtshoorn—are the main draws of the region, but it is the **Swartberg Pass,** rated one of the most spectacular drives in Africa, the **unique sandstone architecture,** and the **small-town Afrikaans ambience** that makes no Garden Route itinerary complete without a sojourn in Oudtshoorn, center of the Klein Karoo.

Fun Fact **Feather Barons & Ostrich Palaces**

It was the ostrich that put the Klein Karoo on the map: During the late 19th and early 20th centuries, when the world decided that ostrich feathers were simply the hautest of haute, Oudtshoorn, where the first ostriches were farmed, found itself crowned the feather capital of the world. Local ostrich farmers, known then as "feather barons," became millionaires overnight, building themselves luxurious "ostrich palaces," clearly identifiable by their sandstone turrets and other baroque touches. Sadly, the boom went bang in 1914, with the sobering outbreak of World War I. The profitable trade in feathers never really recovered, with fickle Dame Fashion seeking her post-war inspiration elsewhere, but with the current health scares surrounding red meat, the ostrich is again enjoying a surge in popularity—it's a delicious and low-fat alternative to beef, and bears absolutely no resemblance to chicken.

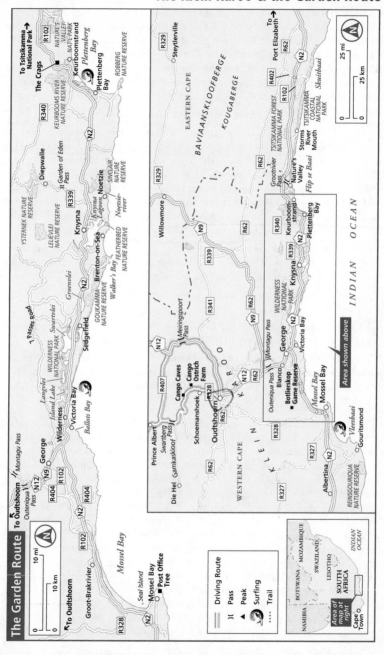

ESSENTIALS

VISITOR INFORMATION   You'll find the **Oudtshoorn Tourism Information Bureau** (© **044/279-2532;** www.oudtshoorn.com; Mon–Fri 8am–5pm, Sat 9am–1pm) on Baron van Rheede Street. The best place to get information in Prince Albert (about the town as well as trips to Die Hel, Karoo National Park, and the Garden Route) is at **Dennehof** (contact Lindsay at © **023/541-1227** or 082/456-8848; princealbert@telkom.co.za)

GETTING THERE   By Plane   There are no scheduled flights here.

By Car   Whichever way you approach it, you'll have to traverse a mountain pass to get to Oudtshoorn. Via the N1 from Cape Town, you'll head south on the R407 to Prince Albert before tackling the majestic Swartberg Pass. Alternatively (and time allowing, preferably), you can come via Calitzdorp (see "The Route Less Traveled," earlier in this chapter). The quickest way to get here is to travel along the N2 to Mossel Bay before heading north over the Robinson Pass (R328/$49), or to George before heading north over the Outeniqua Pass (N12). Oudtshoorn is an hour (88km/55 miles) from Mossel Bay and 45 minutes (55km/34 miles) from George.

By Bus   Intercape and **Translux** travel from Johannesburg daily; Translux travels from Cape Town to Port Elizabeth. The **Baz Bus** operates a shuttle between Oudtshoorn and George. See chapter 2 for regional phone numbers.

By Train   The **Blue Train** stops at Oudtshoorn on its Garden Route Tour (see chapters 2 and 3).

GETTING AROUND   Avis (© **044/272-4727**) has an office on Voortrekker Street. If you need a taxi, contact **DD Transport** (© **044/279-2176**).

SPECIAL EVENTS   Every April, Oudtshoorn hosts the **Klein Karoo National Arts Festival (KunsteFees)** 👁👁👁, one of the biggest and best cultural festivals in South Africa. Contact the Tourism Bureau for more information.

WHAT TO SEE & DO

With the introduction of wire fencing and sweet lucerne, the large-scale domestication of the ostrich first became possible in the 1800s. But it was only when Victorian fashion victims developed an insatiable appetite for ostrich feathers around 1880 that it became a reality, and land values in the Oudtshoorn area shot up overnight. At the height of the feather boom, the so-called feather barons built lavish town houses where they would occasionally overnight before returning to their marble-floored farmhouses.

The best preserved of these "ostrich palaces" (albeit not the grandest) is the **Le Roux Town House,** a satellite of the CP Nel Museum, where you can peruse photographs of other houses that didn't survive the 20th century. Fortunately, more of these magnificent sandstone buildings survived than were knocked down; though most are closed to the public, they're worth taking a walk or drive past (you can pick up a map from the tourism office). Note particularly **Pinehurst** on Jan van Riebeeck Street, now part of a teachers' training college, and the elegant **Mimosa** on Baron van Reede Street. The latter street becomes the R328, which leads out of town to the ostrich farms (see below), the Rust-en-Vrede waterfall (a 74m/243-ft. drop under which you can cool off in summer), and the Cango Caves, Oudtshoorn's biggest attraction after the ostrich.

Arbeidsgenot 👁👁   Arbeidsgenot (meaning "The Pleasure of Work") is not a feather palace, but the humble abode of C. J. Langenhoven, author of South Africa's first national anthem, and his family from 1901 to 1950. It's a delightfully authentic house museum, not least because everything has been left exactly as it was when the man penned his noteworthy novels and poems, and a very tranquil place to spend a half-hour.

217 Jan van Riebeeck Rd. (©) **044/272-2968.** R10 ($1.50) adults, R8 ($1.20) children. Mon–Fri 9:30am–1pm and 2–5pm.

CP Nel Museum ⭐ Located in a handsome sandstone building opposite the Tourist Information Bureau, this old-fashioned museum has many exhibits relating to Oudtshoorn's boom period, as well as photographs of some of the ostrich palaces that never made it past the 1950s. It also houses a synagogue and exhibits relating to Oudtshoorn's once-large Jewish community—in fact, Oudtshoorn was often derisively referred to as "Little Jerusalem" by those envious of the success of the feather merchants, most of whom were Jewish. Admission includes entry to the **Le Roux Town House,** a "mini" feather palace on High Street. Built in 1909, the interior features some original pieces dating back to the Le Roux family's heyday, but the majority of the furnishings—imported from Europe between 1900 and 1920—have been bought and placed *in situ* by the museum.

Corner of Baron van Rheede St. and Voortrekker Rd. (©) **044/272-7306.** R10 ($1.50) adults, R3 (45¢) children under 13. Mon–Fri 8am–5pm; Sat 9am–4pm.

The Cango Caves ⭐⭐ *Kids* The **Cango Caves** were first explored in 1780 by a local farmer who was lowered into the dark, bat-filled chamber now named in his honor. The **Van Zyl Hall,** 107m (351 ft.) across and 16m (52 ft.) high, has some truly incredible million-year-old limestone formations, including the "Organ Pipes." A second chamber was discovered in 1792, and a century later the caves opened as a tourist attraction. Regrettably, they were damaged in the 1960s and 1970s, when the floors were evened out with concrete; ladders, colored lights, and music were installed; and a separate entrance was chipped away for "nonwhites" (who had tours at different times).

Today the caves enjoy a slightly more respectful treatment, with wardens fighting an ongoing battle to keep the limestone formations from discoloring from exposure to lights and human breath (although their running commentary is a tad irritating). There are two tours to choose from: the hour-long "standard" tour, which departs every hour and visits six chambers; and the 90-minute "adventure" tour, which covers just more than 1km (a little over ½-mile), some of which must be crawled (under no circumstances tackle this if you're overweight or claustrophobic; have heart, knee, or breathing problems; or are not wearing sensible shoes and trousers).

Approximately 30km (19 miles) from town on the R328. (©) **044/272-7410.** Standard tour R40 ($5.95); Adventure tour R55 ($8.20). Daily 9am–4pm.

VISITING AN OSTRICH FARM

The ostrich remains the primary source of income for Oudtshoorn, with thousands flocking to see, touch, eat, and (yes) even ride the giant birds. There are some 400 ostrich farms, of which Highgate (incidentally, the biggest ostrich farm in the world), Safari, Oudtshoorn, and Cango all vie for the tourist buck—R32 to R40 ($4.75–$5.95), to be exact—offering more or less the same 45- to 80-minute tour. These include an explanation of ostrich farming (from incubation to tanning), guided tours of the farm, the opportunity to sit on an ostrich, and an ostrich "derby." All offer meals with ostrich on the menu (you usually need to prebook).

Of the farms, **Cango Ostrich Farm** 🐦🐦 ((© **044/272-4623**) is considered by many to be the best, not least because of its location overlooking the beautiful Schoemanshoek Valley. Individuals are not tagged onto large tour groups, and visitors take a brief walk from one process to the next rather than being driven around a large farm. Finally, while you can sit on an ostrich, they are not raced here, saving you the embarrassment of this circus display (if you'd like to see this for anthropological reasons, opt for **Highgate** [© **044/272-7115**], the world's oldest and largest show farm). The 45-minute tours (R36/$5.35) take place daily from 9am to 4:30pm; reserve ahead and enjoy a lunch (or dinner) served in restored laborers' cottages with great views overlooking the valley. For an extra R15 ($2.25) you can also book a wine tasting with your meal and sample the distinctive flavors of the Klein Karoo.

A BREATHTAKING DRIVE 🐦🐦🐦

For many, the greatest highlight of visiting the Klein Karoo is traversing the Swartberg Mountains to Prince Albert, a charming 18th-century Groot Karoo town that lies 100km (63 miles) north.

To reach the **Swartberg Pass** 🐦🐦🐦, a 27km (17-mile) gravel road built more than 100 years ago by master engineer Thomas Bain, take the R328 (also known as Cango Valley Rd.) north from Oudtshoorn. About 1km (a little more than ½-mile) before the road terminates at the Cango Caves, you'll find a turnoff to the west, signposted PRINCE ALBERT. This marks the start of the pass, which soon begins its steep ascent. By the time you reach the summit, you will have enjoyed stupendous views of the Klein Karoo, which lies some 1,220m (4,002 ft.) below. Stop to gird your loins, for the journey has only just begun. The northern descent is hair-raising—10km (6¼ miles) of zigzags, serpentines, twists, and steep gradients on a narrow dirt road with nothing between you and the abyss but a good grip on the wheel. You'll note a turnoff to the west that will take you to **Die Hell (Gamkaskloof)** 🐦🐦🐦. This is another magnificent drive, particularly popular with fynbos lovers, but unless you overnight in one of the rudimentary Cape Nature Conservation cottages, you'll have to return the way you came—set aside most of the day for this detour. For guided hikes in Die Hell, contact **Saxe-Coburg Lodge** (© **023/541-1267**).

The road continues to twist and turn before finally winding its way out of the Swartberg. At this point, you can either go to Prince Albert or turn back into the mountains and return to Oudtshoorn via Meiringspoort. Opt for **Prince Albert** 🐦🐦🐦; the town is an architectural gem, with almost all the buildings preserved and maintained in their original 19th-century form. If you're in need of real tranquillity or wish to wander the streets at sunset to view the mix of architectural styles, consider spending the night—recommendations are listed below; alternatively, contact **Prince Albert's Tourism Information,** Church Street (© **023/541-1366;** Mon–Fri 9am–5pm, Sat 9am–noon).

To return to Oudtshoorn, take the road back to the Swartberg Pass, keeping an eye out for the R407, which takes you east through Meiringspoort. This is another spectacular drive, though this time the views are up.

In prehistoric times, the Great Karoo was a swamp that apparently broke through to the sea at Meiringspoort. The majestic **Meiringspoort Pass** 🐦, a natural ravine created by the course of what came to be known as the Groot River, features soaring cliffs and spectacular rock formations. The 25km (16-mile) tarred road follows and crosses the river several times as it winds along the floor of the gorge.

Finds Olive, Anyone?

Prince Albert has a reputation for producing some of the country's finest olives—it even has an Olive Festival in April. Sample these at **Sampie se Plaasstal**, at the bottom end of Church Street (© **023/541-1345**; daily 8:30am–5pm). Among the other *padkos* (food for the road), all locally produced, are springbok or ostrich pies, dried fruit rolls, biltong, and homemade ginger beer.

WHERE TO STAY
IN & AROUND OUDTSHOORN

De Opstal ✿   Stopping in Schoemanshoek Valley (just outside Oudtshoorn, on the way to the Cango Caves and close to the Cango Ostrich Farm) is an excellent opportunity to get a feel for the rural Klein Karoo. Certainly, if you're interested in Afrikaans "boere" culture, De Opstal rates as one of the most authentic Afrikaans guesthouses in the country. Matilda de Bod is an eighth-generation Schoeman, still living on the original Schoemanshoek Valley farm, though she and her husband, Albertus, now share it with guests. The 1830 farmhouse, stables, and milking parlor have all been converted into en-suite bedrooms, and four more rooms built from scratch. These have the most modern amenities, but my personal favorite is still the huge honeymoon suite (no. 1), with its large bed and fireplace (essential in winter—windows close with shutters rather than glass). Meals are traditional and hearty (foodies would be better off eating at Jemima's; see below), and invariably feature ostrich.

P.O. Box 1425, Oudtshoorn 6620. Schoemanshoek Valley; 12km (7½ miles) north from Oudtshoorn on R328. © 044/279-2954. Fax 044/272-0736. 20 units. R980–R1,200 ($146–$179) double. Rates include breakfast. AE, DC, MC, V. **Amenities:** Dining room/bar/lounge; pool; room service; laundry. *In room:* A/C, TV, minibar, tea- and coffee-making facilities, fireplaces (all but 2 rooms, specify in winter!).

Rosenhof Country House ✿✿   This is the most upscale place to stay in Oudtshoorn: a calm, gracious oasis beautifully furnished with selected works by famous (white) South African artists, and in springtime, a rose-filled garden that saturates the senses. Rooms are built around a courtyard, each with its own entrance. Though each has a different theme, they share the most important characteristics: space, beautiful linens, well-sprung beds, and elegant, traditional taste. The courtyard contains a large pool—a necessity during the searing summer heat. The staff is very eager to please, and despite the hotel's relatively small size, there are such luxuries as room service. Meals are a five-course affair (R160/$24) served in the original homestead, which dates back to 1852. Ingredients are local, with herbs picked fresh from the garden.

264 Baron van Reede St., Oudtshoorn 6620. © 044/272-2232. Fax 044/272-3021. 14 units. R1,450–R1,950 ($216–$291) double; R1,900–R2,800 ($284–$418) suite. Rates include breakfast. AE, DC, MC, V. Children by prior arrangement only. **Amenities:** Dining room; bar, lounge; pool; room service; laundry. *In room:* A/C, TV, minibar, tea- and coffee-making facilities.

PRINCE ALBERT

An excellent alternative to De Bergkant is **Dennehof Karoo Guesthouse** ✿ (© **023/ 541-1227;** http://home.intekom.com/dennehof), a tasteful and tranquil oasis on the outskirts of the village. Book the gorgeously renovated Wagon Shed (R710/$106 double, including breakfast; prices of rooms vary, with The Forge coming in at R460/$69 double). Rea and Lindsay are not only very good at running the guesthouse, but they act as an informal tourism bureau for the area and are keen to ensure that you enjoy your time here. If Dennehof is full, try **Saxe-Coburg Lodge** (© 023/541-1267; www.saxecoburg.co.za; R600–R750/$90–$112 double).

De Bergkant Lodge and Cottages ★★ This guesthouse, recently upgraded, is the best place to stay in town, and offers particularly good value during winter (the best time to visit the Klein Karoo). Situated in a national monument in the Cape Dutch style, with Victorian-style bathrooms and beautifully furnished with antiques, the guesthouse also comprises three rooms built in a Georgian-style building, a 15m (49-ft.) saltwater swimming pool, an outdoor "star bath" (can't recommend this highly enough!), and a new wellness center. Owner Charles offers attentive, intelligent service, with dinners on request. Children are welcome.

5 Church St., Prince Albert. © 023/541-1088. Fax 023/541-1015. www.debergkant.co.za. 8 en-suite rooms. High season R1,400 ($209) double; low season R900 ($134) double. Rates include breakfast. AE, DC, MC, V. Off-street parking. **Amenities:** Dining room; pool; wellness center. *In room:* A/C.

WHERE TO DINE

If you're overnighting in the tiny hamlet of Prince Albert, you have a choice between real traditional Karoo fare (traditional *bobotie*—lightly curried ground beef cooked in a savory egg custard and served with yellow rice, Karoo lamb pie, chicken pie, or Karoo leg of lamb, followed by sticky malva pudding or steamed lemon pudding) served in the campy, over-the-top atmosphere of **Karoo Kombuis** (© 023/541-1110; dinner Mon–Sat; no credit cards; BYOB) or the **Blue Fig** (© 023/541-1900), which serves a slightly more adventurous menu. The latter was under new management at press time, so best to take advice from your host.

Jemima's ★★★ Value SOUTH AFRICAN INNOVATIVE This is not only the best restaurant in Oudtshoorn, but it has regularly featured in the annual top 10 national "Eat Out" awards. Run with flair by sisters Celia and Annette le Roux (who, incidentally, have no formal restaurant training, and who used their parents' home to secure a bank loan), Jemima's typifies sincere Karoo hospitality and laid-back country style. Traditional South African fare is given innovative twists, such as snoek samosas with curried peach salad, ravioli (homemade) with spicy *boerewors* (a uniquely South African mince and pork sausage), a Karoo lamb platter with a mint-flavored *frikkadel* (meatball) in muscatel jus, and ostrich Wellington. This is also the only restaurant in the Klein Karoo where vegetarians are well cared for, with such offerings as fresh pasta (with lemon and Parmesan or chile and garlic) and mushrooms in phyllo pastry served with salsa verde; much of the fresh produce comes direct from the farm where the sisters grew up.

94 Baron van Reede St. © 044/272-0808. Main courses R20–R75 ($3–$11) dinner. MC, V. Tues–Sun 6:30–10pm.

Tips Putting the Karoo into Lamb

Karoo lamb is on just about every menu in the Western Cape, and where better to sample it but here in the little Karoo? In this semi-arid region, farms are the size of small countries, and sheep range far and wide to nibble on wild herbs like *brakbos* and *gannabos* (the equivalent of wild rosemary). The result is tender, herb-infused meat.

Fun Fact **Claim to Fame**

Mossel Bay features in the *Guinness Book of Records* as having one of the mildest all-year climates in the world—it's second only to Hawaii.

ENTERING THE GARDEN ROUTE—MOSSEL BAY

Traveling east on the N2, the first sign of the fast-approaching town of Mossel Bay, unofficial entry point of the Garden Route ("officially" it starts at Heidelberg), is the sci-fi spectacle of the MossGas oil plant on your left. The town does not really improve on closer inspection, but if you're traveling by at noon, it does have a good seafood restaurant (see "Where to Dine," below) and a few interesting attractions.

Mossel Bay is approximately 4 hours from Cape Town on the N2, and 20 minutes from George.

WHAT TO SEE & DO

Mossel Bay was the site of the first European landing on the South African coast, when Bartholomieu Dias, having battled a fearsome storm, tacked in for water and safety in 1488. **The Bartholomieu Dias Museum Complex** (© 044/691-1067) comprises a collection of historic buildings, of which the **Maritime Museum** is excellent. It relates the early Portuguese, Dutch, and British seafaring history (which is a bit text-heavy), and houses a life-size replica of the caravel in which Dias set sail in 1487—it's hard to imagine going where no man has gone before in something that looks like a large toy. The ship on display was built in Portugal and sailed from Lisbon to Mossel Bay in 1987 to commemorate the 500th anniversary of Dias's arrival on southern Cape soil. The museum, located on Market Street, is open Monday through Friday from 8:15am to 5pm, and Saturday and Sunday from 9am to 4pm. Admission is R6 (90¢), R10 ($1.50) to access the ship.

Mossel Bay is also one of the best places along the coast to get up close and personal with a Great White shark (see "Staying Active," earlier in this chapter). If you'd prefer your ocean interlude with a little less adrenaline, contact **Seven Seas** (© 044/691-3371) or **Romanza** (© 044/690-3101) for whale-watching pleasure cruises, or trips to Seal Island; a 60-minute cruise costs approximately R50 ($7.45).

For more information, contact the **Tourism Bureau** (© 044/691-2202; www.visit mosselbay.co.za; Mon–Fri 8am–6pm, Sat–Sun 9am–4pm), located in the historical center, at the corner of Church and Market streets.

WHERE TO DINE

The Gannet *Kids* SEAFOOD   Conveniently located across the road from the main museums and a stone's throw from the Tourism Bureau, The Gannet is an excellent seafood restaurant, but with a small (rather unimaginative) range of pizzas and pastas (lunch), and meat dishes (dinner), even the non–seafood lover won't leave disappointed. The linefish, basted with lemon butter and herbs, and grilled or fried to tender perfection, is so fresh that it's almost moving. The seafood casserole, baked with a creamy wine sauce, is another house specialty; or try the grilled marinated tuna *sosatie,* coated with a mango, pepperdew, and yogurt sauce. Beleaguered parents will be pleased to know the restaurant is also child friendly, with a separate kids' menu. Weather permitting, you can dine alfresco in the garden overlooking the bay, keeping an eye out for whales and dolphins.

Market St., Bartholomieu Dias Museum Complex. ℂ 044/691-1885. Main courses R60–R185 ($8.95–$28). AE, DC, MC, V. Mon–Fri 7am–10:30pm; Sat–Sun 7am–11pm.

GEORGE & WILDERNESS

Halfway between Cape Town and Port Elizabeth, the sprawling city of George won't win any beauty competitions, but it has a majestic mountain backdrop and is the commercial heart of the Garden Route, with the most transport connections and a large choice of restaurants. It's not worth overnighting in this inland town, however, as its attractions are few and far from scintillating, and the coastal town of Wilderness, with a number of pleasant lodging options, is just a 10-minute drive away. From Wilderness, Knysna lies 20 minutes east, while Plettenberg Bay is just under an hour away.

ESSENTIALS

VISITOR INFORMATION   The **George Tourism Bureau** (ℂ **044/801-9295;** www.georgetourism.co.za; Mon–Fri 8am–5:30pm, Sat 9am–1pm) is located at 124 York St. *Note:* It's not essential to stop here; Knysna has an excellent tourism bureau.

GETTING THERE   By Air   You can fly to **George Airport** (ℂ **044/876-9310**) from Cape Town, Johannesburg, or Durban with **SAA** (ℂ **044/801-8434**) or **Nationwide** (ℂ **044/801-8414**) or—since May 2005—budget airline **Kulula.com.**

By Train   Sadly, the intercity trains running between Cape Town and Port Elizabeth have been canceled. If you've got money to burn, board the Edwardian **Rovos Rail** (ℂ **012/315-8242;** www.rovos.co.za), which does the 24-hour run from Cape Town to George—a beautiful route, with a wine or brandy-tasting stop—during the summer months. Tickets are R7,380–R9,900 ($1,101–$1,478) per person, sharing.

By Bus   The intercity buses (**Intercape, Greyhound, Translux,** and **Baz Bus**) travel from Cape Town along the Garden Route to Port Elizabeth. See chapter 2 for regional numbers.

GETTING AROUND   By Car   Choose from one of six companies offering rental cars at the airport, including **Avis** (ℂ **044/876-9314**), **Budget** (ℂ **044/876-9204**), and **Hertz** (ℂ **044/801-4700**).

GUIDED TOURS   By Bus   Eco Afrika (ℂ **044/384-0479** or 082/472-9696; www.eco-afrika-tours.co.za) offers the largest variety of tours, from township visits and golf tours to photographic safaris and adventure tours.

By Train   You can travel between George and Knysna on the **Choo-Tjoe steam train,** one of the region's top attractions; for details, see the "Knysna" section, later in this chapter. Another fun option is to trundle to the top of the scenic Montagu Pass

---

(Fun Fact The Original Snail Mail

Outside the Maritime Museum is the **Post Office Tree,** South Africa's first post office. In 1501 the first of many sailors sent his mail by leaving a letter stuffed in an old boot and tied to what the city fathers claim is this particular milkwood tree. Soon this became an informal postal system, with letters picked up by passing ships and distributed accordingly. Today you can post a letter in a boot-shaped post box and it will be stamped with a special postmark.

in an **Outeniqua Power Van** (© 044/801-8239)—a little motorized trolley used for rail inspections; the trip takes 3 hours (with a 45-min. stop on the mountain for a BYO picnic).

By Air On Air Helicopter Tours (© 082/556-3532; www.onairtours.co.za) offers helicopter charters covering a range of attractions, from the ostrich farms and Cango Caves of Oudtshoorn, to flights over the coast to Knysna, Noetzie, and Plettenberg Bay.

WHAT TO SEE & DO

The best reason to be in George itself is to board the **Choo-Tjoe steam train** that runs between George and Knysna—although you can board in Knysna and do the return journey by road with **Kontours** (© 082/569-8997; see the "Knysna" section of this chapter for details). *Note:* Train spotters and vintage-car lovers could probably spend the better part of the day examining the locomotives and cars in the **Outeniqua Railway Museum,** adjacent to the platform where the Choo-Tjoe and Outeniqua Power Vans depart and arrive.

You are spoiled for choice when it comes to the number of **excellent drives** leading out of George. To do a circular route to Oudtshoorn, take the **Outeniqua Pass** (or R29) to Oudtshoorn, then return via the **Montagu Pass,** a gravel road dating back to 1843. If you're heading to Wilderness or Knysna, consider taking the **Seven Passes Road.** This, the original road linking George and Knysna, lacks the great sea views of the N2, but it takes you through dense indigenous forests, crosses streams via a number of quaint Edwardian bridges, and finally traverses the **Homtini Pass,** another engineering feat by the famous Thomas Baines. Alternatively, head down the N2 for the most direct route to the pretty town of Wilderness—8km (5 miles) away via the **Kaaimans River Pass.**

Wilderness is anything but, with a residential development creeping up the forested hills that overlook the Touw River estuary, and a string of ugly mansions lining the beach; yet it is effectively an island within the national park, and still the smallest and most tranquil of the coastal towns along the Garden Route—hence the proliferation of B&Bs over the years. Set around the mouth of the Touw River, it marks the western end of a chain of lakes that stretches some 40km (25 miles) east, most of which are under the control of the **Wilderness National Park.** Although the beaches along this stretch are magnificent, strong currents regularly claim unsuspecting and inexperienced swimmers. You're better off floating in the waters of the **Serpentine,** the waterway that links Island Lake, Langvlei, and Rondevlei to the Wilderness lagoon. Don't be put off by the tea-colored water or frothy bubbles; these are caused by plant oxides and oxygenation, and the water is perfectly clean.

You can explore the area on foot on a number of trails that take from 1 to 4 hours to walk, or cover some 15km (9¼ miles) of inland waterways in a canoe. **The Wilderness National Park** (reception © 044/877-1197) issues trail maps (for guided canoe trips; see "Staying Active," earlier in the chapter). To reach the park, follow signs off the N2, 2km (1¼ miles) east of Wilderness; should you wish to overnight in the park, see review below. For details, contact the helpful **Wilderness Tourism Information Bureau** (© 044/877-0045; www.wildernessinfo.co.za; Mon–Fri 8am–6pm, Sat 8am–1pm, Sun 3–5pm).

WHERE TO STAY
In George
Fancourt Hotel and Country Club Estate ★★★ *Kids* This is without a doubt the best address in George, and a destination in its own right for keen golfers. Host of

the 2002 President's Cup, Fancourt boasts four excellent golf courses, of which two—designed by Gary Player and consistently rated among the top four in South Africa—are open only to guests. Besides the golf academy there is a fabulous health spa to ease aching shoulders (or nagging golf widows) and four pools to choose from. In fact, you don't have to be a golfer to appreciate the luxurious atmosphere, lovely setting, and helpful staff. Rooms are either in the original manor house or set in the beautifully landscaped gardens. Not much differentiates them, other than price; rooms are smaller in the manor house, but they are closer to all amenities. The luxe two-bedroom Garden Suites or "lodges" are ideal for families. ***Note:* Land's End Guest House** (for contact details, see "In Victoria Bay," below) has purchased a 2-bedroom garden suite on the 18th fairway of the Montagu course, about 250m (820 ft.) from the hotel. The lodge costs R900 to R1,850 ($134–$276, depending on season) a night for two people, representing a great savings. Remember to request that the lodge be serviced on booking.

Montagu St., Blanco, George 6530. ⓒ 044/804-0000. Fax 044/804-0710. www.fancourt.co.za. 100-plus units. R2,930–R3,820 ($437–$570) double; R4,220–R5,860 ($630–$875) 1-bedroom suite; R7,260 ($1,084) 2-bedroom suite; R9,800 ($1,463) presidential suite. Rates quoted depend on season; ask about discounted winter rates. AE, DC, MC, V. **Amenities:** 4 restaurants; 2 bars; 4 (2 heated) swimming pools; 4 golf courses; 4 tennis courts; health and beauty spa; children's programs; room service; babysitting; mountain bikes and 6km (3¾-mile) trail. *In room:* A/C, TV, minibar, hair dryer, tea- and coffee-making facilities.

In Victoria Bay

Land's End Guest House 🏆 *(Finds)*   "The Closest B&B to the Sea in Africa," it trumpets, and at 6m (20 ft.) from the high-water mark, this is no doubt true. Land's End is the last house on the only residential road in Vic Bay (a tiny bay with a sandy beach that lies between George and Wilderness); beyond lie the rocks and the ocean, and beside you is the safest swimming bay for miles around. The guesthouse is run in a very laid-back manner (the proprietor is a surfer) and furnished in a homey fashion, with lovely touches like complimentary sherry. The views from the two self-catering units, each with private deck, are fantastic; try to book these rather than the downstairs rooms. ***Note:*** Land's End also owns a two-bedroom garden suite, "Lodge 743," at Fancourt (see above).

P.O. Box 9429, George 6530. ⓒ **044/889-0123.** Fax 044/889-0141. www.vicbay.com. 4 units. High season R1,000–R1,200 ($149–$179), depending on room; low season: R500–R900 ($75–$134). Half-price for children under 12. AE, MC, V. At the end of Beach Rd., Victoria Bay. **Amenities:** Dining room/bar; watersports equipment rental; laundry. *In room:* TV, minibar, hair dryer, tea- and coffee-making facilities.

In Wilderness

The Dune Guest House 🏆🏆 *(Finds)*   You know you're on holiday when you wake up and hear, smell, and see the ocean from your bed, then slide open your doors, step out onto your private patio, and pad down a short boardwalk onto an almost solitary beach that stretches as far as the eye can see. One of the few B&Bs on the entire coast that is literally right on the beach, The Dune comprises four comfortable en-suite bedrooms, each with semiprivate decks furnished with teak deck chairs. Top choices are White (literally, entirely white) and Africa, the only semi-sea-facing option, but a very stylish room nonetheless. A self-catering apartment is ideal for groups or families. Architecturally, the building is rather charmless, so if you're not set on a sea view or are traveling here in winter, you'd be better of at Moontide.

31 Die Duin, Wilderness 6560. ⓒ/fax **044/877-0298.** www.thedune.co.za. 5 units. R840–R1,150 ($125–$172) double depending on season, R1,250 ($187) apt;. Rates include breakfast. AE, MC, V. Children by prior arrangement only. **Amenities:** Pool. *In room:* TV, minibar, tea- and coffee-making facilities.

Moontide Guest Lodge ★★ *Value*   Situated on the banks of the Touw River, in gardens that flow into its tidal waters, this guesthouse (the only one right on the lagoon) offers one of the best value-for-money options on the Garden Route. The thatched homestead, with separate suites, is set among 400-year-old milkwood trees and an abundance of ferns and flowering plants. All rooms have entrances that lead out into the garden with semiprivate seating areas. Built on stilts among the milk-woods and overlooking the guesthouse and lagoon, the aptly named Treetops is the most private and luxurious (and unbelievably good value); Milkwood, which has a charming private alfresco seating area and very spacious bedroom (with another in the thatch) is another favorite (shower only), as is the cozy Boat House, which has an entrance (and views) right on the lagoon. The recent additions Moonshadow 1 and 2 are also popular; River Suite has a new bathroom. Guests have exclusive use of the lounge, with a large log fireplace and sliding doors leading to the terrace overlooking the tranquil lagoon—shallow but great for swimming, especially when the lagoon is tidal.

Southside Rd. (at the end of the cul-de-sac), Wilderness 6560. © 044/877-0361. Fax 044/877-0124. www.moontide. co.za. 7 units. R500–R900 ($75–$134), depending on season and room. Rates include breakfast. AE, MC, V. **Amenities:** Lounge; boat. *In room:* TV, minibar.

Palms ★★   Palms is Swiss-owned and -managed, and with four hosts to attend to guests' needs, complemented by an enthusiastic staff, service manages to be both attentive and laid-back. Rooms, each with a private entrance from the garden, are spacious and stylishly furnished in crisp whites, deep blues, and black. Green is the other dominant color, supplied by the lush gardens, and the red and pink hibiscus flowers make a stark statement against the black marbled pool. But one of the main reasons to book into the Palms is the restaurant—one of the best in Wilderness, it's often full, and guests obviously enjoy preferential booking. Weather permitting, book a table on the candlelit veranda to enjoy the gardens. The five-course set menu is prepared daily (so guests never get bored). The only drawback here is the lack of views.

Owen Grant St. (opposite the Wilderness Hotel), Wilderness 6560. © 044/877-1420. Fax 044/877-1422. www.palms-wilderness.com. 12 units. R900–R1,020 ($134–$152), depending on season. Rates include buffet breakfast. MC, V. **Amenities:** Restaurant; pool; room service; laundry. *In room:* TV, hair dryer.

Wilderness National Park *Value*   Accommodations in the Wilderness National Park (called **Ebb & Flow** rest camp) offer exceptional value, though some of the ron-dawels in Ebb & Flow North are very rudimentary and share washing facilities. Your best options are in Ebb & Flow South, particularly the timber "forest huts" numbered 24 to 33. These are slightly raised and built right on the Touw River—you can almost cast for fish from your front door. Bear in mind that not all units are en-suite showers, so remember to specify your requirements. All forest huts have kitchenettes and braai areas. Of the four-bed log cabins (better equipped if you prefer to self-cater), nos. 7 to 13 enjoy the best location, on the Serpentine River. All units are serviced daily. There is a rudimentary shop, so you'll have to bring in your own supplies (a large, well-stocked Pick 'n Pay grocery store is situated on the outskirts of George) or dine out.

Off N2, 2km (1¼ miles) east of Wilderness; follow signs. Bookings: P.O. Box 787, Pretoria 0001. Bookings: © 012/428-9111. Fax 021/343-0905. Direct: © 044/877-1197. www.parks-sa.co.za. 45 units comprising 4-bed cottages and forest huts, and 2-bed rondavels, not all with bathrooms. R590 ($88) en-suite cottage; R540 ($81) en-suite forest hut with kitchenette; R170–R320 ($25–$48) huts with communal ablutions and kitchens. Camping from R100–R160 ($15–$24) double. AE, DC, MC, V.

WHERE TO DINE

In George

If the restaurant scene is indicative of a city's cultural pulse, then the opening of the **Conservatory at Mead House,** 91 Meade St. (© **044/874-1938;** Mon–Sat 8:30am–4:30pm), means that George has finally outgrown its backwater status. A large, airy space, attached to a rather nice gift and bookshop, with an array of seating options (couches, armchairs, barstools, dining chairs), the conservatory offers shaded tables spilling out onto the paved lavender garden. It's open all day for confectionary and coffee, but the small lunch menu is extremely tempting, with a variety of garden-fresh salads and tarts, generous sandwiches, quiches, and slightly larger mains like bangers and mash or hearty Irish stew. For dinner, head for the **Reel 'n Rustic,** corner York and Courtenay streets (© **044/884-0707;** closed Sat lunch), which has been reeling in customers for almost a decade with its well-aged steaks and fresh linefish selection.

In Wilderness

If you've had enough of fine dining and the weather is fine, make sure you book for dinner at the wonderfully situated alfresco **Beach House,** where Monica serves up platters of prawns and burgers to her mostly resident backpackers and barefoot surfer-types, sprinkled with a few well-dressed local guesthouse owners. The food may not be that memorable, but the sound and smell of the sea, the quirky service, and the laid-back atmosphere are what beach holidays are all about (© **044/8770549**); get there before the sun sets.

The Palms ★★ FRENCH/INTERNATIONAL   Vying with Serendipity as the most romantic dining experience in Wilderness, but a lot less formal, the Palms offers attentive service yet laid-back atmosphere (Serendipity probably offers better value in terms of creativity, however). Book a table on the candlelit veranda to enjoy the gardens. The five-course set menu is prepared daily (so guests never get bored) but always includes a choice of starters (marinated blue rock cheese on watercress salad, for example, or summer salad with seafood), a soup or small pasta (langoustines on lemon-grass risotto), followed by a palate-clearing sorbet and a choice of mains (baked leg of lamb on mint sauce or grilled Cape sole on fruit chutney butter) and a choice of desserts. Portions are smartly sized so that you don't feel overly full, but if you don't like the choices, you can always opt to replace items from the small a la carte menu.

George Rd., opposite the Wilderness Hotel. © 044/877-1420. Set menu R180 ($27). AE, DC, MC, V. Mon–Sat 7–11pm.

Riverside Kitchen ★★ *Value* SOUTH AFRICAN/ECLECTIC   Located on the banks of the Touw River, in a large double-volume thatch building with tables outside overlooking the river, the Riverside Kitchen is charming, unpretentious, and good value, catering to a wide-ranging clientele, from local farmers and B&B owners to globetrotters. Recommended starters include black mushrooms topped with slices of sliced pear and melted Roquefort cheese, or the hot lychee and prawn salad, with melted Roquefort cheese and sesame-coated prawns, served with a papadum. If you haven't yet tried ostrich, this is the place to do so; chef-patron Roxanne does it to a turn. Order the *espetada*—tender chunks of ostrich meat (do specify ostrich, it's more tender than the beef)—sizzling with herbed butter dripping down its vertical skewer, or coated with a Moroccan rub and served with a quince jelly jus on couscous. Linefish is also recommended—if you're lucky it's *kabeljou,* rolled in herbs and crushed pepper, and topped with peach and ginger salsa.

Pirates Creek (signposted off N2). ℭ **044/877-0900** or 072/124-7375. Main courses R62–R145 (for the seafood platter) ($9.25–$22). AE, DC, MC, V. Tues–Sun 6:30–10pm (daily mid-Dec to mid-Jan); Sun 12:30–3pm.

Serendipity ☆☆ INTERNATIONAL/MODERN CAPE   The only Wilderness restaurant to make it in *Wine* magazine's 2003 top 100 selection, this is the village's fine-dining option—great if you're in a celebratory mood or like your food cordon bleu, but a little uptight if your idea of a holiday is hanging barefoot and fancy-free. Despite its haute credentials, it's very much a family affair: Lizelle is the young ex–Prue Leith chef; husband Rudolf is front-of-house; and the venue, a house on the banks of the lagoon, is Lizelle's parents' guesthouse. Lizelle changes the five-course set menu every week, but expect fresh locally procured ingredients, combined with creativity and skill: caramelized onion and feta tartlet is served with biltong shavings; spring rolls are stuffed with ostrich *bobotie* and served on a banana, coriander, and peanut sambal; kudu (antelope) is wrapped in bacon and served with traditional samp and bean stew, green beans, and fruit jus; and sweet-corn fritters are stacked with roasted tomatoes, baby spinach, and mushroom duxelles. Even the crème brûlée has a twist—it's made with Amarula (a local version of Baileys Irish Cream).

Freesia Ave. (off Waterside Rd.), Wilderness ℭ **044/877-0433**. Set menu R169 ($25). MC, V. Mon–Sat 7pm–late (closed winter months).

SEDGEFIELD & GOUKAMMA RESERVE

The drive from Wilderness to Sedgefield on the N2 is very pleasant, with a series of lakes on the left and occasional glimpses of the ocean on your right. Sedgefield looks very unattractive from the road—a motley collection of shops, estate agents, and service stations—but it's worth turning off and heading for the beach, which is one of the most attractive along this stretch (mostly because the houses are set back behind the sand dunes). One of the best Garden Route beach walks starts here: During low tide, walk westward to **Gericke's Point,** a low hillock of sandstone where locals come to pick fresh mussels.

Next stop is the 2,230-hectare (5,508-acre) **Goukamma Nature Reserve,** which encompasses forests, an estuary, beaches, reputedly the highest vegetated dune in southern Africa, and Groenvlei, or "Lake Pleasant," a freshwater lake. There are a few rudimentary accommodations options and several hiking trails that cover various habitats in the reserve, including a 4-hour beach walk and a short circular walk through a milkwood forest. Admission to the Goukamma Reserve is R18 ($2.70), and its gate hours, accessed via the Buffalo Bay turnoff, are daily 8am to 6pm. For more information, contact ℭ/fax **044/383-0042.**

WHERE TO STAY & DINE

Lake Pleasant Living Exclusive Holiday Suites ☆☆   Arguably the most luxurious hotel this side of Plettenberg Bay (though not when you include guesthouses like Parkes Manor), this is situated on the south bank of Groenvlei, making it one of the few hotels on the Garden Route located in a nature reserve and bird sanctuary. Don't let this mislead you, however; the N2 hum is hardly ever out of earshot. Despite this, the atmosphere is immensely peaceful, and the views across the lake are lovely. The hotel had a substantial upgrade in 2001 and now enjoys all the amenities of a five-star SATOUR–graded hotel—unfortunately, none of the old country-inn atmosphere has been retained, and though decor in rooms and public spaces is perfectly comfortable and tasteful, it all feels a little mass produced. Aside from its proximity to Knysna (a 20-min. drive), the hotel has numerous nature trails, and the beach is 2.5km (1½ miles) away.

Off N2, 16km (10 miles) west of Knysna. P.O. Box 2, Sedgefield 6573. © 044/349-2400. Fax 044/349-2401. www.lakepleasanthotel.com. 36 units. R1,500–R3,200 ($224–$478) double. Rates include breakfast. AE, DC, MC, V. **Amenities:** Restaurant; bar; cigar bar; pools; tennis; spa; room service; babysitting; laundry; horseback riding; canoes; a bird hide. *In room:* TV, A/C, minibar, hair dryer, tea- and coffee-making facilities, under-floor heating.

KNYSNA

The founder of Knysna (pronounced "*nize*-na") was one George Rex. In 1802, at the age of 39, he—having shocked the Cape community by shacking up with a woman "of colour"—purchased the farm, which included the whole basin containing the Knysna lagoon. By the time of his death in 1839, he had engaged in a number of enterprises, the most profitable of which was timber, and had persuaded the Cape authorities to develop Knysna as a port. Knysna's development and the decimation of its forests were well under way. That there are any areas of forests to have escaped the devastation of the 19th century is thanks to far-sighted conservation policies introduced in the 1880s, and today Knysna has the largest areas of indigenous forests left in South Africa. The Knysna elephants have fared less well—attempts to augment their numbers by relocating three young cows from Kruger National Park failed miserably when it was discovered that the last remaining Knysna elephant was also a female. The surviving cows have subsequently been relocated to the Shamwari game reserve in the Eastern Cape. Detractors believed the forest pachyderms to be extinct, and that the only free-roaming elephants left in Knysna were those painted on road markers warning drivers to "beware." Then in October 2000, a 20-year-old elephant bull was spotted—and photographed—deep in the forest, making headlines throughout the Western Cape, and in 2003 author and environmentalist Gareth Patterson set about collecting dung for Lori Eggbert, a scientist from the Smithsonian Institute, to perform DNA tests and hopefully prove his theory that at least 9 or 10 elephants remain at large. Actual sightings have yet to be repeated, however, and you're more likely to spot one if you overindulge in the delicious local beer.

Knysna used to be a sleepy village inhabited only by a handful of hippies and wealthy retirees, but the last decade has seen a tourist boom that has augmented numbers substantially—nowhere is this more evident than on the congested main road that runs through town. Still, Knysna has retained a great deal more of its original village charm than either George or Plettenberg Bay, and remains the emotional heart of the region, with a resident population who actually live here all year-round (unlike Plett, which turns into a ghost town in winter). Its raison d'être is the large tidal lagoon, around which the town has grown, and the towering sandstone cliffs (called the heads) that guard the lagoon's narrow access to the sea. The eastern buttress has unfortunately been developed, but this means you can now overnight and play golf surrounded by a spectacular sea and fynbos environment, and the western side remains untouched—a visit to the Featherbed Nature Reserve should be high on your list of priorities.

ESSENTIALS

VISITOR INFORMATION The **Tourism Information Bureau** (© 044/382-1610; www.visitknysna.com; Mon–Fri 8am–5pm, Sat 8:30am–1pm; hours are extended Dec–Jan) is at 40 Main St. Adjacent is the booking service; contact **Knysna Reservations** (© 044/382-6960; booking@mweb.co.za) for accommodations and other bookings. You can also visit the independent **Central Reservations** (© 044/382-5878 or 082/558-1661; daily 9am–6pm) for advice and bookings.

Road Closures: Avoiding the Queue

At press time the N2 between George and Knysna was undergoing extensive repairs, scheduled to be completed by the end of 2006. Waiting periods of up to 20 minutes can be expected (in 2005 these stretched to 2 hr.). You can call one of the engineers on ℂ **082/555-7817** (Kobus) for a progress report, or simply bypass the N2 by taking a little-used back road: The **Seven Passes,** the original road between George and Knysna, is a wonderful country drive taking you through dense indigenous forest and rolling farmlands, and crossing numerous winding rivers. It takes quite a bit longer but is well worth it, and you can stop for tea at the tea garden 5km (3 miles) after the Big Tree Forest Walk.

GETTING THERE   The closest airports are at **George** (see "George & Wilderness: Getting There," earlier in this chapter) and **Plettenberg Bay;** both are about an hour's drive away. Contact **Budget** (ℂ **044/533-1858**) or **Economic Car Hire** (ℂ **082/ 800-4258**).

GETTING AROUND   For a fun way to get around (not to mention avoid Knysna's seasonal traffic congestion), rent a mountain bike (see "Staying Active," earlier in this chapter). For a taxi, call **Benwill Shuttle** (ℂ **083/728-5181**) or **Glory's** (ℂ **083/226-4720**). To explore the lagoon in a small cabin boat, rubber duck, or speedboat, contact **Tait Marine Boat Hire** (ℂ **044/382-4460;** fax 044/382-7476; www.taitmarine.com).

GUIDED TOURS   **Forest Explorer** (ℂ **083/702-5103**) runs 90-minute (minimum) orientation tours of Knysna, as well as tours of the forests, Belvidere, Noezie, the goldfields, Tstisikamma, Oudtshoorn, and various tailor-made options. For a range of **sailing or ferry tours** of the lagoon, see "Staying Active" at the beginning of the chapter. For a **"Township Trail"** tour that includes a visit to a *sangoma* (healer), a *shebeen* (drinking house), a local rasta community, a "temporary" timber home, and a community project, call the **Heads Adventure Centre** (ℂ **044/384-0831** or 083/ 232-8898).

BOAT TOURS   With comfortable seating and a restaurant/bar on board, the floating double-decker **John Benn Ferry** (ℂ **044/382-1693**) offers a 90-minute trip on the lagoon that costs R75 ($11) for adults, meals and drinks extra. R55 ($8.20) buys you a ticket on their **River Catcher Ferry**—the only ferry licensed to go through the Heads. **Waterfront Ferries** (ℂ **044/382-5520**) runs a number of 90-minute trips as well as a 2½-hour sunset lagoon trip daily; all ferries depart from the Knysna Quays Waterfront. For sailing trips, contact **Spring Tide Charters** to charter the luxury yacht *Outiniqua* for an exclusive, very romantic breakfast, all-day, sunset, or dinner cruise (ℂ **082/470-6022;** www.springtide.co.za; prices on application). Alternatively, hire the services of *The Mistress* (ℂ **082/700-1597;** www.knysnalagoon.com).

ACTIVITIES   The **Heads Adventure Centre** can organize a number of outdoor experiences, from sea kayaking, snorkeling, and scuba diving to canoeing, abseiling, and guided hikes. Contact ℂ **044/384-0831** or 083/232-8898.

SPECIAL EVENTS   Knysna gets very busy during the annual **Knysna Loerie Festival,** held for a few days every May and aimed at the predominantly local gay and lesbian market; and even more so during the **Knysna Oyster Festival** held every July. For information, contact the Tourism Bureau.

WHAT TO SEE & DO IN KNYSNA

Besides the top attractions listed below, one of the first things first-time visitors are usually encouraged to do is take a drive to the **Knysna Heads**, where you can walk right up to the lagoon mouth and watch skippers gingerly navigate the treacherous surf. Stop for tea at the East Head Café, then view the rare Knysna seahorse at the small NSRI aquarium, currently endangered by the ongoing development happening in and around the lagoon.

Exploring the forests is another major drawing card (see below), as are **lagoon-based activities;** several companies run boat trips on the lagoon, home to 200 species of fish and a major supplier of oysters—expect to see this on almost every Knysna menu. (For ferry and sailing options, see "Boat Tours," above.)

Another local product definitely worth trying is the beer. **Mitchell's Brewery,** Arend Street (© 044/382-4685), produces four types of unpasteurized "live" ales, the best of which are Bosun's Bitter and Forrester's Draught. You can either take a 45-minute tour and tasting (Mon–Fri 10:30am) or sample them with your meal at any of the Knysna eateries. Ask for directions or a list of outlets from the Tourism Bureau, or combine an oyster- and beer-tasting with a lagoon trip by boarding the **John Benn Ferry** (© 044/382-1693) and heading for the bar. To reach the closest sandy shore, you'll need to head west to **Brenton-on-Sea,** an endless stretch of sand 16km (10 miles) from Knysna, or, better still, east for **Noetzie Beach**, some 11km (6¾ miles) from town. It's a steep walk down to this beautiful little beach, but a small, very swimmable estuary spilling out into the ocean and five over-the-top crenellated castles overlooking the beach make it more than worthwhile. Knysna lagoon's **Bollard Bay,** accessed from Leisure Isle, is an excellent family beach, with safe swimming in the shallow waters of the lagoon.

Last but not least, Knysna offers some of the best shopping this side of Cape Town, though much of it is very hippie-inspired and craftsy. The exception to this, with its super-sophisticated take on African-influenced homeware and local crafts, is **Am-Wa,** 13 Main Rd., Knysna (© 044/382-0561). The buyer has an exceptionally good eye for what is described here as "original functional art," on a par with anything you'd find in the best of Cape Town's design shops.

THE TOP ATTRACTIONS

Featherbed Nature Reserve   This privately owned nature reserve on the western head of Knysna is a National Heritage Site and home to the endangered blue duiker antelope. Guests are ferried over and then ascend the head in a large open-topped vehicle to enjoy the magnificent views of the lagoon, town, and ocean. Qualified guides then lead the visitors down through milkwood forests and coastal flora onto the cliffs and coastal caves on the 2km (1.25-mile) **Bushbuck Trail** (you can also choose to drive down). Meals are served at the **Tavern;** the buffet is included in your ticket price and focuses mainly on seafood. *Note:* The reserve's peace is seriously compromised during Knysna's busiest season, when additional trips are made.

Ferry leaves from Municipal Jetty, Remembrance Ave., off Waterfront Dr. © 044/382-1693. R235 ($35) adults, R50–R110 ($7.45–$16) children 3–12. Depart daily at 10am (more scheduled, depending on demand; phone ahead). Duration approximately 4 hr. Admission after 2:30pm R120 ($18) adults, R35 ($5.20) children; no food included. Duration approximately 3 hr.

Knysna Forests   These, the last pockets of indigenous forest, are located some distance from the town: **Goudveld State Forest** is 30km (19 miles) northwest of Knysna, while **Diepwalle** is some 20km (12 miles) northeast of town. Goudveld is a mixture of plantation and indigenous forest, making Diepwalle, with its ancient yel-lowwoods, the better option for the purist. Look out for the emerald Knysna Loerie and the brightly hued Narina Trogon in the branches. Diepwalle has three excellent circular trails color-coded with red, black, and white elephant markers. The routes are all 7 to 9km (4¼–5½ miles) long, and the red route is recommended because it features the most water.

Diepwalle: Take the N2 east; after 7km (4¼ miles), turn left onto the R339 for 16km (10 miles) before taking turnoff to Diepwalle. Goudveld: Take the N2 west, turn right into Rheenendal Rd. ⓒ 044/382-9762. R6 (90¢). Daily 8:30am–4pm.

Outeniqua Choo-Tjoe ★★★ Kids
One of the top attractions on the entire Garden Route, the **Choo-Tjoe train** provides some of the best views of the coastline and hidden valleys inaccessible by car. First opened in 1928, the 68km (42-mile) Choo-Tjoe is the last fully operational steam train in South Africa and chugs across the Knysna lagoon into the verdant valleys and lakeside settings that lead to Wilderness, where it traverses the Kaaimans River gorge, past Victoria Bay to George. Most locomotives date back to 1948 (though some are over a century old) with timber-and-leather-fitted carriages dating from 1903 to 1950. Grab a window seat—the views really are spectacular—and settle in for a truly enjoyable excursion. *Tip:* To avoid traveling back the way you came (which will take the whole day), book through **Kontours** (ⓒ **082/569-8997;** R135/$20 adults, R90/$13 children; price includes train journey). Kontours provides a map with places and points of interest as seen from the train, and will pick you up from the George station and return you to Knysna (the reverse by arrangement).

The Station, Remembrance Ave. ⓒ 044/382-1361. R70 ($10) adult one-way, R50 ($7.45) children 3–16. Train departs Mon–Sat 9:45am and 2:15pm; reduced days (Mon, Wed, Fri) during winter. Duration one-way is 3 hr.

Knysna Elephant Park Kids
This "safari," undertaken in four-wheel-drive vehicles that depart from reception every half-hour, is a little better than viewing elephants in a zoo, as you are at least guaranteed an opportunity to touch the elephants that roam the 80-hectare (198-acre) "reserve." The park now has 10 elephants, most of whom were born in Kruger and have been returned—according to the park's promoters—to "the home of their ancestors." For a hefty R980 ($146), you can take an exclusive walk with them through the forests with just a guide for company—"an experience described by many as a lifetime high." One can only wonder what these "many" must have been smoking—possibly their "Friends of the Elephant" certificate, included in the price and made from elephant dung. The R395 ($59) option, in which groups of up to 10 walk with the elephants, after which breakfast or dinner (rice and *bobotie*) is served, offers better value, but it's still to my mind pricey, and children will no doubt enjoy the much cheaper, shorter 45-minute tour more. A far better-value option is offered at **Botelierskip Private Game Reserve** near George (www.legendlodges.co.za), where you can go on a real elephant-back safari, either as a day visitor or overnight; riders must be 6 or older. Cost is R350 ($52) adults, R300 ($45) children.

Off N2, 22km (14 miles) east of Knysna. ⓒ 044/532-7732. 45- to 60-min. tour R100 ($15) adults, R50 ($7.45) kids; R240–R395 ($36–$59) breakfast or evening "safari"; R980 ($146) for exclusive safari. You'll need to book the sunrise and sunset elephant safari in advance. Rates include light breakfast/dinner and membership certificate. Tours daily 8:30am–5:30pm.

WHERE TO STAY
If you'd like to have the lagoon at your doorstep, look into renting an apartment, home, or loft in the attractive **Thesen Island** development (ⓒ **044/302-5735;**

www.theislands.co.za). If you'd like to experience a very different side of Knysna, look into a Knysna home stay and spend the night in the local township with a warm and welcoming family; bookings through **Glendyrr** at ☎ **044/382-5510.** For more long-stay options, contact **Knysna Booking Services** (☎ **044/382-6960;** booking@ mweb.co.za). Note that prices vary considerably depending on season, with most specifying low, mid-, and peak seasons. Low season is usually from May 1 to August 31, with peak or high season usually from mid-December to mid-January.

Belvidere Manor ⭐ Located in the picture-postcard-cute suburb of Belvidere, these detached cottages, situated on lawns that sweep down to the water's edge, are the most upscale places to stay on the actual lagoon (but they're nowhere near as nice as Phantom Forest or Parkes!). The best units remain the original "lagoon" suites—unfortunately, the addition of the cheaper "garden" suites in the manor's back garden turned what used to be a very exclusive retreat into a more run-of-the-mill hotel experience. Even so, the suites, which are, in effect, small cottages, are spacious, tastefully decorated, and fully equipped, should you wish to self-cater. Meals are served either on the veranda of the historic Belvidere House, a national monument, or in the charming pub.

Duthie Dr., Belvidere Estate, Knysna 6570. ☎ **044/387-1055.** Fax 044/387-1059. www.belvidere.co.za. 30 units. High season R1,220–R2,010 ($182–$300) double; low season R1,100–R1,760 ($164–$263) double. Rates include breakfast. AE, DC, MC, V. Children 10 and over. **Amenities:** Restaurant; bar; pool; room service; laundry. *In room:* TV, hair dryer, tea- and coffee-making facilities, fans.

Falcon's View Manor ⭐ Set high up on the hills overlooking the lagoon and surrounded by peaceful gardens, this guesthouse offers a gracious retreat from the hustle and bustle of town. The manor house (ca. 1899) features a wraparound veranda and elegant sitting room, as well as garden- or lagoon-view rooms on the upper level—these are a little fuddy-duddy and small; opt instead for one of the luxurious **garden suites** ⭐⭐, where the generously sized en-suite bedrooms, each comfortably furnished in muted modern colors, lead out onto private terraces overlooking the gardens and pool. Good, old-fashioned dining. A rather self-satisfied and snooty attitude permeates and ruins an otherwise soothing atmosphere.

P.O. Box 3083, Knysna 6570. ☎ **044/382-6767.** Fax 044/382-6430. www.falconsview.com. 9 units. Standard rooms from R1,250 ($187) double; garden suites from R1,600–R1,850 ($239–$276). AE, DC, MC, V. **Amenities:** Dining room; bar; pool; room service; laundry. *In room:* A/C, TV, hair dryer, tea- and coffee-making facilities in garden suites, heated towel rails.

Headlands House ⭐ Although locals are very unhappy at the rate of development on Knysna's previously pristine eastern head, there is at least a good guesthouse from which you can enjoy the stunning ocean and lagoon views. Perched high above the town and overlooking the ocean, all four rooms enjoy breathtaking views, as does the pool. The "honeymoon suite" has sliding doors opening onto one of the most dramatic sea views on the Garden Route and is worth the extra rands. No dining.

50 Coney Glen Dr., The Heads, Knysna 6570. ☎ **044/384-0949.** Fax 044/384-1375. www.headlandshouse.co.za. 4 units. High season R1,100–R2,200 ($164–$328) double; low season R1,100–R1,500 ($164–$224) double. Rates include continental breakfast. MC, V. Children under 10 on request. **Amenities:** Bar/lounge; small pool. *In room:* TV, hair dryer, tea- and coffee-making facilities, heated towel rails.

Inyathi Guest Village *(Value* Located in the heart of Knysna, Inyathi attracts a younger visitor with a great combination of value and taste. Despite its location just off the busy main road, with tourist information and a number of dining options within close walking distance, the village affords a great sense of privacy. Innovatively laid out around a courtyard, many of the double-bedded timber cabins feature beautiful stained-glass windows, and most have a luxurious slipper bathtub. While the rooms are charming and decorated with charm and creativity, they are relatively small—not the sort to lounge around in all day.

52 Main St., Knysna 6570. ⓒ/fax **044/382-7768.** www.inyathi-sa.com. 11 units. R370–R530 ($55–$79) double, depending on season. Rates include breakfast. AE, DC, MC, V. **Amenities:** Bar; babysitting; laundry. *In room:* TV, hair dryer, tea- and coffee-making facilities, fans, heaters.

Lightley's Holiday Houseboats ⓐ ⓚ*ids*   The best way to escape the seasonally congested streets of Knysna is to hire a houseboat and cruise the lagoon. You need no experience to skipper—just switch on and "drive" (navigational video, charts, maps, and instructions are supplied by Lightley's). You can fish for dinner from your boat (fishing rods are hired) or simply chug along to Crab's Creek or Belvidere Manor for a meal. Houseboats come equipped with everything: stove, fridge, hot and cold water, chemical toilet, radio/tape decks, CB radio, electric lights, crockery and cutlery, and barbecues—just remember to pack towels and detergent, and don't run out of fuel. Parents should request a boat with a water slide. Rates quoted are for **Leisure Liners,** which sleep four; **Aqua Chalets** sleep six, are more luxurious, and look better. *Note:* If you'd prefer a more luxurious boat, complete with your own skipper and chef, charter the *Outiniqua* (ⓒ **082/470-6022;** www.springtide.co.za), a 15m (50-ft.) luxury yacht comprising three double bedrooms and a large saloon.

P.O. Box 863, Knysna 6570. ⓒ **044/386-0007.** Fax 044/386-0018. www.houseboats.co.za. 12 houseboats. Low season R752–R1,020 ($112–$152) per day; high season R1,080–R1,500 ($161–$224) per day. MC, V.

Parkes Manor ⓐⓐ   The owners of this national monument have done a great job of transforming it into a gracious English-style country guesthouse, with established trees, green hedges, and manicured lawns (edged with a profusion of colorful beds), creating a delightful foreground to the equally inspiring lagoon views. It will probably be a better option for the older traveler than Phantom Forest; certainly, the accommodations are the best in this "country house" class (superior to Belvidere or Falcon's). All rooms are situated upstairs; huge, comfortable, and elegantly understated, each has access to an outdoor seating area. It is a little close to the N2, so do try to book a garden-facing suite (which are generally bigger and offer much better value); nos. 5 and 7 are particularly recommended. Of the lagoon-facing rooms, no. 3 is recommended. The small size of the guesthouse ensures attentive, personalized service, but it has many hotel-like aspects, such as the new restaurant, **Glenshiel at Parkes,** and a range of treatments at the attached health and beauty center.

1 Azalia St., Knysna 6570. ⓒ 044/382-5100. Fax 044/382-5124. www.parkesmanor.co.za. 8 units. High season R1,616–R1,936 ($241–$2890) double; low season R980–R1,260 ($146–$188) double; Premier suite R1,396–R2,010 ($208–$300). Rates include breakfast. AE, DC, MC, V. Children by arrangement only. **Amenities:** Dining room; bar; pool; room service; laundry. *In room:* TV, minibar, hair dryer, tea- and coffee-making facilities, fans.

Pezula Resort & Spa ⓐⓐⓐ   Perched atop the Knysna East Head cliffs on a links course designed by Ronald Fream and David Dale, this idyllic retreat is not only a recommended option for golfers, but is—together with Phantom (below)—the most luxurious choice in Knysna. Opened in December 2004 by Corinne Harrison (who launched the Saxon in Jo'burg and North Island in Seychelles), it offers superb service levels and tip-top accommodations matched only by the majestic forest and fynbos location (all reasons why it made it into *Condé Nast Traveler*'s 2005 Top 60 Hotels

Hot List). It's modern, with plenty of the currently di rigueur stone and dark slate, adorned with lots of South African art (including a whole lobby devoted to works by Mandela). The restaurant, **Zachary's,** where New York–born chef Geoffrey Murray is at the helm, is yet another reason why golfers aren't the only ones heading up the hill.

Pezula Estate, East Head Cliffs, Knysna. *©* **044/302-3333.** www.pezula.com. 76 units. Suites R3,150–R4,275 ($470–$638), depending on season. Rates include breakfast. AE, DC, MC, V. **Amenities:** Restaurants; pool; golf; tennis; gym; spa; laundry; walking trails; horseback riding; canoes; boat; mountain bikes. *In room:* TV, minibar, hair dryer, DVD, Internet, tea- and coffee-making facilities.

The Phantom Forest Eco-Reserve ★★★ If you prefer a more back-to-nature experience, these are without a doubt the best accommodations in Knysna, particularly if you're looking for a lodging option with strong safari overtones. Located on a 137-hectare (338-acre) nature reserve on a hill overlooking the Knysna River, it offers visitors the chance to explore indigenous forest and estuarine wetland, or just lie back and enjoy being surrounded by it. Meandering boardwalks connect the public spaces to the privately located suites, which are more like luxurious treehouses tucked into the forest canopy. Each of the Classic Suites comprises a large double-volume bedroom with sitting area leading out to a small elevated deck, and a large bathroom (with or without bathtub). One entire wall of each lagoon treehouse is a sheer sheet of glass, affording a stupendous view of the forest and Knysna lagoon shimmering in the distance. The newer Upper Tree Suites have additional luxuries like bathtubs on the deck, while the Moroccan Suites are the biggest. Service is not always up to par (you have to leave your car at the foot of the hill and wait for a vehicle to traverse the steep road; this can take longer than is comfortable), but the incredible setting, charming architecture, and fabulous views more than make up for this. (If you're looking for unparalleled service standards, you're better of at Pezula; see above.)

Off Phantom Pass, 7km (4¼ miles) from Knysna. Mailing address: P.O. Box 3051, Knysna 6570. *©* **044/386-0046.** Fax 044/387-1944. www.phantomforest.com. 14 units. Suites R2,400–R3,200 ($358–$478); ask about winter specials. Rates include breakfast; dinner R225 ($34) per person. AE, DC, MC, V. Children 12 and over. **Amenities:** 2 restaurants; bar; pools (w/incredible views); sauna; massage treatments; laundry; walking trails; canoes; boat; mountain bikes. *In room:* Minibar, hair dryer, tea- and coffee-making facilities, fans.

Rockery Nook ★★★ *Finds* Tucked away on the Knysna Heads, neighboring some enormous holiday houses on the water's edge in "Millionaires Row," the modest but gorgeous Rockery Nook is the best-kept secret on the Garden Route. Behind the walls of this stucco-and-stone beach house, with its sash windows framed by light blue shutters, you'll find an eclectic, super-chic interior with an arty mix of local paintings,

---

Tips **The Best Room in Knysna**

The aptly named "Paradise Room" at **Kanonkop** (*©* **044/382-2374;** www. kanonkoptours.com; R1,490–R2,090/$222–$312, depending on season), a guesthouse on the outskirts of Knysna, will have you wishing your entire holiday could be spent here. Owner Chris Conyers has spared no expense—from maximizing the superb views (including the elevated tub surrounded by elegant travertine) to the rich, sumptuous decor and wonderful personal touches (complimentary biscotti, divine-smelling toiletries, and vegetable crisps—with everything sourced from small local producers). He has succeeded in making you feel on top of the world—literally. Rates include breakfast.

crystal chandeliers, and huge antique armoires. For a family booking a long-stay holiday, the Main House is ideal, with a fully equipped kitchen and pantry, a central dining area with a huge table for entertaining, as well as an airy, sea-facing lounge. Two sea-facing bedrooms (main en-suite) are on the upper ground floor, and a loft upstairs has two bedrooms and a bathroom to share. Eating, sleeping, drinking, and taking an early-morning swim in the lagoon are all you have to think about during your stay.

George Rex Dr.; The Eastern Heads, Knysna Lagoon; Knysna, Eastern Cape. © 083/267-1732. Fax 011/646-9278. www.rockerynook.co.za. Main House (sleeps 13) from R3,800–R5,000 ($567–$746) per day; Fishermans Nook (sleeps 2) and Lover's Nook (sleeps 2) R,700–R1,300 ($104–$194) double (self-catering). No credit cards. **Amenities:** Serviced daily; laundry service available.

Under Milkwood ✦✦ (Kids) This timber village, set under centuries-old milkwood trees, with cobbled streets running past quaint higgledy-piggledy bungalows to a sandy beach and the lagoon, is charming. It's also convenient, with the Knysna Heads, Paquitas, and East Head Café within walking distance. Each two-bedroom chalet (double bed in main bedroom and two single beds in second bedroom) has a fully equipped kitchen and an open-plan lounge, a sun deck, and barbecue facilities. If you want to be right on the beach, ask for a "front" chalet: Sailor's Arms, Sinbad, Manchester, or Bottom. Skylark, Bayview, Curlew, and Schooner, all "hillside" chalets, offer the best value for money but require climbing stairs. Note that the "middle" chalets have the least privacy, and chalets Captain Cat and Schooner have parking places some ways away. Unless you're traveling with kids, peak-season prices do not represent good value.

P.O. Box 179, The Heads, Knysna 6570. © 044/384-0745. Fax 044/384-0156. www.milkwood.co.za. 16 units. High season R1,800–R2,600 ($269–$388) double or 4 persons; low season R650–R950 ($97–$142) double, depending on location. DC, MC, V. **Amenities:** Babysitting; canoes; paddle-skis; sailboard. *In room:* TV, hair dryer, tea- and coffee-making facilities, fan.

WHERE TO DINE

Dry Dock ✦✦✦ SEAFOOD/FUSION A great waterfront location, with plenty of boat action and twinkling marina lights at night. Order the catch of the day, and you'll find it is perfect—not overcooked or tarted up (just a little lemon butter), just simple as fish should be served when fresh (though more complex flavors, like fish preserved with fig preserve and spinach, are also available). The mussels, cooked in cream, pickled ginger, lemon grass, and coriander, are also delicious, as is the tempura Niçoise salad: lightly tempura-battered sugar snap peas, leeks, spinach, and patty pans, finished off with seared tuna, egg, and watercress and dressed with a mustard and pineapple dressing. For those requiring a little redder meat, the options include springbok filet served with deep-fried sweet potato and a chocolate and red-wine sauce. All seafood and produce is locally procured, and fresh fish and shellfish are delivered daily. Ask for a table upstairs or outside on the deck for the best views. *Tip:* If you're in the waterfront for lunch, you might want to check out sister outfit **34° South** (© 044/382-7268) around the corner (also on the water); it's often vibier at lunchtime, and the deli-style food is super-fresh and delicious—it's also a good place to put together a beach picnic.

Waterfront Shop 1, Knysna. © 044/382-7310. www.drydock.co.za. Reservations essential in season. Main courses R48–R486 ($7.15–$73); crayfish R249 ($37). AE, DC, MC, V. Daily 11:30am–10pm.

The Eatery at Mackintosh's ✦✦ (Value) FUSION/DELI If you're self-catering or about to go on a picnic, head for this "fine food emporium" (we're talking truffle oil) and fill a basket with farm-fresh vegetables and fruit, an array of delectable cheeses (many produced locally), pickles, meats, freshly baked breads and pastries . . . or give in to the aroma from the kitchen and sit down at one of the mismatched tables and order the homemade spring rolls (shrimp, crab, pickled ginger, lime, and coriander, served with marinated bean sprouts and wakame seaweed), lamb *tikka* (marinated in fresh papaya yogurt and served with egg noodles, wilted greens, deep-fried vermicelli, mango *achar* [relish], and coriander yogurt), or Spanish squid (pan-fried and served with tomato cilantro, onion, chile, and lime salsa). They also do a mean eggs Benedict. The only drawback is the lack of view (for that, go to sister outfit **34° South;** see above).

Thesen House, 6 Lower Long St. ℂ 044/382-6607. Meals R26–R49 ($3.90–$7.30). DC, MC, V. Daily 7am–5:30pm (kitchen 8am–4pm).

Ile de Pain Bread & Café ☆☆ BREAKFAST/SANDWICHES/SALADS   Atkins-dieters be warned. When Austrian chef-patron Markus Farbinger bakes, bread is all you'll want to eat! Whether it's his fresher-than-fresh potato bread, fluffy croissants, fragrant focaccias, crispy ciabattas, or signature *companion* (half-wheat, half-rye sour-dough made with a 300-year-old starter dough), Markus makes you realize that there is something seriously wrong with the bland stuff you find in supermarkets. Not only is the bread impeccable, but all the produce is free-range and from the farm. Whether you come for breakfast or lunch, you'll be seated at long wooden tables, either under the trees or in the rustic bakery, from where you can choose which of the daily sand-wiches (don't miss the toasted baguette with figs, Gorgonzola, rocket, and balsamic reduction), salads, or sweet treats chalked on the blackboard wall you wish to eat.

10 The Boatshed, Thesen Island. ℂ 044/302-5707. Sandwiches and salads R25–R80 ($3.75–$12). Daily breakfast and lunch.

The Phantom Forest ☆☆☆ PAN-AFRICAN   It's worth dining here just for the primal forest atmosphere and views in this stunning ecoreserve (see "Where to Stay," above), but with residents enjoying first dibs on tables, make sure you book well in advance. Get here early enough to order a predinner drink at the bar, and grab a chair next to the pool to watch as the enormous sky changes into its sunset hues, reflected in the lagoon waters below. At press time, a new chef had taken over, but the six-course table d'hôte dinner, served in a large boma, still changes daily and features a soup, a choice of four starters, sorbet, a choice of four main courses, followed by cheeses and a choice of four desserts. An African blend coffee is served outside around the large bonfire where dinner guests can mingle or simply lose themselves in the flames. With demand outstripping chair space, the team has now opened the new **Moroccan Chutzpah,** an intimate North African–themed venue (also set menu), where colorful cushions, candles, sunken lounges, and hookah pipes set the tone. Both offer a truly romantic dinner experience and are worth the irritation of having to wait to be transported from the base of the hill in the reserve's four-wheel-drive.

Off Phantom Pass Rd. ℂ 044/386-0046. Reservations essential in high season. Set dinner R260 ($39). AE, DC, MC, V. Daily 6:30–8:30pm.

PLETTENBERG BAY & SURROUNDS

Several miles of white sands, backed by the blue-gray outline of the Tsitsikamma Mountains and lapped by an endless succession of gentle waves, curve languidly to create **Bahia Formosa**—the "Beautiful Bay"—as the Portuguese sailors who first set eyes on it named it. Over the years its beauty has inevitably drawn an ever-increasing string of admirers, with some 50,000 of Jo'burg's wealthiest individuals descending on the seaside town of **Plettenberg Bay** every December, augmented by British socialites

Dining with a Local

Persellos (© 044/382-2665), known to the locals as "Mama's," is a real Italian family concern. Mama's sons make the pizzas, her daughters-in-law serve the tables, and in between making the specials, Mama wanders in and out of the kitchen, talking to one and all. Order the calamari: Mama makes the lightest batter for the tenderest calamari, and make sure you ask for her homemade garlic mayonnaise as a dip. **The Bow Tie Chinese Restaurant** (© 044/382-0132) is where Angela Chang serves while her husband quietly cooks behind the counter in the open kitchen. He has a gentle hand, leaving vegetables crisp and sauces subtle; pork with ginger and spring onions or crispy duck in a sweet and sour sauce are delicious. Like Mama's, the decor is simple, so bring your own ambience (and your own wine, if you wish). When we have out-of-town guests who want to be near the lagoon, we take them to the **Dry Dock** (see review, above) at the waterfront for dinner. Or we head to **34° South**—part of the same group as Dry Dock, it's busy and lively, and you can help yourself to a plate of cold mixed deli food, nice for a hot summer's day. If we're in the mood for classic country cooking, we book at **Pembreys** (© 044/386-0005) on Belvidere Road—hey, the food must be good because it's always full! Peter cooks while wife Viv does front-of-the-house duties, offering lots of different choices on a blackboard. If we just want a drink and a good vibe, we go to the **Oyster Catcher at the Waterfront** (© 044/382-9995) on a Sunday afternoon and listen to the live Latin American music. If we feel like listening to a local jazz group, we head to the **Cruise Cafe** (© 044/382-1693) on Friday evenings. Again, it is right on the Waterfront at the Featherbed jetty—you can sit on the large lagoon deck and sip your drink and have a large plate of mixed snacks, and soak up the laid-back vibe that is Knysna.

—Local foodie Jacquie Mansfield spent 25 years in the restaurant business before retiring to Knysna.

here to pay and play the Kurland International Polo Match. But in the off season, when the vast majority of holiday homes stand empty, a far more laid-back atmosphere prevails—though some find the ghost town unsettling, the empty beaches certainly make up for it.

There's not much to do in town itself but laze on the beach; try **Lookout** ✦✦✦, on the eastern side (which enjoys blue flag status), or **Robberg,** on the west. The much smaller **Central Beach,** dominated by the timeshare hotel Beacon Isle, is the area from which most of the boats launch. Sadly, money and taste seem to have enjoyed an inverse relationship in Plettenberg Bay; huge monstrosities line most of the beachfront, particularly Robberg Beach, with the exception being the less developed far-western edge, bordering the reserve. <u>**Robberg Nature Reserve** ✦✦✦ (© 044/533-2125)</u>, the rocky peninsula on the western side of the bay, offers fantastic whale-watching opportunities during the course of a 9km (5.5-mile) trail. The going gets very rocky, so be sure to wear sun protection and good shoes, and try not to time your visit with high tide.

For the less energetic, there are shorter 2½-hour versions; pick up a map from the reserve gate when you pay your R20 ($3) to get in. To find it, follow signs off airport road; the gate is 8km (5 miles) southeast of town. The reserve is open from 7am to 5pm daily; in high season from 6:30am to 7:30pm.

Plettenberg Bay (or "Plett," as the locals call it) is blessed with two estuaries, with the Keurbooms River in the east by far the larger and least spoiled. You can access the **Keurbooms River Nature Reserve** ✿✿ (✆ **044/535-9648;** daily 6am–7:30pm in summer, 7:30am–5:30pm; R5/75¢ in winter) only by water—it's definitely worth paddling upstream to view the lush vegetated banks and bird life, however; keep an eye out for Knysna loeries, kingfishers, and fish eagles. A canoe and permit will run you R40 ($5.95; R140/$21 for a double canoe); both are available at the gate kiosk at the slipway, or from **Aventura Eco.** There is also a highly recommended overnight canoe trail in the reserve—see "Staying Active," at the beginning of the chapter. For R70 ($10) per adult (R35/$5.20 children under 12), you can head upstream without lifting a finger by boarding the **Keurbooms River Ferry** (✆ **044/532-7876;** departs from slipway). Daily scheduled trips, which last approximately 2½ hours, take place at 11am, 2pm, and sundown, and include an optional 30-minute walk or picnic (bring your own food and pack a bathing suit). Beach lovers who find Plett's urbanization depressing should consider spending a day on the relatively unspoiled **Keurbooms Beach** (follow signs off N2). This wide beach shares the same bay and has rock arches and pools to explore, but the swimming is not quite as safe, so take care.

The inland area from Keurbooms River to the Bloukrans River is known as **the Crags**—if you don't mind not being on the beach, it has a few lovely accommodations options, as well as **Monkeyland** ✿ (signposted off N2, 16km/10 miles east of Plett; ✆ **044/534-8906;** open 8am–5pm), a primate sanctuary situated in indigenous forest that houses 13 different species. Saved from laboratories or the illegal pet trade, the majority of these free-roaming primates are either endangered or critically vulnerable. Admission is free, while foot safaris, guided by knowledgeable rangers, cost R90 ($13) adults, R45 ($6.70) children. A little farther east lies **Nature's Valley,** a tiny hamlet on a wide, deserted sweep of beach, and beyond this **Storms River Mouth,** both in the **Tsitsikamma National Park** ✿✿✿—a must on any Garden Route itinerary (see below).

For more information, you could visit the local **Tourism Bureau,** located in Melville's Corner Shopping Centre (✆ **044/533-4065;** admin@plettenberg.co.za; Mon–Fri 8:30am–5pm, Sat 9am–2pm, Sun 10am–1pm); staff members, however, are well meaning but not very switched on.

⌒Moments 3, 2, 1, Aaaaaaa!

If Plett's views aren't enough to take your breath away, remember that the world's highest bungee jump is only a 15-minute drive east on the N2. For R580 ($87), you can have the rare privilege of freefalling for 216m (708 ft.) off the Bloukrans Bridge, and then watch yourself doing it all over again on video (see "Staying Active," at the beginning of the chapter). Booking for this and all other adventure activities in the region can be made through ✆ **083/231-3528** or 042/281-1458.

Sea & Air Safaris

Top on your list of things to do in Plettenberg Bay is a **marine safari** ★★★ in the mammal-rich bay; you'll be provided with plenty of excellent photo ops as well as new insights into the various species' behavior and characteristics. Apart from the Bryde whale, the Indo-Pacific humpback, and the bottlenose and common dolphins who feed in the bay year-round, Plett also enjoys seasonal visits from the Southern Right, humpback, and killer whales during their annual migration (July–Oct)—it's worth booking a "close encounter" trip with a boat licensed to approach the whales up to 50m (164 ft.). Coastal and pelagic bird life and the historical and geological makeup of the bay are also discussed. Tours last approximately 2 hours and cost R300 to R500 ($45–$75); proceeds benefit whale and dolphin research and conservation. The longest-running operators are **Ocean Blue Adventures** (© 044/533-5083; www.oceanadventures. co.za) and **Ocean Safaris** (© 044/533-4963). A noisier way to view Plett's marine mammals—at least for those on the water and ground—is by air. **African Ramble Air Safaris** (© 044/533-9006; www.aframble.co.za) offers 30-minute low-level flights over the bay and up the coast, entering the Knysna estuary through the Knysna Heads, then returning via the forested inland. These require a minimum of two passengers and cost R400 ($60) per person; note that you can charter this five-seater to any of the private game lodges in the Eastern Cape for R5,200 ($776).

WHERE TO STAY

Like Knysna, Plett prices vary considerably depending on the summer or winter season, with December and January considered by most to be peak.

In Plettenberg Bay

The Grand Café and Rooms ★★★ (Value)   The Grand opened late in 2004, and hurrah for that! Stylish, quirky, and classy, like proprietor Gail Behr herself, it provides a modern take on the old-fashioned family hotel; it's by far the most interesting destination in Plett. Located on the high street (conveniently close to everything, and still walking distance to the beach), it's all about easy living, with eight huge suites and an all-day restaurant offering uncomplicated, bistro-style food with an African kick. Each spacious room is individually decorated, all leaning toward a witty, bohemian feel, including extra-high (with footstools), extra-length king-size beds and bathtubs big enough for two; in room no. 6, the free-standing tub is placed, altarlike, in front of shuttered doors that open onto views of Lookout Beach. The downstairs rooms open onto a pool deck; others have their own private courtyard (perfect for honeymooners). Spend the afternoon lying in the sun on comfy, cushioned daybeds overlooking the bay with a cocktail in hand.

Main Road, Plettenberg. © **044/533-3301.** Fax 044/533-3301. www.thegrand.co.za. R1,200–R2,600 ($179–$388) double. Rates include breakfast. (ask about low-season rates). **Amenities:** Dining room; pool; room service. *In room:* TV, DVD/CD players.

Periwinkle Guest Lodge ★ (Value)   This guesthouse is one of a handful that provides guests with excellent access and views of the beach and ocean, which is just across the narrow coastal road that traverses Robberg's beachfront. All rooms are relatively spacious and comfortably outfitted with wrought-iron beds and marine blues, whites, and/or sand colors; each has a small patio or balcony with a varying degree of privacy and views. Room nos. 1, 2, and 5 (particularly no. 2) are luxury rooms that enjoy the best views of the beach and ocean; all of these rooms have fireplaces. Of the standard rooms, no. 6 is the best option, while no. 3 is the proverbial "last chicken in the shop." The open-plan lounge, dining room, and deck are airy, comfortable, and—with wonderful views of the ocean and Robberg peninsula—filled with light. Dinners and lunches by prior arrangement; hosts are happy to make suggestions and arrangements for dining out.

75 Beachy Head Dr., Plettenberg Bay 6600. ©/fax **044/533-1345.** www.periwinkle.co.za. 7 units. High season R850–R1,550 ($127–$231) double; low season R650–R800 ($97–$119) double. Rates include breakfast. AE, DC, MC, V. Children welcome. **Amenities:** Lounge; laundry. *In room:* TV, fridges, hair dryer, tea- and coffee-making facilities, heated towel racks.

The Plettenberg ★★★
Situated on a hill overlooking Lookout Beach, with views all the way to Keurbooms and the blue-gray mountains beyond, this hotel has one of the best vantage points in the country. (Make sure you've booked a room that makes the most of this, as the standard double rooms with views of the parking lot are still pretty pricey and definitely not worth it.) Rooms are individually decorated and differ somewhat in size—the luxury double rooms with sea view are worth the extra R400 ($60). The "Blue Wing" comprises only suites and has beautiful views of the Beacon Isle Beach, but it's situated across the road, and guests occasionally complain of feeling cut off; personally, I would specify a Lookout Beach view. The Plettenberg is a Relais & Châteaux hotel, and as such, you can expect excellent food in the formal dining room. The emphasis is on seafood, but Karoo lamb is also a specialty. Service is attentive, but this is not a place to let your hair down.

40 Church St., Lookout Rocks. Mailing address: Box 719, Plettenberg Bay 6600. © **044/533-2030.** Fax 044/533-2074. www.plettenberg.com. 38 units. High season R2,800 ($418) double with no sea view, R3,700 ($552) luxury double with no view, R4,200 ($627) luxury sea-facing double, R4,800 ($716) suite, R5,800 ($866) suite with sea view; low season R1,375–R4,600 ($205–$687). AE, DC, MC, V. Children 12 and over. **Amenities:** Restaurant; bar; 2 pools (1 heated); spa; business services on request; salon; room service; laundry. *In room:* TV, A/C, minibar (suites only), hair dryer.

Plettenberg Park ★★★ *Finds*
Situated a few minutes from town, perched on the cliffs overlooking the Indian Ocean and surrounded by a private nature reserve, this is without a doubt the most exclusive retreat in Plettenberg Bay, offering unparalleled luxury, privacy, and service. Guests are accommodated in what used to be the owner's holiday house; its northern aspect overlooks a tranquil inland lake and a wild duck sanctuary, and the southern views are of the pounding ocean. A path winds from the elevated timber decks down the cliff face to a tidal pool and private beach, but it's a stiff walk back! A new wing has been built with five new rooms, Jacuzzi, gym, and sauna, but this wing has all the bland aspects of a hotel, so request one of the rooms in the original house and specify the view you'd prefer (sea or lake) when making reservations. There are four choices here: a good-value (small) sea-facing room or three huge sea- or lake-facing rooms, each with its own fireplace and decorated in what has come to be known as the Afro-colonial style (natural materials in neutral, earthy tones; crisp whites; bleached animal skulls). Service is attentive and personal; the chef will even create the daily menu around each person's preferences. If you're looking for a romantic retreat with very little disturbance from the outside world, Plettenberg Park is perfect—the only drawback is that you have to share it at all.

Off the Plett Airport road. P.O. Box 167, Plettenberg Bay 6600. © **044/533-9067.** Fax 044/533-9092. www.plettenberg park.co.za. 9 units. High season R4,540–R5,060 ($678–$755) double; low season R2,720–R4,040 ($406–$603) double. Rates include all meals, (local) drinks, and laundry. AE, DC, MC, V. Children 12 and over. **Amenities:** Dining room; bar; pool; room service; laundry; private beach. *In room:* TV, minibar, hair dryer, video, stereo, fireplaces.

Southern Cross Guest House ⊛   This pale-pink-and-white timber beach house is one of the most beautiful homes in Plettenberg—an American Colonial seaboard-style home that wouldn't look out of place on Long Island. It's also Plett's only guesthouse built right on the beach; a timber boardwalk leads through the vegetated dunes to the sand. Located on the western side of Robberg Beach, close to the reserve, the beach is pretty deserted and provides an excellent sense of getting away from it all. Rooms are extremely tasteful—like the rest of the house, they are decorated predominantly in cool whites with an occasional touch of black or natural wood; bathrooms are spacious, with expensive finishes. The owners (who live upstairs) have definitely bagged the best views, however—all the guest rooms are built around a central grassy courtyard, so none of them enjoys a sea view, and unless you close your doors and curtains, they also lack privacy. Breakfasts are served in the sunny lounge and dining area or on the patio overlooking the beach and sea—bliss on a beautiful day.

2 Capricorn Lane, Plettenberg Bay 6600. ✆ **044/533-3868.** Fax 044/533-866. www.southerncrossbeach.co.za. 5 units. High season R1,190 ($178) double; low season R950 ($142) double. Rates include breakfast. AE, DC, MC, V. **Amenities:** Lounge; laundry. *In room:* TV, hair dryer, tea- and coffee-making facilities.

Around Plettenberg Bay

Some of Plett's best accommodations are found outside of town, surrounded by indigenous bush and forests, beautiful gardens, or riverside settings. The only drawback is that you'll have to drive to the beach.

Hog Hollow Country Lodge ⊛ *Value*   Overlooking the dense indigenous forests that drop away below the lodge and carpet the Tsitsikamma Mountains beyond, Hog Hollow offers charm, comfort, and privacy. Both duplexes and simplexes (recently upgraded to suite status—all now have private lounges and extended decks) are recommended: French doors lead out onto private balconies or decks with hammocks and chairs to soak in the views of the verdant gorge. The "forest" luxury suites are huge, but with no minibar or telephone, it's a long walk to the main house to place a drink or tea order. One of the most charming suites is the "round house"; the en-suite master bedroom with wooden balcony is upstairs, and the lounge with fireplace is downstairs. Hog Hollow is renowned for its food—dinner is a set affair that will run you R175 ($26). Meals are served around the large dining-room table, turning the event into an informal dinner party. The service is excellent.

Askop Rd., The Crags, Plettenberg Bay 6600. ✆/fax **044/534-8879.** www.hog-hollow.com. 12 units. High season R1,275 ($190) double; low season R1,820 ($272) double. Rates include breakfast. AE, DC, MC, V. Closed June. 16km (10 miles) east of Plett signposted off the N2. Children by prior arrangement only. **Amenities:** Dining room; bar; pool; sauna; laundry. *In room:* Hair dryer, tea-and coffee-making facilities, fireplace.

Hunter's Country House/Tsala Treetops Lodge ⊛⊛⊛   Hunter's comprises charming cottages set in beautifully manicured gardens, each individually furnished with antiques, and each with its own fireplace and private patio. This is not a place for modern design enthusiasts—the frills and florals in some of the rooms are almost cloying. Orchard suites offer rather good value when compared with any of the top-end options in this area, premier suites are larger than garden suites but not necessarily better, and classic suites have private pools and outdoor showers. Meals are excellent (both Hunter's and Tsala are Relais & Châteaux members), and the personal, warm, discreet service has earned this luxurious family-run hotel its many accolades. The biggest drawback is that Hunter's offers no views, which is just one reason to bypass the Hunter's turnoff and head straight for Tsala Treetops. Located on the same property (just 500m/1,640 ft. from Hunter's) but with totally separate amenities, Tsala offers a sublime combination of privacy, luxury, and the sense of space that should come packaged with every holiday. Very much in the style of the luxurious safari camps up north, Tsala features a large double-volume open-plan public space surrounded by generous decking, off which the elevated boardwalks connect to 10 privately situated glass and timber "treehouses." These are literally minihouses, with fabulous views of the forested surrounds from every vantage point, including the comfortable lounge (each with fireplace and chess set) and deck with private plunge pool.

10km (6¼ miles) west of Plett, off the N2. P.O. Box 454, Plettenberg Bay 6600. ℭ 044/532-7818. Fax 044/532-7878. www.hunterhotels.com. Tsala 10 units. Hunter's 24 units. Tsala suites R4,580 ($684); Hunter's Orchard suites R1,980 ($296); Garden suites R2,380 ($355); Premier suites R2,780 ($415); Classic suites (including Forest suite) R3,980–R4,900 ($594–$731). All rates include breakfast; call for winter discounts. AE, DC, MC, V. **Amenities:** Dining rooms; bar; lounges; pool; children's "Cub Corner" at Hunter's; concierge; business services; room service; massage; laundry; library. *In room:* TV, minibar, hair dryer, pool (Classic, Forest, and all Tsala suites), fireplaces.

Kurland ⭐⭐⭐ *(Kids)*   Surrounded by paddocks and polo fields, the Kurland vies with Hunter's as the most gracious country hotel on the Garden Route. It's more intimate (only 12 rooms), a little less frilly, and more relaxed (kids are expressly welcome)— which definitely gives it the edge for parents. Rooms are huge (each with a living area, some with private plunge pools) and are comfortably decorated in English country-manor style, with antiques and original oil paintings. Superior rooms have their own swimming pools. Ten suites have loft rooms, with mini-furnishings for children— even an extra pool just for the kids. As with all of these out-of-town options, you have to drive to the beach, but there's plenty to do on the premises—like lying flat on your back on a massage table, lounging around the library, or mounting one of the polo ponies to explore the estate—and meals are of a high standard, just some of the reasons it was placed as a runner-up in *Tatler's* 2002 Hotel of the Year award. Unless you desire a sea view, this is the best option on the Garden Route.

19km (12 miles) east of Plett off N2. P.O. Box 209, The Crags 6602. ℭ 044/534-8082. Fax 044/534-8699. www. kurland.co.za. High season R6,000 ($896) double; low season R4,400 ($657) double. Rates include dinner and breakfast. Ask about low-season specials. **Amenities:** Dining room; bar; 2 pools; tennis; spa; room service; babysitting; laundry; library (w/Internet facilities); horseback riding; mountain bikes. *In room:* TV, minibar, hair dryer, fireplace.

WHERE TO DINE

It's the location rather than the food that draws people to **Lookout Deck** (ℭ 044/ 533-1379), but what a location! Right on the beach, with awesome views across the ocean to the Tsitsikamma Mountains stretching beyond, this is probably the best-placed restaurant on the Garden Route. Enjoy a "sunrise" breakfast on the upstairs deck, or get here for sundown and try the Lookout's famous wild oysters, picked off the Plett coast. Sipping sundowners at Lookout Deck is a hard act to follow, but if you tire of the beautiful views (and the semi-attired *Baywatch*-type babes and bums tossing back Mermaid's Orgasms and Beach Affairs), consider the following.

For sparkling wine and gourmet pizzas, the stylish Plett set head for **Cornutti Al Mare** (ℭ 044/533-1277)—you can't miss it; it's located to the left of the hill you have to drive down to get to Central/Robberg beach, with the facade and balcony covered in hand-painted tiles and mosaics, and great views across the bay from the outdoor tables (book a table indoors next to the fire if you're traveling in winter). Or try the dining room at the new **Grand Café** (see "Where to Stay," above), as much for the fresh, delicious fare (like the fresh wood-baked naan bread, served with smoked salmon, mascarpone, wild rocket, and pesto) as the ambience—where Gail Behr is, socialites from all walks of life are sure to follow. **Blue Bay** (ℭ 044/533-1390) is another stalwart, despite its location in a shopping mall. If you're after a more fine-dining experience, with exceptional elevated sea views, you'd be hard-pressed to beat a table at the **Sand at The Plettenberg** ✦✦ (✆ **044/533-2030**). Or opt for forest surrounds and a more cozy candlelit atmosphere at **Tsala Treetops Lodge** (✆ **044/532-7818**); here the excellent fusion/pan-African table d'hôte menu will run you R225 ($34). And finally, if you're really hungry, **The Islander** (✆ **044/532-7776**) is the place to be. A family-run restaurant, located 8km (5 miles) west of Plett in simple wood-and-thatch buildings, this has been providing diners with a huge buffet covering an incredible array of seafood dishes for almost 20 years. Drawing on island cuisine (Indonesia, Polynesia, Seychelles) as well as Portuguese, Creole, and South African traditions, the buffet costs R135 ($20) per person. *Note:* Lookout Deck and Islander close in winter.

TSITSIKAMMA NATIONAL PARK & STORMS RIVER MOUTH

Starting from just beyond Keurboomstrand in the west, this narrow coastal belt extends 80km (50 miles) along one of the most beautiful sections of the southern Cape coastline, and includes a marine reserve that stretches 5.5km (3½ miles) out to sea. The craggy, lichen-flecked coastline is cut through with spectacular river gorges, and the cliff surrounds are carpeted in fynbos (a beautiful and diverse floral kingdom) and dense forest—the fact that the Otter Trail, which takes in the full length of the coastline, is South Africa's most popular trail gives some indication of its beauty (see "Staying Active," earlier in this chapter, for more information).

Tsitsikamma is roughly divided into two sections: De Vasselot (which incorporates **Nature's Valley**) in the west, and Storms River Mouth in the east. There is no direct road linking them, but it's well worth taking the detour off the N2 and visiting both, though Storms River Mouth is the more awesome sight of the two. To reach Nature's Valley, the only settlement in the park, take the scenic R102 or Groot River Pass. Call in on the ever-helpful Beefy and Tish, who run a local information center from the **Nature's Valley Restaurant, Pub and Trading Store** (✆ **044/531-6835;** beefy@cyberpark.co.za); contact them for anything from a weather report to local B&B or self-catering accommodations options.

To visit **Storms River Mouth,** take the marked turnoff, some 60km (37 miles) from Plettenberg Bay, and travel 10km (6¼ miles) toward the coast. (*Note:* Do not confuse Storms River Mouth with Storms River Village, which is just off the N2 and has nothing much to recommend it.) The gate is open 24 hours, and the entry fee is R20 ($3), kids 2 to 16 R10 ($1.50). You can eat at **Tsitsikamma Restaurant** (✆ **042/281-1190**)—located at the beginning of the walk to the Storms River Mouth, it has one of the best locations on the entire Garden Route, right on the sea, but features pretty standard fare: a variety of linefish, steak, spareribs, and the like. Better to look for the sign just off the N2 (at Tsitsikamma Lodge) for **Fynboshoek Cheese,** where you can enjoy wonderful fixed-menu lunches, with everything on your plate made and grown by resident cheesemaker Alje. With only 20 seats, reservations are recommended (✆ **042/280-3879**).

EXPLORING ON FOOT

With no roads connecting sites of interest, this is, for most, the only way to explore the park (there is also a snorkeling and scuba-diving trail, however; for equipment and a guide, contact **Stormsriver Adventures** [✆ **042/281-1836**], the outfit that offers a host of activities in and around the park, including abseiling into the gorge and black-water tubing down the river). The easiest and most popular trail is the 1km (just more than ½-mile) boardwalk, which starts at the visitors' office and Jabulani, and winds its way along the mountainside, providing beautiful glimpses of the sea and forest, and finally descending to the narrow mouth where the dark waters of the Storms River surge into the foaming sea. This walk also takes you past the appropriately named **Mooi (Pretty) Beach,** a tiny cove where the swimming is safe, though the water can be very cold. Once at the mouth, don't miss the excavated cave with its displays relating to the Khoi *strandlopers* (beachcombers) who frequented the area more than 2,000 years ago. You can cross the suspension bridge that fords the mouth and climb the cliff for excellent ocean views, though it's steep going. To explore the otherwise inaccessible gorge, catch the *Spirit of the Tsitsikamma* ✮, a boat that departs from the old jetty below the suspension bridge from 9:30am to 4pm every 45 minutes for a half-hour journey upstream. The trip costs R40 ($5.95) per person. To find out more about the various trails, pick up a map from the visitors' office (✆ **042/281-1607**) at the rest camp. Hours are from 7am to 6pm daily.

WHERE TO STAY & DINE

Storms River Mouth Restcamp ✮ *(Value)* The S.A. Parks Board is not about to win any architectural awards, but Storms River is their best attempt by far. Almost all the units enjoy good sea views, particularly the "oceanettes." Try to book a ground-floor apartment; in front is a narrow strip of lawn with your own barbecue, and beyond lie the rocks and the pounding surf. You can head off into the forest or walk the rocks; at low tide the rock pools reveal a treasure trove of shapes and colors. The only drawback to staying in the oceanettes is that they are the farthest units from the restaurant, though the short drive, which snakes along the coast, is hardly unpleasant. If you're going to have all your meals at the restaurant, consider staying in the forest huts, particularly nos. 1 and 2, which overlook a burbling stream; keep in mind that the cabins are sweltering hot in peak summer and you share ablutions. Better still is to book one of the following log chalets: Nos. 8 (one bedroom) and 9 (family) are right on the ocean, as are the three honeymoon suites.

Reserve through National Parks Board, P.O. Box 787, Pretoria 0001. ✆ **012/428-9111.** Direct inquiries: ✆ 042/281-1607. www.sanparks.org. 46 units, consisting of 8-bed, 7-bed, 4-bed, and 2-bed log chalets; 3- and 4-bed oceanettes; and 2-bed forest huts with no kitchen or ablution facilities. Rates start at R240 ($36) for forest huts; R430–R780 ($64–$116) double for log cabin; R760 ($113) for family cottage; R350–R650 ($52–$97) for oceanette. 10% discount May–Aug. AE, DC, MC, V. **Amenities:** Restaurant; pool; relatively well-stocked shop; self-service laundry facilities.

5 The West Coast

For many the West Coast is an acquired taste—kilometers of empty, often windswept beaches and hardy coastal scrub, low horizons and big skies, lonely tree-lined dirt roads, and distant mountains behind which lie lush pockets carpeted in vineyards make this a truly off-the-beaten track experience. The main reason most visitors venture up here is to catch the spring flower displays that occur in the West Coast National Park anytime from the end of July to early September; but this aside, there are a few more gems to uncover—like eating fresh crayfish with your feet in the sand or living like the landed gentry at the Melck homestead at Kersefontein.

ESSENTIALS

VISITOR INFORMATION The very helpful **West Coast Peninsula Tourism** (✆ **022/714-2088**) is in **Saldanha,** on Van Riebeeck Street. There's very little reason

The West Coast & Side Trips to the Northern Cape

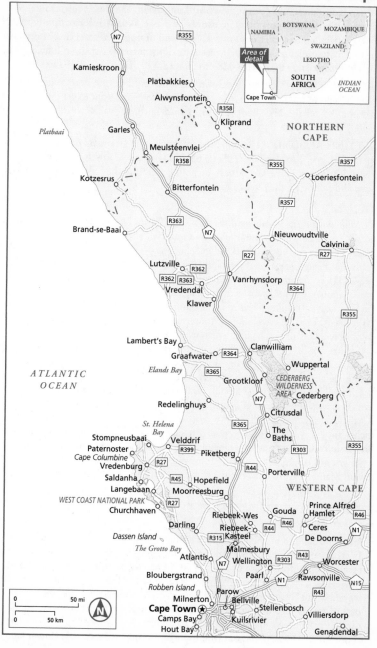

BOTSWANA

NAMIBIA

MOZAMBIQUE

SWAZILAND

LESOTHO

SOUTH
AFRICA

INDIAN
OCEAN

Area of
detail

Cape Town

N7

R355

Kamieskroon

Platbakkies

Alwynsfontein

R358

Kliprand

NORTHERN
CAPE

Platbaai

Garles

Meulsteenvlei

R358

R355

R357

Loeriesfontein

Kotzesrus

Bitterfontein

R357

Brand-se-Baai

R363

N7

Nieuwoudtville

Calvinia

Lutzville

R362

R27

R362 R363

Vredendal

Vanrhynsdorp

Klawer

R364

R355

Lambert's Bay

Graafwater

R364

Clanwilliam

Elands Bay

R365

Wuppertal

ATLANTIC
OCEAN

Grootkloof

CEDERBERG
WILDERNESS
AREA Cederberg

N7

Redelinghuys

R365

Citrusdal

St. Helena
Bay

The
Baths

Stompneusbaai

Velddrif

R355

Paternoster

R399

Piketberg

R303

Cape Columbine

Vredenburg

R27

Porterville

Saldanha

R45

Hopefield

R44

Langebaan

Moorreesburg

WESTERN CAPE

WEST COAST NATIONAL PARK

R27

Churchhaven

Riebeek-Wes

Gouda

Prince Alfred
Hamlet

R46

Darling

Riebeek-
Kasteel

R44

R46

Ceres

N1

Dassen Island

R315

De Doorns

The Grotto Bay

Malmesbury

R303

R43

Atlantis

N7

Wellington

Worcester

Bloubergstrand

Paarl

N1

Rawsonville

N15

Robben Island

R43

Milnerton

Parow

Bellville

Cape Town ★

Stellenbosch

Villiersdorp

Camps Bay

Kuilsrivier

Hout Bay

Genadendal

0   50 mi

0   50 km

N

209

to visit this industrialized town, however; **Langebaan,** the closest town to the West Coast National Park, may be more convenient. The **Tourist Information** (© 022/ 772-1515) is at the corner of Oostewal (the road in from R27) and Bree streets. For up-to-date information on the best places to view flowers at any given time, contact the **Flowerline** at © 083/910-1028 or 021/418-3705 (Mon–Fri Aug–Oct).

GETTING THERE   From Cape Town, take the N1, then turn north onto the R27. If you intend to travel farther north, say, to Cederberg, and want to get there quickly, take the N7 off the N1; this is the main road north to Namaqualand (the flower region) and Namibia.

GETTING AROUND   The only way to explore the area is by car or with a tour operator. **Cape Eco Trails** (© 021/785-5511; ecotrail@mweb.co.za) offers four-wheel-drive tours up the West Coast, including trips into the Kalahari Desert to view game and rafting on the Orange River.

DARLING

A small town a mere 50-minute drive from Cape Town, Darling attracts its fair share of visitors, particularly in September when its **annual wild flower and orchid show** is on— usually held during the third weekend in September—as well as the **Hello Darling Arts Festival** at Pieter Dirk Uys's informal theater and restaurant, **Evita se Perron** (© 022/ 492-2831), on Arcadia Street. Famous for creating the marvelous character of Evita—the tannie (auntie) who held sway over the imaginary homeland of Bapetikosweti, and now the First Lady of Darling—Uys is one of South Africa's most accomplished satirists. He has managed to make even the most conservative South Africans laugh at the country's tragic ironies (not an easy task for a man who dresses in women's clothing).

If you're not here in September, no matter: Evita se Perron has cabaret shows every weekend. Evita presides over many of these, but during her September Arts Festival, she steps aside and showcases the best local talents. You can also sample some of Tannie Evita's traditional fare (try the Madiba lamb curry) at her Station Café after the show. Evita se Dagkombuis (literally "Day Kitchen") serves breakfasts and light meals throughout the day: gay muffins, affirmative tarts, and the self-proclaimed "best toasted sandwiches in the world." To view pure Afrikaans kitsch, take a wander through her **Boerassic Park,** where garden gnomes preside over plastic flowers and political figurines.

To get to Darling, take the R27 (or West Coast Rd., as it's known) and turn off toward Mamre and Atlantis. From Mamre, the road to Darling cuts through fields of

---

Tips Flower-Viewing Tips

It is impossible to predict when each annual flower season will occur, but rainfall is obviously key. Another determinant is temperature, which is why flowers rarely open before 10am and hardly at all on overcast days. Remember that flowers turn toward the sun, so make sure you have the sun behind you when traveling. For the same reason, the flowers are at their best during the hottest part of the day, from 11am to 4pm. The floral carpets are spectacular from the car, but you'll need to stop and walk to marvel at the myriad species—at last count, some 4,000. To find out where the best displays are, call the **Flower Line** (© 083/910-1028).

Fun Fact **Out of Africa**

In one of two leading paleoanthropological theories regarding the origin of man, it is believed that Homo sapiens evolved in Africa about 200,000 years ago, migrating north in successive waves during the Pleistocene ice ages, displacing Homo erectus and Neanderthal man in Europe and Asia. Part of the body of evidence supporting this theory resides in Langebaan Lagoon: The world's oldest fossilized tracks of Homo sapiens—dating back 117,000 years— were discovered here in 1997.

---

wheat and vineyards, and before you know it, you've arrived in town. In Darling, the local **Tourism Information** office (⚹ **022/492-3361;** Mon–Fri 9am–1pm and 2–4pm, Sat–Sun 10am–3pm) staff will happily dispense various maps, details of nearby flower reserves (don't miss the **Tienie Versveld Wild Flower Reserve**), and any other information needed.

WEST COAST NATIONAL PARK ⚹⚹

The West Coast National Park encompasses almost 30,000 hectares (74,100 acres) of wilderness, as well as a 16×4.5km (10×2¾-mile) marine lagoon on which the coastal town of Langebaan is situated. Pack a picnic and head for one of the picture-perfect coves near Preekstoel and Kraalbaai, where the strikingly azure waters gently lap white sands and brilliant green succulents. Be sure to pack a camera and bathing suit. The **Postberg** section, which contains zebra, wildebeest, and gemsbok, is open only in August and September from 9am to 5pm, when the flowers are most spectacular. The community at **Churchhaven** (marked by the Anglican church of St. Peter), which was founded in 1863 by George Lloyd, a deserter from an American merchant vessel, has now closed the road running past it; the only way to gain access is to rent one of its basic self-catering cottages (⚹ **022/772-2799** or 022/772-2489). The hamlet enjoys a unique setting on one of the world's greatest wetlands. Overlooking a blindingly white beach and surrounded by salt marshes, the settlement is visited by more than 140 bird species (including the greater flamingo).

There are two entrances to the park: one off the R27, some 100km (63 miles) north of Cape Town, and the other just south of Langebaan. You can see a good deal of it by entering the one and leaving by way of the other, but make sure you visit the **Information Center** at **Geelbek** (⚹ **022/772-2799**), on the southern tip of the lagoon. Light meals are served, and a number of short trails take you to bird hides overlooking the lagoon—this is particularly rewarding in summer, when the hides provide views of thousands of migrant waders and flocks of pelican, flamingo, curlew, and sandpipers. Admission to the park is R15 to R20 ($2.25–$3) per person, depending on the season. The park is open daily from October 1 to March 31 from 6am to 8pm, from April 1 to September 30 from 7am to 7:30pm. For more information, contact ⚹ **022/772-2144.**

WHERE TO STAY & DINE

The Farmhouse ⚹⚹   With the West Coast National Park right at your doorstep, tasteful decor, and the azure Langebaan Lagoon visible from almost every room, this is by far the best place to stay in Langebaan. The comfortable guest suites, of which 10 have their own fireplace, are very spacious, and it's worth booking a luxury with a sweeping view of the lagoon—ask for room no. 9, 10, or 18. In the cheaper category, room nos. 2 and 4 have the best views. Room no. 12 (R1,010/$151) is spacious and ideal for families—large with a king-size bed and two three-quarter beds. The restaurant, pub, and terrace all enjoy the same beautiful view of the lagoon. A la carte meals include traditional choices like oxtail and chicken pie and, of course, seafood.

5 Egret St., Langebaan 7357. © 022/772-2062. Fax 022/772-1980. www.thefarmhouselangebaan.co.za. 18 units. High season R880–R1,010 ($131–$151) double; low season R560 ($84). Rates include breakfast. AE, DC, MC, V. **Amenities:** Restaurant; bar; pool; access to Langebaan's Country Club facilities. including golf, tennis, and bowls; babysitting; laundry. *In room:* TV, minibar, hair dryer on request, tea- and coffee-making facilities.

Kersefontein ★★ *Finds* This is one of the most authentic, unusual experiences to be had in the country—to be hosted by what is effectively a South African aristocrat in his beautiful Cape Dutch farmstead, a national monument (dating to 1744) on the banks of the Berg River. A 7,000-hectare (17,290-acre) working wheat and cattle farm in the rugged Sandveld, Kersefontein has been owned by the Melck family since 1770, and the sense of history is almost palpable—on the way to the grand dining room, you will pass, for instance, the skull of the last Berg River hippo, shot by Martin Melck in 1876 after it bit his servant. Julian, the eighth-generation Melck, is a bit of a Renaissance man and an eccentric and charming host; it's worth taking the drive up here just to spend an evening in his company (the authentic farm-style food is also delicious). Accommodations are separate from the main house: in either one of the two "African" rooms (top choice, with doors opening onto a small private veranda and sweeping lawns), the Victorian suites (with a communal lounge and a kitchen, should you wish to self-cater), or the self-catering cottage (a personal favorite), situated a short drive away and blissfully tranquil. All have been masterfully decorated by Graham Viney (the man responsible for refurbishing the Orient-Express hotels), utilizing family antiques found in what must be a massive attic! Even if you opt for a self-catering unit, breakfast will be prepared and served at your own dining-room table. It's a 90-minute drive from Cape Town; if you can tear yourself away, the West Coast National Park lies under an hour away.

Box 15, Hopefield 7355. ©/fax 022/783-0850. www.kersefontein.co.za. 4 units. R720–R880 ($107–$131) double. Rates include breakfast. Dinner R140 ($21), including drinks. AE, DC, MC, V. Follow signs off R45 between Velddrif and Hopefield. Children welcome. **Amenities:** Dining room; pub (located in what used to be the old Kersefontein farm bakery); laundry; mountain bikes; boats; ranch riding; private air trips (Julian is also a pilot).

PATERNOSTER & COLUMBINE NATURE RESERVE ★★★

To reach these West Coast gems, stay on the R27 past the West Coast National Park and Langebaan, and then take the R45 west to Vredenburg. Drive straight through this ugly town and take the 16km (10-mile) dirt road to **Paternoster,** a tiny fishing village that—due to strict development guidelines—retains a classic West Coast feel, with almost all of the 2,000-odd residents living in picturesque whitewashed fisherman-style cottages. If you're just here on a day trip, time your visit to stop for lunch at **Voorstrand** ★★★ (© 022/752-2038; daily 10am–10pm). This rustic shack of a restaurant is right on the beach, and you can sit with your feet in the sand while your waitress brings you an ice-cold bottle of wine—when the sun sparkles off the crescent-shaped beach and ocean, the sense of contentment is almost surreal. The small, simple menu is in Afrikaans, but if you're here during November to April there's only one thing to order: succulent crayfish tails (R95–R190/$14–$28, depending on size), served with garlic or lemon butter. Other popular dishes include the Malaysian seafood curry (R50/$7.50) and the "three fish dish"—a good way to sample the linefish caught off this coast. If you can't bear to leave (and believe me, it's hard), book a self-catering cottage—request one right on the beach—through **Lyndré** (© 082/405-8656; R250–R1,250/$37–$187 per night). Or take a look at the **Blue Dolphin** (© 022/752-2001; www.bluedolphin.co.za; R500/$75 double, including breakfast); it, too, enjoys a sublime location on the beach, with lots of nooks to curl up with a book, but the decor is a tad fussy and frilly.

The 263-hectare (650-acre) **Cape Columbine Nature Reserve** (© 022/752-2718; daily 8am–5pm) is home to a wide variety of flowers; the best time to visit is obviously in spring, but the reserve's superb location is a welcome relief from the coastline's ongoing degradation by developers. The campsites (R60/$8.95) are situated right on the sea, and the hikes are beautiful. Try to avoid visiting during school holidays and weekends.

Moments **The West Coast Beach Barbecue**

For dining, a meal at one of the West Coast alfresco restaurants is an unforgettable experience: Sitting on the beach breathing in the aroma of seafood on hot coals and the fresh sea breeze, you drink in the sun and the sound of seagulls, sink deeper in the sand as course after course keeps flowing, and lick your fingers clean (scrubbed mussel shells are often the only cutlery provided). Your only worry will be how you're ever going to manage to save enough space for the crayfish still to come. These eateries are so informal they're hardly restaurants, but if you like casual dining and don't mind sharing your space with strangers, they're well worth trying out. The food, prepared in the manner of one huge beach barbecue, is excellent and usually consists of several kinds of fish cooked in various ways (sometimes with jam, a West Coast specialty); *bokkoms* (salted, dried harders, or small fish) with grapes, mussels, calamari, paella, *waterblommetjie bredie* (waterlily stew); and crayfish. There's also piping-hot white bread baked on the beach and served with fresh farm butter and a number of fruit preserves—this is the killer; you'll want to devour an entire loaf, much to the detriment of the remaining courses. The (on-average) 10-course self-service meal will cost in the region of R120 ($18) per person.

Of the West Coast alfresco "restaurants," **Muisbosskerm** ✸✸✸ (© 027/432-1017) is still the best. Located on the beach 5km (3 miles) south of Lambert's Bay on the Eland's Bay Road (3 hr. from Cape Town), this is where the open-air West Coast restaurant concept was born—for years Edward and Elmien Turner had simply shared their favorite food with friends on the beach, and in 1985 they decided to broaden their guest list. The food is delicious, and you can usually count on a selection of fresh linefish, fresh green mealies, local potatoes and sweet potatoes, seafood *potjies* (pots of stew), curried tripe, *waterblommetjie bredie*, roast lamb, crayfish, mussels, and the legendary West Coast breads and preserves. It's a long drive home after a meal like this, so head for Paternoster, or ask the Turner family to recommend a few accommodations options when you phone for reservations. Booking ahead (for place and times) is essential.

LAMBERT'S BAY

This fishing port, the last bastion of "civilization" on the coast, lies 75km (47 miles) north of Velddrif and 65km (40 miles) west of Clanwilliam. There are two main reasons to visit: to view the colony of birds on Bird Island and feast at one of the coast's best outdoor restaurants.

Bird Island is accessed via a stone breakwater in the Lambert's Bay Harbour. This island houses a colony of Cape gannets, jackass penguins, and cormorants—to be amid the cacophony of a 14,000-strong community all jostling for position on the island is a rare privilege. Alternatively, book a sunset cruise that takes you out to see the marine life of the bay from **Eco Boat Trips** (© 082/922-4334).

6 Cederberg

Around 200km (124 miles) north of Cape Town lies the Cederberg Wilderness Area. This hikers' paradise features majestic jagged sandstone mountains that glow an unearthly deep red at sunset; strange-shaped rock formations that dominate the horizon; ancient San (bushman) rock painting sites; burbling streams in which to cool off; a variety of animals, such as baboon, small antelope, leopard, and lynx; and rare mountain fynbos such as the delicate snow protea and gnarled Clanwilliam cedar. You can drive to a number of designated spots, but the best way to explore this area is on foot.

In keeping with its "wilderness" designation, there are no laid-out trails, though maps indicating how to reach the main rock features—the huge Wolfberg Arch, and the 30m-high (98-ft.) Maltese Cross, as well as to the two main Cederberg peaks—are available. Covering 710 sq. km (277 sq. miles), the Cederberg Wilderness Area is reached via a dirt road that lies halfway between the towns of Citrusdal and Clanwilliam. Of the two, the pretty town of Clanwilliam is the more attractive base, with a few attractions of its own, including the country's main Rooibos tea-processing factory (see "Sampling the 'Erb," below), the Ramskop Wildflower Reserve, and a spectacular drive to the nearby Moravian mission station of **Wuppertal** 🎯🎯. You can camp in the Cederberg or book a self-catering chalet through Cape Nature Conservation, but if you don't want to rough it and are particularly interested in rock art, look no further than the ultraluxurious Bushmans Kloof, northeast of Clanwilliam (see below).

ESSENTIALS

VISITOR INFORMATION The **Clanwilliam Information Centre** (© 027/482-2024; www.clanwilliam.info; Mon–Fri 8:30am–5pm, Sat 8:30am–12:30pm) is opposite the old church hall on Main Street. To camp or walk in the Cederberg Wilderness Area, you will need a permit from **Cape Nature Conservation** in Algeria (© 022/931-2088).

GETTING THERE   By Car Clanwilliam lies just over 2 hours' drive from Cape Town. Head north up the N7; after approximately 160km (99 miles), you'll pass the town of Citrusdal to your left. About 28km (17 miles) farther north on the N7 is the turnoff for Cederberg Wilderness Area; 26km (16 miles) farther is the Clanwilliam, also on your left.

By Bus   Intercape (see chapter 2 for local numbers) travels the N7 to Namibia. Note, however, that unless you have someone to pick you up, you'll be left stranded on the highway.

> ### *Fun Fact* Sampling the 'Erb
>
> **Rooibos** (literally, "red bush," pronounced "*roy*-boss") is a type of fynbos that occurs only in Clanwilliam and the surrounding area. Its leaves have been used to brew a refreshing, healthful drink for centuries but were first exported during World War II, when the Ceylon variety was scarce. Since then it has become popular in the Japanese, German, and Dutch markets, and research shows some amazing health properties. Rooibos is caffeine free, is rich in vitamin C, and contains antioxidants, iron, potassium, copper, fluoride, zinc, magnesium, and alpha-hydroxy acid. Drinking it "neat" is an acquired taste; try it with honey, ginger, and/or lemon; or with milk and sugar. You can sample it at the **Rooibos Ltd factory**, Rooibos Avenue (*©* 027/482-2155), or order it just about anywhere in South Africa. Also recommended is the aptly named Honeybush Tea.

WUPPERTAL ★★★

It's worth visiting this isolated rural community just to travel the 90-minute dirt-road trip from Clanwilliam, with its breathtaking views of the twisted shapes and isolated tranquillity of the northern Cederberg. Once here, you'll feel lost in time: **Wuppertal** looks pretty much the way it did when it was established as a Moravian mission station in the 1830s. In fact, Wuppertal farmers still use sickles to reap, donkeys to thresh, and the wind to sift their grain.

You can't miss the **Tourism Bureau** (*©* 027/492-3410) on the Church Square next to Leipoldt House. This oldest building in the village also houses the **Lekkerbekkie** (little sweet mouth), which serves refreshments. To get to Wuppertal, drive east of Clanwilliam via the Pakhuis Pass on the road to Soetwater. Take the road south some 40km (25 miles) off the Pakhuis Pass Road at the appropriate sign to the Biedouw Valley. From here you have to travel some 30km (19 miles) via the Uitkyk and Kouberg passes.

WHERE TO STAY & DINE

Contact **Cape Nature Conservation** for camping and self-catering information in the Cederberg (*©* 022/931-2088; www.capenature.org.za; R460–R690/$69–$103 for four); **Rietdak**, a thatched cottage 400m (1,312 ft.) from the river, is one of their best self-catering units. If you want to get away from it all, **Tree Tops** (*©* 022/921-3626; R240/$36 double)—four self-catering treehouses on the banks of the Olifants River, close to Citrusdale—is worth looking into. A recommended option in Clanwilliam itself is **Saint Du Barry's Country Lodge** (*©*/fax 027/482-1537), a B&B with five units (R400–R580/$60–$87), each with a television and fridge. But for all-out luxury, with excellent guided tours of Bushmen art, you can't beat Bushmans Kloof.

Bushmans Kloof Wilderness Reserve ★★★   This Relais & Châteaux lodge is by far the most luxurious option in the Cederberg surrounds, with accommodations that are on a par with the best game lodges near Kruger. Located on 8,000 hectares (19,760 acres) stocked with game and filled with flowers in spring, the reserve has more than 125 rock-art sites, and a resident rock-art specialist to explain anything from the mythology to the technique behind this ancient art. Declared a South African Heritage Site, Bushmanskloof—"the world's largest open-air gallery"—is dedicated to preserving the unique biodiversity of the region as well as the history of the San. Early morning rock-art tours provide visitors with insights into this fascinating community, followed by botanical walks, mountain biking, or simply lazing about in the crystal-clear rock pools. Sunset brings game drives in open Land Rovers. The ultraluxurious bedrooms overlook the rolling lawns and river—ask for rooms in River Reeds or Water's Edge. Swimming pools, set above the river, offset the harsh, magical surrounds of the Cederberg beautifully. The lodge is easiest accessed by charter flight; it's a 60-minute flight from Cape Town (its at least 3 hr. by car).

Past Clanwilliam, turn due east for 34km (21 miles) on Pakhuis Pass; entrance is on right. P.O. Box 53405, Kenilworth 7945. Lodge ℂ 027/482-2627, or reservations 021/797-0990. Fax 021/685-5210. www.bushmanskloof.co.za. 16 units. R3,800 ($567) luxury double; R5,000 ($746) deluxe double; R7,000 ($1,045) suite. Rates include all meals, guided rock-art walks, and game drives. AE, DC, MC, V. No children under 10. **Amenities:** 3 dining areas; bar; 4 swimming pools; spa; room service; laundry. *In room:* A/C, minibar.

7 Side Trips to the Northern Cape

A DRIVING TOUR OF NAMAQUALAND

Most of the year the sandveld region north of the Olifants River, a vast semi-arid area known as Namaqualand, sees very little visitors. But come the rains in August or September, the seeds that lie dormant under these dusky plains explode into magnificent multicolored carpets, as 4,000 species burst into vivid bloom. Because of the huge distances to cover to get to Namaqualand (Springbok is some 544km/337 miles from Cape Town), you might want to make sure that the season has begun before you set off on a self-drive tour (though you'll struggle to find accommodations if you don't book well in advance)—note that the season starts on the coast and moves inland. Getting there is pretty straightforward: The area is reached via the N7 highway, which connects Cape Town with Namibia. If you find the distances daunting, note that **National Airways** (ℂ 021/934-0350) will fly you by private charter to **Springbok Airport.**

The seasonal flower displays start quite close to Cape Town (see "Darling" and "West Coast National Park," earlier in this chapter), but you enter the more remote and more spectacular flower region soon after the N7 bypasses Vanrhynsdorp, 283km (175 miles) north of Cape Town. This marks the halfway point between Cape Town and Namaqualand's "capital," Springbok, and while it's strictly still part of the Western Cape, it's well worth planning an overnight stop in the region. To do this, ascend the African plateau by taking the R27 via Van Rhyn's Pass to charming **Nieuwoudtville** 🐾🐾, touted as "the bulb capital of the world" and famed for its white sandstone architecture, or travel farther east to **Calvinia.** If you're traveling in late August, note that the biggest braai (barbecue) in the country—the annual **Hantam Meat Festival**—is held in Calvinia at this time, offering rare tastings of such native delicacies as *kaiings* (salted crackling) and *skilpadjies* (liver in caul fat). To overnight in Nieuwoudtville during flower season, you'll have to reserve long in advance: Try booking **Ystervark Cottage** (ℂ 027/218-1522 or 083/675-1825), a converted stone barn that sleeps two. Contact the **Nieuwoudtville Publicity Association** (ℂ 027/218-1336) for more accommodations options.

For the best tours in this region, conducted in a fantastic old Bedford bus from the 1950s, contact **Neil MacGregor** 🐾🐾🐾 (ℂ 027/218-1200; bookings essential), a third-generation farmer who has hosted the likes of David Attenborough and his BBC team when they were filming *The Private World of Plants* at his farm, Glenlyon. Having traversed the **Knersvlakte** (literally, "Plains of Grinding Teeth"), the first important stop north of Vanrhynsdorp is **Kamieskroon** (174km/109 miles farther on the N7), the last town before Springbok, which lies some 67km (42 miles) farther north on the N7. Kamieskroon is literally a one-horse town, but its claim to fame is the nearby **Skilpad (Tortoise) Wildflower Reserve** ★★★ (© 027/672-1948; daily 8am–4pm in season only). Created by the World Wildlife Fund, and part of the Namaqua National Park, the reserve (18km/11 miles west of town on the Wolwepoort Rd.) catches what little rain blows in off the sea, and is always magnificent during the flower season. The other reason to stop here is the **Kamieskroon Hotel** (© 027/672-1614; kamieshotel@kingsley.co.za). The hotel charges R270 ($40) per person and offers 7-day photographic workshops that could transform the way you look at things. The workshops, co-founded by local photographer Colla Swart and the internationally renowned Canadian photographer Freeman Patterson, cost R6,600 ($985) per person for a 6-day course to R7,700 ($1,149) per person for a 9-day course. *Note:* Try to get your hands on a copy of *Freeman Patterson's Garden of the Gods* (Human & Rousseau), which features the beauty of Namaqualand in full bloom, to whet your appetite for a trip north.

The best place to stay (and eat) in Springbok is the **Springbok Lodge & Restaurant,** on the corner of Voortrekker and Keerom roads (© **027/712-1321;** sbklodge@intekom.co.za; R220/$33 double without air-conditioning and fridge, or R240/$36 double with air-conditioning and fridge). The lodge is clean, but it's far from luxurious. Owner Jopie Kotze, who calls his lodge "a living museum," is a mine of information, and his restaurant walls are lined with photographs and artifacts relating to the area. You can also overnight in self-catering chalets at the top attraction, the **Goegap Nature Reserve** ★★ (© **027/712-1880**), 15km (9¼ miles) southeast of Springbok. The reserve is open daily from 8am to 6pm, though the office closes at 4pm. Admission is R10 ($1.50) adults, R5 (75¢) children.

6

Undiscovered Wilderness:
The Eastern Cape

The country's second-largest province offers a sun-drenched coastline that stretches for 800km (496 miles) from the lush Garden Route to subtropical KwaZulu-Natal, rolling past green hills where villagers live as they have for centuries, and vast plains in the hinterland where the Big 5 again wander. It is that rare combination of undiscovered beauty, enjoyed in solitude. Until recently the Eastern Cape was rarely at the top of the list of holiday destinations, largely because so many of its attractions are off the beaten track, but the large-scale and ongoing rehabilitation of vast tracts of fallow farmland into private game reserves has transformed the region into a must-see destination, not least because these reserves enjoy the additional advantages of being malaria-free and easily accessible—a mere 45- to 90-minute drive from the capital city of Port Elizabeth.

With accommodations as luxuriously appointed as those of their Kruger counterparts, and game rangers on hand to unravel the mysteries of the bush, these reserves are definitely worth exploring, but bear in mind that the terrain—most of which is prickly low-lying scrubland—is not the classic picture-postcard landscape of Africa. However, the sparseness of the vegetation means you're certain to see plenty of game. And the area has its own, strange beauty: You'll treasure forever such sights as a moonlit euphorbia forest, looking more like props from a sci-fi moonscape, or an entire hillside ablaze in orange aloe blossoms.

But the Eastern Cape is also steeped in history: This is the birthplace of some of the country's most powerful political figures, like Steve Biko and Nelson Mandela, and Port Elizabeth was a crucial center of the anti-apartheid movement, with a notoriously deadly security police in close attendance. Today a number of good operators offer excellent township tours that provide an insight into Port Elizabeth's role in South African history, as well as an authentic introduction into traditional Xhosa rites and ceremonies.

English-settler towns like Grahamstown also offer fine examples of colonial-era architecture. Moving north into the thirstlands of the Karoo, you will find vast, uninhabited plains with such atmospheric names as the Valley of Desolation, near Graaff-Reinet, the Eastern Cape's oldest settlement. If you like unpopulated spaces, small towns, and picturesque architecture, this is a highly recommended detour, possibly on a self-drive tour between the Garden Route and Gauteng. Alternatively, opt to explore the coastal attractions, from surfing the perfect wave in Jeffrey's Bay to exploring the aptly named Wild Coast, where you'll find the country's most unspoiled beaches and an exciting new coastal reserve.

1 Port Elizabeth

763km (473 miles) E of Cape Town; 1,050km (651 miles) SW of Johannesburg

The approach to Port Elizabeth, referred to by locals as "P.E." and by a slightly desperate marketing team as "The Friendly City," is somewhat depressing. Factories alternate with brown brick houses on the freeway into town, the ocean breeze is colored by the stench of smokestacks, and a network of elevated highways has effectively cut the center of the city off from the sea.

For most, Port Elizabeth is simply an entry or departure point—usually for a trip up or down the Garden Route, or to visit one of the malaria-free game reserves. If you have a day to kill, take a township tour that covers some of the capital's political history, hang out on Humewood Beach, or amble along the Donkin Heritage Trail to take in P.E.'s settler history. Or, if you're not heading off to a game reserve to overnight, both Addo and Shamwari lie within an hour's drive—a good day-trip option—though not as satisfying as spending a few nights in the bush under a star-spangled sky.

ESSENTIALS

VISITOR INFORMATION Port Elizabeth tourism has been renamed **Nelson Mandela Bay Tourism** (© 041/585-8884; Mon–Fri 8am–4:30pm, Sat–Sun 9:30am–3:30pm), but it's still located in the Donkin Lighthouse Building, Donkin Reserve, central P.E. Possibly more convenient is the **Eas'capism Tourist Information Centre** (© 041/5077912; www.eascapism.com), operating daily from 8am to 7pm from the beachfront entrance to the Boardwalk Casino and Entertainment World.

The 1820 Settlers: Deceit, Despair & Courage

The Industrial Revolution and the end of the Napoleonic wars created a massive unemployment problem in Britain. With their underpopulated colony in southern Africa under threat by the indigenous tribes, the British authorities came up with the perfect solution: Lured by the promise of free land and a new life, 4,000 men, women, and children landed at Algoa Bay in 1820, more than doubling the colony's English-speaking population. Many were tradesmen and teachers with no knowledge of farming, and they were given no prior warning of their real function: to create a human barrier along the Fish River, marking the eastern border of the Cape Colony. On the other side of the river were the Xhosa (pronounced "ko-sa"). The settlers were provided with tents, seeds, and a few bits of equipment, and given pockets of land too small for livestock and too poor for crops. Pestilence, flash floods, and constant attacks by the Xhosa laid waste their attempts to settle the land, and most of them slowly trickled into the towns to establish themselves in more secure trades. Thanks in no small measure to their stoic determination, Port Elizabeth is today the biggest coastal city between Cape Town and Durban, and the industrial hub of the Eastern Cape, with road, rail, and air links to every other major city in South Africa.

Eastern Cape

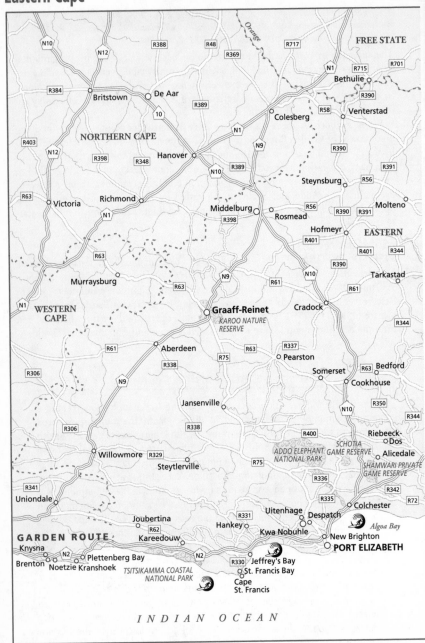

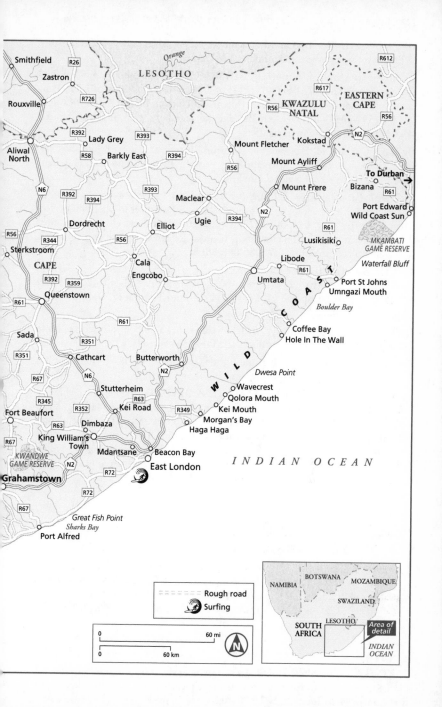

Smithfield · R26
Zastron
LESOTHO
Orange
R612
Rouxville
R617
R726
EASTERN
CAPE
KWAZULU
NATAL
R56
R56
Mount Fletcher Kokstad
N2
R56
R392
Lady Grey R393
Mount Ayliff
R58 Barkly East R394
Aliwal
North
R56
To Durban
N6
R392
R393
Mount Frere Bizana
R61
R394
Maclear
Port Edward
Wild Coast Sun
Dordrecht Elliot Ugie R394
N2
R61
R56
R344
Lusikisiki
MKAMBATI
GAME RESERVE
Sterkstroom
Libode
Waterfall Bluff
CAPE
Cala R61
R392 R359
Engcobo
Umtata
Port St Johns
Queenstown
R61
Umngazi Mouth
Boulder Bay
R61
Sada
R351
Coffee Bay
R351
Cathcart Butterworth Hole In The Wall
R67 N6
N2 Dwesa Point
R345
Stutterheim
Fort Beaufort
R63 Wavecrest
R352 Kei Road R349 Qolora Mouth
R63 Dimbaza Kei Mouth
King William's Morgan's Bay
R67 Town Haga Haga
KWANDWE
GAME RESERVE Mdantsane
N2 Beacon Bay
Grahamstown R72 East London
R72 INDIAN OCEAN
R67
Great Fish Point
Sharks Bay
Port Alfred

WILD COAST

Rough road
Surfing

0   60 mi
0   60 km

N

BOTSWANA
NAMIBIA MOZAMBIQUE
SWAZILAND
SOUTH LESOTHO
AFRICA Area of
detail
INDIAN
OCEAN

GETTING THERE By Car P.E. is on the N2, which runs between Cape Town (7 hr. away; through the Garden Route) and Durban.

By Air Port Elizabeth Airport (✆ **041/507-7319**) is 4km (about 2½ miles) from the city center. **SAA** (✆ **041/507-1111**) and **Nationwide** (✆ **041/507-7290**) fly between P.E. and Johannesburg, Cape Town, and Durban. **British Airways Comair** (✆ **041/581-6055**) flies between P.E. and Johannesburg. Call **Supercab Shuttle** (✆ **041/52-3720**) for airport transfers.

By Bus Greyhound, Baz Bus, and **Translux** all connect P.E. with Johannesburg, Cape Town, and Durban. **Intercape** runs between P.E., Johannesburg, and Cape Town. (See chapter 2 for regional numbers.)

By Train For the ultimate in luxury (with a R22,745/$3,395 price tag!), take the 2-day train trip that runs from Cape Town to P.E. from December to March on the legendary **Blue Train** (✆ **021/449-2672**; www.bluetrain.co.za); see chapter 2 for more details. The national mainline train runs between Johannesburg and Port Elizabeth; for details, call Shozoloza Mail ✆ **086/000-8888.**

GETTING AROUND By Car The best way to explore the Eastern Cape is with your own wheels. **Avis** (✆ 041/581-1306), **Budget** (✆ 041/581-4242), **Hertz** (✆ 041/508-6600), **Imperial** (✆ 041/581-4391), and **Tempest** (✆ 041/581-1256) all have desks at the airport.

By Taxi Hurters Taxi Cabs (✆ **041/585-7344**) has a 24-hour taxi service. **Molo Tours** (✆ **082/970-4037**) offers direct safari transfers to reserves.

By Air Contact **John Huddlestone** (✆ **041/582-2597** or 083/653-4294) for a helicopter trip to any of the reserves, or an aerial tour of P.E.

GUIDED TOURS OF PORT ELIZABETH & BEYOND Besides the highly recommended township tours (see "What to See & Do," below), you can **sail Algoa Bay** on *Spirit of the Millennium,* a gaff-rigged schooner (✆ **041/583-2141**); orient yourself with a 90-minute **Friendly City Tour** (✆ **041/585-1801**); or book a full-day "big-game" excursion with **Pembury Tours** (✆ **041/581-2581**). Pembury also offers 3-day Karoo or 3- to 10-day Garden Route tours. For guided hikes, contact **Eastern Cape Adventure and Hiking Association** (✆ **042/368-3761**).

FAST FACTS: **Port Elizabeth**

Area Code Port Elizabeth's area code is **041.**

Auto Repair Call **AA Breakdown** (✆ **082/16111** or 011/799-1500).

Emergencies For an **ambulance,** call ✆ **10177; National Sea Rescue Institute (NSRI),** call ✆ 041/507-3911; **Police Flying Squad,** call ✆ **10111;** or **police,** call ✆ 041/394-6313. The best private hospital is **Greenacres** (✆ 041/390-7000).

WHAT TO SEE & DO

TAKING A TOWNSHIP TOUR ✿✿✿ To gain real insight into the city, the following tours are highly recommended: If you're prepared to make a night of it, **Mzolifi Quza,** of **Molo Tours** (✆ **082/970-4037;** molotours@signposttravel.co.za), offers one of the best township tours in the country. After visiting an initiation camp (see

Fun Fact **Rites of Passage**

It is not unusual to pass young men covered in white clay on the road—in rural as well as urban areas of the Eastern and Western Cape. These are Xhosa initiates, boys who are about to learn the customs of their clan, culminating in the removal of the foreskin (without anesthetic) to mark their transition to manhood.

"Rights of Passage," above), he will lead you on a tour through the Walmer township, visiting a youth center along the way, before taking you home to enjoy dinner with a Xhosa family. This is followed by a trip to new housing projects and schools and a community choir rehearsal, and ends after a visit to a local *shebeen* (informal drinking house). **Calabash Tours** (© 041/585-6162) offers an excellent morning tour: The 3- to 4-hour "Real City Tour" starts in the city center and looks at Port Elizabeth's history and the forced removal of residents out of the city to coloured and black townships. Xhanpi of **Fundani Tours** (© 082/964-6563) will tailor to your requirements and also offers a 3-day tour that follows the "Footprints of Mandela's Youth." Fundani offers accommodations at a number of Xhosa family homes, and—if the timing is right—can arrange for you to witness a traditional Xhosa ceremony.

A WALK THROUGH SETTLER HISTORY   If you're interested in P.E'.s early history, take the 5km (3-mile) **Donkin Heritage Trail,** a self-guided walk marked with a blue staggered line that takes you past 47 places of historical interest in the old Hill area of central P.E.

You can pick up a map from the tourism office in the Donkin Lighthouse Building, which is in the **Donkin Reserve,** located below Belmont Terrace and Donkin Street—a quaint row of Victorian houses collectively declared a national monument. The reserve was proclaimed an open space in perpetuity by Sir Rufane Donkin, the Cape's acting governor in 1820. Take a stroll to the large stone pyramid monument the governor erected to his late wife, Elizabeth, after whom he also named the city— look for the touching inscription. From here you might want to visit the **No. 7 Castle Hill Museum** ☝ (© 041/582-2515; Mon–Fri 10am–1pm and 2–4:30pm, Sat 10am–1pm; admission R10/$1.50 adults, R4/60¢ children), one of the oldest settler cottages in the city, dating back to 1827.

At the bottom of the hill you can either turn right to browse the **Wezandla Craft Centre** (© 041/585-1185), or turn left to view the pretty **City Hall** and the **City Library,** both on Govan Mbeki Avenue (recently renamed after the father of the current president); it's worth entering the library, a Gothic-Revival building dating back to 1902, to take a look at the stained-glass dome on the second floor.

EXPLORING THE BEACHFRONT   Enjoying an average of 7½ hours of sunshine a day, and lapped by relatively warm waters, Port Elizabeth beaches see a lot of action. The first crescent is **King's Beach;** a safe swimming beach, it has good family facilities, including the **McArthur Baths Swimming Pool Complex** (© 041/582-2282), which stretches south to **Humewood Beach,** the best swimming beach, and proud of its Blue Flag status; opposite is where you will find **Bay World Museum Complex** (© 041/584-0650; daily 9am–4:30pm; R31/$4.60), which houses the **Oceanarium,** a snake park and a museum featuring fossils, scale reconstructions of shipwrecks, and a display on the Xhosa. A little farther along is the beachfront entrance to the **Boardwalk Casino and Entertainment World,** where you'll find a number of restaurants and a cinema. Additional attractions at Humewood include taking a scenic day trip on the **Apple Express** (© **041/507-2333;** R120/$18), a restored narrow-gauge steam train.

To escape the crowds, keep traveling the beachfront road until it becomes Marine Drive, and then take the Sardinia Bay Road to visit the big dunes of Sardinia Bay. This is the start of the **Sacramento Trail** ⚐; call Godfrey Murrell (© **041/373-6794** or 083/463-5546) to explore this 8km (5-mile) coastal walk.

BIG-GAME DAY TRIPS ⚐⚐⚐   The nearest game reserve (a mere 45 min. from the center of town) is **Addo Elephant National Park** (© **042/233-0556;** www.addo elephantpark.com; daily 7am–7pm; R80/$12). Over the past 10 years, the park has grown phenomenally (by some 100,000 hectares/247,000 acres) and currently extends from Darlington Dam in the Karoo all the way to Woody Cape on the coast, including the island groups of St Croix and Bird Island, home to the largest gannet-breeding colony in the world. Although they are in evidence year-round, the most attractive time of the year to visit is in spring, when the harsh Eastern Cape bushveld is softened with flowers, and the gray behemoths can be seen standing in carpets of yellow daisies. Other animals to look for are black rhino, buffalo, lion, hyena, zebra, red hartebeest, eland, kudu, bushbuck, warthog, and a few endemic species such as the flightless dung beetle, found almost exclusively in Addo. To ensure best sightings, head for the watering holes (pick up a map at the entrance). Alternatively, take a guided game drive in an open-topped Land Rover (R140–R220/$21–$33); these take place at sunrise, midafternoon, sundown, or night—the only way to view the nocturnal activities of such carnivores as the black-backed jackal and bat-eared fox.

It was thanks largely to the efforts of visionary Adrian Gardiner that the Big 5 once again roam the Eastern Cape plains. Since stocking **Shamwari,** his 20,000-hectare (49,400-acre) reserve with the Big 5, he has garnered numerous international awards—not only for reintroducing game, but also for the reserve's respectful focus on settler and African culture (he seems set to win more accolades for his work at Bushman Sands; see below). If you don't have the time to overnight, a **day trip** (© **042/ 203-111**) will run you R1,100 to R1,400 ($164–$209). After a buffet-style lunch, visitors are taken to **Kaya Lendaba,** an African art and culture village created by controversial *sangoma* (traditional healer) Credo Mutwa, and the **Born Free centre,** a sanctuary for abused animals, followed by a 3- to 4-hour game drive in which you explore the five ecosystems of the reserve in an open-topped Land Rover with a knowledgeable ranger.

The Crushing of Black Consciousness

Take a detour from the Heritage Trail and visit the sixth floor of the otherwise charmless building located on 44 Strand St.: This is where Steve Biko—the charismatic black-consciousness leader of the 1970s—died while being interrogated by the security police. This, combined with the Soweto uprising, led to the imposition of the arms embargo by the U.N. Security Council. Until the recent Truth and Reconciliation Commission hearings, the official version of events was that Biko slipped and fell, and no one was ever arrested. You can visit the room in which Biko was interrogated; it houses items relating to the man and his past.

Tips **No Oranges, Please . . .**

Be aware that no citrus fruit can be taken into Addo park. Addo elephants regard them as a delicacy, and when they pick up the scent, they can become quite aggressive.

Besides the Big 5, you will no doubt spot plenty of antelope (the reserve has 18 species), giraffe, wildebeest, hippos, and, if you're lucky, cheetah.

Amakhala is another Big 5 reserve, but offering day/night trips for a mere R650 ($97)—the 6,000-hectare (14,820-acre) reserve is also only 45 minutes from the city center (© **042/235-1608;** www.amakhala.co.za). **Schotia** (© **042/235-1436;** www. schotia.com), a small (1,700-hectare/4,199-acre) reserve east of Addo, offers 3- to 4-hour night drives in which you track one of the reserve's six lions on the prowl as well as rhino and hippo. This costs R450 ($67, including transfers from P.E./Addo and supper around the fire) or R750 ($112) if you want to include a game drive through Addo to view buffalo and elephant.

WHERE TO STAY & DINE

Note that the city options are only a 5-minute drive from the airport. Lodges and camps in the options listed under "Tracking the Big 5 in Private Reserves" provide a tranquil alternative to staying in the city, yet are only 45 minutes (Addo) to 90 minutes (Kwandwe) from check-in.

IN PORT ELIZABETH

The two establishments reviewed below are the most stylish options in Port Elizabeth, but if you're about to blow your budget on a luxury reserve, you might want to consider the family-run **Chapman Manor Hotel** (© **041/584-0678;** www.chapman.co. za). A manor house it ain't, but all rooms have sea views, as does the pool, and at R480 ($72) for a double, it's arguably the best deal in town. It also houses a good seafood restaurant called **Blackbeards** (© **041/584-0623;** 6pm–late): Try one of the "brodino" dishes—your choice of fish, combined with mussels and calamari; cooked in a tomato, white-wine, and garlic sauce (herbs are secret); and served in a cast-iron pot. Alternatively, head for the Boardwalk Casino and Entertainment Complex, which has a clutch of recommended eateries: **Kyoto,** for truly excellent Japanese dishes, including super-fresh sushi (© **021/583-1160;** book a booth); **34° South** (© **041/583-1085**), sibling to the hugely popular Knysna restaurant-cum-deli (see "Knysna: Where to Dine," in chapter 5) and serving up delicious deli produce; and **El Greco** (© **041/583-2950**)—don't miss the tender lamb kleftico (Greek casserole). If you're in the mood for something spicy, then make like a local and head for **Natti's Thai Kitchen.** It's in a rather seedy part of town, but Natti (assisted only by her laid-back surfer husband, Mark) has been warming palates here for 8 years (© **041/ 585-4301;** dinner only). And for the best harbor views, head for the appropriately named **Oyster Catcher** (© **041/582-186**).

Hacklewood Hill Country House ✿✿✿ It's almost worth making a special detour to P.E. to stay at what is rather presumptuously called a "country house"— 4 minutes from the airport, Hacklewood is *very* much in the heart of the city, and home to any VIPs visiting P.E. Built in 1898, the gracious Victorian manor house has been artfully converted, with none of the generous spaces of the original home compromised. If you have a thing for bathrooms, these are world class. Each is bigger than most hotel rooms and is furnished with the same class and care as the bedrooms: Victorian bathtubs are set in the center of the room, with comfortable seating provided in deep armchairs, should you wish to converse in comfort. The entire house is furnished with beautiful period pieces, with colors and fabrics evincing exquisite taste, and a staff that's eager to please. The four-course dinners (R185/$28), known as the finest in P.E., are presided over by cordon bleu–trained chef Michael DeReuck.

152 Prospect Rd., Walmer 6065. © **041/581-1300.** Fax 041/581-4155. www.pehotels.co.za. 8 units. R3,200 ($478) double. Rate includes breakfast. AE, DC, MC, V. Children 8 and over. **Amenities:** Dining room/bar; award-winning wine cellar; pool; tennis; transfers by arrangement; business services; room service; laundry. *In room:* A/C, TV, minibar, hair dryer, tea- and coffee-making facilities, heated towel rails.

The Windermere Hotel 𝒜𝒜   Conveniently located one road back from King's Beach, a stone's throw from McArthur Pools, this is the first guesthouse in P.E. to embrace the modern boutique hotel aesthetic, with customized fittings and furniture throughout, much of it designed by Haldene Martin, local *Elle Décor* Designer of the Year. Luxury rooms are huge enough to be termed suites, and furnished with all the modcons needed for a comfortable stay. Book one of the upstairs rooms for views, particularly room no. 3, which has sea vistas from its balcony. Staff members are helpful and willing. Breakfast is served in the dining room, on the deck, or in your room, and a complimentary shuttle service is on hand to take you to the Boardwalk complex, with its many restaurant choices.

35 Humewood Rd., Humewood, Port Elizabeth 6001. © **041/582-2245.** Fax 041/582-2246. www.the windermere.co.za. 8 units. R800–R1,150 ($119–$172) bed and breakfast. AE, DC, MC, V. **Amenities:** Breakfast room; lounge; cocktail deck. *In room:* A/C, satellite TV, DVD player, minibar, hair dryer, IT port.

ADDO ELEPHANT NATIONAL PARK

Addo has continued to expand both its borders and its options, with a few luxury alternatives in addition to the park's rest camp. The pick of the bunch is **Gorah** 𝒜𝒜𝒜 (© **044/532-7818;** www.gorah.com; R2,250–R3,850/$336–$575 double, all-inclusive), a luxury tented camp located in a private concession within the park, with East African–style accommodations that really are in a class all their own. Alternatively, the colonial-style **River Bend Lodge** is situated within a 17,000-hectare (41,990-acre) private concession, with eight luxury rooms displaying exquisite taste and attention to detail (© **042/233-0161;** www.riverbend.za.com; R3,000–R5,000/$448–$746 double, all-inclusive). If you balk at paying these prices, newcomer the **Elephant House** (© **042/233-2462;** www.elephanthouse.co.za; R1,300–R2,150/$194–$321), another eight-roomed luxury lodge close to Addo Elephant park, offers game drives to any of the surrounding game reserves.

Addo Park Rest Camp (Value   Many of these comfortable self-catering cottages have bush views—often with elephants. All units (except for some of the forest huts) are en-suite, though you need to specify whether you want a semi- or fully equipped kitchen, or shared cooking facilities. Unit nos. 1 to 6 (two-bed with communal kitchens) have views of the water hole, as do unit nos. 7 and 8 (six-bed with kitchens); unit nos. 17 to 24 and 29 to 32 (four-bed) have good views of the park. A restaurant serves basic, filling meals—chicken, fish, steaks (including kudu and ostrich), and a few traditional dishes like *umcabosi*, a mix of spinach and pap (maize porridge).

Bookings: S.A. Parks Board, Box 787, Pretoria 0001. © **012/428-9111**. Direct © **042/233-0556**. www. sanparks.org. 42 units: 6-bed cottages, 4-bed cottages, 4-bed forest huts, and 2-bed rondawels. From R729 ($109) double. MC, V. **Amenities:** Restaurant; swimming pool; tennis; store. *In room:* A/C in some units.

TRACKING THE BIG 5 IN PRIVATE RESERVES

The reserves below are given full reviews because they offer exceptionally high standards, but there are a number of new options that might suit your pocket more. The recommended 5,000-hectare (12,350-acre) **Kariega Private Game Reserve** (© **046/ 636-7904**; www.kariega.co.za; R3,600–R4,600/$537–$687 double, all-inclusive) is located in the Kariega River Valley, an 80-minute drive from the city, and near the beaches of Kenton-on-Sea. Of the two lodges, **Ukhozi Lodge** (R4,600/$687 double, all-inclusive) is the more luxurious and exclusive (make sure you book one of the two rooms that come with private plunge pools); **Kariega Lodge** (R3,600/$537 double, all-inclusive) offers better value, particularly for families, with 19 spacious timber chalets, each with its own viewing decks—again, some come with plunge pools at no extra cost, so make sure to book these well in advance.

Alternatively, the 6,000-hectare (14,820-acre) **Amakhala Game Reserve** (© **042/ 235-1606**; www.amakhala.co.za) is a mere 45 minutes from P.E. central, and located just south of Shamwari. Amakhala has five separately owned and privately managed accommodations options, of which **Safari Lodge** (R2,960–R4,700/$442–$701 double, all-inclusive; rates depend on season) is the most luxurious and pricey, with accommodations in six thatched and luxuriously appointed "safari huts." **Leeuwenbosch** offers a more colonial-style experience and good value at R3,900 ($582) double, all-inclusive. But if you are on a real budget, you can't beat Carnavon Dale (R1,050/$157 double), a historic Edwardian-style settler farmhouse dating back to 1857. Finally, golfers should consider the excellent deal to be had at **Bushman Sands** (© **042/231-8000**; www.bushmansands.com; R800–R1,400/$119–$209 bed and breakfast), a 90-minute drive from P.E. Another successful attempt by visionary businessman Adrian Gardiner (of Shamwari fame) to develop sustainable tourism initiatives, this luxury golfing estate and 4,000-hectare (9,880-acre) reserve is centered on the town of Alicedale. Once a thriving railway town, the community was faced with high unemployment when Spoornet moved; with this new project, Gardiner has provided the town with a lifeline.

Kwandwe Private Game Reserve ★★★ Operated by the hugely successful CC Africa (Londolozi, Phinda, to mention but two), Kwandwe should is the first choice for design-conscious visitors to the Eastern Cape. Covering 20,000 hectares (49,400 acres), the reserve has two lodges, Main Lodge and Ecca, as well as Uplands, a gracious 1905 farmhouse that can accommodate six. A member of Relais & Château, it also has the added benefit of 30km (19 miles) of Great Fish River frontage—a big contrast to the slightly arid Eastern Cape environment. Located on the banks of the river, the Main lodge looks like it's been furnished for Karen Blixen: Persian rugs, antique chests and wardrobes, hand-stitched damask linen and cut-glass decanters, African spears, and old-style hunting prints—it's all very *Out of Africa*. The nine luxury suites, each privately situated, feature fabulous views (even from your Victorian tub), indoor and outdoor showers, thatched viewing decks, and private plunge pools. **Ecca Lodge,** completed in December 2003, is situated on rolling slopes overlooking a valley of acacia and aloe trees, offers a more intimate environment (six suites), and is furnished in a more modern and airy style. Besides the de rigueur morning and evening game drives and/or walks, evenings are further augmented by a local historian's fascinating tales about the region—from the period of the Bushmen to the great frontier wars, it makes for fascinating tales. Staff will also arrange excursions to view rock paintings or to the nearby university town of Grahamstown. Kwandwe is a 90-minute drive from the P.E. airport.

Bookings through CC Africa: Private Bag X27, Benmore 2010. ℰ **011/809-4300.** Fax 011/809-4315. www.cc africa.com. 9 units. High season R9,590 ($1,431); low season R5,100 ($761). Rates include all meals, local beverages, game activities, and laundry. Ask about Uplands rates. AE, DC, MC, V. **Amenities:** Dining area/bar/lounge; boma; room service; laundry; game drives; bush walks. *In room:* A/C, minibar, hair dryer, plunge pool.

Lalibela 😸 *Kids*   Although it's not in the same category as Kwandwe or Shamwari, this private game reserve, also located near Grahamstown, is a top choice for beleaguered parents with young children. It leaves parents free to pursue their own game drives or relax at the pool while children are entertained by a specific program developed with those under the age of 8 in mind. From dawn, when the kids are taken to breakfast by their own full-time nanny (included in the price), they are kept busy with conservation projects, mini–game drives (in their own special game vehicle, and kept well away from potentially dangerous encounters), special picnics, and visits to the playground and sandpit. Early afternoon sees parents catch up on all the excitement of the day before the children's activities are again resumed for dinner. Evening is spent sitting in front of the campfire roasting marshmallows and listening to African bush safari stories before bedtime. For those who don't want to be disturbed by children, there are two additional camps, of which **Treetops**—featuring spacious safari tented-style accommodations—is the most exciting. A number of scientific research projects are currently being conducted (in conjunction with Rhodes University) to ensure the future of generations of game at Lalibela, and the wildlife team was proud to announce the discovery of their first litter of lion cubs early in 2005.

Bookings: P.O. Box 13482, Humewood, Port Elizabeth 6013. ℰ **041/581-8170.** Fax 041/581-2332. www.lalibela. co.za. R4,500 ($672) double, all-inclusive; R1,125 ($168) children, all-inclusive including nanny. For specials, check when booking. Rates include all meals, drinks, game drives. AE, DC, MC, V. **Amenities:** Dining room/bar; pool; laundry; cultural dancing performances; game drives; bush walks. *In room:* A/C, hair dryer, tea and coffee in all communal areas.

Shamwari Private Game Reserve 😸😸   This award-winning reserve has a choice of six accommodations options. Aimed at the top-end market are **Eagles Cragg,** comprising nine junior suites, and **Lobengula Lodge,** with six suites. Eagles Cragg suites all have private viewing decks with plunge pools (as do two of Lobengula's junior suites—make sure you bag one of these). These thatched lodges offer the most authentic African-safari experience in the reserve, with huge suites luxuriously furnished in ethnic-chic decor, and great food. However, with only four rooms, **Bushmans River Lodge** (an original 1860 settler farmstead), is the most intimate lodge; as a result, it's extremely popular, so book ahead. Personally, I think **Bayethe,** the new luxury tented camp with nine en-suite tents, offers better value—at least in the hot summer, when you can lounge around your private deck, periodically dipping into your very own plunge pool. If the idea of a tent doesn't appeal, you'll have to settle for **Riverdene,** comprising nine twin rooms (and no private pools!). The least successful (but popular with older clientele, and the only option for parents) is **Long Lee Manor,** a pink Edwardian manor built in 1910, accommodating 36 guests in a more overtly colonial style. It, too, is beautifully furnished and well staffed, but is the most like a hotel and commands the same price as Bayethe, Riverdene, and Bushmans.

Bookings: P.O. Box 32017, Summerstrand, Port Elizabeth 6019. (©) **042/203-1111.** Fax 042/235-1224. www. shamwari.com. High season (Sept–Apr): Lobengula and Eagles Cragg R10,500 ($1,567) suite; Long Lee Manor from R8,650 ($1,291) double; Bushmans River, Riverdene, and Bayethe R8,650 ($1,291) double. Low season: from R5,400–R11,000 ($806–$1,642); some lodges close—check when booking. Rates include all meals, drinks, game drive. AE, DC, MC, V. **Amenities:** Dining room/bar; pool; airport transfers; laundry; television lounge; game drives; bush walks; cultural village; binocular rentals. *In room:* A/C, TV (Long Lee, Bushmans, and Riverdene only), hair dryer.

2 Jeffrey's Bay

75km (47 miles) W of Port Elizabeth

Situated on the 186km (115-mile) stretch between Storms River and Port Elizabeth, this is an easy detour on the way to or back from the Garden Route, particularly if you feel like stopping for lunch at the beach (see "Where to Dine," below). If you're a surfer, however, this coastal town will be a top priority on your itinerary. Considered one of the top three surfing spots in the world, "J-Bay" (as it's affectionately known to locals) shot to international fame in the 1960s cult movie *Endless Summer,* which featured the break at Supertubes—the fastest and best-formed break on the South African coast, as well as "Bruce's Beauties," a rare right-point break you'll find a little farther west, at the quiet coastal hamlet of Cape St Francis.

ESSENTIALS

VISITOR INFORMATION   The **J-Bay Tourism Office** (© 042/293-2588; www. jeffreysbaytourism.com; Mon–Fri 8:30am–5pm and Sat 9am–noon) is on the corner of Da Gama and Drommedaris roads. To find out where the surf is, or for lessons, call **Brenton** at the **South Coast Surf School** (© 083/549-6795; R150/$22 for 2 hr., includes all equipment)—it's never too late to start; some of Brenton's students are in their 50s and 60s.

GETTING THERE   Jeffrey's Bay can be reached only by car or bus; take the turnoff south off the N2. The **J-Bay Sunshine Express** (© 042/293-2221) shuttles between Jeffrey's Bay and Port Elizabeth. **The Baz Bus** (© 021/439-2323) calls in every day on its run between Cape Town, P.E., and Durban.

GETTING AROUND   Once here, you can get around on foot or by car. **Derek** from **Aloe Africa** (© 042/296-2974 or 082/576-4259; aloe@agnet.co.za) offers various adventure activities like surfing, sandboarding, mountain biking, and kloofing (in which you follow a river through a mountain gorge, swimming and clambering your way out).

WHERE TO STAY

The most upmarket option on the final stretch of coast between the eastern end of the Garden Route and Port Elizabeth is the **Beach House** ★★ (© 042/294-1225; www.stfrancisbay.co.za), in St Francis Bay, a small coastal town 20-minutes' drive west of J-Bay. The small thatched lodge (only four rooms) offers 180-degree ocean views, beach access, and luxurious accommodations, at a price: R1,790 to R2,820 ($267–$421) double, including breakfast. In Jeffrey's Bay the best guesthouse is **Diaz 15** (© 042/293-1779; www.diaz15.co.za; high season [Oct–Apr] R1,250–R1,600/ $187–$239 double; low season from R1,000 ($149) double), one of the few along the coast located right on the beach. A well-cropped lawn abruptly dissolves into Main Beach, and the ocean is literally a stone's throw from your sliding windows. Self-catering apartments, tiled in white throughout, are very spacious: Choose between two- and three-bedroom apartments; each bedroom has its own balcony and bathroom, kitchens are open-plan and modern, and living rooms are comfortably furnished with sliding doors opening onto a veranda or balcony. The penthouse (R2,590/$387) and nos. 3, 5, and 10 have the best sea views. Given notice, proprietor Coenie Nel will stock your fridge or serve breakfast, and a good restaurant (Kitchen Windows) is a few minutes' walk away.

WHERE TO DINE

Walskipper ★★ *Kids* TRADITIONAL/SEAFOOD   If you haven't had a chance to sample the open-air West Coast restaurants, Walskipper, run by Grace and Phillip Koornhof, offers a fairly similar experience. Situated right on the ocean, it's a casual affair housed in a simple open-air structure—even the waiters are barefoot. Most dishes are cooked over hot coals, including the ever-popular Walskipper special—a plate of prawns, calamari, mussels, scallops, and crab sticks. Traditional S.A. dishes include oxtail and tomato *bredie*. Guests are seated on rough benches, wine is served in tin mugs and meals come on enamel plates, and chunks of freshly baked bread and jam accompany every meal.

Jeffrey's Bay. Take the road to Aston Bay (next to J-Bay), follow sign to Marina Martinique. ☏ **042/292-0005** or 082/800-9478. Reservations essential. Main courses R48–R65 ($7.15–$9.70). AE, DC, MC, V. Daily noon–9:30pm in season; out of season Tues–Sat noon–9:30pm, Sun noon–4pm.

3 Grahamstown

125km (78 miles) NE of Port Elizabeth

Grahamstown was named after Col. John Graham, who established a garrison here in 1815 with orders to drive the Xhosa eastward over the Fish River—a ruthless expulsion that was to spark the 100-year Frontier War. Reminders of its English colonial past can be seen everywhere: streets lined with charming Georgian and Victorian buildings, the only Victorian camera obscura in the Southern Hemisphere, one of South Africa's oldest English-speaking universities, and a number of highly regarded English-style private boarding schools dating back to 1885. But with the old Fish River frontier a mere 60km (37 miles) east, signs of the impoverished Xhosa community are equally visible, both on the streets and on the hills surrounding the valley.

As something of a microcosm of South Africa's social and economic problems, Grahamstown is certainly worth visiting, and never more so than in July, when the town hosts its 24-year-old arts festival, said to be the biggest in the Southern Hemisphere and second in size only to Edinburgh's.

ESSENTIALS

VISITOR INFORMATION   The helpful Grahamstown tourism is now known as **Makana Tourism** (☏ **046/622-3241;** www.grahamstown.co.za; Mon–Fri 8:30am–5pm, Sat 9am–1pm) and is located at 63 High St.

GETTING THERE   By Car   Take the N2 out of Port Elizabeth; some 125km (78 miles) northeast is the turnoff for Grahamstown.

By Bus   Greyhound and **Intercape** operate daily between Grahamstown and Port Elizabeth. Call ☏ **046/622-2235.** For **Translux** queries, call ☏ **046/622-3241.**

GETTING AROUND   Contact **Beeline** (☏ **082/651-6646** or 082/652-0798) for a taxi.

By Car   You can rent a car from **Avis** (☏ **046/622-8233** or 0800/021-111).

GUIDED TOURS   The best historical tours in Grahamstown are offered by **No. 7 Worcester Street** (© 046/622-2843; www.worcesterstreet.co.za), a guesthouse offering 2 nights accommodations, including all meals plus two excursions with local historian and tour guide **Alan Wyer** (www.alanweyerstours.co.za), for R3,000 ($448) double.

To view examples of Khoisan art, contact **David** (© 082/254-5489).

TOWNSHIP TOURS   Despite Grahamstown's patent lack of industry, people continue to pour in from the former *bantustan* (homeland) of Ciskei. A township tour provides insights into the stark contrasts of this growing community, as well as much-needed income and purpose. An **Umthati Township Tour** ✦✦ with Mbuleli (© 082/979-5906; R150/$22) takes you from Grahamstown into the heart of the Rini township, where 8 out of every 10 people are unemployed. At Umthati's kitchen gardens and education center, you will be served a traditional Xhosa meal (book in advance), learn something about the culture and customs, visit a member's house and local shop, and be taken to the **Egazini Outreach Project** to purchase local crafts from a selection of stimulating heritage crafts and the visual arts (printmaking). Mbuleli will tailor his tour to accommodate the interests of the group, so you can request to attend the local church or even visit the local *shabeen* (informal drinking house) for a drink with the locals.

SPECIAL EVENTS   Grahamstown's **National Arts Festival** (© 046/622-4341; www.nafest.co.za), held every July, is Africa's biggest arts event: Some 1,500 events are staged over 11 days.

EXPLORING GRAHAMSTOWN

Start your tour by driving or walking to the top of Gunfire Hill, where the **1820s Settlers National Monument** overlooks Grahamstown, which is situated in a small valley flanked by hills. To your right you will see Makanaskop, where the Xhosa took their last stand against the British. Enter to view the Cecil Skotnes artworks, then head back down the hill to the **Albany Museum,** on Somerset Street (© 046/622-2312), or the interesting **International Library for African Music** ✦, off Prince Alfred Street (off Somerset). The library houses more than 200 traditional instruments and has thousands of recordings of traditional African music from southern and central Africa, much of it on sale. For an introduction and tour, phone ahead and make an appointment (© 046/603-8557; Mon–Fri 8:30am–12:45pm and 2:15–5pm; free admission). Farther on Somerset Road is the **S.A. Institute for Aquatic Biodiversity** (© 046/636-1002; Mon–Fri 8am–1pm and 2–5pm), where you can view two stuffed specimens of the coelacanth (see "Fishing for Dinosaurs," below).

Moving to the center of town, at the junction of High and Hill streets, you will find the town's most prominent landmark (also the tallest spire in South Africa): the

---

Fun Fact **Bag Ladies**

The **Masithandane Association** owes much of its success to rubbish. Plastic bags—referred to as the new S.A. national flower because of the way they flourish on fences and trees surrounding the townships—are collected by township women, who in return receive a meal. The bags are then skillfully woven by Masithandane members into colorful hats and bags.

Fun Fact **Fishing for Dinosaurs**

In 1938, J. L. B. Smith identified a strange fish species—caught off the East London coast, and sporting six limblike fins—as a coelacanth, a 200-million-year-old species thought to have died out 50 million years ago. The latest catch, made in 2000, was off the coast near St Lucia Wetland Park (see chapter 9 for more on the coelacanth).

Cathedral of St Michael and St George (© **046/622-2445**). Nearby, at the top of Bathurst Street, is the **Gothic-Revival Methodist Commemoration Church** (© **046/622-7210**), which dates back to 1850. Diagonally opposite is a winged statue of peace, dedicated to the men who died in the Anglo-Boer War. Note the inscription; Rudyard Kipling wrote it especially for the memorial.

Next door to the Methodist church are the premises of **T. Birch & Co** (© **046/622-7010**)—an old-style family store—and the **City Hall,** dating back to the 1870s. It's definitely worth purchasing something from Birch's just to watch your money fly across the room—they still use the Lamson trolley system, an overhead cash-delivery system dating back to the 1950s.

Stroll down Bathurst Street to the **Observatory Museum** 🎬🎬, where you can see a 360-degree view of Grahamstown reflected in the restored Victorian camera obscura. The camera, constructed in the mid-1850s, is housed in a custom-designed cupola above the home and shop of the eccentric H. C. Galpin. A watchmaker by trade, Galpin also built a turret housing a clock above his home, the pendulum of which swings in the rooms two stories below. The museum holds interesting exhibits relating to Galpin and his hobbies, as well as early-settler artifacts (© **046/622-2312**; Mon–Fri 9am–1pm and 2–5pm, Sat 10am–2pm; admission R8/$1.20).

WHERE TO STAY & DINE

The dining room at the atmospheric **The Cock House** 🎬 (see below) is where Grahamstown diners go to catch up on a bit of comfort food. Expect home-cooked country-style food, utilizing local ingredients like Karoo lamb, ostrich, and venison. Lunch is served daily, dinner Monday through Saturday (R150/$22 for three courses). **Evolution,** Pepper Grove Mall, African St. (© **046/636-2433**) is, as its name implies, a great deal more modern, with the focus firmly on health-conscious fare (there are even vegan options). Alternatively, head for **La Galleria** 🎬🎬, 13 New St. (© **046/622-2345**; lunch and dinner Mon–Fri). Part of this little gem's charm is the fact that the kitchen is visible from the street—in the afternoon you can look through the window and see pasta drying for the evening meal. Meals start with the antipasto trolley, followed by a typically Italian selection of main courses; try the *barese* (creamed spinach and ricotta with mushroom and bacon) or *pollo cremonese* (chicken breasts prepared with herbs and lemon).

No. 7 Worcester Street is a new guesthouse situated in a beautifully restored Victorian home and currently the most luxurious option in town; rooms are relatively pricey for Grahamstown (R1,500/$224 double), but be on the lookout for regular specials (see "Guided Tours," above) or visit www.worcesterstreet.co.za.

The Cock House 🎬🎬   Built in 1826, this charming two-story settler house (once the home of author Andre Brink) was bought and renovated by owner-managers

Belinda and Peter Tudge in 1991. Very much a country-style inn, this has hosted a number of illustrious guests, like Nelson Mandela, who has stayed here on three occasions. Rooms are tasteful and spacious, though the bathrooms above the public spaces are looking a little tired. Among the rooms in the converted stables, the honeymoon suite is the best.

10 Market St., Grahamstown 6140. ℂ **046/636-1287.** Fax 046/636-1295. www.cockhouse.co.za. 10 units. R730 ($110) double. Rate includes breakfast. (Prices are subject to increase during festival week in July.) AE, DC, MC, V. **Amenities:** Restaurant; bar; laundry. *In room:* TV, tea- and coffee-making facilities, fans.

The Hermitage 🏠🏠 *Value*   If you don't mind being in a B&B (and note that the rooms and the house are large enough for a sense of total privacy), this is one of the best places to stay in Grahamstown. Situated in a beautiful historic home and beautifully decorated by original proprietor Beau Jeffray, The Hermitage has only two rooms. Of the two rooms, the one overlooking the back garden is far larger, with a small sitting room leading out to the tranquil garden.

14 Henry St., Grahamstown 6140. ℂ **046/636-1503.** Fax 046/636-2246. 2 units. R450 ($67) double. Rate includes breakfast. No credit cards. *In room:* TV, fridge, hair dryer, tea- and coffee-making facilities.

4 Graaff-Reinet

254km (158 miles) N/NW of Port Elizabeth

Graaff-Reinet, South Africa's fourth-oldest town, is 837km (519 miles) south of Johannesburg—a good stopover if you're driving down to the Garden Route. Should you have time, try to prolong your stay for a full day. Spend a morning admiring some of the 220 national monuments, and then take one of the worthwhile side trips. This is one of the few towns surrounded by a nature reserve, and you'll find one of the world's best examples of outsider art in the nearby hamlet of Nieu Bethesda.

ESSENTIALS

VISITOR INFORMATION   The helpful **Graaff-Reinet Publicity Association** (ℂ **049/892-4248;** www.graaffreinet.co.za; Mon–Fri 8am–12:30pm and 2–5pm, Sat–Sun 9am–noon) is housed in 13A Church St.

GETTING THERE   By Car   From Johannesburg you travel south on the N1, then take the N9 south at Colesberg to Graaff-Reinet. From Port Elizabeth you take the R75 north, a 3-hour drive.

By Bus   Translux and **Intercape** buses pull in daily from Cape Town, the Garden Route, and Port Elizabeth. See chapter 2 for phone numbers.

GETTING AROUND   The easiest and best way to explore the town is on foot or on a bicycle. For guided tours of the town and surrounds, and bicycle rentals, contact **Karoo Connections Adventure Tours** 🏠 (ℂ **049/892-3978;** karooconnections@ intekom.co.za). They provide the following trips: town and township tours; trips to the Valley of Desolation, Bushman Rock Art, the Owl House, and Karoo Farms; game-viewing drives in the Karoo Nature Reserve; and a number of horseback-riding and hiking tours.

WHAT TO SEE & DO

With more national monuments than any other South African town, the streets of Graaff-Reinet are a pleasure to simply stroll along. Incorporate an informal walking tour with a visit to at least one of the four buildings that comprise the **Graaff-Reinet**

Museum (© 049/892-3801; Mon–Fri 8am–5pm, Sat 9am–3pm, Sun 9am–4pm; admission R16/$2.40). Of these, **Reinet House,** a stately Cape Dutch home facing Parsonage Street, is by far the most interesting. Built in 1812 as the Dutch Reformed Church parsonage, its large, airy rooms display period furniture, a collection of antique dolls, and various household objects. Within walking distance, the **Old Library Museum,** on the corner of Church and Somerset streets, houses a collection of fossilized Karoo reptiles that inhabited the area more than 200 million years ago (see "Fishing for Dinosaurs," above). Other buildings worth noting are the stately **Dutch Reformed Church,** one block up from the Old Library Museum, which dates back to 1886, and the delightful **Graaff-Reinet pharmacy,** a typical Victorian chemist that still operates at 24 Caledon St.

GREAT SIDE TRIPS

Graaff-Reinet lies in the center of the 15,000-hectare (37,050-acre) **Karoo Nature Reserve** (daily dawn–dusk; free admission), the highlight of which is the **Valley of Desolation** ✦✦✦, 14km (8½ miles) from Graaff-Reinet. Sunset is the best time to visit, when the dolomite towers that rise some 800m (2,624 ft.) from the valley below turn a deep red, and the pink light softens the Camdeboo plains. On your return, keep an eye out for the endangered mountain zebra—the Karoo Nature Reserve is one of its last remaining habitats.

Another highly recommended excursion is to **Nieu Bethesda,** 50km (31 miles) northeast of Graaff-Reinet. This typical Karoo *dorp* (small rural town) is charming; modern-day luxuries like electricity are relatively recent phenomena, and donkey carts still a main source of transport, but the main attraction is the **Owl House and Camel Yard** ✦✦✦ on New Street (© 049/841-1603; www.owlhouse.co.za). In her late 40s, after the deaths of her parents, Helen Martins became obsessed with transforming her house into a world of her own making, a project that was to absorb her for the next 30 years. She was obsessed with light: The interior features large reflecting mirrors to maximize this, and every conceivable surface is covered with finely crushed glass, with colors creating large patterns, including a favored sunbeam motif. In the candlelight, the interior glitters like a jewel. Helen Martins's inner vision spread into her backyard, enveloping her in a mystical world of glittering peacocks, camels, mermaids, stars, shepherds, sphinxes, towers, and serpents. Immortalized in the award-winning play and movie *Road to Mecca* (starring Kathy Bates), the house is one of the world's most inspiring examples of Outsider Art. Tours are held from 8am to 6pm daily (9am–5pm June–Sept); admission is R15 ($2.25).

Tea and light meals are available daily at the **Village Inn** (© 049/841-1635), on the corner diagonally opposite the Owl House. There is no official Tourism Bureau, but owner Egbert can assist with just about anything.

WHERE TO STAY & DINE

Andries Stöckenstrom Guest House ✦ The main reason to stay in this listed house built in 1819 is the **food** ✦✦✦—the only way to guarantee a table is to overnight (book no. 6, the largest and most comfortable room). Beatrice is a self-taught chef, but her passion for the medium has rendered her a true artist. Representative of her creative spirit is the appetizer of smoked loin kudu salad or baked fig with Gorgonzola; lightly curried sweet-potato soup with crumbled roasted almonds; or Karoo lamb or deboned quail for a main course. Beatrice constantly darts from the kitchen to ensure that her imaginative meals are to her guests' satisfaction, while

Andre describes them seductively and discreetly keeps topping off wine glasses. A truly marvelous experience—book early.

100 Cradock St., Graaff-Reinet 6280. ©/fax 049/892-4575. 6 units. R1,260–R1,440 ($188–$215) double. Rates include breakfast and dinner. AE, DC, MC, V. **Amenities:** Dining room/bar; limited room service; laundry. *In room:* A/C, hair dryer.

Drostdy Hotel ★ *Value*   The original home and offices of Graaff-Reinet's first magistrate, this elegant Cape Dutch building is in the heart of the historical center. The gracious public spaces are tastefully furnished with antiques and period artworks, and the bedrooms are all situated in the adjacent Stretch's Court—a row of cottages formerly occupied by freed slaves and dating back to 1855. Most of the standard rooms are cramped, and a few have damp walls, making a luxury suite well worth the extra R200 ($30). All the rooms in Ferreira House are charming, particularly no. F3, which has a fireplace and private garden, and no. F5, which is furnished with beautiful antiques. Light meals are served in the garden from 9am to 5pm (the Drostdy's chunky whole-wheat bread is unbeatable). A la carte meals are served in De Camdeboo restaurant, and the seven-course meals (R110/$16) are served in the Old Courtroom; these feature traditional South African dishes such as *boontjiesop* (bean soup), *kerrievis* (curried fish), and Karoo lamb.

30 Church St., Graaff-Reinet 6280. © **049/892-2161**. Fax 049/892-4582. www.drostdy.co.za. R490–R780 ($73–$116) double. AE, DC, MC, V. **Amenities:** Restaurant; bar; pool; room service; babysitting; laundry. *In room:* A/C, TV, minibar, hair dryer, tea- and coffee-making facilities.

5 The Wild Coast ★★

The northernmost section of the Eastern Cape stretches 280km (174 miles) from the Kei River in the south to the mouth of the Mtamvuna River, bordering KwaZulu-Natal. The coast is lush and largely uninhabited, with innumerable rivers spilling into large estuaries; waterfalls plunging directly into the ocean; coastal, dune, and mangrove forests; long, sandy beaches; rocky coves; and a number of shipwrecks, all of which have earned it the name "Wild Coast." This region was part of the former *bantustan* (homeland) Transkei, where any Xhosa that weren't of economic use to the Republic were dumped, and as such it has suffered from overgrazing and underdevelopment and is one of the poorest areas in South Africa. Despite this, the people are incredibly hospitable, and exploring this region will provide you with one of the most unaffected cultural experiences available to visitors in South Africa. Note, however, that much of the coastline is difficult to access—dirt roads are pitted with deep potholes, there is virtually no public transportation, and accommodations options are limited. The exceptions to this are the coast south of Qora Mouth, and the coastal towns of **Coffee Bay** and **Port St Johns** ★.

The only way to reach these coastal towns is via the N2, which cuts through the middle of the hinterland, passing through unfenced green valleys dotted with traditional Xhosa huts and the old Transkei capital of Umtata. The top attraction here is the **Nelson Mandela Museum** ★★★ (© **047/532-5110**; www.mandela-museum. org.za; Mon–Fri 9am–4pm, Sat 9am–noon; free admission). Madiba, the clan name by which Mandela is affectionately known, was born near Qunu, where he still returns for holidays (this is also where he and Oprah Winfrey distributed thousands of Christmas gifts to an overexcited crowd in 2002). The museum is situated in the Bhunga Building, a gracious colonial structure that once housed municipal offices, and comprises several rooms that have been filled with Mandela memorabilia, among them gifts from respectful statesmen, adoring children, and various other admirers. Excellent displays, including posters, videos, and photographs, record the life and works of the greatest statesman Africa has ever known.

ESSENTIALS

VISITOR INFORMATION   There is no central tourism bureau. Contact **Wild Coast Holiday Reservations** (© **043/743-6181;** meross@iafrica.com) in East London, or Ukhenketho **Tourism Port St Johns** (©/fax **047/564-1187**). For information on Wild Coast nature reserves (of which Mkambati is recommended), contact central bookings at © **043/742-4451.**

GETTING THERE & AROUND   By Car   The N2 traverses the length of what used to be called the Transkei, with roads to the coast leading southeast off it. Most roads to the coast are untarred, some are badly marked, and all are time-consuming. Look out for livestock on the road, and don't travel at night. You can also charter a flight from Durban to **Umngazi River Bungalows,** the Wild Coast's best lodging.

By Bus   The **Baz Bus** (see chapter 2 for regional numbers) travels from Port Elizabeth to Durban, with stops at Coffee Bay and Port St Johns.

On Foot   Wild Coast Meander 🎣 (© **043/743-6181;** meross@iafrica.com) offers a 5-day hike that covers 55km (34 miles), from Qora Mouth to Morgan Bay, accompanied by a member of the local community. Hikers ford rivers and traverse isolated beaches, but each night is spent in a hotel. Five days, including accommodations, meals, and transfers from East London airport, costs from R2,400 ($358) for four people.

On Horseback   The 3- to 6-day **Amadiba Trails** (© **039/305-6455;** fax 039/305-6535) is a camping trip completed by foot or on horseback and canoe. You will be accompanied by a local guide, and meals may be enjoyed with members of the local community. Trails (R1,120–R1,650/$167–$246 for 4–6 days by foot, or R2,240–R3,300/$334–$493 for 4–6 days on horseback) start at the Wild Coast Casino, on the border between the Eastern Cape and KwaZulu-Natal.

WHERE TO STAY & DINE

Umngazi (see below) is currently the most comfortable place to experience the rugged splendor of the Wild Coast, but when class outfit Wilderness Safaris (the biggest safari operator in Botswana) elects to open a lodge, you know it's going to be something special. Located relatively near the KwaZulu-Natal border, in the Mkambati Nature Reserve, **Gwe Gwe Lodge** is a new community-based initiative and offers the well-heeled traveler the opportunity to explore one of the most important ecological areas on the planet (Conservation International, WWF, and IUCN have all rated Pondoland as one of earth's critical hotspots). Besides the immense variety of flora, there is the impressive marine life (every year you can witness the "Greatest Shoal on Earth," when millions of sardines migrate, followed by schools of up to 50,000 dolphins and many thousands of sharks) as well as spectacular scenery. Two rivers, over 30 waterfalls (2 of which crash directly into the ocean), and miles of untouched beach—this will be one of the few places in South Africa where you will be able to walk from your room directly onto the beach. Gwe Gwe Lodge is scheduled to open late in 2005, so check out Wilderness Safaris's website (www.wilderness-safaris.com) for details.

Umngazi River Bungalows ★★ *Kids*   If you want to sample the subtropical pleasures of the Wild Coast without roughing it too much, this is the coast's finest and best value-for-money resort—you'll want to stay here for the duration of your holiday. Located just south of Port St Johns, Umngazi is situated in its own private nature reserve, overlooking a large estuary and deserted beach, and flanked by dense coastal vegetation. With a safe lagoon, boats and gillies for hire, river trips, skiing, snooker, a saltwater swimming pool, a host of babysitters, and a separate toddlers' dining room, it offers the perfect family holiday, yet the honeymoon bungalows are private enough for lovers to remain blissfully unaware of the pitter-patter of little feet. (This is, incidentally, where Nelson Mandela chose to spend his first Christmas with wife Graca.) The en-suite bungalows are very basic, with outdoor showers from which you can watch the dolphins surfing—it's definitely worth requesting a sea-facing bungalow (Brazen Head and unit nos. 41–43 are choice). Meals are large buffets and/or table d'hote featuring fresh salads; fish, meat, and chicken; homemade breads; and cheese, all served in the large thatched dining room. The service is generally good, though with English very much a second language, patience is, as always, a virtue.

P.O. Box 75, Port St Johns 5120. ✆/fax **047/564-1115.** www.umngazi.co.za. 48 units. High season R725–R840 ($108–$125) double; low season R700–R810 ($104–$121) double; honeymoon suite R880 ($131). Rates include all meals. AE, DC, MC, V. **Amenities:** Pool; tennis; boating; guided walks; mountain biking; bird-watching. *In room:* Tea- and coffee-making facilities, en-suite bathtubs, fans.

7

Africa's Big Apple: Jo'burg Plus Safari Excursions

For many, Johannesburg, with its heady blend of first and third worlds, is the most exhilarating city in Africa. Sprawling outward from the center of Gauteng, South Africa's smallest and most densely populated province, it makes an ideal base from which to explore the animal-rich nature reserves that lie beyond its business-driven borders. But the city itself is a drawing card. This is, after all, the economic heart of Africa, where the continent's major financial deals are struck. It's a throbbing urban metropolis that is home to a socially vibrant and sassy new African elite, and to thousands more who congregate here from all over the continent in the hopes of finding their own elusive fortune.

Gauteng was literally built on gold—its name, translated from Sotho, means "place of gold"—and it remains a heavily industrialized region in which some seven million people produce almost 40% of the country's GDP. Today you can still descend a working mine shaft to tour the richest bowels of the earth, or step back thousands of years by visiting the Cradle of Humankind, a World Heritage Site where paleoanthropologists continue to unearth clues to mankind's origins. Visitors interested in the country's more recent history should include a visit to the striking Apartheid Museum—which provides poignant insight into what it was like to live under one of the world's most iniquitous systems of

discrimination—and take a tour of Soweto, South Africa's largest "township," inhabited by an estimated two million to four million people, almost all of whom are black—an enduring legacy of the country's separatist history.

Still, most leisure travelers simply use Johannesburg as a gateway to the attractions in neighboring provinces and countries. Of these, Kruger National Park and its surrounding reserves are the best known, so much so that this region enjoys its own separate chapter (chapter 8). Fewer visitors are aware of the Big 5 game reserves closer to Johannesburg, like Madikwe and the Waterberg Mountain region—within easy driving distance, both provide a real sense of being on safari and enjoy the additional benefit of being malaria-free. Madikwe, in particular, has a wonderfully varied terrain that supports what has been dubbed the "Magnificent Seven": In addition to sightings of the Big 5, you stand an excellent chance of seeing cheetah and wild dog, Africa's most endangered predator. Even closer to the city is Pilanesberg National Park—whose nearby neighbor Sun City and the opulent Palace of the Lost City comprise one of the world's glitziest, most over-the-top theme parks.

But if you have a real penchant for solitude, consider venturing even farther northwest, into the vast expanses of Tswalu Private Game Reserve and the Kgalagadi Transfrontier National Park, where the red dunes of the Kalahari Desert support a surprisingly varied—and highly visible—game population. (**Note:** For a comparative overview of all the reserves, go to "Planning Your Safari" in chapter 2.)

1 Johannesburg & Environs

Johannesburg is 1,402km (869 miles) NE of Cape Town; Pretoria is 58km (36 miles) N of Johannesburg

Johannesburg, Jo'burg, Jozi . . . Ever evolving, this vibrant city throbs to a heady, relentless beat, fueled by the paradox of its reputation as a crime hub and the tremendous sociability of its inhabitants. Jozi's diverse population is a considerably better reflection of South Africa's burgeoning hegemonic spirit than you'll encounter anywhere else in the country, with a new black aristocracy creating their own cultural stew in the clubs, bars, and restaurants in this city's more cosmopolitan areas.

But it wasn't always like this. Once rolling bushveld, the "gold capital of the world" was born when a prospector named George Harrison stumbled upon what was to become the richest gold reef in the world in 1886. Within 3 years, these nondescript highveld plains had grown into the third-biggest city in South Africa, and soon Johannesburg, or "eGoli," as it came to be known, would become the largest city south of Cairo. It took only a decade for Jo'burg's population to exceed 100,000, and by 1897 it was producing 27% of the world's gold. The speed at which it grew was due in part to the power and greed of men like Cecil Rhodes—whose diamond mines in Kimberley provided the capital to exploit the rich gold-bearing reefs of the Witwatersrand—and to the availability of cheap labor. Along with other "randlords," as the most powerful consortium of mining magnates was known, Rhodes founded the Chamber of Mines in 1889, which created policies regarding recruitment, wages, and working conditions. In 1893 it institutionalized the "colour bar," which ensured that black men could aspire to no more than manual labor.

By 1895, the ever-expanding mining settlement far outnumbered the original Boer settlers, who had fled here from what they felt to be the oppressive policies of the British in the Cape. Disgruntled by this secondary "invasion," Botha, president of the then South African Republic (ZAR), denied these *uitlanders* (foreigners) the vote and refused to develop an infrastructure to support mining activities. Four years later, the ZAR and Britain went to war, and in 1902 Britain annexed the republic. The British Empire relinquished its hold in 1910 when the Union of South Africa was proclaimed, but for the millions of black migrant laborers who toiled below the earth, working conditions remained relentlessly harsh. By 1946 more than 400,000 black people were residing in and around Jo'burg; in August that year, 70,000 African Mineworkers Union members went on strike over living and working conditions—to no avail, despite the death of 12 men and injuries to over a thousand.

During the 1950s, Johannesburg's uniquely black urban culture was given a name. "Kwela" had its own jazzy sounds, heard in the *shebeens* (drinking houses) of Sophiatown, and a slick, sophisticated style, as evidenced in the pages of *Drum* magazine. But this was also the decade of forced removals, when thousands were dumped into the new suburbs of Soweto, and, consequently, a growth phase for the African National Congress (ANC), which in 1955 proclaimed its Freedom Charter—the basis of the current constitution—in what is now known as Freedom Square.

But it would be another 2 decades before the black majority revolted. On June 16, 1976, police opened fire on a peaceful student demonstration in Soweto and sparked a nationwide riot—South Africa's black youth had declared war on apartheid. Student activism escalated during the 1980s and came to a head during the early 1990s, when political parties jostled for power after Nelson Mandela's release from prison. Some townships were reduced to utter chaos, with a mysterious "third force" (later proven to be state funded) pouring fuel on the flames. Political peace finally came with the 1994 elections, and Jo'burgers returned to their primary pursuit: making money.

For many, however, this remains an elusive goal. South Africa still has the most productive mines in the world, but the size of its gold-mining force has fallen by more than half since 1990. Industries like manufacturing, banking, IT, and media service sectors have shown more consistent growth since the fall of apartheid, but not at a rate that can absorb the sprawling city's burgeoning population. Unemployment has spawned crime that, in turn, has bred a culture of fear, and walled neighborhoods, burglar bars, security guards, and guard dogs are common sights, particularly in the northern suburbs. But Jo'burg's 119-year history is nothing if not unpredictable. Propelled by initiatives like iGoli 2002 and Blue IQ (Gauteng's multibillion-rand investment initiative), Johannesburg's inner city has, according to a 2004 report, enjoyed a huge turnaround, with the general upswing in development led by the Johannesburg Development Agency. And with the emergence of a sophisticated, wealthy black middle class, the city continues to attract entrepreneurs from all over the continent. For every person living in fear, there are a dozen more enjoying the most hip and happening city in South Africa—given a few days, you could be one of them.

ESSENTIALS

ARRIVING

BY PLANE   Most international flights to South Africa arrive in the relatively small but sophisticated **Johannesburg International Airport** (© 011/921-6262, or 086/727-7888 for flight inquiries), recently given a multibillion-rand Afro-chic makeover, and still undergoing runway expansion. If you've arrived early or are waiting for a connection, consider relaxing in one of the Rennies Travel "Premier Club" lounges, which offer the same facilities as a first-class lounge, for a mere R120 ($18; international terminal) or R55 ($8.20; domestic terminal) entry fee. Note that even if your baggage has been checked through to another South African destination, you must pick up your luggage and clear Customs before boarding any connecting flight. The **Gauteng Tourism Authority** has a branch in the airport's International Arrivals hall (© 011/390-3614) and is open daily from 6am to 10pm. Foreign exchange is available 24 hours, and the easiest is to use the ABSA Bank ATM.

The airport is 25km (16 miles) from the city and a 30- to 40-minute drive from the northern suburbs. Taxi lines queue up directly outside the exit; make sure you discuss the price upfront (it should cost you about R250/$37 to get to a Sandton/northern

---

Tips   Need a Jab?

If you plan to travel farther afield in Africa and haven't consulted a doctor, visit the **SAA-Netcare Travel Clinic** in Sandton (© 011/883-3801 or -3802) for up-to-date advice and/or vaccinations. This is also one of the few places in South African where you can purchase a course of Malarone, the best precaution against malaria and one you need start only a day prior to traveling to a high-risk area.

Tips **Staying Safe**

Inevitably, with the promised redistribution of wealth taking longer than many expected, the city is a hothouse for those who have realized that the easiest way to make it is to take it. Carjackings are less common now, but do keep an eye out for suspicious-looking vehicles or persons, and keep your car doors locked and windows up. Don't leave valuables in plain sight in the car, even when you're in it. If your car is bumped from behind and you feel uncomfortable with the situation, don't stop; drive straight to your hotel or call the police on your cellphone (which is something you should keep handy without having it out on display). If you feel the situation is a potentially threatening one, keep in mind that crossing against a red light—carefully, of course—is allowed.

Generally speaking, inconspicuous consumption is the order of the day: People who have nothing worth stealing will not be bothered. Don't carry or wear anything of obvious value when you're exploring the central business district (though some say it's worth carrying a small sum of cash to satisfy a demand), and don't look lost. Hillbrow, Berea, and Yeoville are best avoided unless you're accompanied by a guide who is totally familiar with the area. If you are ever mugged, don't protest—just hand over the goods or money and walk away.

If this sort of talk makes you nervous, it may be wise to tour in a group with a guide (see "Guided Tours," below). Alternatively, you can book one of the lodging options recommended below—which are situated in safe areas—and spend your time sampling the city's many fine restaurants.

suburbs hotel). A cheaper, more convenient option, particularly if you're traveling alone, is the **Magic Bus Shuttle,** in the Multistory Parkade (© **011/394-6902/3;** e-mail them at info@magicbus.co.za before you leave and ask them to meet you with a nameboard). Transfers to the Sandton center take place every 30 minutes and cost R95 ($14) per person; a door-to-door transfer (to your hotel, for example) will cost a little extra.

By Train   Given time, there's nothing better than trundling through the country by train, particularly on the legendary **Blue Train** or the equally (some say more) luxurious **Rovos Rail.** Both roll in to Pretoria via Johannesburg from Cape Town (taking around 28 hr.). Rovos also operates other luxury trips throughout the country and as far afield as Dar es Salaam; see chapter 2 for more details on both. If you like the romance of rail but can't face the steep fares, a good option is to book the **Premier Class** coupe from Cape Town on **Shozoloza Mail,** South Africa's main line passenger services (© **012/334-8459;** www.spoornet.co.za); for departure times and rates, see chapter 2. *Warning:* Because Johannesburg's **Park Station,** corner of Rissik and Wolmarans streets, Braamfontein, is a major center for people arriving from all over Africa, the consequent rich pickings for criminals has made this a dangerous area, so arrange for a hotel transfer from the platform in Pretoria, or inquire about disembarking at Kempton and arranging a transfer from here.

By Car The N1 connects Johannesburg with Cape Town, the N4 with Nelspruit (Kruger gateway), and the N3 with Durban; a recommended route between Johannesburg and Cape Town is to travel along the Garden Route (via Graaff-Reinet; see "The Big Road Trip: Johannesburg to Cape Town" on p. 275). To get to Pretoria from Johannesburg, take the M1 north; this becomes the N1 to Pretoria.

By Bus The intercity buses, **Greyhound, Intercape,** and **Translux** (see chapter 2 for numbers), all arrive at Johannesburg's Park Station. Pretoria's **bus terminal** is on Church Square (© **012/308-0839**).

VISITOR INFORMATION

Besides the office in the airport, the **Gauteng Tourism Authority** has a brand-new **head office** opposite the Market Theatre in Newtown—part of the regeneration of downtown Jozi. At press time, telephone numbers were unavailable, but you can contact their **satellite kiosk** in the Rosebank Mall, near the craft market entrance (© **011/340-9000,** or 011/327-2000 for assistance; Mon–Fri 8am–5pm, Sat–Sun 9am–6pm). It's worth picking up copies of *The Ultimate Guide, What's On in Gauteng,* and the *Gauteng Entertainment Guide,* any of which can give you tips on the city's current and permanent attractions. If you plan to drive yourself, you'd be well advised to pick up *Mapstudio's Rosebank Sandton Guide.* There's also a Gauteng Tourism Authority **satellite office** in Sandton Square, Entrance 6, Shop L31G, near Postnet (© **011/784-9596,** -9597, or -9598; www.gauteng.net; Mon–Fri 9am–6pm, Sat 9am–3pm, Sun 10am–2pm).

Note: At press time, **Pretoria** was in the process of being renamed **City of Tshwane. Tshwane Information Centre** is on Church Square (© **012/337-4337;** www.tshwane.gov.za; Mon–Fri 8am–4pm).

THE NEIGHBORHOODS IN BRIEF

CITY CENTER The streets of the town center (which includes the newly revamped **Newtown** on the northwestern outskirts) and the surrounding inner-city suburbs (**Joubert Park, Hillbrow,** and **Berea**) are lined with skyscrapers, at the foot of which hurrying commuters and shoppers jostle for space with pavement traders. Although the once lily-white north has a preponderance of shopping malls, many Sowetans are geographically still forced to shop in the city center, and many have given up living in shacks to join the African immigrants who've thronged to the inner city, taking over abandoned office blocks and decaying warehouses. The streets are a great deal more lively than those elsewhere in the city, but can be more dangerous—at least on foot. Unless you're accompanied by a guide (see "Guided Tours,"

below), the safest way to get a feel for Jo'burg's center is by driving through it (see map), though the city center's most interesting sights (see "The Top Attractions" and "More Attractions: From African Art to Jo'burg Zoo," later in this chapter) are reasonably safe to visit on your own—the **Carlton Centre** and **Johannesburg Art Gallery** both offer secure parking, and the installation of security cameras at the **Newtown Cultural Precinct** (where many noteworthy attractions are located) has seen a 95% reduction in crime; however, it's still worth being on your guard and not carrying any obviously valuable items with you. Newtown is also one end of Jo'burg's **Cultural Arc,** with the other end at **Constitution Hill,** in **Braamfontein;** the arc represents an area of massive inner-city regeneration where art,

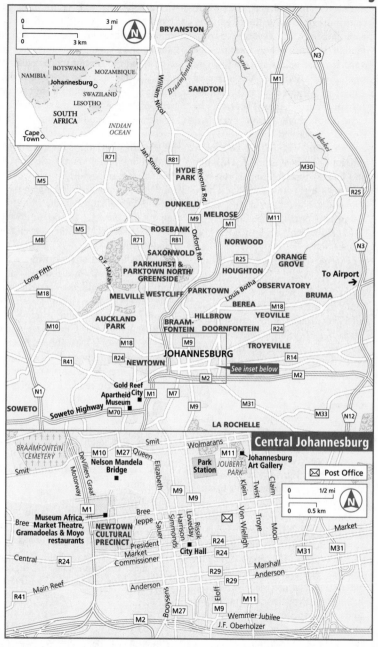

Greater Johannesburg

BRYANSTON

Braamfontein

Sand

Jukskei

SANDTON

SOUTH AFRICA
BOTSWANA
NAMIBIA
MOZAMBIQUE
Johannesburg
SWAZILAND
LESOTHO
INDIAN OCEAN
Cape Town

R71

R81

HYDE PARK

Rivonia Rd.

William Nicol

Jan Smuts

M5

DUNKELD

MELROSE

M9

M1

M11

ROSEBANK

R81

SAXONWOLD

Oxford Rd.

NORWOOD

R25

ORANGE GROVE

M8

M5

R71

PARKHURST & PARKTOWN NORTH/ GREENSIDE

HOUGHTON

D.F. Malan

Long Fifth

MELVILLE

WESTCLIFF

PARKTOWN

Louis Botha

OBSERVATORY

To Airport →

M18

M10

AUCKLAND PARK

BEREA

HILLBROW

YEOVILLE

M18

BRUMA

BRAAM-FONTEIN

DOORNFONTEIN

R24

M18

M9

JOHANNESBURG

TROYEVILLE

R41

R24

NEWTOWN

See inset below

R14

M2

M2

Gold Reef City

Apartheid Museum

M1

M7

M9

M31

M33

N12

N1

SOWETO

Soweto Highway

M70

LA ROCHELLE

N3

M1

M30

R25

N3

Central Johannesburg

BRAAMFONTEIN CEMETERY

Smit

M10

M27

Queen

Wolmarans

Park Station

JOUBERT PARK

M11

Johannesburg Art Gallery

⊠ **Post Office**

Smit

Nelson Mandela Bridge

Devilliers Graaf

Motorway

Elizabeth

M9

M9

Klein

Twist

Claim

M1

Museum Africa, Market Theatre, Gramadoelas & Moyo restaurants

Bree

Bree

Jeppe

Sauer

Simmonds

Harrison

Risik

Loveday

⊠

Von Wielligh

Troye

Mooi

Market

NEWTOWN CULTURAL PRECINCT

President

Market

Commissioner

City Hall

R24

R24

M31

M31

Central

R24

R29

R29

Marshall

Anderson

Main Reef

Anderson

R41

Booysens

M27

Eloff

M9

M11

Wemmer Jubilee

J.F. Oberholzer

M2

architecture, and cultural initiative are contributing to an altogether safer environment for visitors. Braamfontein, a business district on the northern edge of the inner city, is also where you'll find the Witwatersrand University's theater complex and the **Johannesburg Civic Theatre.** The city's central train station, **Park Station,** is also located here.

It's certainly inadvisable to explore the inner-city suburbs of **Hillbrow** and **Berea**—both full to the brim with run-down high-rise tenements. This is where the vast majority of African immigrants arriving in the City of Gold settle down—at least initially, or so they hope.

EASTERN SUBURBS Sadly, a trip to the bars, clubs, and cafes of Rockey Street (around which the once-exhilarating **Yeoville** nightlife centered) may offer an insight into cosmopolitan Africa, but it's still not safe. Gunshots are a regular sound effect (no, it's not part of the soundtrack), and you're likely to feel highly visible and even threatened. A little farther east is **Observatory,** a quiet area with large houses, a few with views (a real luxury in Johannesburg), and one of the best-value accommodations options in Jo'burg (see "Where to Stay," later in this chapter). But note that Sandton's shopping malls and Melville's bars are 18 to 20 minutes away.

Directly east of the city center are **Troyville** and **Bez Valley,** patches of which (like Braamfontein) are inhabited by creative Jo'burgers bored by the seamless high-walled northern suburbs and unable to afford Melville. With no highlighted attractions, tourists seldom find a reason to explore this area, although lunch at the Troyville Hotel is somewhat of an institution.

NORTHERN SUBURBS When the city center slipped into decay (a process,

incidentally, that predates the inauguration of the New South Africa), the financial center effectively relocated to the northern suburbs, and it is here that you'll find the greatest concentration of hotels, restaurants, and shopping malls.

The northern suburb closest to the city is **Parktown,** where the randlords built their Edwardian mansions. Just west of Parktown is **Westcliff,** which, if you can afford it, has the best accommodations option in the city, an elevated cliff-side "village" overlooking the urban forests of Johannesburg—said to be the largest in the world. It's in striking distance of the northwestern suburbs of Melville, Greenside, and Rosebank.

Directly north of Parktown are the well-established, "old-money" suburbs of **Saxonwold** and **Houghton**—the latter is often included in city tours because the house where Mandela and his wife, Graca, stay when they're in town is located here. Nearby are the small, leafy enclaves of **Illovo** and **Melrose;** the latter is where you'll find the Melrose Arch complex, a Eurocentric development where the new elite frequent expensive boutiques. Melrose has some great places to stay and good nightlife options. Next up is **Rosebank,** then **Hyde Park, Sandton,** and **Morningside,** all predominantly white, wealthy, and boring. With its fortresslike homes and gated communities, Sandton is relatively safe but particularly dull at nights, when what little street life there is retreats behind high walls and city malls. Sandton holds the highest concentration of business and retail outlets, but Rosebank offers the best shopping environment.

NORTHWESTERN SUBURBS For a more lively option, head for **Melville** 🎯🎯, northwest of Parktown, and no more than a 15- to 20-minute drive south from Sandton. Adjoining Auckland Park, which is where the SABC (South African Broadcasting Corporation) and the newly formed University of Johannesburg are located, Melville has a bohemian mix of residents, including actors, artists, producers, lecturers, architects, and film crews, and is considered one of the city's most textured suburbs. Come here to drink coffee, dine at one of the many restaurants, or get steeped in the giddy nocturnal meanderings of Melville's dedicated latenight brigade of bar-hoppers, hiphoppers, social players, and cultural activists (see "Johannesburg After Dark," later in this chapter). Aside from a vibrant street life centered primarily along 7th Street, Melville also has the Melville Koppies Nature Reserve (see later in this chapter) close by. In **Milpark,** a short distance from Melville, is the artsy 44 Stanley Avenue development, where a young crowd practices conspicuous afterdark consumption; there are also galleries, stores, and cafes to keep you busy in the day. Dedicated foodies should head for the nearby suburbs of **Greenside** (a short drive west of Westcliff) and **Parkhurst,** both great areas for restaurant browsing.

PRETORIA/TSHWANE An almost uninterrupted ribbon of development connects Johannesburg and Pretoria (a mere 50km/31 miles apart), yet Pretoria's atmosphere is much more laidback, and comparatively dull. Once an Afrikaner stronghold, South Africa's administrative and diplomatic capital has become home to a much more cosmopolitan population since Nelson Mandela was inaugurated the first democratically elected president at its **Union Buildings,** which are the city's most recognizable attraction. The Union Buildings are located in **Arcadia,** the suburb in which most of the embassies and consulates are situated, as well as the Pretoria Art Museum. East of the city are the suburbs of **Sunnyside** and **Hatfield,** home to most of the city's nightlife options and restaurants. Southeast of the center lies the upmarket suburb of **Brooklyn.** Together these suburbs form the nucleus of the "Ambassadorial Belt," named for the many embassies and diplomats housed here. South of the city is the **Voortrekker Monument,** visible for miles around; rent a car or use a tour operator to see sights like this and to visit the **Cullinan Mine.** History buffs, in particular, will find that the city, centered on **Church**

Gone, but Not Forgotten

Sophiatown was once one of the most vibrant black suburbs in the city, where journalists, gangsters, and leaders like Mandela and Sisulu jived to legendary musicians like Hugh Masekela and Miriam Makeba. Considered a criminal and political hotbed, the entire suburb was razed to the ground in the 1950s, rebuilt for poor whites, and crassly renamed Triomf (Triumph) by the apartheid government. The only remaining Sophiatown building is the Church of Christ the King—in a nod to some moral sensibility, apartheid's bulldozers were not allowed to flatten religious buildings—but you can get some sense of what was lost through MuseuMAfricA's displays, which include a re-created shebeen (see "The Top Attractions," later in this chapter). For a specialized tour of Sophiatown, run at certain times of the year, contact the **Parktown and Westcliff Heritage Trust** (© 011/482-3349; Mon–Fri 9am–1pm).

Square, and its outlying areas have enough in the way of cultural and historical sights to fill a day; the area around the Transvaal Museum in **Paul**

Kruger Street serves as a Museum Mall, with paved walkways and signs to direct you to attractions.

GETTING AROUND

Public transport can be unreliable, inflexible, and, after hours, nonexistent. Unless you plan on using a tour operator, Johannesburg is best explored by car, but be warned: Jo'burg drivers are aggressive, as the myriad skidmarks on the roads will attest, and you will need a map. If you intend to stay for a while, it's worth investing in a good one (see "Fast Facts: Johannesburg & Pretoria/Tshwane," below); alternatively, use taxis (see below).

By Car   You can rent a car from **Avis** (① 0861-02-1111 or 011/394-5433; www.avis. com), **Hertz** (① 011/390-9700; www.hertz.com), **Budget** (① 011/394-2905; www.budget.com), or **Imperial** (① 011/0861/13-1000 or 011/574-1000; www.imperial carrental.co.za), all of which have desks in the airport. Of the above, Budget tends to offer the better rates. **Res Q** (① 011/867-6552; www.resqrentacar.co.za) will deliver and collect at the airport, and offers secondhand budget options that have the added advantage of being less desirable to carjackers. **Britz Africa** (① 011/396-1860; www.britz. co.za) specializes in fully equipped four-wheel-drives and camper vans, and will pick you up at the airport. **Southern Motor Group** (contact Neil Kemp at ① 011/621-6352 or 072/119-5957; www.hirealandrover.co.za) rents out a wide range of Land Rovers in good condition; pick up a Discovery from R825 ($123) or a Freelander from R620 ($93) per day.

Parking   Parking on the street can be unsafe in town (park in the Carlton Garage—entrances from Marshall, Main, and Kruis sts.) but shouldn't be a problem in the suburbs recommended below—provided that you never leave anything in the car in open view. Most hotels offer valet parking. When visiting any of the dining and shopping districts, you may need to park on the road; car guards are ubiquitous and it's worth enlisting their services with a friendly hello. Tip car guards at the end of the evening.

By Taxi   Taxis don't cruise the streets, so you'll have to call for one; try **Roses Taxi** (① 011/403-9625; R6/90¢ per km) and **Maxi Taxi** (① 011/648-1212; R6/90¢ per km). In Pretoria, you'll usually find a few **taxis** waiting on the Square, or call **Rixi Mini Cabs** at ① 012/325-8072 or **SA Taxi** at ① 012/320-2075.

GUIDED TOURS

The following recommended operators all travel in comfortable minibus vehicles and cover the city's top attractions, like the Carlton Centre and MuseuMAfricA, with minor variations. Do bear in mind, however, that most are very flexible, so discuss the itinerary upfront and make sure your interests are covered—art lovers may want to ensure that a stop at the Johannesburg Art Gallery is included, and a visit to the Apartheid Museum is definitely worth the extra hour or two (and additional charge) if you are interested in South Africa's turbulent history. Call **Max Maximum** (① 011/938-8703), **Moratiwa** (① 011/869-6629), or **Jimmy's** (① 011/331-6109; www. face2face.co.za). If you want to visit Pretoria, **Ulysses Tours & Safaris** (① 012/663-4941; www.ulysses.co.za) conducts excellent city tours, as well as excursions to nearby sights such as the Cullinan Diamond Mine and De Wildt Cheetah Park.

You Say Pretoria, I Say Tshwane

South Africa's administrative capital was named Pretoria in honor of the Afrikaner hero Andries Pretorius, one of the leaders of the Great Trek, which took place in the 1830s and saw the extermination of large swaths of the indigenous population as the Afrikaners fled the oppressive British to seek out their place in the sun. At press time, the city was in the process of being renamed Tshwane in honor of a black African chief who ruled in precolonial times. Some South Africans are horrified—not least because the change will cost an estimated R1 billion (about $149 million) for changing all maps, signs, and official documents.

Recommended national operators for day or evening trips farther afield (Pretoria, Lesedi, Pilanesberg, Sun City, Kruger National Park) are **Lords Travel & Tours** (© 011/791-5494 or 083/381-1042, reservations 080/020-3861; www.lordstravel. co.za), **Welcome Tourism Services** (© 011/328-8050; www.welcome.co.za), and **Springbok Atlas** (© 011/396-1053; www.springbokatlas.com). Alternatively, check out the following specialized tours:

CRADLE OF HUMANKIND TOURS ★★★ **Palaeo-Tours** (© 011/726-8788; www.palaeotours.com) offers fascinating trips to some of the key sites in what has become known as the Cradle of Humankind, declared a World Heritage Site in 1999 for the significant paleoanthropological and archaeological discoveries made in the area since 1966. The Cradle again made headlines in 2003, when a new dating technique (called burial cosmogenic dating) revealed that the Little Foot Skeleton, found in 1997, is 4.17 million years old—the oldest in South Africa and one of the oldest in the world. Scientists envision that the full Little Foot skeleton will be excavated by September 2005. Guides are paleoanthropology scientists or Ph.D. students who explain the history of evolution while taking you to working excavation sites. The area is some 20 minutes from the city and tours, comprising two site visits, and usually last 5 hours; it may be a good idea to ask for the tour to be extended to include lunch at Cornuti at the Cradle (see "Where to Dine," later in this chapter), possibly followed by a game drive in the Cradle Game Reserve, where you may spot giraffes, rhinos, leopards, and a variety of antelope. Note that all Palaeo-Tours are by arrangement only, so it's worth booking before you leave home.

TOWNSHIP TOURS ★★★ Popular with foreign visitors keen to experience "real" urban life, "township" tourism originated in Soweto (for these, see the box later in this chapter). Township tours offer a fascinating insight into daily life in the segregated black neighborhoods constructed during the apartheid years and the remaining ubiquitous economic contrasts found in the city of gold, like Alexandra, where an estimated 600,000 people live in abject poverty in a 19-sq.-km (7½-square-mile) enclave, just 10 minutes from glitzy Sandton, one of the city's wealthiest suburbs. Among the sights on Alex's "Heritage Trail" tour is the house Mandela lived in when he first came to Johannesburg and the headquarters of the Msomi gang, who terrorized the community in the late 1950s. To arrange a tour, contact the **Alexandra Tourism Association** at © 011/882-3406 or 011/882-0673. Somewhat more organized is the **Parktown and Westcliff Heritage Trust** (© 011/482-3349; Mon–Fri 9am–1pm), which varies its program throughout the year but offers excellent tours through Alexandra, Soweto, and other less-explored neighborhoods.

Tours of the Pretoria townships are not as commercialized as those that visit Soweto, but they can also be a little disorganized—pick up the *Moatwana* brochure from the **Pretoria/Tshwane Information Centre** on Church Square (© **012/337-4337**; Mon–Fri 8am–4pm) to find out more about these tours and operators.

Incidentally, the word *township*—used to denote poor black suburbs—dates back to 1912 and, while commonly used, should ideally be phased out; it's something you may want to discuss with your guide.

MINE & MONEY TOURS ★★★ Underground **operational mine tours** are few and far between these days, largely because of the downturn in South Africa's gold- and diamond-mining industries. If you really want to get under Jo'burg's skin—literally—try contacting Betty Elliot (© **011/498-7100** or 083/263-7776), who may be able to get you on a visit along with an investment group. The tours are physically strenuous and can be psychologically stressful as well; under no circumstances should you attempt one if you are under 16, over 60, or at all claustrophobic. After being given a brief operational and geological overview of the mine in question, visitors are supplied with full underground gear. Keep in mind that conditions 2km (just over a mile) below the surface of the earth are humid and hot, and rock temperatures in working mines can reach 131°F (55°C). Even though refrigerated air is pumped through, air temperatures can exceed 90°F (32°C). After a 1- to 2-hour tour, visitors return to the shaft and shower (towels are supplied). The tour often ends with drinks and snacks, hosted by the mine's management, and costs R550 to R600 ($82–$90) per person. (***Note:*** If an Operational Mine Visit sounds too daunting, you can descend the historic No. 14 shaft at **Gold Reef City;** see "The Top Attractions," later in this chapter).

If Betty cannot assist, you may want to pay a visit to **Cullinan's Premier Mine,** 95 Oak Ave., Cullinan, 50km/31miles east of Pretoria (© **012/734-0081;** booking essential; admission R38/$5.65; tours daily at 10:30am and Mon–Fri at 2pm; no children under 10). Cullinan, yielding an average 2 million carats a year since 1902, is one of the richest diamond mines in the world. Sadly, the mine descent was suspended at press time, but you can still take a 2-hour surface-mine tour, which includes a video of the mining process, a look at the Cullinan Big Hole (40 hectares/99 acres in area and 500m/1,640 ft. deep), displays of uncut diamonds, as well as replicas of the world's most famous diamonds—the Cullinan, Centenary, and Premier Rose were all unearthed here.

SPECIALIST WALKING TOURS ★★★ Beryl Porter loves Jozi with a passion and has set about making its strange beauty more accessible to visitors with a wide

---

Jewel in the Crown

At 3,106 carats, the **Cullinan,** the world's largest diamond, was presented to Edward VII by the Transvaal government not long after its discovery in 1905. It was divided into nine jewels, and the 530-carat Great Star of Africa (the largest cut diamond in the world) and the 317-carat Lesser Star of Africa are now on display in the Tower of London, in the Royal Scepter and Imperial State Crown. You can view a replica of the original at Cullinan's Premier Mine, still one of the most productive diamond mines in the world (see "Mine & Money Tours," above).

selection of walking tours—even glitzy Sandton fascinates her as she enthuses how (while walking to its key sites), within a mere 3 decades, it has been transformed from a sleepy suburb of cow-grazed tracts of land to the new financial center of the city. Personally, I'd opt for a tour of the city center and the nearby Newtown Cultural Precinct, or the derelict attractions of semiseedy Kensington and Troyville and its predominantly Portuguese community (don't miss lunch at the Troyville Hotel, the best and most authentic Portuguese restaurant/bar in the city). Both of these tours last around 3 hours and cost a minimum of R1,200 ($179) for up to 8 participants. Beryl also offers two "dinner-hop" evenings, including one where you kick off from Constitution Hill, travel to the SAB World of Beer for your first course, then sit down for your main at the Rand Club before ending off at the top of Africa's tallest building, the Carlton Centre. Call Beryl at ℂ 011/444-1639 or go to www.walktours.co.za.

ARCHITECTURE & HISTORY TOURS 🛩🛩   In addition to seeing the city center, where century-old relics rub shoulders with sheets of towering glass, make time to view the Edwardian mansions and gardens of Parktown and Westcliff—the very first garden suburbs created by the wealthy randlords, featuring some of celebrated architect Sir Herbert Baker's finest domestic architecture, dating from 1897 to 1905. Though many of the original buildings have been replaced with bland office blocks, it is still well worth exploring. (*Note:* If you want to drive around on your own, you should seek out Ridge Road, particularly **The View** at no. 18, built in 1897; its 1902 neighbor, **Hazeldene,** which also houses **The Herbert Baker** restaurant, ℂ **011/484-6197; Jubilee Road;** and **Rock Ridge Road**—no. 5 was Baker's own residence.) Contact the **Parktown & Westcliff Heritage Trust** (ℂ **011/482-3349;** office hours Mon–Fri 9am–1pm) to find out if it plans to offer any tours of these neighborhoods while you are in the city. The trust also arranges walking or bus tours that cover many other interesting aspects of the city, from "Art Deco and Edwardian Elegance" to "Ghandi's Johannesburg" and "The Jewish Tour." Tours cost R50 to R80 ($7.45–$12) per person.

In Pretoria, specialist **Leone Jackson** offers **Baker's Dozen** 🛩 (ℂ **012/344-3197**), a lecture-type tour that focuses on the mythology and symbols in the work of Sir Herbert Baker (known, together with Lutyens, as the great imperial architect and one of South Africa's most prolific), particularly his Union Buildings, which Leone is passionate about. She also offers in-depth tours of Melrose House. Nicolas Schofield of **The Expeditionary Force** 🛩🛩 (ℂ **012/667-2833**) offers innovative historical tours; he's worth contacting if you're interested in exploring the unofficial version of events.

SPECIAL EVENTS

The city's biggest festival for the performing arts, **Arts Alive** (ℂ **011/838-1383;** www.joburg.org.za/artsalive), takes place in September, with program details available from late June. Globalization has begun to impact the flavor of the festival, with American hip-hop star 50 Cent controversially heading the lineup in 2004. For an authentic take on local culture, note that the highlight of the festival is the Jazz on the Lake Concert, which takes place at Zoo Lake (opposite the zoo). Featuring some of Africa's richest talent, the concert draws a huge cosmopolitan and friendly 300,000-strong audience. To get a sense of South Africa's rapidly growing and very hip Afrocentric fashion scene, book a seat at The Collections during **Jo'burg Fashion Week** (usually end of July). The annual **Dance Umbrella** (ℂ **011/482-4140;** Feb–Mar at various venues) showcases South Africa's not inconsiderable dance and choreographic talents.

FAST FACTS: Johannesburg & Pretoria/Tshwane

Airport See "Arriving," earlier in this chapter.

American Express The head office is in Rosebank at Shop GF03, The Zone, opposite Rosebank Mall (© **011/880-8382**). Hours are Monday to Friday 8:30am to 4:30pm, and Saturday 9am to 12:30pm. There is also an office in Sandton City shopping center, upper level (© **011/883-9009**). For lost or stolen cards, call © **011/710-4747** and ask for the card division.

Area Code Johannesburg's area code is **011**. Pretoria's code is **012**.

Climate Days are usually sunny, with averages of 70°F (20°C). Even winter days are mild (May–Aug), though frost often occurs at night.

Drugstores Drugstores are known as chemists or pharmacies in South Africa. Contact **Daylight Pharmacy,** in Sandton City shopping center (© **011/883-7520;** daily 8:30am–8pm) or **Morningside Dispensary,** corner Rivonia and Allen roads (© **011/883-6588;** daily 8:30am–9pm).

Embassies & Consulates Note that all embassies are in Pretoria (see later in this chapter). Australia, 292 Orient St., Arcadia (© **012/342-3740**); Canada, 1103 Arcadia St., Hatfield (© **012/422-3000**); Ireland, Tulbagh Park, 1234 Church St., Colbyn (© **012/342-5062**); United Kingdom, 256 Glynn St., Hatfield (© **012/483-1400**); United States, 877 Pretorius St., Arcadia (© **012/343-1048**); Zambia, 353 Sanlam Blvd., Hatfield (© **012/342-1541**); Zimbabwe, 798 Merton St., Arcadia (© **012/342-5125**).

Emergencies Dial © **10111** for flying-squad police, or © **999** for an ambulance, or © **082-911** for emergency medical assistance. In case of fire, call © **011/624-2800.** For northern suburbs ambulance or fire emergencies, call © **011/286-6000.** For car breakdowns, call the Automobile Association toll-free at © **0800-01-0101.**

Hospitals Hospitals with 24-hour emergency rooms include **Johannesburg Hospital** (© **011/488-4911**) in Parktown, and **J. G. Strijdom** (© **011/489-1011**) in Auckland Park. To avoid a long wait, you'd be better off at a private hospital like **Morningside Clinic** (© **011/783-8901**), off Rivonia Road, or **Milpark Hospital** (© **011/480-5600**), off Guild Street, Parktown.

Maps You'll find an array of options at CNA/PNA newsagents. The *Witwatersrand Street Guide* is the most comprehensive.

Newspapers & Magazines Good dailies include *The Star* and *The Sowetan.* The weekly *Mail & Guardian* is published every Friday and offers an excellent overview of national events (albeit heavily political) and "what's on" listings. Also now available is the annual *Time Out Johannesburg,* which covers every aspect of the city's leisure life. You can purchase these at local newsagents. **Exclusive Books** is a good national chain of bookstores; branches can be found in the following malls: Sandton City (© **011/883-1010**), The Zone (© **011/327-5736**), Rosebank Mall (© **011/447-3028**), and Hyde Park (© **011/325-4298**).

Post Office Post Office service is generally poor; ask your hotel or guesthouse to deal with any postal items, or use Amex.

WHERE TO STAY

Note: If you're in transit and only here to overnight, a number of good hotels are situated right near the airport; these are described at the end of this section.

The options reviewed below are in areas where you'll be perfectly safe and a short distance of some of the city's best restaurants and shops. All can arrange or offer a shuttle service to and from the airport, 25 to 35km (16–22 miles) away—about a 30- to 40-minute drive. Johannesburg is not a popular leisure destination, and larger hotels generally cater to businessmen; the two most suited to the leisure market (though both with excellent business facilities) are reviewed below.

If you're looking for a more intimate, boutique-style-hotel experience, with personalized service, Johannesburg now also has a fair sampling; the best (Fairlawns, Ten Bompas, and Peech Hotel) are reviewed below. Also worth mentioning in this category is the award-winning **Saxon** in Sandhurst (© 011/292-6000; www.thesaxon.com). Behind an imposing edifice (once the private home of one of South Africa's most successful insurance agents, and where Nelson Mandela wrote *The Long Walk To Freedom* after he split with wife Winnie), the fortresslike house rises from a huge pool floating amid vast green lawns. It's arguably the city's most exclusive hotel (certainly the most expensive)—this is, after all, where the likes of Oprah and Charlize Theron prefer to stay, but unless you're a big name, service does not always match the rate (R4,500–R17,000/$672–$2,537).

On the other end of the spectrum is the small-town bohemian feel of Melville, with lively bars and restaurants within walking distance of most bed-and-breakfasts; here you'll get a real sense of outdoor nightlife (as opposed to the predominantly mall culture of the city). Options are not the most luxurious but have plenty of character.

With Johannesburg becoming an increasingly safer option than it was, say, even 4 years ago, as well as being a truly vibrant and energetic city, it seems unnecessary to stay in Pretoria anymore, but if you have to overnight there for business reasons, I've reviewed a few fine lodging and dining options in a separate box, below.

NORTHERN SUBURBS
Very Expensive

Fairlawns Luxury Hotel 🐾🐾   Located in a peaceful suburb a few minutes' drive from Sandton, Fairlawns, like The Grace, provides generous touches: Complimentary tea trays are delivered to your room on request, rooms have complimentary sherry, cars are cleaned overnight, and shoes left outside the door are shined. But the real reason to stay here are the palatial-size (and -styled) rooms. Decorated by owner Anna Thacker, a master at paint techniques and interior detailing, each room has its own individual theme and personality. Personal favorites include the Swedish (pale blue and gold—beautiful!), the French Provincial, the Bismarck, and the Louis—truly fit for a king. The Africa suite, one wall of which teems with wildlife, is so big you can barely see the TV from the bed. Fairlawns offers a tranquil respite from the city, with a comfortably furnished terrace (where most meals are served; dinner on request) overlooking the lawn and pool. Some people may find it a little too cut off from the action, but with the recently expanded spa facilities, being out of the throbbing city may be just the thing.

Alma Rd., Morningside Manor, Sandton 2052. © 011/804-2540, -2541, -2542, or -2543. Fax 011/802-7261. www. fairlawns.co.za. 19 units. Courtyard wing R2,370 ($354) double; Premier wing R3,520 ($525) double; Presidential suite R17,000 ($2,537). Rates include breakfast. AE, DC, MC, V. Children under 15 discouraged. **Amenities:** Dining room; bar; lounge; pool; golf, tennis, and squash by arrangement; health spa/gym; secretarial services; laundry. *In room:* TV, minibar, hair dryer, safe, tea- and coffee-making facilities.

The Grace ★★★   Devised as a more intimate alternative to the large city hotel, the family-owned Grace, within walking distance of Rosebank's boutiques, galleries, and art cinemas, is a gracious residence that feels more like a London gentleman's club than a 73-room hotel. In stark contrast to the brutal Hyatt (also in Rosebank) or the over-the-top opulence of the Michelangelo, The Grace is designed to human scale, and furnished and finished in tasteful, traditional English style. Wood paneling, floral brocades, generous sofas, gold-framed paintings, and well-thumbed books create a serene, comfortable, and warm atmosphere. The Grace is also generous, with no hidden extra costs—you get complimentary in-room English breakfasts and a selection of complimentary teas, coffee, and cakes (a slice of the *melktert,* a traditional Afrikaans dessert, is a must) served in the library where comfortable sofas invite you to peruse the dailies or books from the ample collection. Small touches like fresh milk and home-baked biscuits, supplied with in-room tea- and coffee-making facilities, as well as the generous size of the comfortable rooms and bathrooms, simply add to this. The service is gracious and personal yet unobtrusive, and the staff do their utmost to ensure your complete comfort, while therapeutic treatments in the spa are the perfect antidote to the pace of the city. The dining room at The Grace enjoys an excellent reputation and is regularly included in critics' selections of Johannesburg's top restaurants. The Grace is a personal favorite, with the best service in the city, but it's worth bearing in mind that for more or less the same money, you could book a luxury room at The Westcliff and enjoy the best views.

54 Bath Ave., Rosebank 2196. ℭ 011/280-7200. Fax 011/280-7474. www.thegrace.co.za. 73 units. R2,700 ($403) double; R3,300–R4,000 ($493–$597) suite. Rates include English breakfast. Children stay free in parent's suite. AE, DC, MC, V. **Amenities:** Restaurant; bar; heated lap pool; spa; access to Virgin Active Health Club; small gym; activity desk; car rental; VIP limousine; business center; salon; room service; babysitting; laundry; rooftop croquet lawn; library; valet parking; mobile phone usage. *In room:* A/C, TV, fax connection, minibar, hair dryer, Internet access, tea- and coffee-making facilities.

The Westcliff ★★★   Clinging to the steep incline of Westcliff ridge, this fully walled hillside "village" is, like the Michelangelo (in Sandton's Nelson Mandela Square; www.lhw.com), a member of Leading Hotels of the World. But while the Michelangelo's focus remains firmly on the business crowd, this caters equally well to the well-heeled leisure traveler (just ask Brad Pitt and the Dalai Lama, who happened to be booked here at the same time in 2004). Understated elegance is the order of the day, particularly in the "tobacco" rooms, and the palatial marble bathrooms are a real treat. Each room is uniquely positioned and sized, so accommodations options vary considerably. Do insist on a room with a view, preferably with a balcony (units in Villa 4, appropriately named "Cliffside," are recommended, particularly nos. 401, 405, 406, 423, or 424; alternatively, try for nos. 105, 201, 503, or 605). Hanging on the lip of the large infinity pool, Johannesburg spreads out before you; as dusk approaches, head for the popular poolside terrace—or adjacent Polo Lounge—and enjoy cocktails while the sun descends and the sky turns pink over the spectacle of the endless forested canopy of the northern suburbs. Later, move upstairs, where a slightly daring menu is served up in rather formal surroundings. Ironically, the hotel's biggest drawback arises from its excellent cliff-side location; in a rather unwieldy arrangement, cars are left at reception and guests are shuttled around by vehicles that regularly traverse the cobbled streets. A complimentary shuttle will take you to the shopping districts of Sandton and Hyde Park, some 15 minutes away; Melville and Rosebank are less than 10 minutes away.

67 Jan Smuts Ave., Westcliff 2193. © **800/237-1236** in the U.S., or 011/646-2400. Fax 011/646-2666. www. westcliff.orient-express.com. 120 units. R2,470–R3,070 ($369–$458) double; R3,650–R7,310 ($545–$1,091) suite; R9,480–R11,950 ($1,415–$1,784) penthouse suite. Children 12–18 pay 50%. AE, DC, MC, V. **Amenities:** 2 restaurants; lounge bar; 2 heated swimming pools; 2 plunge pools; golf (enjoy full membership facilities of a nearby club); tennis court; gym; VIP limousine service; business center; salon; 24-hr. room service; babysitting; laundry; film collection and delivery; the *New York Times* by fax; 24-hour on-call doctor. *In room:* A/C, TV/VCR, fax, minibar, hair dryer, electronic safe, high-speed Internet (charged).

Expensive

Melrose Arch ★★ Jozi's self-proclaimed "hip hotel" is something of a knockoff of the Philippe Starck–Ian Schrager model, and though it's not in the same league, it is filled with flourishes that help make it a celebration of the city's newfound confidence and optimism. It's ideal for the young (or young at heart) traveler looking for some action—you're a stroll from some of the city's hippest restaurants and bars—and has a quirky edge that clearly differentiates it from the more established hotels in the city. The designers have tried to throw in plenty of eye-catching elements, like the entrance lobby floor that constantly changes color, the long drapes that hang from oversize chrome coat hangers, and different "mood" elevators for day and night. Guest rooms feature the latest in stylish technology (like flatscreen TVs) and playful decor: Wooden parquet flooring vies with block-print carpets, glass-top work stations with exposed brick walls, and chintz drapes with Roman blinds—a mishmash of elements sure to disturb the purist but delight the postmodernist. Separated from the bedroom only by a large curtain, the bathrooms feature deep oval tubs and walk-in "rain" showers. **Note:** Unless you prefer to be in a large hotel and within walking distance of excellent nightlife possibilities, you may want to consider the ultrastylish Peech, which is both less expensive and more intimate (reviewed below).

1 Melrose Sq., Melrose Arch, Johannesburg 2196. © **011/214-6666.** Fax 011/214-6600. www.proteahotels.com/ melrosearchhotel. 118 units. Standard room R2,360 ($352) double; Executive room R2,900 ($433) double. AE, DC, MC, V. **Amenities:** Restaurant; 3 bars; pool; golf and tennis privileges; access to nearby health club; 24-hr. room service; laundry; sound room. *In room:* A/C, TV, DVD player/hi-fi, dataport, minibar, hair dryer, safe, tea- and coffee-making facility.

Ten Bompas ★★ (Value South Africa's only city accommodations to be featured in *Design Hotels,* this tranquil urban retreat is something of a Jo'burg legend, with a reputation that has as much to do with its fabulous restaurant, **Sides,** as it does with the fact that this was the city's first boutique hotel. Guest rooms are each individually crafted by a mix of designers, architects, fashionistas, couturiers, and artists—their assignment was to give their own twist on a contemporary ethno-African design. The results are a mixed bag; your personal taste will determine your affection for a particular suite, but all are spacious (each with its own balcony) and extremely comfortable, with big showers that turn into steam rooms at the push of a button. Thanks to its size (only 10 suites), Bompas offers more tranquillity than Fairlawns; it also doesn't have intrusive conferencing facilities. Service is pretty laid-back; you can expect baby champagne in your room after arrival, gallons of complimentary liquor in your minibar (full bottles of Absolut vodka!), and plenty of peace and quiet. The owners of Ten Bompas have lodges in Kruger National Park, The Outpost, and Honeyguide Tented Safari Camps that are worth investigating (see chapter 8).

10 Bompas Rd., Dunkeld West. P.O. Box 786064, Sandton 2146. © **011/327-0650.** Fax 011/447-4326. www.ten bompas.co.za. 10 units. R2,400 ($358) double. Rate includes breakfast, laundry, tea and coffee, and minibar. AE, DC, MC, V. **Amenities:** Restaurant; bar; pool; limousine and chauffeur service; 24-hr. reception; room service; laundry; dry cleaning on request; doctor and dentist on call. *In room:* A/C, TV, CD/hi-fi system, fax on request, complimentary minibar, hair dryer, safe, flashlight (torch), heater, fireplace.

Moderate

The Peech Hotel ★★ *Value*   This fabulous little "hotel," set in a tree-filled, upscale neighborhood, was opened in early 2005 by James Peech, a young creative type from Yorkshire. Swish and sexy, it's clearly styled on the pages of *Wallpaper,* and the ideal hangout for trendy travelers in the hunt for no-frills contemporary style. The emphasis is on in-room comfort (king-size beds, soft white linen, ultra-comfortable mattresses); animal-hide rugs decorate the wooden floors, and large bathrooms with "raindance" showers are a genuine treat. The two guest rooms (ask for room no. 1 or 2) above the lobby are the best in terms of size, while the four garden units have either a small terrace or direct access to the lawn. Wholesome breakfasts and all-day deli-style meals are served in a small open-air dining area, but you're encouraged to go out at night to make your acquaintance with one of the fine restaurants in the area, followed by a visit to a good club (staff will happily arrange transport).

61 North St., Melrose. ⓒ **011/537-9797.** Fax 011/537-9798. www.thepeech.co.za. 6 units. R1,350 ($201) double. Rate includes breakfast, tea, and coffee. AE, DC, MC, V. **Amenities:** Deli-style restaurant; bar; pool; complimentary gym membership; 24-hr. reception; meeting room; laundry on request; library. *In room:* TV, hair dryer, wireless Internet access.

NORTHWESTERN SUBURBS (MELVILLE & PARKWOOD)

If you prefer a modern aesthetic, the most tranquil option in Melville (and with the added benefit of a pool and views of the Melville Nature Reserve) is **Guesthouse 61 On 5th** ★ (ⓒ **011/482-8278;** www.portfoliocollection.com/go/Guesthouse61On5th). Laundry is included in the exceptionally good-value rate (R700/$104 double); airport and city transfers are arranged by your host Marius, and a night guard is on hand to escort you to Melville's nightlife precinct, just a few minutes' walk away. If you'd prefer to be immersed in the ongoing party that happens along 7th Street, **The Space** (ⓒ **083/414-0124;** www.ghasa.co.za) is a B&B with excellent self-catering facilities; reserve the enormous Executive suite for R800 ($119) double; the only potential drawback is that you are very near to the typically loud action. If you're a hippie at heart, look into a stay at **Saffron House.** Located on 4th Avenue, it's an eclectic boho mix of rich colors, paintings, sculptures, mosaics, scatter cushions, and silk drapes; room no. 4 is recommended (ⓒ **011/726-6646;** www.saffronhousebnb.com; from R650/$97 double).

Moderate

The Parkwood ★★   Clearly the Johannesburg B&B/guesthouse scene has come of age with yet another modern boutique-styled option on offer, this time in Parkwood, which is situated a little out of the way but still within striking distance of Melville. Here the architecture, which features plenty of the exposed rough-hewn stone walls that are currently so popular in South Africa, cleverly incorporates indoor and outdoor spaces with foldaway glass doors leading onto an outdoor patio with Moroccan daybeds, all overlooking a skinny lap pool. With a decor that leans toward contemporary African, interiors are sleek and glamorous, with fabrics in warm earth tones; large travertine bathrooms come with Jacuzzi baths, separate showers, and heated towel rails. Healthful breakfasts are served in an informal dining room each morning, and private dinner parties can be arranged given some prior warning.

72 Worcester Rd., Parkwood. ⓒ **011/880-1748.** Fax 011788-7896. www.theparkwood.com. 5 units. R800–R1,400 ($119–$209) double. AE, DC, MC, V. Rates include breakfast. **Amenities:** Dining; pool; laundry. *In room:* TV, minibar, hair dryer, electronic safe, 24-hr. free ASDL connections, under-carpet heating.

A Room with a View & A Hundred Angels ★★ This over-the-top faux-Tuscan manor is the best option in Melville (though if you prefer a contemporary look, opt for The Parkwood or Guesthouse 61 on 5th), with luxury accommodations in 12 varied en-suite rooms occupying two different buildings. Your hostess, Lise, is enthusiastic about her neighborhood and happy to make (good) recommendations; she will also arrange to have you dropped off and picked up (at night it's not advisable to make the 15-min. walk to 7th St.). The lounges and dining-room areas are a bit overdressed, with eclectic objects and furnishings, but somehow it all works, and most of the bedrooms are fabulously comfortable. Try to book a room on the upper floor—these have lovely views, mostly of the Melville Koppies Nature Reserve. The largest rooms are nos. 21, 32, and 33, but personal favorites are room nos. 22 and 23, which have gorgeous views and offer good value.

1 Tolip St., corner 4th Ave., Melville. © **011/482-5435** or 011/726-8589. www.aroomwithaview.co.za. 12 units. R700–R1,300 ($104–$194) double. Rates include breakfast. Children under 10 discouraged. AE, DC, MC, V. **Amenities:** Dining/lounge areas; pool; laundry; day room. *In room:* TV, minibar, hair dryer, tea- and coffee-making facilities, gas fireplaces (in some).

NEAR THE AIRPORT

Bear in mind that Johannesburg and Pretoria are only a 30- to 40-minute drive away. Still, if you have a tight transfer or need that extra half-hour of shut-eye, book into the **Intercontinental Airport Sun** (© **011/961-5400;** www.southernsun.com; R2,200/ $328 double), which is within walking distance of both the domestic and international terminals. A cheaper (in every sense) alternative is the **City Lodge Johannesburg International Airport** (© **011/392-1750;** www.citylodge.co.za; R680/$101 double). Casino lovers with limited time should consider booking into **Caesars Gauteng Hotel Casino** (© **011/928-1000**), which comprises the modestly priced Senator wing (R897/$134 double) and the pricier Emperor section (from R1,730/$258 double); you'll be just 2 minutes from the airport, so you can check in with your airline before returning for breakfast, which is included.

A MOUNTAIN RETREAT

Mount Grace ★★★ It may be a tad off the beaten track, but this romantic retreat is well worth the 1-hour drive from Jo'burg or Pretoria to luxuriate in clear mountain air, relax in the tiptop spa, and savor exquisitely prepared food on a lantern-lit lawn. Besides, some of the region's top attractions are nearby (the Sterkfontein Caves are only 15 min. away, and the De Wildt Cheetah Centre and Lesedi Cultural Village are also within easy striking distance); Mount Grace also makes the ideal stopover if you're traveling to Sun City or Madikwe Game Reserve. All the typical Grace touches are here—spacious, comfortable rooms; friendly, smart staff; understated luxury; and a thorough understanding of how to make guests feel really pampered. Even the thatched-roof Spa at Mount Grace brings a refreshing "healthy hedonism" ethos to spa culture: After unwinding in the Hydrotherapy Spa Garden—steam bath, cold plunge, Jacuzzi, waterfall, reflexology pool, and flotation pool with African music piped in underwater—you'll be served a glass of good South African wine on the spa veranda. Accommodations are stellar: Thatchstone Village rooms overlook garden pathways, Grace Village rooms have patios with garden views, and Treetops Village, set apart from the rest of the hotel in a forested ravine, offers huge luxury suites with balconies or patios. But it's worth asking for 1 of the 10 rooms in Mountain Village, which have private heated plunge pools on balconies overlooking the glittering valley below. From there you can walk down steps carved into the hillside to one of two warmly lit restaurants, with both indoor and outdoor seating.

Mount Grace Country House Hotel, Private Bag 5004, Magaliesburg 1791 (take Rte. 24 northwest from Johannesburg). © 0145/771-350. Fax 0145/771-202. www.mountgrace.co.za. 81 units. Standard double R1,120 ($167); Superior double R1,800 ($269); Luxury double R2,940 ($439). Rates include full breakfast. AE, DC, MC, V. Transportation to and from hotel available. Ask about spa packages. Children 10 and over only. **Amenities:** 2 restaurants; spa cafe; bar and billiards room; 3 swimming pools; tennis; spa; gift shop; mountain biking; croquet lawn; fly-fishing; bird-watching and bird walks; horseback riding, squash, and hot-air ballooning by arrangement; library. *In room:* TV, minibar, hair dryer, safe, tea- and coffee-making facilities, heated towel racks.

WHERE TO DINE

Johannesburg offers a thoroughly eclectic mix of dining possibilities: Just about every national cuisine is represented, so if you have a particular craving, simply ask your concierge or host to point you in the right direction. Alternatively, take your pick from the listings below, all, with the exception of The Cradle, located within reasonable distance from the above accommodations.

If you like cafe society and browsing through menus and venues before deciding on where to hand over your credit card, head for one of the following neighborhoods.

MELVILLE The demand to satisfy Melville's local gourmands is so relentless that one can easily blink only to discover a favorite restaurant along 7th Avenue replaced by another by the time you've opened your eyes. You'll also find the mix of down-at-heel and sophisticated eateries a little confusing at times, since Melville's arty crowd will happily put up with outrageously poor service and crude decor once they've committed to a preferred venue; also keep in mind that Melville's vibrant and varied nightlife options are aimed at attracting the city's trend-setters rather than serious foodies, and that the popularity of 7th Avenue (from early evening till the wee hours) means that it inevitably suffers from congestion. It's worth considering a move to the *très* trendy 44 Stanley Avenue complex, headquarters of the burgeoning Milpark loft district, where you should book at organic-themed **Deluxe** (© 011/482-7795). Back in Melville's 7th Street, opt for **Café Mezza Luna,** 9a, 7th St. (© 011/482-2477) good for springbok carpaccio, ostrich filet, and Frangelica chocolate mousse, or **Soi** (reviewed below) one of the best Asian restaurants in the city. If you're looking for a healthful, popular lunchtime venue, head to **The Service Station,** Bamboo Centre, corner of Rustenberg and 9th streets (© 011/726-1701), where you help yourself to a buffet of salads, Mediterranean mezze, and quiches, and pay by the weight of your plate; after lunch, browse for vino next door at **Wines+,** considered the city's finest wine boutique.

GREENSIDE It's blander than Melville, but the restaurants are of a higher caliber; pick of the bunch is **Yum** (see below). Others worth considering are **Ma Passion,** 36 Gleneagles Rd. (© 011/646-3438), for West African–inspired flavors like chicken with palm nut sauce and cassava leaves; **Icon,** 51 Greenfields Rd. (© 011/646-4162), for superb, simple, contemporary Greek food; and **Karma,** 2 Gleneagles Rd. (© 011/646-8555), serving Indo-Pakistani fare with a Middle Eastern twist (ever tried avocado *korma* or coconut samoosas?). Aside from **Bite** and **Addictions** (reviewed below), more recommended options include entrepreneurial restaurateur Nicky van der Walt's **Circle,** 141 Greenway (© 011/646-3744) and, across the road, **Café Flo,** 116 Greenway (© 011/646-6817), popular for its interesting chalked-up specials (salmon on wasabi mash with watercress sauce) and fabulously innovative pizza combinations (like aubergine and roast lamb); the attached bistro, **Ove Flo** (© 011/486-4576), serves equally delectable dishes.

Doing Business in Pretoria?

Accommodations in the newly renamed Tshwane (formerly Pretoria) are geared very much toward the diplomatic market. So if you're here on business, you'll find a number of options in the "Ambassadorial Belt" (Arcadia, Hatfield, Sunnyside, and the upmarket suburb of Brooklyn); all are, at most, a 10-minute drive from Pretoria's city center. Besides standard hotels (the best of which is the **Sheraton;** specify a room on the fourth or fifth floors with a view of the Union Buildings; look for specials on www.sheraton.com), there are comfortable apartments with hotel-type facilities (like the **Courtyard at Arcadia,** built around a turn-of-the-20th-century manor house; © 012/342-4940; www.citylodge.co.za; R810–R1,250/$121–$187), as well as numerous guesthouses (like the comfortable **Birdwood;** © 012/430-4905; www.birdwood.co.za; R890–R1,450/$133–$216). But if you want to really impress (or are looking for a private, romantic hideaway), book into one of the six opulent guest suites at **Illyria House,** a grand colonial manor house and a favorite of CEOs and state dignitaries from around the world (© 012/344-4641; R2,650/$396 double, including breakfast, or take the all-inclusive option, which includes all meals, spa treatments, tours, and transfers for R7,000/$1,045 double). When it comes to dining, you'll find that most locals are committed carnivores—hence the number of tip-top steakhouses. Of these, **Pachas** (© 012/460-5063), in Club Two Shopping Centre; the **Famous Butcher's Grill** (© 012/347-9970), in Waterkloof Ridge Lifestyle Centre; and **The Grill Club** (© 012/368-1460), in the Menlyn Park Shopping Centre, are all recommended. If you're keen to try traditional *boerekos* (literally "farmer's food," featuring Afrikaans and Malay influences, it is delicious, hearty fare, these days served with some unusual fusion twists), Pretoria has a selection worth driving from Jo'burg for. Of these, **Die Werf Restaurant** 🎔🎔, 66 Olympus Rd., Olympus (© 012/991-1809), and **Moerdijks,** 752 Park St. and Beckett Street, Arcadia (© 012/344-4856) are both highly recommended. Pretoria also has what some consider to be the best French restaurant in the country: **La Madeleine** is on every food critic's top picks list, and international credits include a mention in the *Courvoisier Book of the Best.* The smallish menu changes regularly, with charming Belgian owner-chef Daniel Leusch personally presenting the dishes of the day in a seductively heavy French accent (© 012/361-3667). **Jan Harmsgat Se Kombuis,** 86 Oak Ave., Cullinan (© 012/734-0707), a new restaurant set in the original wine cellar of a farm in the Langeberg foothills, is the place for funky country dining. If you're in the mood for Italian, head to **Ristorante Ritrovo** (© 012/460-4367). Run by father-and-son team Giovanni and Forti Mazzone, this is far and away the best Italian dining in town. (For attractions, see "A Side Trip to Pretoria/Tshwane," later in this chapter.)

NORWOOD   Norwood's post-1990s revival is clearly evident along restaurant-saturated Grant Avenue, the social artery of this predominantly Jewish suburb with a busy village vibe. Bigger than Melville, Norwood has a more mature crowd, with fewer students and more yuppies flaunting their easy style. The area lacks some of Melville's historic ambience, but come here for an evening meal and you're unlikely to miss out on atmosphere. One drawback is that Norwood's not really close to any fabulous accommodations, although it's a relatively easy drive from Melrose Arch, Rosebank, and Observatory. Try **The Barrio** (② 011/728-2577), a kosher restaurant serving sushi and beef carpaccio, or **The Singing Fig,** 44 The Avenue (② 011/728-2434) considered by many (primarily patrons who refuse to dine elsewhere) to be the best restaurant in town. The fare at the Fig is French Provençale with a New World twist: Items like crocodile steak roulade and whiskey-marinated oxtail keep the menu interesting. Flavor of the moment is **Asia D'Afrique** (reviewed below) and, right next door, its cafe stepsister, **Cosmopolitan** (② 011/728-3181), where you can eat ostrich burger with avocado or enjoy a fresh tuna, fig, and quail egg salad. Even if you don't eat in Norwood, be sure to stop in at **meat on grant** (② 011/728-6412), a traditional neighborhood butchery selling the best biltong (jerky) you'll find in Jo'burg.

PARKHURST & PARKTOWN NORTH   These two adjoining neighborhoods represent the city's most relaxed restaurant nexus, and lazy weekend lunches here are tremendously popular with the chic set. Locals flock here (particularly to 4th Ave.), not only for its sidewalk restaurants, but also for its quaint specialty stores—selling anything from Belgian chocolate to African art or English antiques. Recommended restaurants are **Ruby Grapefruit,** 24 4th Ave. (② 011/880-3673), for good sushi; **Cilantro,** 24 4th Ave. (② 011/327-4558), for sublime calamari; and the more fine-dining **Anno Domini,** 4th Avenue and 13th Street (② 011/447-7634), where ex-Savoy chef Aristotle Ravagales serves up contemporary European fare in a romantic atmosphere. **Espresso** ★★ must rate as one of the most popular Italian restaurant groups in the city, featuring some fabulous combinations—try the pear and bleu cheese pizza. There are branches in both Parkhurst, on 4th Avenue (② 011/447-8700), and Parktown North (② 011/880-0920); note that credit cards are accepted at neither. Also in Parktown North, you'll find **Fino Bar and Restaurant,** 19 4th Ave. (② 011/880-6808), with Spanish tapas and an excellent wine list to accompany people-watching.

NORTHERN SUBURBS (PARKTOWN TO SANDTON)

Asia D'Afrique ★★ AFRICAN/ASIAN   Cheekily proclaiming itself the "Ministry of Food and Drink," this Norwood newcomer offers a menu full of creative potential.

Moments Waiter, There's an Elephant in My Soup

Book a table at The Westcliff (② 011/646-2400)—either at the Loggia for breakfast or the three-course luncheon, or the poolside terrace for afternoon tea or sundowner cocktails—and try to spot an elephant. If it isn't pink, you're looking at the Johannesburg zoo's elephant and rhino enclosure, clearly visible from the hotel's elevated position on the cliff. And if the animals are in hiding, never mind—the view of the urban forest, said to be the largest in the world, is astounding.

Understated decor blends Asian zen with African elements—and this is reflected in the mix of food styles, with truly tasty results from chef Wayne Burger. Starters include such exotic fare as sweet-potato and lychee soup, roasted red-pepper parcels (stuffed with wild mushroom ratatouille and glazed Gorgonzola), and a salad of biltong, avocado, Danish feta, and sun-dried tomatoes. Mains sound less interesting but are delicious; try pan-fried ostrich medallions drizzled with an Amarula liqueur demiglaze. Or try oxtail braised in Shiraz sauce with *waterblommetjies* (waterlily stew); it's served in a miniature traditional African iron pot with mash. Finish off with green-tea crème brûlée or traditional African melktart (milk tart) with Kahlúa crème anglaise and green-tea ice cream. ***Note:*** Like all Norwood restaurants that open out onto the sidewalk, it's best visited for dinner, once the daytime business has subsided

41 Grant Ave., corner of Isis St., Norwood. (**011/728-9348.** Main courses R50–R76 ($7.45–$11). DC, MC, V. Tues–Sat noon–midnight; Sun noon–4pm; Mon 6–10:30pm.

Auberge Michel ★★★ FRENCH   Former Soweto resident Michel Morand was born in France, which is where he developed his love of fine cuisine. Now he rubs shoulders with Jo'burg's major players, and some of the country's biggest names come to his classy Sandton restaurant to indulge in superlative French dishes. Formal and gracious, with high-back chairs and stiff napkins, Auberge Michel is the country's first officially rated five-star dining establishment and named one of South Africa's top 10 by critics. Don't pass up chef Frederic Leloup's filet mignon of springbok, served with porcini and artichoke ravioli and a caramelized coffee sauce; the deboned veal tail braised with truffles isn't too shabby, either.

122 Pretoria Ave., Sandton. (**011/883-7013.** www.aubergemichel.co.za. R220 ($33) for a 3-course meal. AE, DC, MC, V. Tues–Fri noon–2:30pm; Mon–Sat 6:30–10pm.

1886 ★★★ CONTEMPORARY   Nicky van der Walt's restaurant in Sandton's stylish new 24 Central complex is where the trendiest crowd—young, upwardly mobile, and mixed—gathers to see and be seen amid the Swarovski crystals, bauble chandeliers, Tretchikoff-inspired wallpaper, and gossamer drapes. Its friendly waiters with names like Steel and over-the-top cheekiness may make you wonder when the floor show is about to begin, but hold on: The real star of this outfit is the outrageously good cuisine. Sushi is on offer and exciting specials keep cropping up, but you shouldn't miss the springbok loin with raspberry jus, duck breast with a teriyaki glaze, or slightly seared yellowfin tuna done with heavenly orange-and-green cardamom. The beef filet and caviar with Marsala and mushroom jus and truffle mash is worth making another trip for. Be warned: The chocolate pudding soufflé is the most decadent dessert in town, closely followed by the berry strudel (served with balsamic and maple syrup ice cream). The wine list is superb, if very pricey.

Tip: This is definitely a weekend venue, so you must specifically reserve in advance for an intimate sofa seat; in truth, the transparent chairs aren't as comfortable as they are interesting to look at.

Shop 8, 24 Central, corner of Gwen Lane and Fredman Dr., Sandton. (**011/884-8240.** Weekend reservations essential. Main courses R58–R85 ($8.65–$13). AE, DC, MC, V. Mon–Sat noon–11:30pm.

La Cucina di Ciro ★★ ITALIAN   Ciro Molinaro's three-star Michelin experience in France's Loire region simply honed his talent for home-cooked Italian fare that locals consider among the best in Jo'burg. It's a totally unpretentious delilike venue (and small, so book), where the focus is firmly on the food: The menu changes weekly, depending on what's in season, but if it's featured, do try the roast aubergine and lentil soup, followed by cannelloni with butternut, sun-dried tomato, and ricotta. The menu usually features at least one fish or meat dish to satisfy the carnivores—and if you're lucky, the salmon and spinach lasagna will be it. In summer, be sure to book a table on the pavement and enjoy the balmy highveld temperatures. *Note:* If you're in the mood for Italian and are based in Sandton, try the authentic fare at **Assaggi** (R), Post Office Centre, Rudd Road, Illova (© **011/268-1370**), where locals congregate not only for the primo pasta, but also to take home jars of tangy sauce from the in-house deli.

17 4th Ave., Parktown North. © 011/442-5346. Reservations essential. Main courses R50–R86 ($7.45–$13). AE, DC, MC, V. Mon–Fri 8am–3:30pm and 6:30–9:30pm; Sat 8am–3:30pm.

Linger Longer (RRR) INTERNATIONAL   In 1976 Walter Ulz opened his restaurant in a Braamfontein prewar rooming house to much acclaim. Thirty years later, having followed big business to the safety of Sandton's suburbs, Ulz is still creating a fine-dining ambience that patrons (who include Nelson Mandela) find hard to leave. Ulz's food is legendary and truly international; while he doesn't attempt to combine different traditions in the same dish ("fusion food is con-fusion," Ulz claims), he certainly adds personal flare. There are a number of solid French classics, but if you want to globe-trot, some good options are the fresh oysters served with seafood ceviche (lime-and-lemon-marinated) on rocket, a rich foie gras terrine with artichoke and green peppercorn, and the veal medallions (stacked with chives, cream cheese, garlic, and fresh basil).

58 Wierda Rd. W., Wierda Valley, Sandton. © 011/884-0465. Reservations recommended. Average main course R135 ($20). AE, DC, MC, V. Mon–Fri 12:30–2pm; Mon–Sat 7–10pm.

Moyo (RR) MODERN PAN-AFRICAN   In a few short years, Moyo has developed into a franchise, with a branch in Stellenbosch, and two more in Jo'burg. It's generally considered the best African restaurant in the country, even if the location—in Eurocentric Melrose Arch—feels decidedly un-African. Frequented by locals and tourists alike, this is a great place to people-watch—even if you don't eat here, come for the mango daiquiris and lounge around in the bar or on the alfresco couches, warmed by wood-burning braziers and blankets in winter. From the waitstaff's bright cerise-pink headdresses to the huge Bushman paintings on the adobelike walls, this is African pastiche with a tongue-in-cheek twist. Popular dishes include fragrant North African stews, slow cooked with ginger, cinnamon, coriander, cumin, and saffron, and served with couscous; the South African venison *bobotie* (a mild, sweetish curry); and the grilled ostrich, prepared with aromatic Ethiopian spices. If you'd prefer something light, the ostrich burger, served on sweet-potato-and-pumpkin bread, is a good option. More than a restaurant, Moyo's is an experience, particularly at night, when music, dance, and other entertainments are on the menu. *Note:* If you're exploring the cultural sights in Newtown, you can take a break and enjoy the same fare at the Market Theatre's branch of Moyo (© **011/838-1715**).

No. 5 Melrose Sq., Melrose Arch. © 011/648-1477 or -1478. www.moyo.co.za. Reservations essential. Main courses R28–R121 ($4.15–$18). AE, MC, V. Daily noon–3pm and 7pm–late.

Sides (RR) (Value) CONTEMPORARY   Yorkshire chef Fred Monaghan's Sides was judged one of the top 10 restaurants in the country in 2004, and deservedly so—who else would combine lime and saffron to make a hollandaise sauce for grilled scallops? Other dishes worth investigating are the oxtail ravioli, homemade sausages, and calves' liver wrapped in Parma ham with fresh sage. But as innovative as the food sometimes

---

Tips **Got a Yen for Sushi or a Thing for Thai?**

If you're in the mood for top-notch Japanese or Thai food, head for Sandton. You'll find what is generally considered to be the city's best Japanese restaurant, **Daruma,** in the Sandton Sun hotel (© **011/780-5157**). **Wangthai,** on the first floor of Sandton Square (© **011/784-8484**), is considered one of the best Thai restaurants in the city; in Pretoria, **Wangthai,** Gramik Office Park, 281 Middel St., Brooklyn (© **012/346-6230**), is another popular favorite.

---

is, the trendy crowd really comes here to be near to the enviable walk-in wine cellar and visit the most talked-about unisex loos in town (edgy music videos play beneath you while you wash your hands); for a reasonably priced, welcoming introduction to Jozi's funky side, come here first.

10 Bompas Rd., Dunkeld W. © 011/325-2442. www.tenbompas.co.za. Reservations recommended. Main dishes R55–R80 ($8.20–$12); 3-course Sun lunch R90 ($13). AE, DC, MC, V. Daily 7am–10:30pm.

NORTHWESTERN SUBURBS (MELVILLE & GREENSIDE)

Addictions ★★ CONTEMPORARY FUSION This intimate restaurant serves delicious, great-value fusion fare: Try the filet with peppercorn and plum sauce with wilted spinach and root vegetables; black cherry duck breast; or ostrich filet rubbed with black pepper and cracked rosemary (it's made with espresso and dark chocolate and is *the* way to have your ostrich). Don't miss the black-pepper or chile ice cream when available. As the name implies, guests return regularly, so book in advance. (Alternatively, if you're in the mood for Asian, grab a table at next-door **Bite;** featuring Japanese, Chinese, and Indonesian cuisines, it has something for everyone, and the prices are good.)

137 Greenway, Greenside. © 011/646-8981. Reservations recommended. Main courses R80–R100 ($12–$15). AE, DC, MC, V. Tues–Sat 12:30–2:30pm; Mon–Sat 6:30–9:30pm.

Soi ★★ (Value THAI/VIETNAMESE Melville's best restaurant is frequented by a devoted local crowd that appreciates the authentic cuisine and stylish lounge filled with modern furniture—perfect for a relaxing pre- or post-dinner cocktail. For one of the hottest mouthfuls in town, try the angry duck, blasted with chiles, but not before you order a variety of starters. The spinach-rolled *meamg khum,* with hints of lemon grass, is recommended, as are the spicy fish cakes and duck salad with bana blossoms. *Tip:* To enjoy your meal in peace, as with any Melville restaurant, take a seat indoors; the sidewalk can be noisy.

Corner of 7th St. and 13th Ave., Melville. © 011/726-5775. Main courses R34–R75 ($5.05–$11). AE, DC, MC, V. Daily noon–2:30pm; Sun–Wed 6–10pm; Thurs–Sat 6–10:30pm.

Yum ★★★ CONTEMPORARY SOUTH AFRICAN Relocation to new premises (just a few meters down the block) has somehow forced the crowds out of hiding and onto the waiting list of this tremendously popular Jo'burg restaurant. For 3 years running, Yum has been voted one of the top 10 in the annual "Eat Out" awards, and is easily considered the best in the city. Owner-chef Dario D'Angeli dazzles with provocative experimentation, producing dishes for the sophisticated palate; his charming mum, Del, greets guests and takes particular pride in running through the specials, her gesticulating fingers capturing the essence of wonderful tastes to come:

Japanese seared beef glazed with honeyed sesame and served with sirloin carpaccio and a sweet chile condiment, or duck livers flambéed in Cassis and served with bitter chocolate pudding. When it comes to mains, there's no beating the tender roast duck: It's deboned, cooked three times to remove excess fat, and served with an apricot glaze and a reduction of molasses and ginger. For a real South African twist on traditional pie, order the *vol au vent*—a stew of ostrich, pork, beef, and venison is reduced and encased in puff pastry; the mouth-watering reduction becomes the sauce for the final product. Yum!

26 Gleneagles Rd., Greenside. ℂ 011/486-1645. www.yum.co.za. Reservations essential. Main courses R95–R150 ($14–$22). AE, DC, MC, V. Tues–Sat 12:30–2pm and 7–10:30pm.

CITY CENTER

Gramadoelas 𝒜𝒜 SOUTH AFRICAN   For nearly 40 years, Eduan Naude and Brian Shalkoff have entertained royals, rock stars, presidents, and audiences from all over Africa in this marvelously cluttered restaurant in Newtown's Cultural Precinct. Not everyone enjoys the food, and the menu sometimes sacrifices excellence in favor of authenticity, but Sen. Hillary Clinton apparently loved the mopani worms *(masonja)*, and the *umnqusho*, a mixture of braised beef shins, beans, and maize, is Mandela's favorite. The *mogodu*, a black tripe and wild African spinach stew, is a hit with those looking for truly traditional fare. For the more timid, there are prawns and the mild Cape-Malay vegetarian and meat curries; ostrich filet and deep-fried crocodile are also worth considering.

Market Theatre Complex, Bree St., Newtown. ℂ 011/838-6960. www.gramadoelas.co.za. Main courses R50–R150 ($7.45–$22). AE, DC, MC, V. Tues–Sat noon–3pm; Mon–Sat 6:30–11pm.

Kapitan's Oriental Restaurant 𝒜 INDIAN   At 90 years, this is Jozi's oldest restaurant—Papa Kapitan, who regularly does the rounds with his wife, fondly remembers Mandela sampling his first Campari here—and it's still going strong. Popular with tourists and businessmen from the nearby Anglo-American and De Beers headquarters (they also love the large selection of Cuban cigars), Kapitan's is where you come for a sense of authentic history (the decor retains its kitsch '50s sensibility), and a fiery curry (the chicken or mutton *vindaloo* is a popular choice) washed down with a local beer.

11A Kort St., Johannesburg. ℂ 011/834-8048. Reservations recommended. Most main courses R35 ($5.20). AE, DC, MC, V. Mon–Sat noon–3pm.

Celeb-Spotting in a Township Tavern

Calvin Klein and Richard Branson are just two of the many luminaries to have signed the walls of **Wandie's Place** 𝒜𝒜𝒜, 618 Makhalamele St., Dube Township, Soweto (ℂ 011/326-1700; www.wandies.co.za), after stopping by to sample the traditional African fare at this legendary township tavern. Even if cow's hooves and sheep's head aren't on the menu—selections change regularly—you'll be sure to discover tasty, exotic flavors you'll be raving about to friends back home. While you're here, do take time to chat to Wandie himself; he may just convince you to forsake your hotel and spend the night in the adjacent guesthouse. *Note:* Wandie's features on the itinerary of practically every Soweto tour.

CITY OUTSKIRTS

The Cradle ✰✰ FRENCH/ITALIAN   Located on the vast nature reserve, The Cradle, part of the Cradle of Humankind World Heritage Site (see "The Cradle: Origin of Humankind," below), is where monied Jo'burgers flee for a country fix in sublime surrounds. The food is good, but it's the views of the reserve that are outstanding—as you tuck into venison curry or tear into grilled ostrich filet with a berry jus, you can watch for passing giraffe, white rhino, zebra, or wildebeest. For a table on the viewing deck outside, however, you'll need to book well in advance; in fact, always phone ahead because the place is regularly booked out for weddings, and during the week, it's available only for groups. If watching doesn't suffice, reserve a Cradle game drive or a bush walk with a ranger (R110/$16 and R40/$5.95, respectively, per person) to explore the grassland plains, or request a visit to one of the Cradle's paleoanthropological digs where excavations are taking place.

Kromdraai Rd. Take R512 to Kromdraai, turn off, then follow signs. ✆ 011/659-1622. www.thecradle.co.za. Reservations essential, particularly for Sun lunch. Main courses R48–R88 ($7.15–$13); Sun lunch fixed-price menu R170 ($25). AE, DC, MC, V. Fri–Sat noon–2:30pm and 6:30–9:30; Sun noon–4pm; Mon–Thurs open only for groups of 20 or more.

WHAT TO SEE & DO
THE TOP ATTRACTIONS

Apartheid Museum ✰✰✰   Many visitors passing through this world-class museum find themselves emotionally unsettled by its meticulous chronicling of apartheid history. Your journey through the modernist concrete structure begins when you are given an entry pass labeling you as either white or nonwhite; you wander through galleries of massive identification cards emphasizing the dehumanizing aspect of racial profiling. A life-size photograph of an all-white race classification board greets you, as do newspaper reports about the board's ridiculous methods (such as sports preferences). It's an emotionally taxing start to a journey that grows in intensity as the history of South African racial segregation and resulting political turmoil is played out in vivid photographs, well-researched textual displays, and gut-wrenching video footage. Besides paying tribute to the triumphs of black political leaders and white liberals who contributed to democracy, several installations and spaces evoke the dreadful horrors of apartheid rule, like the bleak hangman's nooses symbolizing the number of political prisoners executed during apartheid rule until as late as 1989. You can also lock yourself in one of three desperately tiny solitary confinement cells that would have serviced prisoners facing lengthy periods of detention without trial. It's impossible not to be moved by displays, but the museum also chronicles the immense miracle of reform and democratization. Give yourself at least an hour and a half. *Note:* If the history of South Africans struggling against apartheid is of particular interest to you, you may want to visit Kliptown, the site of **The People Shall Govern Exhibition,** part of an Open Air Museum opening mid-2005, and devoted to the story of the Freedom Charter.

6km (3¾ miles) south of city center. Use directions to Gold Reef City (below), or take Boysens Dr. turnoff (off M1) and follow signs. ✆ 011/309-4700. www.apartheidmuseum.org. Admission R25 ($4) adults, R12 ($1.85) children. Tues–Sun 10am–5pm.

Constitution Hill ✰✰   On a hill overlooking the inner city, this is Jo'burg's answer to Cape Town's popular Robben Island attraction, but is a living tribute to the country's fundamental freedoms and human rights, housing South Africa's architecturally provocative **Constitutional Court,** where you can view artworks or—in the spirit of transparency—even attend court hearings. Like Robben Island, this is the site of a prison—the notorious 19th-century **Old Fort,** where brutalities of the worst kind were issued forth on innocents in the name of apartheid; both Nelson Mandela and Mahatma Gandhi were detained here. A guided tour includes **Number Four,** the scene of much human torture and now replaced by an exhibition that attempts to unearth the notion of criminality. A work in progress, involving some of the city's best architects, Constitution Hill centers on **Constitution Square,** a central piazza, where you'll find two stairwells that belonged to the original "Awaiting Trial Block" of the prison; a wall here is filled with a range of comments made by South Africans as the country attained freedom.

Constitution Hill, Braamfontein. ℂ 011/274-5300. www.constitutionhill.org.za. Museum entrance R15 ($2.25) adults. Daily 9am–5pm.

Gold Reef City (Kids)

Six kilometers (3¾ miles) south of the city center, Gold Reef City is built around the No. 14 Crown mine shaft that began operating in 1887 and, by the time of its closure in 1975, had produced over 1,400 tons of gold. A re-creation of the Victorian town of the gold-rush era, the "city" houses a variety of gold-related exhibits and museums, of which the most interesting is the 200m (656-ft.) descent into the old mine shaft, after which you can watch demonstrations of gold being poured and minted. Make sure you time your visit to coincide with a performance by the **gumboot and traditional dancers** ★★—by far the best entertainment on offer (at least for adults). These take place two to three times a day; call for times. Essentially, Gold Reef City is a theme park, and during the school holidays its target audience becomes apparent as teenagers jostle for space on rides like the Anaconda roller coaster and Tower of Terror, and toddlers screech as they trundle past on the Prospector Train. (At press time, however, the proprietors of Gold Reef City were in the process of litigating against an investigative television program for alleging that the rides here are on the verge of falling apart; do check with your Johannesburg hosts what the outcome is.) Adults can take an emotional roller-coaster ride in the adjacent casino, reached via a skybridge, or enjoy jazz along with African-fusion dining at **Back O' The Moon Restaurant** (ℂ 011/496-1423). It's plenty of fun for the family, but for a more exciting experience, visit a *real* mine (see "Mine & Money Tours," earlier in this chapter).

Off Xavier Rd. (off M1), Ormonde. ℂ 011/248-6800. www.goldreefcity.co.za. Admission R80 ($12); includes all rides, shows, and entertainment except mine tour, which costs R50 ($7.45). Free for children under 1.2m (4 ft.). Tues–Sun 9:30am–5pm.

Hector Pieterson Memorial & Museum ★★

Erected in memory of the 1976 student protest, when police opened fire on hundreds of Sowetan schoolchildren who were peacefully demonstrating against the use of Afrikaans as a medium of instruction in their schools. Inside are video footage of the event and many moving photographs taken by brave and talented photographers like Peter Mangubane and Sam Nzima, including the infamous shot of Hector Pieterson—one of the young boys who died in a hail of police bullets—being carried by a young man whose face is contorted in disbelief and pain. Hector's sister runs alongside, her mouth a silent wail of grief. The police reported 59 dead; the actual toll was thought to be closer to 500. Children turned on their parents, something hitherto unheard of in traditional society, and destroyed everything they could belonging to municipal authority—schools, post offices, and the ubiquitous beer halls. The police retaliated with brutal assaults, arrests,

Fun Fact **The Cradle: Origin of Humankind**

"There is more evidence for the origin of humankind in this valley than in any other site in the world," says Dr. Lee Berger, the director of the Wits' (Witwatersrand University) Unit for Research and Exploration in Paleoanthropology. "Who knows what secrets it will still unlock about our common ancestry?" It's incredible to think that 3 million years ago, while cities like New York and London were under permanent ice caps, this very valley was populated with man's ancestors. The **Cradle of Humankind** ✸✸✸, as the valley is now known, first leapt to fame in 1947 when Dr. Robert Broom discovered "Mrs. Ples," the first known adult cranium of an "ape man," dating back 2.5 million years, in the **Sterkfontein Caves.** Named a World Heritage Site because it is one of the most productive paleontological sites in the world, the valley has continued to produce record-breaking finds, including "Little Foot," a complete skull and skeleton found in 1997, in an area still under excavation. In 2003, a team of South African and U.S. scientists, using a revolutionary new dating method, placed the age of Little Foot at 4.17 million years old, a million years older than first thought—fueling one of the most strident debates raging in South African science. These are the most easily accessed hominid digs in the world—ironic, really, considering the fact that, prior to 1994, evolution was a banned topic in South African schools. To visit, see "Guided Tours: Cradle of Humankind Tours," earlier in this chapter.

and killings. These photographs offer a window on the anger, the fear, the aggression, and the grief of these times, after which Soweto and South Africa were never to be the same.

Hector Pieterson Sq., corner of Khumalo and Pela sts., Orlano West, Soweto. © 011/536-0611. Admission R10 ($1.50). Mon–Sat 10am–5pm; Sun 10am–4:30pm.

Johannesburg Art Gallery ✸✸ Predictably, the city's first gallery was financed with the sale of a diamond. In 1904 Lady Phillips, wife of the first chairman of the Rand Mines Company, sold her 21-carat ring to purchase three paintings by Wilson Steer. Over the next 5 years, she wrangled money from her wealthy connections to purchase more artwork, and commissioned Sir Edwin Lutyens to design the elegant building that now houses her collection. It is unfortunate that the gallery lies in the rather seedy center of town, but you should have no problem if you drive in, and secure parking is available. The rather dull Flemish and Dutch collections are made up for by the Brenthurst Collection of African Art, comprising curios plundered by European explorers in the 19th century, and later collections of traditional southern African artworks. Happily, despite ignoring black talent during the apartheid years, the gallery now also has a good selection of South Africa's most renowned, including sculptures by Venda artist Jackson Hlungwani and paintings by Helen Sebidi, Alfred Toba, and Gerard Sekoto. That said, recent remonstrations in the press contend that a lack of artistic direction means that current artists are totally underrepresented.

Klein St., Joubert Park. © 011/725-3130. Free admission. Tues–Sun 10am–5pm. To reach the secure parking: From the M1, take the Wolmarans turnoff and turn left, then right onto Wanderers, and second left onto Bok, which runs into Klein; entrance off Klein.

Soweto: Touring South Africa's Biggest Township

Dispossessed of their land during the 1800s and further reduced to virtual slavery by taxation, thousands of black men were forced to find work in the minefields of eGoli. As more and more settled in inner-city slums, the segregationist government's concerns about the proximity of blacks to white suburbs grew until, in 1930, a solution was found. A farm 11 miles to the southwest of Johannesburg was designated as the new township, and blacks living in and around the city were served with eviction papers. It would now take 3 hours to get to work. There were as yet no roads, no shops, no parks, no electricity, no running water. Public transport and policing were hopelessly inadequate. Not surprisingly, most people refused to move, but in 1933, the government declared the Slums Clearance Act and forcibly evicted blacks from the inner cities. Defeated, these new homeless moved in, and Soweto, acronym for the South Western Township, was born, just 18km (11 miles) from Johannesburg. In 1944 James Mpanza led a mass occupation of open land near Orlando, the original heart of Soweto, and within 2 years, this, the country's first unofficial squatter camp, housed 40,000 people. Rural poverty meant that Soweto remained a magnet for millions searching for a better standard of living, and today Soweto is arguably South Africa's largest city and home to soccer heroes and politicos, record producers and shebeen queens, multimillionaires and the unemployed, murderers and Nobel Peace Prize winners. Population estimates range from two million to four million; with people mistrusting the reasons for compiling a national census, a proper headcount is virtually impossible.

Very few white South Africans venture here for pleasure, despite the warm welcome Sowetans are famous for and the fact that the few *umlungu* (whitey) inhabitants of Soweto say they feel safer here than in the suburbs. For most, however, the crime statistics are frightening: Murders are common, and it is estimated that a rape occurs every 30 minutes. For safety and real insight, Soweto is best visited accompanied by a knowledgeable guide. Most operators cover similar ground: the **Mandelas' old home;** a stop at the **Hector Pieterson Memorial** (see above); a drive down **Vilakazi Street,** the only street in the world to have housed two Nobel Prize winners; **Freedom Square,** where the ANC's Freedom Charter was proclaimed to thousands in 1956; and the **Regina Mundi Church,** the "Parliament of Soweto," where the bullet-marked walls are witness to ex-security-police brutality. Recommended operators are **Jimmy's Face to Face Tours** (© **011/331-6109; 3-hr.** day tours R295/$44, if departing from Jo'burg), the more personalized **Imbiza Tours** (© **011/838-2667;** R300/$45, plus R70/$10 for lunch), and long-standing Sowetan resident Stella Dubazana (© **082/488-1660**), who offers private tours on arrangement. The downside of driving around in a bus armed with a camera is the sense that you are treating people like animals in a reserve. For this reason, you are encouraged to get out of the vehicle and talk to the people on the street. It is, after all, a sense of community that distinguishes life in Soweto from that in Johannesburg or Pretoria.

Lesedi Cultural Village ★★   The Lesedi Cultural Village comprises four totally separate homesteads, inhabited, respectively, by a Zulu, Xhosa, Pedi, and Basotho family, all of whom live here permanently looking after the cows, chickens, and tourists that wander through the veld. The 3-hour tour commences at 11:30am and 4:30pm daily—opt for the latter, as it's a great deal more atmospheric at night. On arrival you are given a welcome drink and a 30-minute presentation on these tribes (as well as a short talk on the Ndebele), followed by a guided walk through the four homesteads, which allows for interesting cross-cultural analysis regarding the architectural and social organization and customs of these groups. The tour does not really cover current lifestyles and customs, so you'll have to ask questions to find out what changes the 20th century has wrought. After this, a traditional singing and dancing session is held in the *boma* (a circular open-air enclosure), and a pan-African buffet meal is served. Lesedi is a commercial venture, but if you're yearning to do the cultural village thing, this is a convenient 45-minute trip from Johannesburg. The easiest way to visit is with a tour operator (see "Guided Tours" at the beginning of the chapter); expect to pay about R700 ($104) for the full experience and transfer.

Off the R512; phone for directions. ✆ 012/205-1394. Tours commence daily at 11:30am and 4:30pm. R170 ($25) for tour only; R260 ($39) for tour with lunch or dinner.

MuseuMAfricA ★   Housed in the old Market Building, and part of the cosmopolitan hub that is the Newtown Cultural Precinct, MuseuMAfricA was opened in 1994 as the first national museum to offer a truly modern take on the complex history of South Africa. The best permanent exhibit is "Tried for Treason," an evocative display using video interviews, old radio broadcasts, newspaper headlines, and photographs to tell the tale of the Treason Trial (1956–61), which put, among others, Nelson Mandela behind bars on Robben Island. "Johannesburg Transformations" includes walk-through re-creations of shacks, a miners' dorm, and a shebeen (illegal drinking house). As you explore these makeshift rooms, you are accompanied by a soundtrack comprising some well-selected numbers from the musical giants that Sophiatown and Soweto spawned, like Miriam Makeba and Hugh Masekela.

121 Bree St., Newtown. ✆ 011/833-5624. Free admission. Tues–Sun 9am–5pm.

MORE ATTRACTIONS: FROM AFRICAN ART TO JO'BURG ZOO

Most city tours kick off from the **"Top of Africa"** ★★ (✆ 011/308-2876; daily 8am–7pm; R7.50/$1.10), and with good reason. The top floor of the 50-story Carlton Centre provides great views of the city, and it has a bar, should you time your visit at sunset (from 5:30pm in winter) and wish to toast the city of gold as it turns pink. Access is relatively easy: From the M1, follow the M2 East/City signs, take the Rissik Street turnoff, continue along Rissik, and turn left into Marshall, where you'll see the parking sign for the Carlton Towers.

⟮*Fun Fact*⟯ **City Limits**

Note how the skyscrapers suddenly fall away a few blocks south of Commissioner Street? This is because gold-mine tunnels run beneath this part of the city, making the ground highly unstable for high-rise construction.

Bridging the Gap

Jo'burg's skyline changed forever in 2003 when Nelson Mandela inaugurated a 284m-long (932-ft.) bridge named in his honor. Providing a welcome link between Newtown Cultural Precinct and Braamfontein's Constitution Hill, the imposing steel-and-concrete landmark is symbolic of the determined efforts to renew the inner city and a towering tribute to the nation's favorite leader.

ARCHITECTURE   Buildings worth noting on a short city central driving tour are the **Rand Club,** Loveday Street (call Tony Thomson at ✆ 011/834-8311 to arrange permission), where the city's mining magnates, or "randlords," used to congregate and compare (bank) notes, as well as the **Magistrate's Court** (West St.), the **Gauteng Legislature** (Harrison St.), the **Public Library** (corner of Market and Sauer sts.), the **Post Office** (corner of Market and Rissik sts.), and the **Rand Supreme Court** (Pritchard St.).

Diagonal Street 𝒶𝒶, where you'll find the old beacon marking the southwest corner of the original farm from which Johannesburg grew, is one of the city's most fascinating. In the shadows of striking skyscrapers—the most impressive of which is **De Beers** or **"Diamond House"** (11 Diagonal St.), which was designed to mimic the facets of the gem upon which the company's fortune was built—are myriad street hawkers and tiny shops selling anything from Sotho blankets to traditional medicine *(muti).* The most famous of these is **Museum of Man and Science,** 14 Diagonal St. (✆ 011/836-4470)—it's worth stopping here to stoop under the herbs, bark, and pungent animal bits that hang like a stalactite forest from the ceiling. The Johannesburg Stock Exchange was located at 17 Diagonal St. until 2000, when it followed the trend started by big business in the late 1980s and relocated to the northern suburbs.

MUSEUMS   Moving west to the **Newtown Cultural Precinct** to view **MuseuM-AfricA** (see "The Top Attractions," above), you may wish to tour the **SAB World of Beer,** 15 President St., Newtown (✆ 011/836-4900; Tues–Sat 10am–6pm; 90-min. tour R10/$1.50), which showcases the hops' heritage, from ancient Mesopotamia to a traditional Soweto shebeen. The nearby **Worker's Library Museum,** 52 Jeppe St. (✆ 011/834-1609; daily 8:30am–4:30pm; free admission), in a national monument that housed approximately 400 municipal workers from 1910, shows the iniquitous living conditions of migrant labor, including a punitive "lock-up" room.

ART GALLERIES   Located near the Rand Club, the **Standard Bank Art Gallery** 𝒶, corner of Simmonds and Frederick streets (✆ 011/636-4231), which displays some of the work of the best contemporary South African artists as well as the World Press photography awards, is a must for art lovers. (Call ahead to arrange off-street parking.) Deep in the bowels of the Johannesburg Civic Theatre (Loveday St.,) in Braamfontein, you can usually catch some innovative artwork in the small gallery space known as **The Premises** (✆ 011/877-6859; Tues–Sat noon–8pm), which is run by one of the city's most prolific art collectives, the Trinity Sessions. The Premises includes an outdoor terrace overlooking a landscaped piazza that suggests the envisioned tone for Johannesburg's rapidly evolving **Cultural Arc**—the area from Newtown to Constitution Hill. Across the piazza are the beautiful new studios of the South African Ballet Theatre.

OUTDOOR PLEASURES   If the concrete jungle starts to get to you, the **Melville Koppies Nature Reserve** has a nature trail that ends at an Iron Age settlement. It's open the first three Sundays of each month (call ℂ **011/788-7571** for times). A guided tour is recommended; call Wendy Carstens (ℂ **011/482-4797**). On the northeast corner of the reserve is the city's **Botanical Garden,** which reputedly has the largest rose garden in Africa, best enjoyed late September. The garden lies on the banks of the Emmerentia Dam; enter off Thomas Bolwer Street. Alternatively, take a stroll or row around **Zoo Lake,** the city's finest park and a great place to take kids. Across the road is the **Johannesburg Zoo,** Jan Smuts Avenue (ℂ **011/646-2000;** daily 8:30am–5:30pm; R30/$4.45 adults, R18/$2.70 children, R10/$1.50 parking), through which you can access the surprisingly popular **Museum of Military History** (ℂ **011/646-5513;** daily 9am–4:30pm; R10/$1.50 adults, R5/75¢ children). Along with examples of tanks and aircraft (a Messerschmitt Me-262 jet is one of only two to have survived), a submarine, swords, guns, uniforms, and medals from both world wars, it houses mementos from every civil war South Africa has fought.

If you've always dreamed of cuddling with a lion cub, the 208-hectare (514-acre) **Lion Park** (ℂ **011/460-1814;** www.lion-park.com; daily 8:30am–5pm; R65/$9.70 adults, R45/$6.70 children) is a 35- to 40-minute drive northwest of Sandton. If you'd like to see more than just lions, the 1,480-hectare (3,700-acre) **Rhino & Lion Nature Reserve** (ℂ **011/957-0109;** Mon–Fri 8am–5pm, Sat–Sun 8am–6pm; R70/$10 adult, R40/$5.95 children under 12), 45 to 50 minutes northwest of Sandton, boasts 30 species. While the buffalo, zebra, wildebeest, and antelope roam free, predators are kept in large enclosures, and it's little more than a comfortable zoo. Be warned, however, that the animals are not as tame as they look: Stepping out of his minibus for a better photo once cost a visitor an arm and a leg—really. If you're there on a Sunday, coincide your visit with the nearby **Heia Safari Ranch** 🏵 (ℂ **011/659-0605;** R160/$24 adults, R80/$12 children, including barbecue), where Mzumba tribal dances take place from 2 to 4:30pm. Unless you're obsessed with spotting lion, the best option of all the above is lunch and a game drive, bush walk, or horse trail at the **Cradle Reserve.**

A SIDE TRIP TO PRETORIA/TSHWANE

Once an Afrikaner stronghold, South Africa's administrative and diplomatic capital has become home to a much more cosmopolitan population since Nelson Mandela was inaugurated the first democratically elected president at its **Union Buildings** 🏵🏵, Meintjieskop Ridge, Arcadia (ℂ **012/325-2000**), a change somewhat symbolized by its hotly contested new name, Tshwane.

With the best views of the city, the Union Buildings are a great place to orient yourself, even though access has become much more restricted since the inauguration of Thabo Mbeki. Probably the best-known creation of prolific "British Imperial" architect

---

Up, Up & Away

Discover the most picturesque part of Gauteng, the **Magalies River Valley,** with **Bill Harrop's "Original" Balloon Safaris** (ℂ 011/705-3201; www.balloon.co.za), also located northwest of Johannesburg. Flights cost R1,995 ($298) per person, last about an hour, and include sparkling wine (served onboard) and a hot breakfast on landing. Flights depart from the balloon launch site at Hartebeespoort Dam.

The Great Toaster

In 1938 the secretive Afrikaner *Broederbond* (brotherhood) organized a symbolic reenactment of the Great Trek and sent a team of ox-wagons from Cape Town to Pretoria to celebrate its centenary. By the time the wagons reached Pretoria, more than 200,000 Afrikaners had joined, all of whom camped at Monument Hill, where the foundation stones for a monument were laid. Ten years later, the **Voortrekker Monument** ☆☆ was completed, and the Afrikaner Nationalist Party swept to power. This massive granite structure, sometimes compared irreverently to a large Art Deco toaster, dominates the skyline at the southern entrance to Pretoria. Commemorating the Great Trek, in particular the Battle of Blood River, fought on December 16, 1838, the monument remains hallowed ground for many Afrikaners. Every year on that date, exactly at noon, a ray of sunlight lights up a central plaque that reads WE FOR YOU SOUTH AFRICA. The "we" refers, of course, to Afrikaners—in the marble frieze surrounding the lower hall depicting the Trek and Battle, you will find no carvings of the many black slaves who aided the Boers in their victory. The museum below has memorabilia relating to the Great Trek; most interesting is the "female" version of the monument frieze—huge tapestries depicting a romanticized version of the Great Trek's social events. Even more interesting than this sanitized take on the pioneer days are the photographs of the "tannies" (literally "aunties," an Afrikaans term of respect) who created these tapestries. They are the perfect foil to the Afrikaner men: ladies plaiting threads while the men wrest with stone in the monument. The Voortrekker Monument and Museum is situated 6km (3¾ miles) south of the city. Call ✆ 012/326-6770 for details, or organize a visit through a tour operator.

Sir Herbert Baker, the buildings—the administrative headquarters of the South African government and the office of the president since 1913—are generally considered his finest achievement. The office-block wings are said to represent the British and Afrikaner people, linked in reconciliation by the curved amphitheater. African natives were, of course, not represented, nor were they allowed to enter the buildings except to clean. In 1994 the buildings and gardens were the scene of huge emotional jubilation as everyone from Castro to Al Gore witnessed the inauguration of Mandela, South Africa's first black president, and African praise-singers in traditional garb exorcised the ghosts of the past. Visitors are allowed to walk along Government Avenue, the road that traverses the facade, but entrance is gained only by those on official business. Anyone interested in a truly in-depth interpretation of the symbols and mythology of the building and its maker should call tour guide Leone Jackson (✆ 012/344-3197).

The rest of Pretoria's **city center** can be explored on foot. The city grew around diminutive **Church Square,** which is surrounded by an array of impressive buildings that were funded by the discovery of gold in 1886; it makes sense to start here. In the center is Anton van Wouw's **statue** of a dour Paul Kruger, facing north (no doubt away from the British). On the southwest corner is the **Old Raadsaal,** completed in 1891; directly opposite are the **Palace of Justice,** on the northwest corner, and the original **South African Reserve Bank** (like the Union Buildings, designed by Herbert Baker). East of this are a number of banks; **Cuthberts Corner,** dating back to 1904 when George Heys (of **Melrose House**) used to run his coaching operation from here; and the neoclassical **Standard Bank,** built in 1935.

After visiting the tourism office, located in the 1896 **Netherlands Bank Building,** pop in at neighboring **Café Riche,** 2 Church Sq. (*©* **012/328-3173**), Pretoria's oldest cafe.

West of the Square, on Church Street, is **Kruger House,** Church Street West (*©* **012/326-9172;** Mon–Fri 8:30am–4:30pm, Sat–Sun 9am–4:30pm). Built in 1884, the house is on every tour group's itinerary, but because most of the furnishings are simply of the period rather than the very things Paul and his wife lived with, the house does little to conjure up the spirit of the man (for this, a guided tour, available for R15/$2.25, is well advised). A boy during the arduous Great Trek north, and present at the Battle of Blood River, this first president of the ZAR (Zuid Afrikaanse Republiek) was known as a pious, stern Calvinist. He was also oddly approachable and would hold court on his veranda, chatting to anyone passing by—provided they were white, of course. Here are personal pieces, including his pipes, spittoons, and the knife he used to amputate his thumb after a hunting accident; but the best exhibit is a photograph of the cantankerous old codger sitting next to the stone lions that still guard the entrance to the house. Opposite is the church in which he preached. Nearby, you'll find **Heroes Acre,** the burial place for a number of historical figures.

Moving east down Church Street, you'll come across **Strijdom Square,** once a fresh produce market, where the ugly bust of even uglier former prime minister J. G. Strijdom, a staunch supporter of white rule in the 1950s, came tumbling down on May 31, 2001, exactly 40 years after South Africa was declared a republic. (The square has come to have a more sinister connotation since 1993, when namesake Barend Strijdom opened fire here on random black targets. Despite showing no remorse, he was subsequently released under political amnesty.)

Five blocks north of Church Square, along Paul Kruger Street, is Boom Street; turn right here for the **zoo** (with 3,500 animals, some of them extremely rare, it's touted as one of the best zoos in the world, where you can catch a cableway across its length, letting you view the animals from the air) or turn left to reach **Marabastad,** where Pretoria's Indian community trades. Alternatively, move south down Paul Kruger to the uninspiring **Transvaal Museum,** Paul Kruger Street (*©* **012/322-7632**); still, **"The Genesis of Life,"** an exhibition relating the development of early man based largely on fossil finds at the Sterkfontein and Kromdraai caves, is interesting. Two blocks west of here, on Schubart Street, is **The African Window,** entered from 149 Visagie St. (*©* **012/324-6082;** daily 8am–4pm), Pretoria's modern cultural history museum, and an attempt to celebrate the diverse cultures that make up the South African community.

How Do Those Cats Survive?

Internationally renowned for its success in both breeding and researching endangered species, the **De Wildt Cheetah and Wildlife Centre** offers an opportunity to observe cheetah, king cheetah, brown hyena, and the African wild dog up close—with between 3,000 and 5,000 left in the world, the latter is Africa's most endangered predator. The 3-hour guided tours are by arrangement only; either set one up as part of a tour or call *©* **012/504-1921** or -1922. De Wildt is 45 minutes north of Pretoria.

Two blocks south of the Transvaal Museum, turning left onto Jacob Mare, you'll find **Melrose House** (© **012/322-2805;** Tues–Sun 10am–5pm), a neobaroque mansion—mixing English Victorian and Cape Dutch styles—built in 1886 for George Heys, who made his fortune in stagecoach transportation. Melrose House has been carefully restored to ensure its authenticity, and the furnishings are little changed since the Heys family lived here.

Art lovers shouldn't miss **The Pretoria Art Museum** ☆☆, Arcadia Park, corner of Wessels and Schoeman streets (© **012/344-1807;** Tues and Thurs–Sat 10am–5pm, Wed 10am–8pm, Sun noon–5pm), which owns over 3,000 artworks and showcases some of South Africa's rich and varied talent in bland spaces that allow the art to dominate. Besides the country's best collection of work by white South African artists (including an even better collection of Pierneefs than the Pierneef Museum on Vermeulen St.), there is a growing representation of black artists, including the celebrated Sekoto and Ephraim Ngatane. The prebooked guided tour is recommended.

SHOPPING—FLEA MARKETS TO HIGH-END CRAFTS

Johannesburg attracts people from all over the continent with one sole purpose: to shop till they drop. To that end, the city has more than 20 malls to choose from, but the best atmosphere by far is found in **Rosebank,** which has plenty of outdoor areas to break the monotony of mall shopping as well as a good selection of essentials such as travel agents and music, book, fashion, and crafts shops (see below). The rooftop at **Rosebank Mall,** which is open every Sunday and public holidays from 9:30am to 5pm, hosts the city's best market. Adjacent to the rooftop market, but open daily, is the worthwhile **African Craft Market** (© **011/880-2906;** 9am–5pm winter, 9am–6pm summer), where you can shop for artifacts and artworks from across the continent.

CITY CENTER & SURROUNDS   The **Newtown Cultural Precinct** has a small market that operates daily, but the best place to look for indigenous handicrafts in Newtown is the shop at the **Bus Factory** ☆☆, 1 President St. (© **011/834-9569;** Mon–Fri 9am–5pm, Sat 10am–4pm), located in a 1930s transport depot that was revamped as part of the regeneration of Newtown. Administered by the Craft Council, under the excellent curatorship of Susan Sellschop, the Bus Factory showcases the finest crafts pieces available in the country. Other places of interest in the city include **Diagonal Street**—look for Sotho blankets—and the **Mai Mai Bazaar** under the M1. The latter sells mostly to the Zulu community, and you're best off visiting here with a guide.

Less than 1km (just over ½-mile) from Newtown (follow Jeppe St. into Fordsburg) is the **Oriental Plaza** ☆ (© **011/838-6752**), a shopping center where Johannesburg's shrewd Indian traders barter and cajole. Look for fabrics, cotton clothing, brasswares, and, of course, spices. This is also a great place to sample *samoosas,* fried meat- or vegetable-filled pastry triangles. A stone's throw from the Plaza is the **Bag Factory,** 10 Minaar St. (© **011/834-9181;** www.bagfactoryart.org.za; Mon–Fri 9am–4pm), an art gallery officially known as the Fordsburg Artists' Studios (FAS); it was a dilapidated ex-bag-factory building until being converted to a multicultural studio facility for professional artists. Standards vary, but visitors are invited to negotiate sales with individual artists.

NORTHERN & NORTHWESTERN SUBURBS   **Rural Craft** ☆☆ (© **011/788-5821**), in Rosebank's Mutual Gardens, Shop 42E (opposite Old Mutual Bank), markets goods on behalf of the Crafts Association of South Africa, and all profits are returned to the communities. Also in Mutual Gardens is **Batanai Artworks** (© **011/880-1004;** www.batanai.co.za), where the talents of a pool of artists from all over southern Africa are showcased. Fashionistas looking for distinctive "where-did-you-get-that?" designer items need to head for The Zone and browse **The Space** ⚓, lower level (© **011/327-3640**); next door is **Sun Godd'ess** ⚓, a small boutique for real African goddesses. Upstairs at **Stoned Cherrie** ⚓, opposite Primi Piatti restaurant (© **011/447-9629**), you'll find more of the best Afro-chic threads in town. Also upstairs at The Zone is **The Y-Store** (© **011/ 887-7070**); it's operated by Y-FM, the country's hippest black urban radio station, and it's where you'll find the clothes and accessories Jozi's trendiest young hipsters are wearing. Right next door is **Compact Disc Wherehouse** (© **011/788-9831**), where staff can assist with a selection of African music.

JOHANNESBURG AFTER DARK
THE PERFORMING ARTS

The **Market Theatre,** on Bree Street, Newtown (© **011/832-1641**), is famous for having spawned a generation of protest theater, and is likely to have a good selection of local talent. The **Johannesburg Civic Theatre,** Loveday Street, Braamfontein (© **011/877-6800;** www.showbusiness.co.za), is one of the largest and most technologically advanced theaters in the country; this is where large-scale musicals, operas, dance, and orchestral music are performed. Also see what's on at Tshwane's **Spoornet State Theatre,** 320 Pretorius St. (© **012/392-4027**): It's a regular venue for some of the country's biggest and most expensive productions, as well as many of the shows overlooked by Johannesburg's Civic Theatre; smaller, more colloquial plays and comedies are also performed here. Back in Jozi, the **Wits Theatre Complex,** corner of Jorissen and Station streets, Braamfontein (© **011/717-1372**), attracts a wide variety of local and international theater talent, including good dance productions; quality varies, so be informed.

Good-quality local productions of major international shows can also be found in some of the city's lavish casinos; best of the bunch is **Pieter Toerien's Montecasino Theatre,** William Nicol Drive, Fourways (© **011/511-1818**), set in a Tuscan-themed casino village. Gold Reef City's **Globe Theatre** (© **011/248-5168**) runs musicals and revues of the chorus-line variety.

For current listings for all these venues and more, check out the daily "Tonight" section in *The Star,* and the weekly *Mail & Guardian* (www.mg.co.za). Tickets for most shows can be booked and paid for by phone; call **Computicket** (© **011/340-8000** or 083-131; www.computicket.com).

THE CLUB, BAR & MUSIC SCENE

In a city where work is everything, social interaction is an important distraction. You'll discover a seemingly endless selection and variety of bars, pubs, clubs, and downright sleazy drinking holes. If you like to club- or bar-hop, several areas have a concentration of options—in fact, cruising from venue to venue is a popular after-dark pastime, spawning the label "Jo'burg Joller" (Johannesburg party-animal), applied to some of the city's BMW- and Mercedes-driving cliques. Many of the larger clubs are in otherwise missable neighborhoods and require some driving to reach. More accessible is the trendy, Eurocentric **Melrose Arch,** a chic playground for Johannesburg's rich and famous and their friends, with stylish restaurants and bars lined up along one street, well lit with plenty of parking. **Melville,** close to central Johannesburg, features a mixed bag of restaurants and bars within walking distance of each other in "old"

Melville (7th St.) or "new" Melville (Main Ave.). Along 7th Street, the evening starts before dark; you can rub shoulders with artists, journalists, and performers at Mozambican-themed **Xai-Xai,** or cross the road to mingle with the black intelligentsia at **Spiro's.** Then enjoy a relaxing cocktail at gay-friendly **Statement, Sixt** next door or mellow **Berlin** before hitting one of the rowdier drinking holes: **Buzz 9, Ratz,** and **Tokyo Star** (off 7th St.) are all popular with students. Note that, in Melville, when the venues fill up, the party simply spills out onto the road, so drive with caution. Between Melville and the city, **The Color Bar** (see below), in Milpark, is one of Jo'burg's best and most sociable watering holes, attracting a truly mixed crowd. **Newtown,** home of the Market Theatre Precinct, is another area where you'll find a host of clubbing options, reviewed below.

If you're a **jazz** aficionado, some names to watch for are Gloria Bosman, African Jazz Pioneers, Feya Faku, the Sheer All Stars, Andile Yenana, Sipho Mabuse, Lulu Gontsana, Bheki Mbatha, Khaya Mahlangu, Barney Rachabane, Oscar Rachabane, Octavia Rachabane, Herbie Tsoaeli, McCoy Mrubata, Zim Ngqawana, Louis Mhlanga, Linda Kekana, Moses Khumalo, and Pops Mohamed.

Kwaito acts to look for are Brothers of Peace (BO), Mandoza, Mafikizolo, Zola, M'Du, Mzekezeke, Kabelo, Mapaputsi, Bongo Maffin, and Mzambiya.

Clubs generally start up at around 11pm and close between 4am and 7am; most offer secure parking for a small donation to the freelance guards who watch over cars while their owners dance the night away.

Northern Suburbs

The Blues Room 🌟🌟   In the heart of Sandton, this upmarket nightclub serves up live blues, jazz, fusion, comedy, and even rock 'n' roll for an older and mostly white crowd. Village Walk Mall, corner Rivonia and Maude sts., Sandown, Sandton. ✆ **011/784-5527.** www.bluesroom.co.za. Cover R50 ($7.45).

Café Vogue 🌟🌟🌟   A trendy crowd flocks to this Rivonia joint on Thursday (R&B and hip-hop), Friday (fusion), and Saturday (disco and French house). The music is fine and the cocktails are cool. Corner of 9th St. and Wessels Rd., Rivonia. ✆ **011/728-3448.** Cover R30–R60 ($4.45–$8.95).

Kilimanjaro 🌟🌟🌟   Africa's hip and well-heeled love to splurge at this ostentatious club; some say it's gotten too big for its boots and already growing out of fashion; catch it before it's gone. It has a restaurant, bars on two levels, and a stage where jazz, kwaito, and other local acts perform over weekends. Melrose Arch, Melrose. ✆ **011/834-9187.** Cover depends on events.

Melville/Milpark

The Color Bar 🌟🌟🌟   You may take a while getting into the groove of the often highly experimental music choices, but it's easy to understand why the young, smart crowd has made this its after-work hangout. Regular parties are a mainstay, with DJs concocting danceable tunes that give world music a house beat. 44 Stanley Ave., Milpark. ✆ **011/482-2038.** www.colorbar.co.za. Fri–Sat cover starts at R40 ($5.95) after 9:30pm.

Oh! 🌟   The best things in this all-week gay bar are the toned barmen who hand over expensive drinks to a crowd of young and middle-aged men. A spiral stairway leads down to an often cramped dance floor where the music is standard (or worse) commercial house. Expect karaoke on Monday, but look for the occasional party hosted by cross-dressing DJ Thelma Klensch. Corner of 4th Ave. and Main Rd., Melville. ✆ **011/482-4789.**

The Big Road Trip: Johannesburg to Cape Town

You have two choices, should you decide to empty your mind and meditate along the long and relatively empty highways that lead between Jo'burg and Cape Town—a great way to see the country, particularly Route B.

Road Trip A: Drive directly south on the N1 to Bloemfontein, enjoying traditional Afrikaans hospitality at **De Oude Kraal,** a 2,400-hectare (5,928-acre) farm just south of the city of Bloemfontein, about 4 hours from Johannesburg (© **051/564-0636;** www.oudekraal.co.za). Spend the next night at the **Lemoenfontein Game Reserve** (© **023/415-2847;** www.lemoenfontein.co.za); look for the signs 4km (2 ½ miles) north of Beaufort West, and take an early-morning game drive before setting off for the final leg to Cape Town. Alternatively, book into one of the large chalets in the gloriously tranquil **Karoo National Park** (© **021/428-9111,** or direct 023/415-2828; www.sanparks.org), which lies just south of Beaufort West and recently saw the reintroduction of rhino. Cape Town lies 4 hours away. **Total driving time: 13 to 14 hours.**

Road Trip B: Time allowing, this is a road trip you will treasure as one of the most memorable you have ever taken, as it takes you through tiny settler towns, Big 5 game reserves, and some of the most scenically beautiful areas of the country. You should, however, set aside at least a week to do this in comfort. The route is as follows: Head south on the N1 as far as Colesberg, then take the N9 to Graaff-Reinet (a 7½-hr. drive), where you overnight before heading to one of the **malaria-free game reserves** near Grahamstown or Port Elizabeth (see chapter 6 for accommodations recommendations from Graaff-Reinet to Port Elizabeth). After 2 nights at the reserve, travel along the lakes and forests of the **Garden Route,** overnighting in Knysna or Wilderness for a few days (see chapter 4). Cape Town is about 4 hours from here; consider taking the longer route through the Swartberg Pass to overnight at **Prince Albert. Total driving time: 17 to 19 hours.**

Trans-Sky Beat Bar It's small and often packed to capacity, but the matchbox dance floor showcases groovy hipsters getting down well into the small hours at this casual Melville restaurant-bar-club; drum 'n' bass Thursdays are popular, while on Friday and Saturday, the beats are house and trance. 7 7th St., Melville. © **083/604-0832.**

Newtown/City Central

Bassline 𝕬𝕬𝕬   This regular hangout for Jo'burg's multiracial intelligentsia used to be in Melville but reopened in Newtown in 2005. A popular live-music venue for local talent, it offers an assorted lineup, ranging from jazz, blues, and rock bands to hip-hop and world artists. 10 Henry Nxumalo St. © 011/838-9145. www.basslinejazzclub.co.za. Cover varies.

Carfax 𝕬𝕬   Set in an old warehouse, this super-cool venue once catered to the most discerning clubbers. You'll still encounter a wide mix of parties, with everything from performance art to French house parties and hip-hop and jungle nights, but its burgeoning popularity means that it's increasingly mainstream and queues can be long. 39 Pim St., Newtown. © 011/834-9187. Cover depends on events.

Heartlands   Once the center of gay party life in downtown Johannesburg, Heartlands closed several years ago when the previous owners were arrested for drug manufacture. This legendary venue was scheduled to reopen at press time, now with four different venues: **Sugar Reef, Cruise, DCM** (or Don't Cry Mama), and the **Rhino Bar.** Expect valet parking, a varied and up-for-it crowd, drag shows, live bands, and long nights of dance-floor mayhem. Braamfontein. www.heartlands.co.za.

Horror Café 🦍🦍   With brilliant decor consisting of horror and science-fiction movie memorabilia, this vibrant nightspot regularly features hip-hop and deep house parties, while reggae, ragga, jazz, world music, and African rhythms are also heard. 15 Becker St., Newtown. ☎ 011/838-6735. Cover R30–R50 ($4.45–$7.45).

Insanity 🦍🦍   Downtown Jo'burg comes alive on Friday with a multiracial crowd grooving to deep house, drum 'n' bass, and hip-hop, as well as graffiti, break-dancing, and skating displays. 248 Jeppe St., Johannesburg Central. ☎ 011/336-1026. Cover from R30 ($4.45).

Kippies 🦍🦍   This small, laid-back downtown venue in the Market Theatre complex—the city's oldest jazz club—gets crowded when big names in South African jazz play to passionate crowds on Friday and Saturday, and sometimes during the week. Market Theatre, Bree St., Newtown. ☎ 011/833-3316. Cover around R40 ($5.95).

Oneonefive 🦍🦍   Located in the center of town, this small but lively venue throbs with drum 'n' bass and deep house on Friday. On Sunday it is Remedy from 7pm to 2am, a gay club night with funky, uplifting vocal and tribal house. It can get a tad rough when the crowd swells to gargantuan proportions; go only if you're seriously into squeezing through an often impenetrable mass of party animals. 115 Anderson St., Johannesburg Central. ☎ 011/331-2878. Cover R50 ($7.45).

2 Sun City & the Palace of the Lost City

187km (116 miles) NW of Johannesburg

Set within the southern border of the Pilanesberg National Park, this glitzy Vegas-style resort is made up of casinos, cinemas, theaters, restaurants, two world-class golf courses, man-made jungles, lakes, and the Palace of the Lost City, the most over-the-top five-star hotel in Africa. Developer Sol Kerzner, the boxer-turned-businessman known locally as the "Sun King," capitalized on apartheid South Africa's stern antigambling laws by situating Sun City in the then homeland of Bophuthatswana, the hodgepodge of inferior land into which the Tswana were forced. As an "independent" state, headed by the corrupt Lucas Mangope, Bophuthatswana was literally a law unto itself, and millions began to swarm to "Sin City," not only to gamble, but to see international acts like Sinatra, George Benson, and Elton John, who ignored the cultural boycott at the time.

EXPLORING THE RESORT

The resort is relatively easy to get around, and shuttle buses are constantly moving from one end to the next. A **"sky train"** takes visitors without cars from the entrance to the entertainment center. Closest to the entrance are the **Kwena Crocodile Sanctuary, Waterworld,** and **The Cabanas,** followed by the tacky **Sun City Hotel, Casino,** and world-famous **Gary Player Golf Club.** Adjoining this club to the north is the more upmarket **Cascades Hotel and Entertainment Centre,** from where you enter the grounds of the **Palace of the Lost City**—for most visitors, the star attraction.

The Palace was built 12 years after Sun City opened, and the sheer magnitude of its opulence is proof of the amount of money taken from those frequenting Sun City's slot machines and tables. Separated from the rest of the resort by **"The Bridge of Time"**—a large stone structure that shudders and rumbles at preappointed times from a mythical earthquake, and is lined with a "guard of honor" of carved elephants—the Palace is entered through the massive Mighty Kong Gates. Looking down on the rivers and jungle vegetation, you truly feel as if you are entering another world; it's hard to imagine that just a decade ago this was nothing but a dusty, rocky plain. From the bridge, you can clearly see the **"Valley of Waves,"** where landlocked Gautengers learn to surf on simulated waves, tan on man-made beaches, and hurtle down steep water-slides, reaching speeds of up to 35kmph (22 mph; note that the Valley is closed in winter). In the distance, overlooking a lake filled with live flamingos, is the majestic Palace, with what seems like an entire jungle of carved animals in attendance. Surrounding the Palace is what must be the most artfully landscaped garden in Africa, featuring 5 trails through 22 different sections of forest. The theme (that of a "lost city" that has been rediscovered and restored) is sometimes carried to ridiculous extremes, but the craftsmanship is world class; the fantasy landscape is quite overwhelming. With Michael Jackson a regular visitor and now the majority shareholder, things can only get weirder.

SUN CITY ESSENTIALS

A number of tour operators offer day trips to Sun City (see "Guided Tours" in Johannesburg and Pretoria, earlier in this chapter). Alternatively, you can fly to Sun City on **SA Airlink** (✆ 011/978-1111), take a **bus** from Johannesburg airport or the Sandton Sun Hotel (✆ 011/780-7800; R200/$30 one-way), or hire a car and drive: It's a 90-minute-to-2-hour drive northwest of Jo'burg. Note that you will need an accommodations reservation number to enter for free; nonresidents pay R55 ($8.20) to enter (of which R30/$4.45 are "Sunbucks," the "local" currency) and, more important, will not be allowed to enter the Palace. Overnighters pay no entry anywhere. Day-trippers can play golf at the **Gary Player Country Club,** host of the Nedbank Million Dollar Tournament, or the **Lost City Country Club,** which Player, incidentally, prefers. For a variety of trips and safaris out of Sun City into the Pilanesberg National Park, see "Pilanesberg Park Essentials," below.

For more information on Sun City facilities, call ✆ **014/557-1544** or 014/557-1000 and ask for the Welcome Centre.

WHERE TO STAY & DINE

There are four accommodations options: the over-the-top Palace, the good-value Cascades, the overrated Sun City hotel, and the family-oriented Cabanas. The Sun City hotel, situated in the same building as the main casino and nightclub, is only marginally cheaper than Cascades, yet is by far the tackiest choice and not reviewed here; it's best avoided unless you're solely here to gamble and want to be as close as possible to the jangling slot machines. All lodgings have a number of restaurant options, from grill rooms and pizza dens to fine-dining rooms.

The Cabanas (Value (Kids   Closest to the resort entrance and overlooking "Water-world" (the resort's largest artificial lake, where a variety of watersports and cruises are offered), these terraced cabanas are designed to appeal to families; ask for a lake-facing unit. Not only is The Cabanas the most relaxed and casual of the hotels, but a fully supervised program of kid activities and facilities is available at Kamp Kwena, on The

Cabanas' lawns. And at 10am and 4pm, kids can witness the free flying display of birds from Animal World. It's the most downmarket option, but guests enjoy access to all the Sun City and Palace facilities, which are immense.

P.O. Box 3, Sun City 0316. © **014/557-1000.** Fax 014/557-1902 or 014/557-1131. 380 units. R1,405–R1,615 ($210–$241) double; R1,785–R2,200 ($266–$328) family rooms. Children under 18 stay free in parent's room. AE, DC, MC, V. **Amenities:** 2 restaurants; 2 bars; massive pool; Gary Player Country Club (includes golf, gym, and spa/salon); minigolf; children's programs; babysitting; laundry. *In room:* A/C, TV, minibar (on request), hair dryer.

The Cascades 🌟🌟 *(Value)*   A comfortable, better value-for-money option than either the Sun City Hotel or the Palace, this is a classic example of early '80s opulence— J. R. Ewing wouldn't look amiss here. All rooms are spacious (many with sunken Jacuzzis in the bedroom) and overlook huge tropical gardens with waterfalls, weirs, lagoons, and shaded walks. If you ask for a room on one of the top floors, you'll have a view of the Gary Player–designed golf course and, beyond, the bushveld plains. The restaurant locations are lovely—the Peninsula is set next to a lake, while the Fishmonger is tucked under a waterfall—but consider dining at the Palace; the walk is short and spectacular.

P.O. Box 7, Sun City 0316. © **014/557-1000.** Fax 014/557-1902 or 014/557-1131. 243 units. R2,370–R2,965 ($354–$443) double; R5,300–R14,400 ($791–$2,149) suite. Children under 18 stay free in parent's room. AE, DC, MC, V. **Amenities:** 2 restaurants; 2 bars; 2 pools; Gary Player Country Club (includes golf, gym, and spa/salon); tennis; concierge; business center; 24-hr. room service; babysitting; laundry. *In room:* A/C, TV, minibar, hair dryer.

Palace of the Lost City 🌟🌟🌟   From the beautiful life-size carvings of animals arching out of fountains and hand-painted domed ceilings, to the tusklike pens in every room, the decor of this fantastical hotel is totally over the top, and a must for anyone even remotely interested in design. Standard rooms are a little disappointing, given the opulence of the public spaces (even the lifts feature exquisite carvings), so make sure you book a lake-facing room, where the view will make up for it. If money is no option, however, you can't beat a suite on the top floor of the Palace—just ask Michael Jackson.

For the best fine-dining experience in Sun City, book a table here at the **Villa Del Palazzo,** which serves northern Italian cuisine in a romance-soaked double-volume room overlooking the water, or the **Crystal Court,** where 7m-high (23-ft.) doors open onto rolling views of the Valley of Waves.

P.O. Box 308, Sun City 0316. © **014/557-1000.** Fax 014/557-1902 or 014/557-1131. 338 units. R4,070–R5,085 ($607–$759) double; R5,925–R40,900 ($884–$6,104) suite. Children under 18 stay free in parent's room. AE, DC, MC, V. **Amenities:** 3 restaurants; bar; (massive) pool; golf; spa/salon; concierge; Internet and business services; 24-hr. room service; babysitting; laundry. *In room:* A/C, TV, minibar, hair dryer.

3 Game Reserves in the Waterberg Mountain Region

Approximately 350km (217 miles) N of Johannesburg

The Waterberg, a 150km-long (93-mile) mountain ridge that rises quite dramatically from the bushveld plains to 2,085m (6,839 ft.) above sea level, is substantially less populated than the big-game country that lies to the east of the Escarpment. With no major roads and only one town (Vaalwater) within a 15,000-sq.-km (5,850-sq.-mile) area, the region is almost totally devoid of humans—and, with no forestry or industry contributing to pollution, it's one of the most pristine wilderness areas in the country. It also offers a more varied terrain than most of Kruger, with majestic mountainscapes and rocky ravines, grassed valleys, and lush riverines. Aside from its proximity (a 2½-hr. drive) to Johannesburg, the reserve is malaria-free, which means

---

⌒ Moments Close Encounter on Horseback

Your horse stops, its ears pricked. It is staring at a large shadow in the trees. The shadow stares back. Although leopard sightings are not common here, they do occur, which is one reason **Equus Horse Safaris** ⭐⭐⭐, P.O. Box 975, Vaalwater 0530 (© **014/721-0063;** www.equus.co.za) expects you to be both fit and, at the every least, a rider capable of trotting and cantering. It's a wonderful way to explore the unspoiled beauty of the Waterberg. Base camp comprises three fully furnished en-suite tents; cost is R1,750 ($261) per rider per night, all-inclusive. **Note:** There is a 95-kilogram (210-lb.) rider weight limit.

---

you don't have to suffer the side effects of medication. Add to this the mountainous landscape and lack of congestion when compared with some of the private game reserves around Kruger, and it becomes a very appealing choice indeed.

Waterberg has three major players. At the southwestern end of the mountain range is the National Parks Board's **Marakele Park** and the adjacent **Welgevonden Reserve**—both feature the Big 5, as well as 16 species of antelope and some 250 species of birds, but Marakele is accessible only by four-wheel-drive vehicles and offers basic accommodations in furnished tents (contact the National Parks Board at © **012/428-9111;** www.sanparks.org). By contrast, Welgevonden, a magnificent 40,000-hectare (98,800-acre) wilderness, has been managed and restocked by a consortium of wealthy concession holders, all of whom have had to develop their camps along very strict guidelines. Vehicles are not allowed off-road, for example, which can be a major drawback if you spot a lion lying 100m (328 ft.) away, and which makes leopard sightings extremely rare. But the high density of animals still ensures good sightings, and the intimacy of the small lodges is most conducive to relaxing. Currently, Welgevonden is experiencing an oversupply of elephant and lion, a problem that will be solved before the end of 2006, when the fence with Marakele will be removed, creating a new super reserve. The planned change should increase sightings of animals, such as leopard, currently limited by excess lion.

Separated from these two reserves by a large area of game and hunting farms is the 35,382-hectare (87,394-acre) **Lapalala Wilderness,** the second-biggest privately owned game reserve in Africa (Tswalu'in the Northern Cape is the largest), and internationally renowned for its black rhino conservation and environmental education efforts—more than 45,000 pupils from all over the world have been hosted by the Lapalala Wilderness School. Lapalala has no lion but is a good budget alternative to those wanting a remote bush experience.

ESSENTIALS

GETTING THERE   By Plane   There are four landing strips on Welgevonden Reserve—your lodge will arrange the 1-hour charter from Johannesburg airport.

By Car   To make the 2½-hour journey, take the N1 north from Johannesburg or Pretoria; take the turnoff for Nylstroom after the toll gates, then head 72km (45 miles) northwest on the R33 for Vaalwater. The main entrance to Waterberg (from where your lodge will arrange a transfer) lies 26km (16 miles) west of Vaalwater, and the entrance to Lapalala is 70km (44 miles) north. Lodges will arrange transfers direct from Jo'burg, too.

VISITOR INFORMATION   For information on **Waterberg Tourism,** you will have to contact the municipality (© **014/717-1344/5**). Geraldine at the **Waterberg Centre** (© **014/755-4189**) has information on the Lapalala area.

GETTING AROUND   At Welgevonden: You leave your car at Main Gate and are transferred by your lodge; twice-daily game drives are offered by all lodges. **At Lapalala:** You can drive to your camp, but once there you have to explore on foot or horseback.

WHERE TO STAY & DINE

Clearwater Lodges, P.O. Box 365, Stellenbosch 7599 (© **021/889-5514**; www. clearwaterlodges.co.za; R7,700/$1,149 double; winter R3,900/$582), a member of Relais & Châteaux, comprises two totally separate camps: **Tsheshepi Lodge,** built next to a stream at the foot of a wall of mountain, is great if you've always wanted to be serenaded by baboons, but it feels cocooned when compared with **Kudu Lodge** 🐾🐾, set in the middle of an open sweet-grass savanna, surrounded by grazing antelope, zebra, and rhino. Here each generously sized chalet has a deck from which you can enjoy the passing parade at the nearby watering hole. Both lodges accept children—a bonus in a malaria-free reserve.

For solitude at an unbelievably low price, **Lapalala,** P.O. Box 348, Vaalwater, Waterberg 0530 (© **014/755-4395**; www.lapalala.com; Wilderness Bush Camps: R390–R440/$58–$66 double, minimum 2 nights; Rhino Camp: R180–R190/$27–$28 per person, minimum six persons) is unbeatable. Lapalala has 10 **wilderness bush camps**—rustic self-catering fully equipped camps located in the bush or next to the river, all with flush toilets. Once settled, you're on your own (not even the cleaning staff intrudes), and because driving in the reserve is not allowed, you won't come across another human until you leave. The presence of crocodiles and hippos means the river should be approached only with extreme caution.

Makweti Safari Lodge 🐾🐾🐾   This intimate stone-and-thatch lodge is, architecturally, the most attractive option in Welgevonden. Over and above the low-key and tasteful use of African artworks and artifacts, you'll find the layout of the boutique-style lodge emphasizes privacy, while the setting—perched on a rocky ravine on the edge of a verdant valley—is fabulous. Warthog, zebra, and other herbivores graze and play around a watering hole adjacent one viewing terrace, while you can enjoy fantastic views of the bush from the tastefully decorated main lounge areas. Accommodations are in generously proportioned chalets, most with king-size beds, small verandas on stilts, and spectacular bathrooms. The beautifully presented meals are accompanied by fine South African wines from less commercial estates and, weather allowing, are served in the boma. Ask for Wayne as your safari guide; he'll go out of his way to make you enjoy your game drives. Wayne is not only knowledgeable about the wilds, but he'll quickly have you believing that he really *does* talk to the animals (just watch how he handles an angry elephant bull that's decided to obstruct the road).

Welgevonden Private Reserve, Limpopo. P.O. Box 310, Vaalwater, Waterberg 0530. © 011/837-6776. Fax 011/837-4771. www.makweti.com. 5 units. Summer R5,900 ($881) double; winter R3,500 ($522) double. Rates are all-inclusive. No children under 12 unless entire lodge is rented out. **Amenities:** Dining area; boma; bar; sala; plunge pool; game drives; bush walks; African art boutique. *In room:* Hair dryer, fireplace, fan, heater.

4 Game Reserves in the North-West

PILANESBERG NATIONAL PARK 🐾🐾

Some 1.4 billion years ago, the Pilanesberg plains were bubbling away in the second-largest alkaline volcano in the world. Today the rim of this ancient crater, eroded by time, forms the natural boundary of undulating Pilanesberg National Park. Typified by concentric rings of rocky hills, and centered on a large hippo- and crocodile-filled lake, Pilanesberg is one of Africa's most picturesque parks and—as it's a mere 90-minute to 2-hour drive—an ideal place to visit if you're stuck in Jo'burg with limited time to go elsewhere.

In 1979, the once overgrazed farmland of Pilanesberg was transformed by Operation Genesis, which saw the translocation of over 7,000 animals into the 58,000-hectare (143,260-acre) reserve. Today it is home to 364 different species, and among its 35 large mammals are the Big 5, as well as leopard, cheetah, and brown hyena. The park's natural beauty, abundance of wild animals, and lack of malaria have made it one of the area's strongest drawing cards, though most visitors here are based at Sun City. Pilanesberg's proximity to Sun City and Gauteng means that its well-maintained network of roads can get very busy, and first-time visitors to the bush should note that this is not the kind of untamed wilderness you'd encounter at, say, Welgevonden (see above) or Madikwe (see below)—and both these reserves are also malaria-free and also relatively accessible—2½ and 3½ hours from Johannesburg, respectively.

PILANESBERG PARK ESSENTIALS

The main entrance and reception are at the Manyane Gate on the park's eastern side. From Sun City, the nearest entrance is Bakubung Gate, west off the resort on the R565. Gates open from 5:30am to 7pm November through January, 6am to 6:30pm September through October, and 6:30am to 6pm the rest of the year. The park can be easily explored in your own car. Entry costs R20 ($3) per adult (R15/$2.25 children); you can purchase a map (R10/$1.50) as you enter, and the roads are in good condition.

To organize 2½-hour safari trips in elevated open-topped vehicles into **Pilanesberg** from neighboring Sun City (R230/$34 adults; R80–R130/$12–$19 children), contact **Gametrackers** (© **014/552-1561**) or book at their safari desk (tel] **014/552-5021**) at the Sun City hotel (if you have your own transport to the reserve gates, the rate is R170/$25, but you should then book through Gametrackers in the reserve at © **014/555-5469;** the pickup point is the Manyane restaurant). Gametrackers also offers 4-hour **walking safaris** accompanied by armed rangers (R250/$37 per person; four-person minimum).

The September 2002 arrival in Pilanesberg of Chikwenya, Sharu, Sapi, Mana, and Michael—five elephants orphaned some 20 years ago in Zimbabwe and subsequently hand-reared—means that Gametrackers can offer 3-hour elephant-back safaris, costing R990 ($148) per person; an elephant "interaction safari" costs R450 ($67) and lasts 90 minutes. The most expensive (and potentially exhilarating) way to see the Pilanesberg is on a hot-air-balloon safari, also offered by Gametrackers; the 4-hour experience includes hotel pick-up, guided transfers through the reserve, a 1-hour balloon trip, sparkling wine, and a full breakfast at a cost of R2,500/$373. To book, call © **014/552-1561** or visit www.gametrac.co.za.

WHERE TO STAY & DINE

It's worth overnighting in Pilanesberg just to have the run of the reserve at dawn, before the day-trippers from Sun City descend. The Bakubung and Kwa Maritane lodges pitch themselves as the park's up-market alternatives, but frankly, they're not recommended. If you're looking for a certain level of luxury but still want to feel as if you're living in the untamed bush, there is only one place in Pilanesberg worth considering.

Tshukudu Bush Lodge ★★★   Climbing the 134 steep steps to the lodge (the luggage is carried for you), you may be forgiven for cursing Tshukudu, or "place of the rhino." Get to the top, however, and the panoramic view alone is likely to replenish your reserves. The setting, atop a *koppie* (hill) overlooking a large open plain and waterhole, provides great views of a variety of game from the dining area/bar platform. The luxury cottages are designed to make the most of the view, with the spacious interior divided into two distinct areas. The bedroom overlooks a small lounge (with fireplace) that opens onto a private balcony overlooking the plain. The sunken bathtub also has a view of the plain so that you won't miss the action just because you happen to be taking a bath. The two standard cabins are basic by comparison and don't have views. Game walks and drives are scheduled daily, and because Tshukudu is located in a private part of Pilanesberg that's inaccessible for Sun City day-trippers, this is a tranquil experience.

P.O. Box 6805, Rustenburg 0300. Guests are transferred from Bakubung Lodge, located just west of Sun City on the southern edge of the reserve. © 014/552-6255. Fax 014/552-6266. www.tshukudulodge.co.za. 7 units. R5,850 ($873) double. Rate includes all meals, drinks, game drives, and bush walks. AE, DC, MC, V. No children under 12. Amenities: Dining room; bar; rock pool; game drives; bush walks. *In room:* Minibar, hair dryer, safe, tea- and coffee-making facility, fireplace.

MADIKWE ✦✦✦

Malaria-free and offering varied and beautiful terrain, this is prime game-viewing turf and a great triumph for wildlife lovers. Fifteen years ago, this 75,000-hectare (185,250-acre) area on the South Africa/Botswana border was overgrazed farmland, but in a far-reaching decision it was proclaimed the Madikwe Game Reserve in 1991, transforming it into South Africa's fourth-largest reserve. Ecologically, Madikwe is better suited to support wildlife than livestock, and within 6 years, 10,000 animals were once again roaming the Madikwe plains in what was dubbed Operation Phoenix, the largest game translocation exercise in the world. The decision to do this here was based on the area's highly diverse ecozones—bordered by the Dwarsberg Mountains in the south and the Marico River in the east, the reserve's rocky hills, perennial rivers, seasonal wetlands, acacia bushveld, savanna grassland, and Kalahari's desertlike sandveld allow it to support an unusual range of animal species. Today it has the second-largest elephant population in the country, and visitors are assured of sighting what they term "the Magnificent Seven" on a 2-night stay. This includes the Big 5 as well as cheetah (very rare in the reserves around Kruger) and wild dogs, Africa's most endangered predator. Commercial expansion over the last 2 years has been rapid, yet Madikwe remains large enough to satisfy visitors starved for solitude, something the more popular Mpumulanga reserves can't always deliver.

MADIKWE ESSENTIALS

Madikwe is some 280km (174 miles) northwest of Johannesburg. There are daily flights to the reserve from Johannesburg; your lodge will arrange air transfers (it's a 45-min. flight). If you have the time, however, a road journey is definitely recommended—with no one else on the road, and surrounded by bush and classic big African skies, the journey alone is a holiday. It's an easy road trip, involving some well-maintained dirt roads to add to the sense of getting away from it all, and takes about 3½ hours from Johannesburg.

WHERE TO STAY & DINE

If both of the lodges reviewed below are full, you'll find exclusivity and comfort at a reasonable rate at **Impodimo Game Lodge** (© 083/411-7400 or 083/561-5355; www.impodimo.com; 8 units; high season/Dec–Apr R4,700/$701 double; low season/May–Sept R3,900/$582). Small and exclusive **Jaci's Tree Lodge** ✦✦ (© 083/700-2071 or 014/778-9900; www.madikwe.com; R3,990–R6,590/$596–$984 double; includes all meals and game activities) comprises eight air-conditioned tree-houses built around giant tambotie and leadwood trees. Its sister lodge, Jaci's Safari Lodge, is right next door and offers tented accommodations without the luxury of air-conditioning. A cheaper in-season option is **Madikwe River Lodge.** The very first lodge to open in Madikwe, it's looking a little rough around the edges, but accommodations are adequate, it's very child-friendly, and it still provides first-class access to the reserve (🕿 **014/778-0891;** www.threecities.co.za; 16 units; R3,300–R3,960/ $493–$591 double; includes all meals and game activities).

Madikwe Hills 🏵🏵   The large, sumptuous guest rooms at this luxury lodge offer stunning views across a vast plain within the Madikwe Reserve. Although divided by name into two lodges, it's basically one property with guest rooms and common amenities linked by wooden pathways; architecturally, the lodge has been imaginatively integrated into the boulder-strewn hilltop, which means that rooms and facilities occur at different levels (let reservations know if stairs and uphill climbs are a worry). Each suite has a large terrace balcony with its own plunge pool; from here you can easily watch animals come to drink at the watering hole that is right in front of the main lodge. Family suites are suitably massive. There's a strong colonial air about the place—you may feel that, despite the majestic views and excellent safari experience, the luxury hotel ambience is just a touch out of place; it's also pricey for Madikwe. **Little Madikwe** forms part of Madikwe Hills but can be turned into a private lodge, inclusive of the magnificent presidential suite.

P.O. Box 612, Hazyview 1242. 🕿 **013/737-6626.** Fax 013/737-6628. www.madikwehills.com. 11 units. R7,800–R8,800 ($1,164–$1,313) double; R11,700–R13,200 ($1,746–$1,970) family suite. Children under 10 are accommodated only in the family suite. Rates include everything except premium wines. AE, DC, MC, V. **Amenities:** Dining area; bar; lounge; pool; spa; gym; curio shop; babysitting; laundry; game drives; bush walks; Internet; library. *In room:* A/C, minibar, hair dryer, safe.

Madikwe Safari Lodge 🏵🏵🏵 *Value*   Although it opened only in late 2004, this lovely property made it onto *Condé Nast Traveler*'s 2005 Hot List. Not surprising: High on style and low on pretense, this lodge consists of three separate camps situated a short distance from one another, but adding tremendously to the level of peace, quiet, and privacy. Drawing inspiration from the turreted anthills that dot the Madikwe landscape, the architect used packed earth, stone, and thatch to fashion a series of organic living spaces offset by simple luxury and great comfort. Interiors combine Afrikaner baroque with cleverly chosen Ndebele artifacts to give the spaces quirky tongue-in-cheek cheerfulness; it's the type of safari lodge that makes you want to explore the property as much as the wildlife. If you're traveling with children, you'll be stationed in West Camp, which has the fewest guest rooms (meaning more privacy); each of the three "camps" has its own unique charms, not least of which are the inspired meals (don't miss the sublime ranger's omelet at breakfast). Game drives are meticulously professional—you'll be driven by young, earnest rangers with a passion for the bush. Operated by renowned CC Africa, this lodge doesn't have quite the same views as the more elevated Madikwe Hills (see above), but offers innovative design, privacy, and good value.

Private Bag X27, Benmore 2010. 🕿 **011/809-4300.** Fax 011/809-4315. www.ccafrica.com. 3 camps, each with 6 units. High season (Oct–Apr) R5,900 ($881) double; low season (May–Sept) R3,700 ($552) double. Rates include all meals, game drives, walks, tea, and coffee. AE, DC, MC, V. **Amenities:** Each camp has its own dining area; bar; lounge; babysitting; laundry; game drives (including separate children's game drives); bush walks. *In room:* A/C, minibar, hair dryer, safe, plunge pool.

5 Game Reserves in the Kalahari Desert

The seemingly endless, hot, and dusty drive from Johannesburg may be arduous, but it's well worth taking time out to include the breathtakingly beautiful Kalahari Desert on your itinerary. The sandveld environment alone is stunning—rust-red Kalahari sand dunes and wispy blonde grasses contrast starkly with huge cobalt-blue skies—yet this harsh and arid landscape supports a surprisingly varied and rich amount of game. Besides the big-maned "Kalahari" lion, you will find cheetah, hyena, elephant, jackal, and the gemsbok, or oryx.

KGALAGADI TRANSFRONTIER PARK 🌟🌟🌟

First proclaimed in 1931, the Kalahari Gemsbok National Park and adjoining Botswana's Gemsbok Park were renamed **Kgalagadi Transfrontier Park** in 1999, formalizing a decade-long joint management arrangement that has ensured that game are free to wander long, ancient migratory routes in search of water. While the Kgalagadi (literally "place without water") is one of Africa's biggest reserves—covering an area of more than 38,000 sq. km (14,672 sq. miles)—most of the established accommodations options are still in the South African region. Of the rest camps, Twee Rivieren is the most developed, and Nossob, on the dry riverbed that creates a natural unfenced boundary between South Africa and Botswana, the most isolated, but it is the tented camps that should be your final destination (see below).

For the best game-viewing opportunities, make sure you rise early (see "Better Wildlife Viewing for the Self-Guide Safari" in chapter 8 for more game-viewing tips), take plenty of extra water, and be prepared to travel long distances—the shortest circular drive is 100km (62 miles) long. Inquire at Twee Rivieren about evening game drives with experienced rangers—these are recommended.

ESSENTIALS

GETTING THERE   By Car   From Jo'burg, it's a 904km (560-mile) drive: Take the N14 to Kuruman, then the R31 to Hotazel, across vast, empty plains to join the R360 for the final leg to the park. You can drive here from Cape Town, taking the N7 north to Springbok, or taking the R27 north from Vanrhynsdorp and Calvinia to Upington. The R360 takes you north to the park. See chapter 2 for rental car details.

By Plane   SA Airlink (© 054/332-2161) flies from Johannesburg and Cape Town to **Upington Airport** (© 054/337-7900). From here you can contact Newton Walker of **Walker Flying Service** (© 082/820-5394) and charter a flight into the park's Twee Rivieren camp (to hire the four-seater craft costs R2,600/$388), where you can pick up a prearranged car (see below). Newton also flies to Tswalu for the same rate.

GETTING AROUND   Avis has a desk (© 054/332-4746) at the Upington Airport and will also drop a car off at the park, should you charter a flight directly there. Unless you intend to enter Botswana or venture to the remote Bitterpan Wilderness Camp, you won't need a four-wheel-drive to travel to and around in the park, despite the fact that most of the roads are dirt.

GUIDED TOURS   Jaco Powell 🌟 (aka Jacels Tours; www.jacelstours.com), an honorary ranger for South African National Parks (SANParks) and a rich source of information on the Kgalagadi, offers fully catered specialist tours in the park as well as other places of interest in the Northern Cape. Contact Jaco at © 082/572-0065 or info@jacelstours.com. Pieter Hanekom's **Kalahari Safaris** (© **054/332-5653** or 082/ 435-0007; pieter@kalahari-safaris.com) organizes a variety of desert safari options, designed to satisfy different budgets.

VISITOR INFORMATION   Direct all booking inquiries to **SANParks,** 643 Leyds St., Muckleneuk, Pretoria (© **012/428-9111;** fax 012/343-0905; www.sanparks.org). The park is quite popular, particularly the tented camps, so book well in advance. The **Visitor's Centre** (© **054/561-2000**) is at Twee Rivieren, the park's headquarters. There is a conservation fee of R120 ($18) per person per day; children pay R60 ($9). Note that you can enter the Botswana side from Twee Rivieren, but you'll need to have a passport, and any information on campsites comes from the **Department of Wildlife and National Parks** in Maun, Botswana (© **267/318 0774**).

WHEN TO GO   Rain falls mainly between January and April. The best time to visit is between March and May (autumn), when it's neither too hot nor too dry. In summer, temperatures may exceed 104°F (40°C). In winter, temperatures at night are often below zero. Note that the park's gate hours vary considerably depending on the season and are strictly adhered to—if you aren't going to arrive between 7:30am and 6pm, call ahead to find out exactly what time the gates close.

WHERE TO STAY & DINE

Given the distances, you'll almost certainly have to book your first night at **Twee Rivieren** ⚐, which, like all the options below, is run by South African National Parks (see "Visitor Information," above, for booking information). Twee Rivieren is just beyond the entrance to the park, which will come as welcome respite from the long road trip since you've more than likely covered vast distances to get here; this is also the only camp with a restaurant, a pool, and air-conditioned units. Each of the self-catering two-, three-, four-, and six-bed chalets, all en-suite, has a fully equipped kitchen and a *braai* (barbecue) area. Each chalet costs a minimum of R430 ($64) a night for two people—best bet is to book a family cottage (R380–R500/$57–$75). Besides the basic restaurant, there is a takeout shop, fuel station, and grocery shop; you can buy supplies like milk, bread, wood, frozen meat, eggs, and tinned food here, but it's best to stock up on a few extras in Upington.

If you decide to head farther into the reserve, consider spending a night or 2 in one of the new wilderness camps: **Urikaruus** ⚐ and **Kieliekrankie** ⚐ are both quaintly designed and less than 2 hours from Twee Rivieren. Each camp features four two-bed units (R630/$94 double) with their own fully equipped (gas-powered) kitchen and bathroom with a shower; linen and towels are provided, but you should stock up on food and bottled water. Urikaruus, which is built on stilts, is situated on the banks of the Auob River and overlooks a busy waterhole. Tented Kieliekrankie feels as though it's in the middle of nowhere, approached via a tunnel dug into the red Kalahari dunes. From either of the wilderness camps, you can follow the course of the dry Auob River— which offers excellent game-viewing opportunities—to **Mata Mata,** which lies 120km (74 miles; 2½ hr.) from Twee Rivieren, or preferably at the nearby **Kalahari Tented Camp.** Mata Mata is a great deal more rustic than Twee Rivieren, and the best accommodations—none of which has air-conditioning—are limited to eight chalets (R380/$57 double); again, the best option is a family chalet, available for R630 ($94). I suggest you simply fill up here (it has a shop stocked with basic supplies and a fuel station) and press on to the relatively swish **Kalahari Tented Camp** ⚐⚐, which lies about 3km (1¾ miles) away. Here you overnight at one of 10 en-suite desert "tents" (sandbag and canvas constructions with amenities like kitchenettes, bathrooms, and ceiling fans; R660/$99 double), or book early for the pick of them all, the honeymoon unit, costing R770 ($115) double. The camp also has four family tents, each sleeping four.

Alternatively, head farther north to the en-suite desert cabins at either **Grootkolk** or **Gharagab**, charming wilderness camps, each with only four units (R630/$94 double); there are private barbecue areas, and at Gharagab you can shower beneath the stars. This is the real deal—gloriously remote and silent, and accessible only by four-wheel-drive vehicle.

TSWALU KALAHARI RESERVE

At 100,000 hectares (247,000 acres), this is the largest privately owned reserve in South Africa and the only place to come if you want to experience the stark beauty of the Kalahari in total luxury.

Initially developed by the late Steve Boler, an ardent hunter, the reserve was filled with species; among the 9,000 head of game that Boler imported to his $6-million enterprise were lion, black rhino, cheetah, leopard, and buffalo. When Boler died, the reserve was taken oven by the wealthy Oppenheimer dynasty, who have since employed experts to help restore the wildlife to its natural state. Many guests report some of their most fascinating animal-viewing experiences here; sightings are excellent as there's no thick vegetation to conceal animals. It is also one of the most sumptuous safari lodges on the continent, with accommodations in thatched stone minihouses on a par with the luxurious lodges in the reserves abutting Kruger. Rooms are expansive and beautifully finished, with indoor and outdoor showers, open fireplaces, and sun decks that look out over the Kalahari. It's pricey, but if you do make it this far away from civilization, there's plenty on offer to make a stay worth your while, such as guided horse rides and a visit to archaeological sites where San rock art can be viewed. You can either stay here en route to the park from Johannesburg or charter a flight in from Johannesburg (R3,575/$534 per person) or Cape Town (R4,675/$698). Tswalu also offers **Tarkuni Lodge,** where friends or family groups can enjoy complete privacy in a remote valley inside the reserve for R25,000 ($3,731) per night.

P.O. Box 1081, Kuruman 8460. © **0861/879-258** or 053/781-9234. Fax 053/781-9238. www.tswalu.com. 10 units. Suite R8,800–R9,300 ($1,313–$1,388) double. Rates include game drives, walking safaris, all drinks, local calls, laundry, valet, and horse riding. Children under 12 stay free if sharing with parents; 50% if not sharing. **Amenities:** Dining area; bar; lounge; boma; heated pool; children's room; gift shop; massage; babysitting; laundry; wine cellar; game drives; bush walks; library. *In room:* A/C, minibar, hair dryer, safe, fireplace.

8

Big-Game Country:
Kruger National Park & Environs

Watching wild animals, dangerous and untamed, in their natural, untouched habitat, brings about a deeply satisfying communion with nature. It's why we South Africans crave the bush. Much of this has to do with sheer size. South Africa has some of the largest tracts of wilderness on the continent, and as political relations in the region have stabilized, this rich heritage has expanded even farther, with fences between South Africa and parks in neighboring Mozambique and Zimbabwe falling away to create the largest conservation area in the world, unfettered by the constraints of human borders. This is where you will find an unprecedented number of lodges offering unparalleled wildlife experiences in some of the most perfect (and ever more luxurious) settings known to man—particularly those able to pay top dollar.

The areas richest in big game (and luxury lodges) are the landlocked provinces of Limpopo and its southern neighbor, Mpumalanga, which together form the northeastern corner of South Africa and share one of the continent's most famous game reserves, the Kruger National Park. Most people come to this region seeking the romance of precolonial Africa, a place where vast plains of bush savanna teem with game, rivers are swollen with lumbering hippos and lurking crocodiles, dense indigenous jungles shroud twittering birds, horizons shimmer with heat, and the nights are lit only by stars and

crackling campfires. This you will find— and more. Here lies the Escarpment, carpeted in the world's largest man-made forests and offering breathtaking drives and views; the Blyde River Canyon, third-largest canyon in the world; the lush subtropical gardens of the legendary Rain Queen; and Stone Age sites and perfectly preserved boomtowns that tell of Mpumalanga's short but turbulent gold rush–era history.

But the primary destination remains Kruger National Park, Africa's greatest game park, and the private game reserves that surround it. Kruger's budget facilities and well-maintained roads make an African safari experience tremendously accessible, but the private game reserves that flank the Kruger's western unfenced borders (as well as the more recent concessions within the park) offer a truly close-up encounter with the Big 5, and are highly recommended despite the steep price tag.

Predictably, even in this scenic environment, you cannot escape the ironies and contrasts that are South Africa: Neighboring some of the world's most luxurious lodges are the economically deprived communities of Lebowa, Gazankulu, and Kangwane. Many here resent what they see as a white man's playground; others are demanding restitution of apartheid-era land grabs in the Land Claims Commission. The challenge is to find a balance between the needs of wildlife, industry, and community, pulling them into a general economic interdependence and prosperity, with Kruger Park at the hub. To a large extent, tourism is doing just that.

1 Staying Active

Principal among the activities on offer within the game reserves are game drives; these safaris typically last 3 to 4 hours and take place in the early morning and evening. If you are staying at a private safari lodge, game drives and bush walks are included in the price; fishing may also be on offer. A few lodges also offer activities like hot air ballooning and even helicopter rides, but always at an extra cost.

Most of the activities listed below are offered outside the game reserves themselves. If you're looking for a one-stop advice and booking shop, contact **Golden Monkey** (© 013/737-8191; www.big5country.co.za), an agent for the largest selection of adventure operators in the Sabie, Graskop, and Hazyview areas, as well as a booking and information agent. Another high-energy outfit offering a range of adventure activities (including mountain biking, river rafting, quad biking, kloofing, and abseiling) is **Induna Adventures** (© 013/737-8308; info@indunaadventures.com).

ABSEILING Choose between an abseil (rappel) down the Sabie waterfall (R150/$22) or a leap off a granite outcrop (R195/$29) before heading into Kruger; bookings are through Golden Monkey (see above).

BALLOONING Take off at sunrise and float over the foothills of the Escarpment, possibly sighting some game, then alight for champagne breakfast at a nearby lodge. Based 10km (6¼ miles) from Hazyview and White River, **Balloons Over Africa** (© 013/737-6950; www.balloonsoverafrica.co.za; R2,040/$304 per person) prides itself on its expertise—the company's chief pilot, Kevin Roberson, is a multiple winner of the South Africa Hot Air Balloon Championships.

BIRD-WATCHING Along with KwaZulu-Natal, this is the prime bird-watching destination in South Africa, providing enormously varied habitats. For expert advice and tailor-made tours to these areas, as well as to other top birding destinations in southern Africa, contact **Lawson's Birdwatching Tours** ✿✿✿ (© 013/741-2458; www.lawsons.co.za).

ELEPHANT RIDING Kapama (© 015/793-1265; www.kapama.co.za) has introduced **elephant-back safaris** ✿✿✿ in its Big 5 reserve located near Hoedspruit; either overnight at its luxury tented flagship, Camp Jabulani, or book a 90-minute ride for R1,250 ($187).

FLY-FISHING Trout fishing ✿✿✿ on the highland Escarpment is well established, with an infrastructure of self-catering cottages, guesthouses, and lodges situated on well-stocked lakes and streams. **Dullstroom** is the unofficial capital of the trout-fishing areas, and rod rental, fees, and accommodations can be arranged through its helpful **Tourist Information Centre** (© 013/254-0254; www.dullstroom.biz). For information on trout fishing in the Letaba area, contact **Magoebaskloof-Byadladi Tourist Association** (© 015/276-4972 or 015/276-5047; www.magoebaskloof.com). Some of the best fishing facilities are on offer at **Craneridge** (© 082/855-5697), some 23km (14 miles) from Belfast.

GOLFING The nine-hole course at **Skukuza** (© 013/735-5543; skukuzagolf@ sanparks.org) is quite possibly the most dangerous course in the world—it is

> ### *Tips* Golfing in the Wild
>
> Golfing in big-game country is not to be taken lightly—a golfer at Hans Meren-sky was trampled to death by an elephant that had broken through the fence from neighboring Kruger. Golfers at these clubs should heed the warning signs posted at water hazards and elsewhere. Should you encounter a large mammal or predator, remain still, then back away quietly—under no circumstances should you run. If the thought of meeting a large pachyderm or leopard in the rough puts you right off course, you can choose a safer scenic route: The 9-hole **Pilgrim's Rest course** (© 013/768-1434) or the more challenging 18-hole championship course at **White River Country Club** (© 013/751-3781) are both popular.

unfenced, and wild animals wander the greens at will. More wild golfing experiences await at the exclusive 18-hole course at **Leopards Creek** ★★★ (© 013/791-2000), co-owned by Jack Nicklaus and Gary Player. Besides the resident leopard, crocs and hippos lurk in the aptly named water hazards. To play here, you'll have to book into the **Malelane Sun InterContinental** (© 013/790-3304). Or book into luxurious **Makalali** (see "Where to Stay & Dine," in "Private Game Reserves," later in this chapter), a private game lodge that lies just under an hour away from the 18-hole **Hans Merensky Country Club** ★★ (© 015/781-3931), which borders Kruger and is often visited by its wildlife.

HELICOPTER TRIPS & SCENIC FLIGHTS   If you fancy flying through cavernous gorges and across verdant valleys, consider getting a bird's-eye view of the region with **Mpumalanga Helicopter Co.** ★★; rates for two passengers start at R4,590 ($685) for the 45-minute scenic Cascades trip; golf packages and fly-in safaris are also available. Book by calling © 084/505-2052 or 013/750-2358, or visit www.mhelicopter.co.za. If you prefer small, single-propeller planes, Dave Gunn of **Airventures** (© 082/600-5388) offers flights out of Dullstroom.

HIKING   The region's myriad **hiking trails** ★★★ offer excellent scenic opportunities. Lodges within the private game reserves in and around Kruger offer **bush walks** ★★ and **on-foot animal tracking** ★★★; check out the options later in this chapter. Ngala, a tented camp in the Timbavati reserve, offers walking safaris for the well-heeled; see "Private Game Reserves: Where to Stay & Dine" later in this chapter; Rhino Walking Safaris (also later in this chapter) offers various combinations of walks and game drives. If you're traveling here via the Panorama Route, note that the region has a number of excellent day trails, most of which are near the Escarpment towns of Sabie and Graskop—the 14km (8.75-mile) **Loerie Trail** (R5/75¢) per person) takes you through some of the region's most attractive surrounds. If you're not that active, stroll the pretty 3km (1.75-mile) **Forest Falls Walk.** If you're traveling through the Letaba area, the 11km (6.75-mile) circular **Rooikat Trail** ★ (© 015/307-4310; R5/75¢), which follows a stream through the forests of Agatha, is highly recommended.

The top overnight hike in the Mpumalanga area is the 5-day **Blyde River Canyon Trail** (R30/$4.45 per person per night), a 65km (40-mile) walk that traverses the full length of the Blyde River Canyon Nature Reserve, descending from the panoramic heights of God's Window to the tranquil waters of the Blyderivierspoort Dam. Hikers' huts are basic: Bunk beds, flush toilets, *braai* (barbecue) sites, pots, and firewood are provided; all else must be carried in (don't forget toilet paper!). The views and vegetation make this one of the most popular trails in South Africa, so book in advance (② 013/759-5341).

South African Forestry (SAFCOL, now marketed in the region as Komatiland Ecotourism) created hiking trails with overnight facilities through some incredibly scenic areas in the Limpopo Province, including the relatively tough 2-, 3-, and 5-day **Magoebaskloof Trails** (highly recommended), and the 2-, 3-, and 5-day **Fanie Botha Trails** (both R52/$7.75 per person per night). For details and bookings, contact ② 012/481-3615 or go to www.komatiecotourism.co.za.

HORSEBACK RIDING **Filly's Way Mountain Horse Trails** (call Mark at ② 082/294-8349; try michelle@slm.co.za) operates in the Tzaneen area and offers hourly rides (from R110/$16 per person) and 2-day rides with overnight camping or lodge accommodations (from R700/$104 per person), as well as fly-fishing trips.

HUNTING Hunting season usually runs from April to September, though some farms enjoy year-round concessions. For more information on procedures and bookings, contact Rian de Lange at the **Mpumalanga Parks Board** (② 013/759-5336); for information on professional hunters and outfitters, contact the **Lowveld Hunting Association** (② 013/752-3575) between 8am and noon.

MOUNTAIN BIKING Sabie is a fabulous area to explore by bike; rent a bike and an experienced guide (R100/$15 per person for 4 hr.) from **Bike Doc** (② 013/764-1034); ask about the Ceylon Trails. If you're traveling in the Letaba area, the exhilarating 19km (12-mile) **Debengeni Downhill** 👣, a forestry road that starts at the top of the Magoebaskloof Pass and plummets down to the Debengeni Falls, is highly recommended for adrenaline junkies. Bikes here are rented by the hotels listed. Within Kruger Park, **Olifants Rest Camp** (see later in this chapter) offers mountain biking, with the added excitement of spotting wildlife en route.

QUAD BIKING BacTrac Adventure Trails (② 082/808-0866) offers excursions on "quad bikes" (four-wheel motorcycles) through the Magoebaskloof forests; unless you really want the T-shirt and a visit to a crocodile farm, the best-value option is the R420 ($63) half-day trip.

RIVER RAFTING River rafting 👣👣👣 takes place on three rivers during the summer months (usually Sept–May). The **Blyde River** 👣 (a few grade IVs, overall grade III) offers the most exciting rafting in this area. This 8.5km (5¼-mile) trip is completed in one (tiring!) day; expect to pay R750 ($112) for a day trip, R1,100 ($164) to overnight. A day trip down the **Olifants Gorge** 👣 (overall grade II, some IV) will run you R450 ($67). The 2-day trip is recommended—approximately 60km (37 miles) long, it passes through spectacular scenery, and the night is spent on a sandy beach flanked by steep mountainside and baobab trees. Expect to pay R1,100 ($164) per person for a 2-day trip and R1,300 ($194) for a 3-day trip. The minimum age is 10, but minors must be accompanied by parents. The tranquil **Sabie River,** ideal for families (ages 6 and up only), offers a 3- to 4-hour trip on flat water (R220/$33), covering some 12km (7½ miles). **Hardy Ventures** (② 013/751-1693, www.hardyventure.com) runs all three rivers, while Wynand from **Otter's Den** (② 083/279-5565) concentrates on the Blyde River and Olifants Gorge.

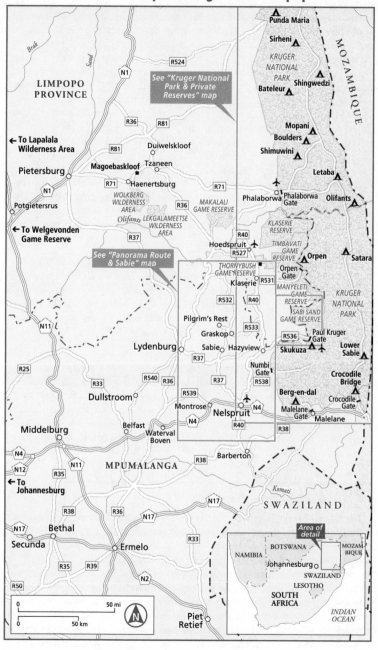

Punda Maria

Sirheni

KRUGER
NATIONAL
PARK

Bateleur
Shingwedzi

Brak

Sand

R524

N1

See "Kruger National
Park & Private
Reserves" map

LIMPOPO
PROVINCE

R36

R81

Duiwelskloof

R81

Magoebaskloof

Tzaneen

Pietersburg

R71

Haenertsburg

WOLKBERG
WILDERNESS
AREA

Olifants

LEKGALAMEETSE
WILDERNESS
AREA

R36

MAKALALI
GAME RESERVE

Mopani
Boulders

Shimuwini

Letaba

Phalaborwa Phalaborwa
Gate

Olifants

KLASERIE
RESERVE

TIMBAVATI
GAME
RESERVE

Orpen

Satara

R71

← To Lapalala
Wilderness Area

N1

Potgietersrus

← To Welgevonden
Game Reserve

R37

Hoedspruit

R40

R527

See "Panorama Route
& Sabie" map

THORNYBUSH
GAME RESERVE

Klaserie

R531

Orpen
Gate

MANYELETI
GAME
RESERVE

SABI SAND
GAME RESERVE

KRUGER
NATIONAL
PARK

N11

R25

R532

R40

Pilgrim's Rest

Graskop

R533

Lydenburg

Sabie

Hazyview

R536

Paul Kruger
Gate

Skukuza

Lower
Sabie

R37

Numbi
Gate

R33

R540

R36

R37

R538

Crocodile
Bridge

Dullstroom

R539

Montrose

Nelspruit

N4

Berg-en-dal

Crocodile
Gate

Malelane
Gate

Malelane

Middelburg

Belfast

Waterval
Boven

N4

R40

R38

N4

N12

N11

R35

← To
Johannesburg

MPUMALANGA

R38

Barberton

R38

R36

N17

N17

N17

Bethal

Komati

SWAZILAND

Secunda

Ermelo

R35

R39

R33

Area of
detail

NAMIBIA

BOTSWANA

MOZAM-
BIQUE

R50

N2

Johannesburg

SWAZILAND

LESOTHO

0   50 mi

0   50 km

N

Piet
Retief

SOUTH
AFRICA

INDIAN
OCEAN

2 Organized Tours

If you don't want to follow the suggestions below for exploring this region in your own car, you may want to consider going with one of these recommended tour operators.

Thompson's Indaba tours (© 013/737-7115; www.indaba.co.za) offers open-vehicle safaris with an experienced game ranger to Kruger—expect to pay R740 ($110) per person for a full day (5 or 6am–5:30pm), or R592 ($88) for a morning; prices exclude meals. Walking safaris in Kruger (weather dependent) will run you R830 ($124). Thompson's also offers night safaris; these take place either in Kapama, which can include an afternoon visit to the Hoedspruit Research & Breeding Centre (R700/$104; dinner included), or in the Sabi Sands (R830/$124), arguably the most game-dense private reserve in South Africa. The Panorama Route tour, with a stop for lunch at Pilgrim's Rest or Graskop, costs R552/$82 per person. (Other tours include Mohololo Centre and Shangana Cultural Village, but if you have your own vehicle, you're better off visiting these places on your own.) Safaris Direct (© 013/737-7945, or cellphone 082/804-5026; www.safarisdirect.co.za) offers similar tours at similar rates—a full-day safari in an open-vehicle will, for instance, cost R710 ($106).

SPECIALIST TOURS

John Williams at Monsoon's African Travel and Adventures (© 015/795-5114 or 083/700-8921; www.monsoongallery.com) will help plan a self-drive itinerary that takes in the less-publicized cultural and archaeological sights in the big-game regions of the lowveld, offering the opportunity to meet many of the artists and craftspeople whose works stock Williams's gallery. He will also assist visitors in visiting the far reaches of the Limpopo Province, an area that is not yet well geared for tourism. For accompaniment by a specialist guide, be sure to make arrangements well in advance.

3 En Route to Big-Game Country

The journey between Gauteng and Kruger—a comfortable 5-hour drive with no major detours—includes some of South Africa's most dramatically beautiful drives, and the surrounds become scenic within 2 hours of leaving Johannesburg. The three routes described below take you from the highveld plateau before dropping, usually quite spectacularly, to the lowveld, much of which is taken up by Kruger National

---

Tips Need to Save Time?

The quickest way to get to the Kruger is to fly directly from Cape Town or Johannesburg to Kruger-Mpumalanga International or the Hoedspruit/East-gate airports; from Johannesburg, you can also fly direct to Phalaborwa air-port, gateway to Central Kruger.

If you plan to drive to Kruger and will be arriving in the afternoon, plot your route so that you enter the park via the gate closest to the camp where you will be overnighting. Gate times are strict, as are the park's rules regarding speed limits—at 50kmph (31 mph), this can make for slow going. It may cause you to arrive at your camp later than you'd planned and find yourself unable to check in—camp admission times are also inflexible. See "Kruger National Park," later in this chapter, for details.

Park and the surrounding private game reserves. The best way to savor the journey is to overnight at one of the many places that lie between 2 and 4 hours away from Gauteng and make the most of the Escarpment's dramatic scenery before setting off for big-game country.

The first, most popular route takes you via the Escarpment towns of Sabie and Graskop (**Pilgrim's Rest** ★ is an optional but recommended side trip) before traversing the Escarpment rim along what is called the **Panorama Route** ★★★—a spectacular half-day drive. This journey will definitely warrant an overnight stay, preferably two, and you are then ideally positioned to enter one of Kruger's southern or central gates.

The second approach is via Machadodorp on the N4, the main artery connecting Gauteng with Nelspruit, the capital of Mpumalanga—this is ideal if you need to enter one of Kruger's southern gates and don't have time to do much sightseeing or overnight along the way.

A lesser-known way to get to central Kruger, but in parts even more scenic, particularly from June to August, is to follow in the footsteps of the Voortrekkers on the Great North Road (N1) as far as Polokwane (ex-Pietersburg), then branch off eastward via the **Letaba/Magoebaskloof area** ★, also known as "land of the silver mist" and "garden of the Rain Queen." This route will necessitate an overnight stay, and you are advised to reserve a room at the **Coach House** ★, P.O. Box 544, Tzaneen 0850 (© **015/306-8000;** fax 015/306-8008; www.coachhouse.co.za), which lies on a 560-hectare (1,383-acre) working fruit and nut farm, and offers excellent amenities (including a full spa and good restaurant), as well as a great location with superb views; it's situated in Agatha, just outside Tzaneen. Rates, including a generous breakfast, are R1,300 to R1,750 ($194–$261) double, R1,850 ($276) suites. Even better views are to be had from the old-fashioned, generous, and friendly **Magoebaskloof Hotel,** off the R71, Magoebaskloof Pass (© **015/276-4776;** fax 015/276-4780; www.magoebaskloof. co.za), which reopened after a devastating fire in 2004; it has been rebuilt with fewer rooms and a slightly more contemporary look, but retains its good value. Meals, ranging from perfect steaks to Sunday lunch buffets, are recommended. Rates are R620 ($93) double, including breakfast.

4 The Escarpment & Panorama Route

This is the most popular route to big-game country, with roads taking you past endless pine and gum forests, pockets of tangled indigenous jungle, plunging waterfalls, and breathtaking views of the subtropical plains. A 4-hour drive from Gauteng, it's an easy escape for Johannesburg's ever-harassed city dwellers, desperate to breathe fresh air and drive around with unlocked doors. Unfortunately, the air is not always that fresh; Mpumalanga's industrial activities are responsible for one of the highest acid rainfalls in the world. This is compounded during the dry winter months, when veld fires are rife, coloring the air with a hazy smog that obscures the views. While this is one reason to consider traveling via the Letaba/Magoebaskloof area, which is generally a great deal greener in the winter, nothing matches the magnificent view of the lowveld plains from the aptly named God's Window, or watching the Blyde River snake through Blyde River Canyon, thousands of meters below. In addition, the region's popularity makes for a plethora of great accommodations options; it's worth noting that, with the exception of Pilgrim's Rest, overnighting in any of the Escarpment towns (as opposed to the outlying areas) would be a mistake—the surrounding forests and farms offer a lot more in the way of views and setting.

In short, the route is as follows: After driving through **Dullstroom,** the highest town on the Escarpment, you drop down the eastern slopes via the scenic **Long Tom Pass** to the forestry towns of **Sabie** and **Graskop.** (Pilgrim's Rest, a restored gold-mining village, lies another mountain pass away and warrants a separate visit of at least a half-day, excluding travel time.) Graskop is the gateway to the **Panorama Route,** a drive that curls along the rim of the Escarpment, with lookout points along the way that provide relatively easy access to some of the most panoramic views in Africa (see "Driving the Panorama Route," later in this chapter). Once past the canyon lookouts, the final descent to the lowveld follows the Abel Erasmus Pass to **Hoedspruit,** which offers easy access to Kruger via the centrally located Orpen Gate, or the private game reserves of Timbavati, Thornybush, and Manyeleti. Or head south to **Hazyview** for access to the Paul Kruger Gate or Sabi Sands Reserve, or complete the loop to return to Sabie or Graskop. *Note:* If you fly directly to Hoedspruit's Eastgate airport, you can still tour the Panorama Route as a day trip—just exclude Dullstroom and Long Tom Pass from the itinerary.

ESSENTIALS

GETTING THERE **By Car** If you're traveling from Johannesburg, take the N12, which joins up with the N4, the main artery between Pretoria and Nelspruit, capital of Mpumalanga. When you reach Belfast (South Africa's coldest town), turn north onto the R540 to Dullstroom and Lydenburg, then take the R37 east to Sabie. From here the R532 runs north through Graskop along the Panorama route.

By Plane From **Cape Town: SA Express** flies daily to Hoedspruit's Eastgate Airport—this is the best airport to fly to if you want to do the Panorama Route as a day trip. From **Johannesburg: SA Express** flies daily to Hoedspruit's Eastgate Airport. Note that you can also fly from Cape Town, Johannesburg, and Durban to the relatively nearby Kruger-Mpumalanga International Airport.

VISITOR INFORMATION **Golden Monkey** (© 013/737-8191) is one of the few centralized sources of information on the Sabie, Graskop, and Hazyview areas. To book accommodations in **Dullstroom,** speak to Les Adams at the local **tourism bureau,** Shop 9, Hugenote Street (© 013/254-0254; www.dullstroom.biz; Mon–Fri 8am–5pm, Sat 9am–5pm, Sun 9am–2pm); she'll also help you out with reliable information on what the town has to offer. In **Sabie:** Contact **Panorama Information,** at Sabie Market Square (© 013/764-1125; www.panoramainfo.co.za; Mon–Fri 8am–5pm, Sat–Sun 9am–1pm). A better service, **Graskop Information,** is offered at Graskop, located in the Spar Centre, Pilgrim's Way (© 013/767-1833; www.wild adventures.co.za; Mon–Sat 8:30am–5pm). In **Pilgrim's Rest:** See "Pilgrim's Rest: Visitor Information," later in this chapter.

GETTING AROUND Most lodges supply transfers from the airport; otherwise, contact **Eastgate Lodge Transfers** (© 015/793-3678; bookings@eastsaf.co.za). For the ultimate transfer, contact **Mpumalanga Helicopter Co.** (© 013/750-2358; www.mhelicopter.co.za). For car rentals, **Avis** and **Budget** have desks at all three airports in the Kruger region; see chapter 2 for contact details.

DULLSTROOM

Many travelers compare a visit to Dullstroom with a stint in the Scottish Highlands; the promise of landing a 6- to 7-pounder in the well-stocked dams and streams of the

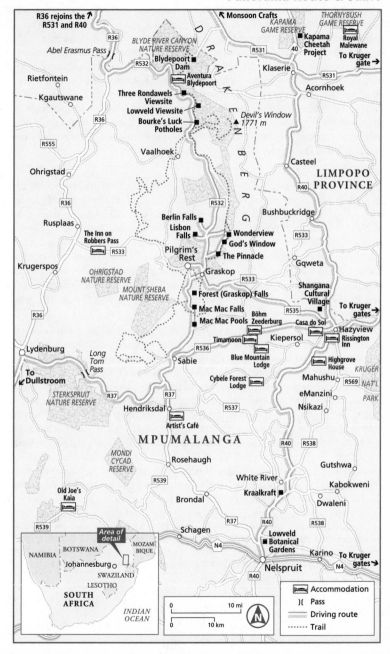

R36 rejoins the
R531 and R40
R36
BLYDE RIVER CANYON
NATURE RESERVE
Abel Erasmus Pass
R532
Blydepoort
Dam
Aventura
Blydepoort
Rietfontein
Kgautswane
Three Rondawels
Viewsite
Lowveld Viewsite
R36
Bourke's Luck
Potholes
Devil's Window
1771 m
R555
Vaalhoek
Ohrigstad
Casteel
LIMPOPO
PROVINCE
R36
R40
R532
Rusplaas
The Inn on
Robbers Pass
R533
Pilgrim's
Rest
Berlin Falls
Lisbon
Falls
Wonderview
God's Window
The Pinnacle
Bushbuckridge
R533
Krugerspos
Graskop
Gqweta
OHRIGSTAD
NATURE RESERVE
R533
MOUNT SHEBA
NATURE RESERVE
Forest (Graskop) Falls
Shangana
Cultural
Village
To Kruger
gates
R36
Mac Mac Falls
Mac Mac Pools
Böhm
Zeederburg
R535
Casa do Sol
Timamoon
Kiepersol
Hazyview
Rissington
Inn
Lydenburg
Long
Tom
Pass
R536
Blue Mountain
Lodge
KRUGER
To
Dullstroom
Sabie
Cybele Forest
Lodge
Highgrove
House
Mahushu
R569
NAT'L
STERKSPRUIT
NATURE RESERVE
R37
R37
eManzini
PARK
Hendriksdal
Artist's Café
R537
Nsikazi
MPUMALANGA
MONDI
CYCAD
RESERVE
Rosehaugh
R40
R538
Gutshwa
R539
White River
Kabokweni
Old Joe's
Kaia
Brondal
Kraalkraft
Dwaleni
R539
R37
R40
R538
Schagen
N4
Lowveld
Botanical
Gardens
Karino
To Kruger
gates
Nelspruit
N4
R40

Monsoon Crafts
KAPAMA
GAME RESERVE
THORNYBUSH
GAME RESERVE
Kapama
Cheetah
Project
Royal
Malewane
To Kruger
gate
40
Klaserie
R531
R531
Acornhoek

Area of
detail
MOZAM-
BIQUE
NAMIBIA
BOTSWANA
Johannesburg
SWAZILAND
LESOTHO
SOUTH
AFRICA
INDIAN
OCEAN

Accommodation
Pass
Driving route
Trail

0   10 mi
0   10 km

N

highveld's best trout-fishing region makes it a popular weekend getaway for urban South Africans. At 2,012m (6,599 ft.) above sea level, this is the highest town on the Escarpment—expect bitterly cold evenings in the winter, and don't be surprised to find fires lit even in midsummer. The town, some 230km (143 miles) northeast of Johannesburg, dates back to the 1880s, when a committee under the chairmanship of Wolterus Dull collected money in Holland to assist Boers who had suffered losses in the First Anglo-Boer War. The town was razed to the ground again by the British in the Second Anglo-Boer War, but despite perennial mist and low temperatures, the townsfolk simply rebuilt it. Its popularity with tourists has seen a huge rise in development in recent years, meaning that there is a greater selection of adventure activities available in the vicinity.

WHERE TO STAY

If you don't want to shell out for Walkersons (see below), **Dullstroom Inn** (© 013/254-0071; from R550/$82 double), a cozy, convivial inn that has been offering succor to travelers for almost a century, is the place to stop. There are fireplaces everywhere downstairs, but heaters, carpets, duvets, blankets, and hot-water bottles help ward off the Dullstroom chill in the rooms. Equally warming is the pub, which can get raucous when the townsfolk gather here over weekends. The inn is also within walking distance of some of the best restaurants in the area; both Mrs. Simpson's and Fibs (see below) are just down the road. Alternatively, try **Peebles Country Retreat** (© 013/254-8000; reservations@peebles.co.za; R500–R900/$75–$134), where accommodations are spacious and amenities plentiful.

Walkersons 🐾🐾   Set amid green, misty surrounds with trout-filled dams and weirs winding their way through the 600-hectare (1,482-acre) estate, Walkersons' grounds are pure Scottish highlands. Inside, the decor only adds to the illusion. From issues of *Majesty* to framed photographs of the Duke and Duchess of Windsor, the Walkersons have striven to create a home reminiscent of English aristocracy. Walls are covered in tapestries and Victorian oil paintings (purchased at Sotheby's, of course), windows are draped in heavy fabrics, floors are carpeted with sisal upon which Persian rugs add color, and all of the rooms have individual antique pieces. Each bedroom is huge, with a king-size bed, a writing desk, and two comfortable chairs facing the fire (lit before you arrive). The lodge offers a full selection of fly-fishing tackle. Note that Walkersons also operates the beautiful **Critchley Hackle** property, located at the edge of a lake and offering 23 neatly appointed rooms with fireplaces; they're good value, from R1,380 ($206) double, including dinner and breakfast.

10km (6¼ miles) north of Dullstroom off R540. © 013/254-0999. Fax 013/254-0262. www.critchleyhackle.co.za. 21 units. R1,980 ($296) double stable room (no fireplace or phone); R2,380 ($355) Highland suite. Rates include dinner and breakfast. Check website or call ahead for specials. AE, DC, MC, V. Children 12 and over welcome. **Amenities:** Restaurant; pub; room service (6:30am–9:30pm); helipad; runway; jogging/hiking trails; bird of prey center; horseback riding; fly-fishing. *In room:* A/C, TV, minibar, hair dryer, tea- and coffee-making facilities, fireplace.

WHERE TO DINE

Husband-and-wife team Natalie and Craig Hutton have opened a modern bistro on Main Street called **2 Chefs** (© 013/254-0920; closed Wed). If the Dullstroom chill has you cold to the bone, nothing but their hot South Indian fish and prawn curry will do. Dullstroom's other two top restaurants are within spitting distance of one another: **Fibs** (which, incidentally, has nothing to do with what the chef has to say and everything to do with the tall tales of the fly-fishermen patrons) is located on

Voortrekker Street in an old general dealer's store, and serves creative delicacies like roasted quail with a grape and tarragon stuffing, and whole trout with fennel and capers. It's open for lunch Tuesday to Sunday, and dinner Tuesday to Saturday; for bookings, call © **013/254-0059.** Named for the famous Wallace, the intimate **Mrs. Simpson's** is owned by culinary duo Bryan and Stephen, who like to experiment with their changing menu; ask for their signature filet, served with a chocolate-chile sauce. Casual, family-oriented options include **The Flying Dutchman** (© **013/254-0939**), the legendary **Harrie's Pancakes** (© **013/254-0801;** see "Sabie & Surrounds: Where to Dine," below) and **Dullstroom Inn** (see above). *Note:* It's worth reserving a table at these establishments on weekends, when Jo'burg's desperados make the 2-hour drive to soak up Dullstroom's country living over lunch before setting off for the traffic jam back home.

LYDENBURG & LONG TOM PASS

Lydenburg, or "place of suffering," was founded by a party of depressed Voortrekkers who, having lost a number of loved ones to a malaria epidemic in nearby Ohrigstad, retreated to its mosquito-free heights in 1849. Happily, "lydenburg" proved to be a misnomer, and today the town has a substantial center, though there's little to see beyond some interesting examples of pioneer architecture. The town is also known for a famed archaeological find: the **Lydenburg Heads,** seven ceramic masks that date back to the fifth century and were discovered in the late 1950s. You can see replicas of the heads (the originals now reside in the South African Museum in Cape Town) at the **Lydenburg Museum** (© **013/235-2213,** ext. 278), situated in the **Gustav Klingbiel Nature Reserve,** 3km (1¾ miles) out of town on the R37. For guided tours (by appointment only), call ahead. Hours are Monday through Friday from 8am to 4pm, Saturday and Sunday from 8am to 5pm; free admission.

From Lydenburg, the R37 east takes you down the **Long Tom Pass** 🜲🜲—at 2,150m (7,052 ft.) the second-highest mountain pass in South Africa. It was named after the Creusot siege guns that the Boers lugged up the pass to try and repel the British forces during the Second Anglo-Boer War (1899–1902). These guns, or cannons, were known as Long Toms because of their extended necks, which could spit a shell 9.5km (6 miles). Near the summit of the pass, at the **Devil's Knuckles,** a Long Tom replica commemorates the 4-day battle that was fought on this mountainside in 1900—the original cannons were destroyed by the Boers to prevent them from falling into British hands. You can still see the holes blasted by the cannons as the Boers retreated down the **Staircase,** a series of hairpin bends that zigzag down the pass.

Continuing east along the R37, passing the turnoff south for Hendriksdal, you come to the small forestry town of Sabie.

SABIE & SURROUNDS

Sabie (pronounced "*sah*-bee") dates to 1871 when a few friends, picnicking at the Lower Sabie Falls, were showing off their marksmanship skills. Bullets chipped the rocks behind the mock targets, revealing a glint of gold, and prospectors promptly followed. The initial boom was short-lived, though the mining industry was still to transform Sabie. The first commercial trees, intended for mine props, were planted in 1876 and today form the heart of what are claimed to be the largest man-made forests in the world. To date, more than a million acres have been planted with pine and eucalyptus, and many of these are destined to prop up shafts in the mines that run deep below Gauteng's surface; treehuggers can find out more at the **Forestry Museum**

(© **013/764-1058;** Mon–Fri 8am–4:30pm, Sat 8am–noon; R5/75¢ adults, R3/45¢ children).

The area surrounding Sabie and Graskop is also renowned for its waterfalls. But if your idea of a waterfall worth detouring is Victoria Falls, give these a miss and head straight for Pilgrim's Rest and/or the Panorama Route. If you visit only one waterfall, consider **Lone Creek Falls,** reached by traveling 10km (6¼ miles) on the Old Lydenburg Road northwest from Sabie. You will pass turnoffs for both the **Bridal Veil** (R5/75¢ per car) and **Horseshoe Falls** (R5/75¢ per car) before reaching the **Lone Creek** gate (R5/75¢ per car). The single cascade plunges 68m (223 ft.) into an attractive pool and is framed by the lush green foliage of a small damp rain forest.

A little farther along the R532, you will see the sign for **Forest Falls** (© **013/764-2423;** R10/$1.50 per person for a permit, obtainable from Forestry Museum); this is an easy 3km (1.75-mile) walk and well worth tackling, time allowing. To view the Lisbon and Berlin waterfalls, take the Panorama Route following the rim of the Escarpment.

WHERE TO STAY

The following establishments are located amid lush plantations, subtropical farms, or indigenous bush, and most feature superb views and luxurious suites—all of which come at a price. For a good budget alternative, check out the **Graskop Hotel** (© **013/767-1244;** www.graskophotel.co.za; R500/$75 double, including breakfast); it's located in the town of Graskop but offers decent decor and good service at a reasonable rate; alternatively, **Bohm's Zeederberg Country House** (© **013/737-8101;** www.bohms.co.za; R840/$125 double, including breakfast), which offers 10 chalets in lush subtropical gardens with great views—ask for no. 5, 6, 10, 11, 12, or 14.

Near Sabie

Blue Mountain Lodge ★★★   Do not book into this 198-hectare (494-acre) estate if your taste runs to spartan minimalism—from the dark timber and mustard-yellow walls of the "Bismarck" to the floral and leopard-print "Fassler," each Victorian Suite has its own unique personality, yet all share a Versace-like opulence. Located in eight separate cottages set below ponds, palms, a pool, a dining terrace, and a grand staircase that sweeps down to more immaculately manicured lawns, Blue Mountain is one of the most romantic, luxurious, and expensive accommodations options on the Escarpment, but don't expect the consistency of service you find for a comparable price in the cities. Over and above the Victorian Suites there are the decadent Manor Houses and the Quadrant Rooms—while the latter are not as pricey, they're very average, so don't book these. Food is yet another reason why Blue Mountain enjoys such an excellent reputation—head chef Elvis Mnisi prepares a new menu every day, a copy of which is delivered to your room in the late afternoon along with canapés and an invitation to predinner drinks.

P.O. Box 101, Kiepersol 1241. (Take the Kiepersol turnoff, 28km/17 miles east of Sabie on the R536, follow for 4km/2½ miles before turnoff.) © 013/737-8446. Fax 013/737-8446. www.blu-mountain.com. 13 units; 2 manor houses. Victorian Suite R2,950 ($440) double; Quadrant Room R2,670 ($399) double; Presidential Suite R4,140 ($618) double. Rates include dinner and breakfast; AE, DC, MC, V. No children under 12. **Amenities:** Restaurant; bar; large pool; room service (6:30am–11pm); same-day laundry. *In room:* A/C, minibar, hair dryer.

Timamoon ★★   It's hard to beat the total peace offered by these four secluded thatched two-bedroom "lodges," located a few minutes' drive from each other. Kruger lies but 40 minutes away, but you'll be hard-pressed to leave your well-appointed and spacious cottage, furnished with artifacts that the owners have collected from years of travel throughout Africa. Each features two en-suite bedrooms with four-poster beds draped in mosquito netting, private plunge pools, and decks overlooking a forested gorge through which the Sabie River cascades. Moon River is built on the lip of the gorge in the style of a Moroccan castle, as is New Moon, which offers better value. Luxurious bathrooms and outdoor showers enjoy similar views. The main drawback is that there's no phone (and no room service), and you have to drive to get to the restaurant, a charming candlelit room built on stilts. Dinner menus are set three-course meals, and any dietary preferences need to be cleared in advance. A good budget alternative is one of the two fully serviced self-catering cottages; although they don't have pools, they are furnished with flair and are extremely spacious. Each features two bedrooms, two bathrooms, a lounge, a private balcony (with wonderful forest views), and a fireplace. Dinner (R120/$18) may be booked at the restaurant a day in advance.

P.O. Box 292, Hazyview 1242. (24km/15 miles east of Sabie, turn off from R536; follow signs for 3km/1¾ miles). (℃) 013/767-1740 or 082/445-3788. Fax 013/767-1889. www.timamoonlodge.co.za. 5 units. 4 lodges: R1,900–R3,200 ($284–$478) double (from R750/$112 per person for 4 people sharing). Rates include breakfast and dinner. Self-catering cottages: R2,400 ($358 double; R1,050/$157 per person for 4 people sharing). Rates include breakfast and dinner. AE, DC, MC, V. No children under 12 in lodges. **Amenities:** Restaurant; private plunge pool (lodges). *In room:* TV (cottages only), minibar (lodges only; cottages on request), hair dryer on request.

Near Hazyview

Casa do Sol 🎐 *Kids*   A charming Mediterranean-style village, complete with cobbled streets, white stucco walls, and terra-cotta roof tiles, set in award-winning tropical gardens behind which stretch 500 hectares (1,235 acres) of indigenous bush, Casa do Sol was established in 1968 and still retains a vaguely 1970s feel, despite regular decor updates. The C and D suites are ideal for families—the D suites are upstairs and feature views of the valley and estate from the private patio. Dinners offer a choice of three starters, three main courses, and a dessert and cheese board; diners are welcome to indulge in all nine courses. This is an all-around excellent hotel, with a good ambience, though it doesn't offer the well-bred intimacy of lodges like Blue Mountain or Cybele.

P.O. Box 57, Hazyview 1242, off the R536, 39km (24 miles) east of Sabie and 5km (3 miles) west of Hazyview. (℃) 013/737-8111. Fax 013/737-8166. www.casadosol.co.za. 54 units. Casa R960–R1,190 ($143–$178) double, depending on season; Villa R1,145–R1,430 ($171–$213); C and D suites R1,550–R1,945 ($231–$290). All rates include breakfast and dinner. Children under 12 R175 ($26); children 12 and over R330 ($49). AE, DC, MC, V. **Amenities:** Restaurant; bar; 2 large swimming pools; all-weather tennis court; 24-hr. room service; babysitting; same-day laundry; horseback riding; bass fishing; trails to view antelope; tours and safaris arranged with recommended operators. *In room:* A/C, TV, minibar (villas and suites), hair dryer.

Cybele Forest Lodge 🎐🎐🎐   Long before crime encouraged Jo'burgers to take regular long-weekend getaways, the rooms at Cybele were booked months in advance, and the way you pronounced the name said a lot about how happening you were (it's pronounced "sigh-*bee*-lee"). Even Capetonians traveled north to sample the legendary cuisine (the lodge is a Yellow Shield member of Relais & Châteaux) and to relax in the subtropical surrounds. Over the years, owners Rupert and Barbara Jeffries have added a number of free-standing suites, the newest being the Forest Suites, with everything from espresso machines and private heated pools to CD and DVD players and fireplaces in the bathrooms. A pool has replaced the farm dam, but the standard of the food and the beauty of the 120-hectare (296-acre) grounds remain unchanged. The original farmhouse, where the lounge and dining room are situated, is wonderful: Rooms are painted in rich, warm colors and are cluttered with an eclectic mix of

Driving the Panorama Route

This drive takes you past the Blyde River Canyon, the third-largest canyon in the world, and the sheer 1,600m (5,248-ft.) drop from the Escarpment to the warm lowveld plains shimmering below. Hot air rising over this wall generates the heavy mists and high rainfall that, in turn, create the unique montane grasslands and riverine forests of the Blyde River Canyon Nature Reserve, which start just north of Graskop before broadening out to include the Blydepoort Dam, 60km (37 miles) north. To complete the Panorama Route as a circular trip (approximately 160km/99 miles), stopping for most of the viewpoints and returning to either Sabie or Graskop, set aside a day.

As you follow the tour below, refer to the "Panorama Route & Sabie" map earlier in this chapter for more information.

To drive this route, take the R532 north out of Graskop before turning right on the R534. The first stop is the **Pinnacle**—a thin 30m-tall (98-ft.) quartzite rock topped with trees that juts below the viewpoint—but **God's Window** ⭐⭐, 4km (2½ miles) farther, which offers the first view of the open lowveld plains, is more impressive. (Wonderview is a variation of this and can be skipped if you're pressed for time.) The looping R534 now rejoins the R532. Turn left and look for the sign if you want to visit **Lisbon Falls,** which drop 37m (121 ft.). To continue on to Blyde River Canyon, turn right onto the R532, taking in the 48m (157-ft.) **Berlin Falls** on the way. If you're ready for refreshments, the **Berlin Peacock Tavern** ⭐ (℗ **013/767-1085**) lies on the way to the Berlin Falls—aside from some spectacularly over-the-top baroque decor, the food is delicious, and according to the visitors' book, even rival lodge-owners visit regularly.

Back on the R532, head north for **Bourke's Luck Potholes** (℗ **013/ 761-6019**). Here gold-digger Bourke predicted that he would strike it lucky, but he found nothing in these large scooped formations, carved by the movement of pebbles and water in the swirling whirlpools created by the confluence of the Blyde and Treur rivers. Bourke was not the last person to be disappointed by the Potholes—it's a long walk to look at them, and they reveal very little. Nor does the visitor center, which, in addition to some dry displays on the geology of the area, features a few dusty stuffed animals that look close to decomposing. The lichen trail is very easy and good for children. Gates open from 7am to 5pm; admission is R20 ($3).

Some 20km (12 miles) north is the lookout for the **Three Rondawels** ⭐⭐⭐, by far the most impressive stop of the entire trip. The name—which refers to the three circular hut-shaped outcrops that are more or less opposite the lookout—does nothing to describe the humbling size of what beckons. A sheer drop threatens to pull you off the precipice; thousands of feet below, the Blyde River snakes its way through the canyon to the tranquil Blyde Dam, embraced by green mountains. Beyond, the great lowveld plains shimmer in the distance.

Tip: If you're feeling thirsty, drop into the **Aventura Blydepoort Resort** (the turnoff is a couple of miles north past the Three Rondawels and clearly signposted; © 013/769-8005), which offers another angle on the Three Rondawels from its terrace; however, much beyond a toasted sandwich is not recommended. (To take a look at its budget self-catering lodging, go to www.aventura.co.za—and ask for a cottage with a view.)

From here you will descend the **Abel Erasmus Pass** before passing through the J. G. Strijdom Tunnel—approximately 20km (12 miles) from here is the turnoff for **Monsoon Gallery** (© 015/795-5114), off the R527. Monsoon carries a fine selection of African crafts, but stock is often limited. You can enjoy a light meal at the adjacent **Mad Dogz Café** (© 015/795-5425) or make an appointment to meet with John Williams (see "Specialist Tours," earlier in this chapter) about archaeological and ecotours.

At this point, you can stay on the R527, heading east for Hoedspruit, if you wish to enter the Timbavati private game reserve, or head for the airport. If not, take the R531 southeast to Klaserie—look for the turnoff to **Aventura Swadini** (© 015/795-5141). From here you can take a 90-minute boat trip on the Blyde Dam to see the mouth of the canyon and look up at the Escarpment towering above (R65/$9.70 per adult, R35/$5.20 children 5–15). The R531 takes you to Kruger to enter via Orpen Gate (the closest to the Satara Rest Camp), or to travel to the Manyeleti or northern Sabi Sand reserves via Gowry Gate. Turn north on the R40 to Kapama, a fenced private reserve and site of the popular **Hoedspruit Research and Breeding Centre for Endangered Species** (© 015/793-1633), also known as the "Cheetah Project." This is also the pickup point for Kapama's exciting elephant-back safaris. The latter is well worth considering: For R1,250 ($187), you get to be transported through big-game country on the back of one of these lumbering giants and learn more about this most intelligent of species; for times and bookings, call Karin at © 015/793-1633. The Cheetah Project is equally educational but far less exhilarating. Guided tours (daily, every hour 8am–3pm) kick off with a video presentation, after which you are driven through the center by a ranger, sighting cheetahs, wild dog, rhino, and various bird species. At 90 minutes, the tour is a tad long, and although one of the cheetahs has been successfully released into the wilds, it still feels a little like a large, comfortable zoo. The tour that takes in the rare Barbary lion—identified by his extended black mane—is more like a traditional game drive (the lions are kept in a 6.8-hectare /17-acre area) but will take 3 hours out of your day.

To return to Graskop, take the R40 south from Klaserie, then follow the R533 from Bosbokrand, climbing Kowyn's Pass to Graskop. (Note that the R40 between Hazyview and Acorn Hoek is unsafe to travel at night when animals wander at will, and a few travelers have been ambushed. During daylight you're more likely to be pulled over for speeding, so take it easy.)

antiques, English country–style fabrics, kilim rugs, and a few African crafts. With upgrades and revamps taking the lodge (and its popular spa) into the 21st century, Cybele remains a place of tranquillity and relaxation. If you expect jump-on-demand service, however, you are likely to be disappointed; this is a mellow retreat that moves at a rural pace—something that may irritate, given the steep price tag.

P.O. Box 346, White River 1240. (Take the Kiepersol turnoff, 28km/17 miles east of Sabie on the R536; follow for 10km/6¼ miles before taking a road to the left marked "whitewaters" and following Cybele signs. Alternatively, follow signs off the R40 between Hazyview and White River.) ℂ 013/764-9500. Fax 013/764-9510. www.cybele.co.za. 12 units. R2,200–R3,780 ($328–$564) double; R3,000–R4,180 ($448–$624) suite; R3,700–R5,700 ($552–$851) Paddock suite; R5,400–R7,200 ($806–$1,075) Forest suite. Rates include breakfast and dinner. Inquire about winter rates. AE, DC, MC, V. No children under 10. **Amenities:** Restaurant; bar; pool; spa; gym; gift store; horseback riding (the surrounds are truly beautiful); hiking trails; trout fishing (tackle is provided). *In room:* A/C (suite no. 14), TV, mini-bar, hair dryer, stereo, fans, fireplaces, private pool (suite).

Highgrove House 🏵🏵

Follow the grand tree-lined driveway and at the end of the cul-de-sac, and you'll find an elegant, old-fashioned country retreat where guests are treated like royalty. "English-country" style is a constant theme in South African decor, but here it is particularly well done: The eight garden suites are decorated in pale, earthy colors and feature separate sitting rooms with log fireplaces and double doors that lead onto verandas with marvelous views over the forest or valley. The slightly pricier Orchard Suites (Orchard 1 is a personal favorite) have private pools and saunas, as well as their own garden. Beautifully presented dinners, prepared by the talented Anna Mahlele under the watchful eye of proprietor Mary Terry, are—together with the meals served at Blue Mountain—considered by many to be the best in Mpumalanga (see "Where to Dine," below). The candlelit atmosphere is romantic but may be a bit stuffy for some vacationers—no jeans or sneakers allowed.

Off R40, 17km (11 miles) south of Hazyview. P.O. Box 46, Kiepersol 1241. ℂ **013/764-1844.** Fax 013/764-1855. www.highgrove.co.za. 8 units. R2,500 ($373) double; R3,000 ($448) Orchard Suite. Rates include dinner and breakfast. AE, DC, MC, V. No children under 14. **Amenities:** Restaurant; bar; pool; limited room service. *In room:* Minibar (Orchard Suites), hair dryer, fireplace, pool, sauna.

Rissington Inn 🏵 ⟨Value⟩ ⟨Kids⟩

Rissington offers unbeatable value, and with Kruger's Phabeni Gate just 10 minutes away, it makes an extremely comfortable base from which to explore Kruger and the Escarpment surrounds. What it lacks in style (the honeymoon suite has a false thatch roof jutting over the bed), the inn makes up for in charm, comfort, and great food. Meals (non-residents should book in advance) are excellent value as well, with most main dinner courses costing about R60 ($9). Of the 10 rooms, Euphorbia (sunset-facing, with a sitting room and a super-king-size bed) and Ivory (a garden view, a deep veranda with built-in day bed, and a super-king-size bed) are recommended. Camelfoot and Sycamore, both spacious and furnished with two queen-size beds, are good choices for families. Proprietor Chris Harvie is known throughout the region for his great hospitality, charming dry humor, and sensible approach to pricing.

1km (½ mile) south of Hazyview, follow signposts off R40. P.O. Box 650, Hazyview 1242. ℂ **013/737-7700.** Fax 013/737-7112. www.rissington.co.za. 7 units. R650–R1,100 ($97–$164) double. Rates include breakfast. Children sharing R120 ($18). AE, DC, MC, V. **Amenities:** Restaurant; bar; pool; room service; laundry; library. *In room:* Hair dryer.

WHERE TO DINE

Sabie is the town with the most restaurants, but only one is worth stopping for: **Country Kitchen,** 78 Main St. (ℂ **013/764-1901**) may lack atmosphere, but the food, prepared by Hilton-trained Edmund Idzik, is excellent (try the stir-fried crocodile spring rolls with coriander, papaya, and mango, followed by pan-fried medallions of ostrich in a port-wine sauce, to finish with the popular Sabie River Mud Pie, a delicious chocolate dessert served with Amarula cream). For a more rural ambience, the **Artists Café,** a "trattoria" in the middle of nowhere, is well worth the detour. Owners Leon and Hetta have been developing their kitchen garden to ensure that most of the vegetables served are fresh-picked daily; in keeping with the simple food, the atmosphere in the restaurant is casual—chairs are mismatched, dishcloths serve as napkins, and walls are covered with local artworks as well as crafts from across Africa, most of which are for sale.

Note also that many of the places listed in the "Where to Stay" section, above, are renowned for their fine cuisine and romantic atmosphere. Besides **Blue Mountain Lodge,** which offers alfresco dining at its most romantic (make sure to get here before dark to enjoy a drink on the deep verandas overlooking the lush, manicured gardens of this 200-hectare/494-acre estate), **Highgrove** is definitely worth considering; five-course dinners (R180/$27 per person) are served in a candlelit fine-dining atmosphere (dressing up is, however, required) and the menu may include goat's cheese and tomato soufflé served with hazelnut and Parmesan sauce, followed by East Coast sole baked with bay leaves and oregano. The Relais & Château **Cybele Forest Lodge** (see above) is another romantic fine-dining dinner experience; you can also opt for a light lunch in their gardens (R25–R115/$3.75–$17)—the vegetables are homegrown, the house salad is picked fresh daily, and the pasta is homemade.

When in **Graskop,** tasting one of **Harrie's Pancakes**—thick crepes filled with trout mousse and horseradish, or butternut with cumin and bleu cheese sauce, or green fig preserve and pecan nuts and cream or ice cream, to mention but a few—is as high on the priority list as visiting the nearby Escarpment attractions (© **013/767-1273**). And for a truly unusual evening, give Bevvie a call and book an evening at her **Thistle's Country Kitchen** (© **082/467-5276**). A very intimate affair, this spot comprises only three tables, each seating four to eight and personally attended to by Bevvie Myberg, Graskop's one-woman wonder, who cooks, waits, and washes in her home-style restaurant.

When in the **Hazyview** area, you'll find great-value home-cooked fare, served in a truly laid-back atmosphere, at **Rissington Inn**—order comfort dishes like the smoked-trout cheesecake or the beef stroganoff; Chris also serves up the most delicious filet this side of Hazyview. And if you're interested in sampling traditional African fare accompanied by some superb singing and dancing by local Shangaan people, book an "Evening Festival" at the nearby **Shangana Cultural Village** (see below).

And if you're traveling anywhere near Whiteriver, make sure you schedule a stop at **Salt** (© **013/751-1555**), the new sister restaurant opened by Dario de Angeli, the man behind the award-winning Yum in Johannesburg (see chapter 7).

PILGRIM'S REST

The village of Pilgrim's Rest was established in 1873 after Alex "Wheelbarrow" Patterson discovered gold in the stream that flows past what was to become the first goldrush town in South Africa. Having struck out on his own to escape the crush at Mac Mac, he must have been horrified when within the year he was joined by 1,500 diggers, all frantically panning to make their fortunes. A fair number did, with the largest nugget weighing in at 24 pounds, but by 1881, the best of the pickings had been found, and the diggings were bought by the Transvaal Gold Mining Estates (TGME). A century later, the village still looked much the same, and the entire settlement was declared a national monument, with the Works Department and Museum Services put in charge of restoring and preserving this living museum.

If you're looking for historical accuracy, then you'll find Pilgrim's Rest overcommercialized; the town's streets are probably a great deal prettier than they were at the turn of the 20th century, and the overall effect, from the gleaming vintage fuel pumps to the flower baskets, is a sanitized, glamorized picture of life in a gold-rush town. As theme parks go, however, Pilgrim's Rest is a pleasant experience. Most of the buildings line a single main street, and the architecture is of the quaint Victorian variety prevalent in so many of colonial Africa's rural towns—walls are corrugated iron with deep sash windows, and corrugated-iron roofs extend over large shaded *stoeps* (verandas).

ESSENTIALS

GETTING THERE   Travel north from Sabie on R532. The R532 meets with the R533 in a T-junction; head northwest on R533 for 15km (9¼ miles). Pilgrim's Rest is 35km (22 miles) north of Sabie and about 360km (223 miles) northeast of Johannesburg.

VISITOR INFORMATION   Contact the **Tourist Information Centre** (© 013/768-1060; daily 9am–7pm) and, if possible, ask for the information officer. The center is clearly marked on the main street; staff will supply free town maps as well as tickets to the museums, and will book tours for you.

GETTING AROUND   Pilgrim's Rest has no street numbers; it's literally a one-horse town, with buildings stretched along a main road. Uptown, or Top Town, is literally the higher (and older) part of the main road, while Downtown stretches below the turnoff into town. Most of the tourist sights are situated in Uptown, as is the tourist office. For guided tours, contact John Pringle (ex–information officer for the town) at © 083/522-6441.

WHAT TO SEE & DO

St. Mary's Anglican Church, seen overlooking the main street as you enter town, is where sinners' souls were salvaged. Higher up the hill, the evocative **Pilgrim's Rest Cemetery** ⚬⚬ is definitely worth a visit. Besides the tombstone simply inscribed ROBBERS GRAVE—easily identified because it is the only grave that lies in a north-south direction—the many children's graves are moving testimony to how hard times really were, and the many nationalities reflect the cosmopolitan character of the original gold-rush village.

The three museums in town, the **Dredzen Shop and House Museum,** the **News Printing Museum,** and the **House Museum,** can all be visited with the ticket sold at the Tourist Information Centre (R10/$1.50 adults, R5/75¢ children under 13), but none of these house museums feels particularly authentic; furnishings and objects are often propped haphazardly and look much the worse for wear.

The **Alanglade Museum** ⚬⚬ (no phone; R20/$3), which used to house the TGME's mine manager and his family, is more interesting. Although the furnishings, which date from 1900 to 1930, are not original, they have been selected to represent the era and are maintained with more care than those in the house museums. It is set in a forested grove 1.5km (about 1 mile) north of town. Tours are offered at 11am and 2pm Monday through Saturday, and must be booked half an hour in advance from the Pilgrim's Rest Tourist Information Centre.

Don't leave town without popping in to The Royal Hotel's **Church Bar** ⚬ (the tiny building used to be a church in Mozambique before it was relocated here, thereby answering the prayers of the thirsty Pilgrims of Mpumalanga).

WHERE TO STAY

District Six Miners' Cottages *(Value)* The District Six cottages date back to the early 1920s. Set high up on the hill overlooking the town, these spartan accommodations have lovely views from their verandas and are serviced daily. Each has two bedrooms, a living room, a bathroom, and a fully equipped kitchen. Not surprisingly, these cheap, charming cottages are popular during school holidays—so make sure to book ahead. Keys are collected at The Royal Hotel.

Public Works Private X516, Pilgrim's Rest 1290. Book in advance; there is no on-site office. © **013/768-1261.** Fax 013/768-1113. 6 units. R280 ($42) for 4-bed and R420 ($63) for 6-bed cottage. No credit cards.

The Royal Hotel The Royal first opened its doors in 1873, and more than a century later, it's still going strong—this is one of the most charming places to overnight on the Escarpment. Besides the 11 original hotel rooms, which are arranged around a small courtyard behind the reception area, the hotel has grown to include 39 rooms located in buildings adjacent to the hotel, all dating back to the turn of the 20th century and impeccably restored and furnished in the Victorian style. The relatively small bedrooms feature brass beds, many of them four-poster, wooden ceiling fans, marble-and-oak washstands, and ball-and-claw bathtubs. This is not a luxurious experience, however—the mattresses are a little monastic, and corrugated-iron houses can become bitterly cold in winter. The honeymoon suite, situated in the Bank House, is the only room with a fireplace, and during June and July, when temperatures drop close to freezing, it's worth booking well in advance.

Main Rd., Uptown, Pilgrim's Rest 1290. © **013/768-1100.** Fax 013/768-1188. www.royal-hotel.co.za. 50 units. R940 ($140) double. Rate includes breakfast. Ask about winter specials. AE, DC, MC, V. **Amenities:** 2 restaurants; bar; golf, tennis, horseback riding, and trout fishing can be arranged; babysitting; laundry. *In room:* Hair dryer.

WHERE TO DINE

You'll find a number of places to eat and drink all along the main road, but for quality home-style country cooking, and lovely views, your best bet is **Inn on Robber's Pass**, off the R533, 15km (9¼ miles) from Pilgrim's Rest (© **013/768-1491**), though you'll have to drive to get there.

5 Kruger National Park

Southern (Malelane) gate: 428km (265 miles) NE of Johannesburg; Northern (Punda Maria) gate: 581km (360 miles) NE of Johannesburg

Proclaimed by South African president Paul Kruger in 1898, this jewel in the South African National Parks crown stretches 381km (236 miles) from the banks of the Crocodile River in the south to the Limpopo River in the north, and covers almost 2½ million hectares (6.2 million acres).

Even more impressive than its size, however, is the diversity of life the Kruger sustains: Sixteen ecozones (each with its own geology, rainfall, altitude, and landscape) are home to more than 500 bird species and 147 mammal species, including some 2,000 lions, 1,000 leopards, 1,800 rhinos, 8,000 elephants, and 15,000 buffaloes. Cheetahs, wild dogs, hyenas, zebras, giraffes, hippos, crocodiles, warthogs, and a large number of antelope also roam Kruger's open plains and waterways. The rich plant life varies from tropical to subtropical; almost 2,000 species have been identified, including some 450 tree and shrub species and 235 grasses. The opportunity to see wildlife is superb—many people report seeing four of the Big 5 (the most elusive being leopard) in 1 day.

Kruger National Park & Private Reserves

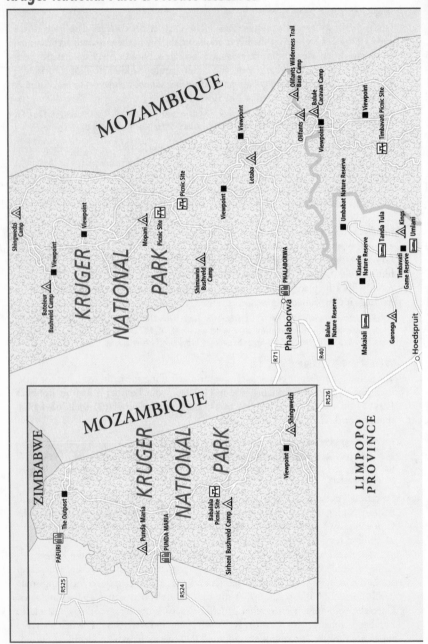

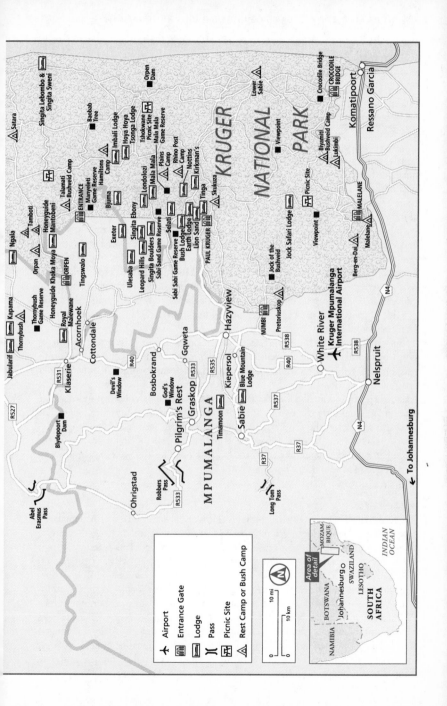

(*Fun Fact* **Going to the Dogs**

While most tourists love chasing after lion and leopard, it takes a small scruffy dog with rather powerful jaws to excite a ranger: The wild dog is Africa's rarest and most endangered predator.

Kruger also has a number of archaeological sites, the most interesting being Thulamela, a 12th-century stone-walled village overlooking the Luvuvhu River in the north. Others include the Stone Age village at Masorini and San engravings and paintings found at the Crocodile Bridge hippo pool or on the Bushman and Wolhuter trails. Historical sites relating to early European explorers and Kruger's beginnings are also dotted throughout the park.

In 2002, ecodiplomacy reached new heights when the fences between the Kruger and Zimbabwe's Gonarezhou National Park and Mozambique's Gaza Reserve were removed, effectively bringing into being the 37.5 million–hectare (92.5 million–acre) **Great Limpopo Transfrontier Park,** or, simply, **Limpopo Park,** as the park is currently referred to, the biggest conservation area in the world. (Though interestingly enough, attempts to get animals, particularly elephants, to relocate to the Mozambican side of the border have been futile; even animals moved there at great cost are soon seen back on the South African side.)

But excitement over the Kruger's expanding borders has to some extent been tempered by concerns over the current disputes before the country's Land Claims Commission, charged with returning land appropriated from its original owners under apartheid governance. Thus far, only one of these claims has been settled: The Makulele people, located in the northern region of the park, have been awarded a large tract of land and have come to an amicable agreement whereby a private lodge (The Outpost; see later in this chapter) is administered on behalf of the Makulele by independent concession holders. Once the contract expires, the lodge reverts to the Makulele, who are also employed by the lodge. Hopefully, this will, in fact, prove to be an exercise in sustainable development.

ESSENTIALS
ARRIVING
BY PLANE   There are three airports in the Kruger vicinity: Kruger-Mpumalanga International Airport (near White River and Hazyview, southern Kruger), Eastgate Airport (Hoedspruit, southern/central Kruger), and the Kruger Park Gateway Airport (Phalaborwa, central Kruger). **From Cape Town: SA Express** (www.saexpress.co.za) flies daily to Hoedspruit's Eastgate Airport. **SA Airlink** (www.saairlink.co.za) flies daily to the relatively nearby Kruger-Mpumalanga International—as does **Nationwide** (www.flynationwide.co.za), but you'll have to stop in Johannesburg for at least 20 minutes to pick up passengers. **From Johannesburg:** SA Express flies daily to Hoedspruit's Eastgate Airport; SA Airlink and Nationwide fly daily to Kruger-Mpumalanga International. SA Airlink also flies daily from Johannesburg into Kruger Park Gateway Airport. **From Durban:** SA Airlink flies Sunday through Friday to Kruger-Mpumalanga airport.

BY CAR   The park has nine entrance gates, most a comfortable 5- to 6-hour drive from Johannesburg or Pretoria. The closest gate, Malelane, is 428km (265 miles) from Johannesburg, while Punda Maria (the farthest) lies 581km (360 miles) northeast. The southern gates: **Malelane, Crocodile Bridge, Numbi, Phabeni,** and **Paul Kruger.** The central gates: **Orpen** and **Phalaborwa.** The northern gates: **Punda Maria** and **Parfuri.** Allow sufficient traveling time to the park; entrance-gate hours (see "Fast Facts: Kruger National Park," below) are strictly adhered to. Note that officials recommend using the new Phabeni Gate from a safety and ease-of-access point of view.

VISITOR INFORMATION   All inquiries and applications should be made to **South African National Parks (SANParks),** P.O. Box 787, 643 Leyds St., Muckleneuk, Pretoria (© **012/428-9111;** fax 012/426-5500; www.sanparks.org; Mon–Fri 7:30am–5pm, Sat 8am–2pm). Or you can e-mail them at reservations@sanparks.org for short-notice bookings (3 days or less in advance). You can also phone the park directly at © **013/735-4000** or 013/735-4246. The park's headquarters is situated at Skukuza Rest Camp, located in the southern section, on the banks of the Sabie River (see later in this chapter).

GETTING AROUND   **By Car**   **Avis** has a desk at the Eastgate Airport (© **015/ 793-2014**), at the Kruger-Mpumalanga airport (© **013/741-1087**), and at Phalaborwa's Kruger airport (© **015/781-3169**). **Budget** operates from the Kruger-Mpumalanga airport (© **013/741-3871**) and Phalaborwa's Kruger airport (© **015/ 781-5404**). It's exciting to explore the park at your own pace in a rental car, but at least one guided game drive in an open-topped vehicle is recommended (see "Organized Tours," at the beginning of the chapter). Also see "Guided Game Drives & Walks," below—these take place in a variety of vehicles and are organized by Kruger officials.

WHEN TO GO

Each season has advantages. Between October and March, when summer rains (often in the form of dramatic thunderstorms) have transformed the dry landscape into a flowering paradise, the park is alive with baby buck and migratory birds, but at the same time, temperatures can soar above 105°F (40°C), dropping to 68°F (20°C) in the balmy evenings. The dense, junglelike foliage hides game, and the malaria risk is at its highest. In the winter, when water is scarce and the plant life dies back, animals are easier to spot, especially at water holes and riverbeds. Because this is the most popular season, however, be prepared to share your sightings with other motorists. The days are warm, but temperatures can drop close to freezing at night, and units are not heated. Try to avoid going during the school holidays, particularly in winter, when the park is packed to capacity.

Tips   Saving You Time and Money

Expressions of Africa (© **011/978-3552;** www.saexpress.co.za), a division of SA Express, caters to travel agents and individuals wanting to fly in to safari destinations throughout southern Africa. Work out a rough itinerary and contact them directly for the best deals on flights and possible savings on accommodations.

FAST FACTS: Kruger National Park

Admission Hours **For the Park**   Entrance gates open from January to February from 5:30am to 6:30pm, March from 5:30am to 6pm, April from 6am to 6pm, May to July 6am to 5:30pm, August to September 6am to 6pm, October from 5:30am to 6pm, and November to December from 5:30am to 6:30pm.

For the Rest Camps   The gates follow the same hours, except in the summer months (Nov–Jan), when they open an hour earlier (that is, 4:30am). Camps are fenced off to protect residents from predators. If you're changing rest camps, try not to travel more than 200km (124 miles), to ensure you get to your new camp before gates close. Operating hours for camp receptions are 8am to 5:30pm; shops 8am to a half-hour after camp gates close; restaurants 7 to 9am, 12 to 2pm, and 6 to 9pm.

Bank & ATM Networks   There is a bank and ATM at Skukuza, and an ATM at Letaba.

Driving Rules   Unlike private game reserves, where rangers are free to drive off road, everyone at Kruger drives on roads; the public drives on approved roads only. The speed limit is 50kmph (31 mph) on paved roads, 40kmph (25 mph) on gravel roads, and 20kmph (12 mph) in rest camps. If photographs of fatally maimed animals don't help ensure that these speeds are adhered to, speed traps do. Stay in your vehicle unless you're at a designated picnic site.

Fees   SANParks charges a **daily conservation fee** for each person entering the park; at press time, this was R120 ($18) per adult and R60 ($8.95) per child. If you plan to spend more than 6 nights in Kruger and/or visit other national parks in South Africa, it may be worth purchasing a **Wild Pass,** which starts at R795 ($118) for a 10-day card; other benefits include a 5% discount on park accommodations.

Fuel   Every rest camp has a fuel/petrol station. You must pay in cash.

Malaria   While certain areas of Kruger are soon to be removed from the list of malaria areas, the risk of infection remains, and it is a deadly disease you really want to avoid. The highest risk is between October and May, during which time a course of prescription antimalaria drugs is advised (for more information, see chapter 2).

Medical Emergencies   There is a doctor in Skukuza (✆ **013/735-5638**). If you need help during the night, drive to the camp gate and beep your horn. The closest hospitals are in Nelspruit, Hoedspruit, and Phalaborwa.

Money   South African rand, traveler's checks, Visa, MasterCard, Diners Club, and American Express are accepted. Foreign currency can be exchanged at all rest camps.

Reservations   Preference for choice units is given to written applications (this includes fax and e-mail) received 13 months in advance. Pay your deposit as soon as possible to ensure the booking—this can be done over the telephone with a credit card.

Safety   Don't let the tarred road fool you—once you've left the safety of your fenced-off rest camp, you really are in the wilds. *Under no circumstances* should you leave your vehicle unless at a designated site (see "Designated Pit Stops & Picnic Sites," below, or get a map from a rest camp shop); one ranger who left his game drive to "relieve" himself didn't survive to do up his zipper, so make sure to take care of any bathroom business before leaving camp. When in camp, try not to be frightened by spiders and other small insects you may encounter; unlike mosquitoes, they can do you no harm. Snakes are a rare occurrence in camps; if you do spot one, alert reception. (See chapter 2 for more safety tips on safaris.)

EXPLORING THE PARK

SANParks officials make no bones about the fact that their main concern is wildlife; Homo sapiens are a necessary nuisance. Although an effort is made to service visitors' needs, such as providing escorted night and day drives (highly recommended unless you're going on to a private game reserve), the rules (like gate-opening times) are inflexible, the staff can be bureaucratic, and, because services are geared toward the South African self-catering market, you're pretty much expected to toe the line. Here's how.

THE LAY OF THE LAND

Despite its many defined ecozones, to the untrained eye, much of the park looks the same, with a major portion covered with a large shrublike tree called mopane. You'll find the most variation in the south and far north of the park—old bush hands, in fact, divide the park into three distinct regions: The south they call the "circus"; the central area, the "zoo"; and the north, the "wilderness." These are apt descriptions, particularly in the winter months, when the human and animal population soars in the water-rich south, while the less-accessible north remains a calm oasis.

Southern Kruger supports some of the richest game concentrations in Africa, which, in turn attracts the most people. The busiest—and often very rewarding—road linking Skukuza to Lower Sabie Rest Camp is often referred to as **Piccadilly Highway,** and motorists have been known to jostle each other to get a better view of lions and even create traffic jams around great sightings.

The **central area** still features a wide variety of species, particularly around Satara Rest Camp. A little more laid-back, with fewer camps, but with a reputation for the highest concentration of lions, this area continues to attract its fair share of tourists.

Most of the 7,500-odd resident elephants are found north of Olifants rest camp, but mile after mile of dense mopane scrubland makes even these huge animals difficult to see. The **northern part** of the park is probably not the best destination for a first-time visitor, unless it's combined with a sojourn in the south, but this wilderness area has definite advantages for real bush lovers, not least because there are fewer people. As you travel farther north, the mopane is broken by the lush riverine vegetation of the Shingwedzi, the baobab-dotted sandveld, and finally, the tropical floodplains that lie between the Luvuvhu and Limpopo rivers. This northernmost part of the park is, in fact, at the crossroads of nine of Africa's major ecosystems, and the countryside is full of contrasts. Spend at least 5 days in the Kruger if you include the north in your itinerary.

DESIGNATED PIT STOPS & PICNIC SITES

The designated sites dotted throughout the park are *the only places visitors are allowed to get out of their vehicles.* Maps, available at all rest camp shops, will indicate where these are located, as well as the types of facilities each has. (These may include restrooms, boiling water, barbecues, seating, shade, telephones, educational displays, and shops manned by attendants who sell wood, hot refreshments, and cold drinks.) The two best-equipped and most popular sites are **Nkulu,** on the Sabie River between Skukuza and Lower Sabie (that is, off Piccadilly Hwy.), and **Tshokwane,** named after an elephant bull that frequents the area. The shop here sells everything from scones to brandy. Less busy, and with good game- and bird-viewing opportunities, are **Orpen Dam,** an elevated picnic spot overlooking the water, east of Tshokwane; and **Parfuri,** considered the best picnic site in the park, but located in the far north.

GUIDED GAME DRIVES & WALKS

Even if you're self-driving, a guided game drive is a good way to get oriented; it also allows you to travel park roads that are usually inaccessible to tourists and have the animals around you identified by experienced rangers without having to look it up in a book. Sadly, the major rest camps provide these in large 23- to 46-seat vehicles; the only way to avoid the potential noise and obstructed views is to book into one of the recommended bush camps, where game drives take place in 10-seaters (See "Where to Stay & Dine," below).

The best option, offered almost everywhere, is a **sunrise drive** ⭐⭐⭐ (R115/$17 per person at rest camps, R145/$22 at bush camps), which departs any time from 4 to 6am (30 min. before gates open). There are also **morning drives** at Lower Sabie rest camp (R200/$30 per person) and **midmorning drives** (R100/$15) at Letaba Restcamp that depart at a more civilized hour, but with less potential for game activity. The 3-hour **sunset drives** (R115/$17 per person at rest camps; bush camps R145/$22), departing 2 hours before the gates close, are popular, but the 2-hour **night drive** ⭐⭐⭐, departing 2 hours after the gates close, is the one to make sure you're on; note that these are available only at Letaba, Mopani, Olifants, and Satara rest camps (R100/$15), and at Shimuwini and Sirheni bushveld camps (R145/$22). Outside the concession areas, this is the only way to see the Kruger at night, giving visitors an opportunity to view the nocturnal activities of such animals as bushbabies, porcupines, civets, hyenas, honey badgers, and aardvarks. Be warned, however, that nocturnal animals are shy, and on a bad night sightings can be frustratingly rare. You can book any of these drives when making your accommodations booking—particularly advisable for early-morning and night drives and during school holidays.

To appreciate one the country's more authentic culinary experiences, you may enjoy a **bush braai,** offered by a few of Kruger's rest and bushveld camps. These barbecues under the stars are a sociable way to conclude late-afternoon game drives; **Bush "breakfasts,"** where you break for a sandwich-type meal in the bush, are less agreeable; cost for either is approximately R330 ($49) per person, but you need to confirm availability and price when booking.

If being restricted to a vehicle undermines your appreciation of the bush, **morning walks** ⭐⭐⭐ (R220–R250/$33–$37 per person), usually lasting 3 to 4 hours, with a maximum of eight people, are offered at selected rest camps and bushveld camps—these, too, are recommended. If you don't mind the heat, **afternoon walks** ⭐ (R175/$26) are another option.

For private tour operators offering full-day and half-day game drives in the park (the advantage of these trips being that they cater to fewer people), see "Organized Tours," at the beginning of this chapter.

WILDERNESS TRAILS ★★★

These 3-night, 4-day trails (R2,240/$334 per person for the duration), catering to a maximum of eight people, offer an opportunity to experience the real essence of the African bush in Kruger at an extremely affordable rate. Although you are unlikely to see quite as much big game on foot (and you may spend a lot of time hoping you don't), and you won't get as close to most animals as you can in a vehicle (animals don't associate the smell of gasoline with humans), you will be introduced to the trees, insects, and animals that make up the surrounding bush under the protection of an armed and experienced ranger. The emphasis is on reconnecting with the wilderness in some elemental way rather than ticking off species, but rangers are armed for a reason.

As yet, there has never been a human fatality on any of the Kruger trails, and considering the caliber of the rangers on hand, it is unlikely to ever occur, but do follow their instructions—given at the start of each trail—closely.

The locations of the base camps—comprising thatched A-framed two-bed huts with reed-walled, solar-heated showers and a shared flushing toilet—have been selected for their natural beauty. Note that, unlike the trails offered in KwaZulu-Natal's Hluhluwe-Umfolozi reserve, you'll return to the same base camp every night. Besides bedding, towels, cutlery, and food, the park supplies rucksacks and water bottles. Drinks (which you must supply) are kept cold in gas fridges. Age limits are 12 to 60 years, and a reasonable degree of fitness is required—you will be covering from 8 to 15km (5–9¼ miles) a day.

You have seven trails to choose from: The **Napi, Bushman,** and **Wolhuter** are all situated in the southwestern section, known for white rhino, granite hills, and Bushman rock paintings. The **Metsi-Metsi,** which overlooks a small waterhole, and the **Sweni,** which overlooks the marula and knobthorn savanna, are in the central area, known for its lions. **Olifants Trail** ★, which overlooks the perennial Olifants River, west of its confluence with the Letaba, is particularly scenic and one of the most popular. **Nyalaland,** situated in the pristine northern wilderness among the sandveld's fever tree and baobab forests, is a favorite of birders. But even if you're not a birder, the vegetation and views more than make up for the relative lack of game.

Reservations often need to be made a year in advance, but cancellations do occur. For bookings, call ✆ **012/426-5111;** for more information, check the park's website or request a brochure—see "Essentials," above, for contact details.

WHERE TO STAY & DINE

SANParks runs its camps like large hostels, and although many South Africans share a certain nostalgia in coming back year after year to find the same impala-lily and bird fabric on every curtain, cushion, and bed; *Custos Naturae* stamped on every sheet; and the kudu crest embossed on every soap—it's not everyone's idea of a relaxing holiday. If, however, you are prepared to rough it a little, the en-suite accommodations—situated throughout the park—are scrupulously clean, relatively comfortable, and, for the most part, unbelievably cheap. They are also remarkably varied, with a collection of rest camps, satellite camps, bushveld camps, and bush lodges (the latter is suitable only for large groups). Of these, the bushveld camps are highly recommended—with only 7 to 15 units, they offer a great deal more privacy than the large rest camps (Skukuza, the largest, has more than 200 chalets), and the game drives offered by the park are in smaller vehicles. You will, however, have to do your own cooking when the camp gates are locked at night—only the rest camps have restaurants.

Tips **Better Wildlife Viewing for the Self-Guide Safari**

1. **Purchase a detailed map** that indicates all rivers, dams, dirt roads, lookout, and picnic points. These are available at all rest camp shops. Though the tone is a little schoolmarmish, the illustrated *Make the Most of the Kruger* will tell you what ecozone you're in and which species you should look out for, and point out the geology and historical sites. The *Find It* booklet is a shorter version.

2. Between picnic spots there are no restrooms, fuel stops, or shops, so **plan your journey along the way** and make sure you have something to drink and eat in the car, should you wish to stay with a sighting for some time.

3. **Be there at the right time.** The best times to view wildlife are in the early morning and late afternoon; animals don't move much in the heat of the day. So try and set off as soon as the camp gates open (4:30–6:30am, depending on the season). Hopefully, camp gate hours will be extended in the near future.

4. You're bound to bump into something if you **follow a river.** Traffic allowing, always stop on bridges when crossing and look for crocodiles, herons, leguaans (large amphibious lizards that can grow up to 3m/10 ft.), hippos, and so on. In winter you are almost always assured of seeing animals at a water hole or dam; just park your car and wait.

5. **Spot a spotter.** A stationary car with binoculars pointed in a certain direction is an obvious clue. It is not considered bad form to ask what they have spotted (but you're unlikely to get a polite answer if you obscure their view).

The good news is that the park—realizing that its prowess lies in conservation, not accommodating discriminating guests—has awarded concessions to private operators, who have over the past year built superluxurious lodges; the bad news is that staying there won't come cheap. If you're not prepared to shell out for these yet want a certain level of luxury (we're talking double beds and bathtubs), you will (aside from Skukuza's new riverside bungalows) have to stay in one of the hotels or guesthouses situated on Kruger's periphery and enter the park daily. Only 10 minutes from the Phabeni Gate, Rissington Inn is a recommended option (see "The Escarpment & Panorama Route: Sabie & Surrounds: Where to Stay: Near Hazyview," earlier in this chapter), as is **Buhala Country House,** 10 minutes from the Malelane Gate, with excellent views overlooking the banks of the Crocodile River. With only 10 bedrooms, and no children under 10 allowed, this is a truly tranquil option; rooms are elegant and cool (iron beds, white linen, thatched ceilings), and dining is superior to anything you'll find in the rest camps. Like Rissington, Buhala will organize tours of the Escarpment as well as safaris into the park (© 013/792-4372; www.buhala.co.za; from R1,540/$230 double, including breakfast). Another country-style option near the Malelane gate is **River House,** Visarend Street, Malelane (© 013/790-1333; R1,796/$268 double, with dinner and breakfast), a well-nurtured home; where owners Johan and Duffy offer 12 en-suite bedrooms, each with its own balcony overlooking the

6. **Appreciate the rare.** Most first-time visitors want to tick off the Big 5, but it's worth finding out more about other species. Sighting a wild dog becomes that much more exciting when you know there are fewer than 400 left in the park.

7. **Bring a good pair of binoculars** and drum up some enthusiasm for the vegetation—that tree you stop to admire may reveal a leopard.

8. **Drive slowly**—sharing the shadow of the tree you just whizzed past could be a pride of lions. (The recommended speed for viewing is 25kmph/16mph.)

9. Dirt roads give a great sense of adventure, but **don't shun the tar roads:** Besides being quieter, less dust makes for tastier grass verges.

10. **Consult the animal-sightings book** at your rest camp reception area—many animals are territorial and don't cover huge distances. Some experts advise that you concentrate on a smallish area, getting to know the movements of the animals, rather than driving all over the park.

11. Animals have the right of way on the roads. If a group of elephants is crossing, **keep a respectful distance,** switch the car off, and wait. If you're lucky enough to spot a black rhino (which has a hooked lip rather than the wide, square lip of the white rhino), be *very* wary.

12. **Never feed the baboons and monkeys** that hang out at picnic sites; this is tantamount to signing their death warrant as they then become increasingly aggressive and have to be shot.

13. Most important, **be patient.** The only way you'll ever witness a kill, or any interesting animal interaction, is by watching a situation unfurl.

Crocodile River. The **Malelane Sun Hotel** is even closer to the gate and offers all the comforts and anonymity of a hotel chain at a relatively reasonable price; with access to the exclusive 18-hole Leopard's Creek course, this is a good choice for golfers (© **013/790-3304;** www.southernsun.com; R1,500/$224 double, including breakfast). Farther north, right outside the Paul Kruger gate (the closest entrance to Skukuza), is **Protea Hotel Kruger Gate** (© **013/735-5671;** www.proteahotels.com), another comfortable option if you'd prefer not to be in the park itself, though this basically a faceless hotel experience.

Note: If you're traveling during the summer, especially with kids, make sure to book into a camp with a swimming pool: Berg-en-Dal, Lower Sabie, Pretoriuskop, Mopani, Skukuza, or Shingwedzi.

PRIVATE CONCESSIONS

Using the model so successfully initiated by the Botswana government, the new Kruger concessions—effectively areas in which operators enjoy sole traversing rights—are awarded for a 20-year period on the condition that camps should in no way disturb the environment (hence the fact that most camps are raised off the ground). In keeping with the kind of service offered in the unfenced private reserves that flank the Kruger, rangers within most of these concessions can drive off-road to track or view animals from a close-up perspective, but it's worth noting that some animals found off-road in Kruger are often not as acclimatized to vehicles as those that roam across the unfenced private reserves neighboring Kruger (see "Private Game Reserves," later in this chapter). Competition for these tenders was understandably stiff, and the operators chosen all come with experience, utilizing the best in the business to establish these camps. As these are run similarly to the luxury lodges in the private reserves, the reviews of the best are posted below.

PARK REST CAMPS

If you're on a budget, the most popular accommodations in Kruger are the main rest camps, which offer a variety of cottages, bungalows, huts, and safari tents. All units are sparely furnished and semiserviced (that is, beds are made and floors are swept, but you'll have to do your own washing up). Water is scarce, so "en-suite" usually means flushing toilet, sink (often in the bedroom), and shower. The bigger camps are like small suburbs and are designed to encourage interaction among guests (units are close together and often emulate the old Voortrekker *laager,* a circle, facing inward), so there is little privacy. Try to book a river-facing unit (assuming there is one) or check to see whether you can book a perimeter unit; these face into the bush, albeit through a fence.

The three- to six-bedroom guest cottages represent the top accommodations option in each rest camp. It's well worth investigating these if you're traveling with friends, as they offer the most privacy and small luxuries (like a bathtub).

The restaurant food (usually a three-course set menu, with minimum choice, or buffet) varies between edible and filling. A soup starter may be followed by goulash, baked fish, chicken casserole, lamb chops, overdone roast beef, and the like, and desserts are of the "ice cream with chocolate sauce" ilk. Breakfast will run you R45 ($6.70), lunch R65 ($9.70), dinner R85 ($13). The service varies from well meaning to indifferent, and the (usually overlit) atmosphere is nonexistent—far better to barbecue, which is what most visitors do. Most basics such as milk, bread, butter, wood, dishwashing liquid, tea, tinned products, cereal, cold drinks, firelighters, and wood can be purchased from the camp shop, but don't expect anything fresh, or "delicacies" like olive oil, balsamic vinegar, or fresh fruit. Meat is frozen, and potatoes, tomatoes, and onions are usually the only vegetables available. Vegetarians and epicureans are advised to shop at a supermarket in one of the Escarpment towns before entering Kruger. The wine selection in the camp shops can be surprisingly good, however—if you don't know what you're looking for, choose one of the Nederburgs, an old standby.

Note: You can reserve accommodations in the park with a MasterCard, Visa, or a euro credit card.

The Top Rest Camps

Berg-en-Dal 🐾🐾 This is one of Kruger's newer rest camps and, as such, is rather different from its predecessors: Gone are the characteristic round rondawels, and walls are finished in ugly brick face. Perhaps this is supposed to reflect the granite surrounds—besides

---

⒯Tips **Camps for Travelers with Disabilities**

Facilities for travelers with disabilities are available at Crocodile Bridge, Berg-en-Dal, Lower Sabie, Skukuza, Satara, Olifants, Letaba, Mopani, Shingwedzi, Pretoriuskop, and Tamboti.

being the ideal habitat for leopard and rhino, Berg-en-Dal's hilly terrain comes as some relief to the reserve's mostly flat bushveld. The family cottages and two exclusive guest-houses (try to book no. 26) are a great deal more spacious than the bungalows (of which, the "perimeter" bungalows offer the chance of spotting wildlife through the fence), and each unit has an enclosed patio and braai area, offering a sense of privacy that is lacking in so many of the other camps. These are also the only accommodations with double beds. The indigenous gardens are also very attractive. Where the trail leaves the river and follows a narrow path through dense bush, Braille signs are set out to guide the visually impaired past plants and animal skulls on display. The dam sees much wildlife activity, although you may have to sit on one of the benches and wait for it: Crocodiles lurk—and hunt—in its waters. This is one of the few camps to offer bush braais.

Enter through Malelane Gate, southern Kruger. ✆ **013/735-6106.** Fax 013/735-6104. 88 units. Bungalows R480–R530 ($72–$79) double; family cottages R895 ($134) for 4 people; guesthouses R1,665 ($249) for 4 people. **Amenities:** Restaurant; pool; information center; shop; laundromat; game drives; bush walks; bush braais; fuel; camping.

Letaba ✿ This rest camp is set in elephant country, just where the mopane terrain starts to become monotonous. The location, along a large bend of the Letaba River, sees plenty of activity, particularly in the winter. The nearby Engelhardt and Minger-hout dams are also excellent game sites, and the gravel road that follows the Letaba River is worth exploring. Letaba is also one of the few camps in Kruger to offer **night drives** and **bush braais.** Unfortunately, very few of the units have views, but the restaurant has one of the best; eat lunch while watching various plains animals wandering down for a drink. Accommodations are in thatched units set in gardens that are shaded by well-established apple leaf trees, acacias, mopane, and lala palms—ask for a bungalow on the perimeter fence, as game often venture quite close. Better still, the pricier Fish Eagle and Melville guesthouses have good views and plenty of space. Furnished safari tents are a budget alternative, but, as with the five huts, you'll have to share bathrooms and kitchen facilities.

Enter through Phalaborwa Gate, central Kruger. ✆ **013/735-6636.** Fax 013/735-6662. 125 units. Huts R285 ($43) double; safari tents R240 ($36) double; bungalows R435–R515 ($65–$77) double; cottages R895 ($134) for 4 people; guesthouses R1,665 ($249) for 4 people. All but huts and tents en-suite. **Amenities:** Restaurant; bar; information center; shop; laundromat; game drives and walks; fuel; bush braais and breakfasts.

Lower Sabie ✿✿✿ Overlooking the banks of the Sabie River, with large lawns and mature trees, this is one of Kruger's most pleasant camps, particularly if you manage to bag one of the units with a waterfront view (nos. 11–24 or 73–96; nos. 3–10 also have river views, but they are a little too close to the camping and caravan area, which can be noisy during school vacations). In the camping area there are 24 East African–safari style tents; all feature twin beds, en-suite shower and toilet, and an outdoor "kitchen" (hot plate, fridge, barbecue)—make sure you bag one with a riverside view. Just about every animal has been spotted drinking along the riverbanks, and at night (if you switch your fridge off), you'll fall asleep to the grunting of hippos. Elephants are often found just west of the camp, and with two dams in the immediate vicinity, Lower Sabie provides an excellent base for observing wetland birds. Every unit has a braai, but most have no cutlery or crockery, though the basics can be rented for a small fee from reception. Once again, there is no privacy, as most units share walls, but the 9pm curfew keeps things quiet. Stroll along the paved walkway that overlooks the Sabie River at night with a torch: The red eyes you light up probably belong to hyenas, lured by the smell of braaiing meat.

Fun Fact Chewing Up the Scenery

An elephant consumes up to 200 kilograms (480 lb.) of vegetation daily; a herd thus has a huge, potentially destructive impact on the landscape. This is why elephant numbers need to be controlled, by either culling or translocation. Elephants are extremely sensitive animals, however, and actively mourn the death of a family member, performing intricate burial ceremonies. When clans reunite, they make a great show of affection, "kissing" (probing each other's mouths with their trunks) and trumpeting their joy. To find out more about this amazing species, book a 90-minute **elephant safari** (© **015/793-1633**) or stay at **Camp Jabulani**, located at Kapama, a Big 5 fenced private reserve near Hoedspruit (www.kapama.co.za).

Enter through Crocodile Bridge Gate, southern Kruger. © **013/735-6056** or 013/735-6062. 119 units. Huts R130–R225 ($19–$34) double; safari tents R395–R425 ($59–$63) double; bungalows R475–R505 ($71–$75) double; family bungalow/cottage R865–R885 ($129–$132) for 4 people; guesthouse R1,665 ($249) for 4 people. All but the huts en-suite. **Amenities:** Restaurant; pool; shop; laundromat; game drives and walks; fuel.

Olifants ⭐⭐⭐   Situated on a hilltop 100m (328 ft.) above the banks of the Olifants River, with views of the vast African plains that stretch beyond to the hazy Escarpment, this smallish camp is a favorite, and you'd be well advised to book as soon as you read this. Unit nos. 1 to 24, which are situated along the camp's southwest perimeter, not only have the most spectacular views of the river and the animals that are constantly in attendance, but are also the most private—it's almost worth rearranging your trip until one is available! One feels less caged in here than at Kruger's other camps; while all camps are surrounded by wire fencing to keep predators out, the sudden drop below Olifants' bungalows means that the expansive views are totally uninterrupted. Like many of the Kruger units, the veranda incorporates both kitchen and dining area, and it's the place where you drink it all in. Families note that there are two-bedroom bungalows with river views (it'll cost just R700/$104 for two adults and two children). Throughout the day, animals drink from the pools, watched by basking crocodiles. Birds—in particular, eagles—wheel below, searching for prey, and it feels as if you're quite literally on cloud nine. This is also currently the only camp offering mountain biking as an alternate bush experience.

Enter through Phalaborwa Gate, central Kruger. © **013/735-6606**. Fax 013/735-6609. 109 units. Bungalows R440–R660 ($66–$99) double; guesthouses R1,665 ($249) for 4 people. **Amenities:** Restaurant; shop; laundromat; shop; game drives; mountain bike trails; fuel.

Punda Maria ⭐⭐ *Finds*   Very few people have the time to travel this far north, just one of the reasons why Punda Maria—which is close to the Zimbabwean border—is the number-one choice for wilderness lovers. Built in the 1930s, this small thatched and whitewashed camp retains a real sense of what it must have been like to visit Kruger half a century ago. All units have fridges, but you must specify one with kitchen facilities if you don't want to live on restaurant food. The area does not support large concentrations of game, but it lies in the sandveld where several springs occur, and borders the lush alluvial plains, making it a real must for birders. A nature trail winds through the camp, and the area surrounding the camp is scenically splendid. Head north to the Luvuvhu River, the only real tropical region of the park, to spot a variety of birds, including the colorful Narina trogon. Overlooking the river is one of Kruger's most interesting archaeological sites, **Thulamela.** A little farther east along the river is the most beautiful picnic site in Kruger, **Parfuri,** which lies under massive thorn, leadwood, and jackalberry trees, with water constantly on the boil for tea.

Enter through Punda Maria Gate, northern Kruger. © **013/735-6873.** Fax 013/735-6894. 31 units. Safari tents R450 ($67) double; bungalows R435–R480 ($65–$72) double; family bungalow R820 ($122) for 4 people. All en-suite. **Amenities:** Restaurant; pool; shop; laundromat; game drives; fuel; bush braais.

Satara 🛖 The second-biggest and one of the three most popular camps in Kruger (the others being Skukuza and Lower Sabie), Satara is located in one of the finest game-viewing areas in the park. The rich basaltic soils support sweet grasses that attract some of the largest numbers of grazers (such as buffalo, wildebeest, zebra, kudu, impala, and elephant), which, in turn, accounts for what is considered to be the largest lion population in the park. Just as well, for the setting and housing are rather disappointing: five massive *laagers,* each 25-rondavel strong, with verandas all facing inward. The best options are the units in semicircles that face the veld (nos. 161–179), though you have to look at it through an electrified fence. The road just south of Satara toward Gudzani Dam is famously beautiful, with wonderful river views in summer, and the area around Tshokwane is said to have the highest concentrations of lions in the world.

Enter through Orpen Gate, central Kruger. © **013/735-6306.** Fax 013/735-6304. 166 units. Bungalows R475–R535 ($71–$80) double; luxury bungalows R725 ($108) double; cottages R915 ($137) for 4 people; guesthouses R1,665 ($249) for 4 people. All en-suite. **Amenities:** Restaurant; shop; laundromat; game drives and walks; fuel; bush braais.

Skukuza 🛖🛖 Just east of the Paul Kruger Gate, you will find Skukuza, so-called capital of Kruger. Skukuza (or "he who sweeps clean") refers to Kruger's first warden, Stevenson-Hamilton, who set up his base camp here. Today Skukuza accommodates some 1,000 people in prime game-viewing turf. This is an ideal spot for first-time visitors, though it would be a pity if this were your only experience of the park because it really is like a small town. Besides the people and cars, there is the noise of the occasional charter planes landing, though this doesn't seem to distract the many visitors strolling along the wide walkway that follows the course of the Sabie River. Accommodations are in a range of thatched en-suite units, the best of which are the luxury riverside bungalows. These bungalows (book nos. 88–96) were rebuilt after the 2000 floods and offer the best riverfront views; they're furnished with luxuries such as a double bed, a fully fitted kitchen, and satellite TV. There is still no overture to privacy, with bungalows approximately 10m (33 ft.) apart. All other units have fridges on their small verandas, some with hot plates and cooking equipment. For the budget-conscious, there are furnished East African–style tents, but you have to share bathrooms and kitchen facilities with the hordes of campers and RV drivers who descend on the camp, particularly in June/July and December/January.

Enter through Paul Kruger Gate, southern Kruger. © **013/735-4152.** Fax 013/735-4054. 238 units. Safari tents R240 ($36) double; bungalows R480–R515 ($72–$77) double; luxury bungalows R800–R920 ($119–$137) double; cottages R885 ($132) for 4 people; guesthouses R1,665 ($249) for 4 people. **Amenities:** Restaurant; bar; pool; golf; information center; car rental; shop; laundromat; library; game drives; bush walks; airport; bank; post office; doctor; fuel.

Other Camps

Among the other camps to choose from, tiny **Balule** (© **013/735-6606;** rates start at R165/$25) is ideal for the hard-core bush enthusiast; it has no shops, restaurants, or electricity—and the six huts have no real windows, let alone fans or air-conditioning,

Tracker Tips

Of course, you can't expect to know in a few days what professional trackers have gleaned in many years of tracking animals or growing up in the bush, but nature does provide a myriad of clues for the amateur tracker.

1. **Look for "hippo highways."** Hippos don't pick up their feet when they move; they drag them, so if you see a trail of trampled grass leading to a water hole, it's likely a hippo has been there, going to and from the water (where it stays during the heat of the day) to the grass it feeds on. Don't tarry on a hippo highway; once they set off down their well-trodden paths, very little will stop them.

2. **Use your nose.** Elephant urine has a very strong scent; waterbuck have a distinctive musky smell.

3. **Train your vision.** Vultures wheeling above may indicate the presence of predators, as may fixed stares from a herd of zebra or giraffe. A cloud of dust usually hovers over a large herd of moving buffalo. And of course, paw prints provide vital information, not only to what has passed by (you should purchase a wildlife guidebook to recognize the differing imprints), but how recently it was there—the latter a skill, frankly, that takes years of experience to hone.

4. **Examine trees.** For instance, bark and branches sheared off trees or trees rubbed raw are evidence that elephants have passed by—they eat the bark and use trees as scratching posts. And certain trees attract specific species—giraffe, for example, love to browse the mopane.

5. **Listen to the sounds of the bush.** The lead lioness makes a guttural grunt to alert her pride. Baboons, monkeys, squirrels, and birds give raucous alarm calls in the presence of predators. Kudus bark when frightened.

6. **Look for droppings and dung.** Elephant dung is hard to miss—extra-large clumps full of grass and bark—while a trail full of fresh black, pancakelike dung marks the passing of a herd of buffalo. A good wildlife guidebook will have illustrations of many species' dung.

7. **Watch bird behavior.** Follow the flight of oxpeckers, and you're likely to locate a herd of Cape buffalo; oxpeckers survive off the ticks and other insects that cling to the buffalo hide. Cattle egret dine on the insects and earthworms kicked up by grazing herbivores.

making them unsuitable for high summer no matter how much you want to get back to basics. **Crocodile Bridge** (© **013/735-6012;** rates start at R250/$37 double for a safari tent, R525/$78 double for a bungalow) is much too close to civilization, across the river from the farms that neighbor Kruger, and you might just as well be there, ensconced in a comfortable guesthouse. **Mopani** ⛺ (© **013/735-6536;** rates start at R480/$72 double) is the most modern camp in Kruger and one of the few camps with a swimming pool. Book one of the popular units with dam views (nos. 9–12, 43, 45, 47–54, and 101–102). **Orpen** (© **013/735-6355;** R225/$34 double for a hut, R905/$135 for a family-size cottage) is one of the Kruger's smallest camps and enjoys a reputation for fine sightings—lions, leopards, and wild dogs are regularly seen in the area. **Pretoriuskop** (© 013/735-5128) is Kruger's oldest camp and can house nearly 350 guests; bunga-lows, some of which have double beds, start at R445/$66 double. It's a popular camp, but consider stopping only 1 night here—it's only 8km (5 miles) from the Numbi Gate, and most people prefer to go deeper into the bush. **Shingwedzi** (© 013/735-6806; double-bed bungalows go for R445/$66 double) is a medium-size rest camp on prime elephant territory with old-style accommodations and a pool. **Tamboti** (© 013/735-6355; rates start at R245/$37 double) is Kruger's answer to the East African safari, and comprises 40 tents located among apple leaf, jackalberry, and sycamore fig trees; 10 of these tents are fully equipped (R555/$83 double). The camp is one of Kruger's most popular, however, mostly because of its location on the banks of the Timbavati River; animals, particularly elephants, are attracted by the promise of water.

Bushveld Camps

The five bushveld camps are much smaller than the major rest camps and provide a greater sense of being in the bush. They have no restaurants or shops, however, so you must do your own cooking, and any last-minute shopping will have to be done at the nearest rest camp. On the plus side, most of the en-suite units are more spacious than rest-camp options and feature well-equipped kitchens with braai (barbecue) spots. Only residents are allowed to travel the access road, which makes these an excellent get-away-from-it-all option. Best of all, the game drives are in vehicles that accom-modate 8 to 10 people. You pay a little more for the seclusion—rates range from R755 to R895 ($113–$134) for two to four persons—but it's still a bargain.

The centrally located **Talamati** ★★★, close to the Orpen Gate (© 013/735-6343), and southern **Biyamiti** ★★★, close to the Malelane Gate (© 013/735-6171), are the most popular, located as they are in Kruger's game-rich areas. Shimuwini, Bateleur, and Sirheni are all located in the northern section of the park. **Shimuwini** ★★, which is reached via the Phalaborwa Gate (© 013/735-6683), and **Sirheni** ★★, halfway between Shingwedzi and Punda Maria (© 013/735-6860), both have scenic waterside settings that attract a variety of game and birds, and offer night drives. **Bateleur** ★★ (© 031/735-6843) is the oldest bushveld camp and—with only 7 thatched units rather than the usual 15—the most intimate. The closest gate to Bateleur is Phalaborwa. For more information, contact Kruger reservations (see "Visitor Information," earlier in this chapter).

⟨Fun Fact⟩ The Mightiest Bite

- The term **"Big 5"** originated in the days when Africa's big game was hunted by gun rather than camera, and referred to the most dangerous animals when wounded: lions, leopards, elephants, black rhinos, and buffaloes.
- The docile-looking **hippo** is responsible for more human deaths than any other mammal in Africa.
- The most dangerous wildlife in Africa is not much bigger than an eyelash—check under "Fast Facts: Kruger National Park," earlier in this chapter, for tips on protecting yourself from malaria-carrying **mosquitoes**.

CAMPING

Campsites (R105/$16 double) are available at **Balule, Berg-en-Dal, Crocodile Bridge, Letaba, Malelane, Maroela, Lower Sabie, Pretoriuskop, Punda Maria, Satara, Shingwedzi,** and **Skukuza.** Every site has a braai (barbecue) and many also have electricity; you will need to bring in all your own equipment, however, including a tent (see Skukuza, Letaba, or Tamboti for furnished tents). Campers enjoy shared bathrooms (shower/toilet blocks) and kitchens, and have access to all rest-camp facilities.

6 Private Game Reserves

Flanking the western section of Kruger Park and covering over 150,000 hectares (370,500 acres) are South Africa's most famous private game reserves, owned by groups of freehold landowners and concession-holders with traversing rights. Because most of the fences that separated the private reserves from Kruger have been taken down, animals are to some extent able to follow natural migratory routes, and you will find as many species in these reserves as you will in Kruger. Unless you're staying at a luxury lodge in a private concession, that, however, is where the similarity ends.

The difference between a visit to a Kruger Park Rest Camp and a private lodge is so big as to be almost incomparable. Not only do the luxurious accommodations options offer supreme privacy and make the most of the bushveld surrounds, but visitors are taken in open-topped and elevated Land Rovers to within spitting distance of animals by Shangaan trackers and armed rangers, who give a running commentary on anything from the mating habits of giraffe to the family history of a particular lion. Animals in these reserves, particularly Sabi Sand, are so used to being approached by vehicles that they almost totally ignore them—you can trail a leopard at a few feet without it so much as glancing backward. Two-way radios between rangers, many of whom are allowed to traverse on each other's land, ensure good sightings, although these can be somewhat marred when three or sometimes four vehicles (the maximum lodges allow) converge on the same spot.

The 2- to 4-hour game drives take place in the morning and again in the late afternoon and evening, with stops in the bush for a hot drink and muffins in the morning (particularly in winter) and cocktails in the evening. It can be bitterly cold in the winter, and you may want to opt instead for an escorted walk after breakfast—another service included in the rate.

In addition to pursuing animals off-road through the African bush, these private reserves offer unfenced accommodations of luxuriously high standards. Equally high end is the cuisine—as all meals are included in the rate, this is certainly not the time to go on a diet. Breakfasts feature a selection of cereals and fresh fruit, yogurt, and freshly baked bread and muffins. Hot breakfasts are cooked to order and usually comprise eggs, sausage, bacon, and tomato, or omelets. A few lodges offer variations like eggs Benedict or eggs Florentine. Lunch is the lightest meal, usually a buffet with interesting salads and cold meats. Breakfasts are served late (after the morning game drive, which usually ends at about 10am), so some lodges prefer to skip lunch altogether and serve a high tea at 3pm, with quiches, sandwiches, and cakes. From there you depart on a 3- to 4-hour evening game drive, traveling with a spotlight in the dark, tracking nocturnal creatures on the move. You will more than likely be expected to dine with your game-drive companions (if this is a problem, alert the staff in advance, and alternative arrangements will be made). Dinners feature grilled or

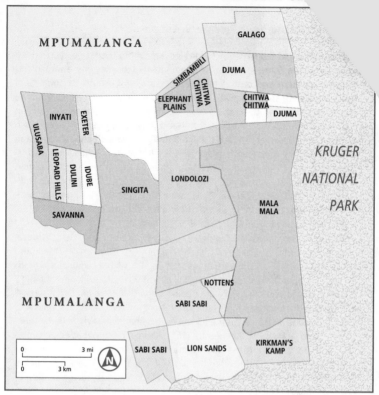

roasted meat, giving visitors an opportunity to taste at least one species spotted earlier that day—kudu, springbok, impala, and warthog are particularly popular. Lodges cater to dietary requirements but require advance warning, as supplies take time to arrive in the bush. If you're a vegetarian or keep kosher, notify the lodges prior to your arrival. Almost every lodge rotates dinners from their dining room to the ever-popular open-air *boma* (an open-air enclosure lit with a large fire), and some even offer surprise bush dinners, with a game drive concluding at a serene spot where tables have been set up under trees or in a riverbed.

The drawback to all this? A hefty price tag. If you've come to South Africa to see big game, however, it's definitely worth delving a little deeper into your savings and spending at least 2 nights in a private game reserve, preferably 3. Prices (which are often quoted in U.S. dollars and include all meals, game drives, bush walks, and occasionally your bar bill) do vary considerably (from season to season, for example), and it is possible to find affordable options, the best of which are described below (see Umlani and Honeyguide, in particular).

Note: An admission fee is charged at the entrance gates of some of these reserves, not all of which accept credit cards, so carry cash. The fee at Timbavati, for example is R75 ($11) per car and R90 ($13) per adult entering the reserve; Sabie Sand charges R60 ($9) per vehicle. You may also have to pay a small conservation levy at the lodge.

our Private Reserve

ew concessions located within the Kruger, you'll need
najor private reserves that border one another and
entral section. They are, from south to north, **Sabi**
Timbavati. None of these reserves is fenced off from the
or Kruger, which allows a seamless migration of animals through an area roughly the size of Massachusetts—and growing bigger every year. Each of these three reserves features the **Big 5 (lion, leopard, elephant, rhino, and buffalo),** as does **Thornybush,** a relatively small reserve almost surrounded by Timbavati, but currently still fenced. Another private reserve in the region worth considering is **Makalali,** a large buffalo-free reserve that lies within striking distance of Kruger's central Phalaborwa Gate. To make an informed decision about which reserve to visit and for more private reserves and lodges, you'll need to page to chapters 2, 5, 7, 9, 10, and 11.

Each private reserve has a number of luxury lodges or camps that share traversing rights on land, thereby increasing the range of their vehicles. Many also report major sightings to the other reserves. In fact, with a cumulative 6 hours of every day spent tracking game, you will almost certainly see four of the Big 5 during a 3-night stay (the most elusive being leopard). Bear in mind that you will enjoy yourself a great deal more (and irritate your ranger less) if you spread your focus to include an interest in the myriad species that make up life in the bush.

Sabi Sand ★★★, a 66,000-hectare (163,020-acre) reserve that encompasses the southern lowveld, is the most game-rich area in the country, and most guests leave having sighted all of the Big 5—indeed, after 3 decades of intensive safari action, animals here have practically been born to the clicking of cameras, making them the easiest to track and approach in Africa. Sabi Sand, then, has become known as the continent's most exclusive reserve, with the largest number of luxury camps. Chief among these is the attention-grabbing **Singita,** which has replaced MalaMala as *the* name to drop in informed company (note that at press time, **MalaMala** was undergoing an extensive upgrade). Not only does Singita offer top-notch game-viewing, but in 2004 it was once again crowned Best Destination in the World by *Condé Nast Traveler,* a distinction it has earned in no less than five top international travel polls. The standards of service and luxuriousness of the accommodations at Singita are incomparable, and—like ever-popular **Londolozi**—it offers excellent game-viewing with attentive and very knowledgeable rangers. So renowned is Sabi Sand that it even attracted billionaire tycoon Richard Branson, who purchased **Ulasaba** (© **011/705-1809**; www.ulusaba.com), in the western sector of the reserve, apparently because his wife liked the view; it's now something of an over-the-top bush resort with some cringe-worthy design ideas.

During the apartheid era, when black people were not allowed to vacation in Kruger, **Manyeleti** ★—the region just north of Sabi Sand—was considered "their" reserve, and a visit to the original Manyeleti Rest Camp makes the most basic Kruger camp look like a luxury option. Officially, it's actually still a poorly run 23,000-hectare (56,810-acre) public reserve (administered by the Limpopo provincial government), within which private companies operate a few key concessions; its border with Kruger Park is unfenced, so animals can roam freely between the reserves. While other lodges—like luxurious **Tintswalo** ⭐ (© **011/464-1208** or 015/793-9013; www.tintswalo.co.za)—have opened their doors in the Manyeleti, the good-value **Honeyguide** (see later in this chapter) remains the recommended choice, particularly if you're keen on a more authentic bush experience. Note that operators in Manyeleti are restricted in the areas in which they may drive off-road in pursuit of game.

Timbavati ⭐⭐, the 65,000-hectare (160,500-acre) reserve located alongside Kruger's central section, first became famous for the white lions that resided here (all were captured and taken to the Johannesburg zoo to "protect" them). Although it offers a comparable game experience to the much-vaunted Sabi Sand, the vegetation is less arresting, and rhino are scarce. Animals are almost as habituated to vehicles here as at Sabi Sand, and you can get within a few feet of large predators. The main reason to choose Timbavati over Sabi Sand is that it has far fewer camps and fewer people, and, like Manyeleti, the rates are generally friendlier, particularly at Umlani, one of the most authentic bush experiences in the area.

Bordered in the north and west by Timbavati, the 14,000-hectare (34,580-acre) **Thornybush** ⭐⭐ game reserve is currently still a fenced reserve. It boasts a high percentage of lion, but the thicket-type vegetation is not as conducive to sightings of varied species. The best reason to choose this reserve is **Royal Malewane,** a lodge that offers unbelievably luxurious accommodations and superb style; suites are on par with Singita but at a slightly reduced price.

If you're not hung up on ticking off the Big 5, the **Makalali** ⭐ conservancy, which lies farther north and is cut off from Kruger, extends over 10,000 hectares (24,700 acres) and has lions, leopards, rhinos, and elephants. The area is also of geological interest, with quartz rock crystals strewn throughout the area. The long-term plan is to keep increasing the conservancy, eventually creating a corridor connecting it to Kruger. In the meantime, it, too, offers relatively reasonable rates.

Note: For visitors with limited time or those unwilling to risk malaria, the 40,000-hectare (98,800-acre) **Welgevonden** ⭐⭐ and 35,382-hectare (87,394-acre) **Lapalala** reserves lie only a 3-hour drive north of Johannesburg (see chapter 7); if you are planning a second visit to South Africa or are keen to combine a visit to one of the above reserves with one that has a totally contrasting biome, the other Big 5 private reserves worth considering are **Madikwe** ⭐⭐⭐, which covers more biomes than Kruger, thereby offering a greater variety of species, and **Tswalu Kalahari Reserve** ⭐⭐, a beautiful desert reserve and the largest private reserve in southern Africa (see chapter 7). KwaZulu-Natal's reserves include **Phinda** ⭐, **Mkuze Falls** ⭐, and **Ndumo** ⭐, and offer subtropical vegetation and abundant birdlife (see chapter 8). Whatever you do, don't miss an opportunity to visit the reserves in Botswana's **Okavango Delta** ⭐⭐⭐—the "original Eden" (see chapter 11).

GETTING THERE

The closest international airport is Johannesburg, from where it's a 5- to 7-hour drive to this region, depending on which route you choose (see the Panorama, Lowveld, and Letaba routes, earlier in this chapter). Alternatively, you can fly directly from Johannesburg, Cape Town, or Durban—see "Kruger National Park: Essentials," earlier in this chapter. All camps and lodges will organize pickups from any of these airports, as well as arrange transfers by air or land to or from competitors.

WHERE TO STAY & DINE

Increasingly, visitors to Africa's safari meccas are placing a premium on sophisticated luxury and designer bush experiences that enhance the traditional game-viewing phenomenon; you can expect to find some of the finest lodges in the world in the private lodges within and abutting Kruger. Because lodges and camps need adequate warning to stock up on fresh produce (remember, all meals are included in the rates below), transfers need to be prearranged; special dietary requirements also need to be sorted well in advance. And because many are extremely popular, booking ahead is essential. Although winter is the best time to view game, many lodges experience a seasonal drop-off and reduce prices from May to August—some by as much as 50%.

IN KRUGER

In addition to the top concessions reviewed below, another option is the upscale **Tinga Private Game Lodge** (© 013/735-5810 or 0861/505-050; www.tinga.co.za), which operates two luxury lodges: Narina and Legends, both in the vicinity of Skukuza. Legends opened on the banks of the Sabie River in mid-2004 and comes with a great deal of promise. Grand without being overly decadent, it aims high with its colonial-style villas; each has a private lounge, a large bathroom with double showers, and its own heated plunge pool. It's pricey (from R12,000/$1,791 double), but good deals are frequently found on the Internet. If you're traveling in 2006, look for **Royal Makulele,** another new concession from Wilderness Safaris (www.wilderness-safaris.com), one of Africa's best safari operators. Divided between two smaller camps, the lodge will comprise 12 luxury thatched rooms, each with its own pool, *sala* (small shaded pavilion), and outdoor shower; game activities are expected to be top-notch.

Hamiltons Tented Camp ₭₭ (Value)   A far cry from the tents in the days of Hemingway and Blixen, these modern tented camps provide every comfort needed (bedside lamps, king-size beds, crisp white linen, flushing toilets, outdoor showers and

---

(Moments **Wish You Were Here**

It's 5am. The phone rings. It's the lodge manager. He politely asks how you slept, then requests that you do not leave your room as planned. There has been a leopard kill meters from your chalet. He apologizes for the inconvenience and informs you that an armed ranger will be along shortly to escort you to the dining room for coffee before you depart on your early-morning game drive. This seldom happens, but every so often it does. Lodges in private reserves are not fenced off from predators, so you are advised to exercise extreme caution—under no circumstances are guests, whatever their age, to walk about unaccompanied after dark.

Tips   Kidding Around

Bear in mind that many camps and lodges do not welcome children; over and above a concern for other guests' peace is the belief that the bush holds too many inherent dangers, not least of which is the ever-present threat of malaria (see "Fast Facts: Kruger National Park," earlier in this chapter). Even if they are allowed, young children may not go on game drives or dine in the outdoor boma, and you will have to sign an additional indemnity form. One lodge that actively encourages children, with a separate child-friendly program, is **Londolozi** (see later in this chapter).

slipper baths with hot and cold running water) yet still offer a sense of authenticity and close communion with the bush. The best camp in the Imbali concession (the two other components—Imbali Main Camp and smaller Hoyo Hoyo—are not in the same class), Hamiltons comprises six luxury en-suite canvas-walled units; these are set on stilts with wooden floors and private viewing decks with an outside shower overlooking the Ngwenyeni Dam. Tents are privately situated and linked via raised timber walkways to the open tented lounge and dining room and pool. Hamiltons' size makes this an ideal camp for anyone wanting to escape the rat race. The nearest gate for access to Hamilton's is Orpen, 50km (31 miles) away.

Booking office in U.S.: ℂ **305/792-0172.** In S.A.: ℂ **086-1000-333.** www.threecities.co.za. 6 units. R7,040–R8,800 ($1,051–$1,313) double. AE, DC, MC, V. No children under 8. **Amenities:** Dining/bar area; boma; pool; butler/room service; laundry; game drives; bush walks. *In room:* A/C, fans.

Jock Safari Lodge ★★ *(Value)*   This was the first private lodge in Kruger to open in December 2001, and, having carved a name for itself as a warm, convivial camp, elegant and tasteful yet without pretensions of grandeur, it made *Condé Nast Traveler's* Hot List in 2003. The large thatched bungalows, situated for maximum privacy, each feature great bushveld views, tasteful furnishings, and large bathrooms with tubs and indoor as well as outdoor showers; each unit has its own *sala* (a shaded outdoor lounge) overlooking the river, and there are fireplaces for winter. Scattered between the main lodge and the guest suites are a series of ox-wagons intended to recall the gold-prospecting adventures of the 19th-century pioneers. The lodge is situated in the south, at the confluence of the Mitomeni and Biyamiti rivers, where herds of antelope and elephant gather to cool off or quench their thirst. It's also easily accessed from the Malelane and Skukuza gates (a 30-min. drive from the Kruger-Mpumalanga airport to the gate, then a 90-min. drive through the park). The only possible drawback is its size (at 6,000 hectares/14,820 acres, this is Kruger's smallest concession), but given the density of game, you don't need to travel far to start ticking of species. Winter rates are excellent.

P.O. Box 781, Malelane 1320 ℂ **013/735-5200.** Fax 013/735-5944. www.jocksafarilodge.com. 12 units. Summer R6,500 ($970) double; winter rates on request. Rate is all-inclusive except for imported wines and spirits. Children under 12 pay 50%. AE, DC, MC, V. **Amenities:** Dining area; bar; boma; pool; wellness center; shop; room service; babysitting; laundry; game drives; bush walks; valet on request. *In room:* A/C, minibar, hair dryer, fireplace.

The Outpost ★★★ *(Value)*   Listed as one of the 101 Best Hotels Worldwide in *The Tatler* 2005 Travel Guide, The Outpost is an ultramodern lodge set atop a hill in the most untouched region of northern Kruger, overlooking a magnificent riverine. An oasis of calm (it's a good 120km/74 miles from the nearest town), the property oper-ates on an area covering more than 23,600 hectares (58,292 acres), and is now effec-tively owned by the Makulele people, who won the first land claim in Kruger. The local people also contribute to the daily running of the lodge, making this a landmark exer-cise in sustainable development. Cantilevered out of a rocky mountainside, it offers a combination of chic minimalist design and unimpeded nature; the 12 en-suite guest "spaces" ("rooms" would be misleading) designed by Italian-born architect Enrico Daf-fonchio, are constructed of steel, canvas, and aluminum, and are completely open to the elements except for the rock face they appear to grow out of. Like those at Singita, each offers unparalleled views, this time of the surrounding floodplains of the Limpopo and Luvuvhu rivers—a richly textured terrain of ancient baobabs, thorny acacias, and lush palms. For the ultimate view, reserve "space 12," a good 5-minute walk along a raised walkway from the open bar, dining, and pool area. The only drawback is the rela-tive remoteness of the lodge and the fact that game here is less dense than in the more crowded, southern regions of Kruger. But this also means there are fewer vehicles, which heightens the sense of total escape. That said, at press time, Wilderness Safaris was about to open its new **Pafuri Lodge** on the same concession.

P.O. Box 786064, Sandton 2146. ℂ 011/341-0282. Fax 011/341-0281. www.theoutpost.co.za. 12 units. R4,600 ($687) double, all-inclusive. AE, DC, MC, V. **Amenities:** Dining room; bar; pool; laundry; library; wine cellar; game drives; bush walks; river safaris. *In room:* A/C, stocked cooler box.

Rhino Walking Safaris 🐾🐾 This award-winning private concession shares a bor-der with MalaMala in the Sabi Sand reserve, renowned for the density of its game and lush vegetation. Although the area is a massive 12,000 hectares (29,640 acres), it is a restricted wilderness concession, meaning that off-road game drives are not allowed. Instead, the focus is on game walks and luxury sleep-outs, offering a much-needed break from the monotony of most other safari lodge schedules. There are two lodges, **Rhino Post** 🐾🐾, where a morning walk is combined with an afternoon drive, and **Plains Camp** 🐾, where you'd better be prepared for 4 to 5 hours of bush walking per day. Guests are also given the opportunity to overnight at the camp's "sleep-out digs" deep in the bush (70 min. on foot from Plains Camp), where tents have been erected on decks high up on stilts at a watering hole. You need carry only a few clothes and toiletries; all other necessities are provided. Back at Rhino Post, accommodations are neat and functional. Set on raised wooden decks with private terraces overlooking the Mutlemuve River, the thatched guest rooms have canvas walls that allow the sounds of the bush to penetrate at night; bathrooms feature tubs, double basins, and an out-door shower. Public areas are elegant and simple, comprising wood and packed-stone walls, and include an inviting glass-walled wine cellar.

Reservations: P.O. Box 1881, Jukskei Park 2153. ℂ 011/467-1886. www.rws.co.za. Rhino Post 8 units. R5,000–R5,800 ($769–$8,660) double. Plains Camp 4 units. R3,900–R4,700 ($582–$701) double. Packages available.

Horny Misconception

It is a common misconception that white and black rhinos are differentiated by skin tone. Actually, the white rhino gets its name from a flippant English adop-tion of the Afrikaans word for the animal. The Afrikaans name for the species is *wyd* (meaning "wide" and pronounced "white"); it refers to the shape of the jaw rather than color.

AE, DC, MC, V. No children under 12 at Plains Camp or on bush walks. Children under 12 pay 50% if sharing. **Amenities:** Dining area; bar; pool; gym; curio shop; library; wine cellar; game drives; bush walks. *In room:* Minibar, hair dryer, safe, tea- and coffee-making facility.

Singita Lebombo & Sweni ✦✦✦   When Lebombo opened in March 2003, it immediately became the last word in designer safari experiences, wowing fashion-conscious travelers and chalking up awards while gracing its way into the pages of chic magazines and coffee-table tomes. A year later, Lebombo received a smaller neighbor: **Sweni,** named for the beautiful river over which its six fabulous suites look. The lodges feature almost identical sumptuous accommodations. Dramatic wraparound glass walls and massive glass sliding doors open onto outdoor showers and private balconies; in summer you can even sleep here, under the stars. Constructed of saligna wood, raised on stilts, and laid out in a tasteful open plan, with enormous room-dividing curtains and sapling ceilings, this is the most modern camp in Africa, featuring fabulous home-grown furniture—designed by local craftspeople working in concert with funky young designers—contrasted with retro-modernity (think *Wallpaper* magazine). The whole effect is more Afro-Euro chic boutique hotel than game lodge. There's an emphasis on fun and relaxation; rooms are stocked with board games and treats to occupy you between meals (which are superb). Yet despite the experimental design and unashamed New York loft atmosphere, the bush is always close at hand: Situated in a 15,000-hectare (37,050-acre) concession in a remote eastern section of Kruger National Park bordered by Mozambique, the camp is elevated on a sheer cliff, with stunning views of the Lebombo Mountains and surrounding bushveld plains. In comparing the two, Lebombo is lighter, brighter, and quite dramatic in its proportions, while Sweni is inspired by earthier tones and is far more intimate; catering to a maximum of 12 guests, it has a more homey atmosphere and additional touches that improve on Lebombo's original design (Sweni's suite no. 5 is a personal favorite, while at Lebombo you should ask for a suite close to the river for maximum privacy). Between Lebombo and Sweni is Singita's unique "Village," comprising a spa, a state-of-the-art gymnasium, wine-tasting facilities, and some of the best shopping you'll find anywhere.

P.O. Box 23367, Claremont 7735. ✆ **021/683-3424.** Fax 021/683-3502. www.singita.co.za. Sweni: 6 units. Lebombo 21 units. R13,600 ($2,030) double, all-inclusive (except French champagne and spa treatments). No seasonal discounts. AE, DC, MC, V. Children over 10 only. **Amenities:** Each lodge has dining areas; bar; lounges; boma; pool; room service; laundry; Internet terminal; library; wine cellar; game drives; bush walks (The Village features a spa; gym; craft and gift stores; art gallery; wine-tasting venue). *In room:* A/C, minibar, hair dryer, safe, tea- and coffee-making facilities.

IN SABI SAND

At press time, **MalaMala,** arguably Africa's most famous private game reserve, was undergoing an extensive and much-needed upgrade. With their new **Rattray's Lodge** (R11,390/$1,700 double, all-inclusive except for beverages), featuring eight luxurious suites overlooking the Sand River, as well as the five suites currently being built at **Sable Camp,** the Rattrays are hoping to finally keep abreast of developments at Londolozi, Sabi Sabi, and Singita. Catching up will be long haul, though; check out www.malamala.com to see how they're doing.

Djuma Vuyatela ✦✦ (Value)   Like many of the lodges in Sabi Sand, Djuma actually comprises three separate camps, including **Galago,** a self-catering single unit lodge, and **Bush Lodge,** but it is **Vuyatela** ✦✦, the flagship, which is really worth considering. Pricier than its good-value counterparts, Vuyatela is also the youngest of the properties and the more exciting option, thanks to design exuberance. A celebration and fusion of southern African culture, the lodge is fashioned from architectural materials similar to those used in villages and townships—adobe mud-pack walls are offset by corrugated iron, for instance—and the crafts and artworks reflect African-style pop art, of which the Coca-Cola bottle chandelier is a particularly fine example. Accommodations comprise eight thatched chalets, each with a generous bedroom, dressing room and bathroom, separate lounge, and large private deck with small plunge pool and shower. The cuisine reflects the lodge's pan-African theme. Djuma is very much owner-managed, which means that service is excellent, and the game-viewing is pure Sabi Sand. Djuma has access to more than 9,000 hectares (22,230 acres), of which it owns 7,000 (17,290 acres), making it one of the largest landowners in the Sabi Sand Reserve. As Djuma can be accessed only via the northerly Gowrie Gate, reached via 55km (34 miles) of harrowing dirt road, you should definitely consider flying in on the Djuma Shuttle, a fly-in package arranged through the lodge.

P.O. Box 338, Hluvukani 1363. (✆) 013/735-5118. Fax 013/735-5070. www.djuma.co.za. Vuyatela 8 units; Bush Lodge 8 units; Galago 5 units. High season Vuyatela R7,900 ($1,179) double; Bush Lodge R5,500 ($821) double; Galago R600 ($90) per person, minimum of 6. Low season (winter) Vuyatela R5,300 ($791) double; Bush Lodge R3,960 ($591) double. Rates include all meals, drinks (at Vuyatela), game drives, and bush walks. Children under 12 pay 50%. AE, DC, MC, V. **Amenities:** Dining room; bar/lounge area; boma; pool; game drives; bush walks; cultural village visit. Vuyatela: Gymnasium; room service; massage; laundry; Internet library; small aquarium. *In room:* A/C, minibar (Vuyatela only), hair dryer, Internet connection (Vuyatela only).

Exeter ⭐⭐ Argentine owner Stephen Saad has transformed the three lodges in the Exeter stable (**River Lodge** ⭐, **Dulini** ⭐, and **Leadwood Lodge** ⭐⭐) into high-end design-conscious Afro-chic hideaways, though some of the ultramodern, Eurocentric furnishings may disturb safari purists. River Lodge offers eight suites and is the closest to a bush experience, but this does not mean forgoing private plunge pools, inside and outside showers, and luxurious living quarters done out in reds, blacks, grays, and whites; large glass walls and huge screened doors look out onto views of the river. Shades of ocher and clay, taupe and teak bring a slick, sophisticated look to the huge double-volume lounges, and dining areas are huge, magnificent open-sided rooms with views of the nearby Sand River—a beautiful place to enjoy meals or schmooze. More romantic is Dulini, which caters specifically to couples and has only six guest suites; children under 12 are not accepted. Utterly private (with very exclusive rates) are the four huge Leadwood suites, located in stone buildings with fireplaces. It's worth knowing that Exeter has also taken over **Kirkman's Kamp** (ex-MalaMala), which lies farther south. Originally established in the 1920s, it retains its colonial flavor and is functional rather than luxurious, despite having facilities like tennis courts; with 18 cottages, it precludes privacy but is an affordable way to access some of the best game-viewing areas in Kruger.

P.O. Box 360, Umhlanga Rocks 4320. (✆) 031/583-2840. Fax 031/583-2848. www.exeterlodges.com. 36 units. High season double River Lodge R7,200 ($1,075); Dulini R7,900 ($1,179); Leadwood R5,200 ($776); Kirkman's Kamp R5,600 ($836). Low season River Lodge R5,400 ($806); Dulini R5,900 ($881); Leadwood R5,200 ($776); Kirkman's Kamp R4,600 ($687). Rates include all meals, game drives, and bush walks. AE, DC, MC, V. **Amenities:** Dining room; bar; boma; pool; gym; game drives; bush walks; wine cellar (Leadwood); tennis courts (Kirkman's). *In room:* A/C, minibar, hair dryer, safe, tea- and coffee-making facilities.

Leopard Hills ⭐⭐ Like Exeter and Ulusaba (Virgin billionaire Richard Branson's neighboring lodge), Leopard Hills (named for the leopard born where the kitchen is now) traverses the busy, animal-rich western sector of the Sabi Sand. Some say it offers the best game-viewing in the greater Kruger region (imagine four of the Big 5, plus cheetah, all on one morning drive!). Not only does Leopard Hills offer excellent accommodations, but it's built on a hilltop, with views of the African bush savanna that go on forever. You can enjoy these views from the public areas as well as from five of the well-proportioned suites (specify savanna views), which are tasteful and generous, with wraparound glass frontages opening onto private sun decks, each with its own plunge pool. The muted cream, white, tan, and brown African-themed decor is executed with a mixture of rough untreated timber, bamboo, concrete, sisal, and leopard-print fabric, used sparingly. A fully stocked wine cellar, fine cuisine, and very well-maintained library with a cozy fireplace and more fabulous views complete the picture. Specially designed Land Rovers provide absolute comfort as you traverse the 10,000 hectares (24,700 acres) to which Leopard Hills has access, and although this sector sees a fair amount of traffic, sightings are limited to a maximum of three vehicles. There is now also a spa *sala*, where you can enjoy aromatherapy treatments while you drink in the views.

P.O. Box 612, Hazyview 1242. ⓒ **013/737-6626.** Fax 013/737-6628. www.leopardhills.com. 8 units. R10,800 ($1,612) double; winter R8,400 ($1,254). AE, DC, MC, V. Children stay on request. **Amenities:** Dining area; bar; lounge; boma; pool; gym; spa treatments; room service; laundry; library w/TV, DVD/VCR/CD players; game drives; bush walks. *In room:* A/C, minibar, hair dryer, safe, tea- and coffee-making facilities.

Lion Sands Ivory Lodge ★★   With only 3,500 hectares (8,645 acres) of prime game country to itself, you might expect Lion Sands to be slim on sightings, but given the fact that no fences separate it from neighboring Kruger (Skukuza airstrip is just 20 min. away) and accommodations overlook the Sabi River, then **Ivory Lodge** turns out to be an ideal place to watch animals while you cool off in your very own rim-flow plunge pool or have a closer look with the telescope on your private terrace. The ultra-chic guest suites, housed in thatched chalets, are decorated according to a strict ebony-and-ivory theme; cream-toned walls, floors, and fixtures are offset by black furnishings and cushions. An extensive bathroom, with an egg-shaped stone tub and an outdoor shower in its own garden, adds to the sense of luxury. Some guests may be disturbed by the open entrance area separating the bedroom from the living area, but despite the obvious danger of predator intrusion, staff quickly assure you that "only leopards have access to the terrace." Privacy is key; morning tea is delivered through a service hatch, and spa treatments are taken in-room—in fact, you need never leave your suite at all, even at meal times (reserve the "Peregrine" suite for ultimate privacy). Even the safari vehicles are designed for exclusivity, accommodating only six passengers and carrying game and birding books and hot-water bottles in winter. Such exclusivity comes at a price, of course. This is one of the most expensive safari lodges in the country, though regular specials are often available on the Web (www.africanpridehotels.com); in 2005 the winter rate was R5,600 ($836) double! *Note:* Lion Sands' **River Lodge** is far less exclusive, with 20 small, hotel-like rooms, and rates (R7,700/$1,149 double, including meals and game drives) that are easily matched by far-superior establishments such as Exeter's River Lodge or Djuma Vuyatela.

P.O. Box 30, White River 1240. ⓒ **013/735-5000.** Fax 013/735-5330. Reservations: P.O. Box 2667, Houghton 2041. ⓒ **011/484-9911** or -9916. www.lionsands.com. 6 units. R14,000 ($2,090) double. AE, DC, MC, V. No children under 12. **Amenities:** Dining area; bar; lounge; boma; pool; spa treatments; board room; curio shop; library; wine cellar; Internet; game drives; bush walks; clay pigeon shooting; nature and stargazing talks. *In room:* A/C, minibar, hair dryer, safe, Internet connectivity, CD player, tea- and coffee-making facility, fireplace, plunge pool, telescope.

Londolozi ★★★   Famed for its leopards, this superb safari camp began life as a diminutive hunting lodge in the 1920s. In the '70s, when the Varty brothers inherited land, they turned to conservation and began offering basic safaris to wildlife enthusiasts. Today Londolozi has evolved into four separate luxury camps—**Pioneer, Founder,**

Bateleur ⭐⭐⭐, and **Tree** ⭐⭐⭐—and offers such a high standard in accommodations, cuisine, and game-viewing that it has become the model upon which all subsequent luxury lodges were based. While neighboring Singita (reviewed above) is overtly design conscious, Londolozi retains a distinctly understated yet luxurious, safari-inspired look; restrained elegance is achieved through tasteful and functional design choices that never overwhelm your primary motive for being here: to view game.

The vegetation surrounding the camps (which are built on the banks of the Sand River and within walking distance, but out of sight of one another) is the closest to jungle you'll find in the predominantly bushveld savanna. The best value-for-money option is the Bateleur chalets, with large granite en-suite bathrooms and beautifully appointed bedrooms—mood lighting is controlled from a bank of switches and dimmers—and a king-size bed overlooking a totally private timber deck with your own plunge pool. (Chalets at Pioneer and Founder camps cost the same but have no pools.) If money is no object, the Tree Camp's suites are the most intimate choice (the camp is half the size of the others), but Bateleur's Granite Suites deserve a special mention—book no. 1 and you'll find yourself swimming in a private pool that drops onto the boulders that form the Sand River banks, close enough to hear the river running from your bath. Londolozi is a Relais & Châteaux lodge, which sets high standards for both accommodations and cuisine; particularly enjoyable are barbecues in the boma, where you'll also be entertained by a homegrown choir. (Pioneer is also increasingly popular for its interactive cooking evenings.)

Having set the standard, Londolozi remains one of the top (and most expensive) lodges in southern Africa. Bear in mind, however, that Londolozi's size may compromise the sense of exclusivity that such high prices demand, particularly when all four camps are full. But with more than 15,000 hectares (37,050 acres) to traverse, there are excellent game-viewing opportunities, not least of which is finding the famed Londolozi leopards, who are relaxed enough to allow prolonged viewing sessions that leave even the most amateur photographer satisfied.

Private Bag X27, Benmore 2010. ☎ **011/809-4300.** Fax 011/809-4315. www.ccafrica.com. Pioneer Camp 6 units. Founder's Camp 6 units. Bateleur Camp 12 units. Tree Camp 6 units. Chalets high season R11,600 ($1,731) double; low season R7,150 ($1,067) double. Suites R13,600 ($2,030). AE, DC, MC, V. Children under 11 pay 50%. **Amenities:** Each camp offers its own dining area; bar; boma; pool; room service; babysitting (no children at Tree); laundry; game drives; bush walks. *In room:* A/C, minibar, hair dryer, fireplace (only suites at Pioneer Camp), plunge pool (at Bateleur and Tree camps only).

Notten's Bush Camp ⭐ *(Value)*

Wedged between MalaMala and Sabi Sabi, this small camp—the cheapest fully catered option in the Sabi Sand reserve—is an oasis of calm. Gilly and Bambi Notten have created a home-away-from-home atmosphere (lions are framed next to family photos), and if the number of repeat visits is anything to go by, it's a winning formula. The raised open veranda, where the substantial high tea buffets and generous breakfasts are served, provides a wonderful view of the water hole and surrounding grass plain where just about every mammal under the African sun has been spotted. Most of the guest chalets are tiled with attractive slate and warmed with sisal carpets; two of these have indoor as well as outdoor showers. Large sliding doors open onto private verandas; room nos. 2, 4, and 5 enjoy the best views. Comfortable furnishings are offset by the fact that rooms have no electricity; showers are heated by an old donkey boiler. Note that if luxuries like air-conditioning leave you cold, Umlani's huts (see below)—which go for a similar price—give an even greater sense of being in the bush. Notten's food is better, however: home-cooked cuisine that's refreshingly unfussy and totally delicious. In place of lunch, there's usually a high tea, and dinners are sumptuous three-course affairs. The major drawback here is that because of the camp's size (some 3,500 hectares/8,645 acres), you may not spot as much game as on neighboring territories.

P.O. Box 622, Hazyview 1242. Ⓒ **013/735-5105** or 013/735-5750. Fax 013/735-5970. www.nottens.com. 6 units. R5,000 ($746) double; low-season rates available on request. Rate includes meals, game drives, and bush walks. AE, DC, MC, V. Children over 8 only. **Amenities:** Dining area; bar; lounge; boma; pool; therapeutic treatments; game drives; bush walks. *In room:* Fan.

Sabi Sabi ★★ Clearly covetous of the attention lauded upon Singita's contemporary aesthetic, safari stalwart Sabi Sabi expanded to include its now rather popular and pricey **Earth Lodge.** Having recently bought Londolozi's Safari Lodge, Sabi Sabi seems set to further increase guest capacity. With a quarter of a century in the safari business, Sabi Sabi hardly needs to impress anybody, but this has clearly been the aim with Earth Lodge, where the architects' mandate was to build a thoroughly modern lodge for the new millennium. The entire lodge looks as if it has been built into the earth, with one of the most spectacular open-air entrance foyers in Africa. Even though they photograph well, rooms are less impressive (certainly when compared with those at Singita or Royal Malewane), with dark interiors, tiny plunge pools, and hard, modern edges. Besides Earth Lodge, the larger **Bush Lodge** has also been completely rebuilt and offers generous dark-gray, ocher, and cream suites set amid gardens and furnished with plush colonial-style and Balinese pieces, with African artifacts and kilim rugs adding warmth. But you still feel as if you're in a hotel, with units too close together for privacy. For this you'd be better off booking into the pleasantly refurbished **Selati Lodge**. Previously a hunting lodge and named after the famed turn-of-the-20th-century railway line that ran through the area and into Kruger Park, this elegant lodge is filled with vintage railway memorabilia, antiques, and old sepia-tone photographs depicting those early days. The thatched free-standing chalets are spacious and beautifully furnished, with dark stinkwood beds offset by swathes of white mosquito netting—for a little extra, it's worth booking the ultraluxe honeymoon suite.

P.O. Box 52665, Saxonwold 2132. Ⓒ **011/483-3939.** Fax 011/483-3799. www.sabisabi.com. Bush Lodge 25 units. Selati Lodge 8 units. Earth Lodge 13 units. Bush Lodge R8,800 ($1,313) double; presidential suite R11,400 ($1,701). Selati R9,900 ($1,478) double; presidential suite (own Land Rover and ranger) R11,800 ($1,761); honeymoon suite: R10,800 ($1,612). Earth Lodge R11,200 ($1,672) double; presidential suite (own butler, Land Rover, and ranger) R22,400 ($3,343). Rates include all meals, local beverages, game drives, and bush walks. AE, DC, MC, V. No children under 13 at Selati or Earth. Special rates for children apply. **Amenities:** Dining area; bar; boma; pool; room service; laundry; IT center (Bush and Earth); game drives; bush walks. Earth and Bush Lodge also offer spa; small gym; IT center; wine cellar. *In room:* A/C, minibar, hair dryer, safe.

Singita Ebony & Boulders ★★★ Awards and accolades for Luke Bailes's sumptuous private game reserve keep flooding in; Singita has again been awarded top honors as the Best Destination in the World by *Condé Nast Traveler*, and now also by *Travel+Leisure*. Frommer's has rated this lodge as the best in the country since 1998. While you might find it difficult to leave your room at Londolozi, here it is virtually impossible. Why bother when you can take a dip in your own personal plunge pool or enjoy a massage or pedicure on your private deck, watching the wildlife on the open plains beyond the river? But do try to take in at least one game drive. The quality of the game-viewing is superlative; Singita not only enjoys traversing rights to more than 18,000 hectares (44,460 acres), but also ensures that you're well taken care of by eloquent game rangers who are impeccably well versed in their craft. You will be enlightened and entertained in an easy, effortless manner throughout your stay.

Singita is separated into two lodges, **Boulders** and **Ebony,** each with its own large, open main lounge. Each of the suites in the contemporary-styled Boulders Lodge is the size of a small house and features a massive Balu teak deck and private rim-flow plunge pool, sliding floor-to-ceiling glass walls, a stone fireplace, en-suite bathroom with Victorian-style bath with uninterrupted views, a beautifully furnished lounge, and a king-size bed dressed in embossed linen. Colors are earth tones and textures are organic, combining stone, polished concrete, timber, granite, and ceramics with soft fabrics in muted browns offset by crisp white. Ebony Lodge features the same standard of luxury, service, and privacy, but the decor has an African colonial theme, lending a somewhat more homey sensation to the overall design—plus, the atmosphere is a few degrees more relaxed. Most of the accommodations here overlook the Sand River, but for more privacy and space, definitely opt for suite no. 7, 8, or 9.

A Relais & Châteaux lodge, Singita offers superb dining at all meals; three-course lunches use the freshest of ingredients to fashion creative takes on traditional Cape dishes like *bobotie* (meat pie), and dinners always feature a vegetarian option. Wine tastings (largely South African wines) in Boulders' handsome wine cellar are popular ongoing events. The Singita staff is one of the friendliest around, and the vibe is a happy one, without the imperiosity of luxe resorts elsewhere in the world.

P.O. Box 23367, Claremont 7735. (*) 021/683-3424. Fax 021/683-3502. www.singita.co.za. Ebony Lodge 9 units. Boulders Lodge 9 units. R13,600 ($2,030) double, all-inclusive (except French champagne). No seasonal discounts. AE, DC, MC, V. Children over 10 only. **Amenities:** Dining room; bar; lounge; spa; gym; home and curio shop; salon; room service; laundry; Internet; library; 12,000-bottle wine cellar; game drives; bush walks. *In room:* A/C, minibar, hair dryer, safe, tea- and coffee-making facilities, fireplace, private pool.

IN MANYELETI

Honeyguide Tented Safari Camps ★★ (Value Honeyguide's tented camps offer some of the best value-for-money game experiences in the country and tend to attract a young, occasionally raucous crowd. Relaxed safari chic comes close to describing the informal minimalism of **Mantobeni Tented Camp,** with Morris chairs, leather couches, cotton sheets, old-style lanterns, and damask linen suggesting a modest degree of *Out of Africa* styling. Guests are accommodated in East African–style tents, set on raised wooden decks with lovely concrete bathrooms featuring double showers and partially sunken tubs. Set in a riverine forest, most of the 12 tents overlook a riverbed (usually dry) or the water hole; it's a good idea, however, to reserve tent no.1, which enjoys more privacy and is likely to be farther away from loud neighbors. The central lounge/dining and lazing area is relatively sparsely furnished, and tents can become quite hot in summer—most of your attention should be diverted toward the narrow, elegant pool. Early-morning drums alert you to the dawning game drive, and tea is brought to your tent—a luxury even the most upmarket camps don't always offer. Five minutes away, the 12 en-suite tents at Honeyguide's **Khoka Moya Tented Camp** offer almost exactly the same experience, but the tents (this time set on concrete slabs) are slightly more spacious, and the somewhat more elegant bathrooms don't have tubs. Khoka Moya's more contemporary furnishings include large plush ottomans and beanbags around the fire. Most important, Khoka Moya allows children, making it great for families, while Mantobeni is more suitable for romance.

P.O. Box 786064, Sandton 2146. (*) 011/341-0282. Fax 011/341-0281. www.honeyguidecamp.com. Mantobeni 12 units. Khoka Moya 12 units. R4,600 ($687) double; winter R3,600 ($537) double. AE, DC, MC, V. **Amenities:** Dining room; bar; lounge; boma; pool; game drives; bush walks. *In room:* Standing fan.

IN TIMBAVATI

Kings Camp 🐾🐾   This is an ideal place to find yourself if your idea of "roughing it" is letting the butler have the afternoon off. While Tanda Tula (reviewed below) provides a more authentic bush experience, accommodations at Kings Camp are pure luxury (far better value than CC Africa's main Ngala camp). Actually, it's hardly a "camp" at all; the large, private, thatched chalets are arranged at the edges of a well-tailored lawn with a pool and various cozy and comfortable lounge-cum-viewing areas. On your personal terrace, you can sip martinis or lounge on a hammock just meters from the animal-rich Timbavati bush, while in your suite you're cocooned in traditional luxury. Rooms are air-conditioned and spacious, with comfortable furnishing and fittings; bathrooms are large, with his and hers outdoor showers. Even the game drives are decidedly genteel, with repeated reminders to mind the thorns as you drive through the bush. Upon returning from a grueling early evening of tracking leopard, lion, and buffalo, your bedroom will be filled with a herbal scent and your bath drawn piping hot. Kings Camp is an excellent place for virgin bushwackers determined to track the Big 5, learn about every leaf and smell along the way, and keen to listen to vivid wildlife tales at a communal dinner table, where meals are of a high standard.

Seasons in Africa, P.O. Box 19516, Nelspruit 1218. ℃ **013/755-4408.** Fax 013/752-5842. www.kingscamp.com. 10 units. R5,900 ($881) double; R4,400 ($657) in winter. Rates include meals, wildlife activities, tea, and coffee. Children under 12 pay 50% if sharing with 2 adults. AE, DC, MC, V. **Amenities:** Dining room; bar; lounge/viewing deck; pool; therapy tent; gym; TV and DVD room; shop; limited room service; babysitting; laundry; library; game drives; bush walks; 24-hr. doctor on call. *In room:* A/C, minibar, hair dryer, safe, tea- and coffee-making facility.

Ngala Tented Safari Camp 🐾🐾🐾 *(Kids)*   Conservation Corporation (CC Africa) is

one of southern Africa's premier safari operators, with a variety of camps and lodges operating to varying standards; they have two operations in the Timbavati, one of which is this highly recommended camp, comprising six deluxe en-suite tents on the banks of the Timbavati River—it delivers a superb bush experience, with operating rights within 14,000 hectares (34,580 acres) of land providing one of the best game-viewing experiences outside of Sabi Sand. By contrast, don't be tempted by the "luxury" lodging at the **Ngala Main Camp,** which is overpriced (R6,840/$1,021 in peak season), with thatched cottages that are cramped and too stacked on top of one another to provide a relaxing experience or any sense of privacy; in fact, it's more like a small hotel than a safari. Note that Ngala offers a highly recommended 3-day walking safari for R6,450 ($963).

Private Bag X27, Benmore 2010. ℃ **011/809-4300.** Fax 011/809-4315. www.ccafrica.com. Main Camp 21 units. Tented Camp 6 units. Tented Camp R9,590 ($1,431). Main Camp R6,840 ($1,021) double; R3,210 ($479) in winter. All rates include meals, game drives, and bush walks. Children under 11 pay 50%. AE, DC, MC, V. **Amenities:** Boma/restaurant; bar; lounge; pool; game activities; babysitting; laundry. *In room:* Hair dryer.

Tanda Tula 🐾🐾   One of the very first luxury tented camps in the Kruger area,

Tanda Tula gives a real sense of being in the heart of the bush. The en-suite safari-style tents, erected on timber deck floors, offer all the comforts of a well-furnished room, while the tent walls do nothing to filter out the sounds of the wilds. The 12 tents are all privately situated, each with its own furnished *stoep* (veranda); try to reserve tent no. 1 for the best view (or no. 10 as an alternative). Bathrooms have Victorian tubs and outdoor showers. Because the surrounding bush is quite dense and rooms are not as luxurious as its competitors, you're more likely to spend time in the elegant and comfortably furnished open-sided lounge and dining area, which leads out onto the lawns and pool. This is where drinks are served, as well as lunch, and at night a huge fire is lit, even if dinner is served in the adjacent boma. Weather permitting, breakfasts are served in the bush, and braais (barbecues) are regularly held on the riverbed. Tanda Tula means "to love the quiet," and the team does everything possible to ensure that you can do just that. Game drives cover a potential 20,000 hectares (49,400 acres), providing Tanda Tula with access to the largest area in Timbavati, and you'll likely spot at least three of the Big 5 in 1 day.

P.O. Box 32, Constantia 7848. © 021/794-6500. Fax 021/794-7605. www.tandatula.co.za. 12 units. High season (Dec–Mar) R7,000 ($1,045) double; low season (Apr–Nov) R5,400 ($806). Rates are all-inclusive. AE, DC, MC, V. No children under 12. **Amenities:** Dining area; bar; lounge; boma; pool; laundry; game drives; bush walks; bush breakfasts; riverbed braais. *In room:* Hair dryer, fan.

Umlani Bushcamp *Kids* Offering one of the most authentic bush experiences, Umlani (place of rest) is a personal favorite. Not only does it offer a relatively affordable alternative to the luxury lodge, but it's a really relaxed camp, the kind of place you sit with your toes in the sand listening to the sounds of the bush (rather than the hum of the pool filter)—it has no formal gardens and very few staff, the en-suite huts are relatively basic, and at night the camp is lit only by firelight and paraffin lamps. Accommodations are in thatched, bamboo-wall en-suite rondavels (circular huts), which now have screen windows and a few shelves. No official camp guards are there to escort you in the evenings as you follow the flame-lit sandy walkway to your bed; suddenly, the huts, which in the light of day seem a little too on top of each other, are reassuringly close. During the day, as you swing in the hammock waiting for a predator to come padding down the dry Nshlaralumi riverbed, the tranquil camp is far too relaxed to promote paranoid feelings. Nina, Don, and Dave are the laid-back hosts who manage this rustic haven; it's definitely the place to come if you're young or want to bring children (it has three family huts). Every effort has been made to retain a sense of what it's like to camp in the middle of the bush; there's even a stilted tree-house overlooking a water hole where you can spend the night with only the sounds of nocturnal animals for company. The limited set menu (advise of dietary preferences ahead of time) is of the home-cooked variety. Umlani is small, but with traversing rights to parts of Tanda Tula, it effectively covers 10,000 hectares (24,700 acres) and regularly has good sightings. *Note:* Even though there is no electricity, it is possible to charge camera batteries here.

P.O. Box 11604, Maroelana 0161. © 012/346-4028. Fax 012/346-4023. www.umlani.com. 8 units. R3,740 ($558) double; 3-night special R9,570 ($1,428) double; Winter (May–June) R2,700 ($403) double. Rates include all meals, drinks, game drives, and bush walks. Children under 12 pay 50%. AE, DC, MC, V. **Amenities:** Dining room; bar; boma; pool; shop; small library; game drives; bush walks; bush breakfasts; microlighting and ballooning by arrangement.

IN THORNYBUSH

Royal Malewane It's difficult to imagine that anything would be too much trouble for the gracious staff at Liz Biden's much-lauded luxury lodge. Here you are warmly received and—at every turn—reminded to relax, unwind, and soak up that rarest of pleasures, absolute tranquillity. Like Singita, the aptly named Royal Malewane offers such sumptuous accommodations that you will be hard-pressed to leave your suite, even for game drives. Elevated walkways are the only link between the wonderfully private thatched suites set on stilts right in the midst of the bush, each with a huge open-plan bedroom/sitting room with fireplace and equally enormous bathroom. Whether you're lying draped in Ralph Lauren linen in the antique canopied king-size bed, or luxuriating in the elegant claw-foot bathtub or huge open shower, floor-to-ceiling windows provide wonderfully unobscured views of your private outdoor terrace with outside shower and gazebo, and, beyond, the bush. Here antelope, warthog, rhino, and giraffe regularly come to graze, while an elephant may arrive to use your private rim-flow plunge pool as a convenient watering hole. The lounge and dining areas are similarly decorated in modern colonial style, and the boma, which, unlike most, is open, affording a view of the bush, is one of the best dressed in Kruger. Chef John Jackson conjures up remarkable meals, including a sumptuous Bedouin-themed affair served in the bush; but don't be surprised if, immediately after dessert, you're whisked away on an impromptu game drive, prompted by roaring lions. For the ultimate honeymoon or getaway destination, you don't get any better than the palatial Royal and Malewane Suites, where up to four guests can enjoy the same unfettered luxuries visited upon regulars Elton John and U2's Bono; besides 25,489 sq. km (2,368 sq. ft.) of living space, you enjoy the personal attentions of a 24-hour private butler, private chef, and masseur. With traversing rights on 11,500 hectares (28,405 acres) and some of the top trackers in South Africa, the lodge also offers excellent game-viewing opportunities—elephant and lion are easily seen within the hour. For all its superlative luxury, it's a remarkably unpretentious lodge, and arguably *the* ultimate luxury safari destination.

P.O. Box 1542, Hoedspruit 1380. Ⓒ **015/793-0150.** Fax 015/793-2879. www.royalmalewane.com. 6 units. R10,900–R11,900 ($1,627–$1,776) double; Royal and Malewane Suites R38,500 ($5,746) for 4 people. Rates include all meals, local beverages, game drives, and bush walks. AE, DC, MC, V. **Amenities:** Dining room; lounge/bar; boma; bush and theme dinners; spa w/heated lap pool, aromatherapy, massage, and body and beauty treatments; gym; gift shop; room service; laundry; Internet access; library; game drives; bush walks. *In room:* A/C, minibar, hair dryer, safe, tea- and coffee-making facilities, fireplace, plunge pool; Royal & Malewane Suites include TV, CD/DVD player, full kitchen, private chef, private butler, private masseuse; Royal Suite includes laptop, fax/printer.

IN MAKALALI

Makalali Game Lodge ★★ *Value* Makalali means "place of rest" in the local Shangaan language, and you can expect plenty of rest in what *Tatler* magazine once voted the "Most Innovatively Designed Hotel in the World." Aiming for a sensual bush experience with something seemingly inspired by Antoni Gaudí, architect Silvio Rech has combined architectural styles from all over Africa—shaggy East African roof thatching adorns mud and stone walls, while rugged North African–inspired turrets create a mythical village palace sensibility. Makalali consists of four camps—each with its own swimming pool, boma, and lounge and dining area—situated on various points of the Makhutswi River, which flows for approximately 8 months of the year. Rooms are huge and totally private; each features a fireplace as well as a *sala,* joined to your hut via a boardwalk, where you can arrange to have a romantic dinner. Try to book a room in the uniquely situated camp 4, where the rooms are most dispersed and you reach your public areas via a swingbridge—*very* romantic. Don't get stuck with room no. 3 in camp 4 (adjacent the staff village) or room no. 4 in Camp 1; the latter is too close to the kitchen—which, incidentally, produces wonderful food.

P.O. Box 809, Hoedspruit 1380. Ⓒ **015/793-1720.** www.makalali.co.za. Or book through Three Cities in U.S.: 305/792-0172. www.threecities.co.za. 4 camps each with 6 units. R5,680 ($848) double. Rate includes meals, game drives, and laundry. Children under 12 pay 25%. AE, DC, MC, V. **Amenities:** Each camp includes dining area; bar; lounge; boma; pool; room service; babysitting; laundry; game drives; bush walks. *In room:* A/C (Camp 4), hair dryer, safe, phones (in Camps 1–3), fans.

9

Kingdom of the Zulu: KwaZulu-Natal

Demarcated in the west by the soaring Drakensberg Mountains, its southern tip and eastern borders lapped by the warm Indian Ocean, the densely vegetated KwaZulu-Natal is often described as the country's most "African" province. Its subtropical latitude translates into long, hot summers—at times oppressively humid—and balmy winters, while the warm Mozambique current ensures that the ocean is never more than 2° to 3° cooler than the air. These sultry conditions have not gone unnoticed by its landlocked neighbors, resulting in an almost unbroken ribbon of development along the coastal belt south of the Tugela River, a region dubbed "the Holiday Coast." In its center is Durban, the busiest port in Africa, and enjoying a revival as a tourism hub for locals in search of affordable beach-based holidays and international travelers looking for good-value safaris, the most accessible of which lies only 45 minutes west of the city center.

Durban has a unique energy that continues to spawn some of the continent's most creative trendsetters, but it is the region north of the Tugela River, known as Zululand, where the amaZulu rose to power during the early 19th century under the legendary ruler Shaka, that draws most international travelers. Traditional ways still play a major role in contemporary life here, and visitors are welcomed at special events such as

sangoma initiation ceremonies and annual reed dances. Zululand is also home to the majority of the KwaZulu-Natal game reserves, some of Africa's oldest wildlife sanctuaries. Given the difference in vegetation, they make a recommended addition to a safari in Kruger or Botswana. A mere 3 hours' drive north of Durban, you can see the Big 5 at Hluhluwe-Umfolozi Game Reserve or at one of the nearby private reserves—this is one of the few places in the world where you can track a pride of lions in the morning, then spend the afternoon cruising the lush waterways of the Greater St Lucia Wetland (a World Heritage Site) for hippo and croc, or diving the rich coral reefs off Sodwana Bay. If you have time, join the privileged few who have explored the rich marine life and pristine coastline that lies north of Sodwana, from beautiful Mabibi to the even more secluded Rocktail Bay. The more intrepid nature lover should head even farther, to Kosi Bay, in the far northern corner of the province. Inland lie Mkuze and Ndumo, the country's premier bird-watching reserves, while to the west lie the famous battle sites of the many wars fought among the Zulu, British, and Boers in the 19th century.

Pride of place for those who enjoy walking must, however, go to the soaring Drakensberg Mountains, or "Barrier of Spears," as the amaZulu called them. Site

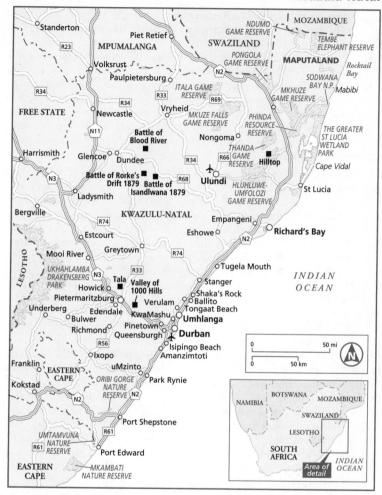

of more than 35,000 ancient San rock paintings, thought to be the mostly densely concentrated area on the African continent, the Drakensberg was declared a World Heritage Site in 2000, bringing a much-deserved focus to southern Africa's most majestic mountainscape.

1 Staying Active

BIRD-WATCHING Two of South Africa's best bird-watching destinations—the Mkhuze and Ndumo reserves—are located here. Contact Peter at **Lawson's Bird-watching Tours** ✦✦✦ (© 013/741-2458; www.lawsons.co.za), which operates throughout southern Africa and invariably includes both reserves in its fully catered bird-watching safaris. A 4-hour drive from Durban, **Mkhuze** has very basic facilities (it has no restaurant, but the small Rhino Diner serves simple "pub grub" style dishes, for example), but the park is magnificent (see "Zululand: Tracking down the Big 5 in Zululand: The Greater St Lucia Wetland Park," later in this chapter). Do ensure that your itinerary includes the laid-on luxuries of **Ndumo Wilderness Camp,** on the border between KwaZulu-Natal and Mozambique. The camp is located in the exquisite Ndumo Game Reserve, an area often compared with the Okavango Delta (in Botswana), with pans and jungle teeming with more than 400 bird species—60% of South Africa's birdlife. The camp opens only on the request of a professionally guided group numbering eight or more persons, and offers eight well-appointed en-suite safari tents, each situated on a raised wooden deck and linked by a boardwalk under a canopy of giant fig trees.

HIKING   The wilderness trails in **Umfolozi Game Reserve** 🦏🦏🦏, in which you track game on foot, are considered the best in the country, superior even to those in Kruger. You can choose the type of hike you prefer, based on your fitness level and personal comfort, but the **Traditional Trail,** in which all your gear is carried by donkeys, is recommended, although a fair degree of fitness is required. The **Summer Bushveld** trails, in which you have a chance to relax between the morning and afternoon walks, are worth asking about if you're not such a keen walker. For more information, call ✆ 035/550-8478 or visit www.kznwildlife.com; for bookings, call ✆ 033/845-1000. See also "Zululand: Tracking down the Big 5 in Zululand: Hluhluwe-Umfolozi Game Reserve," later in this chapter. The **Mziki Trail** 🦏🦏 (located in the Mfabeni area) in the Greater St Lucia Wetland Park comprises three 1-day loops of 10 to 18km (6¼–11 miles). Accompanied by an armed field ranger, you explore the park's estuary shore, dune forests, and coastline, with the chance to see elephant, buffalo, hippo, and crocodile; for bookings, call ✆ 035/590-9002 or e-mail rossouwd@kznwildlife.com. The 3km (1.75-mile) circular guided **Mkhuze Fig Forest Walk,** through one of the area's rarest and most attractive woodlands, is also recommended; to arrange, this call ✆ 035/573-9004. Kosi Bay's 4-day **Kosi Bay Hiking Trail** 🦏 takes in all four lakes, coral reefs, pristine beaches, and the country's largest mangrove forest; to arrange this, call Frances Randall at ✆ 082/829-8281. Of the many trails traversing the Drakensberg, the **Giant's Cup Hiking Trail** 🦏🦏 (located in the Cobham area), a 3- to 5-day self-guided clearly marked hike that takes you past caves with San paintings, crystal-clear rivers, pools, and deep grass valleys, is recommended for relatively inexperienced hikers. For detailed information about the Drakensberg trails and/or bookings, contact KZN Wildlife (✆ 033/845-1000; www.kznwildlife.com).

SURFING   To rent a surfboard and arrange lessons, contact **Surf Zone** (✆ 031/368-5818) in the Ocean Sports Complex, on Marine Parade in Durban. Good surf spots around the city are North Beach and the adjacent "Bay of Plenty." Check out Green Point, Scottburgh, the Spot, Warner Beach, and Cave Rock; the latter has an excellent right reef break.

SWIMMING   Dolphin Encounters (✆ 011/462-4551) offers 4-day swimming-with-dolphin packages just north of the KwaZulu-Natal border—visitors must arrange to travel to the Kosi Bay border post (4-hr. drive from Durban). With warm water year-round, the entire coast is popular with swimmers, and shark nets protect the main swimming beaches from Port Edward to the Tugela; note, however, that many beaches shelve suddenly into deep surf, with strong undertows—swim only

Moments Sangomas at Dawn

Walk along a Durban beach at dawn, and you may see a group of Zulu *sangomas* (traditional healers), their beads and buckskin adornments covered in brightly colored cloth, wading into the ocean to collect seawater, to be used in *muti* (traditional medicines) to protect crops. An estimated two-thirds of South Africans regularly consult sangomas, and recently even large pharmaceutical companies have been tapping into their knowledge of the medicinal properties of plants.

where signs indicate safety, or where there are lifeguards. (Keep an eye out for Portuguese man-of-war jellyfish as well.)

WHITE-WATER RAFTING **Umko** offers a full day (R495/$74) on the Umkomaas River, considered one of the best commercial-run rivers in South Africa (up to grade-5 rapids). These can be extended into 2-day trips; call Dave at © **083/270-0403.**

2 Durban

1,753km (1,087 miles) NE of Cape Town; 588km (365 miles) SE of Johannesburg

The Union Jack was first planted in Durban's fertile soil in 1824, a year after George Farewell fortuitously happened upon its harbor. It was only after the fledgling settlement was formally annexed in 1844, however, that the dense coastal vegetation was gradually consumed by buildings with broad verandas and civilized with English traditions such as morning papers, afternoon tea, and weekend horse racing.

Sugar was this region's "white gold," with large fortunes made by the so-called sugar barons. The most famous of these was Sir Marshall Campbell; today his home, housing the Campbell Collection, is one of Durban's star attractions, and one can still travel along the beachfront in the two-wheeled "rickshaws" he introduced to the city in 1893. The world's voracious appetite for sugar was also responsible for the strong Indian influence on Durban's architecture, cuisine, and customs—during the 19th century, thousands of indentured laborers were shipped in from India to work the sugar plantations, and today Durban houses the largest Indian population outside of India.

South Africa's third-largest city, Durban attracts the lion's share of South Africa's domestic tourists and offers a completely unique atmosphere. On the surface is the creeping sense of decay typical of places in which the constant presence of humidity brings about a kind of torpor, yet get under the skin and you'll find a city pulsating with promise—and not only among real estate agents exhilarated by the property boom that has followed urban beachfront rejuvenation projects like the R21.5-million ($3.2-million) Wilson's Wharf, the R750-million ($112-million) uShaka Marine World theme park, and the R1.5-billion ($224-million) Suncoast Casino. There's a general sense of pride in Durban's ability to consistently birth some of the country's greatest creative talents. From traditional pottery and beadwork to cutting-edge fashion and interior design, Durban cooks.

It's certainly worth scheduling 2 days here before heading north for the game parks and marine reserves of Zululand, or west to the Drakensberg. If you're interested in the region's arts and crafts, make it a priority to visit the Durban Art Museum, the

KwaZulu-Natal Society of the Arts (NSA) Gallery, and the BAT Centre. But to experience the essence of South Africa's most multicultural city, take a guided walking tour of the Indian District, where Indian dealers trade in everything from spices and sari fabrics to fresh fish and meat, while Zulu street hawkers ply passersby with anything from haircuts to *muti*—baboon skulls, bits of bark, bone, and dried herbs—used to heal wounds, improve spirits, ward off evil, or cast spells. Or just take a stroll along Battery Beach, where the Shembe may be conducting a baptism while surfers look for the perfect wave, or a group of Hindus may be lighting clay votive lamps while a Zulu *sangoma* tosses in an offering to the ancestors. It is a bizarre and wonderful city, a truly African city, undergoing its own little renaissance. And with plans for a new international airport at La Mercy taking shape, Durban looks set to give lily-white Cape Town a real run for its money.

ESSENTIALS

VISITOR INFORMATION   You can make all your travel arrangements at the Tourist Junction, where **Durban Africa** (② **031/304-4934;** www.durbanexperience. co.za; Mon–Fri 8am–4:30pm, Sat 9am–2pm) is located, as is a branch of **KwaZulu-Natal Wildlife (KZN Wildlife)** and Tourism KwaZulu-Natal. The Tourist Junction is in the Old Station Building (160 Pine St.). For details on local events, pick up a free copy of *What's On in Durban and KwaZulu-Natal.* *Note:* If you plan to travel north to the Zululand reserves and beyond, **Camera Africa** is a recommended agent that specializes in the Zululand area (② **031/266-4172;** www.camera-africa.com).

GETTING THERE   By Plane   Durban International Airport is 15km (9¼ miles) south of the city center, but plans are afoot to relocate to La Mercy (about 35 min. north) and rename it King Shaka International Airport. Until then, most flights remain domestic. For arrival and departure information, call ② **031/451-6666;** for reservations, call **SAA** (② **031/250-1111**). Taxis are always lined up outside, or you can use the **airport bus service** (② **031/465-5573**) to the SAA building on Aliwal Street. For 24-hour service, call **Super Shuttle** (② **0860/333-444**).

By Train   The **Trans-Natal** from Johannesburg pulls into Durban Station (② **086/ 000-8888**), on NMR Avenue, above the bus service terminal.

By Bus   Country-wide operators **Greyhound, Intercape,** and **Translux** (see chapter 2 for contact information) all arrive and depart at the station complex. The **Baz Bus** has an office at Tourist Junction and does drop-offs at hostels.

By Car   The N2 from Cape Town runs parallel to the coast as far as Zululand; the N3 to Johannesburg meets the N2 at Durban.

WHEN TO GO   The best time to visit is from February to mid-May, when it's not too humid. Temperatures range from 61°F to 73°F (16°C–25°C) in winter (May–Aug) and 73°F to 91°F (23°C–33°C) in summer (Sept–Apr).

GETTING AROUND   By Car   The city center is relatively small, but to explore farther afield, you're best off renting a car. A number of companies have desks at the airport—contact **Avis** (② **031/408-1282**) or **Budget** (② **031/408-1809** or 031/304-9023; the latter usually offers a slightly better rate). For a cheaper deal, call **Windermere Car Hire** (② **031/312-0339** or 082/454-1625) or **Maharani** (② **031/368-6563**).

By Bus   The city center, beachfront, and Berea are serviced by **Mynah** buses (② **031/309-5942**); trips cost from R1.50 (20¢). You can catch the **Umhlanga**

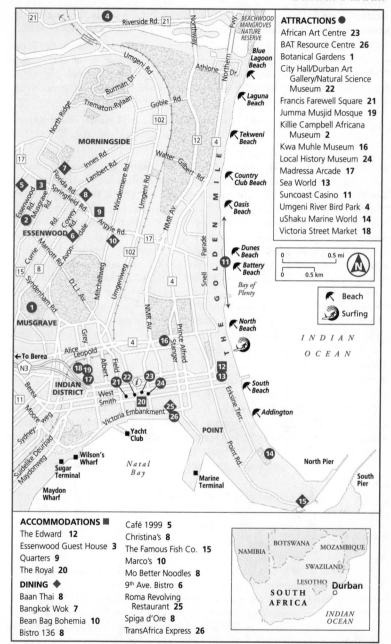

ATTRACTIONS ●

African Art Centre **23**
BAT Resource Centre **26**
Botanical Gardens **1**
City Hall/Durban Art
  Gallery/Natural Science
  Museum **22**
Francis Farewell Square **21**
Jumma Musjid Mosque **19**
Killie Campbell Africana
  Museum **2**
Kwa Muhle Museum **16**
Local History Museum **24**
Madressa Arcade **17**
Sea World **13**
Suncoast Casino **11**
Umgeni River Bird Park **4**
uShaku Marine World **14**
Victoria Street Market **18**

```
0          0.5 mi
0      0.5 km
```

🏄 Beach
🏄 Surfing

ACCOMMODATIONS ■

The Edward **12**
Essenwood Guest House **3**
Quarters **9**
The Royal **20**

DINING ◆

Baan Thai **8**
Bangkok Wok **7**
Bean Bag Bohemia **10**
Bistro 136 **8**

Café 1999 **5**
Christina's **8**
The Famous Fish Co. **15**
Marco's **10**
Mo Better Noodles **8**
9th Ave. Bistro **6**
Roma Revolving
  Restaurant **25**
Spiga d'Ore **8**
TransAfrica Express **26**

Express (📞 **082/268-0651**) to Umhlanga Rocks. For coaches to the South Coast, contact **Margate Mini Coach** (📞 **039/312-1406**) or **U Tour** (📞 **031/368-2848**).

By Taxi   The three-wheeled Asian-style *tuk tuks* queue all day on Marine Parade and will take you anywhere between the beach and central Durban, as will **Bunny Cabs** (📞 **031/332-2914**) and **Eagle Taxis** (📞 **031/337-8333**), both reputable cab companies. **Super Shuttle** (📞 **0860/333-444**) offers a personalized transfer service to any destination in KwaZulu-Natal.

GUIDED TOURS   On Foot   Historical Walkabout and **Oriental Walkabout** 🎯🎯 walking tours (both R50/$7.45) can be arranged through **Durban Africa** (📞 **031/304-4934**).

By Bus   The **Durban Ricksha Bus** (📞 **083/289-0509**) is an open-topped double-decker bus that offers a 2½-hour guided city tour every Tuesday, Thursday, and Sunday afternoon (R40/$5.95). The most authentic city tour is offered by **Tekweni Ecotours** 🎯🎯🎯 (📞 **031/312-8727**). The full-day tour takes in the multicultural sights of the city and the harbor before moving on to the township of Cato Manor, where a local guide takes you on a short walking tour that ends at a *shebeen* (informal bar) where you enjoy a meal with members of the community; the cost is R380 ($57), including transport, drinks, and dinner. Best of all, a percentage of the tour price is reinvested in the community. **Strelitzia Tours** (📞 **031/266-9480**) offers 3-hour Durban City tours (R230/$34), as well as a number of tours farther afield—the Midlands Meander (R730/$109) and Sani Pass (R995/$149) are both highly recommended. Strelitzia Tours can also arrange special-interest tours for golfers, divers, and deep-sea fishermen. **Stud Farm Tours** (📞 **031/314-1579**) is a day trip to the top stud farms (R250/$37), located in the scenic Midlands, and includes a lunch at a top country hotel.

By Boat   Board the luxury charter yacht *African Queen* (📞 **032/943-1118** or 082/961-4313) for a cruise, and set sail for the north coast. Trips last 3 hours and cost R150 ($22) per person. Less romantic is the engine-powered **Sarie Marais Pleasure Cruisers** (📞 **031/305-4022**), a ferryboat that does 30-minute harbor cruises and 90-minute "deep-sea" cruises (R50/$7.45) every 30 minutes. **Adventure Ocean Safaris** (📞 **082/960-7682**) is the only licensed boat-based whale-watcher in the Durban area. For more boating options, contact the **Durban Charter Boat Association** (📞 **031/301-1115**).

By Air   Nac Helicopters (📞 **031/564-0176**) offers a variety of trips, from a 30-minute flight around greater Durban and a 1-hour trip along the coast and the Valley of a Thousand Hills, to golf trips, Drakensberg tours, and game tours.

CITY LAYOUT   Sightseeing in the city can be divided into roughly four areas. The **city center** encompasses the buildings and memorials surrounding Francis Farewell Square, as well as the Indian District, the latter best explored with a guide on foot (see above). The **"Golden Mile,"** the beachfront that forms the eastern arm of the city, runs south from Blue Lagoon Beach and terminates in Durban Point, where uShaka Marine World leads the regeneration of this previously underutilized harbor area. Stretching eastward from here is the **Victoria Embankment** (or Esplanade); running at more or less 90 degrees to the Golden Mile along the harbor's edge, it creates the city's southern border—this is where you will find the BAT Centre (overlooking the Small Craft Harbour) and, a little farther along, Wilson's Wharf. On the western outskirts of the city lies **the Ridge,** as Durbanites refer to the wealthy colonial-era suburbs, like Berea, with elevated views of the city and harbor. This is where you will find most of the city's best guesthouses—a good place to base yourself, not least because this is also where you'll find the city's most centralized restaurant and nightlife precinct.

FAST FACTS: Durban

American Express Located in "The Vibe" East Coast Radio House, Umhlanga Rocks Drive (© **031/566-8650**; Mon–Fri 8am–5pm, Sat 8:30–11am).

Area Code Durban's area code is **031**.

Emergencies For an **ambulance,** call © **10177** and ask to be taken to the casualty unit at **Entabeni Private Hospital** (© 031/204-1300). Staff will also treat nonemergencies. **Police:** © 300-3333; **Flying Squad:** © 10111; **SAP Tourist Protection Unit:** © 031/368-4453; **Fire brigade:** © 031/309-4341; **NSRI** (sea rescue): © 031/361-8567; **Rape Crisis:** © 031/312-2323.

Pharmacy Late-night chemists include **Medicine Chest** (© **031/305-6151**), 155 Berea Rd., and **Day-Night Pharmacy** (© **031/368-3666**), 9A Nedbank Circle, corner of Point and West (the latter has free delivery).

Safety Malaria was pushed north to Zululand by development and pesticides, with no reported incidences in Durban in more than 50 years. If you plan to travel into northern Zululand, a course of antimalarial drugs is necessary (see chapter 2). Like any large city where a large percentage of the population is poor, Durban is troubled by street crime. The display of wealth is unwise anywhere in the city or beachfront, and visitors are advised to do their explorations of these areas during the day.

Weather For a weather report, call © **082/231-1603**.

EXPLORING THE CITY

CITY CENTER   If you're interested in taking a look at the city's Indian District, it's probably best (and certainly safest) to call and book an **Oriental Walkabout** ★★ through **Durban Africa** (© **031/304-4934**). Walking tours start at the Tourist Junction, where you can take a look at the African Art Centre (see "Shopping for African Craft & Design," below); both are housed in the Old Station Building at 160 Pine St. Alternatively, head for nearby Francis Farewell Square, to the **City Hall** (1910), a stone-for-stone replica of the City Hall in Belfast, Ireland. The City Hall's first floor houses the **Natural Science Museum** (© **031/311-2256**). The usual array of very dead-looking animals is useful as a crash course in wildlife identification if you're traveling north, and kids will also appreciate the gross-out qualities of the "Kwanunu" section, where the insect displays include some large, truly revolting roaches. One floor up, you'll find the excellent **Durban Art Gallery** ★★ (© **031/311-2264;** Mon–Sat 8:30am–4pm, Sun 11am–4pm; free admission). Back in the 1970s, this was the first national gallery to recognize African crafts as art, and today it has arguably the most representative and exciting collection of traditional and contemporary South "Africana" art in the country (see "Discovering Zulu History ," later in this chapter, for more).

East of the City Hall, facing Aliwal Road, is the **Old Court House,** home of Durban's local-history museum (© **031/311-2229;** Mon–Sat 8:30am–4pm, Sun 11am–4pm; free admission). The first public building erected in Durban (1866), this is a lovely example of the Natal Verandah style, and today houses a rather dry collection of exhibits, focusing on 19th-century history. Wander past the costumes worn by the disparate groups that made up Durban society for over 200 years (look for the bead-work items). A few of Gandhi's artifacts are also housed here (see "The Making of Mahatma: Gandhi's Turning Point," below). A great deal more stimulating is the **Kwa Muhle Museum,** an annex of the Local History Museum (© **031/311-2233;** same hours), a 10-minute walk north up Aliwal Road to where it intersects with Ordnance Road. Certainly, anyone interested in South Africa's history of race relations should view the exhibition titled the "Durban System," which provides a graphic explanation of how the "System," a municipal race policy that evolved in Durban in the early 1900s, granted itself sole monopoly on the brewing and distribution of beer (provided traditionally by women), which it sold through "African-only" beer halls. Proceeds were, in turn, used to finance the administration and control of black labor in this very building—these were the offices of the Bantu Administration Board, where the city's black inhabitants were "processed."

THE GOLDEN MILE BEACHFRONT   The Portuguese explorers who first laid eyes on Durban's beachfront must have been a poetic lot, and their description— "sands of gold"—has stuck long after the high rises and concrete promenades dwarfed the beaches. Unphased by the urban backdrop, Durbanites from all walks of life still head here at the drop of a hat. Ask any local which city beach is their favorite, and you'll get a different answer from each one. Some (usually the girls) love **Blue Lagoon** (located in the far north of the Golden Mile) for romantic early evenings, one describing it as "a soulful place, where you can take in the salty sea air and meditate on the incoming tide of the Umgeni River mouth and the distant misty afternoon view of Durban's beachfront skyline." It's apparently a great bird-watching spot, too—no pun intended; look for the wading giant goliath herons and, if you're lucky, the majestic African fish-eagle. If this kind of talk turns you on, follow the Umgeni west to nearby **Umgeni River Bird Park** (© **031/579-4600**)—rated as one of the best of its kind, with more than 300 species from around the world housed in large aviaries, and planted with palms, cycads, and other tropical plants. Surfers (and a host of others) head for **Battery and North Beach,** the latter now overlooked by the new **Suncoast Casino & Entertainment World**—which, aside from the casino, contains cinemas and restaurants, including the popular **Havana Grill and Winebar,** which has a deck area a stone's throw away from the sea.

THE POINT & VICTORIA EMBANKMENT   The star attraction here (particularly for families) is the new **uShaka Marine World** 𝕽𝕽, located at The Point. Set over 16 hectares (40 acres), this waterfront theme park incorporates a spanking-new underground aquarium—one of the world's biggest (tailing Atlantis, Beijing, San Diego, and Orlando) and featuring the largest collection of sharks in the Southern Hemisphere. There are also dolphin and seal stadiums, a snorkel lagoon, and a "Wet 'n Wild" world—slides and rides to keep the kids happy for the entire day. And uShaka is justifiably proud of the fact that every drop of water pumped into its system returns cleaner than when it came in. If you've done Disney, keep moving along the Esplanade, where you'll definitely want to turn off into the Small Craft Harbour to shop for crafts at the **BAT Centre** ⋆⋆ or have a meal at the **TransAfrica Express**—not only to sample the wonderful African-influenced menu, but to chill with the sun sparkling on the harbor; this is also the best place to hear live Afro-jazz over the weekends (usually Fri, but call ahead to confirm). A little farther along is **Wilson's Wharf,** Durban's mini-waterfront complex, replete with numerous bars and restaurants overlooking the harbor, another good place to sink into a beer when the sun starts to go down.

BEREA   This gracious old suburb is home to the **Campbell Collections** ⋆⋆⋆, arguably Durban's top attraction. Housed in Muckleneuk, the neo–Cape Dutch home that sugar baron Sir Marshall Campbell built for his family in 1914, it gives one a great sense of what it must have been like to live in colonial splendor high up on the Ridge, with sweeping views from the upstairs rooms of the harbor below. Tours take in the gracious gardens and the Cape Dutch furniture and artwork collected by Campbell's son (whose private hunting farm became what is today the private game reserve MalaMala), as well as the extensive Africana library and ethnological artifacts collected by his daughter, "Killie" Campbell. Killie was a voracious collector of traditional utensils, ornaments, art, musical instruments, sticks, and various items of beaded clothing (don't miss the necklace of British redcoat buttons worn by Zulu warriors as a sign of bravery). Today her collection, known as the **Mashu Museum of Ethnology,** corner of Marriott and Essenwood roads (© **031/207-3432;** mchunum@ ukzn.co.za), is considered one of the country's finest groupings of African artifacts. Tours of the Campbell Collections and the Mashu Museum of Ethnology are by appointment only.

SHOPPING FOR AFRICAN CRAFT & DESIGN

The **African Art Centre** ⋆⋆⋆ (© **031/304-7915;** Mon–Fri 8:30am–5pm, Sat 9am–1pm), conveniently located on the first floor of the Tourist Junction, is the best place to start browsing for woodcarvings, ceramics, beadwork, baskets, tapestries, rugs, fine art, and fabrics, created by predominantly Zulu craftsmen and artists. The Centre sources the best work from a wide variety of artists, and staff members are usually extremely knowledgeable and helpful about the products and their creators. It's worth buying at least one item here—proceeds are reinvested in the development of local talent. If this whets your appetite, a visit to the **KwaZulu-Natal Society of the Arts (NSA) Gallery** ⋆⋆⋆, at 166 Bulwer Rd., Glenwood (© **031/202-3686;** Tues–Fri 9am–5pm, Sat 9am–4pm, Sun 10am–3pm), is a must. The excellent exhibitions feature artists from different cultural and ethnic backgrounds and may include paintings, mosaics, beadwork, lithograph, and embroidery. The adjacent shop has a wide variety of visual arts, including works by master craftspeople, and the alfresco Arts Café serves light meals and some of the best coffee in town.

It can't really compete in terms of variety, but the **BAT shop** ⋆ © **031/332-9951;** Mon–Fri 9am–4:30pm, Sat–Sun 10am–3:30pm) in the **BAT Resource Centre,** Small Craft Harbour, 45 Maritime Place (© **031/332-0451;** www.batcentre.co.za), offers relatively good prices and a harborside setting. Established in 1995, this innovative community arts center is a pleasant place to shop, with several art studios where you can watch artists at work, a few shops (**Bayside Gallery** [© **031/368-5547;** Tues–Sun 10am–4pm] has a good selection of South African talent), and a great restaurant. Plan your visit for a Friday afternoon, hang around until the harbor lights come on, and then soak up some good local jazz. (Note that another BAT Centre shop is now open in the Drakensberg.)

If you're looking for quirky, funky clothing and accessories, visit the **Durban Designer's Emporium,** at 77A Musgrave Rd. (© **031/201-2783**), where you'll find a great selection of top local labels—Durban is, after all, considered to be the spawning ground for South Africa's most creative clothing designers (a claim that's hotly contested by Capetonians, of course). Another hot Berea spot is **St Verde** (© **031/ 2019176**); Neville Trickett transformed what used to be a dilapidated electrical substation into a trendy cafe/shop—a great place to browse if you're looking for local talent but are tired of obviously African-looking merchandise. On Saturday you can move on to the **Essenwood Flea Market,** held in the adjacent Berea Park (look for Nicola Jaffer's Free Spirited Designs). Lastly, if you've got your second wind and are still on the lookout for souvenirs, **Springbok Art and Jewelers** (© **031/304-8451**), located in the Workshop, a shopping center on Aliwal Street, claims to offer the largest selection of African masks in the country.

HEADING NORTH UP THE HOLIDAY COAST

Durban's coastline is a 5-hour drive from dry, dusty Jo'burg, and even less from the Free State. With every middle-class family demanding its place in the sun, this subtropical belt south of the Tugela River has been swallowed up by condominiums, timeshares, brick-face homes, and tatty caravan parks, ruining, at least for nature lovers, almost the entire "Holiday Coast." Thankfully, there are a few areas where the lush coastal vegetation hides all signs of human habitation—from the beach, at least. The fecund vegetation is, in fact, the saving grace of this coastline; wild banana trees and masses of flowering shrubs and trees, often alive with monkeys, do much to soften concrete lines. Unless you're traveling to or from the Eastern Cape, wish to dive the Aliwal Shoal, or are here on a golfing vacation, the 160km (99-mile) South Coast stretch, incorporating the "Hibiscus Coast" and the "Strelitzia Coast," is best avoided in favor of the slightly less developed North Coast.

The most popular seaside suburb on the North Coast is **Umhlanga Rocks** (pronounced "*um*-shlung-ga"), a 20- to 30-minute drive north of the city center. Originally part of Marshall Campbell's sugar estate, it is now simply an extension of Durban, with well-developed facilities, safe bathing areas, and plenty of accommodations options. The region's **Sugar Coast Tourism Association** (© **031/561-4257;**

Fun Fact **The Making of Mahatma: Gandhi's Turning Point**

On June 7, 1893, a young lawyer named Mohandas Gandhi, recently arrived in Durban, found himself stranded at the nearby Pietermaritzburg Station after being ejected from a whites-only first-class carriage. He spent the night mulling the incident over in the waiting room, and, according to the great man himself, "[his] active non-violence started from that day." Mohandas (later to become Mahatma) was to spend the next 21 years peacefully fighting the South African laws that discriminated against Indians before leaving to liberate India from English rule. If for some reason you find yourself in Pietermaritzburg, you can visit the platform where Gandhi was unceremoniously tossed (at the seedy end of Church St.), the **Gandhi statue** (near the City Hall end of Church St.), or the **Natal Museum,** 237 Loop St. (www.nmsa.org.za), which has a few exhibits relating to the man.

Mon–Fri 8am–4:30pm, Sat 8am–1pm) is also situated here, on Chartwell Drive. If you're tired of sunbathing and swimming, the one noteworthy place worth visiting in Umhlanga is the office of the **Natal Sharks Board** (© 031/566-0400; www.shark. co.za). One of the most prestigious centers for shark research in the world, the board offers informative audiovisual presentations about these awesome predators—up to 14 species swim off this coast. Get there for the first showing at 9am, or at 2pm, and you can watch one of the sharks—who are regularly caught in the shark nets—being dissected. Currently the most viable protection for swimmers, these controversial nets are responsible for the deaths of hundreds of sharks as well as numerous rays, dolphins, and endangered turtles. You can also catch a ride on a **Sharks Board** boat to observe firsthand how the meshing crews go about servicing the shark nets; trips are 2 hours and need to be prebooked (© 082/403-9206).

Sibaya is a new casino just beyond Umhlanga (© 031/508 5002); it's Zulu-ethnic on a palatial scale. A re-created Zulu village offers insight into how Zulu communities lived many decades ago—and still do in remote corners of the country—while the thatched-roofed restaurant, **Sondela Tavern,** offers Zulu food with a contemporary twist. You see it all as either a kind of "living museum" or simply rather tacky.

If you're looking for uncrowded beaches, you'll have to head farther north, beyond Ballito to **Zimbali Lodge** (see below), the Holiday Coast's premier resort. Even farther north, **Blythedale** (roughly 25km/16 miles north of Ballito and 70km/43 miles north of Durban) has a total ban on high-rise construction—making this the best-preserved beach on the Holiday Coast. Some 13km (8 miles) farther, the tiny hamlet of **Zinkwasi** is the least developed beach resort on the North Coast and marks the end of the Holiday Coast. If you plan to spend time in this area, contact the **Dolphin Coast Tourist Information** (© 032/946-1997; fax 032/946-2434) in Ballito.

WHERE TO STAY

Unlike the lodgings in Cape Town and along the Garden Route, most hotels here have a year-round rate, though there's no harm in asking for a discount during the winter months. The center of town is only 17km (11 miles) from the current airport, so it's not necessary to book into an airport hotel to catch a late-night or early flight—besides, all the establishments listed will arrange airport transfers. Hotels line the beachfront, but in Durban itself you're better off in a great guesthouse—the best tend to be concentrated on the Ridge, with views overlooking the city and harbor. Besides Essenwood (see below), you might want to take a look at **164 Guesthouse & Bar,** another gorgeous homestead dating back to the 1920s, located in nearby Musgrave (© 031/201-4493; www.164.co.za; from R490/$73 double). If you really do prefer hotels, The Edward is still the most charming hotel on the beachfront (at least it has character, even if the Protea chain has drained it of quality); alternatively, opt for the **Royal** (© 031/333-6000; www.theroyal.co.za). Given that it's a member of The Leading Hotels of the World, the Royal's rates (R740/$110 double, including breakfast, in May 2005) offer remarkable value, and it's within walking distance of many of Durban's top attractions (as well as the Tourist Junction and African Art Centre). It also offers terrific views of the busy port and city, and features very high levels of service, with every staff member primed to make you feel special (though as a training hotel, things can, and do, go awry at times). People keen on a beach-based stay usually book into a hotel in Umhlanga Rocks, but better by far is **Zimbali Lodge,** which is about 35 to 40 minutes north of the city center, and much classier than anything you'll find in Umhlanga. Or, for the ultimate in safari luxury, at a fraction of the usual price, head for **Tala Private Game Reserve,** a wildlife conservancy that lies a mere 45 minutes west of Durban. See below for reviews of both.

DURBAN

The Edward 🏵🏵 *Kids*   The grand dame of Durban's beachfront, The Edward has played host to princes and presidents, field marshals and millionaires, and movie stars and holy men since the 1920s, though its current incarnation as part of the Protea chain has drained it of some of its charm. Its position on the Golden Mile beachfront and proximity to the city sights (it's a 10-min. stroll to the center) is still ideal, however. This is also a good family hotel, particularly considering that children sharing the spacious sea-facing double, with a bay window overlooking the beachfront, and two double beds, stay free. If you like your space, the deluxe suite has a separate lounge with a dining room table, a writing desk in the bay window, and a separate balcony— ask for room no. 211, and you'll have the pleasure of knowing how the Dalai Lama enjoyed his stay in Durban. Meals are served in the **Brasserie,** which isn't going to win any culinary awards; best to dine at one of the recommendations below.

149 Marine Parade, Durban 4000. ℂ 031/337-3681. Fax 031/332-1692. www.proteahotels.com. 101 units. R850 ($127) non-sea-facing double; R1,050 ($157) sea-facing double; R1,550 ($231) suite. AE, DC, MC, V. **Amenities:** Restaurant; bar; pool; business services; room service; babysitting; laundry. *In room:* A/C, TV, minibar stocked on request, hair dryer, tea- and coffee-making facilities.

Essenwood Guest House 🏵🏵 *Value*   If you don't enjoy the anonymity of a hotel and would like to experience firsthand what it's like to live in the most sought-after residential area in Durban, then Essenwood Guest House is ideal. A rose-tinted colonial homestead built in 1924 in a large tropical garden with a pool, this was originally the family home of one of Durban's sugar barons. Paddy and John, themselves former sugar-cane farmers, have restored the house, furnished it with tasteful antiques and artworks, and—thankfully—opened it to guests. The six spacious suites have views of the city and distant ocean; request one of the four with private, broad verandas. The city center and Morningside's restaurants are a mere 5-minute drive away. Dinners can be served by prior arrangement.

630 Essenwood Rd., Berea 4001. ℂ/fax 031/207-4547. www.essenwoodhouse.co.za. 6 units. R640 ($96) double. Rate includes breakfast. AE, DC, MC, V. Children 12 and over only. **Amenities:** Pool; laundry. *In room:* A/C, TV, minibar, hair dryer on request, tea- and coffee-making facilities.

Quarters 🏵🏵   Comprising four Victorian houses set on fashionable Florida Road, Quarters is a classy, boutique-style guest lodge—the best-dressed joint in town. Walls feature striking black-and-white photographs of South African life by Angela Shaw. All rooms are relatively spacious and have queen-size sleigh beds, and are double-glazed to eliminate neighborhood noise, though this is scant protection from the sound of the person above flushing his/her toilet—ask for a room on one of the top floors. Bathrooms are big and well designed; specify shower or bathtub. The **Brasserie** has a small but good menu; alternatively, some 30 restaurants lie within a 5km (3-mile) radius, many within walking distance.

101 Florida Rd., Durban 4001. ℂ 031/303-5246. Fax 031/303-5269. 24 units. R1,100–R1,160 ($164–$173) double. Rates include breakfast. AE, DC, MC, V. Children by prior arrangement only. **Amenities:** Restaurant; bar; business services; room service; laundry. *In room:* A/C, TV, hair dryer, tea- and coffee-making facilities.

NORTH OF DURBAN

Zimbali Lodge 🏵🏵🏵   Opened in 1998 to much acclaim, Zimbali (a 35-min. drive north of Durban) has brought some much-needed class to the Holiday Coast.

Surrounded by secluded indigenous coastal forest, with a private access beach, the lodge is inspired by the architecture of tropical climates, with local influences including the nearby sugar baron estates and Indian temples. The opulent interior (decorated by the same team responsible for the Palace of the Lost City) is arguably the country's finest example of Afro-colonial chic style. From staircases to trusses, beds to deck chairs, each item is beautifully crafted and custom made. Set on a bluff, the buildings (including the rooms, which are situated in the gardens surrounding the lodge) overlook a natural lake, surrounded by forested hillsides and, beyond, the ocean. A large number of activities are on offer, including the Tom Weiskopf–designed 18-hole championship golf course, with a new golf course planned for completion in 2007. A selection of villas offering two- to six-bed luxury self-catering accommodations are scattered around the estate.

P.O. Box 404, Umhlali 4390 (off M4 just before Ballito). ✆ 032/538-1007. Fax 032/538-1019. www.suninternational. com. 76 units. R3,010 ($449) double; R5,900 ($881) suite; R1,500–R6,000 ($224–$896) villas. Ask about winter specials; children's rates by arrangement. AE, DC, MC, V. **Amenities:** Restaurant; bar; pool; golf; tennis; spa; bicycles; room service; laundry; private beach; horseback riding. *In room:* A/C, TV, minibar, hair dryer, tea- and coffee-making facilities.

WEST OF DURBAN

Tala Private Game Reserve ★★★ *Value*   Ideally located for an overnight getaway, this 3,000-hectare (7,410-acre) wildlife conservancy is a mere 45 minutes' drive from the bright lights of Durban. In a mixed landscape of acacia thornveld, open grassland, and lush wetland, only two of the Big 5 roam (buffalo and rhino), but the reserve has a variety of buck (including the rare sable antelope), hippo, giraffe, and well over 300 bird species. But the real reason to come here is the flagship Leadwood Lodge, which offers all the luxury of a truly top-end game lodge with one digit missing from the price tag. Built by a team of artisans with locally sourced shale, and decorated by the award-winning Boyd Ferguson (who put Singita on the map), the design combines stone, earth, water, glass, and wood. The decor, based on an ethic of "nothing straight, nothing painted," is an eclectic merging of antique and organic Africa. You can choose between the two rooms in the main lodge (very good value) or the six privately situated luxury cottages—all with lounge area and a large open-plan bathroom with an outdoor shower romantically tucked away in the bush, and similarly well appointed in solid hardwood and subtle colors. The 90-minute game drives are with an experienced guide and tracker, and guided horseback rides and walks along the many trails are an exciting way to explore the reserve and its flora and fauna.

P.O. Box 13665, Cascades, 3202. ✆ 031/781-8000. www.tala.co.za. 8 units. R3,000 ($448) double; R4,800 ($716) cottage. Rates include all meals and game activities. Ask about winter specials. AE, DC, MC, V. **Amenities:** Restaurant; bar; heated pool; library; game drives and walks; horseback riding. *In room:* Minibar, hair dryer.

WHERE TO DINE

Combine temperate weather with panoramic sea views, Victorian with Art Deco architecture, and Indian, African, and colonial flavoring, and you start to realize what it is that makes Durban's restaurant scene so interesting and varied. Luckily for the first-time visitor, much of it is concentrated on Windermere and Florida roads, both in Morningside, a residential suburb on the western outskirts of town, as well as in Musgrave on the Berea. The following suggestions were compiled by local foodie Ingrid Shevlin, who contributes to the annual *Eat Out* magazine.

WINDERMERE ROAD   Two options are worth trying here. Starting at the bottom end of Windermere, you'll find **Bean Bag Bohemia** ★★, no. 18 (✆ 031/309-6019).

Located in a stylish old Durban home and hugely popular with the social arty set, this is the place to come and greet and meet the locals. On the ground floor is a buzzy bar and cafe-style eatery that never seems to sleep, while a more fine dining–oriented restaurant on the first floor serves innovative contemporary fusion food. If you're into a more laid-back vibe, head to the bottom end of Windermere and Florida roads to **Marco's,** no. 45 (© **031/303-3078**), where Luciana Conte cooks pasta just like Mama did and offers a family-style welcome.

FLORIDA ROAD Book a table on the veranda overlooking Florida Road at **Baan Thai,** no. 138 (© **031/303-4270**) a dependable Thai restaurant; or check out what's up at neighbor **Christina's** 😿😿, no. 134 (© **031/303 2111**), an internationally respected training school and restaurant run by Christina's daughter Michelle, who has revamped the restaurant to create a look that is very chic, very contemporary. Her food is consistently good and reasonably priced. Just a few paces away is **Bistro 136,** no. 136 (© **031/303-3440**), where Swiss-trained chef/patron Willi serves up classic Continental fare. Farther up Florida road you'll find **Spiga D'Ore** 😿😿 (© **031 303 9511**), a vibrant, family-owned Italian eatery that spills over onto the pavement; the food here is good and cheap. It's open till late and is so popular you may have to wait for a table. If you're in the mood for light Asian, head straight for **Mo Better Noodles** 😿😿, Shop 5, Florida Centre, 275 Florida Rd. (© **031/312-4193**), a noodle bar serving consistently good Thai-style food. The menu is small, but a long list of daily specials keeps regulars loyal. Farther along the Ridge, in the mainly residential enclave of the Berea, you'll find real Thai food, prepared by genuine Thai chefs, at **Bangkok Wok** 😿, no. 440 (© **031/201-8557**). Its modest menu is augmented by a long list of daily specials.

FOR FOODIES Perhaps it's the year-round balmy weather, perhaps it's the casual laid-back atmosphere that pervades the city, but Durban has fewer fine-dining outlets than other cites. For the traveling foodie looking for something special, reserve a date at the following two restaurants. (Also check out the prime picks from the wealth of Indian fare available in a city in "King of Curry," below.) Ranked among the best in the city, **9th Avenue Bistro** 😿😿😿, in the Avonmore Centre, not far from the buzz of Florida Road (© **031/312-9134**), is where award-winning chef/owner Carly Goncalves serves superb modern bistro fare. The menu is small and changes according to what's available seasonally, but expect the likes of butternut ravioli with Madeira cream sauce; pear and Gorgonzola salad with candied pecans; and fresh Scottish salmon served with roasted garlic mash, grilled courgette, a tomato-thyme jam, and saffron and lemon. Another popular choice is **Cafe 1999** 😿😿😿, high up on the Berea in the Silvervause Centre (© **031/202-3406**), where chef Marcelle Labuschagne and her partner Sean Roberts, who handles the front of house, wow with food inspired by the cuisines of the Middle East and Pacific Rim: Spanish meatballs in white wine, lime prawn tails with wasabi mayo, or butternut ravioli with Gorgonzola and walnuts. Best of all, most menu items are offered in "tidbit" (R14–R45/$2.10–$6.70) or "bigbit" (R19–R74/$2.85–$11) portions, so you can taste to your stomach's capacity. The only downside is the noise levels—if you're looking for a quiet tête-à-tête, this is not the spot for you.

TABLE WITH SEA VIEW, PLEASE If you've ever thought the world revolved around you, **Roma Revolving Restaurant** 😿😿, John Ross House, Victoria Embankment (© **031/337-6707**), is the place to prove it. Enter John Ross House from a slightly seedy side alley off the Victoria Embankment, whoosh up 32 floors in the

Durban after Dark: Getting Down with a Durbanite

I always find time for a wave at either **Battery Beach** or **North Beach.** There's ample parking and it's the best way to end the day, watching the light fade on one of the many ships moored in the bay of one of Africa's biggest man-made harbors. After this I might take a cruise past the Esplanade to sink a cold beer at the **Bat Centre** (particularly on Fri, where sundowners mix with live jazz and *maskanda*—Zulu folk music) or to a bar at **Wilson's Wharf,** or head straight back up to the Berea and grab a table at the unassuming **Mo's Noodles** on Florida Road, which serves delicious Southeast Asian dishes, and where you can sit outside still in your beach attire. Just up the road and around the bend is Durban's favorite ice cream shop, **Mozarts,** which has a dizzying selection of gelato and sorbets produced by Chaco Kember, who has been making ice cream for 26 years.

Amble back down Florida Road to the **Zeta Bar,** 285 Florida Rd. (© 031/312-9436), a relaxed old colonial home where you can get a comfortable table on the veranda and take cover from a tropical evening downpour. It has a mixed crowd that heaves and hums. If you find yourself tapping your feet, the **Reform Club,** 198A Florida Rd. (© 031/303-1802), a chic, intimate house club that gets bums shaking and eyebrows winking, is just a 5-minute walk farther down Florida Road. Indian owned, it has a largely black/Indian crowd and a lovely easy atmosphere with an outside balcony overlooking Florida Road. If you're still up for it, head down Florida Road through the lights to **Bean Bag Bohemia,** 18 Windermere Rd. (© 031/309-6019), where you will be happily met by the loyalist punters who get everything they desire right there. If it's a Saturday night, it's downhill all the way to **330,** 330 Point Rd. (© 031/337-7172), a Durban institution (imported to London), for hard-core house music and another late night. Top it off with an early-morning body surf at Battery Beach, while the sun rises over the warm Indian Ocean and the sangomas baptize their flock.

—*David Allardice, born-and-bred Durbanite*

small lift, and you'll step directly into a plush 1970s haven. The Roma revolves completely every 60 minutes, providing great views of the city, harbor, beachfront, and the Berea from every table. Best of all, the classic Italian fare is good, and the gnocchi is legendary. For a more one-dimensional but no less spectacular take on Durban, head south down Point Road to the **Famous Fish Co.,** Kings Battery North Pier (© 031/368-1060). Seated right at the harbor entrance, diners on the deck are often mere meters away from the towering tankers that enter and depart Africa's busiest harbor. If you're not in the mood for seafood or want to browse for great crafts, head for the BAT Centre, where **TransAfrica Express** 🖈🖈 (© 031/332-0804) offers a stunning view of the Small Craft Harbour and the chance to dine under the stars. Inspired by the tastes of Africa, the food is innovative, even edgy, but still accessible to Western palates. For a range of dining-with-a-view options, head farther along the Embankment to **Wilson's Wharf,** at the southern end of Durban's bay, where you can choose among seven restaurants (including a good sushi bar), all with decks overlooking the harbor. **Suncoast Casino,** overlooking Durban's North Beach, is a casino and family-entertainment center rolled into one; the best option here is **Havana Grill and Wine Bar** ✿ (© **031/337-1305**), which offers top-quality steaks as well as interesting seafood and vegetarian options. Both the terrace and the smoking area are a mere stone's throw away from the warm waters of the Indian Ocean. In Umhlanga, head for the Beverly Hills Hotel, to **The Sugar Club** ✿✿, a stylish, luxurious alternative offering fine-dining contemporary cuisine by award-winning executive chef Gerard van Staden, as well as views over the sea.

KING OF CURRY　If Durban curry has one common characteristic, it is that it is hot, damn hot, so don't attempt this particular brand if you have a delicate stomach. Most locals say that **Saagries** ✿✿✿, Marine Parade Holiday Inn (© **031/332-7922**), is the best place to try the local curry—though it does offer regional Indian food, it's best known for its traditional Durban curries (only for asbestos-coasted tongues, mind you) and signature dishes such as crab curry. The lush and plush decor, old-style service, and superb food attract a clientele that ranges from Zulu royalty to celebrities. For an experience that feeds most of the senses, try **Jaipur Palace** ✿, 3 Riverside Complex, NorthWay, Durban North (© **031/563-0287**), where the decor is grand (large carved entrance doors, marble-inlaid floors, chandeliers), the service superb, and the North and South Indian cuisines good. The reasonably priced buffet (lunch R55/$8.20; dinner R90/$13) allows you to sample the flavors of a number of Indian regions in one go. Or head down to Greyville, to 20 Windermere Rd., where **Vintage** (© **031/309-1328**), a popular Indian restaurant located in a renovated old Berea home, serves up a selection of North and South Indian food; don't pass up the butter chicken—it's one of the best in town.

3 Zululand

Cross the Tugela River (88km/55 miles north of Durban), traditionally the southern frontier of Zululand, and it soon feels as if you've entered a new country. Passing a largely poor, rural population through KwaZulu-Natal's Big 5 reserves and coastal wetlands, you are now traveling the ancestral lands of the Zulu, and the designated Zulu "homeland" prior to 1994.

Most visitors to Zululand spend at least 2 days in or near Hluhluwe-Umfolozi, the province's largest game reserve. Run by KwaZulu-Natal Wildlife, it is home to the Big 5 and has the most sought-after wilderness trails in the country. In addition, its proximity to Durban (less than a 3-hr. drive) makes it one of South Africa's most accessible Big 5 game reserves, and its varied vegetation and top-value accommodations make for an experience to rival the Kruger National Park.

If, however, your idea of the "wild life" is pausing in your pursuit of lion with a drink poured by your personal ranger, there are now a number of private reserves to cater to your every need. Lying north of Hluhluwe and close to (in the case of Phinda, part of) the Greater St Lucia Wetland, these luxurious private game reserves are close enough to the coast to add diving with dolphins, sharks, and a magical array of tropical fish to your Big 5 experience—the combination of big game, lagoon, and beach is, in fact, one of the major benefits of choosing a safari in KwaZulu-Natal.

The first area in South Africa to be declared a World Heritage Site, the Greater St Lucia Wetland Park is a top destination for South Africa's divers, fishermen, and birders, as well as the rare loggerhead and leatherback turtles that have been returning to these

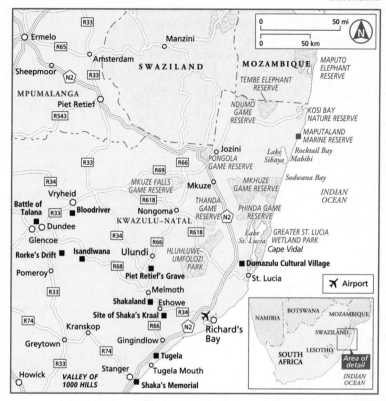

beaches to breed every summer for thousands of years. Encompassing the foothills of the Lebombo Mountains, wetlands, forests, lakes, and the coastal coral reefs, the park is quite literally a paradise, but unless you opt for luxury lodgings or visit during school term, you will have to share it with the hordes who similarly appreciate its natural bounty. Which is why you're best off traveling farther north to Mabibi and Rocktail Bay, the real highlight of the KwaZulu-Natal coast, where a handful of guests find themselves alone on a stretch of pristine beach that stretches for hundreds of miles, untainted by human habitation.

For those with more time, a sojourn in the far northeastern corner, where a chain of lakes empty into the beautiful Kosi Mouth, is also recommended. You will, however, need to rent a four-wheel-drive (or set off on foot) to explore this as-yet-untouched coastline, one of the three richest floristic areas in Africa.

ESSENTIALS

VISITOR INFORMATION The best regional office to visit en route from Durban is **Eshowe Publicity** (© **035/474-1141;** Mon–Thurs 7:30am–4pm, Fri till 3pm) on Hutchinson Street. For information on the Hluhluwe region, call the **Hluhluwe Information Office** (© **035/562-0353**). For information on the Greater St Lucia Wetland Park, call the **St Lucia Publicity Association** (© **035/550-4059**).

For specific information on the provincial game reserves, contact **KwaZulu-Natal Wildlife** (℃ **033/845-1000;** www.kznwildlife.com).

GETTING THERE **By Air** The quickest way to get to Zululand is to fly to Richard's Bay Airport with **SA Express** (℃ **035/786-0301**) from Johannesburg.

By Car The N2 leading north out of Durban traverses the Zululand hinterland; east lie the Greater St Lucia Wetland Park, Phinda private game reserve, and the birding reserves (Ndumo and Mkuzi); west lie Hluhluwe and most of the Zulu museums and cultural villages. From Gauteng, take the R29 through Piet Retief to Pongola; this becomes the N2 south.

By Bus Contact **Greyhound** or **Translux** (see chapter 2 for regional numbers) to travel to Richard's Bay from Durban or Johannesburg, respectively.

SAFETY Northern Zululand (Ndumo, Kosi Bay, Rocktail Bay) is a high-risk malarial area, and there is a medium-to-low risk in the Greater St Lucia Wetland Park, depending on the time of the year. For the most up-to-date advice, contact your doctor (also see chapter 2).

GETTING AROUND **By Car** There is virtually no public transport in Zululand, so once here you'll have to contact a tour operator, rent a car, or arrange a transfer with **Thompsons Hluhluwe Shuttle** (℃ **035/562-3002**). (Private reserves like Rocktail Bay supply their own transfers from Richard's Bay.) To explore Kosi Bay on your own, you'll need to rent a four-wheel-drive. Car rental can be arranged through **Avis** (℃ **035/789-6555,** or 035/789-3097 for 4WD) or **Imperial** (℃ **035/786-0309**). Both have desks at the airport.

GUIDED TOURS Ex-mayor of Eshowe and proprietor of local Eshowe hangout the George Hotel, **Graham Chennells** ★★★ offers the most authentic and exhilarating opportunities to see contemporary Zulu life in Africa (*National Geographic* has commissioned no less than three film shoots of his tours.) Guests are provided with a Zulu guide (Walter Cele or Victor Mdluli), who will then introduce them to friends in the broader community. On most weekends, Graham can arrange attendance at either a Zulu wedding, coming-of-age celebration, sangomas' healing rituals, or traditional church services, and guests are treated as part of the extended family. For more information, go to www.eshowe.com, or call the George Hotel, 36 Main St., Eshowe (℃ **035/474-4919** or 082/492-6918). For guided tours of the Zululand reserves, contact **Umhluhluwe Safaris** (℃ **035/562-0414**); choose between night, half-day, and full-day game drives in Hluhluwe-Umfolozi, Mkuzi, and the St Lucia Wetlands. **Brett Adventure Tours** (℃ **032/456-3513** or 083/744-8288) specializes in a variety of Zululand experiences, from golfing to visiting Maputaland and Zulu villages. (For tour operators departing direct from Durban, see "Durban: Essentials," earlier in this chapter.)

SPECIAL EVENTS On February 23, Sangoma Khekheke's **Annual Snake Dance,** attended by 1,000 people, is held. September also sees **King Shaka Day Celebrations** and the **Zulu King's Reed Dance**—here some 15,000 maidens congregate to dance for King Goodwill Zweliteni. Most of October is taken up with the **Prophet Shembe's celebrations,** with Sundays seeing some 30,000 people participating in prayer dancing. During the first week in December, the King's first **"Fruit Ceremony"** must be held before the reaping of crops can begin. To arrange attendance at any of these, contact Graham Chennells (see "Guided Tours," above).

DISCOVERING ZULU HISTORY

The proud amaZulu have fascinated Westerners ever since the first party of British settlers gained permission to trade from the great Zulu king Shaka, known as "Africa's Napoleon" for his military genius. As king, he was to unite the amaZulu into the mightiest army in the Southern Hemisphere and develop new and lethal fighting implements and tactics, including the highly successful "horns of the bull" maneuver to outflank the enemy. In 1828, Shaka was murdered by his half-brothers Mhlangana and Dingaan, and Dingaan was crowned king.

Distrustful of the large number of "white wizards" settling in the region, Dingaan ordered the massacre of the Trekker party led by Piet Retief, whom he had invited—unarmed—to a celebratory banquet at his royal *kraal* umGungundlovu. (A kraal is a series of thatched beehive-shaped huts encircling a central, smaller kraal, or cattle enclosure.) Dingaan paid heavily for this treachery at the **Battle of Blood River** (see "A Brief History of the Battlefields," later in this chapter), where the Zulu nation suffered such heavy casualties that it was to split the state for a generation. In 1840, Dingaan was killed by his brother Mpande, who succeeded him as king.

The amaZulu were reunited again under Mpande's eldest, Cetshwayo, who, having, in turn, murdered a number of his siblings, became king in 1873 and built a new royal kraal at Ulundi. Though by all accounts a reasonable man, Cetshwayo could not negotiate with the uncompromising English, who now wanted total control of southern Africa, with no pesky savages to destroy their imperialist advance on the gold fields. In 1878 the British ordered Cetshwayo to disband his army within 30 days, give up Zululand's independence, and place himself under the supervision of an English commissioner. This totally unreasonable ultimatum, designed to ignite a war, resulted in the **Battle of Islandwana** and England's most crushing defeat (see "A Brief History of the Battlefields," later in this chapter). Nine months later, on July 4, 1879, 5,000 British redcoats under a vengeful Lord Chelmsford advanced on Ulundi and razed it to the ground. A captured King Cetshwayo was exiled to Cape Town and later England; he was reinstated as a puppet in 1883. This was to be the last Anglo-Zulu battle; the might of the Zulu empire had finally been broken.

The area known today as Emakhosini, "Valley of the Kings," has applied for status as a World Heritage Site; in the meantime, you can visit Dingaan's homestead at **uMgungundlovu** (or "secret place of the great elephant"), part of which has been reconstructed and features 200-year-old artifacts; there is also a memorial to Piet Retief and his 100-strong delegation (© **035/450-2254;** daily 9am–4pm). You can also visit a reconstruction of the royal kraal at **Ondini,** near Ulundi. To get here, take the R68 off the N2 to Eshowe, stopping to visit the **Zulu Historical Museum** and the **Vukani Collection** first (see reviews below), or to meet Graham Chennells at the George Hotel for his highly recommended tours of the region (see "Guided Tours," above). To reach uMgungundlovu, take the R34 to Vryheid and look for the turnoff on your left.

Fort Nongqayi Museum Village ★★★ (Finds

While Westerners head for the many cultural villages dotted throughout Zululand, many urban Zulu parents bring their children to the **Vukani Collection** to gain insights into the rituals, codes, and crafts of the past. This is the finest collection of Zulu traditional arts and crafts anywhere, and a visit here is essential for anyone interested in collecting or understanding Zulu art, particularly traditional basketware (not least to browse the hand-picked selection of art and basketware in the museum shop). Another highlight of the collection are the pots made by master potter Nesta Nala (her work is sold in international galleries through-out the world for increasingly vast sums). Nesta walks for miles to find just the right clay before grinding and mixing, then sunbaking her paper-thin shapes and firing them in a hole in the ground. Pots are finally rubbed with fat and ashes, applied with a river stone. Keep an eye out for another award-winner, Allina Ndebele, whose tapestries are inspired by Zulu myths and legends as told to her by her grandmother. Besides the collection, you can visit the **Zulu History Museum,** housed in **Fort Nongqayi** (1883), where the Natal "Native" Police were garrisoned. This museum traces the history of the fort and the virtual enslavement of the Zulu as a result of a poll tax; it also houses a good beadwork collection, dating back to the 1920s, and a collection of John Dunn's furniture—the son of settlers, Dunn became King Cetshwayo's political advisor and was the only white man to become a true Zulu chief. Embracing Zulu polygamy by taking 49 wives, he almost single-handedly spawned Eshowe's "coloured" community. Having taken in the **Zulu Missionary Museum** in the chapel, you might be in need of refreshment—take a seat in the **Adams Outpost,** housed in an 1887 settler's house. (*Note:* Booking ahead is essential so that a museum guide can be arranged.)

Nongqayi Rd. (marked off the R68), Eshowe. ℭ 035/474-2419, ext. 247. Vukani Collection ℭ 035/474-5274. R20 ($3) adults, R4 (60¢) children. Daily 7:30am–4pm.

TRACKING DOWN THE BIG 5 IN ZULULAND

If you're looking to tick off the Big 5, your KwaZulu-Natal options have broadened considerably since 2000. Run by the KwaZulu-Natal Nature Conservation Services, **Hluhluwe-Umfolozi** is, at 96,453 hectares (238,824 acres), by far the province's largest Big 5 reserve and offers excellent value and even better accommodations than the Kruger. It is also open to day as well as overnight visitors, which gives you the flexibility to, say, base yourself in the **Greater St Lucia Wetland Park,** where you are closer to both the ocean and the estuary, and visit Hluhluwe as a day-tripper. Twenty kilometers (12 miles) north of Hluhluwe lies the new 5,000-hectare (12,350-acre) **Thanda Private Game Reserve.** Modeled on the luxury lodges surrounding Kruger, the reserve will have you wanting for nothing and—if you opt for the tiny tented camp—provides one of the most exclusive bush experiences in southern Africa. There's more laid-on luxury to be had at **Mkuze Falls Private Game Reserve**—a private reserve that comprises more than 17,000 hectares (41,990 acres) and is one of the best-value Big 5 reserves in the country—and nearby Amakhosi Lodge, in the 10,000-hectare (24,700-acre) **AmaZulu Private Game Reserve.** Phinda Private Game Reserve's camps—particularly Vlei—offer the most stylish bush accommodations in the province, but note that for this kind of money you could be staying in a top-notch lodge around Kruger. Finally, there are the beautiful coastal reserves, where you can stay at **Thonga Beach Lodge** or **Rocktail Bay,** both of which offer a chance to explore the coastal forest, laze away the days snorkeling and scuba-diving in tropical waters, and perhaps witness one of nature's most primeval miracles. From October to February, the large leatherback turtle (weighing in at 600kg/1,320 lb.) and its slightly smaller relative, the loggerhead turtle, travel thousands of miles, using ancient navigational techniques to return to the precise beach they were born, heaving themselves ashore to produce the next generation—a cycle some believe dates back more than 6,000 years.

HLUHLUWE-UMFOLOZI GAME RESERVE ★★

Established in 1895, Hluhluwe-Umfolozi (pronounced "shloe-shloe-whee"), once separate reserves, is one of the oldest wildlife sanctuaries in Africa. United in 1989, when the land between them was proclaimed the "Corridor Game Reserve," the reserve today covers 96,453 hectares (238,239 acres) and is the provinces' premier wildlife destination, and the second-most-popular park after Kruger. Though only a twentieth of the size of its Mpumalanga competitor, the reserve is home to a large variety of wildlife, including the Big 5, cheetah, hyena, wild dog, wildebeest, giraffe, hippo, zebra, and a large variety of antelope. Certainly, this is the best place in the world to spot rhino, particularly white (or square-lipped) rhino, which KwaZulu-Natal Wildlife single-handedly brought back from the brink of extinction. Many consider its unique combination of forest, woodland, savanna, and grasslands, and its hot, humid, wet summers, the "real" Africa—well worth visiting in addition to Kruger.

Treks along the **wilderness trails** ⊛⊛⊛ are conducted by rangers from March to November in the 25,000-hectare (61,750-acre) Umfolozi wilderness, once the royal hunting grounds of King Shaka. Access to this area is permitted only on foot, helping to make this some of the most pristine bush territory in the world. Unlike in Kruger, where walkers return to the same bush camp every night, provisions and luggage are carried by donkeys to new sites, providing hikers with a sense of heading deeper into the jungle. Book trails well in advance through **KZN Wildlife** (see "Staying Active: Hiking," earlier); cost is R2,480 ($370) per person (4 nights all-inclusive), and R1,400 ($209) per person (2 nights).

VISITOR INFORMATION   Open daily March through October from 6am to 6pm, and November through February from 5am to 7pm. Admission is R35 ($5.20) per person. Guided 2-hour walks (R100/$15) take place in the early morning and afternoon, as do the 3-hour game drives, early morning or evening (R150/$22); these are open to residents only. For more information, call **Hilltop Camp** (✆ 035/562-0848) or **Umfolozi Camp** (✆ 035/550-8477).

GETTING THERE   The reserve lies approximately 280km (174 miles) north of Durban, with two entrances leading off the N2. The quickest way to get to Hilltop Camp is via Memorial Gate, 50km (31 miles) north of Mtubatuba (Hilltop is approximately 30 min. from here), but if you want to enter the park sooner, enter via Nyalazi

---

Fun Fact **The Great White Rhino Recovery**

The recovery of the world's white rhino population—from fewer than 100 individuals in the 1920s to more than 7,000 worldwide today—is largely due to the efforts of the **KwaZulu-Natal Wildlife** (formerly the KwaZulu-Natal Nature Conservation Services). Early conservation efforts ensured a steady increase in numbers at Hluhluwe-Umfolozi, giving rise to Operation Rhino in 1961, whereby surplus numbers of white rhino were relocated to other protected areas and to private land. By 1997 this worldwide distribution had reached a total of 3,912, and white rhino numbers had increased to such an extent that it was the first species to be removed from the World Conservation Union's Endangered List in 1994. There are hopes of the same success with the extremely rare black rhino (the same color, incidentally, but slightly smaller and with a distinctive hooked lip). There are currently only 2,640 black rhinos in the world, of which almost half are in South Africa; most are in KwaZulu-Natal, which has the world's second-largest population (after Namibia).

Gate (turn off on the R618 at Mtubatuba). Adhering to the 40kmph (25 mph) speed limit, it's about a 50-minute drive to the camp. The third entrance, Cengeni Gate, is approached from the west, 30km (19 miles) from Ulundi. To drive from Cengeni to Hilltop, allow 3 hours.

Where to Stay & Dine

Of the two public rest camps in Hluhluwe-Umfolozi, **Mpila,** an unfenced camp located in Umfolozi, offers, for the most part, basic accommodations (shared kitchen facilities and ablutions), but if you're prepared to self-cater, you may want to ask about one of the two-bedroom cottages or (en-suite and electrified, but shared kitchen) tents. The Mpila camp shop provides basic provisions; a pool is planned by late 2005, as well as an additional five en-suite tents and 12 twin-bed thatched huts. **Hilltop,** in the Hluhluwe section, is rated as one of the best public camps in the country; it's a good base not just for the reserve, but also for day forays to Mkuzi or Lake St Lucia (2 hr. from Hilltop).

Note: Also available are a number of houses, which KZN Wildlife calls **lodges,** that are situated in secluded areas picked for their natural beauty. These are unfenced, necessitating the protection of an armed ranger for bush walks; most also have a resident cook (though you may have to provide ingredients; check beforehand), or you may choose self-catering. These lodges (sleeping six to eight) are available only for single bookings, making this option suitable for a group or family, or a couple prepared to pay a little extra for total privacy. For more information on these, take a look at www.kznwildlife.com, write to bookings@kznwildlife.com, or call ℂ **033/845-1000.**

Hilltop Camp ☆ 𝓥𝑎𝑙𝑢𝑒   Appropriately named, this KZN Wildlife camp commands lovely views of the surrounding hills and valleys, and offers a variety of accommodations options. Pick of the bunch are the two-bed en-suite chalets (all feature bar fridges and tea- and coffee-making facilities; Zone has an equipped kitchenette) and the four-bed chalets (all with equipped kitchens). For some of the best locations, request nos. 10 to 14, 28 to 33, or 44 to 49. The shop sells basic provisions (frozen meat, fire lighters, liquor, camera film), but it's worth stocking up in Durban or dining at the restaurant. If *nyala* steak is on the menu, order it; the meat of this shy, pretty antelope is delicious, and you're unlikely to find it elsewhere. Hilltop also has a lodge that is fully catered and hosted, suitable for a group or family, and two bush lodges where a cook is made available upon request.

KN NCS, P.O. Box 13053, Cascades 3202. Reservations ℂ **033/845-1000.** Fax 035/845-1001. www.kznwildlife.com. (Direct inquiries, but no bookings, ℂ **035/562-0255).** 70 units, consisting of 2-bed huts (no bathroom), 2-bed rondawels, 2- and 4-bed chalets, and a 9-bed lodge. From R280 ($42) double; R480 ($72) for 2- or 4-bed fully equipped chalet. AE, DC, M, V. **Amenities:** Restaurant; bar/lounge; pool; babysitting; limited laundry; fax; fuel station.

THE GREATER ST LUCIA WETLAND PARK ☆☆☆

From the Mfolozi swamps in the south, this park—declared a World Heritage Site in December 1999—stretches 220km (136 miles) northward to Mozambique, incorporating the **St Lucia Game and Marine Reserves, False Bay Park, Cape Vidal, Sodwana Bay,** and **Mkhuze Game Reserve.** Covering 254,500 hectares (628,615 acres), it encompasses five distinct ecosystems, including one of the three most important wetlands in Africa, mangrove forests, the dry savanna and thornveld of the western shores and the vegetated sand dunes of the eastern shores, the Mkuze swamps (home to over 400 bird species, including the rare Pel's fishing owl), and the great estuary and offshore coral reefs.

Tips **How to Avoid Becoming Dinner**

Always keep a distance of about 3m (9¾ ft.) from the water's edge—remember that crocodiles can remain underwater for up to 2 hours, in only a foot of water, so don't assume you're safe just because there's no sign of 'em. If you see a V-shape on the surface of the water moving toward shore, get away fast; if the critter actually gets hold of you, try to locate its eyes and stick your thumbs in as deep as they'll go.

The most easily accessed aspect is Lake St Lucia. A 38,882-hectare (96,039-acre) expanse of water dotted with islands, it supports an abundance of wildlife, including Nile crocodile, hippo, rhino, elephant, buffalo, and giraffe, as well as a host of water-birds, including pelican, flamingos, herons, fish eagles, kingfishers, geese, and storks. The lake is flanked on the west by typical bushveld terrain and on the east by the high-est forested dunes in the world. These, incidentally, contain large deposits of titanium and zirconium, and conservationists waged a long-running war with mining consor-tia over their fate, a battle they thankfully won.

The easiest way to explore the lake is to catch a ride on the 85-seater **Santa Lucia** ✿✿✿ (bookings advisable; ✆ 035/590-1340). The 90-minute guided tours depart daily at 8:30am, 10:30am, and 2:30pm, and cost R80 ($12). If you're there on a Friday or Saturday, take the 4pm sundowner cruise; there's a fully licensed bar on board. The launch point is clearly marked off the R618 east, which leads to St Lucia Village, located at the mouth of the St Lucia Estuary. Top attraction here is the informative **Crocodile Centre** ✿✿, McKenzie Street (✆ 035/590-1387; daily 7:30am–4:30pm; R20–R25/$3–$3.75, depending on day). There are literally hun-dreds of crocodile parks throughout the country, but this is by far the best—the only recognized crocodile research facility in South Africa. Get there at 2pm on a Satur-day for a snake presentation, followed by feeding time for the crocs at 3pm. The cen-ter houses all of the African species of crocodile—though you'll certainly spot at least one of the estimated 2,000 Nile crocs that lurk in the lake if you take a cruise on the *Santa Lucia*—swimming in the lake, understandably, is strictly prohibited. The cen-ter also has a good restaurant that specializes in—you guessed it—crocodile.

The only other reason to find yourself in St Lucia Village is because you're on your way to **Cape Vidal** ✿ (direct ✆ 035/590-9012; KZN Reservations ✆ 033/845-1000), a 2-hour trip north to the coast. Besides the Umvubu Forest and Imboma trails, which take you over the tallest vegetated dunes in the world, the offshore reef at Cape Vidal makes the sea safe for swimming and ideal for snorkeling, and a whale-watching tower provides an excellent view of passing marine mammals (including 18m /59-ft. whale sharks). The beaches are also now off-limits to four-wheel-drives, making for a relatively untouched paradise. Day-visitor numbers to Cape Vidal are restricted to 120 vehicles, so it's worth considering an overnight at the camp. Comprising 18 five-bed and 11 eight-bed log cabins (from R444/$66 double), all well equipped for self-catering (stop for provisions in St Lucia Village) and relatively privately situated, this is one of the best value-for-money options in the area. The log cabins are all a stone's throw from the beach and the warm ocean, but the large dune precludes any sea views, and the dune forest makes for a slightly gloomy atmosphere.

Birders should include a visit to **Mkhuze Game Reserve** ⓚ (ⓒ **035/573-9004;** 5am–7pm; R35/$5.20 per vehicle, and R35/$5.20 per person), which is connected to the coastal plain via the Mkuze River. Reached via the N2 (take the Mkuze Village turnoff; the Emshopi Gate entrance is 28km/17 miles farther), this reserve has 430 species of bird on record, which is indicative of the varied vegetation and landscape. Maps are issued at the reception office; don't miss the two bird hides at Nsumo Pan, where you can picnic and watch the changing spectacle on the waterway. This is also the start of the 3km (1.75-mile) circular guided (R60/$8.95) **Mkhuze Fig Forest Walk,** one of the area's rarest and most attractive woodlands.

Last, but certainly not least of the Greater St Lucia Wetland Park attractions, is **Sodwana Bay** ⓚ, South Africa's diving mecca. Here the warm Agulhus current brings in some 1,200 varieties of fish, second in number only to Australia's Great Barrier Reef. This is the best place in the country to become a qualified diver, but if you just want to snorkel, head for Jesser Point.

Where to Stay & Dine

The only dining options are in St Lucia Village, but don't expect miracles—you're a long way from civilization: **Quarterdeck** (ⓒ 035/590-1116), on McKenzie Street, is reputable and known for its seafood. If you're cooking, buy fresh fish from the **Fishing Den** next door; they also sell tackle and bait.

There are a few B&B and hotel options in St Lucia Village, but the village itself holds few attractions; much better to stay in one of the privately owned lodges on the western shore. The best by far is the exclusive **Makakatana Bay Lodge** (ⓒ **035/550-4189;** www.makakatana.co.za), situated in the heart of the St Lucia Wetland Reserve and comprising six privately located suites overlooking the lake, with a variety of activities on offer—from mokoro canoe safaris through the wetlands or snorkeling the coastline, to full-day safaris in nearby Hluhluwe-Umfolozi and Zulu dancing at Dumazulu. The all-inclusive rate (all meals and game activities) is R3,738 to R4,300 ($558–$642) double, R3,988 to R5,300 ($595–$791) honeymoon suite. If this strikes you as steep, check out the larger **Hluhluwe River Lodge** (ⓒ **035/562-0246;** www.hluhluwe.co.za). With 12 thatched chalets, the lodge offers much the same by way of activities, for slightly less money (from R2,998/$447 double, including all meals and activities; R2,170/$324 double, including breakfast.) Also worth considering is **Falaza Game Park,** with gorgeously outfitted en-suite tents, located on the western dunes of False Bay (ⓒ **035/562-2319;** www.falaza.co.za; R1,200/$179,

---

╭ Fun Fact   Curse of the Coelacanth?

Thought to be extinct until 1938, when one was caught off the Eastern Cape coast, the coelacanth are closely related to the first fish that came ashore to live on land 360 million years ago. Sightings are still incredibly rare, and when three of these 400-million-year-old dinosaurs of the deep were discovered off the coast of St Lucia in November 2000, several diving expeditions were arranged in an attempt to film a living specimen. Since then, three members of the coelacanth expedition have died while diving. Admittedly, deep dives are dangerous (coelacanths swim at depths of 150–585m/500–1,950 ft.), but these events have begged the question: Is this the curse of the coelacanth?

including breakfast and dinner; R1,500/$224 all-inclusive). Divers who want to concentrate on underwater game should take a look at **Sodwana Bay Lodge** (© 035/571-6000; www.sodwanadivelodge.co.za).

Another option is to hire a **self-catering unit** within the reserve from **KwaZulu-Natal Wildlife**—the best camps are at Cape Vidal, Charters Creek, and Sodwana Bay. To find out more about these, or to check out the other options within the reserve, contact **KZN Wildlife,** P.O. Box 13053, Cascades 3202 (for reservations, © 033/845-1000, fax 033/845-1001; for inquiries, © 033/845-1002; www.kznwildlife.com). If you're still stumped for accommodations, call **St Lucia Tourism,** an informal bureau run by volunteers, at © **035/590-1247.**

PHINDA PRIVATE GAME RESERVE

Adjoining Mkhuze Game Reserve in the south, the 17,000-hectare (41,990-acre) Phinda covers seven ecosystems, including sand forests, mountains, wetlands, and river valleys, and is home to the Big 5. Wildlife numbers are not as abundant as in Mpumalanga, but most visitors (who have to overnight to gain access) are here for the exceptional range of experiences available—referred to as **Phinda Adventures,** these include diving expeditions to the coral reefs at nearby Mbibi and Sodwana, flights over the surrounding Maputaland wilderness (including to Lake Sibaya, the largest freshwater lake in Africa), deep-sea fishing, black rhino trailing in Mkuzi, turtle-tracking, and canoeing and cruising the Mzinene River. Phinda also offers the most stylish bush accommodations in KwaZulu-Natal.

Phinda Lodges ⓇⓇ   When CC Africa launched **Forest Camp** in 1993, the zenlike glass boxes—each privately located within a torchwood tree forest, and constructed with minimum impact on the environment—were lauded as the most stylish bedrooms in Africa, though some found the forest a bit gloomy. **Mountain Camp** is the oldest and least modern of the camps but is the most family friendly, and has excellent views of the distant Lebombo Mountains and surrounding plains. The pick of the bunch are the modern glass boxes at Vlei Camp (pronounced "flay"): six glass-fronted timber dwellings on stilts located a discreet distance from one another, each with a private plunge pool overlooking marsh and woodland. Equally exclusive, but a bit more hippie, **Rock Camp** consists of six adobe-like chalets built into the mountainside, also with private plunge pools, and overlooking a watering hole. The latest additions are **Phinda Zuka,** comprising four chalets, with a sole-use price of R14,750 ($2,201) per night, and **Phinda Getti,** a four-bedroom house that will set you back R20,000 ($2,985) for the night.

Private Bag X27, Benmore 2010. © 011/809-4300. Fax 011/809-4315. www.ccafrica.com. Rock and Vlei 6 units each. Forest 16 units. Mountain 20 units. Rock and Vlei R9,590 ($1,431); Forest and Mountain R5,210–R8,130 ($778–$1,213), depending on season. Rates include all meals and activities within the reserve. AE, DC, MC, V. **Amenities:** Dining room; bar; pool; room service; babysitting (Mountain and Forest only); laundry; airport transfers from Richard's Bay; game drives; guided bush walks and the Phinda Adventures (see above); Zulu village visits. *In room:* A/C, minibar.

MKUZE FALLS GAME RESERVE

Mkuze Falls (not to be confused with the KZN Wildlife–owned Mhkuze reserve) is a 10,000-hectare (24,700-acre) private game reserve with all the luxuries and exclusivity associated with the upmarket reserves flanking Kruger, and home to the Big 5. As such, it is providing stiff competition to the much pricier Phinda (located some 90 min. south, in the Greater St Lucia Wetland Park), but Phinda's camps still have the edge when it comes to accommodations. Note that there is yet another Big 5 Mkuze option you might want to consider, with rates often coming in even lower than Mkuze Falls Lodge: **Amakhosi Lodge,** situated in the **AmaZulu Private Game Reserve,** comprises six River Suites, each with lounge and deck overlooking the Mkuze River. Rates start from R,4000 ($597) double, including all meals, local beverages, and game drives (© **034/414-1157;** www.amakhosi.com).

Mkuze Falls Lodge ★★ *Value* Some may find the fake elephant tusks surrounding the headboard a little over the top, but no one complains about the generous size of the chalets, the private plunge pools, or the views—each of the nine stilted and thatched units, connected via boardwalk, enjoys lovely views of the Mkuze River and the surrounding plains, which support a variety of game. Accommodations options have now been extended with the creation of a tented lodge, accommodating a maximum of 10 guests in luxury East African–style safari tents. As is the case in most private reserves and lodges throughout southern Africa, the daily highlights are the early-morning and evening game drives in open-topped vehicles with experienced rangers at the wheel.

Off R66. P.O. Box 238, Pongola, Zululand 3170. © **034/414-1018.** Fax 034/414-1021. www.mkuzefalls.com. High season (Aug–Apr) chalets R6,000 ($896) double; tents R4,200 ($627). Low season chalets R3,360 ($501) double; tents R2,640 ($394) double. Rates include all meals, game drives, and bush walks. AE, DC, MC, V. Mkuze Falls is close to the southern border of Swaziland and a 4½-hr. drive from Durban. **Amenities:** Restaurant; bar; lounge; room service; laundry; game drives and walks; air and road transfers. *In room:* Private deck w/plunge pool.

THANDA PRIVATE GAME RESERVE

Located just 23km (14 miles) north of Hluhluwe, this new Big 5 reserve, rehabilitated by the visionary Dan Olofsson, is a 2-hour drive from Richards Bay airport (or you can utilize the reserve's private airstrip). As such, it's the most easily accessed of the Big 5 private reserves here and is aiming high, with ultraluxurious accommodations, equally high service standards, and a sublime stretch of Zululand bushveld. Hard to believe that a decade ago this was cattle farmland. Today not only the Big 5, but wild dog and cheetah roam the reserve, and guests are offered the opportunity to add dolphin encounters and scuba-diving to their game-viewing experiences (at press time, the reserve had a very agreeable package deal with Thonga Beach Lodge; see "Coastal Reserves: Mabibi, Rocktail & Kosi Bay," below).

At Thanda (which means "love" in Zulu) the focus is also very much on providing guests with a unique cultural experience—from Vula Zulu, the traditional Zulu homestead you are invited to visit (the highlight of which is seeing its 100 Zulu *impis* dancing, creating a thunderous beat) to the Zulu bedtime story placed on your pillow overnight, you will leave with a newfound respect for this proud nation. And no doubt delighted that Thanda is a shared community project, enjoying the full backing of King Goodwill Zwelithini—besides the employment opportunities, a percentage of proceeds is directly paid to the local community.

Thanda Bush Villas & Tented Camp ★★ *Value* With the tented camp offering all the luxuries that you'd never associate with camping, it's a good-value option, but if money is no object, the huge and luxurious villas are the ultimate. In a nod to Singita, decor is African modern (chandeliers made from high-gloss dried seeds, curtains from wire threaded with tiny stones, stone fireplaces). Each villa has a large four-poster bed with the by now de rigueur private plunge pool (heated here) and huge viewing deck with thatched *sala* and circular daybed from which to enjoy the sublime views. Discreet, thoughtful service and an excellent wellness spa complete the picture.

P.O. Box 652585, Benmore, 2010. ℂ **011/704-3115.** Fax 011/462-5607. www.thanda.co.za. Villas 9 units. Tented camp 4 units. High season villas R7,000 ($1,045) double; tented camp R3,600 ($537). Low season villas R6,300 ($940) double; tents R2,640 ($394) double. Rates include all meals, game drives, and bush walks. AE, DC, MC, V. **Amenities:** Restaurant; bar; lounge; wellness center; room service; laundry; game drives and walks; air and road transfers. *In room:* Private deck w/plunge pool.

COASTAL RESERVES: MABIBI, ROCKTAIL & KOSI BAY

Home of the Tonga and Mabudu peoples, the northeastern corner of KwaZulu-Natal is the most remote part of the province, with large tracts accessible only by four-wheel-drive vehicles. Combined with the total ban on vehicles on the beach and outboard motors at sea, this inaccessibility has protected it from development, and the coastline is absolutely pristine. A minimum stay of 3 days is needed to really validate the effort it takes to get here—but you'll find plenty to do, like sunbathing, snorkeling, fishing, bird-watching (60% of the birds occurring in South Africa have been recorded here), canoeing the lakes (avoiding hippo and croc!), sampling the local *ilala* palm wine, and just getting to know the flora; almost 7,000 species grow in this region alone.

South Africa's largest freshwater lake, Lake Sibaya, lies only 10km (6¼ miles) north of Sodwana; but if you're headed for Rocktail or Kosi Bay, this is a major detour by road, and there's nothing much to do here but bird-watch or canoe. This in itself may be a major benefit—besides, on the west side of Sibaya is **Mabibi,** one of the most remote and beautiful stretches of beach in Africa.

The **Kosi Reserve** is about 15km (9¼ miles) northeast of Kwangwanase via a dirt road. You will, however, need a four-wheel-drive vehicle (and guide) to get to the mouth (some 5km/3 miles from the camp), where one of the most impressive views in the country overlooks Kosi Bay (in reality, an estuary), laced with intricate Tonga fish traps and unchanged for centuries. Turning back, you can see each of Kosi's four lakes, linked by narrow channels, extending inland for some 20km (12 miles). **Lake Amanzamnyama (dark waters)** is the most southerly lake, fringed by large subtropical swamp and raffia palm forests, and accessible only by canoe or guided hike—the best way to explore the area. Hikers should ask about the 1-day guided hike through the forest and lagoon to the beach (R40/$5.95) or the 4-day guided **Amanzamnyama Trail,** which takes in the four lakes as well as coastal dunes, raffia forests, coral reefs, and beaches. Contact F. B.Coetze (ℂ **035/5920-0414**).

Note: Northern Maputaland is a malarial area, and you're advised to start taking medication beforehand (see chapter 2 for more information on malaria), though autumn and early winter are low risk, and the weather is still balmy. Best times for diving are November to February.

Where to Stay & Dine

If you'd like to overnight overlooking Sibaya, **Sibaya Lake Lodge** offers all the comforts and total peace (ℂ **011/616-9950;** www.lakesibaya.co.za; R2,450/$366 double, all-inclusive). To overnight amid a milkwood forest overlooking the coral-sand beaches of Mabibi, book into **Thonga Beach Lodge** ★★★ (ℂ **035/474-7100;** info@isibindiafrica.co.za; R3,600–R4,480/$537–$669)—vying with Rocktail Bay as the most romantic destination along the coast. Besides offering snorkeling and diving (diving currently takes place in nearby Rocktail Bay), the managerial couple Laurence and Zoe, both of whom are enthusiastic and incredibly knowledgeable about the area, offer guided beach or forest walks, sundowner trips on Lake Sibaya, dolphin-encounter boat trips, turtle tracking, and Sea Spa treatments. The lodge will arrange transfers from anywhere in Zululand or the Richards Bay airport; if you want to get there on your own, you will need a proper 4×4 to traverse the sand.

If you wish to stay near the river mouth that empties into Kosi Bay, your best bet is in one of the **KZN Wildlife huts** (© 033/845-1000; www.kznwildlife.com; R472/ $70 double), but you will also need a four-wheel-drive vehicle to get here; the last 4km (2½ miles) of road are sand; alternatively, try **Kosi Bay Lodge,** which is 15km (9¼ miles) from the beach (© 035/592-9561; nwkosibay@mweb.co.za); self-catering units start at R390 ($58) double; it's R1,020 ($152) for a double, full-board.

Rocktail Bay 𝒦𝒦𝒦   This is a castaway fantasy come true: 10 thatched en-suite chalets (small but adequate, and very simply decorated) raised on stilts into the forest canopy, each with its own wooden deck and within close walking distance of the beach. There are no telephones, TVs, or radios to disturb, and—with the exception of guests—no one to bump into on the 60km (37-mile) shoreline. A charming lounge/ pub area has a small plunge pool, and all meals are served around a communal table in the dining area. The food is simple but well cooked. Lunches are light and feature salads and quiches, and dinners are a sit-down three-course affair with limited choice (anything from roast lamb to pan-fried fish). With advance notice, any dietary needs will be taken into consideration. A boardwalk winds from the lodge through the dune forest to the beach and ocean, which appear totally deserted.

Armed with flippers and snorkel, you discover a world of color beneath the water's surface. Nature walks, four-wheel-drive treks, and picnics to Black Rock (another excellent snorkeling spot) are arranged, and in summer there are sea turtle expeditions. This is a highly recommended experience for stressed city dwellers. Note that you not need a four-wheel-drive vehicle to get here—best to arrange a transfer from a nearby spot or from Richard's Bay airport.

Wilderness Safaris, P.O. Box 78573, Sandton 2146. © 011/883-0747. Fax 011/807-2110. www.wilderness-safaris. com. 10 units. R3,620–R4,340 ($540–$648) double, depending on season. Rates include all meals and activities. AE, DC, MC, V. **Amenities:** Lounge/pub; private decks; en-suite facilities.

4 The Battlefields

Ladysmith 251km (156 miles) NW of Durban; Dundee 320km (198 miles) N of Durban

Most of the battles fought on South African soil took place in the northwestern corner of KwaZulu-Natal, where the rolling grasslands were regularly soaked with blood as battles for territorial supremacy would, in turn, pit Zulu against Boer, Brit against Zulu, and Afrikaner against Brit. The official Battlefields Route covers 4 wars, 15 towns, and more than 50 battlefields, and includes numerous museums and memorials to the dead and victorious; but few would argue that the heroic Anglo-Zulu battles that took place on January 22, 1879, at Isandlwana and Rorke's Drift—immortalized in the movie *Zulu,* starring Michael Caine—are the most compelling, and best for those with limited time.

Another site worth investigating is that of the Battle of Blood River, which took place 41 years earlier, this time between the Trekkers and the Zulus. This victory was to validate Afrikaner arrogance and religious self-righteousness. Visitors should also visit Ladysmith to immerse themselves in the siege that jump-started the Second Anglo-Boer War—it would take the world's mightiest nation 3 years and thousands of pounds to defeat some of the world's smallest, and embroil some of the century's giants, like Winston Churchill and Gandhi.

This is one area where a guide is almost essential, and top of the line is David Rattray (see below), who offers an award-winning performance that regularly reduces onlookers to tears. If, however, you are eager to tackle a self-guided tour but are unfamiliar with the historical background of the wars, a brief chronological account is supplied below.

ESSENTIALS

VISITOR INFORMATION   Contact Karin van Tonder, the KZN **Battlefields Route Secretary** (© 082/802-1643), and she'll direct you to the information officer in charge of each of the 15 battlefields towns. The main centers are **Dundee** (Rorke's Drift and Isandlwana), **Ladysmith** (Second Anglo-Boer War), and **Vryheid** (Battle of Blood River). The **Ladysmith Tourism Information Bureau** (© 036/637-2992; www.ladysmith.co.za) is particularly helpful.

GETTING THERE   By Car   It takes around 3½ hours by car from Durban to get to the battlefields, 4½ hours from Jo'burg. You have a choice of a number of routes. If you're interested in Zulu culture, travel to or from Durban via Eshowe.

By Bus   Greyhound and **Translux** (see chapter 2 for regional phone numbers) both travel through Ladysmith daily.

GUIDED TOUR   Exploring with a guide is definitely recommended. The best, David Rattray, is based at his lodge at **Fugitive's Drift** (© 034/642-1843; see also "Where to Stay & Dine," below). A consummate storyteller, Rattray may err a tad on the historical side, but his detailed research on the individuals who fought on both sides of the Anglo-Zulu War humanizes the battles, and even those who hate history are enthralled. If he is not available, his handpicked staff members are well versed and rehearsed in the inimitable Rattray style. Space allowing, nonresidents may join these tours at a cost of R570 to R600 ($85–$90), depending on season.

Other guides worth mentioning are **Prince Sibusiso Shibe,** the local historian working with Thompson's Tours (© 031/250-3100 or 083/967-6347); **Rob Gerrard,** resident historian and Fellow of the Royal Geographical Society, based at Isandlwana Lodge (see "Where to Stay & Dine," below); **Pat Rundgren** (© 082/690-7812), an avid researcher and collector based in Dundee; and natural scientist **John Turner** (© 035/835-0062), who combines battlefield tours with trips to nearby reserves such as Hluhluwe-Umfolozi, where he puts his degree in animal behavior to excellent use.

THE TOP ATTRACTIONS

Isandlwana Battlefield ★★   Other than the rather beautiful "Zulu-necklace" monument, and the many white painted rocks, there is not much here to evoke the 1879 battle of Isandlwana, but with a good guide, you may be able to hear the sound of 20,000 Zulu warriors chanting *"zee, zee, zee"* like angry bees amassing, before attacking with the Zulu deep-throated war cry *"uSuthu, uSuthu, uSuthu,"* and ultimately delivering the most crushing defeat the mighty British Empire was to suffer in Africa—at the hands of "savages armed with sticks." The white cairns mark the places where British soldiers fell and were buried. The British were horrified to find their men disemboweled—proof, they thought, of the savagery of the Zulu. In fact, the Zulus were honoring the men by setting their spirits free.

Off the R68 between Nqutu and Babanango. © 034/271-8165. R15 ($2.25) adults. Mon–Fri 8am–4pm; Sat–Sun 9am–4pm.

A Brief History of the Battlefields

The first major battle in this area took place some 48km (30 miles) east of Dundee, at what came to be known as **Blood River**. Following the treacherous murder of Retief and his men (see "Discovering Zulu History," earlier in this chapter), and Dingaan's ruthless persecution of white settlers, Trekker leader Andries Pretorius moved an Afrikaner commando of 464 men to a strategic spot on the banks of the ironically named Ncome (Peace) River, where he created an impenetrable *laager* (a circular encampment of wagons, with oxen in the center) with 64 ox-wagons, and prayed for victory. On behalf of the Afrikaner nation, Pretorius made a solemn vow to God that, should they survive, Afrikaners would hold the day sacred in perpetuity. On December 16, 1838, the Zulus attacked. Three times they were driven off by fire before Pretorius led a mounted charge. Eventually, the Zulus fled, leaving 3,000 dead and the river dark with blood. Not one Boer died, giving rise to the nationalistic Afrikaner myth that their Old Testament God had protected them against invincible odds, proving that they were indeed the chosen race. Today December 16 remains a national holiday (though renamed Day of Reconciliation), and visitors can view the eerie spectacle of a replica laager, 64 life-size ox-wagons cast in bronze, at the original site of **Blood River Battlefield**. The site is off the R33 and is open daily 8am to 5pm.

Zulu might rose again under Cetshwayo. This clearly did not fit in with British imperialist plans, and, having delivered a totally unreasonable ultimatum, three British columns under an overconfident Chelmsford marched into Zululand in January 1879. On January 21, Chelmsford set up temporary camp at **Isandlwana Hill** and, believing that the Zulu army was elsewhere, took a large detachment to support a reconnaissance force, leaving the camp defenseless. Six kilometers (3¾ miles) away, 24,000 Zulu soldiers sat in the long grass, waiting silently for a signal. At about 11:30am the following day, a British patrol inadvertently stumbled upon them, and the Zulu warriors quickly surrounded the patrol, chanting their famed rallying cry, *"uSuthu"* (oo-*soo*-too).

Ladysmith Siege Museum 🏛🏛   If your interest lies in the battle between the Boers and the British, this is an essential stop. Displays and photographs vividly depict the wars that so greatly affected 20th-century South Africa, as well as the appalling conditions at the end of the siege, when 28 to 30 people died daily. On Keate Street is the **Cultural Centre and Museum** (Mon–Fri 9am–4pm; R2/30¢ adults), where you can listen to the sweet a cappella sounds of **Ladysmith Black Mambazo,** the best-selling group that shot to fame with the record *Homeless*.

Murchison St. (the main road running through Ladysmith), next to the Town Hall. ✆ **036/637-2992.** R2 (30¢). Mon–Fri 9am–4pm; Sat 9am–1pm.

Rorke's Drift 🏛🏛   Located in the reconstructed hospital where 100 men holed up for 12 hours and successfully warded off 4,000 Zulus led by Cetshwayo's brother

Two hours later, 1,329 of the 1,700 British soldiers were dead. Survivors fled across **Fugitive's Drift,** where more died, but two men made it to the nearby mission station called **Rorke's Drift,** where a contingent of 139 men, of which 35 were seriously ill, were waiting with provisions for Chelmsford's return. With seconds to spare, the men barricaded themselves behind a makeshift wall of army biscuit boxes, tinned meat, and bags of maize meal, and warded off the 4,000-strong Zulu onslaught. The battle raged until dawn, when the Zulus finally withdrew. Despite incredible odds, only 17 British soldiers died at Rorke's Drift, and 11 Victoria Crosses were awarded— more than at any other battle in British history. Six months later, on July 4, 1879, the Zulus suffered their final defeat at Ondini.

A year later the British would begin a new brawl, this time with the Afrikaners, and although a peace treaty was signed in March 1881, it sowed the seeds for the Second Anglo-Boer War, a 3-year battle that captured the world's attention and introduced the concept of guerrilla warfare. On October 20, 1899, the first battle was pitched on **Talana Hill,** when 14,000 Afrikaners attacked 4,000 British troops. The Brits managed to repel the attackers, and on November 2, the little town of Ladysmith was besieged by the Afrikaners for 118 days. Thousands died of disease, trapped without access to clean water, and more fell as the British tried to break through the Afrikaner defenses. (Winston Churchill, covering the war for the *London Morning Post,* narrowly escaped death when the train he was traveling on was blown up by Boer forces some 40km/25 miles south of Ladysmith.)

The most ignominious battle during this time took place on **Spioenkop** (literally, Spies Hill) when Boers and Brits battled for this strategic position until both sides believed they had lost. The British were the first to withdraw, leaving the astonished but triumphant Boer in force on this strategic hill (off the R600). Two years later, following the scorched-earth policy of the British—when hundreds of acres of farmland were burnt, and Afrikaner women and children were placed in concentration camps where they perished from malnourishment and disease—the Boers acceded defeat.

Dabulamanzi, this is the most evocative interpretation center on the route. Realistic scenes are augmented by battle sounds and electronic diagrams. An added bonus is the adjoining **ELC Craft Centre** ⊛ (✆ **034/642-1627**), where you can browse for textiles, carpets, tapestries, and pottery.

Off the R68, 42km (26 miles) from Dundee on the road to Nqutu. ✆ **034/642-1687.** R15 ($2.25) adults. Mon–Fri 8am–4pm; Sat–Sun 9am–4pm.

WHERE TO STAY & DINE

Fugitive's Drift Lodge ⊛ is owned by David Rattray—generally considered the finest battlefields guide in South Africa. Situated within a 2,500-hectare (6,175-acre) nature reserve in the heart of battlefield country, it features a variety of spacious rooms; book room no. 6 if you'd like to see what happens when a group of top British interior and product designers collaborate with local Zulu craftworkers, though Nicci Rattray has, in fact, incorporated many of these items into her other rooms (© **034/642-1843** or 034/271-8051; www.fugitives-drift-lodge.com; R2,390–R3,980/$357–$594 double, depending on season; includes all meals). If you'd like to stay in stylish accommodations at a more reasonable rate, you may be better off at neighboring **Isibindi Lodge** (for reservations, © **035/474-1504,** or direct 034/642-1620; www.zulunet.co.za; high season [Oct–Apr] R1,760–R2,150/$263–$321 double, including all meals and a game drive). The rooms at Isibindi take a traditional Zulu beehive hut as their departure point and must rate as one of the most successful blends of Western and African architecture in Zululand. Alternatively, **Isandlwana Lodge** (for reservations © **011/537-4620,** or direct 034/271-8301; www.isandlwana.co.za; R2,380–R2,940/$355–$439 double, depending on season; includes all meals) is very much an elegant Afro-colonial lodge and the closest to a hotel experience in the area. The lodge occupies a great location overlooking the historic battlefield and offers a host of activities, including a Zulu Village "Safari" in which a licensed Zulu guide takes visitors to a local church, home, clinic, and sangoma.

5 The Drakensberg Mountains

The Drakensberg extends from just north of Hoedspruit in the Northern Province 1,000km (620 miles) south to the mountain kingdom of Lesotho, where a series of spectacular peaks some 240km (149 miles) long creates the western border of KwaZulu-Natal—it is this border that most refer to when they speak of the Drakensberg. Known as uKhahlamba (Barrier of Spears) to the Zulus, they were renamed "Dragon Mountains" by the Trekkers seeking to cross them. Both are apt descriptions of South Africa's premier mountain wilderness—the second-largest range in Africa and, thanks to the haven it provided for the ancient San people, the largest open-air gallery in the world, with more than 35,000 images painted at 600 sites.

The main range falls within the uKhahlamba-Drakensberg Park, a 243,000-hectare (600,210-acre) semicircle that forms the western boundary of the province. Of this, the northern and central sections are most spectacular, with majestic peaks surrounding grassed valleys fed by crystal-clear streams and pools—a hiker's paradise. But you don't have to be a keen and fit walker to appreciate the San rock paintings, or spot rare raptors, or simply enjoy the chance to breathe the air in the aptly named Champagne Valley or Cathedral Peak. To enjoy the benefits of this World Heritage Site, all you need is a couple of days, a car, and the following information.

ESSENTIALS

VISITOR INFORMATION   Northern Berg: The Drakensberg Tourist Information (© **036/448-1557;** Mon–Fri 9am–4pm; www.drakensbergtourism.com) is based in Tatham Road in Bergville, which you have to pass to access the Royal Natal National Park. **Central Berg:** If you're traveling to Cathedral Peak, take time to visit the informal bureau at **Thokozisa Centre,** off the R600, 13km (8 miles) from Winterton (© **036/488-1207**), where you can grab a bite to eat and browse for local crafts. Much of the Berg falls under the protection of **KwaZulu-Natal Wildlife,** so inquiries may also be directed to its head office by visiting www.kznwildlife.com or calling © **033/845-1000.**

GETTING THERE   By Car   Roads to the Berg all branch off west from the N3 between Maritzburg and Ladysmith. Take the R75 west to Winterton (for Cathedral

The Drakensberg

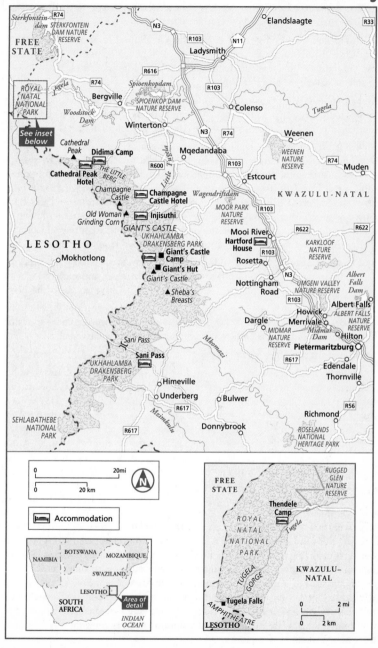

Peak or Giant's Castle); farther north is Bergville for the turnoff to the Royal Natal National Park.

By Bus   Most hotels offer transfers from the **Greyhound** or **Translux** terminals in Estcourt and Ladysmith (see chapter 2 for regional phone numbers). There is, however, no transport to any of the **KwaZulu-Natal Wildlife** properties, and you won't be able to explore the area in full.

GETTING AROUND   There are no connecting road systems, making long, circuitous routes necessary to move from one part of the Berg to the next. It's best to base yourself in one or two areas: Stay at Royal Natal or Cathedral Peak, followed by a night at Giant's Castle.

On Foot   Walks range from a few hours to several days. Detailed maps are available at Parks Board camps, the departure point for all of the best hikes. The most popular book is still David Bristow's *Drakensberg Walks: 120 Graded Hikes and Trails in the Berg* (Struik), which is light enough to carry and is available from the Parks Board shops. Because winter snows and summer rainfalls can put a damper on hiking expeditions, the best times to explore the Berg, as locals call it, are spring and autumn. (For more information, see "Staying Active: Hiking," earlier in this chapter.)

By Plane   Starlite Aviation ((*C* 082/572-3949; berg@starheli.co.za) operates from Champagne Sports Resort and offers rides with champagne sunset cocktails in the mountains. Guests staying at the Cathedral Peak Hotel have access to the hotel's helicopter.

GUIDED TOURS   Stef Steyn ((*C* 033/330-4293; www.kzntours.co.za) specializes in guided hikes in the Drakensberg (also in the Cederberg in the Cape).

EXPLORING THE DRAKENSBERG

The **Northern Drakensberg** is dominated by the **Amphitheatre,** a dramatic wall of rock that is some 8km (5 miles) long, flanked by the Sentinel (3,165m/10,381 ft.) and Eastern Buttress (3,047m/9,994 ft.). Falling within the 8,000-hectare (19,760-acre) **Royal Natal National Park,** it's the most awesome rock formation in the Drakensberg and the most photographed. This is where you'll find **Mont-aux-Sources,** at 3,282m (10,765 ft.), the country's highest peak, and source of five of South Africa's major rivers, including the Tugela. The 6-hour **Tugela Gorge Walk** will take you past the base of the **Tugela Falls,** where the Tugela River plunges 948m (3,109 ft.) from the plateau, its combined drop making it the third-highest falls in the world, and affords marvelous views of the Amphitheatre. Entrance to the Royal Natal ((*C* **036/438-6303**) costs R25 ($3.75), and it opens at 6am and closes at 6pm (10pm if you are staying at Thendele).

If you don't feel like walking the 6-hour round-trip, you can take a look at it from the top by traveling north on the R74 and taking the Oliviershoek Pass past the Sterkfontein Dam until you get to a T-junction where you turn left onto the R712, following the signs to Witsieshoek Mountain Resort. Just before the resort, take the road marked SENTINAL CAR PARK, the departure point for the steep 2-hour hike to the summit of Mont-aux-Sources via chain ladder. Anyone with a reasonable degree of fitness can complete this, a fact attested to by the unfortunate litter along the way. The views, litter notwithstanding, are stunning.

Central Drakensberg comprises four distinct areas: the beautiful **Cathedral Peak** in the north; followed by relatively populated **Champagne Valley,** where most of the

Berg resorts are based; **Injisuthi,** an isolated wilderness ideal for hikers, and at 3,459m (11,346 ft.), the Berg's highest peak; and **Giant's Castle,** famous for its San Rock paintings. The easiest mountain to climb (a 9-hr. round-trip) is Cathedral Peak (3,004m/9,853 ft.), which, conveniently, has the best hotel in the Drakensberg at its feet. The more hard-core hiker in search of solitude should opt for **Giant's Castle Game Reserve,** where the Injisuthi and (relatively luxurious) Giant's Castle camps serve as the departure point for numerous trails, serviced by overnight huts and caves. The reserve is open daily April through September from 6am to 6pm, and October through March from 5am to 7pm; admission to Giant's Castle is R25 ($3.75) per person, to Injisuthi R20/$3 per person. Initially established to protect the eland, Africa's largest antelope, the Giant's Castle reserve is today one of the few places where you'll see the rare **lammergeyer,** or "bearded vulture" (occurring only here and in the Himalayan foothills). Visitors keen to spot the lammergeyer—thought to be an evolutionary link between the vulture and the eagle—should visit the **Lammergeyer Hide** ✷ (© **036/353-3616;** www.drakensberg-tourism.com; R115/$17 per person, minimum four persons; R400/$60, maximum six persons; May–Sept only; advance reservations are essential). Visitors are driven in a four-wheel-drive to the hide early in the morning, and meat and bones are laid out to attract the birds.

WHERE TO STAY & DINE

Hikers wanting to overnight in the mountains must book their huts and caves through the KwaZulu-Natal Wildlife office closest to the trail; the camps below are the best bases for walking—hikes start literally from your front door. *Note:* There is an entry fee (R25/$3.75) into all the parks.

If you don't like hotels, **Cathedral Peak** is a comfortable good-value alternative; using the Drakensberg caves as their departure point, KZN Wildlife developed **Didima Camp** ✷ in 2002, with each of the 63 comfortably outfitted two-bed chalets shaped to resemble a cave (R720/$107 double). Should you wish to self-cater, there are also two four-bed chalets and a three-bedroom lodge; all units are equipped with satellite TV and fireplaces. There is also a restaurant, bar, and lounge, as well as a San Art Interpretive Centre.

If you decide to visit the Ardmore Studio (on the R600, which leads to Champagne Castle), stop at **Thokozisa Mountain Café** ✷, 13km (8 miles) from Winterton (© **036/ 488-1273**), for a light meal made with organic produce; a little farther is the **Nest** (© **036/468-1068**), where filling food (roasts, cottage pie) is served in a rather fusty atmosphere. Should you wish to overnight in Champagne Valley, the old-fashioned **Champagne Castle Hotel** (© **036/468-1063;** fax 036/468-1306; www.champagne castle.co.za; also off the R600; R410–R715/$61–$107, depending on the season) is closest to the mountains and enjoys the best views, though it's nowhere as remote or charming as Cathedral Peak.

Giant's Castle (see below) is one of KZN Wildlife's flagship rest camps, but if you'd prefer to stay in the lap of luxury and visit the San paintings at Main Caves as a day visitor, **Hartford House** (© **033/263-2713;** www.hartford.co.za; from R880/$131 double) in nearby Mooi River is one of the top country lodges in South Africa. The historic homestead and luxuriously appointed cottages are absolutely beautiful, and the cuisine, prepared by Jackie Cameron, is superb.

Cathedral Peak ✷✷✷ *Kids*   This is without a doubt the best option in the Drakensberg. The only hotel situated in its own valley, at the base of the mountains within the Natal Parks' protected area, it offers great views, comfortable rooms, a super-friendly staff, and a relaxed atmosphere. Even getting here is a good experience, on a road that provides charming vignettes of rural bliss. Book a luxury room; they cost very little more and are the most modern, with French doors opening onto the gardens, and some with excellent views of the mountains. The varied facilities also make this one of the best family resorts in the country. Trails start from the hotel, and maps are provided. The 11km (6.75-mile) Rainbow Gorge round-trip is recommended. Meals are huge buffets with a large variety of dishes. Some are exceptionally tasty; others suffer from standing around. But there is at least something for everyone, including finicky kids.

P.O. Winterton, KwaZulu-Natal 3340. © **036/488-1888.** Fax 036/488-1889. www.cathedralpeak.co.za. 90 units. R1,090–R1,140 ($163–$170) double; R1,370–R2,850 ($204–$425) suite. All rates include dinner and breakfast. Children under 10 sharing R250–R390 ($37–$58). AE, DC, MC, V. All routes clearly signposted from Winterton. **Amenities:** Dining room; bar; pool; (9-hole) golf; tennis; babysitting; hiking; bowling; squash; volleyball; horseback riding; helicopter trips. *In room:* TV.

Giant's Castle 🐾 The camp's proximity to the Lammergeyer Hide ensures its popularity, but the camp itself is one of the best in the KZN Wildlife stable. Comprising 37 comfortable two-bed self-catering cottages (equipped with cutlery, crockery, bedding, and fireplaces); a private, upmarket six-person lodge (chef included); four larger two-bedroom chalets; and four three-bedroom chalets; as well as the three-bedroom Rock Lodge, which has a truly exceptional and private setting, Giant's Castle is definitely worth including on your Drakensberg itinerary. All units are well equipped for self-catering, but a fully licensed restaurant and bar with viewing deck make it unnecessary. A shop offers basic provisions, but visitors planning to self-cater should stock up before arriving.

Bookings through KwaZulu-Natal Wildlife (see "Visitor Information," above). Direct © **036/353-3718.** 44 units, consisting of 2- and 4-bed chalets, 6-bed cottages, and a 6-bed lodge. From R630–R692 ($94–$103) double; R1,998 ($298) lodge. AE, MC, V. **Amenities:** Restaurant; bar; shop; San paintings; lammergeier hide; filling station.

Thendele Hutted Camp 🐾🐾 Situated deep within the Royal Natal National Park, with awesome views of the Amphitheatre, these units enjoy the best location of all the KwaZulu-Natal Wildlife camps, but the fact that the camp has no restaurant could be a drawback. There's a shop with basic provisions, but for fresh supplies, stock up in Bergville. Another option will be the restaurant at the Orion Mount-au-Sources hotel, which is about 15 minutes away, but note that you must get back to camp before 10pm, when the gates close. Upper camp has slightly more modern units, but for totally unobstructed views of the Amphitheatre, book cottage no. 1 or 2, or the wonderfully situated three-bed lodge—they're more expensive (more bedrooms) but worth the extra money.

Reservations through KwaZula-Natal Wildlife (see "Visitor Information," above). Direct © **036/438-6411.** 29 units, consisting of 2- and 4-bed bungalows, 2- and 4-bed cottages, and a 6-bed lodge. From R600–R910 ($90–$136) double. AE, MC, V.

10

Thundering World Wonder: Victoria Falls & Vicinity

When explorer David Livingstone became the first white man to set eyes on the falls, he famously described the crashing waters as exuding such power that they must have been "gazed upon by angels in their flight," and promptly named them for his queen. A century and a half later, the might and influence of the British crown has waned, but the waters of the Zambezi River continue to draw travelers to witness the spectacle as they plummet some 100m (328 ft.; twice the height of Niagara) into the Batoka Gorge.

Straddling the western border between the beautiful, poverty-stricken states of Zimbabwe and Zambia, Victoria Falls is justifiably called one of the Wonders of the Natural World, and spans almost 2km (a little more than 1 mile), making it the largest show of its kind on earth. The sight of more than 9 million liters of water crashing down into the Batoka Gorge is one not easily forgotten; on a clear day, the veil of roaring spray can be seen from up to 80km (50 miles) away, and the rain forest that clings to the cliffs opposite the falls in the Victoria Falls National Park is nourished by this perennial spray. It is this phenomenon that gave the falls its local name: *Mosi-Oa-Tunya*—literally, "the smoke that thunders."

People come here not only to immerse themselves in the spectacle of the falls, but also to partake in the varied adventure activities, from bungee jumping off the bridge between Zimbabwe and Zambia to surfing the most commercially challenging rapids in the world—not for nothing has this area been dubbed the adrenaline capital of southern Africa.

If, however, your idea of the ideal Vic Falls trip is to soak up the scenery and then simply return to your lodge and kick back with a gin and tonic, admiring the bushveld savanna while watching elephant and crocodile patrolling the great Zambezi, rest easy: Accommodations on both sides of the falls will provide this—and more.

1 Orientation

VISITOR INFORMATION & TOUR COMPANIES

In Zambia With tourism to the falls a growing concern, the **Zambia National Tourism Board** is doing its best to maintain an up-to-date website (www.zambia tourism.com). The largest operator, specializing in the full spectrum of adventure activities as well as transfers on both sides of the falls, is **Safari Par Excellence** (© 260\3/32-0606; www.saf-par.co.za). The Zambia office is located at Zambezi Waterfront Lodge, located off Mosi-Oa-Tunya Road, halfway between Livingstone and the Vic Falls bridge; if you're traveling from South Africa, contact the local representative, **Maplanga Africa** (© 27/11/794-1446; www.maplanga.co.za), in advance.

Tips **Country Codes**

This chapter contains phone numbers for three countries. So that you'll know which country each is in, all phone numbers in this chapter start with the country code as well as the local code. Phone numbers starting with **263** are in Zimbabwe, those starting with **260** are in Zambia, and those beginning with **27** are in South Africa. The Zimbabwean telephone exchange is temperamental (make that hair-tearingly frustrating), and you will find that at certain times of the day it is impossible to get through to any number you dial. E-mail, strangely, almost always works, although addresses change frequently.

If you're considering a more substantial safari adventure into Zambia (highly recommended, by the way—the country is relatively undiscovered and the bush truly wild), you should consider contacting the London-based **Zambia Safari & Travel Company** (www.zambezi.com).

In Zimbabwe Poor tourist numbers in the village of Victoria Falls means that hotel staff and private operators will bend over backward to assist you (this in no way includes staff at **Victoria Falls Publicity Association,** however, who are likely to be on lunch break at any time). For the best advice, try the travel and adventure center at **Ilala Lodge** (see "Where to Stay & Dine," later in this chapter), the efficient **Backpacker's Bazaar,** Shop 5, Victoria Falls Centre (© **263/13/45828;** backpack@africa online.co.zw or bazaar@mweb.co.zw), or **Shearwater Adventures,** Sopers Arcade, Parkway Drive (© **263/13/44-471** or 263/13/43-392; www.shearwateradventures.com).

For more essential information on Vic Falls, including getting there, travel documents, health, and more, see chapter 2.

GETTING THERE
BY PLANE
From Botswana Victoria Falls is a convenient place to end a tour of the Okavango Delta and Chobe in Botswana; the easiest way to get there is to charter a flight to Kasane (gateway to Chobe) and then arrange for a road transfer: Kasane is no more than a 40-minute drive from the falls. Alternatively, have your charter company fly you to Livingstone, the town nearest the falls on the Zambian side, from Maun or Kasane.

From Johannesburg With the majority of visitors now more likely to arrive on the Zambian side of the falls, the most convenient connection is with Nationwide Air, which flies daily directly from Johannesburg to Livingstone. Alternatively, catch the daily British Airways flight to Victoria Falls International Airport (even if you're heading for the Zambian side, it's relatively easy to arrange a transfer and only an hour away; see "Visas," under "Fast Facts: Victoria Falls & Livingstone," below). South Africa Airways also flies this route, but at press time at a higher rate. See "Getting There," in chapter 2, for contact details.

Most hotels offer a complimentary shuttle from the airport; arrange this in advance. If you have to make a visa payment at the airport in Zimbabwe, make sure you have the correct amount or you will be given change in Z$ (see "Money Matters," below).

Please note that you will have to pay a US$30 departure tax when you leave Zimbabwe; make sure that this is included in your ticket, or have the cash on you.

BY TRAIN

If you fancy chugging to the falls in style, consider the **Shongololo Express** "Southern Cross Adventure," a 16-day train tour from Johannesburg, with days spent touring sites in Swaziland, Mozambique, Kruger, Zimbabwe, Livingstone, and Botswana's Chobe National Park (© **27/11/781-4616;** www.shongololo.com; US$2,685–US$5,653 per person).

GETTING AROUND

Because hiring a car is impractical and taxis outside towns are few and far between, the most convenient way to get around is to have your hotel or lodge arrange transfers, or book a hotel within walking distance of the falls (there are a number of options in Vic Falls Village on the Zimbabwean side, and the Royal Livingstone and Zambian Sun are within ambling on the Zambian side). **Safari Par Excellence** (see "Visitor Information & Tour Companies," above) offers prearranged transfers anywhere, as well as a shuttle service from both airports and Victoria Falls Village to their Waterfront Lodge (on the Zambian side), where many of the adventure activities take place.

Victoria Falls Village is a very small town, with most attractions (including the falls) within walking distance or, at worst, a short taxi ride away. Taxis are relatively cheap (make sure you negotiate the price upfront), but almost all of the hotels and lodges offer a shuttle service to the falls and around town. Biking is a great way to get around; some of the hotels have bicycles for loan or should at least be able to point you in the direction of a decent rental agency (there are a number of options in Park Way Drive in Vic Falls Village). Cycling from Vic Falls Village to Livingstone, the nearest town on the Zambian side, should take you about an hour. Renting a car is unnecessary and, with the fluctuating fuel prices (increases of 100% are not uncommon) and ongoing fuel shortages, risky; so it's far better to take advantage of the numerous outfits offering overnight safaris in appropriate vehicles within Zimbabwe, as well as to

---

Tips Money Matters

Exchange rates within Zimbabwe fluctuate according to the whims and fancies of aging President Robert Mugabe, and bank rates in no way reflect the full devaluation of the Z$ (for example, the real value of US$1 at press time was believed to be around Z$13,000, yet Zimbabwean banks supplied local currency at a rate of US$1 to Z$6,500). Because nearly every rate is quoted in US$ and many operators don't accept credit cards, it is imperative that you carry foreign currency on your trip to Zimbabwe. Visitors are advised not to exchange foreign currency because almost any foreign currency (US$, pounds, rands) will translate into several hundred thousand Zimbabwean dollars, which will not only be difficult to carry, but are ultimately worth little. For the same reason, use your credit card in Zimbabwe only if you're being charged in US$, or you may be charged at the undervalued bank rate. Don't let the bank rate tempt you into changing money in black-market dealings, however—at best, you'll wind up with a fistful of newspaper; at worst, in jail.

Tips **The Best Times to Come**

The falls are most impressive from January to April after the summer rains, when up to 700,000 million cubic liters (182,000 million gal.) per minute rush over the 100m-high (328-ft.) lip into the gorge below. The spray can become so thick during this time, however, that it obscures the view. From May, nights can be cold, but it starts to warm up by the end of August. By September and October, at the end of the dry season, the flow is down to about 3%, but the view is clearest.

Zambia, Botswana, and Namibia. If you remain determined to go it alone, **Budget** (© 263/13/42-243) usually offers the best rates, or book a four-wheel-drive from **United Touring Company,** 7 Park Way (© 263/13/44-267, -772, or -297). United Touring also offers information on out-of-town transfers.

BY BOAT
Breakfast, lunch, bird-watching, and sunset river cruises are operated by a number of companies. All cruises take place on the calmer, game-rich waters above the falls and are usually in large, twin-deck boats—a wonderful way to enjoy the water wildlife, such as hippos, elephants, and aquatic birds, though you'll probably also see plenty of other tourists. One of the oldest operators is **Dabula,** represented by the South African–based **African Adrenalin** safari company (© 27/11/888-4037; www.african adrenalin.co.za). Sunset cruises cost, on average, US$25 to US$35; shop around for the best prices. If you're averse to crowds, it's worth inquiring about the cruises offered on smaller (maximum eight people), shallower, propeller-free **"jet boats";** they're a bit more expensive but quieter, and can explore places larger boats can't get to. (Also see "Canoe Safaris," later in this chapter.)

BY TRAIN
A 1922 Class Ten steam locomotive, operated by **Victoria Falls Safari Express** (© 263/13/42229; www.steamtrain.co.zw), crosses the mighty Zambezi via the Victoria Falls Bridge—do the bridge run for US$51 to US$58, or travel between Victoria Falls and Livingstone for US$126, including lunch or dinner. Booking is essential—most trips are confirmed only with 20 clients.

FAST FACTS: **Victoria Falls & Livingstone**

Banks Almost everyone prefers foreign currency, and the bank exchange rate in Zimbabwe is never an accurate reflection of the devaluation of the Z$ (see "Money Matters," above). If you really do need local currency in Victoria Falls, there are a few local banks along Livingstone Way. Try **Zimbank, Barclays,** or **Standard Chartered.** Bank hours are usually Monday to Tuesday and Thursday to Friday from 8am to 3pm (Zimbank stays open till 4pm), Wednesday 8am to 1pm, and Saturday 8 to 11:30am. On the Zambian side, you can buy **kwacha** (Zambian currency) at most hotels, or make use of one of the facilities (including an ATM) at The Falls casino and entertainment center, near the border.

Business Hours Shops are generally open Monday through Saturday from 8am to 5pm (some close Sat evening), and Sunday mornings. Activity centers and markets are open daily; many close only when the last traveler leaves.

Climate The most comfortable temperatures are between April and September, but this is not necessarily the best time to view the falls. See "The Best Times to Come," above.

Crime Despite the land-grab crisis elsewhere in Zimbabwe, the falls remain largely unaffected and relatively safe. Following the fatal stabbing of a visitor in January 2003, hoteliers in Victoria Falls instituted a Tourism Police service, with guards patrolling the main drag. Avoid petty crime by not flashing valuables, and stay in groups, particularly at night; also stay clear of deserted areas, including the banks of the Zambezi. Bear in mind that Livingstone is a much larger town than Victoria Falls, and many people live here to cash in on tourists; be alert and don't walk around alone.

Currency See "Money," in chapter 2.

Doctor **In Livingstone:** Contact Dr. Shafik, 49 Akapelwa St. (© **260/3/32-1130** or -1320). **In Victoria Falls:** Contact Dr. Nyoni at the **Victoria Falls Surgery,** West Dr., off Park Way (© **263/13/43356;** Mon–Fri 9:15am–4:30pm, Sat 9:15am–12:30pm, Sun 10–11am; after hours © **263/13/43380** or 263/11/404949).

Drugstore Drugstores are called chemists or pharmacies. **In Livingstone:** Visit **Moore Chemist** on Akapelwa Street (© **260/3/32-1640**). **In Victoria Falls: Victoria Falls Pharmacy** is located in Phumula Centre, Park Way (© **263/13/44403;** Mon–Fri 9am–6pm, Sat–Sun 9am–1pm). A drugstore in the Kingdom Hotel is open daily.

Electricity Electricity in southern Africa runs on 220/230V, 50Hz AC, and sockets in Zimbabwe and Zambia take flat-pinned plugs. Bring an adapter/voltage converter; note that some bush camps have no electricity.

Embassies & Consulates All offices are located in capital cities of Harare (Zimbabwe) and Lusaka (Zambia); if you have any diplomatic problems, speak to your hotel manager and ask him/her to contact your country's local representative.

Emergencies Your hotel or lodge is your best bet for the safest medical and emergency care. Alternatively, contact **Medical Air Rescue Service,** a 24-hour emergency evacuation service (© **263/13/44764**). For an **ambulance,** call © **994;** for the **police,** call © **995;** to report a **fire,** call © **993;** for **general emergencies,** call © **999.**

Health **Malaria** Consult your physician before leaving about starting a course of antimalarial prophylactics. If you suspect you have malaria, get to a doctor immediately for a test. For more information, see "Health, Safety & Insurance," in chapter 2.

Language English is widely spoken in the tourist regions of both Zimbabwe and Zambia.

Taxes Sales tax is 15% in Zimbabwe; 17.5% VAT is charged in Zambia—check that this is included in the price.

Telephone This chapter contains codes for three countries. See "Country Codes," above. For tips on making international and local calls, see chapter 2.

Time Zone Both Zimbabwe and Zambia are 5 hours ahead of GMT, or 7 hours ahead of Eastern Standard Time.

Tipping For a meal, leave 10%; for small services such as hotel porters carrying your bags, tip US$1 to US$3 or the equivalent.

Visas Note also that if you intend to fly into Victoria Falls Village, only to transfer by road to a lodge on the Zambian side of the falls (less than 1-hr. drive), these lodges can usually obtain a visa waiver (a savings of US$40 for U.S. citizens, £35 for U.K. citizens, and US$25 for others). Passport details must be given to the lodge at least 48 hours prior to arrival. If you are based at Victoria Falls, you will need a multiple-entry visa if you also want to make the worthwhile trip to view them from the Zambian side (at present US$45; £70 for U.K. citizens); a single-entry visa (US$30–US$55, depending on your nationality). For a day trip to Livingstone, purchase a day visa to Zambia for US$10 at the bridge.

Water Tap water is generally considered safe, but it's worth asking first. You're often better off drinking the bottled water provided in your hotel room, since local water is less processed and may be richer in mineral content than your stomach is used to.

Wildlife Keep your eye out for elephant and hippo when you're out walking, cycling, or canoeing—do not block their routes; it's best not to turn around, but back away slowly. When driving on highways that are part of national parkland, never speed, and keep a watchful eye out for animals emerging from the bush to cross the road. Note that baboons are a nuisance on both sides of the falls. Keep food out of sight and remember that—like all wild animals—they are unpredictable and potentially dangerous.

2 What to See & Do

The area is famous for its myriad adventure activities and offers excellent wildlife-viewing opportunities, but when all is said and done, it's the falls that are the star of the show.

SOAKING UP THE FALLS

There are two great vantage points, each offering a different angle, and it's worth covering them both, which will take at least half a day. Break your return journey by stopping for a sumptuous high tea at the Victoria Falls Hotel—a real highlight.

The Victoria Falls National Park ★★★ The Victoria Falls National Park—which some say affords the best vantage point of the falls—is a 2,340-hectare (5,780-acre) narrow strip that runs along the southern bank of the Zambezi River and protects the sensitive rain forest around the falls. You will almost certainly get drenched by the permanent spray, so rent a raincoat or umbrella at the entrance (or just relish the experience and take a change of clothes). Remember to put your camera in a waterproof bag. A clearly marked trail runs through the lush and fecund rain forest (look out for the aptly named flame lilies), with side trails leading to good viewing points of the falls. Head down the steep stairs to **Cataract View** for views of

Devil's Cataract ⭐⭐; this is also where you'll find the unremarkable statue of David Livingstone. The final viewpoint, nearest the falls bridge, is called **Danger Point**— here you can perch right on the edge of a cliff and peer down into the abyss. When the moon is full, the park stays open later so that visitors can witness the lunar rainbow formed by the spray. Not only is it a beautiful sight, but the experience is untarnished by the sounds of helicopters and microlights, which can be something of a noise nuisance during much of the day.

You don't need a guide to visit the falls. Many unofficial guides stand near the entrances, but unless you want to learn more about the rain forests (in which case, hire a guide from a reputable company), chances are that they won't be able to show you anything other than the direction of the path. Livingstone Way leads from the Victoria Falls Village directly to the entrance.

No phone. US$20 adults, children half-price. Daily 6am–6pm, later during full-moon nights, when entry is US$40.

Mosi-Oa-Tunya ⭐⭐⭐ *Value*   The Zambian side offers a more spectacular vantage point than its Zimbabwean counterpart during high water (Apr–June), when the view is less obscured by spray. Here the focus is on seeing the main gorge and Eastern Cataract; you can also walk (or scramble, rather) across to a vantage called Knife Edge, where you will stand suspended above the churning waters of Boiling Pot—a vicious rapid most rafters get to know a little too intimately. *Warning:* There are no fences on this side of the river—every year, one or two people slip on the wet rocks attempting

---

Curious about Curios? Getting Crafty about Crafts

With a long tradition of carving and weaving in the area, you will find a plethora of arts and crafts available on both sides of the falls. Besides cruising the streets of Livingstone for a relatively authentic big-town African experience, you can browse the woodwork, masks, handcrafted jewelry, sculptures, and other trinkets at the **craft market** that borders the entrance to Mosi-Oa-Tunya (off Livingstone Rd.). In Zimbabwe, shopping can be memorable for the simple persistence of cash-starved stall owners ready to part with finely crafted wood carvings, woven baskets, and traditional Zimbabwean batik fabrics for rock-bottom prices. Some salesmen will even offer to exchange their handicrafts for a pen or other such "luxury" that has become difficult to find in Zimbabwe. This can be an intimidating experience, as desperation (you may represent the only chance of a meal for weeks to come) can result in some pushy behavior and even sometimes fights between the hawkers. Another reason to stop and think before you drive prices down is the fact that cheap curios are putting pressure on the hardwood forests and may mean that these desperately poor people end up chopping down a tree for a couple of bucks. If you're into more serious articles (Zimbabwean sculptors are world-renowned for their soapstone creations), consider visiting **Falls Craft Village**, Stand 206, Soper's Crescent, off Livingstone Way (© **263/13/4309**; daily 8:30am–4:30pm), a complex consisting of the reconstructed huts of five different Zimbabwean tribes from the 19th century, with numerous shops and stalls; or **Soper's Curios**, 1911 Adam Stander Rd., Victoria Falls (© **263/13/4361**; daily 8am–6pm), which has been trading in Zimbabwean artifacts since 1911, and where you can find excellent wood and soapstone carvings, though at relatively inflated prices.

Zimbabwe

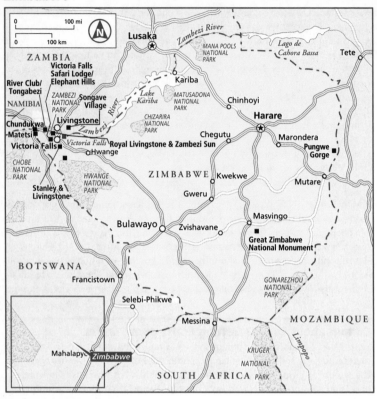

to get that extra special photograph or experience. If you don't recover your footing, the chance of survival is nil.

Entrance off Livingstone Rd. No phone. US$10. Year-round daily 6am–6pm.

VIEWING WILDLIFE

Despite the commercialism of Vic Falls Village, the falls remain surrounded by dense bush, and you can start your African safari right here. You have to venture only a few miles upstream from the river along Zambezi Drive to take a look at the **Big Tree,** a 1,500-year-old baobab (if you're lucky, you'll see elephants, too), or take a guided **Zambezi river walk** (see "Staying Active: Bush Walks," below) to view species like hippo and crocodile. **Backpacker's Bazaar** (see "Visitor Information & Tour Companies," earlier in this chapter) also arranges morning, afternoon, and night drives to Zambezi National Park, Mosi-Oa-Tunya Park, and Hwange, as well as full days in Chobe, Botswana. If you want to spend the day game-viewing in Chobe, the best tour is one that travels in a loop, allowing you to cover more terrain; **Matopo Tours** (**© 263/13/42209** or 263/91239311) in Vic Falls Village can arrange this for US$120, including lunch.

For safaris by canoe, plane, helicopter and horse- or elephant-back, see "Staying Active," below.

A BIT OF HISTORY

Scottish explorer David Livingstone may have been the first white man to view the falls, but archaeological digs show that human occupation of the area dates back 2 million years before. Much of this Stone Age evidence is on-site in the **Livingstone Museum**, Mosi-Oa-Tunya Rd., next to the post office (*C* **260/3/32-4428**)—Zambia's oldest and largest. The archaeological exhibits are augmented with historical artifacts, from ancient Tonga drums (the original telephone), to black-and-white photographs from the turn of the 20th century. If you're interested in African culture, take time out to visit the 700-year-old traditional **Mukuni Village** (off Mosi-Oa-Tunya Dr., on the way into Livingstone)—where Livingstone obtained traversing permission from Chief Mukuni in the mid-1800s. The tree under which Livingstone awaited an audience with the chief still provides shade for those wishing to do the same.

3 Staying Active

Most of the hotels will arrange reservations and give advice on activities, but for the widest range of activities listed below, visit **Safari Par Excellence** (www.safpar.com), which has branches in Zimbabwe (Phumula Centre, Park Way Dr.; *C* **263/4/70-0911**) and Zambia (Waterfront; *C* **260/3/32-1629**), and in South Africa (*C* **27/11/794-1446**); alternatively, contact **Backpacker's Bazaar** in Vic Falls Village. For details, or more options, see "Visitor Information & Tour Companies," earlier in this chapter.

ABSEILING, GORGE SWING & "FLYING FOX" Rappel down a 50m (164-ft.) drop into the Batoka Gorge, then tackle the gorge swing or traverse the "flying fox." Attached to the world's highest commercial high wire, the gorge swing allows you to experience freefall for 70m (230 ft.), then swing over the Zambezi churning 120m (394 ft.) below. "Flying fox" is one of the world's longest cable slide lines, whereupon you more or less fly, fully harnessed to the cable, above the Zambezi rapids at speeds of up to 105kmph (65 mph). Cost is US$80 for a half-day, US$95 for the full day, and you can do any activity as often as you want.

BUNGEE JUMPING The checklists of most adventure-sportsmen aren't complete until they've done the heart-stopping 111m (364-ft.) bungee off the Vic Falls Bridge, stopping about 10m (33 ft.) from the boiling waters in the Batoka Gorge. Jumps are done daily (9am–1pm and 2–5pm); the first jump costs US$75 (US$105 for tandem). Note that jumps may be delayed during the months of heavy spray (Mar–June).

BUSH WALKS "Walking with lion cubs" is a new activity in which you actually walk the bush with a lion cub between 5 and 18 months old, affording you a unique opportunity to interact with the king (in-waiting) of the jungle, accompanied by an armed guide; book through Safari Par Excellence (US$100; see above). You can do the **Zambezi River walk** (take the river path from just outside the Falls National Park fence upstream to Zambezi River Lodge) without a guide, but frankly, it's not safe to wander it on your own. **Robin Brown** (*C* **263/11-605063;** www.cansaf.com) will accompany you on a variety of expeditions, from 2-hour bush walks to 2-night walking safaris, as well as canoe safaris.

CANOE SAFARIS Canoe safaris offer a more sedate option than rafting, with the added bonus of seeing hippos, elephants, and crocodiles while you paddle the broad expanse of the Upper Zambezi. There are no (or very small) rapids on this trip, so you won't get your hair wet, though be aware that hippos do occasionally upend

> **Fun Fact** **Courtin' the Zambezi River God**
>
> Every year Nyaminyami, the Zambezi River god, claims one or two of the 40,000 lives that hurtle down his course. It is said that by wearing his serpentlike image around your neck, you will escape harm. Hundreds of hawkers in and around the falls make a living selling Nyaminyami pendants, which forever brand you as a brave warrior who has ridden the mighty Zambezi River.

canoes (in which case, your guide will whisk you aboard almost immediately). **Sunset cruises** are particularly recommended (US$35). Contact Robin (see above) or book through the one of the adventure outfits.

ELEPHANT-BACK SAFARIS 🐘 A number of companies now offer elephant-back safaris, so you might want to compare costs before booking. Safari Par Excellence, which offers rides on both sides of the falls, charges US$100 for a 2- to 3-hour amble, breaking for a light lunch along the way.

FLYING 🐘🐘🐘 Take to the skies on a microlight or ultralight flight—both are quieter than helicopter or fixed-wing flights, and you'll be sailing a great deal closer to nature (and, for that matter, the wind). Ultralights, considered marginally safer than microlights, cost US$100 for 30 minutes. **Batoka Sky** (book through any of the adventure-activity operators; see above) operates tricycle-style microlight flights from Zambia and charges US$80 for 15 minutes. You can't take a camera (if you drop it, it may stop the engine below), so Batoka has a camera attached to the wheels; your pilot will take a photograph of you at the most appropriate moment—flying past the falls.

For helicopter trips, book through an adventure center or direct with the **Zambezi Helicopter Company** (© 263/13/45806; helicopters@shearwater.co.zw; US$85 for 15 min.); for fixed-wing flights, book with **Southern Cross Aviation** (© 263/13/44618 or 263/13/44456; sca@zol.co.zw; US$65 for 25-min. scenic flight). **United Air Charter** (© 260/3/32-3095 or 263/11/407573; www.uaczam.com) offers scenic flights (US$115 for 20 min.) over the Zambezi and the falls in a vintage Tiger Moth biplane; flights leave from Livingstone International Airport.

GOLFING The 6,786-yard **Elephant Hills Intercontinental** course is at times just a stroke from the roaring Zambezi River, and the constant presence of the falls—not to mention wildlife—makes this Gary Player–designed course one of the most interesting in Africa. For details, contact Elephant Hills Intercontinental (© 263/13/44793).

HORSEBACK SAFARIS 🐎 **Zambezi Horse Trails** (© 263/13/44611) provides riders with an opportunity to get closer to game than they can on foot or in a car. Rides are led by an experienced guide with an extensive knowledge of the flora and fauna of the area, and take place on 30,000 hectares (74,100 acres) of the Matetsi River Ranch, which borders the Zambezi National Park. Experienced riders can choose among half-, full-, or multiday riding safaris (US$65–US$90). Novices are taken on a 2-hour ride (US$45) into areas where potentially dangerous animals like elephant are avoided. Alternatively, if you stay at **Chundukwa** (see below), you can hire the owner's horses for guided game-viewing trips along the river.

SKYDIVING 🐘🐘 If you think bungee-jumping is for babies, a tandem skydive—accelerating toward Victoria Falls before enjoying a restful 5-minute parachute ride—is for you. Gary Wellock of **Skydive Zimbabwe** (© 263/11/60-1340) is the person to contact; weather permitting, you'll be whisked up to 2,700m (9,000 ft.), ready for the most exciting outlook on the falls.

QUAD-BIKING   If you enjoy your adrenaline rush with the ground firmly beneath you, why not explore the terrain around the Batoka Gorge on a four-wheel motorbike? **Batoka Sky** (see above) caters to experienced riders as well as first-timers (US$55–US$115).

WHITE-WATER RAFTING ✦✦✦   Operators pride themselves on offering the best commercially run rapids in the world. You need to be reasonably fit (not only to deal with the grade 3–5 rapids, but also for the 230m/754-ft. climb out of the gorge at the end of a tiring day). You should also be a competent swimmer. Don't worry if you haven't done anything like it before—organizers offer dry-ground preparation before launching onto the water, and the safety and guiding standards are excellent; note that this does not prevent unforeseen disasters—several adventurers recently lost their lives when their raft got too close to the falls. The best time for rafting is when the water is low and the rapids impressive, in September and October. (Apr–May, when the water is particularly high, some rafting companies close altogether.) You should be aware that there *is* a certain level of danger and that the rapids claim a few lives every year, though these are usually kayakers. The safest option is to get on a boat that has an oarsman who guides you along the safest path, but the alternative, where everyone in the group has his or her own paddle, is much more fun, despite the fact that—or in large part because of it—you'll definitely end up in the water. River-boarding is the most hair-raising way to brave the rapids—alone, on a boogie board, you literally surf the waves created by a selection of grade 3–5 rapids. Most river-rafting companies offer an optional half-day rafting, half-day boarding experience. The kings of the river are **Raft Extreme** (© **260/3/32-3929;** www.raftextreme.com) and **Safari Par Excellence** (see above). Both offer trips from the Zambian side—though it's a bit of an effort to go across the border, these trips have the added advantage of including a few extra rapids, and they also begin right beneath the falls. Zambian guides are also usually the longest-serving guides and are, therefore, very familiar with what can be a dangerous river. Expect to pay US$100 for a half- or full day. Prices include lunch, drinks, and all equipment. On the Zimbabwe side, you can book your rafting or riverboarding through **Shearwater Adventures** (see earlier in this chapter)

While you're drifting down the river, keep an eye out for *taita* falcons. These rare, swift-flying birds nest in the cliffs and can sometimes be spotted from the water swooshing in and out of updrafts.

4 Where to Stay & Dine

The instability of the Zimbabwean economy and political unease has resulted in a downturn in tourism on the Zimbabwean side of the falls, while across the bridge, in Zambia, business is booming. The truth is, there is no reason for visitors to stay away from Zimbabwe's Victoria Falls Village: It is as peaceful as ever, with great accommodations options and often offering better value for money. But the suffering under Mugabe's rule is palpable. His recent Operation Murambatsvina (literally translated as "Drive Out Trash") resulted in a great many innocents, including staff working at hotels in Vic Falls Village, losing their homes and being "relocated." For most visitors flying to the falls, staying in Zambia is currently the norm.

IN ZAMBIA

If you're looking for the most authentically "Out of Africa" experience, just a stone's throw (well, a 10-min. drive) from the falls, look no further than The River Club. Note that Chundukwa's operating company, Maplanga, has several other budget properties in and around the falls worth investigating (details below).

Chundukwa *Value* Located rather a long way (30km/19 miles upstream) from Vic Falls, the rustic Chundukwa Tree Lodge comprises four stilted reed chalets that literally hang over the Zambezi River; their water-hugging position makes them ideal for birders, and elephants from the Zambezi National Park (which lies directly opposite the river) are often seen as they swim to the river islands. Chundukwa is a great place for quiet mediation, with compact, simply furnished guest rooms (very basic bathrooms, but hot running water). Owner Doug Evans is a retired Zimbabwe conservation officer with a penchant for polo cross (on polo days you can hear the horses thundering over the pitch)—you can hire his horses for guided game-viewing trips along the river.

Bookings through Maplanga, P.O. Box 2331, Honeydew 2040, South Africa. (C)/fax **27/11/794-1446.** www.maplanga. co.za. 4 units (plus self-catering bush camp). From US$250 double. Rate includes full board, airport transfer, and one activity per day. MC, V. **Amenities:** Dining room; bar; pool; boat trips; horseback riding; fishing; trips to Victoria Falls and various adventure activities.

The River Club *★★★* A neighbor to Tongabezi (see below), with even better views, this romantic retreat on the banks of the Zambezi is the most overtly colonial of the Zambian lodges, and a top choice. (Even its history smacks of "white mischief": The property's original owner killed his wife after she allegedly had an affair with a local priest.) Set amid wonderful gardens, the main house has been rebuilt but is filled with period pieces that evoke a distinctly Edwardian atmosphere, and is managed by a delightful Anglo-French couple. Meals are elegant affairs, particularly dinners, when you're waited on hand and foot by staff in white uniforms and red fez hats, after which you may choose to take a drink in the library, partake of a game of moonlit croquet, or flop into your huge bed, romantically swathed in mosquito nets. During the day, enjoy a rejuvenating riverside massage treatment. The open-sided split-level bungalows are built overlooking the Zambezi; the Victorian bathrooms, which are almost within touching distance of the river, are a real highlight. For the most spectacular views, request the "Edward" guest suite.

Bookings through S.A.: (C) **27/11/883-0747.** Lodge: 260/97-771032. Fax 27/11/883-0911. www.wilderness-safaris.com. 10 units. High season (July–Oct) US$730 double; midseason (Apr–June and Nov) US$540; low season US$390. Rates are all-inclusive except for premium-brand alcohol imports. All adventure activities arranged at extra cost. MC, V. **Amenities:** Dining room; lounge; pool; bush golf; laundry; library; sunset cruises; trips to Mosi-Oa-Tunya National Park, Livingstone and Railway Museum, croc farm, Jewish tour and local African village; croquet; boule; canoeing; fishing. *In room:* Hair dryer, safe, fans.

Royal Livingstone *★★* **& Zambezi Sun** Within spitting distance of the border, on the banks of the Zambezi, is the massive Sun International hotel and entertainment complex, incorporating the two hotels as well as **The Activity Centre,** an adult playground with a small casino, shops, eateries, offices, and banking facilities. The single biggest reason to book into this flashy resort is its proximity to the falls—the park entrance is within easy walking distance (100m/328 ft. from the Zambezi Sun), so you can visit as often as you want. The downside is that they're often filled to capacity with tour groups, who share access to all facilities, so there's little chance for privacy other than in your room—all the more reason to book at the more exclusive Royal Livingstone, where all accommodations overlook the river and are more luxurious and spacious (book the second floor for better views). Service levels at Livingstone are also excellent—even if you arrive in a dilapidated taxi from Kasane, looking as if you've lived in the bush for a week, you'll be treated like royalty. (For better value, not to mention a more memorable experience, book The River Club; see below.)

Mosi-Oa-Tunya Rd., P.O. Box 60151, Livingstone, Zambia. ℂ 260/3/32-1122. www.suninternational.com. Zambezi Sun (212 units) from US$400 double; Royal Livingstone (173 units) from US$600 double. Rates include breakfast. AC, DC, MC, V. **Amenities:** 2 restaurants; 2 pools; Activity Centre (see above); transfers; laundry; 10% discount on all adventure bookings done through hotel; sundowner deck. *In room:* A/C, TV, minibar (Livingstone only), hair dryer, safe, tea- and coffee-making facilities.

Tongabezi 🐾🐾   Situated 20km (12 miles) upstream from the falls, and overlooking a broad expanse of the Zambezi, Tongabezi Lodge is set in a grove of African ebony trees. Guests can choose to stay in one of the thatched cottages, each with a private veranda overlooking the river, but you should ideally reserve one of the huge "houses"—particularly **Tree House** 🐾🐾🐾, which has recently been made over; carved out of the rock, it is completely open to the elements, the mighty Zambezi River just meters from your bedroom and sumptuous bathroom (with tubs low enough to feel as if you're almost part of the river). For the ultimate in romance, ask for a "sampan dinner" (included in the rate), where guests can indulge in a private candlelit dinner on a raft, and waiters bring the courses by canoe. For those who don't mind roughing it a bit (flushing toilets and running cold water, but hot bucket showers and candles only), a night at the satellite **Sindabezi Island Camp** is a must. Located on an island 3km (1¾ miles) downstream, the five small thatched chalets with roll-down canvas walls have wonderful views of the river and its banks.

During the low-water season (July–Mar), Tongabezi also organizes trips to and champagne lunches on **Livingstone Island** 🐾🐾🐾, perched right on the edge of the falls. They can also arrange for you to overnight here—an unbelievable privilege, especially during full moon when there's a lunar rainbow.

Private Bag 31, Livingstone. ℂ 260/3/32-3235 or 260/3/32-4450. Fax 260/3/32-3224. www.tongabezi.com. Tongabezi 9 units. Sindabezi 4 units. Tongabezi cottages US$628–US$800 double; Tongabezi houses US$778–US$996 double; Sindabezi chalets US$658 double. Rates are fully inclusive (excluding premium wines, champagne, and liqueurs). MC, V. No children under 7 at Tongabezi; no children under 14 at Sindabezi. **Amenities:** Dining areas; bar; pool; (grass) tennis; laundry; library; bush/gorge walks; canoeing; fishing; bird walks; game drives; visit to Zambian side of falls; sunrise and sunset boat cruises; village tours.

IN ZIMBABWE

On the Zimbabwean side, **Matetsi Water Lodge** should top your list if you'd like to combine the falls with some serious game-viewing, while the **Victoria Falls Hotel** is best for convenience (it's almost on top of the falls!) and the glam and old-world charm of its public spaces. If you want to score a good deal, **Elephant Hills Resort,** located 4km (2½ miles) from the falls, with good service and a wide range of amenities (including the area's only 18-hole golf course, designed by Gary Player), is very eager for your business, so don't be afraid to request an elephantine discount. Rooms in the River View Wing are your best option (ℂ **263/13/44793;** www.suninternational. com; currently from US$278 double).

Ilala Lodge 🐾   This small, pleasant thatched hotel offers midrange accommodations an easy 10-minute walk from the falls. It's put together very much along an African theme, with thatched roofs, colonial-era paintings and fabrics, cane furniture, and views of the lawn and thick bush of the National Park. Guest rooms are—like those at Victoria Falls Hotel (reviewed below)—small. The hotel is not completely fenced in, so don't be surprised if you hear the sounds of elephants feeding outdoors at night. Best of all, the food at the **Palm Restaurant** enjoys a good reputation and is full most nights of the week—even if you don't stay here, it's worth taking a table (see below).

411 Livingstone Way. Box 18, Victoria Falls. ☎ 263/13/44737/8/9, or 888/227-8311 from the U.S. Fax 263/13/44417. 32 units. US$294–US$420 double, including breakfast. Children under 12 pay US$63 if sharing with parents. DC, MC, V. **Amenities:** Restaurant; bar; pool; gift shop; room service (7am–10pm); laundry; travel, adventure and safari center. *In room:* TV, hair dryer.

Matetsi Water Lodge ★★★ *Value* Located 40km (25 miles) upstream from the falls, on 73,500 hectares (181,545 acres) with access to the adjacent Zambezi National Park, this highly recommended lodge comprises three small, separate camps (each with six suites), built right on the Zambezi River. A stay here really combines a safari experience with a visit to the falls, which is at least 45 minutes away, so this is not an ideal choice if you're planning to spend only 1 night. Previously a hunting-concession area, Matetsi is now home to herds of buffalo, elephant, and sable antelope, as well as predators like lion, hyena, and leopard, all of which range freely throughout the vast, unfenced area. Each privately located and luxurious suite—with teak fittings, canopied king-size beds, enormous bathrooms—has its own plunge pool and deck overlooking the river and its wildlife (similar accommodations in South Africa and Botswana would cost double). Morning and evening meals are served on teak decks beside the river, under ancient trees, while wholesome lunches are brought to your chalet in specially designed wicker baskets. Guests enjoy access to morning and evening game drives, boat cruises, canoeing, fishing, and guided bush walks. (Note that there are plans to reopen the slightly less glamorous **Matetsi Safari Camp** at the end of 2005; here luxury en-suite tented accommodations overlook an open grassland that attracts a variety of game.)

Reservations through CC Africa: Private Bag x27, Benmore 2010, S.A. ☎ 27/11/809-4300. Fax 27/11/809-4315. www.ccafrica.com. Water Lodge 18 units. Safari Camp 12 units. High season (July–Oct) US$500 double; low season US$410. Rates include all meals, all game activities, shuttle, and laundry. MC, V. **Amenities:** Dining room/bar; room service; babysitting; laundry; morning and evening game drives; boat cruises; canoeing; fishing; guided bush walks. *In room:* A/C, minibar, hair dryer, safe.

Stanley & Livingstone ★★★ Tranquil, luxurious, elegant, but slightly soulless, the Stanley & Livingstone offers the most expensive and exclusive accommodations in Zimbabwe. Each of the 16 luxurious, ultraspacious suites opens onto an elegantly furnished, private veranda; decor consists of elegant period furnishings and colonial-style fittings like ball-and-claw bathtubs. Only 10 minutes from the falls and 2 minutes from Zambezi National Park, it's located in its own 2,400-hectare (5,928-acre) private reserve (the restaurant and bar overlook a water hole that attracts a variety of species), with a choice of game drives, bush walks, or fishing part of the package. Service and dining are excellent. It's certainly a good option if you like opulence and prefer colonial styling, but do consider Matetsi's less uptight Water Lodge camp before booking here.

Reservations: Rani Africa, Box 2682, Witkoppen 2068. ☎ 27/11/467-1277. Fax 27/11/465-8764. www.raniresorts. com. 16 units. Bed and breakfast US$588 double; all-inclusive rate US$858 double. AE, MC, DC, V. Children under 12 by arrangement only and pay 50% if sharing with parents. **Amenities:** Dining room; bar; pool; complimentary shuttle to village and airport; room service; laundry; game drives; bush walks; fishing; canoeing; shop; wine cellar. *In room:* A/C, TV, minibar, safe, tea- and coffee-making facilities, scale.

Victoria Falls Hotel ★★ Having entered its second century of operation, this colonial-style hotel is the most genteel accommodations option in the village. It's located in a prime spot overlooking the Victoria Falls Bridge, within walking distance of the falls. A member of Leading Hotels of the World, it was built in 1904 in the imperial manner for Cecil Rhodes's Cape-to-Cairo railway. The hotel is all columns, arched loggias, and broad verandas, while wall-mounted hunting trophies and decorous chandeliers suggest the overstated opulence of a bygone age; only recently have collar-and-tie dining rules been relaxed. If your budget can handle the extra cost, the deluxe rooms (with views of the spray and bridge) and suites are definitely worth it; standard rooms are tiny. Enjoy drinks and high tea served on a generous, sweeping terrace with excellent views—a must even if you're not staying here. A path through the gardens leads to the falls, and a 30-minute trail descends into the gorge to the river. David Livingstone enthusiasts should inquire about the excellent talks given by Russell Gammon. Service is well meaning, but it's not uncommon to wait 20 minutes for a beer. A conference center is, unfortunately, in the making.

Mallet Dr., Box 10, Victoria Falls. (*) 263/13/44751. Fax 263/13/42354. S.A. central reservations (*) 27/11/886-3430/1. www.victoriafallshotel.com. 180 units. Standard room US$326–US$358 double; deluxe room US$366–US$408 double; suite US$549–US$816. Rates include breakfast. AE, DC, MC, V. **Amenities:** 3 restaurants; 2 bars; various lounges; pool; tennis; spa; playground; salon; room service; babysitting; laundry; chapel; reading room; library with faxed international newspapers; Internet. *In room:* A/C, TV, hair dryer.

Victoria Falls Safari Lodge (*)(*) Just 3km (1¾ miles) from the village, this hotel is set high on a plateau that overlooks the plains of the Zambezi National Park and is surrounded by views of unspoiled bush. Constructed on 11 levels, much like an open-plan thatched treehouse, the colorful interiors feature ethnic touches, like African drums hanging from the ceiling. Overlooking a very productive water hole, the balcony has been described as one of the best places in Africa to breakfast, with everything from elephant to buffalo quenching their thirst in full view. All rooms have glass doors that open onto private west-facing balconies, offering views of the bushveld sunsets; standard rooms are a bit cramped, so opt for a deluxe unit (or the privacy and space of Matetsi). Beds are draped with mosquito nets and covered in crisp white linen; bathrooms are small but have tubs and showers. Guests must be accompanied by guides when walking outside the perimeters of the resort, a reminder of how close to nature you are. Nearby, families can opt for a two-bedroom self-catering chalet at **Lokhutula Lodges** (US$120–US$200), part of a timeshare development. This is also where you'll find **The Boma.**

Squire Cummings Rd., Box 29, Victoria Falls. (*) **263/13/32014.** Fax 263/13/3205. Bookings through RSA: (*) **27/31/310-3333.** www.threecities.co.za. 72 units; Lokhutula Lodges 37 units. High season (July–Dec) US$370–$440 double; low season US$308–US$370 double. AE, DC, MC, V. **Amenities:** 2 restaurants; bar; 2 pools; beauty/health spa; game room; activities desk; complimentary shuttle to the falls; 2 gift shops; room service; babysitting; laundry; library; TV lounge; game drives; nature walks; animal hide. *In room:* A/C, minibar (suites and deluxe rooms only), hair dryer, safe, tea- and coffee-making facility.

11

Original Eden: Botswana

by Keith Bain

Largely untouched by human hand, Botswana is home to one of the world's great natural phenomena, the tranquil Okavango Delta, a 15,000-sq.-km (5,850-sq.-mile) inland flood plain that fans out in the northwestern corner of the country, creating a paradise of palms, papyrus, and crystal-clear channels and backwaters. Set in a massive sea of desert sand, this fragile wonderland of waterways, islands, and forests is an oasis for wildlife, drawn to its life-giving waters from the surrounding thirstlands. Here, the evening air is filled with the sounds of birds calling, frogs trilling, and antelope rustling in the reeds. Wildebeest, hartebeest, buffalo, and zebra roam the islands; elephants wade across channels guarded by hippos and crocs; and predators rule the night.

But it is not only animals and birds that are attracted to this huge, verdant oasis. Because the area is so sensitive, the Botswana government operates a policy of low-volume, high-income tourism, making southern Africa's premier wilderness destination a pricey holiday destination—but this doesn't stop people from flocking to one of the world's most game-rich and unspoiled wilderness areas. To service these visitors, scores of safari companies have been established in and around the delta, particularly in the Moremi Game Reserve, situated in the northeastern sector of the delta. Because it is both expensive and complicated to travel independently in Botswana (huge

distances are involved and the road network is poor) and almost impossible in the delta itself, visitors are advised to contact one of these companies to arrange their trip. Most offer full-package holidays that cover the delta and surrounds, and will organize everything for you, including flights, transfers, accommodations, and game-viewing trips.

Bear in mind that if you do a whistle-stop visit, flying in one night and out the next day, you will be disappointed. The delta has its own unique moods and rhythms, and a varying landscape: To experience these, you should plan to spend 3 nights here, preferably 4.

But there is more to Botswana than the delta. To the northeast lies Chobe National Park, a 12,000-sq.-km (4,680-sq.-mile) home to some 100,000 elephants. To the southeast are the spectacular Makgadikgadi and Nxai pans, where the space is so vast that, it is said, you can hear the stars sing. Most safari companies include the Chobe and its surrounds on their itineraries, and some venture south into the endless horizons of the Kalahari pans.

Like so many of Africa's wilderness areas, the delta is under threat from human need. A shortage of good grazing on adjacent lands makes the lush grass in the delta a standing temptation to stock farmers, especially in times of drought. The demands of Botswana's diamond-mining industry and the ever-expanding town of Maun (principal jumping-off point for the delta), both thirsty for water, pose an ongoing threat to the delta's precious liquid reserves, as does the proposed dam at Popa Falls, Namibia. All of which means that, if you want to experience the untamed Africa of our ancestors, a trip to Botswana should enjoy the highest priority.

1 Orientation

VISITOR INFORMATION

Botswana's **Department of Tourism** has a website (www.botswanatourism.org), but not all of the information is up-to-date. You can e-mail (dwnp@gov.bw) or call the department at ℂ 267/395-3024, but far better to contact one of the **Botswana Tourism Representatives:** U.S. travelers should contact **Kartagener Associates Inc.,** 631 Commack Rd., Suite 1A, Commack, NY 11726 (ℂ **631/858-1270;** fax 631/858-1279; www.kainyc.com); U.K. travelers should contact **Southern Skies Marketing** (ℂ **44/1344/298-980;** www.southern-skies.co.uk). For more information on the region, often aimed at budget or self-drive travelers, read some of the useful features published in *Getaway,* Africa's largest-circulation travel magazine; look them up on **www.getawaytoafrica.com** and click on "Botswana." If you're considering a self-drive safari, you will need to contact the **Department of Wildlife and National Parks** (ℂ **267/397-1405;** www.botswanatourism.org). For essential information on Botswana, including getting there, travel documents, health, and more, see chapter 2.

GETTING THERE

BY PLANE   **Air Botswana** (www.airbotswana.co.bw; see chapter 2 for more contact details) flies directly from both Johannesburg and Cape Town to **Maun,** which is the jumping-off point for most destinations in the Okavango Delta. Prices vary greatly depending on the month you fly, but in May 2005, a return ticket from Johannesburg cost R2,760 ($412)—and from Cape Town R2,440 ($364). Most operators will arrange for you to fly into Maun and then transfer you to your delta camp by charter flight; make sure this is part of the package, or bank on paying between US$90 and US$180, depending on where in Botswana you need to be. To reach Chobe National Park (or Victoria Falls), you will fly to **Kasane,** then transfer by air or road; again, your operator or lodge should arrange this pickup.

GETTING AROUND

BY PLANE   With large wilderness areas, much of it inaccessible by car, this is the most sensible way to get around. From Maun, visitors usually join overland safari operators or fly in light aircrafts into their camps. There are many charter companies operating out of Maun: **Sefofane** (ℂ **267/686-0778**) is one of the biggest; other operators include **Mack Air** (ℂ **267/686-0675;** mack.air@info.bw) and **Delta Air** (ℂ **267/686-1682**). Each leg of your journey will cost upward of US$90 (one-way). Unless you're claustrophobic, this is a very exciting way to travel: Views of the delta and Botswana's untamed wilderness are spectacular. The plane (which may be anything from a 6- to a 12-seater) often has to buzz the airstrip to clear it of herds of grazing animals, and the "departure/arrivals" lounge may be a bench under a tree.

BY CAR   Traveling under your own steam at your own pace could be the adventure of a lifetime, but you won't necessarily save money and it will certainly impact your time. Your best option is to concentrate on one area—say, Chobe—and hire a fully equipped four-wheel-drive and camping vehicle (fitted out with tables, chairs, cutlery,

---

Tips   **Lightening Your Load**

At press time, the luggage weight restriction for these light charter aircraft remains a meager 10 to 12 kilograms (22–26 lb.) per person. Bitter complaints from many travelers has meant a reconsideration of this limitation, and as a result, some companies will be allowing up to 20 kilograms (44 lb.) of luggage—but at the expense of an extra passenger, so ticket prices are likely to increase. If you're leaving from and returning to Johannesburg, you can transfer any essentials to a small soft-sided bag and store your heavy bags in the very convenient luggage-storage facility in the Jo'burg airport (Maun and Kasane airports also have luggage-storage facilities, but at this time we don't recommend using them). Also check with your safari operator or ground handler to see what services they provide—a number of them will store your luggage at their offices in Maun or Kasane while you're on safari.

---

and bedding). Safer still is to take a guided self-drive trip, which lets you enjoy the experience of driving through Botswana but safely under supervision. Both are offered by **Britz** in South Africa (© 011/396-1860; www.britz.co.za; see "Getting Around" in chapter 2 for rates). In Botswana, try **Avis** (© 267/391-3093 or 267/397-5469), which has desks in the airports in Maun (© 267/686-0039) and Kasane (267/625-0144). To **rent a car,** you must be 25 or older. Your home driving license is good for 6 months (as long as it's in English). If you need tents and cooking equipment, make arrangements through **Kalahari Canvas** (© 267/686-0568), which is also near the airport.

WITH A PACKAGE TOUR   In Botswana it really is worth using an established operator to make your bookings, or at least compare package prices before booking—going it alone can be as expensive as buying a car from spare parts. Packages include, among other things, transport to the lodge or base camp; accommodations; food, soft drinks, and, in many cases, all alcoholic drinks except for imported liquors; game-viewing, fishing, and photographic expeditions; professional guides; boat hire; and mokoro trips (sometimes you pay extra for park entry fees). See recommended operators under "Specialist Safaris & Operators," below.

BOTSWANA BUSH CAMPS: WHAT TO EXPECT

ACCOMMODATIONS   A holiday spent in Botswana, and particularly in the delta area and its surrounds, is not a traditional "hotel" experience (though the Orient-Express group comes pretty close!)—operators are awarded a mere 5-year concession by the Botswana government and must leave no permanent mark on the land, so camps are generally raised and built with thatch, timber, and/or canvas. The managers of these camps, many of them husband-and-wife teams, put a high premium on hospitality, however, whether your choice is comfortably rustic or luxuriously colonial. Even in the tented camps, accommodations are in generously sized en-suite safari tents, and the food, while usually prepared in tented bush kitchens, is of a very high standard. In most camps, laundry is done by hand on a daily basis.

Visitors to the delta should bear in mind at all times that they are in a wilderness area: Most of the camps and lodges are unfenced, and dangerous animals roam through them. Stay alert and never wander the grounds without a guide or ranger after dark. For more details, see "Health, Safety & Insurance," in chapter 2.

Botswana

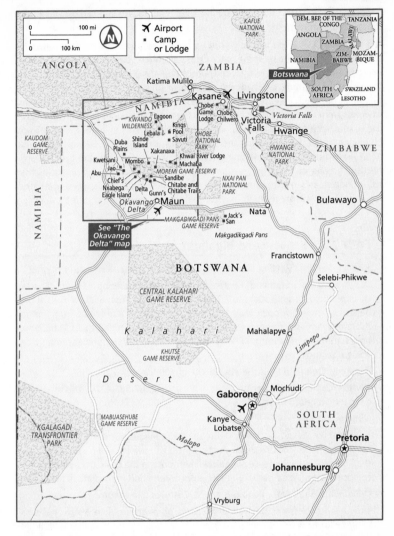

DINING Botswana doesn't have an ethnic cuisine to call its own, and food in the camps and lodges is generally designed to appeal to a wide range of cosmopolitan tastes. Although standards vary, most pride themselves on serving wholesome, home-baked fare, and, in the lodges and fixed camps, kitchens can be surprisingly sophisticated. Some, like Orient-Express, employ chefs who design menus of international standard. Expect the choice of a full English or continental breakfast, including fresh fruit, imported at great expense. Morning and afternoon tea are institutions at most lodges. Game is served in some lodges (although not in those situated in game reserves), so more adventurous diners can experiment with crocodile steaks, gemsbok (oryx) filets, and the like.

South African beers and wines are available in all lodges and camps, and in many camps are included in the rates.

A TYPICAL DAY You will be woken up early, just before sunrise, with coffee or tea to warm you before the morning game drive. It is often very cold; remember to take a warm jacket, but don't forget a hat and sunscreen—the sun can get downright fierce by the end of the morning, especially in the summer. (In some camps, breakfast is followed by a walk or a mokoro trip along the channels, with lunch served on an island some-where far from the camp.) After lunch, guests have the afternoons to rest before regroup-ing around 4pm for the afternoon game drive, which often includes a stop at a scenic (and open) spot for a sundowner and some snacks as the sun sets. In most camps, after-noon drives turn into early-evening drives where a spotlight is used to help you spy on nocturnal creatures. Once back at the camp, you share cocktails and dinner with your fellow lodge mates, often communally at a big, candlelit table on a raised open-air din-ing area. When you are ready to retire, a guide escorts you back to your room or tent.

FAST FACTS: Botswana Highlights

Airport See the "Getting There" sections in this chapter as well as in chapter 2.

Banks **In Maun: Standard Chartered** and **Barclays** are both open Monday through Friday from 8:30am to 2:30pm, and Saturday from 8:30am to 10:45pm. Banks are generally open Monday, Tuesday, Thursday, and Friday from 9am to 2:30pm; Wednesday from 8:15 to noon; and Saturday from 8 to 10:45am. Shop hours are Monday through Friday from 8am to 1 or 2pm, and Saturday from 8:30am to 1pm.

Currency One pula (P) is the equivalent of 100 thebe.

Dentist Call the **Delta Dental Clinic in Maun** (✆ 267/686-4224); the offices are near the Standard Chartered Bank.

Directory Inquiries Dial ✆ 192.

Doctor If you need a doctor in Maun, the **Delta Medical Centre** is on the Tsheko-Tsheko road, which runs through the center of town (✆ 267/686-1411). Note that, should you experience a medical emergency in the bush, the operators and camps recommended below will take appropriate and immediate action.

Documents See "Entry Requirements & Customs," in chapter 2.

Drugstore Drugstores are called chemists or pharmacies in Botswana. **Oka-vango Pharmacy** (✆ 267/686-0043) is on Maun's main street, in the Lewis Build-ing opposite Riley's garage complex.

Electricity As in the rest of southern Africa, you'll need an adapter/voltage con-verter. Botswana uses 220/240V 15/13-amp plug sockets. Plugs are 2- and 3-pin, round and flat. Remember that many bush camps do not have electricity, but run on generators.

Embassies & Consulates Note that all offices are in Gaborone. **U.S. Embassy** ✆ 267/395-3982; the after-hours emergency telephone number is ✆ 267/357-111. **British High Commission** ✆ 267/395-2841. **Canadian Consulate** ✆ 267/390-4411.

Language English is the official language and is widely spoken; Setswana is the national language, spoken by the Batswana people, who make up 50% of the population.

Safety Consult your physician (or a travel-health specialist) before leaving about starting a course of antimalarial prophylactics, and note that children under the age of 12 are generally not allowed in game lodges unless special arrangements have been made with the management. For more information, see "Health, Safety & Insurance," in chapter 2.

Taxes Sales tax is 10% and is included in all prices quoted in this chapter, unless otherwise indicated.

Telephone Phone calls can be made from any post office or business that provides office services. Public call boxes are found in towns. Remember, this chapter lists numbers for Botswana and South Africa, indicated by their country codes. Botswana has no regional or town codes. There are no telephones in the delta. The camps communicate with Maun and each other via radio, and can transmit emergency messages this way. If you do have a satellite phone, you will be asked to keep it switched off.

To call southern Africa from another country: Dial the international access code (United States or Canada 011, United Kingdom or New Zealand 00, Australia 0011), plus the country code (**27** for **South Africa, 263** for **Zimbabwe, 267** for **Botswana,** and **260** for **Zambia**), plus the local number minus the 0 at the beginning of the city/area code. **To make an international call:** Dial 00, wait for a dial tone, then dial the country code (United States or Canada 1, United Kingdom 44, Australia 61, New Zealand 64), the area code, and the local number. **To make calls within Botswana:** Drop the 267 country code; there are no area codes. **To charge international calls:** The toll-free international access code for **Sprint** is ✆ **0800/180-280.** At press time, there was no international access code for AT&T and MCI.

Time Zone Botswana is 2 hours ahead of GMT, or 7 hours ahead of Eastern Standard Time.

Tipping Tipping at bush and delta camps is at guests' discretion, but a good rule of thumb is $5 to $10 per person per day, to be shared among the staff. The average for guides is $5 to $10 per day.

Water Water in all the camps is drinkable, but most camps/lodges do supply plenty of bottled mineral water. There is some disagreement about the safety of water in the smaller towns—to be on the safe side, drink bottled water or bring along a purification system.

When to Go Most operators consider the winter months (July–Oct) as high season; it's cooler, and the delta is usually flooded.

2 Specialist Safaris & Operators

You'll have no trouble finding safari operators or packages, which run the gamut to suit a range of interests and pockets, from fly-in safaris to luxurious lodges to all-hands-on-deck-type trips with nights under canvas.

MOBILE SAFARIS: MOVING BETWEEN CAMPS

Most people with limited time opt for fly-in "mobile safaris" (in other words, moving between camps). Bear in mind that one of the best ways to appreciate the broad changes of landscape in Botswana is to plan a trip that comprises the delta (try to visit both a "wet" and "dry" camp), Chobe, and the Kalahari. Depending on your budget and what you want out of your trip, mobile safaris range from basic participation tours, where you will, for instance, be expected to erect your own tent, to the ultra-luxurious, where the only time you lift a finger is to summon another cold drink. Participants are transported in a suitably modified open vehicle (or mokoro), and camp or lodge overnight at predetermined destinations before flying to the next camp. For contact information for the following operators, see "Safari Operators Specializing in

---

Safari Operators Specializing in Botswana

- **Abercrombie & Kent** www.abercrombiekent.com. **In the United States:** 1520 Kensington Rd., Oak Brook, IL 60523-2156; ✆ 800/-554-7016 or 630/954-2944. **In South Africa:** Sanctuary Lodges, P.O. Box 782607, Sandton 2146 (✆ 27/11/781-0740).

- **Bush Ways Safari** www.bushways.com. **In Botswana:** Private Bag 342, Maun (✆ 267/686-3685).

- **Conservation Corporation Africa (CC Africa)** www.ccafrica.com. **In South Africa:** Private Bag X27, Benmore 2010 (✆ 011/809-4300). **In Botswana:** ✆ 267/661-979; Maun: 267/686-1979; Kasane: 267/625-0119.

- **Hartley's Safaris** www.hartleys.co.za. **In South Africa:** P.O. Box 69859, Bryanston 2021 (✆ 27/11/467-4704).

- **Ker & Downey** www.kerdowney.com. **In the United States:** 6703 Highway Blvd, Katy, TX 77494 (✆ 800/423-4236 or 281/371-2500). **In Botswana:** P.O. Box 27, Maun (✆ 267/686-0375; fax 267/686-1282).

- **Kwando Safaris** www.kwando.co.za. **In Botswana:** P.O. Box 550, Maun (✆ 267/686-1449).

- **Maplanga** www.maplanga.co.za. **In South Africa:** ✆ 27/11/794-1446 or 082/570-2896.

- **Moremi Safaris & Tours** www.moremi-safaris.com. **In South Africa:** P.O. Box 2757, Cramerview 2060 (✆ 27/11/465-3842).

- **Okavango Tours & Safaris** www.okavango.com. **In the United Kingdom:** Marlborough House, 298 Regents Park Rd., London N32TJ (✆ 44/020/8343-3283). **In Botswana:** P.O. Box 39, Maun (✆ 267/66-0220).

- **Orient-Express Safaris** www.orient-express-safaris.com. **In South Africa:** P.O. Box 786432, Sandton 2146 (✆ 27/11/481-6052).

- **Penduka Safaris** www.penduka.com.na. **In Namibia:** P.O. Box 90387, Windhoek (✆ 264/61/23-9643).

- **Uncharted Africa Safari Co.** www.unchartedafrica.com. **In South Africa:** P.O. Box 78465, Sandton 2146 (✆ 27/11/895-0862).

- **Wilderness Safaris** www.wilderness-safaris.com. **In South Africa:** P.O. Box 78573, Sandton 2146 (✆ 27/11/807-1800).

Botswana," above. For separate reviews on top camps, "owned" by these operators, see "Where to Stay & Dine," later in this chapter.

Abercrombie & Kent ⭐⭐⭐   This top-end operator now has four permanent camps in Botswana (Baines', Stanley's, Chief's, and Chobe Chilwero, all reviewed below)—needless to say, you'll want for nothing. **Sanctuary Lodges and Camps,** a division of A&K, will not only handle your bookings, but also set up an itinerary that suits you.

Bush Ways Safaris ⭐ *Value*   This operator offers small and custom participation tours, themed around certain animals and best suited for more adventurous travelers who want a really authentic experience. Guests stay in small dome tents and travel overland in an open Land Rover. Several itineraries are offered, taking in all parts of Botswana, including Chobe, Moremi, the delta, Makgadikgadi, and the Kalahari. Cost for the 15-day Lion Trail trip through northern Botswana is US$2,040 per person, including food and activities. Shorter trips are also available.

Detour ⭐ *Value*   Cape-based operator Shawn Petre will arrange a variety of itineraries to suit your time frame, all of them offering very good value, like the 7-day camping trip covering Moremi, Savuti, Chobe, Kasane, and Livingstone (Vic Falls) for US$1,200, or 3 days of camping in the delta for US$300. For contact details, see "Delta on a Budget," later in this chapter.

Mike Penman's Wild Lifestyles ⭐⭐⭐   Voted one of the top 15 safari guides in the world by *Condé Nast Traveler,* Penman—who has produced and facilitated a number of wildlife documentaries—offers private (usually no more than four guests), custom-made tented safaris, aimed particularly at people with an interest in photography or filmmaking. For contact information, see "Photography & Film Safaris," below.

Orient-Express Safaris ⭐⭐⭐   Orient-Express has three camps in Botswana: two in the delta and one in Chobe. In true Orient-Express style, it offers top-of-the-range luxury, with a reduction in rates kicking in for 4 or more nights. Four nights moving from camp to camp costs US$2380 to US$3,310 per person (depending on season), including everything but your ticket to Maun.

Penduka Safaris ⭐   Based in Namibia but one of the most established mobile safari companies in Botswana, Penduka offers fully catered and serviced camping trips in campsites situated throughout most parts of the country. Its 14-day overland trip through northern Botswana costs US$3,350 per person and takes in the Okavango Delta, various game parks, the Chobe River, the Makgadikgadi and Nxai pans, and Victoria Falls. A 5-day exploration of the Moremi is US$1,300, while 9 days in central Kalahari costs US$2,500 per person.

Uncharted Africa Safari Co. ⭐⭐   This is the foremost operator in Botswana's Kalahari region. Besides the luxurious "HQ" camp (Jack's Camp; see later in this chapter), you can ask for mobile expeditions into the desert, as well as trips north to the delta and Chobe, though that area is better serviced by Wilderness Safaris.

Wilderness Safaris ⭐⭐⭐   This South Africa–based company, the world's first recipient of *National Geographic Traveler*'s World Legacy Award for sustainable ecotourism, is the best all-around operator in northern Botswana, offering superb service, from silky-smooth transfers (they have their own charter air company) to exceptional standards in guiding. It also owns the most camps in the delta and offers three categories to suit various budgets: vintage, classic, and premier. The popular 11-day Jacana Safari offers

---

Fun Fact   **Boating, Botswana Style**

No trip to the delta is complete without a trip in a *mokoro,* a narrow, canoe-like boat propelled by a human poler. Traditionally, they were made out of hollowed tree trunks, but for environmental reasons, many camps now use mokoros made from fiberglass. These are silent craft, enabling you to get close to birds and animals, and ideally suited to the shallow waters of the delta.

---

a combination of cross-country drives and light aircraft transfers, providing access to the prime areas of northern Botswana (Okavango Delta, Linyanti, Chobe National Park, and Victoria Falls) with accommodations in premier and classic camps. Prices start at US$4,000 per person sharing. The 11-day Mopani Safari follows the same itinerary but includes accommodations in the vintage and classic camps (comfortable en-suite tents, but quite basically outfitted in relation to premier camps); expect to pay upward of US$1,500, depending on the season.

MOKORO AND ISLAND CAMPING EXPEDITIONS

The cheapest and one of the most adventurous ways to enjoy the delta is to pack a sleeping bag and join a mokoro trip through the islands, accompanied by a poler with an intimate knowledge of these waters. Okavango Tours & Safaris specializes in mokoro camping trips and also runs the best-value tented camp in the delta: Oddballs (for more, see "Delta on a Budget," later in this chapter).

ELEPHANT-BACK SAFARIS

Abu Camp is for many the highlight of a trip to Africa, and the best place in the world to experience a safari on the back of a pachyderm. The chief elephant is Abu, star of such motion pictures as *The Power of One, Circles in the Forest,* and Clint Eastwood's *White Hunter Black Heart,* who leads a herd of 12 African elephants, comprising 5 adults and 7 youngsters ranging from 4 months to 40 years of age. See "The Okavango Delta & Moremi Game Reserve: Where to Stay & Dine," later in this chapter.

HORSE SAFARIS

Limpopo Valley Horse Safaris 𝒜𝒜   This outfit runs 7-day wilderness safaris, where each night is spent at a different camp within the Mashatu Game Reserve; the focus is often on riding with the vast elephant herds. The first night—always a Sunday—is spent at **Fort Jameson,** a rustic camp with double safari tents that include en-suite flush toilets and hot-water showers. The next nights are spent in bush camps comprising dome tents, stretchers, and sleeping bags. There are bucket showers and long drops. The horses have been individually selected for temperament and rideability, but, again, you need to be experienced. For visitors with less time, try the Limpopo Safari option of being based at Fort Jameson, with two rides per day; there is no minimum stay.

P.O. Box 55514, Northlands, Johannesburg 2116. ℂ 27/11/442-2267. www.lvhsafaris.co.za. Wilderness safari US$280–US$310 per person per night; Limpopo Safari US$240–US$275 per person per night. AE, DC, MC, V. Rates are all-inclusive except for beverages. No children under 16.

Okavango Horse Safaris 𝒜𝒜𝒜   These safaris are run in a private concession in the western delta bordering Moremi Game Reserve, and take you deep into the wetlands. Expect to spend between 4 and 6 hours a day in the saddle. Minimum riding ability required is a mastery of the basics, including an ability to trot for stretches of 10 minutes at a time and—even more important—the ability to gallop out of trouble! The maximum weight limit is 95 kilograms (210 lb.), and riders over 90 kilograms (200 lb.) pay 50% more for an extra horse. The tack is English style, and each saddle has a seatsaver for comfort. Trail riders move from **Kujwana Camp** (spacious safari tents with shower en-suite and flush toilets) to **Moklowane** (tents have bucket-and-pulley showers and safari toilets) to **Fly Camp** (dome tents with camp beds, long drop toilets, and bucket showers). A maximum of eight riders is taken, and the safaris last between 5 and 10 days. Besides horse rides, guests are treated to game drives, bush walks, and mokoro trips, which helps keep things varied and interesting. The camps are closed December through February.

Private Bag 23, Maun. (C) **267/686-1671.** Fax 267/686-1672. www.okavangohorse.com. For a 5- or 10-night safari combining 2 or 3 camps, the rate is US$650 per person per night June 1–Oct 31. Low season (Mar–May and Nov) US$560 per person per night. Rates are all-inclusive. Air transfers are US$270 per person return from Maun. There is a 50% single supplement for people unwilling to share, and a 50% weight supplement for riders over 90kg (200 lb.). No credit card facilities. Children are accepted if they are strong, confident riders.

CYCLING SAFARIS

Mashatu (★★) Radio-linked groups of cyclists set out at dawn and again at dusk on mountain bikes in search of animals; visits to the ruins of 600-year-old settlements on the reserve are included. The program is entirely flexible and can be adapted to the needs and skills of the particular cyclists; game drives can also be included. These safaris are offered in the winter months of April through September, and are conducted from the Mashatu Tent Camp for a minimum of 10 guests and a maximum of 14 guests at no additional charge. For fewer than 10 guests, there is an additional charge of $9 extra per cycle. For more information, call (C) **27/11/442-2267** or 0861-SAFARI (fax 27/11/442-2318; www.mashatu.com).

WALKING SAFARIS

CC Africa Expeditions (★★★) One of Africa's best safari operators runs a 12-day adventure experience that includes a walking safari in northern Botswana's Linyati Private Game Reserve. The expedition sets out from Kasane and includes 10 nights of wilderness camping, taking in the Savute Channel, the Moremi Wildlife Reserve (where game-viewing is from a vehicle), and the Okavango Delta, where mokoro trips add to the experience. Rates start at US$3,315 per person sharing, and include charter flights between the regions; minimum age is 16. For contact details, see "Safari Operators Specializing in Botswana," earlier in this chapter.

Join the No. 1 Ladies Detective

Zimbabwean author Alexander McCall Smith's best-selling novels about Mma Ramotswe, the fictional proprietor of Botswana's No. 1 Ladies' Detective Agency (also the title of the first novel in the series), are so popular that readers have clamored to explore the locations featured in the books. Picking up on the idea, Ker & Downey now offers **Mma Ramotswe's Botswana Tour,** which leaves from the U.S.; covers the Botswana capital of Gaborone, the Okavango Delta, and Victoria Falls; and gets you back stateside in just 14 days. For contact details, see "Specialist Safaris & Operators," earlier in this chapter, or write to info@kerdowney.com.

Ker & Downey ★★ K&D offers "Footsteps across the Delta"—a 3-day expedition where a maximum of nine guests make their way by foot and mokoro from camp to camp. The emphasis is on enjoying the slow pace of the delta—the maximum distance each day is about 6km (3¾ miles), and you can travel light; while you cover the distance, the camp staff transports baggage and camp essentials. Accommodations are in twin-bedded en-suite tents. The cost is upward of US$395 per person sharing; minimum age is 12. For contact details, see "Safari Operators Specializing in Botswana," earlier in this chapter.

PHOTOGRAPHY & FILM SAFARIS

Mike Penman's Wild Lifestyles ★★★ These highly adventurous yet comfortably tented safaris focus on learning about wildlife while affording you the best opportunities to capture the experience on film. Penman has been involved in conservation, photography, and filmmaking in Botswana for 15 years (both producing his own documentaries and helping independent filmmakers and major TV networks), and he personally conducts safaris into Moremi, the delta, Kalahari, Makgadikgadi, Nxai Pans, and Drotsky's Caves. Penman is known for his bold approach to lions and ability to get right into the mix of things, placing you in a great position to capture the moment. Other, tamer photographic and birding safaris with professional guides are offered by Wilderness Safaris (see "Specialist Safaris & Operators," earlier in this chapter).

P.O. Box 66, Maun, Botswana. ℂ 267/686-3664. Fax 267/686-1045. www.wildlifestyles.com. Mobile safaris cost US$395–US$545 per person per day, depending on the season.

CULTURAL SAFARIS

If you're interested in Bushman (or "San") culture, make sure you spend a few nights with **Uncharted Africa Safari Co.** in the Kalahari (see Jack's and San Camp, and Planet Baobab, later in this chapter). Uncharted will also, along with operators like **Moremi Safaris & Tours,** organize a visit to the **Tsodilo Hills** (in the northwest, near the panhandle), where you can view some 3,000 rock paintings. The paintings are known for their fine clarity and wide variety, and trips can be made by air or four-wheel-drive. There is also a traditional village in the foothills. For contact details, see "Specialist Safaris & Operators," earlier in this chapter.

Visitors to the delta can now also immerse themselves in Bushman culture and folklore by spending a night at **Gudigwa,** a 100% Bushman-owned camp that opened in 2003. The Gudigwa community (a settlement of some 800 "Bukakhwe" Bushman) is indigenous to the Okavango Delta, and though these people differ physically somewhat from the Bushman tribes of the Kalahari, their traditional ways of living off the land are very much the same. Guests are accommodated in one of eight large grass huts, all en-suite and comfortably furnished. The camp is situated 5km (3 miles) from the community so as not to disturb its daily life, but visitors are invited to walk with representatives to learn more about the bush, be it medicinal uses of plants, game tracking, or how to discover underground water. In the evenings, villagers perform traditional dances and songs, and tell animated stories in their mother tongue—strangely melodious and known for the complexity of its "clicks." The camp (www.gudigwa.com) is marketed on the Bukakhwe's behalf by **Wilderness Safaris** (see "Specialist Safaris & Operators," earlier in this chapter); cost during high season (July–Oct) is US$850 per room; April to June is $500. Rates are all-inclusive.

3 The Okavango Delta & Moremi Game Reserve

Located in the northwestern corner of the country, this region is for most the highlight of a trip to Botswana, particularly during the winter months (starting in July), when the "flood" turns it into an aquatic paradise. The northeastern segment of the delta has been set aside as the Moremi Game Reserve, a 1,800-sq.-km (702-sq.-mile) expanse of wilderness extending across both wetland and dry terrain. This is known as the "Predator Capital of Africa," and you are almost guaranteed daily sightings of lion and leopard. *Note:* Keep in mind that until new regulations come into force, camps *inside* the Moremi Game Reserve (a national park) are not allowed to have night game drives or drive off designated roads to follow game. Camps that border the reserve aren't bound by those regulations.

The delta originates in Angola, to the northwest, from where the Okavango River flows southward for 1,300km (806 miles) into the Kalahar. Thanks to the same geological activity that caused the Great African Rift Valley, the delta is more or less contained by fault lines between which the crust has sunk and filled up with sediment. It is into this bowl that the Okavango seeps, rather than making its rightful way to the sea. The annual southward flow of water is precipitated by the rainy season in the north, which begins in the Angolan uplands between January and March, and usually arrives at its southernmost point—the delta—around June or July, when the water spreads out to form innumerable pools, channels, and lagoons.

WHERE TO STAY & DINE

At press time, Wilderness Safaris was preparing to open two new camps in the Okavango Delta region; the new **Vumbura Camp** replaces the old Vumbura Plains Camp from May 2005 and will be run as a "premier camp," so you can expect sheer luxury and top-notch service in a concession highly regarded for the quality of its game-viewing; rates start at US$2,400 double. Opening in mid-2005 is **Seba Camp,** with rates

---

Moving Through Maun

The small but sprawling town of Maun is the regional center of Ngamiland (northwestern Botswana) and the gateway to the Okavango Delta. As the starting point for most trips into the delta, Maun has an airport, a few shopping areas, banks, a number of hotels and lodges, and a plethora of safari tour operators, most of which are based or represented here. Maun operates principally as a service center for the safari industry and not as a tourist attraction in its own right, so there isn't much to do or see, and you'll more than likely be transferred directly to your wilderness camp. If for some unforeseen reason you do have to spend the night in Maun, book into **Cresta Riley's Hotel** (© 267/686-0204; www.cresta-hospitality.com; from US$352 double), situated on the main road and within walking distance of the airport. Rooms are basic but comfortable, and its shady gardens are reminiscent of the times when this was a popular watering hole for travelers coming in on the dusty road from Francistown.

starting at a more affordable US$860 double. *Note:* Most rates quoted include transfers from Maun, but do check up front to be sure. Also, most of the camps quote their rates in U.S. dollars.

Abu Camp 🏕🏕🏕 Touted by many as the ultimate Okavango experience, this camp—in a fabulous game-rich concession in a riverine forest in the western part of the delta—lets you explore the waterways of the region on the back of an elephant. Elephants not only cope in water and sand with equal ease, but they also get very close to other game, and guests are transported in comfortable, custom-made saddles. Accommodations include five extremely luxurious, custom-designed en-suite tents, furnished with kilim rugs and mahogany sleigh beds, and raised on teak decking with a private viewing platform overlooking a lagoon. Situated across the lagoon from the tents is the two-bedroom Villa, which was recently featured in *Travel + Leisure*'s list of 50 Most Romantic Places on Earth; the copper bathtub is the ideal after-safari soaking experience. The minimum stay is 3 nights; maximum number of guests 12.

Bookings through Wilderness Safaris (see "Specialist Safaris & Operators," earlier in this chapter). Direct ℭ 267/ 686-1260. www.abucamp.com. 6 units. R5,825 ($890) per person all-inclusive Maun-Maun package. AE, DC, MC, V. The camp is closed during the wet season between mid-Dec and the end of Feb. There are no seasonal discounts. Accounts must be settled electronically prior to visit. No children under 12. **Amenities:** Dining area; bar; lounge; pool; laundry; library; elephant safaris; game drives; nature walks; birding; mokoro trips.

Baines' Camp 🏕🏕 Named for artist-explorer-anthropologist Thomas Baines, this is a personal favorite, not least because the camp retains a colonial exclusivity with only five guest chalets. Each is privately situated and linked by a raised wooden walkway, with private terraces that look out onto the wilderness (ask for a view of the waterway) and spacious, well-laid-out bathrooms (no tubs, though). On arrival you find yourself in a tranquil, tastefully decorated lounge built around a massive tree and overlooking a permanent waterway where noisy hippos play and wallow; they will keep you entertained for hours. The camp is also structurally unique: All the walls are constructed of recycled aluminum cans (collected during an environment-awareness campaign by Maun schoolchildren), packed with elephant dung, and then plastered. Nearby, the more established **Stanley's Camp** 🏕 is a tented operation that is somewhat less luxurious and exclusive (there are eight tents), but with cheaper rates (US$680–US$1,020 double). The same activities are on offer at both properties (they also share an airstrip, where herds of game gather regularly to graze), and one great drawing card is the Elephant Experience, a morning in which you spend intimate time with the pachyderms.

Reservations: Sanctuary Lodges & Camps. ℭ 27/11/781-1497. Fax 27/11/787-7658. www.sanctuarylodges.com. Or book through Abercrombie & Kent (see "Specialist Safaris & Operators" earlier in this chapter). 5 units. High season (July–Oct) US$1,360 double; low season (Nov–June) US$780 double. All-inclusive, except for Elephant Experience, which costs US$235–US$295 per person. MC, V. Children 9–11 must share with an adult. No children under 9. **Amenities:** Dining area; bar; lounge; pool; laundry; library; game drives. *In room:* A/C, minibar, hair dryer, safe, emergency telephone.

Chief's Camp 🏕🏕🏕 This luxury camp, opened by Abercrombie & Kent in 1999, is without a doubt one of the most luxurious in the delta (vying with Mombo and Jao). It's also situated in the exclusive Mombo Concession of the Moremi Game Reserve, and is regarded as the ultimate destination for predators in the delta; with 52 different lions identified in a 9km (5½-mile) radius and almost daily leopard sightings, it's not called the "Predator Capital of Africa" for nothing. Since the camp opened, both white and black rhino have also been introduced into the area. Game drives are conducted in open vehicles in the early morning and late afternoons (night drives are not allowed because it's in a national park). One of the main reasons to

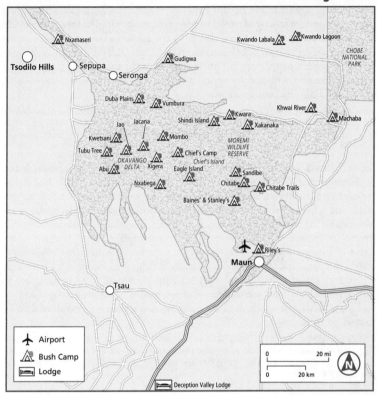

book here is that it offers the experience of both a wet and dry camp: From June to October, when the floodwaters arrive, mokoro activities are also offered; this is also the time to book soothing spa treatments in the *sala* (pavilion) alongside the pool. Accommodations are typical Abercrombie & Kent, with only 12 luxurious tents, each furnished with large twin beds and comfortable armchairs, and featuring spacious, well-equipped bathrooms and private viewing decks sheltered by jackalberry and sausage trees.

Reservations: Sanctuary Lodges & Camps. ℭ 27/11/781-1497. Fax 27/11/787-7658. www.sanctuarylodges.com. Or book through Abercrombie & Kent (see "Specialist Safaris & Operators," earlier in this chapter). 12 units. High season (July–Oct) US$1,470; low season (Nov–June) US$880. MC, V. No children under 9. **Amenities:** Dining area; bar; lounge; pool; spa treatments in high season; craft shop; laundry; library; game drives; seasonal mokoro trips. *In room:* Ceiling fan, hair dryer, safe, emergency telephone.

Chitabe and Chitabe Trails 🛡🛡 Situated on an island alongside the Moremi Game Reserve, with classic Okavango scenery of palm trees and open seasonally flooded plains, Chitabe is part of Wilderness Safaris' "classic" collection, offering good comfort and excellent game drives with seemingly endless sightings of giraffe, zebra, various antelope, and an outstanding variety of birds. But don't be surprised when your ranger suddenly announces that there's been a special sighting (such as an African wild dog kill) and high-tails it to the scene. **Chitabe Trails** offers a slightly more rustic experience, but it's also more intimate, with only five en-suite tents with wooden floors and metal-framed four-poster beds under a canopy of trees. Designed for families with children, tent no. 8 has an extra bedroom and an outdoor shower. A few minutes away, in a similar setting, **Chitabe** main camp is an eight-tented camp with tents built on wooden decks linked by raised wooden footbridges; the public areas have thatched roofs. Guests have the option of spending a night sleeping under the stars in one of the camp's hides—a recommended authentic bush experience.

Book through Wilderness Safaris (see "Specialist Safaris & Operators," earlier in this chapter). High season (July–Oct) US$1,190 double; low season US$860. Rates are all-inclusive. MC, V. Children between ages 8 and 12 are permitted, but parents must book private game-drive vehicle. **Amenities:** Dining area; bar; lounge; pool; laundry; game drives; bush walks. *In tent:* Safe, ceiling fans.

Duba Plains 🐾🐾 Located in the farthermost reaches of the delta, Duba is another of Wilderness Safaris' "classic" camps, best known for its lion and buffalo interactions. Situated in a 35,000-hectare (86,450-acre) private reserve, with breathtaking grass plains and gin-clear freshwater pools, it is particularly suited to people who want a comfortable but not stuffy experience. A small camp (only six tents, each with wooden floors, fine linens, and a veranda overlooking the floodplains) offers excellent value in terms of game-viewing: It is known for its large herds of buffalo (1,500–3,000), which, in turn, attract lions—it's not unusual for guests to see up to 15 lions a day! Guests may choose among game drives (it's a private reserve, so night drives are also on offer), mokoro rides (dependent on flood waters, best usually May–Oct), and walking safaris. Guiding standards are excellent, and rangers will go out of their way to track particular species.

Book through Wilderness Safaris (see "Specialist Safaris & Operators," earlier in this chapter). High season (July–Oct) US$1,440 double; low season US$1,100 double. Rates all-inclusive. MC, V. No children under 8. **Amenities:** Dining room; bar; pool on a raised terrace overlooking the plains; curio shop; laundry; small library; game drives. *In tent:* Safe, ceiling fan.

Eagle Island Camp 🐾🐾🐾 This camp, made up of 12 luxury tents, each with a private deck facing the lagoon, is located at Xaxaba, an island refuge deep in the Okavango. Accommodations are pleasantly spread out for privacy, while the secluded Fish Eagle Bar is the ideal romantic hideaway after a day of game-viewing. Besides affording you all the luxury you'd expect from the Orient-Express group, this is the ideal destination for birders. Set among the floodplains (the camp is navigable only by mokoro during the rainy season), Eagle Island enjoys a high concentration of fish eagles and other bird species, including kingfishers, herons, cormorants, pelicans, darters, and storks. To augment your water-based game activities, game flights in light aircraft are also available on request, and Orient-Express regularly transfers guests from here to **Khwai**, its "dry" camp in neighboring Moremi, and **Savute Elephant,** its Chobe camp; both are a 25-minute flight away.

Book through Orient-Express Safaris (In South Africa, call ☎ 011/274-1800; www.orient-express-safaris.com). 12 units. From US$1,006 double, depending on the season. Rates are all-inclusive. AE, MC, V. No children under 12 except by prior arrangement. **Amenities:** Dining area; bar; heated pool; shop; laundry; book and video library; airstrip; light-aircraft safaris; game drives; mokoro trips; hiking. *In room:* A/C, hair dryer, minibar, safe, intercom.

Jacana Camp 🐾 For much of the wet season, this "vintage" Wilderness Safari operation is, like Eagle Island, accessible only by boat or mokoro. Offering the most rustic experience available within the massive Jao concession, Jacana consists of just five en-suite stilted tents—these are comfortably furnished (albeit relatively basic) and overlook a watery expanse, which is where most of your focus will be. The bar, lounge, and recently renovated upstairs dining area offer a relaxing space in which to enjoy the ever-changing moods of delta.

Book through Wilderness Safaris (see "Specialist Safaris & Operators," earlier in this chapter). High season (July–Oct) US$1,190 double; low season US$860. Rates are all-inclusive. MC, V. Children 8–12 are permitted, but special arrangements must be made with management for private vehicles. **Amenities:** Dining area; bar; lounge area; pool; crafts shop; laundry; boat and mokoro trips; game drives; bush walks; fishing. *In room:* Safe, tea- and coffee-making facility, ceiling fan.

Jao Camp ⭐⭐⭐   Named after a local chieftain, Jao Lodge is one of Wilderness Safaris' top camps, the others being Mombo and the recently renovated King's Pool. Located in one of the finest concessions in the delta, it covers 60,000 hectares (148,200 acres) and borders the Moremi Game Reserve, experiencing huge fluctuations in water levels, with views and game experiences ever changing, depending on the time of year. But location aside, it is—from a style and luxury point of view—one of the most gorgeous camps in the delta, with Indonesian influences (suites are based on the Balinese long-house), a perfect match for the overall African ethos. The camp was designed by renowned architect Silvio Rech (Makalali, Ngorongoro), and it's one of his most restrained efforts: There's a zenlike simplicity and airy elegance that really soothes—the natural qualities of materials (from rich rosewood floors to white Indian cotton sheets) dominate in both color and texture, and neatly offset the great views. The eight suites are arranged along a long, raised wooden footbridge, ensuring fantastic privacy. Built on stilts alongside a lily-speckled waterway, each suite has a large private viewing deck, a *sala* for afternoon siestas, a beautiful open-air shower, and spacious living areas with open-plan en-suite bathroom.

Book through Wilderness Safaris (see "Specialist Safaris & Operators," earlier in this chapter). High season (July–Oct) US$1,740 double; other US$1,200. Rates are all-inclusive. MC, V. Children between ages 8 and 12 are permitted, but special arrangements must be made with management for private vehicles. **Amenities:** Dining area; bar; lounge area; 2 pools; spa and salon; crafts shop; laundry. *In room:* A/C, hair dryer, 2 safes, tea- and coffee-making facility, ceiling fans.

Khwai River Lodge ⭐⭐⭐   This is one of the oldest lodges in Botswana, opened in 1968 by Harry Selby (who, incidentally, worked for Philip Percival, immortalized by Hemingway as "Pop" in his *Green Hills of Africa*) and adjacent to Moremi. Today it the Orient-Express Group's most popular camp and arguably the most lavish lodge in the delta, with luxurious facilities that include air-conditioned tents, a heated swimming pool, and a video library. The camp—comprising 15 large twin-bedded tents, each with generous bathroom (his and her vanity units, and so on) and a private deck furnished with hammocks for comfortable eyeballing of the resident hippo and croc—is built in the shade of indigenous leadwood and fig trees, and overlooks the Khwai River floodplain, where you are likely to see large numbers of elephant. Your chances of spotting lion, hyena, wild dog, and leopard are equally high.

Book through Orient-Express Safaris (see "Specialist Safaris & Operators," earlier in this chapter). 15 units. US$1,006–US$1,500 double, depending on the season. Rates are all-inclusive. AE, MC, V. No children under 12 except by prior arrangement. **Amenities:** Dining and lounge areas; bar; heated pool; shop; room service, laundry; book and video library; VHS video and monitor; airstrip; game drives; boat and mokoro trips. *In room:* A/C, minibar, hair dryer, safe, fan, intercom.

Kwetsani Camp ⭐⭐   Situated in the stunning 60,000-hectare (148,200-acre) Jao Concession area to the west of Mombo and Moremi Game Reserve, this camp features five cute treehouse chalets built on stilts under thatched roofs and linked by raised walkways. Designed similarly to Jao (although far less ostentatiously), Kwetsani is much smaller and enjoys an intimate, relaxed atmosphere; dedicated guides make exploration of the varied terrain memorable, and besides mokoro and boat trips, night drives are available. Built on a heavily wooded island with mangosteen and fig trees, it is particularly beautiful from May to September, when the water levels are at their highest, but the game-viewing is best from October to April, when the flood plains are dryer. Guests wanting a "rougher" bush experience are able to book a night in an animal hide at nearby Jao camp.

Book through Wilderness Safaris (see "Specialist Safaris & Operators," earlier in this chapter). High season (July–Oct) US$1,190 double; other US$860. Rates are all-inclusive. MC, V. Children 8–12 are permitted only if they are in a group with a private vehicle. **Amenities:** Dining area; bar; lounge; pool; laundry; game drives; boat and mokoro trips. *In room:* Safe, tea and coffee station, ceiling fan.

Mombo and Little Mombo ★★★   Seasoned Botswana travelers keep coming back to the Mombo camps, not least because they are situated in the best game-viewing area in the delta (it's one of Botswana's top wildlife documentary locations and has hosted *National Geographic* and BBC shoots). The camps are located on an island at the northwestern tip of Chief's Island, deep within the Moremi Game Reserve in an area where dense concentrations of plains game congregate. It is not unheard of to see 12 mammal species—from your veranda! Predators, including all the big cats, are frequently sighted; the area is especially good for leopard. Mombo is the most sought-after (and expensive) lodge in Botswana, and represents true Okavango luxury; made up of two camps—comprising three and nine tents, respectively—Mombo accommodations are in elegantly furnished tented rooms (all natural materials and white cotton) the size of small houses. These have blond-wood floors, ragged thatch roofs, and large-screen sliding walls that open completely onto large wooden verandas with shaded *salas* and open-air showers. Suites are connected by a long walkway more than 1.8m (6 ft.) off the ground; this allows game to wander freely through the camp. Meals are first-rate and plentiful, and you dine in beautiful open-air pavilions.

Book through Wilderness Safaris (see "Specialist Safaris & Operators," earlier in this chapter). Mombo 9 units. Little Mombo 3 units. US$2,400–$2,670 double. Rates are all-inclusive. MC, V. No children under 8; July 1–Oct 31 age limit increases to 12. **Amenities:** Each camp has a dining room; bar; lounge areas; 2 pools; curio shop; game drives. *In room:* Hair dryer, safe.

Nxabega Okavango Safari Camp ★★   Situated deep in the delta, in a private concession in permanent waters on the western border of Moremi Game Reserve, the camp has the feel of a gentlemen's club, with burnished teak, crisp white linen, soft kudu-hide headboards, parchment lampshades, and dressing tables resplendent with leather boxes. The 10 safari-style en-suite tents are on raised wooden platforms with private verandas and feature all the comforts—but at night the sounds of nature (frogs, insects, and scurrying mammals) may have you reaching for a flashlight. This is one of two properties (the other is Sandibe, reviewed below) owned by CC Africa, renowned for the luxury of their safari lodges throughout the continent. Besides well-chosen settings, they're known for excellent food and attentive service, which isn't always evidenced here.

Book through CC Africa (see "Specialist Safaris & Operators," earlier in this chapter). High season (June–Oct) US$1,080 double; low season US$860. Rates are all-inclusive. There is a single supplement. DC, MC, V. Children welcome. **Amenities:** Dining room; lounge w/bar; pool; curio shop; laundry; interpretive center; airstrip; game drives; mokoro and boat trips; bush walks. *In tent:* Hair dryer, safe, standing fan.

Sandibe Safari Lodge ★★★   This is certainly the better of CC Africa's two Botswana camps (choose it for the better views alone), with only eight African-style

Value Delta on a Budget

Oddballs Palm Island Lodge is not only one of the best-known camps in the delta, but it also offers one of the best deals, with rates starting below US$200 per person per night. The emphasis is very much on the young and fun, with a great viewing deck furnished with mattresses and cushions—ideal for lounging and watching the sun set over Chief's Island. Accommodations are in dome tents set on raised platforms; mattresses, pillows, and a light are provided—you'll have to pack your own sleeping bag and towels; ablutions (hot showers, flush toilets) are communal. Mokoro camping trips are a highlight of the Odd-balls experience—you set off at dawn with your personal guide/mokoro poler and camp out in privacy in the game reserve; all provisions and equipment (tents, cookery, and such) are provided. It's accessible only by air, so you'll have to charter a flight from Maun, 20 minutes away; flights and accommodations can be arranged through San Francisco–based **Africa Travel Resource** (_©_ **866/ 672-3274** or 831/338-2383; www.africatravelresource.com) or **Island-safari.com** (_©_ **866/254-1428** in the U.S.), which specializes in discounted travel to the delta and runs 4- or 5-day mokoro safaris with Oddballs as your base (5-day mokoro safari, including transfers, will set you back roughly US$800). Also look at South Africa–based **www.detourafrica.co.za**: At press time, a 3-day all-inclusive camp-ing trip (maximum of nine guests) in the delta and/or Moremi cost US$300. Private charters are available for the more romantically inclined.

chalets, each with great outdoor showers, classy colonial-style fittings and furnishings, and its own large private deck (furnished with hammocks) overlooking game-rich grassy plains. CC Africa is particularly renowned for the quality of its guides, and Sandibe is an excellent game-viewing area on the southern border of the Moremi Game Reserve (20km/12 miles from Chief's Island) and adjacent to the Santantadibe river system, offering exclusive access to a vast area that includes permanent water. Sandibe offers land and water activities as well as bush walks and night drives.

Book through CC Africa (see "Specialist Safaris & Operators," earlier in this chapter). High season (June–Oct) US$1,080 double; low season US$860. Rates are all-inclusive. DC, MC, V. Children welcome. **Amenities:** Dining/lounge area; bar; pool; curio shop; laundry; game drives; bush walks; mokoro and boat trips. _In room:_ Hair dryer, safe.

Shinde Island Camp _✦✦_   On a lush palm island in the heart of the northern delta, Shinde is Ker & Downey's most luxurious Botswana camp, surrounded by waterways that teem with birds and game. With only five twin-bed en-suite tents, each furnished with understated elegance, the camp is extremely relaxing, with wooden decks that blend in beautifully with the environment. From the veranda of your tent, you can watch game moving across the plains and listen to the sounds of woodpeckers tapping in the trees. Activities include game drives, powerboat excursions, guided walks, fish-ing, and mokoro safaris. You can also hire a private section of Shinde known as **The Enclave,** where three tents are reserved for the use of a private party; the minimum stay here is 3 nights, and you get your own dining area, bar, lounge, and staff, includ-ing a top-notch guide. Offering very much the same facilities in a totally different set-ting is Ker & Downey's **KananaCamp** _✦✦_, situated in the southwestern part of the delta at the edge of the Xudum River; rates are slightly more affordable (US$820–US$990)—some guests prefer this option for its brighter lounge and dining area, and more open feel. Also, if you're keen for a more authentic safari and don't mind rough-ing it a bit, inquire about their **Footsteps across the Delta,** a walking safari with real tents, bucket showers, and long-drop loos.

Book through Ker & Downey (see "Specialist Safaris & Operators," earlier in this chapter). Shinde: 5 units. High sea-son (July–Oct) US$1,100 double; shoulder season (Mar–June and Nov) US$900 double. The Enclave: US$2,835–US$3,625 inclusive of all 3 units. DC, MC, V. No children under 10. **Amenities:** Dining area; bar; lounge/library; pool; gallery shop; laundry; game drives; bush walks; boat and mokoro trips; fishing.

Xakanaxa Camp ✿   Situated within the Moremi Game Reserve, 50km (31 miles) to the west of Khwai, Xakanaxa (pronounced "ka-*ka*-ni-ka") offers year-round boat-ing trips and extensive nature drives into good game country; bird-watching is par-ticularly good. The camp has two sections (one has 16 beds; book ahead for one of the tents in the more intimate 8-bed camp) comprising safari-style tents with very basic en-suite facilities (loo, shower, basin). There is no electricity, so a stay here offers a real bush experience, with candles and lanterns the only source of light. Certainly not the most luxurious option, but shoulder season offers good value.

Book through Moremi Safaris & Tours (see "Specialist Safaris & Operators," earlier in this chapter). 12 units. High sea-son (July–Oct) US$1,270 double; shoulder season (Apr–June) US$790; low season (Nov–Mar) US$600. AE, DC, MC, V. **Amenities:** Both camps have dining and lounge areas; pool; laundry; game drives; boat and mokoro trips.

4 Chobe Region ✶✶✶

The far northern region of Botswana, comprising the Chobe National Park, Chobe Forest Reserve, Linyati and Savuti Channels, and Kwando Wilderness, is almost as popular as the delta, and justifiably so. Chobe National Park alone covers some 11,000 sq. km (4,290 sq. miles) of northern Botswana and offers extreme contrasts and a variety of wildlife experience, but the major drawing card here is elephant: The area harbors a large proportion—some 100,000—of Botswana's elephant population (the largest in the world). In the dry season, the Chobe River is the only major source of water north of the Okavango, so game travels here from great distances, which, in turn, ensures a large lion population, and the area is alive with birds (more than 460 different species, in fact). The nearby Savuti area, located in the west-central region, was once submerged beneath an enormous inland sea and connected to the Okavango and Zambezi rivers, but that was eons ago and today it's a relatively harsh wilderness landscape. Game-viewing is at its peak at the end of the rainy season, when large num-bers of zebra and wildebeest move through the area from the Linyati farther west to the sweeter grasses on offer in the Mababe Depression to the south. Other wildlife you'll see here are giraffe, buffalo, tsessebe, and large prides of lion and hyena.

ESSENTIALS
VISITOR INFORMATION   See "Visitor Information," at the start of the chapter. For information and reservations, go to "Specialist Safaris & Operators," earlier in the chapter, or one of the camp listings below.

GETTING THERE   **By Plane**   **Kasane International Airport** (✆ **267/625-0133**) is 3km (1¾ miles) from the entrance to Chobe National Park. **Air Botswana** has con-nections from Gaborone, Maun, and Johannesburg. See "Getting There: By Plane," in chapter 2 for more information on flying into Botswana.

By Car   From Victoria Falls, there's a road heading southwest to Kasane, a 40- to 45-minute drive away. See "Viewing Wildlife" in chapter 10 for operators specializing in transfers and day tours to Chobe.

GETTING AROUND   Again, it is recommended that you prearrange all transfers, including a possible trip to Vic Falls, with your lodge or safari operator.

WHERE TO STAY & DINE

Just a few minutes from Kasane International Airport, Chobe National Park's 35km (22 miles) of river frontage is conveniently close to the Zimbabwe and Zambia borders, making Victoria Falls day trips possible. As a result, it's a tourist-heavy area, and with the exception of the superb Chobe Chilwero and Orient-Express's swish Savute Elephant Camp, we recommend that you opt for one of the lodges situated on private reserves in and around the greater Chobe region; access is typically by charter plane (from either Kasane or Maun), which can be arranged when booking your accommodations.

NEAR KASANE, ALONG THE CHOBE RIVER

Chobe Chilwero 🌟🌟🌟   One of Botswana's most luxurious safari lodges, this Abercrombie & Kent–affiliated property overlooks the Chobe River and is just a few minutes from the main gates of Chobe National Park. Organized activities include game drives into the park, sunset boat cruises along the Chobe River (weather dependent), and day trips to Victoria Falls—this is the place to stay if you want to include a trip to the falls without overnighting. Accommodations are in spacious, high thatch-roofed private cottages with massive bathrooms that feature sunken hand-hewn tubs, indoor and outdoor showers, and Molton Brown toiletries. A private garden and/or private balcony provides wonderful views over the Chobe River islands and flood plains as far as Namibia. *Note:* The lodge offers good value from December to June.

Reservations: Sanctuary Lodges & Camps. (C) 27/11/781-1497. Fax 27/11/787-7658. www.sanctuarylodges.com. Or book through Abercrombie & Kent (see "Specialist Safaris & Operators," earlier in this chapter). 15 units. High season (July–Oct) US$970 double; low season (Dec–June) US$670 double. Rates are all-inclusive. DC, MC, V. **Amenities:** Restaurant; lounge; pool; spa and beauty treatments; gift shop; library; wine cellar; Internet access; game drives; boat trips; tours to Victoria Falls; fishing. *In room:* A/C, hair dryer, safe.

LINYATI & SAVUTI CHANNEL AREA

Kings Pool Camp 🌟🌟🌟   Substantially upgraded in 2003, this is Wilderness Safaris' premier camp in the Chobe region, and arguably the best (certainly the priciest). Located in a private reserve in the Linyanti/Savuti Channel area, just outside the western boundary of the Chobe National Park, this is prime elephant country (it's not unusual to see 800 elephants in a single day!). Each of the nine large suites, built on raised teak decks, features the ultimate in luxury: a private plunge pool and *sala* (small pavilion) with wonderful views of the Kings Pool Lagoon—this waterway has great birdlife, and hippos, crocodiles, bushbuck, impala, elephant, and sable are all seen from the rooms and private pools on a regular basis. Game-viewing activities include drives in open four-wheel-drive vehicles, night drives, walks with a professional guide, and cruises along the Linyanti River in a double-decker boat (water levels permitting). A cheaper alternative is its **Savuti Camp,** which is also open in summer (see below).

Book through Wilderness Safaris (see "Specialist Safaris & Operators," earlier in this chapter). High season (July–Oct) US$1,740 double; other US$1,190–$1,200 double. Rates are all-inclusive. MC, V. Children 8–12 are permitted through arrangement with management. **Amenities:** Dining; bar; lounge; pool.

Savute Elephant Camp 🌟🌟   This distinguished Orient-Express lodge, incidentally chosen as the second-best camp in Botswana by *Travel + Leisure* in 2005 (after Mombo), is situated in the heart of the Chobe National Park, in the arid regions of the Kalahari sandveld. It's accessible only by chartered light aircraft, so a stay here allows you to experience the impact that scarcely occurring water has on drawing wildlife—particularly, of course, elephant. Expect the standard Orient-Express luxury: Accommodations are in air-conditioned tents with large private viewing decks. *Note:* Due to its location within the Chobe reserve, night drives and walks are not allowed.

Book through Orient-Express Safaris (see "Specialist Safaris & Operators," earlier in this chapter). 12 units. From US$1,006–$1,500 double, depending on the season. Rates are all-inclusive. AE, MC, V. No children under 12 except by prior arrangement. **Amenities:** Dining and lounge areas; bar; heated pool; shop; room service, laundry; book and video library; VHS video and monitor; airstrip; game drives. *In room:* A/C, minibar, hair dryer, safe, fan, intercom.

Savuti Camp ★★ *(Value)* If you haven't yet spotted lion, this tented camp, built along the Savute Channel, lies in a region known for its large number of predators— it's possible to see wild dog, lion, and leopard in 1 day. Activities include game drives, night drives, and walks. The channel has been dry for some years, but the grasslands here make great game-viewing, and the water hole in front of the camp is very productive. Accommodations are in five large walk-in tents; ask for one of the two rooms with dramatic bathrooms that open onto the channel.

Book through Wilderness Safaris (see "Specialist Safaris & Operators," earlier in this chapter). High season (July–Oct) US$1,050 double; Apr–June and Nov US$740 double; Dec–Mar US$500 double. Rates are all-inclusive. MC, V. No children under 8. **Amenities:** Dining area; bar; plunge pool.

KWANDO WILDERNESS

Kwando Lagoon & Labala ★★ *(Kids)* The remote Kwando concession sprawls over more than 232,000 hectares (573,040 acres), making it one of the largest privately run wildlife areas in Africa. Noted for its large herds of elephants, especially during the winter months, the area, which has some 80km (50 miles) of river frontage on its eastern boundary, also attracts big numbers of large cats, buffalo, kudu, and tsessebe. If you want to spot Africa's rarest predator, the wild dog, this is the place to come, especially around the middle of the year, when a pack returns to den here for 2 to 3 months (they've been returning to Kwando for 8 years now); the lion here are also famous for their spectacular kills. With more than 320 species of birds recorded, this area is understandably popular with birders. And, thanks to specialist guides for families (ask for Lisa and Charles), it's popular with parents as well. Kwando Safaris runs two luxury tented camps on the Kwando River: **Lagoon** and **Labala**—although they're just 30km (19 miles) apart, the area is so wild that the trip takes 2 hours. Lagoon Camp is more intimate, accommodating only 12 guests in stilted en-suite safari tents with hot running water, flush loos, and double basins. Labala offers similar lodging but features Victorian bathtubs and open-air showers, as well as private sun decks. Both camps offer morning and night drives as well as boat cruises and fishing expeditions to catch the famed tiger fish. A number of the guides are keen, award-winning photographers.

Book through Kwando Safaris (see "Specialist Safaris & Operators," earlier in this chapter). Lagoon Camp 6 units. Lebala Camp 8 units. Dec–Mar US$610 double; Apr–May US$900 double; June–Oct US$1,350. AE, DC, MC, V. Rates are all-inclusive. **Amenities:** Dining area; lounge; pool; craft shop; laundry; game drives; guided walks; mokoro and boat trips; fishing.

5 The Dry South: Makgadikgadi & Nxai Pans

The Kalahari, one of the longest unbroken stretches of sand in the world, reaches across the center of Botswana, north into Zaire, and south to the Orange River in South Africa. On its northern edge are the enormous complexes of the Makgadikgadi Pans and the relatively small but no less interesting Nxai Pans, characterized by ancient baobabs and large camelthorn trees. Game migrates between the two throughout the year: In the dry season (Apr–Nov), Makgadikgadi is best; during the rains (Nov–Mar), the animals—which include springbok, gemsbok (oryx), red hartebeest, blackbacked jackal, and, occasionally, cheetah and lion—move northward to Nxai.

The Makgadikgadi Pans are a vast (12,000-sq.-km/4,680-sq.-mile) game-filled expanse of flat, seasonally inundated land. When the pans fill with water after the rains, they host countless migratory birds, most notably huge flocks of flamingos. This is the place to go to experience space at its purest: The horizons seem endless. At night, above the pie-crust surface of the pans, the stars shine with a vibrancy unequalled anywhere else in the world.

ESSENTIALS

VISITOR INFORMATION   The best safari operator here is Uncharted Africa—see "Safari Operators Specializing in Botswana," earlier in this chapter. For campsite reservations and more information, contact the **Department of Wildlife and National Parks** (www.botswanatourism.org).

GETTING THERE   By Plane   Your best bet is to fly to Maun and arrange a transfer with a tour company that arranges tours (see "Getting Around," below) in the area, or deal directly with Uncharted Africa. Note that rates here exclude transfers to camps; this should cost about US$170 one-way.

By Car   It is not a good idea to venture onto the pans without a guide or a four-wheel-drive vehicle. You will find both in the towns of Gweta and Nata. These towns can be reached in 2 days from South Africa in a normal two-wheel-drive vehicle, and can be a useful stopover if you're driving to Maun.

GETTING AROUND   On a Guided Tour   For custom-made tours in the pans, contact Uncharted Africa Safari Co., Moremi Safaris & Tours, Bush Ways, Penduka (see "Safari Operators Specializing in Botswana," earlier in this chapter, for contact details), or one of the other overland operators listed.

WHERE TO STAY & DINE

Deception Valley Lodge ★★   This small lodge—comprising five thatched units with Victorian-style bathrooms, outdoor showers, and a comfortable lounge—is situated near the northern border of the massive Central Kalahari Reserve and offers an excellent base from which to explore this vast, arid wilderness. Accommodations, done out in the hues and tones of the desert, are raised on stilts and linked to the lodge by walkways; from the deck you can gaze over the vastness of the Kalahari, which you can also explore on afternoon and night drives when guests are taken out in search of lion, cheetah, leopard, various desert antelope, and the occasional brown hyena. Of particular interest are the guided walks with traditional Bushmen, providing an opportunity to experience how they draw on ancient knowledge to survive the inhospitable conditions of this dry wilderness.

P.O. Box 70378, Bryanston 2021, South Africa. **27/11/706-7207.** Fax 27/11/463-8251. www.islandsinafrica.com. 5 units. High season (July–Oct) US$990 double; low season (Nov–June) US$720 double. Rates are all-inclusive. AE, DISC, MC, V. No children under 12. **Amenities:** Dining/lounge area; pool; curio shop; library; game drives; nature walks. *In room:* Minibar, hair dryer, ceiling fan.

Jack's Camp ★★★   Voted one of the top-10 honeymoon destinations in the world by the South African editions of *Elle* and *Men's Health,* as well as "Best Safari Camp" by both the *London Sunday Times* and *UK Vogue,* Jack's Camp is the place to go to experience the Kalahari in style. Deep in the desert, at the edge of the world's largest saltpans, accommodations comprise 10 en-suite open-air safari tents, and styling is Bedouin-meets-Africa, with Persian rugs and teak furniture providing a counterpoint to the endless desert surrounds (visible from the privacy of your own veranda). If you grow bored of lolling about on antique rugs, you can head out for game drives, walking safaris with Bushmen trackers, or explorations of remote archaeological sites and geological features. December through April sees the spectacular migration of massive wildebeest and zebra herds, followed by hungry predators. Besides trips in custom 4×4s, winter guests are taken across the saltpans on quad bikes, a highly recommended adventure. This can include a trip to **San Camp,** another tented camp, with less luxurious facilities (there's no electricity and you'll have to make do with bucket showers and long-drop toilets, although the Honeymoon tents have four-poster beds), that is situated close to the surreal rock formations known as Kubu Island. During the dry months when San Camp is operational, you can spot such desert creatures as the aardvark and aardwolf.

Both camps have an outstanding staff, including qualified zoologists and biologists, Bushman trackers, and charming and well-trained local guides. All have been thoroughly trained by the very glamorous owner Ralph Bousfield (the camp is named for his father), whose 13-part Discovery Channel series has made him one of the most famous guides in Botswana. *Note:* The camp has no electricity (lighting is fueled by paraffin) and no pool.

Book through Wilderness Safaris or Uncharted Africa Safari Co. (see "Specialist Safaris & Operators," earlier in this chapter). Jack's Camp 10 units. US$1,280 double. San Camp 6 units. $990 double; closed Nov–March. Rates are all-inclusive. Children pay full price. AE, MC, V (only cash is accepted in camp; telegraphic transfer preferred). **Amenities:** Mess tent; drinks tent; tea tent; laundry; library; museum; game drives; game/nature walks; cultural/historical tours; quad biking.

Planet Baobab (★ (Value) Imagine a giant anthill with a Planet Hollywood look-alike sign, a bar with a beer-bottle chandelier, and funkily decorated mud and grass huts in a grove of eight ancient baobab trees. If you don't mind roughing it, Planet Baobab provides a fun base for younger budget travelers to explore the fascinating Makgadikgadi Pans. Guided walks with the San to find out more about the plants and trees of this fascinating area are offered, as are trips over the salt pans in four-wheel-drive quad bikes during the dry season. Although you can opt to stay in a Bushman grass hut, you'll be better off in one of the traditional Bakalanga mud huts, which have private bathrooms. Meals are available, but you can also buy or bring your own provisions and make use of the shared kitchen.

Besides walks with guides (trained at Jack's Camp), guests can choose to be taken to the Kalahari Surf Club for a night in the pans. Planet Baobab is accessible by road; it's off the main road to Maun, 15 minutes from Gweta.

Book through Wilderness Safaris or Uncharted Africa Safari Co. (see "Specialist Safaris & Operators," earlier in this chapter). 14 units. Mud hut $82 double; family hut $116; grass hut $42 double; camping $7 per person. Meals, drinks, and activities are extra. Ask about the 3-day, 2-night itinerary. MC, V. **Amenities:** Dining area; bar; pool; laundry; camping facilities; communal kitchen; expeditions; guided walks; quad biking.

Appendix:
South Africa in Depth

South Africa's northeastern border (formed by the Limpopo River) is some 2,000km (1,240 miles) from the Cape's craggy coastline, while the semi-arid West Coast is more than 1,600km (992 miles) from the subtropical East Coast. A vast country with an immensely varied terrain, it supports a rich diversity of animals, birds, and plants, and offers a correspondingly diverse range of experiences. Historically, too, the contrasts are great: Some of the world's oldest hominid remains—dating back some 4 million years—make this one of the cradles of civilization, yet it was only a decade ago that the country emerged from the dark shadow of an oppressive policy that made it the pariah of the modern world. Born with the dawning millennium, South Africa has one of the most progressive constitutions in the world, yet the majority of its people still live in crippling poverty. Fortunately, its unique combination of natural beauty, varied wildlife, sunshine, good value, and comfortable infrastructure has meant that South Africa has emerged as one of the world's fastest-growing tourism destinations, which, in turn, is providing much-needed economic growth. So, not least of the many reasons to visit is the very warm welcome you can expect from its citizens.

1 The Natural Environment

Geographically, much of South Africa is situated on an interior plateau (referred to as the **highveld**), circled by a coastal belt that widens in the eastern hinterland to become bush savanna, or **lowveld.** It is on these undulating plains that you will find some of South Africa's most famous game reserves.

CAPE FLORAL KINGDOM One of six floral kingdoms in the world, the Cape Floral Kingdom covers an area of some 69,930 sq. km (27,273 sq. miles), yet its plant diversity is comparable to that found in the 51.8-million-sq.-km (20-million-sq.-mile) Boreal Kingdom, which covers all of Europe, North America, and northern Asia. This high concentration of unique plant species makes the Cape as important an area of conservation as the Amazon Basin.

The delicate inhabitants of the Cape Floral Kingdom are referred to as *fynbos*

(literally, "fine bush," pronounced "*feign-borse*")—an evergreen vegetation characterized by the ability to thrive in nutrient-poor soil and survive the Cape's windy, baking summers and cold winters. Thought to be the oldest floral kingdom in the world, and certainly the most diverse, three-quarters of fynbos species are found nowhere else—and many grow only in one valley.

MOUNTAINS South Africa's most famous landmark is the flat-topped **Table Mountain** in Cape Town: At a mere 1,086m (3,562 ft.), it's no giant, but it remains the most climbed mountain in South Africa. Most hikers agree that there is nothing to beat the sheer majesty of the **Drakensberg,** however, recently declared a World Heritage Site for the many San rock paintings it harbors.

DESERT South Africa has no true deserts, but much of its vast hinterland is arid—and, with only two major rivers (the

Moments Truth + Guilt + Apology = Reconciliation?

Following South Africa's first democratic elections in 1994, the **Truth and Reconciliation Commission (TRC)** was formed to investigate human rights abuses under apartheid rule. The many victims of apartheid were invited to voice their anger and pain before the commission, headed by Archbishop Desmond Tutu, and to confront directly the perpetrators of these abuses in a public forum. In return for full disclosure, aggressors, regardless of their political persuasion, could ask for forgiveness and amnesty from prosecution. Although many white South Africans went into denial, many more for the first time faced the realities of what apartheid meant. Wrenching images of keening relatives listening to killers, some coldly, others in tears, describing exactly how they had tortured and killed those once officially described as "missing persons" or "accidental deaths" were broadcast nationwide. Those whom the commission thought had not made a full disclosure were denied amnesty, as were those who could not prove that they were acting on behalf of a political cause. While some found solace in the process, many more yearned for a more equitable punishment than mere admission of wrongdoing.

Twenty-seven months of painful confessions and $25 million later, the commission concluded its investigation, handing over the report to Nelson Mandela on October 29, 1998. But the 22,000 victims of gross human rights violations had to wait until April 2003 to hear that each would receive a one-time payment of R30,000 ($4,478), a decision that was greeted with dismay by the victims. In contrast, big business (and most whites) were relieved to hear that the government had rejected the TRC's proposed tax surcharge on corporations, as well as the threatened legal action driven by New York

Vaal and Orange), a rapidly increasing demand for water, and a decreasing water table, a water shortage is likely to be the number-one problem the country faces in the 21st century. There are two distinct semidesert regions. Beyond the mountains and valleys of the southwest corner of the Cape is the **Karoo.** Like Namaqualand in the Northern Cape, famed for its daisy carpets, the Karoo also flowers in spring. The second semidesert region lies in the northwest: the painterly landscape of the **Kalahari,** with broad swaths of gold and red sand dunes and cobalt-blue skies.

COAST The country has almost 3,200km (1,984 miles) of coast and two oceans to explore. Due to the warm Mozambique Current, the **Indian Ocean** in the east and south is better for swimming. The majestic **yellowwoods** and **stinkwoods** grow along the Garden Route, as do the **cycads,** often known as fossil plants because they have remained unchanged since the Jurassic era.

Moving northward along the West Coast, the coastal strip abutting the cold **Atlantic Ocean** is increasingly sparse and harsh. It is here, in the semidesert called **Namaqualand,** that an annual miracle occurs—the first spring rains. When these fall in August or September, the seemingly barren earth is transformed into a dense carpet of **flowers** stretching as far as the eye can see.

lawyer Ed Fagan and others in American courts against companies that had benefited from apartheid, opting instead for "cooperative and voluntary partnerships." Mbeki emphasized that the TRC was not expected to bring about reconciliation but was "an important contributor to the larger process of building a new South Africa."

While it is true that the commission effected a more accurate rendition of recent history, its focus on an individualized rather than a collective approach to human rights abuses under apartheid demanded little by way of white acknowledgement of collective guilt for the suffering their fellow citizens endured. It is against this backdrop that the **Home for All** campaign was begun in 2000. Initiated, ironically enough, primarily by whites involved in the liberation struggle, the campaign was launched to indicate the willingness of white South Africans to accept that they had personally benefited from apartheid, with signatories pledging to use their skills and resources to contribute to "empowering disadvantaged people, and promoting a nonracial society whose resources are used to the benefit of all its people."

But apologies come hard in South Africa: According to "Reconciliation Barometer," published by the Institute for Justice and Reconciliation, only 22% of whites believe they had benefited from apartheid, and only 29% believe that they should apologize. While it is laudable of the government to "build on the future rather than dwell any further on the past," it is feared that as long as this kind of complacency rules the hearts of the privileged minority, South Africa's democracy remains fragile indeed.

2 South Africa Today

by Richard Calland, Executive Director,
Open Democracy Advice Centre

South Africa is stable, but not yet tranquil. The stability comes from the increasingly self-confident economy, with steady growth—as high as 5.2% in the last quarter of 2004—and relatively low inflation, and from the rapidly maturing constitutional democracy, with its internationally admired, state-of-the-art constitution. But the lack of tranquillity can be seen in the intemperate language of political spats, in the wafer-thin skins of many leading political figures, and in chronic, structural inequalities and poverty.

When broadly defined, South Africa's unemployment is as high as 41%—a figure disputed by the much-respected and popular finance minister, Trevor Manual, whose response was to argue that if unemployment were this high, "we would have a revolution on our hands." Of course, he is partly right: There is a significant *informal* economy. But the fact remains—modest growth notwithstanding—that changes in technology and the global economy have resulted in a net loss of jobs since 1994.

President Thabo Mbeki is painfully aware of this "two nations, two economies"—a theme that peppers his speeches (and his tongue is as sharp as his mind; he is an active participant in the more rancorous public disputes). In 2004 Mbeki returned to office for a second term with an increased majority, having won almost 70% of the vote. Mbeki and his party appeared in full control of their destiny, and well on course. Yet you wouldn't have known it from the president's weekly writings in his now-legendary "Letter from the President" on the ANC's website (www.anc.org.za). Indeed, for a political barometer, there is no better place to start. Having first challenged the patriotism of the giant mining conglomerate Anglo American, Mbeki then took on another South African totem—Archbishop Desmond Tutu, above whom only Nelson Mandela stands in the nation's affection and esteem. Tutu had complained that the ANC leadership was too sensitive to criticism and too quick to sanction and crush internal dissent within its own ranks. In the minds of most commentators, Mbeki's coruscating response to Tutu, containing a vicious personal attack, only proved Tutu's case.

Mbeki is the one of most influential politicians of his generation—globally. His vision of an "African Renaissance" and the economic program of development that accompanies it (known as Nepad) has begun the gigantic task of changing the relationship between the West and Africa. Mbeki is a masterful tactician and a brilliant diplomat: While much attention has focused on the failure of his so-called "quiet diplomacy" with Zimbabwe, his government has facilitated a number of successful negotiations elsewhere on the continent, including the Great Lakes region, Sudan, and the Ivory Coast. South Africa—by far the biggest economy in Africa—is fast learning how to use its power to greatest effect.

Mbeki is also a very able "CEO" of government. His administration has been far more efficient than that of his predecessor, Nelson Mandela. On the government website you will find that each of his cabinet ministers has been assigned targeted goals, with quarterly reports providing refreshingly candid assessments of progress. Yet Mbeki is often considered somewhat "obscure." Certainly, he can be enigmatic—his eccentric opinions on the linkage between HIV and AIDS have greatly undermined international confidence in his judgment. But what other head of state every week provides his or her citizens with up to 3,000 words of insight into the current thinking on the issues of the day?

With Mbeki and his party so dominant, much of the political action pivots around the question of the succession to

Dateline

- **Circa 8000 B.C.** Southern Africa is believed by many paleontologists to be the birthplace of man, with hominid remains dating back some 3.5 million years. Millions of years later, the pastoral KhoiKhoi (Hottentots), joined even later by the Bantu-speaking people (blacks), arrive to displace the hunter-gatherer San (Bushmen).

- **A.D. 1488** Bartholomieu Dias is the first white settler to round the Cape, landing at Mossel Bay.
- **1497** Vasco da Gama rounds the southern African coast, discovering an alternate sea route to India.
- **1652** Jan van Riebeeck is sent to set up a supply station for the Dutch East India Company. Cape Town is born.
- **1659** The first serious armed conflict against the KhoiKhoi

occurs; the first wine is pressed.
- **1667–1700** First Malay slaves arrive, followed by the French Huguenots.
- **1779** The first frontier war between the Xhosa and settlers in the Eastern Cape is fought. Eight more were to follow in what is now known as the Hundred Years War.
- **1795** The British occupy the Cape for 7 years and then hand it back to the Dutch.

Mbeki. The criminal trial of Shabir Shaik, a businessman with close connections to Deputy President Jacob Zuma at the start of 2005, raised questions about Zuma's judgment and fitness to succeed Mbeki. Factions rotated around the issue; the left of the ANC wants Zuma because he will give them more "space," while the Mbeki wing distrusts his lack of intellectualism.

Indeed, to understand South African politics, you have to understand "the alliance" between the ANC as a political party, the South African Communist Party (SACP), and COSATU (the umbrella trade union federation). The opposition parties are increasingly irrelevant, as the 2004 election result showed— bereft of ideas, short of strategic and tactical wit, and apparently unable to tap into a new market of younger voters, many of whom worryingly choose *not* to register to vote. As a footnote, 2004 also heralded the final demise of the party of apartheid, the National Party, consigned to the dustbin of history a mere 10 years after the advent of democracy.

Applying its 100-indicator Democracy Index, independent think tank the Institute for Democracy in South Africa (www.idasa.org.za) recently scored South Africa's democracy at 63%. As the Institute concluded: "Pretty good after barely more than a decade," though it added an important rider: "Largely united, but tragically still deeply unequal, South Africa enters its second decade of democracy, strong and confident, but with profound questions to be resolved . . . having laid such a foundation, it must be used as springboard for the full emancipation of South Africans."

3 A Look at the Past

Like all history, South Africa's biography depends very much on who is recounting the tale. Under the apartheid regime, children were taught that in the 19th century, when the first pioneering Voortrekkers made their way north from the Cape Peninsula, and black tribes were making their way south from central Africa, southern Africa was a vast, undiscovered wilderness. Blacks and whites thus conveniently met on land that belonged to no one, and if the natives would not move aside for the trinkets and oxen on offer, everyone simply rolled up their sleeves and had an honest fight—which the whites, who believed they enjoyed the special protection of the Lord, almost always won. Of course, for those who pursued the truth rather than a nationalistic version of it,

- 1806 Britain reoccupies the Cape, this time for 155 years.
- 1815 Shaka becomes the Zulu king.
- 1820 The British settlers arrive in the Eastern Cape. In KwaZulu-Natal, Shaka starts his great expansionary war, decimating numbers of opposing tribes and leaving large areas depopulated in his wake.
- 1824 Port Natal is established by British traders.
- 1828 Shaka is murdered by his half-brother, Dingaan, who succeeds him as king.
- 1834 Slavery is abolished in the Cape, sparking off the Great Trek.
- 1835–45 More than 16,000 bitter Dutch settlers head for the uncharted hinterland in ox-wagons to escape British domination.
- 1838 A party of Voortrekkers manages to vanquish Zulu
forces at the Battle of Blood River.
- 1843 Natal becomes a British colony.
- 1852 Several parties of Boers move farther northeast and found the Zuid Afrikaansche Republiek (ZAR).
- 1854 The Boer Independent Republic of the Orange Free State is founded by another party of Boers.

continues

the past was infinitely more complex—not least because so little of it was recorded.

FROM APES TO ARTISTS Some of the world's oldest hominid remains have been found in South Africa, mostly in the valley dubbed the **Cradle of Humankind** in Gauteng. These suggest that man's earliest relatives were born here more than 3 million years ago.

The country also harbors the oldest fossil evidence of Homo sapiens, this time in the Eastern Cape. The finding proved that man, his brain now much larger, was padding about in South Africa 50,000 to 100,000 years ago. But for many, the most arresting evidence of early human activity in southern Africa are the many **rock paintings** that the San hunter-gatherers (or Bushmen, as they were dubbed by Europeans) used to record events dating as far back as 30,000 years. The closest living relative of Stone Age man, a few small family units of San, still survive in the Kalahari Desert; but the last San artist must have died over a hundred years ago, as the most recent rock painting dates back to the 19th century.

From these drawings we can deduce that Bantu-speaking Iron Age settlers were living in South Africa long before the arrival of the white colonizers. Dark-skinned and technologically more sophisticated than the San, they started crossing the Limpopo about 2,000 years ago, and over the centuries four main groups of migrants settled in South Africa: the **Nguni**-speaking group, of which the Zulu and Xhosa are part, followed by the **Tsonga, Sotho-Tswana,** and **Venda** speakers. **Trading centers** were developed, such as those near Phalaborwa, the remains of which can still be seen in Kruger National Park.

By the 13th century, most of South Africa's eastern flank was occupied by these African people, while the San remained concentrated in the west. In Botswana, a small number of the latter were introduced to the concept of sheep- and cattle-keeping. These agrarian groups migrated south and called themselves the **KhoiKhoi (men of men),** to differentiate themselves from their San relatives. It was with these indigenous people that the first seafarers came into contact. The KhoiKhoi saw themselves as a superior bunch, and it must have been infuriating to be called Hottentots by the Dutch (a term sometimes used to denigrate the Cape Coloured group, and still considered degrading today).

THE COLONIZATION OF THE CAPE When spice was as precious as gold, the bravest men in Europe were the Portuguese crew who set off with **Bartholomieu Dias** in 1487 to drop off the edge

---

- **1858** The British defeat the Xhosa after the "Great Cattle Killing," in which the Xhosa destroy their crops and herds in the mistaken belief that with this sacrifice their ancestors will destroy the enemy.
- **1860** The first indentured Indian workers arrive in Natal.
- **1867** Diamonds are found near Kimberley in the Orange Free State.

- **1877** The British annex the ZAR.
- **1879** Anglo-Zulu War breaks out, orchestrated by the British.
- **1880–81** First Anglo-Boer War is fought. Boers defeat British.
- **1883** Paul Kruger becomes the first president of the ZAR.
- **1886** Gold is discovered on the Witwatersrand.

- **1899–1902** The Second Anglo-Boer War. British defeat Boers.
- **1910** The Union of South Africa proclaimed. Louis Botha becomes first premier. Blacks are excluded from the process.
- **1912** The South African Native National Congress is formed. After 1923 this would be known as the African National Congress (ANC).

of the world and find an alternative trade route to the Indies. Dias rounded the Cape, which he named **Tormentoso ("Stormy Cape"),** after his fleet of three tiny ships battled storms for 3 days before he tacked back to what is today known as Mossel Bay. Suffering from acute scurvy, his men forced him to turn back soon after this.

It was 10 years before another group was foolhardy enough to follow in their footsteps. **Vasco da Gama** sailed past what had been renamed the Cape of Good Hope, rounding the East Coast, which he named Natal, and sailed all the way to India.

The Portuguese opened the sea route to the East, but it was the Dutch who took advantage of the strategic port at the tip of Africa. In 1652 (30 years after the first English settled in the United States), **Jan van Riebeeck,** who had been caught cooking the Dutch East India Company books in Malaysia, was sent to open a refreshment station as penance. The idea was not to colonize the Cape, but simply to create a halfway house for trading ships. Van Riebeeck was given strict instructions to trade with the natives and in no way enslave them. Inevitably, relations soured—the climate and beauty of the Cape led members of the crew and soldiers to settle permanently on the land,

with little recompense for the KhoiKhoi. To prevent the KhoiKhoi from seeking revenge, Van Riebeeck attempted to create a boundary along the Liesbeeck River by planting a bitter-almond hedge—the remains of this hedge still grow today in the Kirstenbosch Gardens. This, together with the advantage of firepower and the introduction of hard liquor, reduced the KhoiKhoi to no more than a nuisance. Those who didn't toe the line were imprisoned on **Robben Island,** and by the beginning of the 18th century, the remaining KhoiKhoi were reduced to virtual slavery by disease and drink. Over the years, their genes slowly mingled with those of slaves and burghers to create a new underclass, later known as the Cape Coloureds.

In 1666, the foundation stones for the **Castle of Good Hope** were laid, and still more elements were added to the melting pot of Cape culture. Van Riebeeck persuaded the company to allow the import of **slaves** from the Dutch East Indies; this was followed by the arrival of the **French Huguenots** in 1668. Fleeing religious persecution, these Protestants increased the size of the colony by 15% and brought with them the ability to cultivate **wine.** The glorious results of their input can still be enjoyed in the valley of **Franschhoek (French corner).**

- **1913** The Native Land Act is passed, limiting land ownership for blacks.
- **1914–18** South Africa declares war on Germany.
- **1923** Natives (Urban Areas) Act imposes segregation in towns.
- **1939–45** South Africa joins the Allies in fighting World War II.
- **1948** D. F. Malan's National Party wins the election, and the era of apartheid is born.

Races are classified, the passbook system is created, and interracial sex is made illegal.
- **1955** ANC adopts Freedom Charter.
- **1956** Coloureds lose the right to vote.
- **1958** H. F. Verwoerd, the architect of apartheid, succeeds D. F. Malan and creates the homelands—territories set aside for black tribes.

- **1959** Robert Sobukwe forms the Pan African National Congress (PAC).
- **1960** Police open fire on demonstrators at Sharpeville, killing 69 people. ANC and PAC banned. ANC ends its policy of peaceful negotiation.
- **1961** South Africa leaves the Commonwealth and becomes a republic. Albert Luthuli awarded Nobel Peace Prize.

continues

The British entered the picture in 1795, taking control of the Cape when the Dutch East India Company was liquidated. In 1803 they handed it back to the Dutch for 3 years, after which they were to rule the Cape for 155 years.

One of their first tasks was to silence the "savages" on the Eastern Frontier—these were the **Xhosa,** part of the Nguni-speaking people who migrated south from central Africa. Essential to the plan was the creation of a buffer zone of English settlers. Between 1820 and 1824, thousands of artisans and soldiers were off-loaded in the Eastern Cape, issued with basic implements, tents, and seeds, and sent off to deal with the Xhosa. Four frontier wars followed, but it was the extraordinary **cattle-killing incident** that crippled the Xhosa: In 1856 a young girl, Nongqawuse, prophesied that if the Xhosa killed all their cattle and destroyed their crops, the dead ancestors would rise and help vanquish the settlers. Needless to say, this did not occur, and while four more wars were to follow, the Xhosa's might was effectively broken by this mass sacrifice.

THE RISE OF THE ZULU & AFRIKANER CONFLICTS At the turn of the 19th century, the **Zulus,** the Nguni group that settled on the east coast in what is now called KwaZulu-Natal,

were growing increasingly combative as their survival depended on absorbing neighbors to gain control of pasturage. A young warrior named **Shaka,** who took total despotic control of the Zulus in 1818, raised this to an art form—in addition to arming his new regiments with the short stabbing spear, Shaka was a great military tactician and devised a strategy known as the **horns of the bull,** whereby the enemy was outflanked by highly disciplined formations that eventually engulfed them. This was used to great effect on tribes in the region, and by the middle of the decade, the Zulus had formed a centralized military state with a 40,000-strong army. In a movement known as the **Mfecane,** or forced migrations, huge areas of the country were cleared. People were either killed or absorbed by the Zulus; many fled, creating new kingdoms such as **Swaziland** and **Lesotho.** In 1828 Shaka was murdered by his two brothers, one of whom, Dingaan, succeeded him as king.

On the Cape, British interference in labor relations and oppression of the "kitchen Dutch" language infuriated many of the Dutch settlers, by now referred to as *Afrikaners* (of Africa), and later, *Boers* (farmers). The abolishing of slavery in 1834 was the last straw. Afrikaners objected to "not so much their

- **1963** Nelson Mandela and others sentenced to life imprisonment in the Rivonia sabotage trials.
- **1970s** Worldwide economic and cultural boycotts are initiated in response to South Africa's human rights abuses.
- **1976** Police open fire on unarmed black students demonstrating against use of Afrikaans as a teaching medium; the Soweto riots follow.

- **1977** Black-consciousness leader Steve Biko dies in police custody.
- **1980–84** President P. W. Botha attempts cosmetic reforms. Unrest escalates. Bishop Tutu, who urges worldwide sanctions, is awarded the Nobel Peace Prize.
- **1985** State of Emergency declared, gagging the press and giving security forces absolute power.

- **1989** F. W. de Klerk succeeds P. W. Botha.
- **1990** de Klerk ends the State of Emergency, lifts the ban on the ANC, and frees Mandela.
- **1993** de Klerk and Mandela are awarded the Nobel Peace Prize.
- **1994** The first democratic elections are held, and on May 10 Mandela is sworn in as the first black president of South Africa. De Klerk and

freedom" as one wrote, "as their being placed on an equal footing with Christians, contrary to the laws of God and the natural distinction of race."

Some 15,000 people (10% of the Afrikaners at the Cape) set off on what is known as the Great Trek, and became known as the *Voortrekkers,* or "first movers." They found large tracts of unoccupied land that, unbeknownst to them, had been cleared by the recent Mfecane, and it wasn't long before they clashed with the mighty Zulu nation, whom they defeated in 1838 at the **Battle of Blood River.** A century later, this "miraculous" victory was to be the greatest inspiration for Afrikaner nationalism, and a monument was built to glorify the battle. Today the **Voortrekker Monument** is still a place of pilgrimage for Afrikaner nationalists and can be seen from most places in Pretoria.

The Boers' victory was, however, short lived. The British, not satisfied with the Cape's coast, annexed Natal in 1845. Once again, the Voortrekkers headed over the mountains with their ox-wagons, looking for freedom from the British. They founded two republics: the **Orange Free State** (now the Free State) and the **South African Republic** or **Transvaal** (now Gauteng, the North-West, Mpumalanga, and the Northern Province). This time the British left them alone, focusing their attention on places of more interest than a remote outpost with only 250,000 settlers. Needless to say, the 1867 discovery of **diamonds** in the Orange Free State and, 19 years later, **gold** in the Transvaal, was to change this attitude dramatically.

GETTING RICH & STAYING POOR

In both the diamond and the gold fields, a step-by-step amalgamation of individual claims was finally necessitated by the expense of the mining process. In Kimberley, **Cecil John Rhodes**—an ambitious young man who was to become obsessed with the cause of British imperial expansion—masterminded the creation of **De Beers Consolidated,** the mining house that to this day controls the diamond-mining industry in southern Africa. (It is worth noting that the discovery of diamonds was also the start of the labor-discrimination practices that were to set the precedent for the gold mines and the coming apartheid years.) The mining of gold did not result in the same monopoly, and the **Chamber of Mines,** established in 1887, went some way to regulate the competition. **Paul Kruger,** president of the South African Republic, became a spoke in the wheel, however. A Calvinist preacher and survivor of the Great Trek, he did not intend to make things easy for the mostly British

Thabo Mbeki become joint Deputy Presidents.

- **1995** Truth and Reconciliation Commission created under Archbishop Desmond Tutu.
- **1997** South Africa's new constitution, one of the world's most progressive, comes into effect on February 3.
- **1998** Truth and Reconciliation Commission ends. U.S. gives Mandela the Congressional Gold Medal.

- **1999** The second democratic elections are held. The ANC gets 66.03% of the vote; Thabo Mbeki becomes president.
- **2000** UNESCO awards five sites in South Africa World Heritage status. The Kgalagadi, Africa's first Transfrontier Park, which connects vast wildlife tracts between Botswana and S.A., is created. UNAIDS reveals that South Africa has the largest

AIDS population in the world. National Conference on Racism is held.

- **2002** Reversal of AIDS policy; government acknowledges the usefulness of anti-retroviral drugs but fails to roll out national treatment program.
- **2004** The ANC, with Thabo Mbeki at the helm, wins the country's third democratic election with a landslide 70% victory.

entrepreneurs who controlled the gold mines. He created no real infrastructure to aid them, and *uitlanders* (foreigners) were not allowed to vote. Britain, in turn, wanted to amalgamate the South African colonies to consolidate their power in southern Africa. (British forces had attempted to annex the Transvaal in 1877, just after the discovery of diamonds, but they had underestimated Paul Kruger; in 1881, after losing the first Anglo-Boer war, they restored the Boer republics' independence.) In 1899, when the British demanded full rights for the *uitlanders,* Kruger responded by invading the coastal colonies.

At first the second **Anglo-Boer War** went well for the Boers, who used hitherto unheard of guerilla warfare tactics, but the British commander **Lord Kitchener** soon found their Achilles' heel. Close to 28,000 Boer women and children died in Kitchener's concentration camps, and his scorched-earth policy, whereby their farms were systematically razed to the ground, broke the Boer spirit. Ultimately, Britain would pit nearly half a million men against 88,000 Boers. In 1902 the Boer republics became part of the Empire—the Afrikaner nationalism that was to sweep the country in the next century was fueled by the resentments of a nation struggling to escape the yoke of British imperialism.

OPPRESSION & RESISTANCE   The years following this defeat were hard on those at the bottom of the ladder. Afrikaners, many of whom had lost their farms, streamed to the cities, where they competed with blacks for unskilled jobs on equal terms and were known as "poor whites." Black South Africans had also suffered during the Anglo-Boer War (including the loss of some 14,000 in the concentration camps), but in later years, when Afrikaner fortunes turned, this was neither recognized nor compensated. With the creation of the **Union of South Africa** in 1910, the country joined the British Commonwealth of Nations and participated in World War I and World War II. Back home, loyalties were divided, and the Afrikaners were bitter about forging allegiances with a country they had so recently been at war with. In 1934 a new "purified" **National Party (NP)** was established, offering a voice for the "poor white" Afrikaners. Under the leadership of Dr. D. F. Malan, who swore he would liberate the Afrikaners from their economic "oppression," the NP won the 1948 election by a narrow margin—46 years of white minority rule were to follow before internal and international pressure would finally buckle the NP's resolve.

One of the first laws that created the segregationist policy named **apartheid** (literally, "separateness") was the **Population Registration Act,** in which everyone was slotted into an appropriate race group. This caused the greatest problem for those of mixed descent (see "The Coloured Class: Rise & Demise of a New 'Race,'" below). One of the most infamous classification tests was the pencil test, whereby a pencil was stuck into the hair of a person of uncertain racial heritage. If the pencil dropped, the person was "white"; if not, they were classified "coloured." In this way, entire communities, even families, were torn apart. This new group, dubbed the Coloureds, enjoyed slightly more privileges than their black counterparts—a better standard of housing, schooling, and job opportunities—an overture to their white ancestors. Interracial sexual relations, previously illicit, were now illegal, and the Group Areas Act ensured that families would never mingle on the streets. The act also required the destruction and relocation of total suburbs, none of which was white. The **Bantu Education Act** ensured that black South Africans would never challenge the better-educated white

South Africans for jobs. During this time, the majority of English speakers condemned the policies of what came to be known as the Afrikaner NP; but because they continued to dominate business in South Africa, the maintenance of a cheap labor pool was in their interests, and life was generally too comfortable for most to do anything. Change came inevitably from the nonwhite quarters.

By the mid–20th century, blacks outnumbered whites in the urban areas but resided "unseen" in **townships** outside of the cities. Their movements were restricted by **pass laws;** they were barred from trade union activities, deprived of any political rights, and prohibited from procuring land outside of their reserves or homelands. **Homelands** were small tracts of land, comprising about 13% of the country, where the so-called ethnically distinct black South African "tribes" (at that time 42% of the population) were forced to live. This effectively divided the black majority into tribal minorities.

The **African Nationalist Congress Party (ANC)** was formed by representatives of the major African organizations in 1912, but it was only in 1934 that it was to find the inspired leadership of **Anton Lembede, Oliver Tambo, Walter Sisulu,** and **Nelson Mandela,** who formed the **ANC Youth League** in this year. The ANC's hitherto passive resistance tactics were met with forceful suppression in 1960 when police fired on unarmed demonstrators in **Sharpeville,** killing 67 and wounding 200. It was a major turning point for South Africa, sparking violent opposition within and ostracism in world affairs.

In 1963 police captured the underground leaders of the ANC—including the "Black Pimpernel," Nelson Mandela, who was by now commander-in-chief of their armed wing, **UmkhontoWe Sizwe ("Spear of the Nation").** In what came to be known as the **Rivonia Trial,** Mandela and nine other leaders received life sentences for treason and were incarcerated on **Robben Island.** The imprisonment of key figures effectively silenced the opposition within the country for some time and allowed the NP to further entrench its segregationist policies. But it wasn't all clear sailing: Hendrik Verwoerd, the cabinet minister for Bantu Affairs under Malan and the man who was named "the architect of apartheid," was stabbed to death one morning in the House of Assembly—and strangely, not for political reasons; the murderer insisted that a tapeworm had ordered him to do it. In 1966 B. J. Vorster became the new NP leader. He was to push for the independence of Verwoerd's black homelands, which would effectively deprive all black people of their South African citizenship, as well as enforce the use of Afrikaans as a language medium in all schools. Ironically, the latter triggered the backlash that would finally end Afrikaner dominance.

SOUTH AFRICA GOES INTO LABOR On June 16, 1976, thousands of black schoolchildren in **Soweto** took to the streets to demonstrate against this new law, which for the many non–Afrikaans speakers would render schooling incomprehensible. The police opened fire, killing, among others, 13-year-old **Hector Pieterson,** and chaos ensued, with unrest spreading throughout the country. The youth, disillusioned by their parents' implicit compliance with apartheid laws, burned schools, libraries, and *shebeens,* the informal liquor outlets that provided an opiate to the dispossessed. Many arrests followed, including that of black-consciousness leader **Steve Biko** in the Eastern Cape, who became the 46th political prisoner to die during police interrogation. Young activists fled the country and joined ANC military training camps. The ANC, led by Oliver Tambo, called for international sanctions—the world responded with economic, cultural, and sports boycotts, and awarded the Nobel Peace Prize to **Archbishop Desmond Tutu,** one of the strongest campaigners for sanctions. The new NP premier, **P. W. Botha,** or, as he came to be known, *"die Groot Krokodil"* ("the great crocodile"), simply wagged his finger and declared South Africa capable of going it alone despite increasing pressure—in the words of Allen Boesak, addressing the launch of the United Democratic Front, the students of Soweto wanted *all* their rights, they wanted them *here,* and they wanted them *now.* The crocodile's bite proved as bad as his bark, and his response was simply to pour an ever-increasing number of troops into townships. In 1986 he declared a **State of Emergency,** thereby giving his security forces unlimited power to persecute the opposition, and effectively silencing the internal press.

The overwhelming majority of white South Africans enjoyed an excellent standard of living, a state of supreme comfort that made it difficult to challenge the status quo. Many believed the state propaganda that blacks were innately inferior, or remained blissfully ignorant of the extent of the human rights violations; still others found their compassion silenced by fear. Ignorant or numbed, most white South Africans waited for what seemed to be the inevitable civil war, until 1989, when a ministerial rebellion forced the intransigent Botha to resign, and new leader **F. W. de Klerk** stepped in. By now the economy was in serious trouble—the cost of maintaining apartheid had bled the coffers dry, the Chase Manhattan Bank had refused to roll over its loan, and sanctions and trade-union action had brought the country's economy to a virtual standstill. Mindful of these overwhelming odds, de Klerk unbanned the ANC, the PAC, the Communist Party, and 33 other organizations in February 1990. Nelson Mandela—imprisoned for 27 years—was released soon thereafter.

BIRTH OF THE "NEW SOUTH AFRICA" The fragile negotiations among the various political parties were to last a nerve-racking 4 years. During this time, right-wingers threatened civil war, while many in the townships lived it. **Zulu nationalists,** of the **Inkatha** party, waged a low-level war against ANC supporters that was to claim the lives of thousands. Eyewitness accounts were given of security force involvement in this black-on-black violence, with training and supplies provided to Inkatha forces by the South African Defence Force. In 1993 **Chris Hani,** the popular ANC youth leader, was assassinated. South Africa held its breath as Mandela pleaded on nationwide television for peace—by this time, there was no doubt as to who was leading the country.

On April 27, 1994, **Nelson Mandela** cast his first vote at the age of 76, and on May 10 he was inaugurated as South Africa's first democratically elected president. Despite 18 opposition parties, the ANC took 63% of the vote and was dominant in all but two provinces—the Western Cape voted NP, and KwaZulu-Natal went to Buthelezi's Zulu-based Inkatha (IFP) Party. Jubilation reigned, but the hangover was bad. The economy was in dire straits, with double-digit inflation, gross foreign exchange down to less than 3 weeks of imports, and a budget deficit of 6.8% of GDP. Of an estimated 38 million people, at least 6 million were unemployed and 9 million destitute. Ten million had no access to running water, and 20 million no electricity. The ANC had to launch a program of "nation-building"— attempting to unify what the NP had spent a fortune dividing. Wealth had to be redistributed without hampering the ailing economy, and a government debt of almost R350 billion ($52 billion) repaid.

Still, after 300 years of white domination, South Africa entered the new millennium with what is widely regarded as the world's most progressive constitution, and its murky history was finally held up for close inspection by the Truth and Reconciliation Commission, the first of its kind in the world (see "Truth + Guilt + Apology = Reconciliation?" earlier in this chapter). South African sports heroes, barred from competing internationally for 2 decades, added to the nation's growing pride, winning the Rugby World Cup in 1995 and its first gold Olympic medals in 1996. Augmenting these ideological and sporting achievements were those that have happened on a grassroots level: 1999, when the ANC won the second democratic elections with a landslide victory of 66.03% of the vote, saw a change in ANC leadership style, with new president **Thabo Mbeki** centralizing power and focusing on delivery rather than reconciliation. "Africa," Mbeki promised, "will prosper." By the end of 2000, more than 1 million houses had been completed, 412 new telephone lines installed, 127 clinics built, and 917,220 hectares (2,265,533 acres) of land handed over to new black owners. Some 37,396 households had benefited from land redistribution, and water supply had increased from 62,249 recipients in 1995 to a whopping 6,495,205. Black-owned business grew

significantly, and an estimated four million blacks comprised half of the top earners in the country. But with unemployment estimated at between 30% and 40%, the concomitant rise in crime was hardly surprising. The specter of AIDS was also stalking South Africa, and by 2000 it would find itself with the highest HIV-positive population in the world. Equally distressing was the continued divide between black and white incomes, reinforcing South Africa's strange mix of first- and third-world elements, and prompting Mbeki's controversial "two nations" speech in which he stated that "the failure to achieve real nation-building was entrenching the existence of two separate nations, one white and affluent, and the other black and poor."

But despite these problems, the fiscal discipline that the ANC has pursued has resulted in a robust economic outlook in 2003, with crime either stabilized or reduced, and the delivery of basic services and education extended to the majority of citizens. But the reduction of unemployment levels and concurrent poverty alleviation remain challenges that have not been adequately met. That the New South African nation was born in peace was a miracle, but many feel the ANC will need another to meet its campaign promise of "a better life for all."

4 The Rainbow Nation

South African stereotypes are no simple black-and-white matter. Historically, the nation was made up of a number of widely different cultural groups that under normal circumstances might have amalgamated into a singular hybrid called "the South African." But the deeply divisive policy of apartheid only further entrenched initial differences.

At a popular level, Mandela appeared as the architect of the post-1994 "nation-building," utilizing this rainbow myth to

capture the hearts and minds of black and white South Africans alike. Despite the ANC government's stated objective to end racial discrimination and develop a unique South African identity, this "rainbow nation" remains difficult to define, let alone unify. Broadly speaking, approximately 76% of some 38 million people are black, 12.8% are white, 2.6% are Asian, and 8.5% are "coloured" (the apartheid term for those of mixed descent as well as for some 200,000 Cape Malays;

The Coloured Class: Rise & Demise of a New "Race"

Afrikaans-speaking people of mixed descent—grouped together as a new race called "the coloureds" during the Population Registration Act—were perhaps the most affected by the policies of apartheid. They were brought up to respect their white blood and deny their black roots entirely, and the apartheid state's overture to the coloureds' white forefathers was to treat them as second in line to whites, providing them with a better education, greater rights, and more government support than black people. The destruction of their sense of self-worth was made evident when the "New Nationalist Party" (NNP) won the 1994 election race in the Western Cape (where the majority of this group resides). In 1999 the Democratic Party, which had absorbed the NNP, again won the elections in the Western Cape. Voting back into power the selfsame racist party that had created their oppressive new identity was seemingly a direct result of the false sense of hierarchy that apartheid created. Fear of *"die Swart Gevaar"* (an NP propaganda slogan meaning "the Black Danger") is slow to dissipate, and despite calls within the coloured ranks to do away with the label entirely, many still believe that whites are innately superior to blacks and that the coloureds are in a class of their own.

see "The Coloured Class: Rise & Demise of a New 'Race,'" below). Beyond these are smaller but no less significant groups, descendants of Lebanese, Italian, Portuguese, Hungarian, and Greek settlers, as well as the 130,000-strong Jewish community. The latter, in particular, has played an enormous role in the economic and political growth of South Africa, as is evidenced at the Jewish Museum in Cape Town.

In an attempt to recognize this cultural diversity, the government has given official recognition to 11 languages: Zulu, Xhosa, Afrikaans, English, Sotho, Venda, Tswana, Tsona, Pedi, Shangaan, and Ndebele. Television news and sports are broadcast in the four main language groups, English, Nguni (Zulu and Xhosa), Afrikaans, and Sotho. But while languages provide some clue as to the demographics of the population, particularly where a specific language user is likely to live (another apartheid legacy),

they give no real idea of the complexity of attitudes within groups—for instance, urban-born Xhosa males still paint their faces white to signal their transition to manhood, but unlike their rural counterparts, they may choose to be circumcised by a Western doctor. A group of Sotho women may invest their *stokvel* (an informal savings scheme) in unit trusts, while their mothers will not open a bank account. And an "ethnic" white Afrikaner living in rural Northern Cape will have very little in common with an Afrikaans-speaking coloured living in cosmopolitan Cape Town.

Despite continued poverty, it is the previously disadvantaged who show the most optimism for the future. Proof that life has improved for the majority of the population is not always easy to find, but in the "City of Gold," the black middle class is growing, and it is the "buppies" (black-up-and-coming) who frequent the previously whites-only shopping malls.

Even among the new elite, however, there are those who feel that the New South Africa is taking too long to deliver on its promises. "There is no black in the rainbow," an embittered Winnie Madikizela-Mandela said. "Maybe there is no rainbow nation at all." Hardly surprising, really. Years of fragmentation have rendered the nation cautious, suspicious, and critical—a recent survey shows that only 12% of whites have contact with other racial groups outside the workplace, and more than 80% of blacks have never shared a meal with a white person. South Africans are still molded by the social-engineering experiment that separated them geographically and psychologically. For a new, shared South African identity to emerge, it will take time, enough at least for the colors to mingle.

5 South African Cuisine

Visit at least one restaurant that specializes in South African cuisine, and you will sample a new and truly delicious selection of dishes—for, contrary to popular belief, South Africans can cook up a storm.

The most basic African foodstuff is **corn,** most popularly eaten as *pap,* a ground maize porridge, or the rougher wholegrain *samp,* and served with a vegetable- or meat-based sauce. Traditionally, cows were kept as a sign of wealth and slaughtered only for special occasions, but now cheap cuts like liver, heart, and brisket are popular, along with chicken. Popular vegetables include pumpkin, cabbage, carrots, wild spinach, and potatoes.

Easiest on the newly initiated palate are the **Cape Malay dishes,** characterized by sweet aromatic **curries.** These include *bobotie,* a delicious baked meatloaf, mildly curried and served with chutney, and *bredie,* a tomato-based stew. Another Cape delicacy not to be missed is *waterblommetjie bredie,* or waterlily stew, usually cooked with lamb. Many South African menus also feature **Karoo lamb,** favored because the sweet and aromatic herbs and grasses of this arid region flavor the animals as they graze, and **ostrich,** a delicious red meat with no cholesterol.

Your dessert may be ***melktert,*** a cinnamon-flavored custard tart of Dutch origin, or ***koeksisters,*** plaited doughnuts, deep-fried and dipped in syrup.

On the East Coast, Durban is famed for its **Indian curries,** whose burn potential is indicated by such ingenious names as Honeymooners' Delight (hot) and Mother-in-Law Exterminator (damn hot!). The coastline supplies seafood in abundance: fish, abalone, mussels, oysters, crabs, squid, langoustines, and the Cape's famous rock lobster (crayfish), but for a uniquely South African–flavored seafood feast, you'll need to head for one of the West Coast beach restaurants. Here **snoek,** a firm white fish, is traditionally served with *konfyt* (fruits preserved in sugar syrup, from the French *confit,* a legacy of the French Huguenots).

Look for the spiraling smoke trailing over suburban fences and township yards each weekend, when throughout the country South Africans barbecue fresh meat over coals. The ubiquitous ***braaivleis*** **(barbecues)** or ***tshisanyamas*** (literally, "burn the meat") feature anything from ostrich to *boerewors;* the latter, a coriander-spiced beef and pork sausage, is arguably South Africa's staple meat.

Index

THE NEW TRAVELOCITY GUARANTEE

EVERYTHING YOU BOOK WILL BE RIGHT, OR WE'LL WORK WITH OUR TRAVEL PARTNERS TO MAKE IT RIGHT, RIGHT AWAY.

*To drive home the point,
we're going to use the word "right" in every single sentence.*

Let's get right to it. Right to the meat! Only Travelocity guarantees everything about your booking will be right, or we'll work with our travel partners to make it right, right away. Right on!

Here's a picture taken smack dab right in the middle of Antigua, where the guarantee also covers you.

The guarantee covers all but one of the items pictured to the right.

For example, what if the ocean view you booked actually looks out at a downright ugly parking lot? You'd be right to call – we're there for you. And no one in their right mind would be pleased to learn the rental car place has closed and left them stranded. Call Travelocity and we'll help get you back on the right track.

Now, you may be thinking, "Yeah, right, I'm so sure." That's OK; you have the right to remain skeptical. That is until we mention help is always right around the corner. Call us right off the bat, knowing that our customer service reps are there for you 24/7. Righting wrongs. Left and right.

Now if you're guessing there are some things we can't control, like the weather, well you're right. But we can help you with most things – to get all the details in righting,* visit **travelocity.com/guarantee.**

*Sorry, spelling things right is one of the few things not covered under the guarantee.

I'd give my right arm for a guarantee like this, although I'm glad I don't have to.